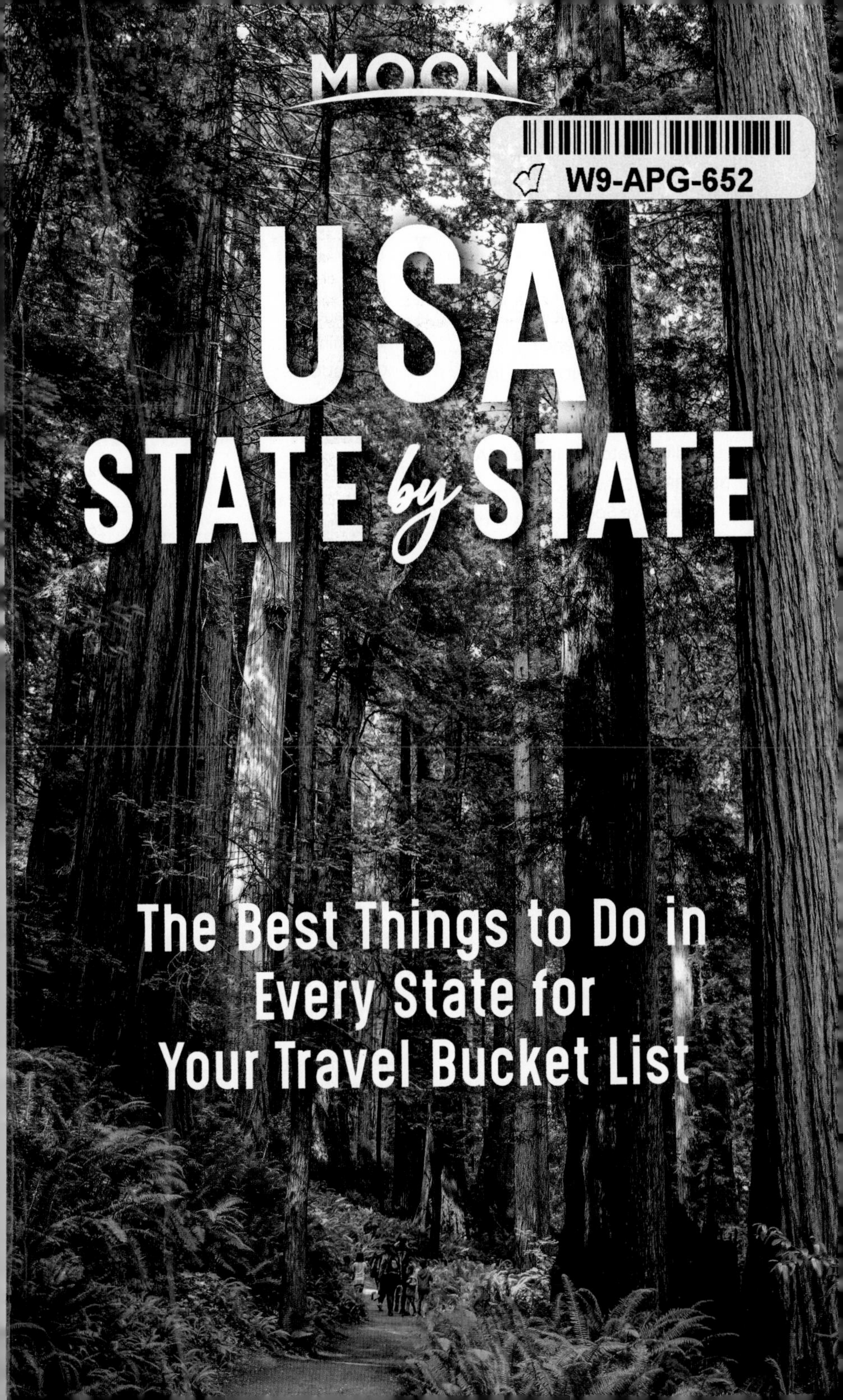

# MOON

**W9-APG-652**

# USA
# STATE by STATE

The Best Things to Do in
Every State for
Your Travel Bucket List

# CONTENTS

Although every effort was made to make sure the information in this book was accurate when going to press, research was impacted by the COVID-19 pandemic and things may have changed since the time of writing. Be sure to confirm specific details, like opening hours, closures, and travel guidelines and restrictions, when making your travel plans. For more detailed information, see page 766.

**PHOTOS (TOP TO BOTTOM):**
CANYONLANDS NATIONAL PARK, UTAH
QUINAULT RAIN FOREST, WASHINGTON
TALLGRASS PRAIRIE NATIONAL PRESERVE,
    KANSAS
RAINBOW ROW IN CHARLESTON, SOUTH
    CAROLINA
PEARL HARBOR, HAWAII

# Best OF THE USA

Welcome to the United States, this big, beautiful, diverse, and complicated country. Covering 3.8 million square miles (9.8 million square kilometers) and home to more than 330 million people, the United States has long been called an experiment: an experiment in democracy, an experiment in the idea that ingenuity and hard work are the main keys to success, an experiment in governing a vast land and diverse populace. The United States revealed on a journey through its best sights and activities is at once fun and full of complexity.

This is a country whose industry and natural resources made it an economic powerhouse, but today protects for future generations hundreds of millions of acres of land—from the remote wilderness of the Gates of the Arctic to the wetlands of the Everglades. Its culture, embodied in its food, music, art, and festivals, draws from the influence of many cultures, of those who make this a nation of immigrants, of those who were enslaved, and of those who are indigenous to the continent. You can taste this influence in fry bread tacos, dance to it in New Orleans jazz, and see it in the quilts, jewelry, and handicrafts made by artisans across the country. And it's in getting to know the nation's heroes, from activists fighting for freedom to groundbreaking musicians, that it's possible to see the great potential of this country, held in its people.

Experiencing the best of the United States can inspire, change perspectives, transform—and hopefully encourage us all to keep contributing to making this country's great experiment a success.

BALLOON FIESTA, ALBUQUERQUE, NEW MEXICO

# TOP 10 Experiences

## MARVELING AT ALASKA'S ACTIVE GLACIERS

Whether you're ice-climbing on Matanuska Glacier or watching glacial ice dropping into the sea, these remnants from another time in the earth's geologic history inspire awe (page 44).

## MAKING A FOOD PILGRIMAGE TO NEW ORLEANS

Beignets, po'boys, gumbo, crawfish...if there's one city in the United States to travel to for the food, it's New Orleans (page 646).

1

### SAVORING THE NEW FOOD CREATIONS AT THE IOWA STATE FAIR

State fairs are famous for serving any and all imaginable foods on a stick, but don't miss trying food vendors' latest creative innovations—they may become your next craving (page 308).

### SNORKELING THE WARM, CLEAR WATERS OF MAUI

Colorful fish, the occasional ray, and elusive turtles inhabit the underwater world off Maui's shores (page 734).

### EXPERIENCING THE CHICAGO SKYLINE

The indelible buildings of this "city of broad shoulders" can be admired from a Chicago Architecture Center boat tour, the public art-filled playground of Millennium Park, or the Skydeck of the second tallest building in the country (page 364).

6

## WATCHING THE SUNRISE OVER BRYCE CANYON

Seeing the early morning light hitting the orange rock formations in the Bryce Amphitheater is a moment of wonder (page 140).

## SEEING OLD FAITHFUL ERUPT

Yellowstone National Park's most famous geyser shoots up to 8,400 gallons (31,707 litres) of hot water at 90-minute intervals (page 218).

7

 **WALKING THROUGH TIMES SQUARE
ON A SUMMER NIGHT**

It's hot, perhaps sticky, and crowded, but inching through the multitudes
gathered against the backdrop of bright neon advertisements conveys
the energy of the United States' largest city, and perhaps the United
States itself, like nothing else (page 495).

 **JOURNEYING THROUGH U.S. HISTORY
AT THE NATIONAL MUSEUM OF AFRICAN
AMERICAN HISTORY AND CULTURE**

You can see and feel the story of the United States—the triumphs, progress, sorrows, and horrors—unfold at this absorbing museum (page 566).

 **DRIVING THE KANCAMAGUS HIGHWAY
IN THE FALL**

New England is known for its riot of fall colors, and this twisting road
through the White Mountains shows off some of the best (page 437).

# *Best* NATURAL WONDERS

### NIAGARA FALLS
**New York**

While not the tallest in the United States, the trio of cascades that make up Niagara Falls flow with a dramatic volume (page 499).

### PICTURED ROCKS
**Michigan**

Washed in shades of pink, red, and green, these famous bluffs are sculpted into caves, arches, and castle-like turrets (page 389).

### BIG SUR COAST
**California**

With rugged green hills tumbling over craggy cliffs overlooking the crashing

▲ BIG SUR COAST, CALIFORNIA

▼ NIAGARA FALLS, NEW YORK

▲ PICTURED ROCKS, MICHIGAN

waves of the Pacific, the Big Sur coast-line is epic (page 97).

## THE BADLANDS
### South Dakota

Once at the bottom of an inland sea, the Badlands hold geologic history in their layers and folds, which turn pink and yellow at sunrise or sunset (page 250).

## CRATER LAKE
### Oregon

This sapphire-blue lake sits in the heart of a sunken volcano (page 74).

▲ BADLANDS NATIONAL PARK, SOUTH DAKOTA

▲ OLYMPIC NATIONAL PARK, WASHINGTON

## MAMMOTH CAVE
### Kentucky

Mammoth Cave is the longest known cave system in the world (page 602).

## TALLGRASS PRAIRIE
### Kansas

One of the last expanses of tallgrass prairie is preserved in the Flint Hills of Kansas (page 286).

## BIOLUMINESCENT BAYS
### Puerto Rico

In these bays—of which Puerto Rico has three of the five in the world—tiny organisms light up the water at night (page 751).

## OLYMPIC NATIONAL PARK RAIN FORESTS
### Washington

"Rain forest" often brings to mind the tropical rain forests of the Amazon, but the Pacific Northwest has temperate rain forests, with two of the most stunning in Olympic National Park (page 61).

## ANTELOPE CANYON
### Arizona

The light shining through the shafts of this slot canyon make its red twists and twirls even more beautiful (page 133).

# MUSIC ACROSS AMERICA

From West Coast hip-hop and rap to New Orleans jazz to Puerto Rican salsa and reggaeton, the United States is home to many musical genres, and music is arguably one of the country's best cultural contributions to the world. Here's a list of places to go for some of the country's best-known genres.

## BLUES

If blues is your thing, then there are two must-go places in the South: **Memphis** (page 617), the birthplace of the blues, and the **Mississippi Delta** (page 704), where you can dive deep into the history of the blues and its seminal figures.

## JAZZ AND ZYDECO

Best known for jazz, **New Orleans** (page 638)—and its clubs and streets that host a wide range of genres—should be on any music lover's travel list. Even outside its most famous city, Louisiana heralds its musical traditions, such as zydeco in the **Acadiana** region (page 643).

## COUNTRY AND BLUEGRASS

**Nashville** (page 617) is where country music is made, and the honky-tonks on Broadway are where to go see it live. **Kentucky** (page 606) is the birthplace of bluegrass music, with spots to hear it that range from front porches to concert halls.

## SALSA

The party district Calle San Sebastián in **San Juan** (page 755), Puerto Rico, combines live salsa music with lots of dancing.

## INDIE ROCK AND JUST ABOUT ANYTHING ELSE

No list of music destinations would be complete without **Austin,** which is billed as the "Live Music Capital of the World." Indie rock, reggae, punk, country, and other bands take the stage at the Texas capital's more than 100 venues (page 168).

JAZZ BAND PLAYING IN THE FRENCH QUARTER OF NEW ORLEANS, LOUISIANA

# *Best* MUSEUMS AND CULTURAL CENTERS

## METROPOLITAN MUSEUM OF ART

**New York City, New York**

Perhaps the most famous museum in the country, the Metropolitan Museum of Art houses one of the world's largest and most diverse collections (page 503).

## ROCK AND ROLL HALL OF FAME

**Cleveland, Ohio**

This "school of rock" holds a dizzying array of rock memorabilia for a complete immersion in musical history (page 399).

## CHICKASAW CULTURAL CENTER

**Sulphur, Oklahoma**

Exhibits at this campus dedicated to Chickasaw history and culture include fine art and artifacts and a re-created village (page 301).

## NATIONAL BASEBALL HALL OF FAME AND MUSEUM

**Cooperstown, New York**

This museum dedicated to the favorite national pastime is a place of homage for baseball fans everywhere (page 501).

▼ METROPOLITAN MUSEUM OF ART, NEW YORK CITY

▲ THE HEARD MUSEUM, PHOENIX

## ART INSTITUTE OF CHICAGO
### Chicago, Illinois

This stunning selection of famous and familiar works include such icons of U.S. art as *American Gothic* and *Nighthawks* (page 370).

## FREER AND SACKLER GALLERIES
### Washington DC

These connected Smithsonian museums display an impressive array of Asian art (page 567).

## LOS ANGELES COUNTY MUSEUM OF ART (LACMA)
### Los Angeles, California

Arguably the best museum on the West Coast, this complex of buildings houses fine and decorative art and artifacts from around the world (page 95).

## NATIONAL CIVIL RIGHTS MUSEUM AT THE LORRAINE MOTEL
### Memphis, Tennessee

The pursuit of equality for all continues, and this unforgettable museum traces where we've been and what we've achieved (page 616).

## HEARD MUSEUM
### Phoenix, Arizona

The Heard Museum holds a large collection of artistic, ceremonial, and daily-life artifacts from both ancient history and modern Native American communities (page 123).

# *Best* BEACHES

With beaches along the Pacific and Atlantic Oceans, as well as the Gulf of Mexico, the Caribbean, and the many interior lakes and rivers, the United States has many spectacular stretches of sand.

## KA'ANAPALI BEACH
### Maui, Hawaii

It's impossible to say which of Hawaii's beaches is the most beautiful, but this one is definitely a contender (page 738).

## PLAYA LUQUILLO
### Puerto Rico

This crescent-shaped beach is a perfect spot to lay out under the palm trees (page 749).

## ZUMA BEACH
### Malibu, California

Zuma Beach is a quintessential Southern California stretch of sand (page 91).

## BAHIA HONDA STATE PARK
### Big Pine Key, Florida

The three gorgeous beaches at this state park are great for lounging, and you can snorkel right off the shore (page 722).

▼ KA'ANAPALI BEACH, MAUI

▲ WILD PONIES ON ASSATEAGUE ISLAND

## GULF SHORES PUBLIC BEACH
### Gulf Shores, Alabama

The sugary sands at Gulf Shores make it one of the best beaches along the Gulf Coast (page 693).

## CITY BEACH
### Coeur d'Alene, Idaho

This scenic beach along Coeur d'Alene Lake draws crowds for swimming and relaxing (page 188).

## ASSATEAGUE ISLAND NATIONAL SEASHORE
### Assateague Island, Maryland

With a 37-mile (59-kilometer) beach, this park protects dunes and wetlands that harbor hundreds of bird species and wild ponies (page 555).

## COAST GUARD BEACH
### Cape Cod, Massachusetts

Cape Cod draws beachgoers from New England and beyond, and Coast Guard Beach is one of the best on the peninsula (page 457).

## HOLLAND STATE PARK
### Holland, Michigan

Weekends bring hundreds of sunbathers to this lovely and accessible beach on the Lake Michigan shore (page 395).

## LONG BEACH ISLAND
### New Jersey

This barrier island hosts some of the Jersey Shore's best surfing beaches (page 512).

# WILDLIFE-WATCHING IN THE USA

The United States spans a number of ecosystems, resulting in much biodiversity. Here is a short list of fun, unique, awe-inspiring, or symbolic animals to watch for in your travels across the country.

## BISON

**Yellowstone National Park** in Wyoming is the best place to see the West's iconic animal (page 218).

BISON IN YELLOWSTONE NATIONAL PARK

## SANDHILL CRANES

The **Platte River** in central Nebraska sees 80 percent of the entire world's sandhill crane population during their annual seasonal migration (page 272).

## FIREFLIES

Associated with summer evenings, fireflies can be seen in the warm, humid parts of the country. Around mid- to late May, seeing these beetles becomes even more amazing as they light up synchronously during their mating season. Head to **Congaree National Park** (page 667) in South Carolina and **Great** **Smoky Mountains National Park** (page 616 and 652), which spans North Carolina and Tennessee, to catch this phenomenon.

## ORCAS

In Alaska, **Prince William Sound** (page 48) is the best place to see these distinctive black and white marine mammals. In the Lower 48, Washington's **San Juan Islands** (page 58) are the summer home of about 80 orcas.

## AMERICAN ALLIGATORS

These fierce-looking reptiles live in wetland environments, so you'll almost surely see them in Florida's **Everglades National Park** (page 714). Other prime gator-spotting opportunities are also in the South, in places such as the **Okefenokee National Wildlife Refuge** (page 685) in Georgia or on a **Louisiana swamp tour** (page 638).

ALLIGATOR IN A LOUISIANA SWAMP

AMERICAN BALD EAGLES, ALASKA

## BALD EAGLES

You can see the country's national bird in **Alaska** (page 50), where thousands live throughout the state. Nevada's only nesting bald eagles are in **Lahontan State Recreation Area** (page 118), and several nesting pairs live in Ohio's **Ottawa National Wildlife Refuge** (page 407).

## GRIZZLY BEARS

**Katmai National Park and Preserve** in Alaska is the best place to see these charismatic brown bears (page 45).

## MOOSE

**Maine** (page 424) has the highest population of these gangly quadrupeds in the Lower 48 states. **Isle Royale National Park** (page 394) in Michigan is also a great place to spot moose.

## MANATEES

The **Crystal River National Wildlife Refuge** in Florida is one of the best places in the country—and the world—to see manatees (page 723).

## WILD HORSES AND PONIES

Wild horses are a popular attraction at some barrier islands in the southeastern United States, such as the **Outer Banks** (page 653) in North Carolina and **Cumberland Island** (page 679) in Georgia, while wild ponies can be seen on **Assateague Island** (page 555) in Maryland.

MANATEE IN CRYSTAL RIVER, FLORIDA

# *Best* BRIDGES

## GOLDEN GATE BRIDGE
### San Francisco, California

This iconic landmark of California—and the United States—is named after its location, not its color, which is a reddish orange (page 90).

## BROOKLYN BRIDGE
### New York City, New York

An engineering marvel at the time it was built, this span affords pedestrians and bicyclists excellent views of the New York skyline (page 498).

## EDMUND PETTUS BRIDGE
### Selma, Alabama

This historic bridge is symbolic for its role in the Selma to Montgomery march for voting rights, one of the seminal events of the Civil Rights Movement (page 696).

## MACKINAC BRIDGE
### Michigan

This scenic suspension bridge connects Michigan's two peninsulas (page 385).

▼ BROOKLYN BRIDGE, NEW YORK CITY

## ARTIST'S COVERED BRIDGE
### Newry, Maine

The Sunday River Bridge earned its evocative nickname because it has appeared in so many paintings (page 424).

## CHAIN OF ROCKS BRIDGE
### St. Louis, Missouri

This bridge features an unusual bend that was too difficult for motorists to navigate. Today, it's used by pedestrians and bicyclists (page 322).

▲ CHAIN OF ROCKS BRIDGE, MISSOURI

## MILE HIGH SWINGING BRIDGE
### Grandfather Mountain, North Carolina

This footbridge on the highest peak in the Blue Ridge Mountains is a mile above sea level (page 658).

## NEW RIVER GORGE BRIDGE
### New River Gorge National Park, West Virginia

This vehicle bridge above the New River opens once a year for daredevil activities (page 536).

▼ NEW RIVER GORGE BRIDGE, WEST VIRGINIA

# SUPERLATIVE SPOTS

Here are a few of the biggest, tallest, and other superlatives within the United States.

- BIGGEST CITY:
  New York, New York
- TALLEST MOUNTAIN:
  Denali, Alaska
- BIGGEST LAKE:
  Lake Superior
- TALLEST BUILDING:
  One World Trade Center, New York
- LONGEST RIVER:
  Missouri River
- OLDEST CITY:
  St. Augustine, Florida
- LOWEST POINT:
  Badwater Basin, Death Valley, California
- LONGEST SINGLE-CABLE TRAM:
  Sandia Peak Tramway, New Mexico
- DEEPEST CANYON:
  Hells Canyon, Oregon and Idaho
- HIGHEST PAVED ROAD:
  Mount Evans Scenic and Historic Byway, Colorado

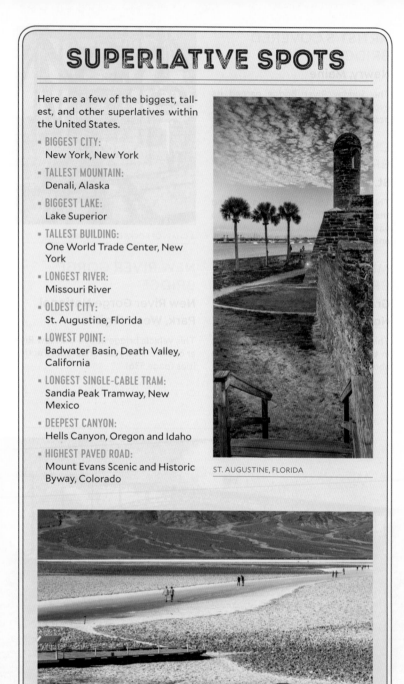

ST. AUGUSTINE, FLORIDA

BADWATER BASIN, DEATH VALLEY

# Best HISTORIC HOMES

Across the country, there are numerous ways to learn about our past. These homes capture history at an intimate, individual level.

## JOHNNY CASH BOYHOOD HOME
### Dyess, Arkansas

See the home that the future Man in Black grew up in, set up to reflect the 1940s (page 631).

## MARTIN LUTHER KING JR. BIRTH HOME
### Atlanta, Georgia

Part of the Martin Luther King Jr. National Historic Site, this home is where the civil rights leader came into the world (page 678).

## THE BREAKERS
### Newport, Rhode Island

This most ostentatious of Newport's Gilded Age mansions was the summer home of Cornelius Vanderbilt and resembles an Italian palazzo (page 469).

## IVY GREEN
### West Tuscumbia, Alabama

Helen Keller's birth home still has the water pump where the future advocate for blind and deaf rights learned to spell out "water" from her teacher, Anne Sullivan (page 697).

## BANDELIER NATIONAL MONUMENT
### New Mexico

It's possible to climb inside some of the cavates carved into Frijoles Canyon that served as homes for the Ancestral Puebloans who lived in what is now New Mexico (page 159).

## HARRIET TUBMAN HOME
### Auburn, New York

Tour the home where the famous Underground Railroad conductor lived after the Civil War (page 504).

## SEQUOYAH'S CABIN MUSEUM
### Sallisaw, Oklahoma

This one-room cabin was the home of the creator of the Cherokee system of writing (page 299).

## LYNDON B. JOHNSON NATIONAL HISTORICAL PARK
### Hill Country, Texas

This two-site park preserves the 36th president's childhood home and the ranch that was his Texas White House (page 171).

## MAGGIE L. WALKER HISTORIC SITE
### Richmond, Virginia

This 28-room Victorian mansion was the home of the first Black woman in the United States to found a bank and holds many of her belongings as she left them (page 585).

# EATING YOUR WAY THROUGH THE USA

Sampling the range and diversity of food in the United States could take a lifetime. Many books are dedicated solely to food in the United States, so this list is hardly comprehensive—it's just a starting point.

## BARBECUE

There are many barbecue styles across the country, and we love them all.

- TEXAS: The focus of Texas barbecue is smoking the meat with the right kind of wood for the perfect amount of time, and purists of this form would never consider adding sauce (page 176).

- KANSAS CITY: This barbecue style features slowly smoked meat slathered in a tomato-based sauce (page 318).

- MEMPHIS: The barbecue in Memphis is known for being tangy and sweet (page 622).

- NORTH CAROLINA: Two styles vie for dominance in North Carolina. Eastern-style uses a thin vinegar and pepper sauce, while Lexington-style sports a thicker, sweeter, but still vinegar and pepper-based sauce (page 660).

- SOUTH CAROLINA: Although all variants of barbecue sauce can be found in the state, South Carolina's signature contribution is a hot, sweet mustard-based sauce (page 673).

## BEEF SANDWICHES

The hamburger might be the food most associated with the United States, but across the country, there are varied preparations of beef served between bread.

- RUNZA AND BIEROCK: Nebraska and Kansas have different names for this spiced beef, cabbage, and onion sandwich (page 281 and 292).

- ONION BURGER: Oklahoma's variation on the burger adds thin pieces of grilled onion to the beef, which gives the patty a savory crust (page 304).

- PHILADELPHIA CHEESESTEAK: Last but not least, Philly's style of beef sandwich uses slices or chunks of meat, rather than ground, with the signature layer of cheese (page 530).

## BURRITOS AND TACOS

Several areas are known for Mexican food, whether authentic or with a regional spin.

- SAN FRANCISCO: The Mission burrito, essentially an incredibly large version of the tortilla-wrapped oblong dish, is a specialty in this Northern California city (page 102).

- TUCSON AND NOGALES: The cuisine styles of Northern Mexico, such as machaca, fill the burritos and tacos of southern Arizona (page 135).

- CHICAGO: The nation's third-largest city is home to the largest Mexican American population outside California and the Southwest, with the taquerias in the Pilsen neighborhood to show for it (page 372).

## FRY BREAD TACOS

A major element of Native American cuisine, fry bread is a round of deep-fried dough. When it's topped with ground meat, cheese, lettuce, and other fixings, it becomes the dish with names such as

Indian tacos, Navajo tacos, or Hopi tacos. Try them in **New Mexico** (page 163) and **Arizona** (page 136).

## VIETNAMESE FOOD

Warm, savory pho noodle bowls and other Vietnamese specialties can be found across the United States. Try them in **New Orleans** (page 647), **Oklahoma City** (page 304), and **Maui** (page 742).

## PIZZA

Just as there are barbecue rivalries, pizza is also a subject of much debate across the country.

- CHICAGO: Also called deep-dish, this style of pizza is thick. The mozzarella is packed on the dough and a topped with a layer of tomato, rather than the other way around (page 371).

- NEW YORK CITY: The big-as-your-head slice is ubiquitous, but for a sit-down meal, there's the crispy-thin, coal-oven pies (page 507).

- NEW HAVEN: New Haven, Connecticut, has its own style, called apizza. A thin, hand-tossed dough is baked in a coal-fired oven and, in the plain version, topped with olive oil, crushed tomatoes, and pecorino cheese (page 487).

## BEER

Beer can wash down any of the foods above, and craft brews in particular are only gaining in popularity. Here are a few hot spots for the beer enthusiast.

- PORTLAND: Known as Beervana, Oregon's biggest city is the epicenter of the country's craft brewing revival (page 84).

- DENVER: The capital of Colorado has 125 breweries and tap rooms, and one of the founders of its first brewpub went on to become governor of the entire state of Colorado (page 231).

- MILWAUKEE: Big time players like Miller and Pabst hail from this Wisconsin city, but craft brews are also part of the scene here (page 359).

CRAFT BEER TASTING IN DENVER, COLORADO

## WINE

Wine regions can be found around the country, and many feature family-owned vineyards producing a few varietals. Here are two famous wine-producing areas to visit.

- CALIFORNIA: Ever since that famous blind taste test against French wines, California's wine country, particularly Napa Valley, has been on the global map, with chardonnay and cabernet sauvignon as two of its famous varietals (page 101).

- NEW YORK: Called the "Napa Valley of the East," the Finger Lakes region combines beautiful fall colors with more than 100 wineries (page 508).

WINE TASTING IN NAPA, CALIFORNIA

# Best for PHOTOS

The United States is full of photogenic spots. Some are iconic, others are whimsical, and still others are simply breathtaking. Here are 10 places where you'll want to have your camera ready.

## MORMON ROW
### Wyoming

These rustic buildings set against the Teton Mountains make for a dramatic photo (page 219).

## MONUMENT VALLEY
### Arizona

The rock formations of Monument Valley Navajo Tribal Park are icons of the Southwestern United States (page 127).

## MARTIN LUTHER KING JR. MEMORIAL
### Washington DC

This powerful monument is striking at any time, but for a few weeks in the spring, cherry blossoms can pop into the frame (page 570).

## STATUE OF LIBERTY
### New York

This gift from France serves as a symbol of the United States and can be photographed from land or on a boat (page 498).

## DELICATE ARCH
### Utah

This natural stone arch stands in a magnificent setting atop gracefully curving slickrock (page 140).

## THE ENCHANTED HIGHWAY
### North Dakota

A clear blue sky is the perfect background for this series of whimsical sculptures (page 253).

## CANNON BEACH
### Oregon

The sea stacks at Cannon Beach are the most recognizable landmark along Oregon's Pacific Coast Highway (page 78).

## RAINBOW ROW
### South Carolina

These nine pastel mansions in Charleston are among the most photographed in the country (page 669).

## CADILLAC RANCH
### Texas

Route 66 is full of photo ops, and this art installation featuring 10 Cadillacs tipped nose-first into the ground makes a memorable image (page 173).

## GREAT RIVER ROAD
### Wisconsin

The Great River Road follows the Mississippi River from Minnesota to Louisiana, but Wisconsin's stretch, especially the portion north of La Crosse, is well-known for its scenery (page 355).

**PHOTOS (TOP TO BOTTOM):**
MORMON ROW, WYOMING
MONUMENT VALLEY, ARIZONA
CANNON BEACH, OREGON
CADILLAC RANCH, TEXAS

# WEST COAST

◄ TAFT POINT, YOSEMITE NATIONAL PARK

# THE WEST COAST
## State by State

### ALASKA

**Why Go:** The pristine landscapes of the country's largest state hold glaciers, fjords, grizzly bears, bald eagles, and the tallest mountain in the United States.

### WASHINGTON

**Why Go:** The Evergreen State earns its nickname from its famous rainy weather—the Olympic Peninsula is the rainiest place in the United States—and the resulting lush greenery in the western side of the state.

### OREGON

**Why Go:** Oregon's diverse landscapes encompass the low-key cool of Portland, the myriad waterfalls of the Columbia River Gorge, dry high deserts, and much more.

### CALIFORNIA

**Why Go:** Southern California captures the imagination with its sunny beaches and nearly year-round beach weather, while heading north leads to dramatic coastal landscapes, massive granite rock formations, and the iconic Golden Gate Bridge.

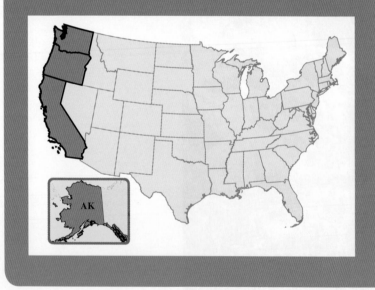

# West Coast ROAD TRIP

You can travel up the coast from **San Diego, California,** through **Portland, Oregon,** to **Seattle, Washington,** on a three-week journey that spans almost 2,000 miles (3,220 kilometers). This road trip stokes the imagination like few other journeys. The highway is framed by golden sands and turquoise waters, bordered by emerald rainforests, and capped off with kaleidoscopic sunsets and indigo night skies.

## SOUTHERN CALIFORNIA

**San Diego to Santa Barbara: 3 Days / 215 miles (346 kilometers)**
Before starting the drive, spend the morning in **San Diego,** then head north to the famous **Orange County beaches** along CA Highway 1, arriving in Los Angeles at the end of the day. Spend a full day in **Los Angeles,** checking out **Griffith Park, LACMA,** or both. The next day, leave Los Angeles on Highway 1, passing through **Santa Monica** and **Malibu** before merging with U.S. 101 to reach **Santa Barbara.**

## CENTRAL CALIFORNIA

**Santa Barbara to San Francisco: 3 Days / 382 miles (608 kilometers)**
Wake up in Santa Barbara, and spend the morning strolling along the coastline path and exploring the beachside city. Head up the coast on U.S. 101 to **San Luis Obispo** for the night. The next day, take Highway 1 out of town and through a series of small coastal towns. North of Cambria, you'll get your first taste of the famous **Big Sur** coast. Head to **Julia Pfeiffer Burns State Park** for the classic view of **McWay Falls.** Spend the night in Big Sur. Finish the jaw-dropping Big Sur coast drive the next morning, spending the afternoon in **Carmel** and **Monterey.** From Monterey to **San Francisco,** Highway 1 takes about 3 hours and U.S. 101 takes about 2 hours.

## NORTHERN CALIFORNIA

**San Francisco to Crescent City: 4 days / 415 miles (668 kilometers)**

HOLLYWOOD SIGN, LOS ANGELES, CALIFORNIA

DENALI MOUNTAIN, ALASKA

Spend a full day in **San Francisco,** making sure to ride a cable car and eat a Mission burrito. In the morning, drive out of the city on U.S. 101, over the **Golden Gate Bridge,** then follow signs out to Highway 1 and keep going north. Near Point Arena, head inland for some wine-tasting in the **Anderson Valley** and spend the night in nearby **Mendocino.** From there, spend two days wending your way up the northern California coast on U.S. 101, making sure to visit a couple parks in the **Redwood National and State Parks** complex. Spend your last night in California in the northern town of Crescent City.

## OREGON

**Crescent City to Astoria: 3 days / 465 miles (750 kilometers)**
From Crescent City, keep heading north on U.S. 101 into Oregon, enjoying the most scenic stretch of the Oregon coast to **Gold Beach.** Overnight in **Yachats.** The next day, make a detour inland at Newport to reach **Portland** around mid-day. Spend the night and have a lazy morning hanging out in the city. Turn back toward the coast to see **Haystack Rock** at **Cannon Beach,** and end up in **Astoria** for the night.

## WASHINGTON

**Astoria to Seattle: 4 days / 430 miles (705 kilometers)**
Cross the Columbia River into Washington, winding along U.S. 101, until you reach **Lake Quinault,** where you'll spend the night. Wind around **Olympic National Park** and visit the park's **Hoh Rainforest, Lake Crescent,** and **Hurricane Ridge** before calling it a day in **Port Angeles.** In the morning, head out to Seattle, where you'll overnight and spend the next day. Be sure to see **Pikes Place Market** and have a nice meal at one of the city's chef-driven restaurants.

## DRIVING TO ALASKA

**6-7 days**
To make an epic trip even more epic, you could keep driving north to Alaska, which requires crossing an international border into Canada. Take one day for driving from Seattle to **Vancouver,** British Columbia (145 miles/233 kilometers), and exploring. Then it's two days to drive from Vancouver to **Dawson Creek,** British Columbia (740 miles/1,190 kilometers), your entry point to the **Alaska Highway.** The section of the Alaska Highway from Dawson Creek to **Whitehorse,** Yukon (914 miles/1,471 kilometers), takes at least another two days. From Whitehorse, the most direct route to Alaska is to continue on the **Alaska Highway** (187 miles/460 kilometers, 1 day) to the border, or you can take the **Klondike Highway** to **Dawson City,** Yukon (333 miles/536 kilometers, 2 days), which links to **Tok,** Alaska (185 miles/300 kilometers, 1 day) via the spectacular **Top of the World Highway.**

GOLDEN GATE BRIDGE, SAN FRANCISCO, CALIFORNIA

# ALASKA

S teep-walled fjords, charismatic bears, soaring eagles, breaching whales, and glaciers creeping down the side of a mountain and into the sea are some of Alaska's grandest sights. But there's so much to Alaska that it can't possibly be summed up in just one image—and every part of the state is a little bit different.

In Southeast Alaska the evergreen rainforest dominates the landscape and totem poles stand silent witness to the passage of time. Southcentral Alaska and the Interior are a road-tripper's dream, clad in boreal forest. Southwest Alaska offers some of the state's best bear and bird-watching. In Arctic Alaska, people are outnumbered by the caribou that migrate between their winter ranges and summer breeding grounds.

As amazing, exotic, and even otherworldly as Alaska's pristine landscapes may be, the "peoplescapes" are just as special. Alaskans are known for being warm and friendly despite—or perhaps because of—cold winter temperatures.

AREA: 663,268 square miles / 1,717,856 square kilometers (1st)

POPULATION: 731,545 (48th)

STATEHOOD DATE: January 3, 1959 (49th)

STATE CAPITAL: Juneau

CARIBOU WITH DENALI MOUNTAIN IN THE BACKGROUND

## ORIENTATION

Southeast Alaska, also known as the **Inside Passage,** is the block of islands and strip of land that border the Canadian province of British Columbia. The capital, **Juneau,** is located here, and this region is the main destination of cruises to Alaska. Southcentral Alaska borders the Yukon and is the home of **Anchorage, the Kenai Peninsula,** and **Prince William Sound.** West of the Kenai Peninsula is the **Alaska Peninsula,** which then breaks apart into the **Aleutian Islands** that trail out toward Russia. North of Anchorage is **Denali National Park** and to the north of that is **Fairbanks.** North of Fairbanks and west of Denali are the vast, remote landscapes of the **Arctic.**

## WHEN TO GO

Summer high season for most of the state is **mid-June** through **early September.** Traveling in high season means you'll have the best weather, the richest landscape, more touring and wildlife-viewing opportunities, and the most services available—along with the highest prices. You can save money—and still have a great time—during the **spring** and **late-summer** shoulder seasons (May and September). In Southcentral and Interior Alaska, spring may not start as early as May, but the rainforests in the southeast are always green. An increasing number of tourists are coming in **winter** to watch the aurora borealis and the Iditarod sled dog race.

# HIGHLIGHTS

## ALASKA NATIVE HERITAGE CENTER

8800 Heritage Center Dr., Anchorage; 907/330-8000 or 800/315-6608; www.alaskanative.net

Almost every community in Alaska has some sort of cultural center dedicated to showcasing—and nurturing—the unique Alaska Native culture in that region of the state. But if you can only visit one such center, make it the Alaska Native Heritage Center in northeast Anchorage.

This enormous center pools information on each of the five distinct cultural regions throughout the state, with performances of traditional dancing, videos on various aspects of Native culture, and guided tours through life-size re-creations of Alaska Native village sites.

The excellent gift shop includes quite a bit of traditional Alaska Native art, and you can sometimes see artisans demonstrating their crafts or teaching them to the next generation. Every so often there are open-enrollment classes where the public can learn traditional arts, too.

THE ALASKA NATIVE HERITAGE CENTER

# ALASKA

**CHUKCHI SEA**

Utqiaġvik

Wainwright

Smith Bay

Harrison Bay

**N O R T H   S L O P E**

Coville River

Point Hope

**RUSSIA**

Kivalina

Noatak

*Noatak National Preserve*

Anaktuvuk Pass

*Gates of the Arctic National Park and Preserve*

*Cape Krusenstern Natl Mon*

Shishmaref

Kotzebue

Kiana

*Kobuk Valley National Park*

Ambler

Shungnak

**B R O O K S**

Kobuk River

Kotzebue Sound

Noorvik

Selawik

*Bering Land Bridge National Preserve*

**BERING STRAIT**

Date Line

Monday

Brevig Mission

Teller

**S E W A R D**
**P E N I N S U L A**

Buckland

Huslia

Sunday

Gambell

Savoonga

St. Lawrence Island

Nome

Koyuk

Elim

Nulato

Galena

Tanana

Minto

*Norton Sound*

Stuart Island

Unalakleet

Nenana

Anderson

*Tanana River*

Stebbins

**SOARING OVER DENALI NATIONAL PARK ON A FLIGHTSEEING PLANE** ⊙

*St Michael Island Nat'l Park*

St. Michael

Healy

Emmonak

Kotlik

Yukon River

*Denali National Park and Preserve*

Alakanuk

McGrath

Denali ▲

Scammon Bay

Mountain Village

St. Mary's

**A L A S K A**

Talkeetna

Hooper Bay

Chevak

Marshall

Russian Mission

Aniak

Willow

Newtok

Wasilla

Tununak

Nelson Island

Kasigluk

Tuluksak

Nunivak Island

Napakiak

Bethel

**ALASKA NATIVE HERITAGE CENTER**

Anchorage

Chefornak

Tuntutuliak

Eek

*Lake Clark National Park and Preserve*

Chugach State Park

Kipnuk

Kongiganak

*Kuskokwim River*

Soldotna

Sterling

Kwigillingok

Quinhagak

*Kenai National Wildlife Refuge*

Cohoe

Seward

*Kuskokwim Bay*

Happy Valley

*Kenai Fjords National Park*

New Stuyahok

Anchor Point

Homer

Togiak

Seldovia

Kenai Peninsula

Manokotak

Dillingham

**WALRUS ISLANDS STATE GAME SANCTUARY** ★

Naknek

Afognak Island

King Salmon

*Fort Abercrombie State Historical Park*

**GETTING A GLIMPSE OF ALASKA'S CHARISMATIC BEARS** ⊙

*Katmai National Park and Preserve*

Port Lions

*Shelikof Strait*

Kodiak

**B R I S T O L   B A Y**

Kodiak Island

**KODIAK MILITARY HISTORY MUSEUM**

**KODIAK BROWN BEAR CENTER**

Port Moller

*Aniakchak Nat'l Monument and Preserve*

**A L A S K A   P E N I N S U L A**

Chirikof Is

**A L E U T I A N   I S L A N D S**

Akutan Island

Unimak Island

King Cove

Sand Point

Akutan

Unimak Pass

Unga Is

Unalaska

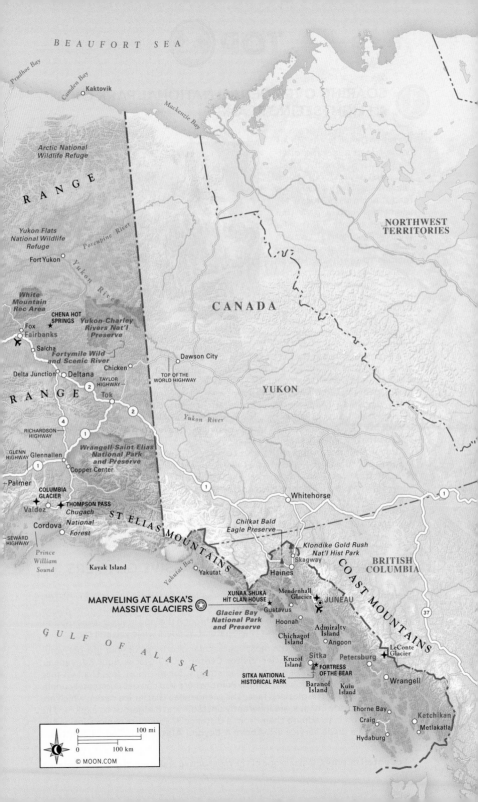

BEAUFORT SEA

Prudhoe Bay
Camden Bay
Kaktovik

Mackenzie Bay

Arctic National
Wildlife Refuge

RANGE

NORTHWEST
TERRITORIES

Yukon Flats
National Wildlife
Refuge

Fort Yukon

Porcupine River

Yukon River

CANADA

White
Mountain
Rec Area

CHENA HOT
SPRINGS

Yukon-Charley
Rivers Nat'l
Preserve

Fox
Fairbanks

Salcha

Fortymile Wild
and Scenic River

Dawson City

Delta Junction  Deltana

Chicken

TOP OF THE
WORLD HIGHWAY

YUKON

RANGE

2

TAYLOR
HIGHWAY

Tok

4

2

Yukon River

RICHARDSON
HIGHWAY

1

GLENN
HIGHWAY    Glennallen

Wrangell-Saint Elias
National Park
and Preserve

1

Copper Center

Palmer

COLUMBIA
GLACIER

THOMPSON PASS

Valdez

Chugach

Whitehorse

1

Cordova

National

Forest

Chilkat Bald
Eagle Preserve

SEWARD
HIGHWAY

Prince
William
Sound

ST ELIAS MOUNTAINS

Klondike Gold Rush
Nat'l Hist Park

Kayak Island

Yakutat Bay

Yakutat

Skagway

BRITISH
COLUMBIA

Haines

MARVELING AT ALASKA'S
MASSIVE GLACIERS

XUNAA SHUKA
HÍT CLAN HOUSE

Mendenhall
Glacier

JUNEAU

COAST MOUNTAINS

Glacier Bay
National Park
and Preserve

Gustavus

Hoonah

GULF OF ALASKA

Chichagof
Island

Admiralty
Island

Angoon

37

Kruzof
Island

Sitka

FORTRESS
OF THE BEAR

Baranof
Island

LeConte
Glacier

Petersburg

SITKA NATIONAL
HISTORICAL PARK

Kuiu
Island

Wrangell

Thorne Bay

Craig

Ketchikan

Hydaburg

Metlakatla

0                    100 mi
0                    100 km

© MOON.COM

# TOP 3

## 1 SOARING OVER DENALI NATIONAL PARK ON A FLIGHTSEEING PLANE

A visit to Denali National Park is the trip of a lifetime, offering the easiest possible access to a vast swath of trackless wilderness. There's only one road, running just 92 miles (148 kilometers) into a park that measures almost 9,500 miles (24,604 kilometers) square. Renowned for its stellar opportunities to see bears, moose, caribou, Dall sheep, and wolves in the wild, the park's pristine scenery is set against the backdrop of the Alaska Range and 20,310-foot (6,190-meter) **Denali,** the highest mountain in North America.

FLIGHTSEEING, DENALI NATIONAL PARK

Any trip into Denali National Park will be a phenomenal sightseeing adventure. But if you really want to see the park—and Denali, the mountain—at their best, take a flightseeing trip. Even the most jaded Alaskan will subside into awe when "The Great One" is front and center in the windshield. Many flightseeing operations also include a landing on a nearby glacier, so you can get out and walk on ground that only the world's most intrepid explorers have ever reached by other means. This is truly a once-in-a-lifetime splurge that everybody should experience.

Only a few carriers are authorized to make glacier landings in Denali National Park, most of which depart from **Talkeetna.** The only provider that can depart straight from the park entrance is **Fly Denali** (907/683-2359 or 877/770-2359; www.flydenali.com). **Temsco Helicopters** (907/683-0683; https://temscoair.com) offers helicopter tours, which allow for lower and slower views than a plane, including glacier landings near the park, tundra landings just outside the park, and helicopter-supported hiking.

## 2 MARVELING AT ALASKA'S MASSIVE GLACIERS

It's unknown exactly how many glaciers there are in Alaska, but 616 are officially named, and some estimate there are as many as 100,000 in total. Think of the glacier as a giant scouring pad that's carving its way through the land in super-slow motion. A trip to Alaska is a chance to visit these natural wonders while you still can.

- **Mendenhall:** For some of the most spectacular photo ops of your life, get yourself to the **Mendenhall Glacier Visitor Center** (6000 Glacier Spur Rd., Juneau; 907/789-0097; www.fs.usda.gov). Head straight for the short, less than 0.1-mile (0.16-kilometer) walk down to **Photo Point,** where you can get completely unobstructed views of the glacier's face. The Mendenhall Glacier **ice caves,** which are featured in many images, are inherently unstable and dangerous to explore. The safest option is to admire them from a distance; if you must explore inside the caves, hire a guide service like **Above & Beyond Alaska** (907/364-2333; https://beyondak.com).

- **LeConte:** LeConte Glacier is one of the most active and studied glaciers in Alaska.

MENDENHALL GLACIER

Both **Whale Song Cruises** (207 N. Nordic Dr., Petersburg; 907/772-9393; www. whalesongcruises.com) and **Tongass Kayak Adventures** (907/772-4600; www. tongasskayak.com) offer tours to see the glacier.

- **Columbia:** The tidewater Columbia Glacier is one of the fastest-moving glaciers in the world. It drops about 13 tons (11 metric tons) of ice into the water every day, and tour companies, like **Lu-Lu Belle** (Kobuk and Chitina; 800/411-0090; https:// lulubelletours.com), mostly based in Valdez, navigate the surrounding icebergs to get you as close as (safely) possible to the face.

 ## GETTING A GLIMPSE OF ALASKA'S CHARISMATIC BEARS

If there's one animal that people associate with Alaska, it has to be the bear. Alaska has three types of bears: **black bears, brown bears/grizzly bears** (actually the same species), and **polar bears.** Seeing one is a guaranteed adrenaline rush. You'll find bears all over Alaska, but the ideal place for a bear-viewing trip is a coastal location where food is plentiful and the human presence is carefully managed.

The most iconic destination for bear viewing is **Katmai National Park and Preserve** (www.nps.gov/katm) in Southwest Alaska. But this is far from the only place you can go to see brown bears playing, tending their young, and feeding on fish. A multiday trip to the remote **Kodiak Brown Bear Center** (877/335-2327; https://kodiakbearcenter.com) lets you observe the largest brown bears in the world in a small group setting.

BEARS, KATMAI NATIONAL PARK

Bear viewing is also a popular activity in Southeast Alaska. **Admiralty Island,** near Juneau, has one of the world's highest concentrations of brown bears; in fact, the bears outnumber the humans. If you'd rather see bears in a somewhat more controlled setting, **Fortress of the Bear** (4639 Sawmill Creek Rd., Sitka; 907/747-3550 or 907/747-3032; www.fortressofthebear.org) is an educational center that rescues orphaned bears.

If you want to see polar bears, very best chance of spotting is on a trip to the tiny village of **Kaktovik** in the **Arctic National Wildlife Refuge.**

# *Best* ROAD TRIP

Because Alaska is so big and the logistics of transport are challenging, it can take three weeks to hit the highlights. To plan a shorter trip, choose one region. South-central Alaska and the area around Anchorage form the heart of Alaska's rudimentary road system, which means it's much easier to get around on your own schedule; that said, the distances between towns often come as a huge surprise to visitors—for example, it takes most people 8 hours to drive from Anchorage to Fairbanks. Interior Alaska is a mix of easy road access (primarily around Fairbanks) and remote communities, which can be reached only by air.

**DAY 1** Visit the **Alaska Native Heritage Center** just outside **Anchorage;** you can easily spend most of the day at this precious testament to Alaska Native culture. Look for a hike in nearby **Chugach State Park,** then enjoy dinner in one of Anchorage's excellent restaurants before you turn in for the night.

THE HARBOR IN HOMER

**DAY 2** Get up early to make the scenic 5- to 6-hour drive to **Homer** for an overnighter. Once you arrive, explore the town's art galleries, gift shops, and restaurants.

**DAY 3** Hop on a half-day **fishing trip**—after all, Homer is considered the halibut capital of the world. Afterward, make the 4.5-hour drive to **Seward** to spend the night.

HUMPBACK WHALE

**DAY 4** From Seward, take a half-day sightseeing cruise through **Kenai Fjords National Park.** Drive back to Anchorage (2.5 hours) via the scenic **Seward Highway.**

**DAY 5** There's no rush today, as long as you make the 2.5-hour drive north from Anchorage to quirky little **Talkeetna** in time to spend the afternoon exploring the shops along Main Street.

**DAY 6** Drive another 2.5 hours north to **Denali National Park and Preserve** and spend the day exploring the park's three visitors centers and hiking or flightseeing. Turn in early at your hotel or campground near the park entrance after a long day.

VISITORS AT THE BASE OF DENALI MOUNTAIN

**DAY 7**
Make the 2.5-hour drive north to **Fairbanks.** Start with a relaxing day trip to **Chena Hot Springs,** before returning back to this charming town to experience its art, music, and food scene.

**DAY 8**
Today, make the beautiful 6.5-hour drive southeast to **Valdez** along the **Richardson Highway.** If you want to check another national park off the list, stop by the **Copper Center Visitor Center** (Mile 106.8 Richardson Highway, Copper Center) of **Wrangell-St. Elias National Park and Preserve** (www.nps.gov/wrst), the largest U.S. national park.

**DAY 9**
From Valdez, take a tour to the awesome nearby **Columbia Glacier** or an unparalleled whale-watching trip in **Prince William Sound.**

**DAY 10**
It's about a six-hour drive back to **Anchorage** or **Fairbanks** to catch your flight back home.

COLUMBIA GLACIER, PRINCE WILLIAM SOUND

## KLONDIKE GOLD RUSH NATIONAL HISTORICAL PARK

A large amount of Alaska's past and present has been shaped by the lust for a particular mineral—gold. It was the Klondike gold strike of 1896—in Canada, not Alaska—that really ignited gold fever. An estimated 80,000 people participated in the rush to the Klondike, using several routes through Alaska to get there. Many of the people who came rushing for gold were turned around by conditions and weather, and if they missed the last steamboat to the continental United States, they'd have to wait out the winter. Towns began to spring up to provide services to the miners.

Klondike Gold Rush National Historical Park is Alaska's most-visited national parkland, drawing about a million visitors every year. For all intents and purposes, **Skagway** is the park—or at least the eight blocks of boardwalked downtown are. The **National Park Service's Klondike Gold Rush National Historical Park Visitor Center & Museum** (2nd Ave. and Broadway, Skagway; www.nps.gov/klgo) offers more detailed information on area trails and historic sights, along with activities including walking tours of Skagway's historic district and nearby **Dyea,** a ghost town that once served gold-hungry miners.

Other parts of Alaska were also developed as a result of gold strikes. By 1899, news of a gold strike on the **Seward Peninsula** sent thousands of people flocking to the area in a single week. Thus **Nome** was born. **Fairbanks** came to be thanks to a strike by an Italian immigrant in 1902. Gold fever also spurred the spread of transportation networks, including the **Alaska Railroad. Anchorage** started as a railroad construction camp. World War II put a stop to the mining-motivated exploration of Alaska.

## SMALL TOWNS

Every Alaska town is surrounded by spectacular natural beauty. But it's their determinedly individual nature, combined with a "play hard, work

# *Major* CITIES

**ANCHORAGE:** Almost half of Alaska's 731,000 people live in Anchorage, which offers delightful sightseeing and great insight into some of Alaska's most charming quirks.

**JUNEAU:** With a population of about 33,000, Juneau is Alaska's second-largest city and the capital. Soaring mountains, massive ice fields, and a distinct absence of local interest in being connected to a highway system mean you can only reach Alaska's capital by sea or air.

**FAIRBANKS:** The state's third-largest city with a population of about 32,000, Fairbanks has become quite a hip place in the past few years. Today, Fairbanks is full of art, music, and creativity.

hard" attitude that kicks into overdrive during long summer days, that really makes them special.

- **Petersburg** was founded by Norwegian fishermen. It remains a hardworking fishing community to this day, and visitors love that authenticity and the lack of the glitzy shops that often accompany cruise ports.

- **Ketchikan** houses the state's highest concentration of totem poles and an impressive stretch of local shops and artists overlooking picturesque Creek Street, where the historical houses stand on stilts over the water.

- **Sitka** is a beautiful port city with locally owned shops, great fishing and whale-watching, and a phenomenal historical park where you can walk the trails among totem poles or visit with Alaska Native artisans as they demonstrate their art.

- **Homer** packs some of the state's best artists, food, and fishing all into one place.

- **Talkeetna** remains the idealized standard of quirky Alaska towns. Visitors often come here just to wander Main Street, but don't miss out on a chance to ride the fabled Hurricane Turn Train.

- **Nome** is worth a visit to see the Iditarod finish in March. By summer, this is a lovely community for birding and road trips.

## WHALE-WATCHING

Don't miss the **orcas** and **humpback** whales in Southeast Alaska. It's impossible to mistake the sight of an orca's tall, black-and-white dorsal fin cutting through the water, or humpback whales' eye-catching behavior, from breaching to sky hopping, lobtailing, tail-slapping, and flipper-slapping.

Orcas live throughout Alaska's waters, with **Prince William Sound** providing some of the best viewing. Perhaps the very best place in all of Alaska to watch humpback whales is in **Frederick Sound,** just north of Petersburg. When you take a July whale-watching tour in Frederick Sound, your boat may be surrounded by more than a dozen humpbacks feeding, diving, and even breaching. Sometimes you'll see orcas, porpoises, and other marine mammals, too.

Both **Whale Song Cruises** (207 N. Nordic Dr., Petersburg; 907/772-9393; www.whalesongcruises.com) and **Tongass Kayak Adventures** (907/772-4600; www.tongasskayak.com) offer whale-watching tours.

KETCHIKAN

# ALASKA NATIVES

In Alaska, the Indigenous tribes are known collectively as Alaska Natives. The capitalization is important: "Native" or "Alaska Native" designates a person with blood that is Indigenous to Alaska; "native" without the capital "N" simply means the person was born here.

Some of the tribes in Southeast Alaska describe themselves as Indians, and some of the northern and northwest Alaska Native tribes choose to describe themselves as Eskimos, reclaiming what has been used as a derogatory term and turning it into a point of pride. So how do you know if it's okay to call someone an Eskimo or an Indian? Listen to how they refer to themselves, or just ask. As long as you approach the conversation with good intentions and open curiosity without making assumptions, people will usually appreciate your inquiry and respond in kind. When in doubt, the umbrella term "Alaska Native" is entirely appropriate and correct.

TOTEM POLES AND CLAN HOUSES

There are five main Alaska Native cultural regions:

- **Iñupiaq and St. Lawrence Island Yupik** occupy Arctic and northwestern Alaska. Many of them still live a hunting and gathering lifestyle that's heavily dependent on animals like the whale, walrus, seal, caribou, and fish, although they're more likely to use snowmobiles instead of dogsleds and rifles instead of harpoons.

- **Yup'ik or Cup'ik** (depending on which dialect of the language they speak) were a migratory people, traveling in small groups of extended family to follow the animals and plants that made up their food sources. Many Yup'ik and Cup'ik people still live subsistence lifestyles today; the modern villages used to be seasonal settlements they used in their travels.

- **Unungan and Sugpiaq,** perhaps better known by their Western names Aleut and Alutiiq, were sophisticated seafarers, using enclosed, split-bow kayaks and larger, open, skin-covered boats for hunting and transport. Unungan and Sugpiaq communities stretched all the way down through the Aleutian Islands, Kodiak, and a little bit of the Southcentral Alaska shoreline around Prince William Sound.

- **Athabascan** people traditionally lived in Interior Alaska along major rivers, moving nomadically to follow the seasons and their food sources. Materials such as birch bark, moose hide, and cottonwood were used to make canoes for traveling on water; sleds and snowshoes were used to travel on snow, and dogs were used as pack animals.

- **Eyak, Haida, Tsimshian, and Tlingit** cultures have a strong, shared heritage. Each of these cultures has a complex social system: creating a societal structure that cleverly kept people from accidentally marrying one of their own relatives. The artwork of all four cultures includes the distinctive totem poles and clan houses that most people associate with Southeast Alaska.

# THE WONDERS OF ALASKAN WILDLIFE

Alaska offers many opportunities to view wildlife, unparalleled almost anywhere else in the world. Bears and whales may be the most iconic, but moose, walrus, caribou, and bald eagles are also among the most sought-after sightings. Even beyond these, the list of wildlife that you might see on your trip is lengthy: Dall sheep, mountain goats, musk oxen, wood bison, wolves, foxes, sea lions, seals, sea otters, and salmon.

## MOOSE

Moose, the largest members of the deer family, range throughout all of Alaska. The Alaska-Yukon subspecies is the biggest of them all, with females typically weighing up to half a ton while males may weigh up to 1,600 pounds. The most common places to see them are where their favorite willow, aspen, and birch browse occur. There's no single best place for seeing moose, although they do seem to cluster particularly around **Anchorage.**

## WALRUSES

Walruses are one of the species being heavily affected by climate change. They depend on sea ice as a resting place or haul-out while foraging, and the ice is thinning and drifting away from the relatively shallow areas where they can feed. If you want to see this fragile species in the wild, you can visit as many as 14,000 walruses at a time in one place—**Walrus Islands State Game Sanctuary,** seven rugged, remote islands in northern Bristol Bay.

## CARIBOU

Every year, caribou migrate en masse from their winter ranges to summer calving grounds. Each band of caribou has set migration routes that they've traveled for hundreds of years, and Alaska Native lifeways were often built around that migration. Caribou live throughout the state, except for Southeast Alaska and most of the Aleutian Islands. **Denali National Park** offers some of the best potential for viewing caribou.

## EAGLES

You'll find both **bald** and **golden eagles** in Alaska, although bald eagles are by far more common, with an estimated 30,000 throughout the state. From October through February, thousands of eagles congregate to feed in the open water of the **Chilkat Bald Eagle Preserve.** You can live in Alaska for decades and never see a golden eagle—so if you do see one, you're very lucky! Your best odds are at the **Gunsight Mountain Hawkwatch** (https://hawkwatch.org), which takes place in early to mid-March.

## FISHING

You'll find spectacular fishing throughout the state. **Salmon** season is in July and August, while **halibut** fishing is good during May and June. Some of the best places to fish or book a fishing trip include:

- **Homer** is quite rightly called the halibut fishing capital of the world.
- **Valdez** makes a great place to fill your freezer with halibut, lingcod, and salmon.
- **Petersburg,** a town founded on fishing, is known for saltwater salmon and halibut fishing trips.

- **Kenai River** offers the most iconic freshwater fishing in Alaska.

# BEST SCENIC DRIVES

The best way to see some of Alaska's most beautiful scenery is on a road trip.

## SEWARD HIGHWAY

Route 1 and Route 9

This 127-mile (204-kilometer) National Scenic Byway from **Anchorage** to **Seward** offers sweeping views of beautiful mountains and seaside scenery, Alaska-style; depending on the season, it can be full-on summer at highway level while snow- and glacier-clad peaks loom in the near distance.

Perhaps one of the most amazing things about this drive—after the phenomenal views, of course—is that for almost its entire length, you're driving through the protected public lands of first **Chugach State Park**, then **Chugach National Forest** and **Kenai National Wildlife Refuge**. That makes for a profusion of beautiful scenery, surprising wildlife-viewing opportunities (keep an eye out for Dall sheep and mountain goats on the cliffs), too many lovely wooded campgrounds to list, and lots of great hiking trails too. For a detailed breakdown of mile-by-mile attractions on this and other Alaska highways, the best reference is **The Milepost** (themilepost.com).

This narrow, two-lane highway is as dangerous as it is beautiful, with lumbering RVs and many blind corners. When you just can't help but slow down to admire the views, pull off to one of the many rest stops and look your fill from there. And if you have more than five cars stacked up behind you, pull over to let them pass.

## VALDEZ FROM FAIRBANKS OR ANCHORAGE

It takes six-plus-hours to drive to Valdez from either Fairbanks, via the **Richardson Highway**, or from Anchorage, via the **Glenn Highway** and the Richardson Highway. While the first couple hundred miles (320 kilometers) are pretty, it's the last 26-mile (41-kilometer) drive through **Thompson Pass** and **Keystone Canyon**—which helps earn Valdez its nickname as "land of the waterfalls"—that will really take your breath away.

## TOP OF THE WORLD HIGHWAY

Open seasonally, the Top of the World Highway runs 185 miles (297 kilometers, about a 6-hour drive) north from **Tok** (rhymes with "poke") and east into Canada's **Dawson City**. Tok sits in an incredibly scenic spot between the **Alaska Range** and the **Tanana River** and its isolated location makes it a great place for viewing the **northern lights.** The first 77 miles (123 kilometers) to the community of Chicken is along the **Taylor Highway,** a designated National Scenic Byway through the "Fortymile" region that so inspired Jack London.

# BEST PARKS AND RECREATION AREAS

## GLACIER BAY NATIONAL PARK

1 Park Rd., Gustavus; www.nps.gov/glba

Encompassing an enormous 3.3 million acres (1.3 million hectares) of land and water, Glacier Bay National Park is larger than the state of Alabama. Its craggy, snowcapped mountains, towering spruce and cedar trees, and rich waters are hardly unique in Alaska, but this park is remarkable for the particularly pristine waters and lands. Glacier Bay is one of the largest protected biosphere preserves in the world. This is one of the best places in the state to sea kayak. Cruise ships do visit the bay, but they never dock, and access during peak months is controlled by a free permit system, resulting in unparalleled solitude.

This place is also a rich, integral part of the Tlingit Alaska Native tradition, and park officials work closely with the tribes. One of their most notable successes was the August 2016 opening of the **Xunaa Shuká Hít clan house,** the first permanent clan house in Glacier Bay since Tlingit villages were destroyed by a rapid glacier advance more than 250 years ago.

## SITKA NATIONAL HISTORICAL PARK

Visitors center at 103 Monastery St., Sitka; 907/747-0110; www.nps.gov/sitk

Come to Sitka National Historical Park to see the past, present, and future of the area's Alaska Natives. Traditionally, totem poles were allowed to fall and decay in the natural course of events, but with the increasing understanding that historic poles must be preserved as part of a cultural legacy, a number of Tlingit and Haida totem poles were brought here to be preserved.

You can walk miles of **Totem Trails** around the park buildings to see historic totem poles set against the area's rich greenery, or even walk to the remains of a wooden fort (the Kiks.ádi fort site) where the Tlingit people of this area staged their last open resistance against the Russians in the 1804 Battle of Sitka. Visit the **Southeast Alaska Indian Cultural Center** (accessed through the park visitors center) to watch Alaska Native master craftspeople demonstrate their art in its full cultural context.

# FESTIVALS AND EVENTS

## THE NORTHERN LIGHTS

The enchanting phenomenon known as the northern lights, or aurora borealis, is caused by charged particles from the sun striking Earth's atmosphere. The lights occupy an important place in the legends and mythology of every culture that evolved under their gaze. They've been viewed as healing spirits, the dancing spirits of our ancestors, animal spirits dancing in the sky, or human spirits playing ball.

Whatever their spiritual implications, the northern lights are beautiful. Unfortunately, the lights are unpredictable and only visible when skies are dark and clear (**Oct.- Apr.** are the best months), so there's no guarantee you'll see them while you're here—but if you take three or four days and use the following tips, you'll have great odds.

## A PLETHORA OF NATIONAL PARKS

Alaska is home to eight national parks; that doesn't even include national forests, national historic sites, and national wildlife refuge. Besides Glacier Bay National Park and Denali National Park, there's also:

- **Gates of the Arctic National Park** (www.nps.gov/gaar) is a vast, untouched wilderness that spans about 8.4 million acres (3.3 million hectares).

- **Katmai National Park and Preserve** (www.nps.gov/katm), known for bear-viewing, also offers phenomenal sea kayaking, world-class fishing, and the stunning Valley of 10,000 Smokes.

- **Kenai Fjords National Park** (www.nps.gov/kefj) was named for its deep, steep-walled, narrow inlets gouged by ancient glaciers.

- **Kobuk Valley National Park** (www.nps.gov/kova) is most notable for its 25 square miles (64 square kilometers) of massive sand dunes, which can reach as high as 100 feet (30 meters).

- **Lake Clark National Park and Preserve** (www.nps.gov/lacl) is most famous for three things: brown bear viewing, fly-fishing, and the cabin of naturalist Richard Proenneke.

- **Wrangell-St. Elias National Park and Preserve** (www.nps.gov/wrst) covers 13.2 million acres (5.3 million hectares) of pristine wilderness, a magnet for mountaineers, birders, wildlife watchers, and serious backcountry hikers.

- Plan your visit in **Nome, Fairbanks,** or a community farther north (like **Utqiaġvik**); all three are at a high enough latitude to see the lights overhead. You might still see the lights in more southerly parts of Alaska, but

IDITAROD

they're more likely to shine low on the horizon and may even be blocked by mountains.

- Get as far away as you can from the city lights and any other light pollution. The darker the sky, the clearer your view of the lights will be. That's one reason why **Chena Hot Springs** (Mile 56.6 Chena Hot Springs Rd., Fairbanks; 907/451-8104; https://chenahotsprings.com) near Fairbanks is such a good place for viewing the northern lights. It's 60 miles (96 kilometers) out of town and offers heated viewing areas where you can watch for the lights all night long.

- Ask for a **wake-up call.** Most hotels under the **"aurora oval"** (the latitude at which the aurora shines overhead) will happily let you know if the aurora comes out. You can also check the University of Alaska Fairbanks Geophysical Institute's aurora **forecast** (www.gi.alaska.edu/auroraforecast).

## IDITAROD

https://iditarod.com; Mar.

The 1,000-mile (1,609-kilometer) Iditarod sled dog race from Willow to Nome—arguably Alaska's most famous winter event—draws competitors from across the nation and the world. This race actually starts twice. The real race starts in **Willow** on Sunday of the first full weekend in March. The day before, however, there's a carnival-like ceremonial start in **Anchorage.** Teams start downtown and run 11 miles (17 kilometers) through town on a mix of city streets, multiuse trails, and dedicated mushing trails. Each team carries an "Iditarider"—a passenger in the sled—and the mushers often dress in costumes, fly flags that announce their country of origin, and throw dog booties or candy to children along the route. Bring a folding camp chair and get there early to stake out the best viewing spots.

It's impossible to predict exactly when the front-runners will finish, but for the last couple of decades, the winner has reached **Nome** in eight or nine days. The current record for fastest finish is 8 days, 3 hours, 40 minutes, and 13 seconds, set by Mitch Seavey in 2017.

# BEST FOOD

## SEAFOOD

If there's a single defining cuisine in Alaska, it's seafood. The sort of fresh, wild-caught seafood that people pay high prices for in the Lower 48 is downright commonplace here, and you'd be hard-pressed to find a restaurant that can't serve at least one excellent seafood dish during the summer. Popular items include crab (king, snow, and Dungeness) and salmon.

- **Tracy's King Crab Shack** (300 S. Franklin St., Juneau; 907/723-1811; http://kingcrabshack.com) offers king crab by the leg and an award-winning crab bisque.

# BEST SOUVENIRS

One of the best souvenirs you can back with you from Alaska is a piece of authentic **Alaska Native artwork.** The trick is making sure you're not bringing home something mass produced, or an imitation. Look for the **Silver Hand sticker** or tag, which signifies that the artist is in fact Alaska native, or the **Made in Alaska sticker,** which means that the product was made or assembled in the state. A few great places to buy beautiful, traditional Alaska Native artwork are the **Alaska Native Heritage Center** and the **Southeast Alaska Indian Cultural Center.**

- **Alaska Salmon Bake in Pioneer Park** (2300 Airport Way, Fairbanks; 907/452-7274 or 800/354-7274; www.akvisit.com) is an all-you-can-eat seafood feast with king salmon, beer-battered cod, and an optional add-on of Alaskan snow crab.

- **Louie's Restaurant** (Uptown Motel, 47 Spur View Dr., Soldotna; 907/283-3660; www.louiessteakandseafood.com), located in a town 75 miles (120 kilometers) north of Homer, cooks up great freshly caught seafood. If you've never had a salmon steak before (a thick slab of meat cut crosswise through the body of the salmon, instead of filleted along its length), this is the place to try it.

## THAI FOOD IN FAIRBANKS

Nobody knows exactly why, but the Interior town of Fairbanks, with around 32,000 people has about 20 Thai restaurants, all of them successful, and doesn't seem to have hit the saturation point yet. The three most popular are **Pad Thai** (3400 College Rd.; 907/479-1251; www.padthai907.com), **Thai House** (412 5th Ave.; 907/452-6123; thaihousefairbanks.com); and **Lemongrass** (388 Old Chena Pump Rd.; 907/456-2200; www.lemongrassalaska.com).

# MAJOR AIRPORTS

- **Ted Stevens Anchorage International Airport:** ANC; 5000 W International Airport Rd.; http://dot.state.ak.us/anc

- **Fairbanks International Airport:** FAI; 6450 Airport Way; www.dot.state.ak.us/faiiap

- **Juneau International Airport:** JNU; 1873 Shell Simmons Dr.; https://beta.juneau.org/airport

# MORE INFORMATION

## TRAVEL AND TOURISM INFORMATION

- **Alaska Travel Advice:** www.alaska.org

- **The Milepost:** https://themilepost.com

- **Alaska State Parks:** http://dnr.alaska.gov/parks

## NEWSPAPERS

- *Anchorage Daily News:* https://adn.com

# WASHINGTON

From towering Mount Rainier to the rain-soaked Olympic Peninsula, from cool alpine lakes to the to the shores of the Pacific Ocean, mountains and water make up the essence of Washington State, which is located on lands shared among 36 Native American tribes. The state has other worthy allures—charming towns, exceptional food and wine, world-class cultural institutions, and Seattle, its forward-thinking capital city—but you haven't made the most of your visit until you've been up on a mountainside (whether you get there by car or bike, or on foot) and out on the water (by ferry, kayak, or whale-watching cruise).

Of course, in the western part of the state the water is bound to find you whether you like it or not. There are two ways to contend with the notorious rainfall. You can either embrace it like a local—bring your waterproof shoes and hat and go about your business—or come in the summer, when the clouds disappear, the temperatures remain mild, and the place feels a lot like Eden.

AREA: 71,362 square miles / 184,827 square kilometers (18th)

POPULATION: 7,615,000 (13th)

STATEHOOD DATE: November 11, 1889 (42nd)

STATE CAPITAL: Olympia

▲ HURRICANE RIDGE IN OLYMPIC NATIONAL PARK

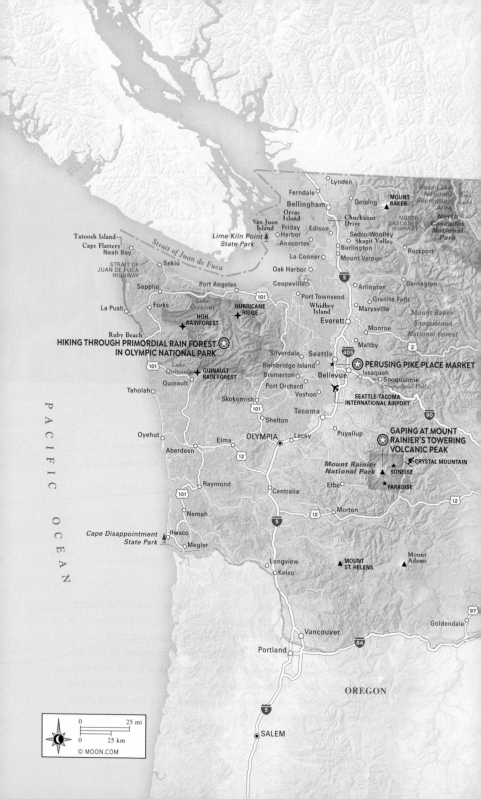

# WASHINGTON

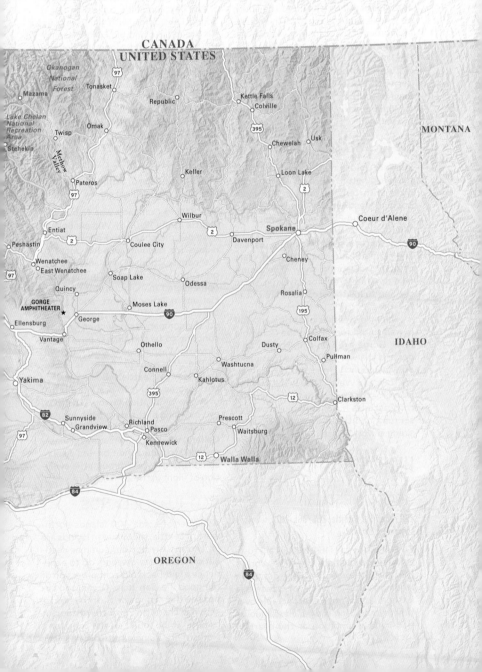

BRITISH
COLUMBIA

CANADA
UNITED STATES

MONTANA

Okanogan
National
Forest

Mazama

Tonasket

97

Republic

Kettle Falls
Colville

Lake Chelan
National
Recreation
Area

Twisp

Omak

395

Chewelah

Usk

Stehekin

Methow
Valley

Pateros

Keller

Loon Lake

97

2

Wilbur

Spokane

Coeur d'Alene

Peshastin

Entiat

2

Coulee City

2

Davenport

90

Wenatchee
East Wenatchee

Soap Lake

Odessa

Cheney

97

Quincy

Moses Lake

90

Rosalia

GORGE
AMPHITHEATER

George

195

Ellensburg

Vantage

Othello

Dusty

Colfax

IDAHO

Yakima

Connell

Washtucna

Pullman

395

Kahlotus

12

Clarkston

82

Sunnyside

Richland

Prescott

97

Grandview

Pasco

Waitsburg

Kennewick

12

Walla Walla

84

OREGON

84

## ORIENTATION

Washington's major metropolis of **Seattle** is tucked between the **Olympic Peninsula** to the west and the **Cascade** mountain range to the east. The U.S.-Canada border is about three hours north of Seattle. **Mount Rainier** and **Mount St. Helens** lie to the south of Seattle, and the much of the southern border of the state is marked by the **Columbia River.** East of the Cascades, the landscape changes to mostly desert, with **Spokane** sitting near the border with Idaho. East of the Columbia River in southern Washington are **Walla Walla** and the wine-producing **Yakima Valley.**

## WHEN TO GO

**Summer** (mid-June-Sept.) is prime time for Washington. The days are long and clear, with temperatures in the most popular destinations rarely climbing above the mid-80s. Summer is also the time when all of nature seems to be open for business. Mountain passes and high-altitude hiking trails are clear of their last spring snow. The sunny, mild days are great for kayaking. Up in the San Juans the orca pods are out in full force.

The mild weather of **spring** and **fall** is well suited for visiting the Columbia River Gorge area on the Oregon border and the warmer regions that make up wine country, from the Yakima Valley to Walla Walla. They won't be mistaken for the Rockies, but come **winter,** the Cascades have numerous downhill ski runs, and the state's cross-country skiing is world-class.

# HIGHLIGHTS

## SPACE NEEDLE

400 Broad St., Seattle; 206/905-2100; www.spaceneedle.com

The 605-foot-tall (184-meter-tall) tower that was built for the 1962 World's Fair has become Seattle's definitive landmark. It's a piece of space-age kitsch that has grown respectable over time, symbolizing the guileless, innovation-minded ambition at the heart of some of Seattle's greatest successes, from software to grunge rock.

Experiencing the Space Needle means taking the 41-second elevator ride up to the 520-foot-high (158-meter) observation deck. As you walk around the outdoor deck you can see the towers of downtown; the docks of Elliott Bay and ships traversing Puget Sound; Lake Union, with glimpses of little Green Lake and big Lake Washington beyond it; and, along the horizon, the Olympic and Cascade mountain ranges, dominated by majestic Mount Rainier. The deck is open until midnight, and the nighttime view has the romantic allure of a landscape covered in twinkling lights. For the best of both worlds, come at sunset.

## MUSEUM OF FLIGHT

9404 E. Marginal Way S, Seattle; 206/764-5720; www.museumofflight.org

The Boeing Company was founded in Seattle in the 1910s by William Boeing, a timber merchant who applied techniques for building wooden boats to the construction of airplanes. Boeing grew into a world leader in the development and manufacture of commercial and military aircraft, and though the corporate offices are now in Chicago, the company's production facilities continue to be the largest private employer in Washington State.

The Museum of Flight is closely linked to Seattle's Boeing legacy but goes beyond it to present a broad overview of aviation history. The most eye-catching of the six exhibition spaces is the glass-walled, light-filled **Great Gallery,** which has 39 historic planes—restored to mint condition—on display, constituting a walk through the evolution of flight in the 20th century.

## SAN JUAN ISLANDS

A cluster of some 400 islands northwest of Seattle, the San Juan Islands are an enormously popular summer destination where city dwellers go to experience a laid-back, old-school version of the good life. **San Juan, Orcas,** and **Lopez** see the vast majority of the tourist activity. There isn't a chain restaurant or hotel to be found on the San Juans. Nor is there a single traffic light. Many

SNOQUALMIE FALLS

lodgings consider it a point of pride not to have TVs or telephones in their guest rooms. Ferries (206/464-6400; www.wsdot.wa.gov/Ferries) to the San Juans depart from **Anacortes;** ferry and accommodations reservations are essential in the summer.

Whale-watching is one of the most popular and distinctive activities in the San Juans. Three resident orca pods, comprising about 80 whales, make the area waters their summer home. The staff at the **Whale Museum** (62 1st St., San Juan Island; 360/378-4710, ext. 30; www.whalemuseum.org) recommends that visitors watch from shore, which has the double advantage of costing nothing and not disturbing the animals. The best viewing points are **Lime Kiln Point State Park** and the **American Camp** in **San Juan Island National Historical Park,** both which have broad vistas overlooking the Haro Strait where the whales often feed. If you choose to take a tour, the museum strongly encourages using an operator that's a member of the **Pacific Whale Watch Association** (www.pacificwhalewatchassociation.com) and adheres to federal regulations, which dictate that boats remain at least 200 yards (182 meters) from the whales and stay out of their line of travel.

## SNOQUALMIE FALLS

6501 Railroad Ave., Snoqualmie

A mile (1.6 kilometers) north of downtown Snoqualmie, east of Seattle, massive Snoqualmie Falls plunges 270 feet (82 meters)—a hundred feet (30 meters) farther than Niagara. It's Washington's most famous waterfall, attracting some 1.5 million visitors annually, and identifiable from the opening credits of TV show **Twin Peaks.** A paved, wheelchair-accessible path leads less than 100 yards (91 meters) from the parking lot to the upper viewing platform. A wide, sometimes steep 0.7-mile (1.1-kilometer) trail leads down to another viewing area at the base of the falls. Once you're down there it's impossible to miss the massive workings of a power plant, built along the river in 1910. Back up at the parking lot, there's a gift shop and espresso stand, and you're right next door to the **Salish Lodge,** known as the Great Northern Hotel to **Twin Peaks** fans, where you can have an indulgent meal or spend the night.

## MOUNT ST. HELENS

Visitors come to Mount Rainier to revel in nature's tremendous beauty. They come to Mount St. Helens to marvel

# TOP 3

## 1 GAPING AT MOUNT RAINIER'S TOWERING VOLCANIC PEAK

360/569-6575; www.nps.gov/mora

Mount Rainier is the most impressive geographical landmark in the Pacific Northwest. With an elevation of 14,410 feet (4,392 meters), it's the tallest peak in the row of volcanic mountains stretching from California to Canada that make up the Cascade Range. It has the fifth-highest elevation of any mountain in America's Lower 48 states, and it's by far the most topographically prominent. That means, in layman's terms, that it has the greatest rise in elevation from its base—over 3,000 feet (914 meters) higher than the second peak on the list, California's Mount Whitney. It's also the most heavily glaciated, with 25 glaciers covering 35 square miles (90 square kilometers), giving it a stately white cap.

SUMMER WILDFLOWERS AT MOUNT RAINIER NATIONAL PARK

The sheer size of Mount Rainier can take your breath away. On land, the white peak is visible all the way from Oregon and Canada. Throughout much of Washington it dominates the horizon. Seattleites even celebrate clear, sunny weather by saying, "The mountain is out today."

Mount Rainier National Park exhibits abundant and varied natural beauty—old-growth forests, waterfalls, alpine lakes, fields of brilliant wildflowers—but one of the main reasons to visit is to ramp up that level of awe the peak inspires. When you're at the **Paradise** and **Sunrise** areas—the two highest points in the park reachable by car—the towering summit feels just beyond your grasp, despite the fact that it's still 8,000-9,000 feet (2,430-2,740 meters) above you. Both areas have visitor centers from which ranger-led nature walks depart daily in summer. Note the Sunrise area is open only in summer.

## 2 PERUSING PIKE PLACE MARKET

Pike Pl. between Pike St. and Virginia St., Seattle; 206/682-7453; www.pikeplacemarket.org

Pike Place Market is Seattle's most charming and enduring landmark. Over the course of a century, what started as a produce market has evolved into a warren of shops and stands supplying the city with not just vegetables but also fresh fish, meat, and flowers, as well as specialty foods, snacks, and souvenirs. Though it can feel like a movie set, it's still the real deal. The produce, fish, meat, and flowers available are of high quality, the prepared foods are delicious and diverse, and quirky, one-of-a-kind shops are tucked away in the more remote corners.

The market is bigger than it appears at first glance. It consists of 22 buildings covering about 10 acres (4 hectares). All told there are some 250 stores, 100 fruit and vegetable stands, 200 craft vendors, and 30 restaurants. (Though fish is central to the market's identity, there are only four fresh-seafood retailers.) The epicenter is beneath the big neon **Public Market sign** and clock in the **Main Arcade,** at the point where Pike Street meets Pike Place. Under the sign you'll find **Rachel the Pig,** the market's bronze mascot, and about 100 feet (30 meters) up Pike Street near the corner of 1st Avenue is the **market information booth,** where you can get

PIKE PLACE MARKET

a map and a list of merchants. Some areas of the market, including the **Main Arcade** and **North Arcade,** are busier than others. Likely there's a line out the door at the **original Starbucks.** To find more elbow room, take the ramp to the floors below, known as the **Down Under,** where quirky retail shops sell, among other things, art, antiques, comic books, and model cars.

 ## HIKING THROUGH PRIMORDIAL RAIN FOREST IN OLYMPIC NATIONAL PARK

www.nps.gov/olym

The Olympic Peninsula feels like God's terrarium: perpetually damp and mind-blowingly fertile, with trees as tall as skyscrapers. The region is so lush, it feels like if you took a nap by the side of the trail, you'd wake up covered in moss.

The **Hoh Rain Forest** is the most popular place to explore the peninsula's lush environment, but **Quinault Rain Forest,** located around Lake Quinault in the western section of the peninsula's Olympic National Park, is just as impressive. Easy trails include the 0.8-mile (1.28-kilometer) **Hall of Mosses Trail** starting from the Hoh Rain Forest Visitor Center and the 0.5-mile (0.8-kilometer) **Rain Forest Nature Trail** on the south side of Lake Quinault.

PATH THROUGH QUINAULT RAIN FOREST

# *Best* ROAD TRIP

**DAY 1** Head to the impressive **Museum of Flight** to the south of the central Seattle on your way into town from Sea-Tac airport, then enjoy a meal in the city.

**DAY 2** Seattle is a big, dynamic city with enough historical and cultural attractions to keep you busy for a month. Get the classic sightseeing experience by visiting **Pike Place Market** and the **Space Needle**.

**DAY 3** From Seattle a 2-hour drive will get you to the White River entrance at the northeast corner of **Mount Rainier National Park**. A pretty, winding road climbs to the **Sunrise** area, the highest point on the mountain accessible by car. In the late afternoon drive to the **Crystal Mountain** (33818 Crystal Mountain Blvd.; 360/663-2262; www.crystalhotels.com) ski resort, where you'll be spending the night.

**DAY 4** Head back into the park and make the drive around to the other side of the mountain, stopping along the way for a short hike on the **Grove of the Patriarchs Trail** (just west of the Stevens Canyon entrance station), which is like a museum of old-growth trees. The road west from there is another gorgeous drive, eventually climbing to the **Paradise** area, where there's an impressive visitors center and a classic cedar lodge. Have dinner at the **Paradise Inn,** located within the national park. You can bed down there, too (reservation essential).

**DAY 5** It's a 3-hour drive to **Lake Quinault,** located at the southern end of **Olympic National Park**. The **Quinault Rain Forest** surrounding the lake is home to some of the tallest trees in the world, several of which are easily accessible on short roadside trails. For your overnight stay you have the option of a national park lodge on the lake or one of several modest hotels in the area.

SEATTLE'S SPACE NEEDLE

SUNRISE AREA OF MOUNT RAINIER NATIONAL PARK

DECEPTION PASS BRIDGE

**DAY 6** It's a 45-minute drive to **Ruby Beach,** a classic example of Washington's misty, pebble-strewn coastline, studded with haystacks (giant rock formations). From here, U.S. 101 heads back inland and turns north; after a 75-minute drive you reach glacier-carved **Lake Crescent,** the most beautiful lake in the state. Stay in the national park lodge here, or get a jump on the next day's driving by heading east another half hour to **Port Angeles.**

**DAY 7** In the morning, head up to the only part of the Olympic Mountains accessible by car: **Hurricane Ridge,** an hour's drive from Lake Crescent or 35 minutes from Port Angeles. Fields filled with wildflowers offer vast vistas of the Strait of Juan de Fuca and the neighboring Olympic peaks. Then, come back down to sea level on the 90-minute drive to the charming town of **Port Townsend** at the northeast corner of the peninsula. You'll find lots of good dining options here. From Port Townsend take the 35-minute ferry ride (206/464-6400; www.wsdot.wa.gov/Ferries) to **Whidbey Island.** (You can reserve a place on the ferry.) Spend the night in the old fishing town of **Coupeville.**

**DAY 8** Drive north from Coupeville and over the picturesque bridge at **Deception Pass** to the town of **Anacortes,** a 45-minute trip, and catch the ferry to **San Juan Island.** The 75-minute cruise through the archipelago is a beautiful way to get into the San Juans state of mind. On San Juan Island, **American Camp** and **Lime Kiln Point State Park** are good spots for whale-watching from the shore. Spend a quiet night on the island.

**DAY 9** Take an early afternoon ferry back to Anacortes. If traffic is clear it's about a 3-hour trip from there back to Seattle.

at nature's tremendous destructive power.

On May 18, 1980, Mount St. Helens, after sitting dormant for more than a century, erupted, sending ash 15 miles (24 kilometers) into the sky and triggering the largest landslide in recorded history. The impact was like a blitz of atomic bombs, and the devastation was total. In one day the volcano lost 1,300 feet (396 meters) in elevation. Today, decades after the eruption, St. Helens and the surrounding area are still in the early stage of recovery.

**Johnston Ridge Observatory** (24000 Spirit Lake Hwy., Toutle; 360/274-2140; www.fs.usda.gov/mountsthelens), named for Dr. David Johnston, a geologist who died in the eruption, has a prime location looking directly into the crater and the moonscape-like desolation that surrounds it. Inside the observatory are first-rate exhibits, including a model of the volcano that shows how the eruption progressed. A large theater shows two short, engaging films. Every visitor should plan to see at least one.

## HURRICANE RIDGE

Olympic National Park; 360/565-3130; www. nps.gov/olym

One of Olympic National Park's most scenic and visited areas, Hurricane Ridge towers 5,200 feet (1,585 meters) over the Strait of Juan de Fuca. Eight day hikes begin from the **Hurricane Ridge Visitor Center,** ranging from short, paved paths to 8-mile (12.8-kilometer) descents into the neighboring valleys. But even if you never set foot on a trail, it's worth the trip up just for the views of the snowcapped peaks from the visitor center observation deck. This is also an easy place to have wildlife encounters. Black-tailed deer frequently meander down to the parking lot, and you might spot a marmot along the quarter-mile (0.4-kilometer) meadow path adjacent to the visitors center.

Hurricane Ridge Road and the visitors center are open daily mid-May-mid-October and Friday-Sunday the rest of the year, so long as the road up is passable. In winter, to find out if the road is open, call 360/565-3131.

KAYAKING ON LAKE CRESCENT

## LAKE CRESCENT

Olympic National Park; 360/565-3130; www.nps.gov/olym

Lake Crescent is the place to go if you're looking for beauty and tranquility in Olympic National Park without having to rough it. The glacier-carved lake is gorgeous, 12 miles (19 kilometers) long and over 600 feet (182 meters) deep, surrounded by old-growth forest that ascends steep ridges to the horizon. The water is translucent turquoise green, made clear by a lack of nitrogen, which inhibits the growth of microalgae. At points along the lake's surface you can see down to a depth of 60 feet (18 meters).

The view from the water's edge is reason enough to pay Lake Crescent a visit. If you spend some time here you can get out on the water in kayaks, rowboats, and paddleboards, which are available to rent; you can fish; and though the water is cold, you can swim in summer.

## CAPE FLATTERY

Cape Flattery marks the northwesternmost point of the contiguous United States. A visit here is more than a novelty—it's also an opportunity to hike one of the most scenic short trails (0.75 miles/1.2 kilometers) in the state. An undulating path, made easier to navigate by cedar boardwalks, goes through old-growth Sitka spruce, with vibrant green ferns carpeting the sun-dappled forest floor, and takes you out onto the cape, where there are coves to either side. From observation platforms, you can look down on the waters of the Pacific crashing around sea stacks and into caves. The woods and surrounding waters teem with life, from swifts, loons, puffins, and cormorants to seals, otters, sea lions, and, in spring, gray whales. At the end of the trail an observation deck gives you a view half a mile (0.8 kilometers) out to Tatoosh Island, where a lighthouse, built in 1857 and now unmanned, still stands. To your left is the Pacific, to your right the entrance of the Strait of Juan de Fuca, and behind you all of America.

## STEHEKIN

The isolated hamlet of Stehekin (steh-HEE-kin) sits at the northwest end of **Lake Chelan,** where it can be reached only by boat, foot, or private plane. It's a beautiful place that feels removed from the rest of the world. The town is also a launching point for treks into the heart of the **North Cascades National Park Complex,** which includes North Cascades National Park and Ross Lake and Lake Chelan National Recreation Areas.

The name Stehekin (an Indian term meaning "the way through") is a good fit for this mountain gateway. The town came into existence in the late 1880s when prospectors arrived in search of gold and silver. They didn't find enough to establish a large mine, and as a result there wasn't the impetus to connect Stehekin to the outside world by road. Today it's home to fewer than 100 permanent residents, but it has all the basics, including a post office, convenience store, restaurant, and grade school, as well as a bakery and an outdoor supply shop that operate only in summer.

A couple of historic sites are part of the Stehekin experience. Three and a half miles (5.6 kilometers) up the main road you'll encounter the **Old Stehekin Schoolhouse,** a character-rich log building that functioned as Stehekin's school from 1921 to 1988. A side road near the schoolhouse leads to **Buckner**

# *Major* CITIES

**SEATTLE:** Washington's major metropolis has a uniquely Pacific Northwest take on city life. In the booming, bustling urban core, historic Pioneer Square and Pike Place Market overlook Puget Sound, and the Space Needle offers panoramas of the city. Surrounding the city center is a cluster of laid-back residential neighborhoods studded with cultural attractions and an exceptional collection of urban parks. The city also boasts some of the country's best restaurants.

**SPOKANE:** Located near the Idaho border, Washington's second-largest city feels as much a part of the Rockies as the Pacific Northwest. It has the friendly, laid-back atmosphere of an overgrown town, with an easily walkable downtown surrounded by quiet residential neighborhoods and, beyond that, the vast countryside.

**TACOMA:** Washington's third-largest city is located 30 miles (48 kilometers) south of Seattle. Once known for its paper mills (most of which have closed) the city now boasts an impressive collection of museums, a revitalized downtown, and a lively theater district.

---

**Homestead and Orchard** (http://bucknerhomestead.org), where 15 structures, the oldest dating from 1889, sit in the midst of an apple orchard that still bears fruit. The Stehekin area and its rustic resorts are also popular with hikers of all levels, with trails running along the water and up into the mountains.

**Lake Chelan Boat Company** (1418 W. Woodin Ave., Chelan; 509/682-4584; http://ladyofthelake.com) has two boats that make the 50-mile (80-kilometer) voyage between Chelan and Stehekin: the 285-passenger **Lady of the Lake II,** which makes the trip in 4 hours, and the 130-passenger **Lady Express,** which gets there in 2.5 hours.

## GORGE AMPHITHEATER

754 Silica Rd., George; 509/785-6262; www.gorgeamphitheatre.net

Located along the Columbia River Gorge, the stunning Gorge Amphitheatre is Washington's premier performance venue. It's worth the effort to get here. The outdoor amphitheater overlooking the river canyon is a beautiful natural setting for a show, especially when enhanced by a summer sunset, and the acoustics are great. Each summer the venue, which seats 20,000, hosts music festivals and headliner rock and pop acts. Major events fill

motels as far away as Wenatchee, so reserve ahead.

# BEST SCENIC DRIVES

## MOUNTAIN LOOP HIGHWAY

About an hour north of Seattle via I-5, the Mountain Loop Highway (not to be confused with the much larger Cascade Loop) is the easiest way to get a taste of the North Cascades on a day trip from the city. The entire loop, which runs through the towns of **Granite Falls** and **Arlington** to the west and **Darrington** to the east, is 95 miles (152 kilometers) long; the main attraction is the scenic 54-mile (87-kilometer) segment on the loop's south and east sides, between Granite Falls and Darrington. This section has the scenic virtues of a hiking trail, with old-growth forest, creeks, lakes, rocky bluffs, and looming peaks all visible from your car seat. The road goes through a corner of the massive **Mount Baker-Snoqualmie National Forest,** with turnouts along the way for camping, picnic sites, and some wonderful mountain hiking trails.

Note that some sections of the drive are gravel, impassable in snow, and closed throughout winter.

# STRAIGHT OF JUAN DE FUCA HIGHWAY

## Route 112

Leaving **Port Angeles,** the Straight of Juan de Fuca Highway (Route 112) parallels the coast, passing a couple of tiny fishing villages but mainly threading through forest and skirting the shoreline. Along the highway there's no town with a population over 1,000. More seals live in this part of the strait than people. The beautiful drive includes lots of curves, especially on its western reaches. Heed the speed limit and be sure to give any logging trucks you encounter a wide berth.

The 20 miles (32 kilometers) of highway between **Sekiu** and **Neah Bay,** where the drive ends, make for one of the most dramatic shoreline drives in Washington, as the road winds along bluffs with beautiful views. About halfway between the two towns is **Shipwreck Point,** a 472-acre (191-hectare) conservation area encompassing an easily accessible beach and second-growth Douglas fir, cedar, spruce, and hemlock. It's a good place to pull over for beachcombing, as there are tide pools as well as views across the strait to Vancouver Island, and the possibility of spotting migrating whales offshore. Farther along the highway, just outside the border of the Makah Indian Reservation, look for **Salt and Sail Rocks,** two sea stacks jutting out from the water. They're favorite places for gray whales to feed.

WILDCAT COVE ALONG CHUCKANUT DRIVE

# CHUCKANUT DRIVE

### Route 11 between Burlington and Bellingham

Heading north up the coast from the Skagit Valley, you enter one of the most scenic stretches of highway in the state—Chuckanut Drive. This 21-mile (33-kilometer) section of Route 11 was built as part of the now-defunct Pacific Highway that once stretched along the coastline from Canada to California. It leaves I-5 just north of **Burlington** on an arrow-straight path across the valley. If you're making the drive from south to north, the first point of interest is the town of **Edison,** a 2.5-mile (4-kilometer) detour west off the highway. Just a few blocks long, it's become a haven for artists and other creatives. Get out of your car to look around at shops, galleries, and restaurants in this fun and novel place.

A short distance north from the Edison turnoff the highway runs headlong into the **Chuckanut Mountains,** which hover over Puget Sound. This is where the memorable driving begins. The road doesn't have a straight stretch for 7 miles (11 kilometers) as it swoops and swerves along the bluffs above the water. Much of the way you're surrounded by woods, but there are scenic turnouts and other breaks between the trees where you can take in grand views across the water to Anacortes, Guemes Island, and, farther north, the San Juans. Ultimately the road winds up in Fairhaven, a pleasant old section of **Bellingham.**

# NORTH CASCADES HIGHWAY

### Route 20 between Burlington and Mazama

Driving through the **North Cascades National Park Complex** is a popular tourist activity, largely because most of it is accessible only on foot or by boat. The portion of Route 20 running between **Burlington** to the west and **Mazama** to the east is known as the North Cascades Highway, and it's the only road crossing the park. At its western end, it follows the Skagit River through flat farmland, but you can see your craggy destination in front of you—the sawtooth peaks of the North Cascades.

As the North Cascades Highway climbs into the park area it becomes a

NORTH CASCADES HIGHWAY

spectacular scenic drive through the heart of the northern Cascades range. One hundred and twenty miles (193 kilometers) later you'll find yourself on the other side, having navigated the beautiful curves of the well-maintained highway up through the North Cascades National Park Complex, into the Okanogan National Forest, over 5,477-foot (1,669-meter) Washington Pass, and down to the Methow Valley.

Note that this is a seasonal trip. When there's a risk of avalanches, usually November-April, the road closes from Ross Dam to the eastern side of Washington Pass.

# BEST PARKS AND RECREATION AREAS

Washington is a veritable outdoor playground. In addition to three national parks—**Mt. Rainier, Olympic,** and **North Cascades,** which is most commonly explored via a drive on the North Cascades Highway—state parks and other recreation areas show off the diversity of the terrain, which stretches from the orca-inhabited Pacific to Cascade mountain peaks.

## LIME KILN POINT STATE PARK

1567 West Side Rd., San Juan Island; 360/378-2044; http://parks.state.wa.us/540/Lime-Kiln-Point

Lime Kiln Point State Park, on San Juan Island, has 1.5 miles (2.4 kilometers) of trails that take you along the rocky bluffs above Haro Strait, through stands of madrona trees (recognizable by their tawny peeling bark), past a postcard-worthy lighthouse, and to the hulking abandoned kiln that gives the park its name. The easy trail is also the best on-land location for spotting orcas in the San Juans. There are several **whale-watching lookout points** along the trail, and the lighthouse serves as a viewing station for statisticians recording the traffic of both orcas and boats. Stick your head in the door and they'll be happy to tell you about recent sightings and show off the orca version of a family photo album. Even if you don't see any whales, you'll still get a beautiful view across the strait to Vancouver Island.

## CAPE DISAPPOINTMENT STATE PARK

44 Robert Gray Dr., Ilwaco; 360/642-3078; http://parks.state.wa.us/486; Discover Pass required for parking

The 1,882-acre (761-hectare) Cape Disappointment State Park, where the mighty Columbia River crashes into the Pacific, is one of the jewels of the Washington State Park System. You'll find wooded trails, sandy coves, dramatic vistas of the Pacific and the mouth of the Columbia, the **Lewis and Clark Interpretive Center** (360/642-3029; http://parks.state.wa.us/187), two historic lighthouses, good fishing, and campsites, yurts, and cabins for overnight stays.

## MOUNT BAKER AND HEATHER MEADOWS

If it weren't for Mount Rainier, Mount Baker (the northernmost of the Cascade volcanoes), would be Washington's iconic peak, and the area around it is a prime location for outdoor recreational activities.

Originating in Bellingham, the incredibly scenic **Mount Baker Highway** (Route 542) ends 57 miles (91 kilometers) away at 5,140-foot (1,566-meter) **Artist Point.** It's the only alpine area in the North Cascades accessible by car, and the surrounding area, **Heather Meadows,** delivers incredible vistas, enjoyable picnic sites, and a multitude of hiking trails to explore in late summer, from the easy mile-long (1.6-kilometer) **Artist Ridge Trail,** with views to Mount Rainier on clear days, to the **Lake Ann Trail,** an 8.5-mile (13.6-kilometer) round-trip above one of the Cascades' most beautiful high-country lakes. At the handsome stone **Heather Meadows Visitor Center** (no phone, July-Sept.), built in 1940, rangers provide information and advice.

ARTIST POINT, MOUNT BAKER HIGHWAY

# FESTIVALS AND EVENTS

## SKAGIT VALLEY TULIP FESTIVAL

www.tulipfestival.org; Apr.

Spring brings blooming flowers to the Skagit Valley, north of Seattle—especially notable during the Skagit Valley Tulip Festival, which takes place throughout the month of April. Get a glimpse of the beautiful fields of flowers simply by crisscrossing the country roads between Mount Vernon and La Conner. There's also a full calendar of events, with Washington Bulb Company's **RoozenGaarde** (15867 Beaver Marsh Rd., Mount Vernon; 360/424-8531; www.tulips.com) and Skagit Valley Bulb Farm's **Tulip Town** (15002 Bradshaw Rd.; 360/424-8152; www.tuliptown.com) hubs of activity. **Tip:** Though the festival spans all of April, the fields are usually more spectacular earlier in the month. If you want to see flowers without the festival trappings, come during the last week of March, when early blooms pop into view.

# BEST FOOD AND DRINK

## SEATTLE'S CHEF-DRIVEN CUISINE

According to Charles Cross, iconic Seattle journalist and biographer of Kurt Cobain, "Food has become the new rock and roll in Seattle. Our chefs are

SKAGIT VALLEY TULIP FESTIVAL

the current grunge stars." It's true. In restaurant kitchens all over the city, young tattooed chefs prepare inventive, meticulously executed meals. The most successful have built multirestaurant mini-empires that boldly encompass a variety of cuisines. Below are some of these top chefs' most notable restaurants. Check their websites for others.

- **Tom Douglas** (www.tomdouglas.com): **Dahlia Lounge;** 2001 4th Ave.; 206/682-4142; www.dahlialounge.com

- **Ethan Stowell** (www.ethanstowellrestaurants.com): **How to Cook a Wolf;** 2208 Queen Anne Ave. N; 206/838-8090

- **Renee Erickson** (www.eatseacreatures.com): **The Walrus and the Carpenter;** 4739 Ballard Ave. NW; 206/395-9227; www.thewalrusbar.com

## COFFEE

Maybe it's the cloudy weather, short winter days, or long hours put in by many tech workers; whatever the reason, there's more coffee consumption—and more coffee shops—in Seattle than any other U.S. city. A place exists to fit every mood, from homey to high-tech, laid-back to obsessively exacting. Standout shops include **La Marzocco Cafe & Showroom** (472 1st Ave. N; 206/388-3500; www.lamarzoccousa.com), located in the performance space of KEXP, Seattle's iconic indie radio station, and **Caffè Ladro** (www.caffeladro.com), a local favorite with eight locations.

## WALLA WALLA WINERIES

With pedestrian-friendly, tree-lined streets, cute locally owned shops, and an abundance of inventive restaurants, Walla Walla is unquestionably Washington wine country's most tourist-friendly town. There are more than 100 wineries in and around town to choose from, but what makes tasting here particularly enjoyable is the wide range of experiences you can have. Some, such as **Mark Ryan Winery** (26 E. Main St.; 509/876-4577;

www.markryanwinery.com) and **Maison Bleue** (20 N. 2nd Ave.; 509/525-9084; www.mbwinery.com) have boutique-like tasting rooms downtown, while others are set in vineyards with views of the Blue Mountains on the horizon. There's also a group of about 20 wineries, including **Dunham Cellars** (150 E. Boeing Ave.; 509/529-4685) and **Tamarack Cellars** (700 C St.; 509/526-3533; http://tamarackcellars.com), that occupy the grounds of Walla Walla's old World War II-era military airport, which makes for a novel touring destination. No matter the atmosphere, the wine you're sampling is likely to be good. The bar for quality is set high here.

Pick up a downtown walking-tour map at the **Walla Walla Visitors Kiosk** (26 E. Main St.; 509/525-8799; www.wallawalla.org; May-Sept.). You can also learn a lot by discussing the subject with locals. Hotel clerks, restaurant servers, bartenders—everyone has a favorite winery.

# MAJOR AIRPORTS

- **Seattle-Tacoma International Airport (Sea-Tac):** SEA; 800/544-1965 or 206/787-5388; www.portseattle.org/sea-tac

# MORE INFORMATION

## TRAVEL AND TOURISM INFORMATION

- **Washington Tourism Alliance:** www.experiencewa.com
- **Washington State Parks & Recreation Commission:** http://parks.state.wa.us

## NEWSPAPERS AND MAGAZINES

- *The Seattle Times:* http://seattletimes.com
- *Seattle Magazine:* www.seattlemag.com
- *Seattle Met:* www.seattlemet.com

# OREGON

Truly epic in its breadth, Oregon's landscape is diverse and dramatic. A broad deep-green swath, lush with farmland and studded with old-growth Douglas firs, runs between the rugged Pacific coast and the volcanic peaks of the Cascades. Farther east, you'll find high desert, mountains, and deep river canyons—spectacular country that's largely unexplored by visitors.

**AREA:** 98,381 square miles / 254,805 square kilometers (9th)

**POPULATION:** 4,217,737 (27th)

**STATEHOOD DATE:** February 14, 1859 (33rd)

**STATE CAPITAL:** Salem

But Oregon is much more than a scenic abstraction. The state is on the traditional lands of the Burns Paiute, Chinook, Clatsop-Nehalem, Coos, Lower Umpqua, Siuslaw, Coquille, Cow Creek Band of Umpqua, Fort McDermitt Paiute, Shoshone, Grand Ronde, Klamath, Siletz, Umatilla, and Warm Springs people. In few places has human civilization meshed so agreeably with the natural environment. Oregonians are fiercely proud of their state, its culture, and its open spaces. Equal to the great outdoors, the arts are cherished and draw crowds by the multitudes. The state also celebrates its historical heritage, ethnic makeup, and straightforward high spirits with a thousand festivals.

ECOLA STATE PARK, OREGON

## ORIENTATION

**Portland** sits a little east of the Oregon coast, which stretches from **Astoria** in the north to **Brookings** and the California border to the south. The **Columbia River** forms much of the state's border with Washington and its gorge, along with **Mount Hood,** form a lovely outdoor recreation area east of Portland. **Ashland** and **Crater Lake National Park** anchor southern Oregon. The state capital of **Salem** and **Eugene** lie in the **Willamette Valley** in almost a straight line south of Portland. The **Oregon Cascades** sit to the east of the Willamette Valley in central Oregon, near **Bend,** and divide the wetter west from the drier east. The **Wallowa Mountains** are located in the state's northeastern corner, near **Hells Canyon** and the border with Idaho.

## WHEN TO GO

Although **summer** weather is usually beautiful, June can be cloudy and cool in the Willamette Valley. When the Willamette Valley heats up, the coast usually remains cool, with morning fog. **Spring** is ideal for touring eastern Oregon, unless you want to make it all the way to the top of Steens Mountain, which is usually closed by snow until early July.

**Autumn**'s first rains appear in September. Even after the rains start, remember that cloudy days with scattered rain are the norm, and that "sun breaks" are common. Although the mountainous parts of the state accumulate huge amounts of snow during the **winter,** snowfall is rare on the coast and in the western valleys. Wintertime temperatures are usually above freezing, though the dampness can make it seem colder.

# HIGHLIGHTS

## PORTLAND ART MUSEUM

1219 SW Park Ave., Portland; 503/226-2811; www.portlandartmuseum.org

The Portland Art Museum encompasses two grand structures along the South Park Blocks, the original Pietro Belluschi-designed building from 1932 and the adjacent and imposing Portland Masonic Temple, which together offer 112,000 square feet of galleries housing 42,000 objects. Dating from 1892, it's the oldest art museum on the West Coast and houses Oregon's most significant art collection, including a noteworthy Asian art collection and an excellent Pacific Northwest Native Art collection.

## INTERNATIONAL ROSE TEST GARDEN

400 SW Kingston Ave., Portland

Encompassing 4.5 acres (1.8 hectares) of roses, manicured lawns, other formal gardens, and an outdoor concert

INTERNATIONAL ROSE TEST GARDEN

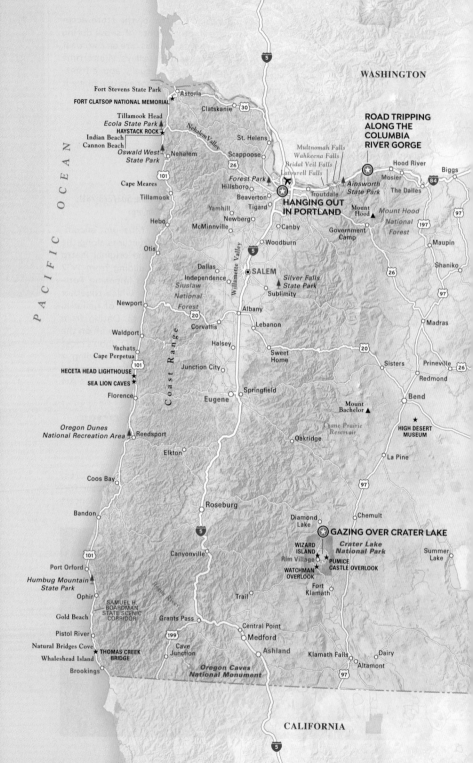

WASHINGTON

Fort Stevens State Park
**FORT CLATSOP NATIONAL MEMORIAL** ★  Astoria
Clatskanie
Tillamook Head
*Ecola State Park* ▲  St. Helens
**HAYSTACK ROCK** ★
Indian Beach  *Nehalem Valley*
Cannon Beach  Scappoose
*Oswald West*  Nehalem
*State Park* ▲

**ROAD TRIPPING
ALONG THE
COLUMBIA
RIVER GORGE**

Cape Meares

*Multnomah Falls*
*Wahkeena Falls*
*Bridal Veil Falls*
*Latourell Falls*    Hood River
Mosier    Biggs
*Forest Park* ▲  The Dalles
*Ainsworth
State Park* ▲

Tillamook
Hebo

Hillsboro
Beaverton
Tigard   Troutdale
**HANGING OUT
IN PORTLAND**

Mount
Hood ▲  *Mount Hood
National
Forest*

Yamhill
Newberg    Canby
McMinnville    Woodburn

Government
Camp

Maupin

Otis

Dallas    **SALEM**
Independence   *Silver Falls
State Park*
*Siuslaw
National
Forest*   Sublimity

Shaniko

Newport   Albany
Corvallis   Lebanon
Waldport   Halsey
Yachats   Sweet
Cape Perpetua   Home
**HECETA HEAD LIGHTHOUSE** ★   Junction City

Madras

Sisters   Prineville
Redmond

**SEA LION CAVES** ★
Florence   Springfield
Eugene   Bend

Mount
Bachelor ▲
*Oregon Dunes
National Recreation Area* ▲   Reedsport
*Crane Prairie
Reservoir*   **HIGH DESERT
MUSEUM** ★

Oakridge
Elkton   La Pine

Coos Bay

Bandon    Roseburg   Chemult

Diamond
Lake   **GAZING OVER CRATER LAKE**

Port Orford    Canyonville
**WIZARD
ISLAND** ★   *Crater Lake
National Park*
*Humbug Mountain
State Park* ▲   Rim Village ★
**WATCHMAN** ★ **PUMICE
OVERLOOK** **CASTLE OVERLOOK**

Ophir
**SAMUEL H.
BOARDMAN
STATE SCENIC
CORRIDOR**
Gold Beach   Fort
Klamath

Summer
Lake

Trail
Pistol River
Natural Bridges Cove   Grants Pass
**THOMAS CREEK
BRIDGE** ★   Central Point
Whaleshead Island   Medford
Brookings   Cave
Junction   Ashland   Klamath Falls   Dairy
Altamont
*Oregon Caves
National Monument*

*Rogue River*

CALIFORNIA

PACIFIC OCEAN

*Coast Range*

*Willamette Valley*

*Nehalem Valley*

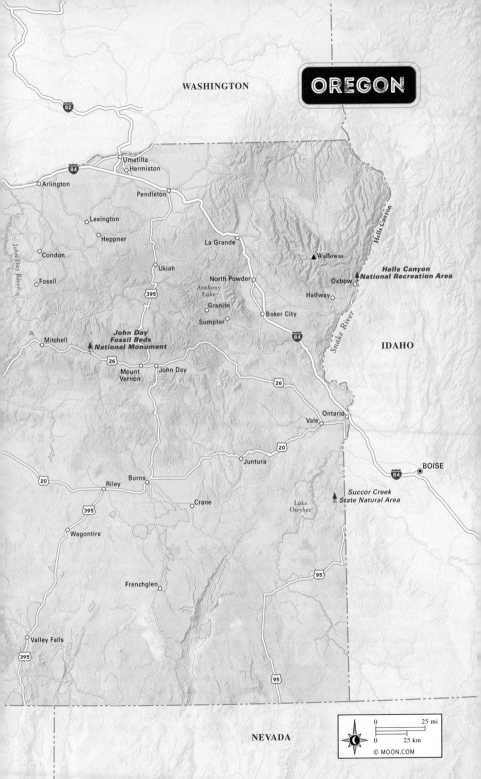

WASHINGTON

# OREGON

82

Umatilla
Hermiston
Arlington
84
Pendleton

Lexington
Heppner
La Grande

Condon
Ukiah
Wallowas
Hells Canyon
National Recreation Area

Fossil
395
North Powder
Oxbow
Halfway

*John Day River*

Anthony Lake
Granite
Baker City
84

**John Day**
**Fossil Beds**
**National Monument**
Mitchell
26
Sumpter

Mount Vernon
John Day
26

*Snake River*

**IDAHO**

Ontario
Vale
20

Juntura

20
Riley
Burns

395
Crane
*Lake Owyhee*

84
**BOISE**

Wagontire

**Succor Creek**
**State Natural Area**

Frenchglen

95

Valley Falls
395

95

**NEVADA**

0          25 mi
0          25 km

© MOON.COM

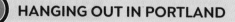

# TOP 3

## 1 HANGING OUT IN PORTLAND

This friendly, flannel-clad, rain-scrubbed city has vaulted to a new place in the popular culture firmament, becoming a major trendsetter in cuisine, wine, arts, design, and up-to-the-second lifestyles. Portland has a population of 2.4 million, but its easygoing and quirky spirit makes it feel like a much smaller town.

PEARL DISTRICT OF PORTLAND

The city is home to many unique institutions and sights worthy of your itinerary. To truly capture Portland's allure, though, you need to do some serious hanging out. Portland's pedestrian-friendly **downtown** is dotted with green spaces, museums, cafés, and bars. The **Pearl District** is an upscale shopping and dining neighborhood, home to many of the city's top galleries and restaurants. This is where you'll find **Powell's City of Books** (1005 W. Burnside St.; 503/228-0540 or 800/878-7323; www.powells.com), which takes up three stories on a whole square block. With their kick-back vibes, the southeast neighborhoods of the **Hawthorne and Belmont Districts** are good places to sip coffee and people-watch. Be sure to stop by a **craft brewpub** or two, and if you're in town on a Saturday, head to the **Portland Farmers Market** (www.portlandfarmersmarket.org). And in true Oregon fashion, hanging out often involves outdoor recreation. Portland's **Forest Park** is the largest urban wilderness in the United States, with more than 70 miles (112 kilometers) of trails.

## 2 GAZING OVER CRATER LAKE

541/594-3000; www.nps.gov/crla

High in the Cascades lies the crown jewel of Oregon: Crater Lake, the country's deepest at 1,943 feet (592 meters). It glimmers like a polished sapphire in a setting created by a volcano that blew its top and collapsed thousands of years ago. Crater Lake's extraordinary hues are produced by the depth and clarity of the water, and its ability to absorb all the colors of the spectrum except the shortest wavelengths, blue and violet, which are scattered skyward.

Begin your adventure in Crater Lake National Park by circling the lake on the 33-mile (53-kilometer) **Rim Drive** (divided into West Rim and East Rim Drives). Start with a walk along the paved path at **Rim Village**—morning views from this path are especially lovely—and then hop in the car. It's best to drive clockwise around the lake; this makes it easier to pull off at the many viewpoints. **Watchman Overlook** offers good views of **Wizard Island** and is the trailhead for **Watchman Peak,** the hike to do if you only do one. At **Pumice Castle Overlook,** you'll spot the bright-orange "castle" jutting out from the cliff wall. From another overlook, the **Phantom Ship** island looks tiny in this big lake; it's really 170 feet (51 meters) tall. If you want to reach the lake itself, there's only one way to get there: a hike down the steep 1.1-mile-long (1.7-kilometer) **Cleetwood Cove Trail.** Once you've reached the shores, you can go for a swim or take a **boat tour.**

CRATER LAKE AS VIEWED FROM THE RIM OF THE CRATER

## ROAD TRIPPING ALONG THE COLUMBIA RIVER GORGE

To Native Americans, the Columbia River Gorge was the great gathering place. To visitors today, the Columbia River's enormous canyon carved through the Cascade Mountains is one of the Pacific Northwest's most dramatic and scenic destinations. The river, over a mile (1.6 kilometers) wide, winds through a 3,000-foot-deep (914-meter) gorge flanked by volcanic peaks and austere bands of basalt. Waterfalls tumble from the mountain's edge and fall hundreds of feet to the river.

The best way to experience the area is via a drive along the **Historic Columbia River Highway;** the old highway's sections from **Troutdale** to **Ainsworth State Park** and **Mosier** to **The Dalles** attract millions of motorists annually. One worthy stop along the route is the **Vista House Visitors Center at Crown Point** (40700 E. Historic Columbia River Hwy.; 503/344-1368; www.vistahouse.com), a distinctive octagonal structure with an observation deck. As you continue driving, you'll pass many more scenic lookout points, many with trailheads where you can stretch your legs and explore. **Hood River,** an outdoorsy little town about halfway between the **Bridge of the Gods** (which crosses over the Columbia River into Washington State) and The Dalles, is a good place to stop for a meal. You'll be captivated by the many waterfalls along the roadside: Latourell Falls, Bridal Veil Falls, Wahkeena Falls, Horsetail Falls, and the most famous of them all, **Multnomah Falls.** Plunging 620 feet (188 meters), the highest drop in the state, Multnomah is one waterfall you can't miss.

CROWN POINT AND THE COLUMBIA RIVER GORGE

# *Best* ROAD TRIP

**DAY 1** Fly into **Portland International Airport.** Spend the afternoon strolling around downtown, visiting **Powell's City of Books** and the **Pearl District.** Spend the night at downtown and dine on Pacific Northwest cuisine at **Higgins.**

**DAY 2** Head northwest from Portland on U.S. 30 to **Astoria** (98 miles/157 kilometers; 2 hours). Explore this historic town at the mouth of the Columbia River, including a visit to the replica of **Fort Clatsop.** Then continue south for 25 miles (40 kilometers; 40 minutes) to **Cannon Beach,** where you'll find one of Oregon's iconic views: **Haystack Rock** rising up in the water, close to shore.

**DAY 3** Head south out of town on U.S. 101 and stop for a walk at **Oswald West State Park,** where you can follow a short trail through an old-growth forest to Short Sands Beach to watch the surfers. Then drive down the coast as far as **Yachats** (120 miles/193 kilometers; 3 hours) and spend the night. Stop at **Yachats Brewing** (348 U.S. 101 N.; 541/547-3884; http://yachatsbrewing.com) for a beer and a plate of pickled veggies.

**DAY 4** Spend the morning exploring the tide pools and old-growth forest around **Cape Perpetua.** Take a tour of **Sea Lion Caves** (or just peer down from the road with your binoculars). Make the 4-hour drive to **Ashland,** arriving in time to have dinner before attending a world-class play.

APPROACHING POWELL'S CITY OF BOOKS

HAYSTACK ROCK AT CANNON BEACH

OSWALD WEST STATE PARK

**DAY 5** From Ashland, backtrack a bit through **Medford** to drive up the Rogue River on Highway 62 to **Crater Lake National Park** (77 miles/123 kilometers; 1.5 hours). Take a driving tour around the lake, and then spend the rest of your day in the park hitting some hiking trails or taking a boat tour. Spend the night at **Crater Lake Lodge** (866/292-6730, www.travelcraterlake.com), if you snagged a reservation months ahead of time.

**DAY 6** Head north on U.S. 97 to **Bend** (90 miles/144 kilometers; 2 hours), visiting the **High Desert Museum** and sampling a few stops on the Bend Ale Trail. In the late afternoon, drive up to **Mount Hood** (115 miles/185 kilometers; 2.5 hours) and spend the night at **Timberline Lodge**.

**DAY 7** Hike along the **Ramona Falls Trail** (or spend the morning skiing—even in August), and then head north to **Hood River,** where you can start your drive back to Portland along the **Columbia River Gorge**. Give yourself more than the 2 hours that the 70 miles (112 kilometers) would take if you don't stop—because you'll want to make at least a few stops at viewpoints and scenic waterfalls.

MULTNOMAH FALLS

venue, the International Rose Test Garden is wedged onto the steep slopes of the West Hills in Washington Park. In addition to intoxicating scents and incredible floral displays, the garden also offers the classic view of Portland—Mount Hood rising above the downtown office towers. Today, the rose garden features over 10,000 rose bushes of 650 varieties, both old and new. A charming annex to the rose garden is the **Shakespeare Garden,** which includes only herbs, trees, and flowers mentioned in Shakespeare's plays.

## PORTLAND JAPANESE GARDEN

611 SW Kingston Ave., Portland; 503/223-1321; www.japanesegarden.com

Just up the slope from the rose gardens, the Portland Japanese Garden is a magical 5-acre (2-hectare) Eden with tumbling water, bonsai, and elaborately manicured shrubs and trees. Winding paths link six separate gardens. Architect Kengo Kuma designed the striking on-site Cultural Village in modern Japanese style, with a courtyard and dry-stacked rock wall, a gallery, a library, and a café.

## LAN SU CHINESE GARDEN

239 NW Everett St., Portland; 503/228-8131; www.lansugarden.org

The Lan Su Chinese Garden is a formal Chinese garden built in the style of the Ming Dynasty. The block-square green space is the result of a joint effort between two famed gardening centers, Portland and its Chinese sister city, Suzhou. Over 60 landscape designers and craftspeople from Suzhou lived and worked in Portland for a year to complete the gardens, which are the largest traditional Chinese gardens in the United States. Nearly all the materials and tools used were also brought from China, including roof and floor tiles, all the hand-carved woodwork, the latticed windows, and over 500 tons (453 metric tons) of Swiss cheese-like Taihu granite boulders.

# *Major* CITIES

**PORTLAND:** Graced by the presence of the Columbia and Willamette Rivers and nearby Mount Hood, Portland is the state's green urban core. Just north of downtown, you'll find the vibrant Pearl District. To the west, Washington Park is home to rose gardens; trails here connect to Forest Park, the nation's largest urban forested park. Cross the Willamette River to the east side to explore thriving neighborhoods.

**SALEM:** Oregon's capital serves as a reminder of the state's pioneer tradition and legacy of progressive legislation. Downtown Salem has had a bit of a renaissance in recent years; after visiting the capitol, walk a few blocks west past lovely old buildings, shops, and restaurants toward the Willamette River.

**EUGENE:** Oregon's third-largest city and home to the University of Oregon offers a laid-back Pacific Northwest version of urban sophistication. The Willamette River curves around the northwest quarter of the community, and from an elevated perch you can see the Coast and Cascade Ranges beckoning you to beach and mountain playgrounds little more than an hour away.

## CANNON BEACH AND HAYSTACK ROCK

Cannon Beach is an extremely popular resort town on Oregon's North Coast. An enclave of tastefully weathered cedar-shingled architecture, Cannon Beach is chockablock with art galleries, boutiques, and upscale lodgings and restaurants.

At the beach itself, **Haystack Rock,** looms large above the long, broad stretch of sand. This is the third-tallest sea stack in the state, measuring 235 feet (71 meters) high. As part of the Oregon Islands National Wildlife Refuge, it has wilderness status and is off-limits to climbing. Puffins and other seabirds nest on its steep faces. Flanking the monolith are two rock formations known as the Needles.

One of the most photographed views of Haystack Rock is from Ecola Point in **Ecola State Park,** located 2 miles (3.2 kilometers) north of Cannon Beach. The southward view takes in famous sea stacks and the overlapping peaks of the Coast Range extending to Neahkahnie Mountain. From Ecola Point, a steep, narrow road and a similarly steep trail lead north to horseshoe-shaped **Indian Beach,** the starting point for the 2.5-mile (4-kilometer) Clatsop Loop Trail up to **Tillamook Head,** considered by Lewis and Clark to be the region's most beautiful viewpoint.

## SEA LION CAVES

91560 U.S. 101, Florence; 541/547-3111; www. sealioncaves.com

The only U.S. mainland rookery of Steller sea lions (*Eumetopias jubatus*), Sea Lion Caves is home to a herd that averages 200 individuals, although the numbers change from season to season. These animals occupy the cave during the fall and winter, which are thus the prime times to visit. In summer you may not see any sea lions in the cave, but might spot them with binoculars on the rocks outside the cave. In addition, California sea lions (*Zalophus californianus*), common all along the Pacific coast, are found at Sea Lion Caves late fall-early spring. Enter Sea Lion Caves through the gift shop on U.S. 101, and a steep downhill walk leads to an elevator that drops an additional 208 feet (63 meters). After exiting the lift, you'll see sea lions on the rock shelves amid the surging water inside the enormous cave. A set of stairs leads up to a view of **Heceta Head Lighthouse** through an opening in the cave.

## HIGH DESERT MUSEUM

59800 U.S. 97 S., Bend; 541/382-4754; https://highdesertmuseum.org

The High Desert Museum is an excellent indoor-outdoor museum where you can observe otters at play, porcupines

HIGH DESERT MUSEUM

## SAMUEL H. BOARDMAN STATE SCENIC CORRIDOR

The stretch of highway from **Brookings** to **Port Orford** along Oregon's south coast is known as the "fabulous 50 miles" (80 kilometers). Some consider the dozen miles (19 kilometers) of coastline just north of Brookings, encompassed by Samuel H. Boardman State Scenic Corridor, to be the most scenic in Oregon—and one of the most dramatic meetings of rock and tide in the world. You'll want to have a camera close at hand and a loose schedule when you make this drive, because you'll find it hard not to pull over again and again, as each photo opportunity seems to outdazzle the last.

Eleven named viewpoints have been cut into the highway's shoulder. **Natural Bridges Cove,** which overlooks several rock archways framing an azure cove, is worth a stop, as is **Thomas Creek Bridge,** the highest bridge in Oregon. **Whaleshead Island** viewpoint, another great stop, offers vistas and trails to an enchanting preserve, while **House Rock,** the site of a World War II air-raid sentry tower, has a trail that goes down to the water.

## CASCADE LAKES HIGHWAY

Hwy. 46

The Cascade Lakes Highway, a.k.a. Century Drive or Highway 46, is an 89-mile (143-kilometer) drive leading to more

sticking it to each other, and birds of prey dispassionately surveying the scene. More exhibits cover contemporary Native American life, the development of the West, photography, native plants, and other small critters.

## ASTORIA

Located at the mouth of the mighty Columbia River, Astoria is the oldest permanent U.S. settlement west of the Rockies. The best introduction to the area is the 360-degree panorama from atop the 125-foot-tall (38-meter) **Astoria Column** (2199 Coxcomb Dr.; 503/325-2963; www.astoriacolumn.org) on Coxcomb Hill, the highest point in town. The column is covered in friezes with scenes depicting the history of the Pacific Northwest. Another highlight is **Fort Clatsop National Memorial** (92343 Fort Clatsop Rd.; 503/861-2471; www.nps.gov/lewi), a replica of Lewis and Clark's 1805-1806 winter camp that offers a fascinating glimpse into frontier life.

# BEST SCENIC DRIVES

The entire Oregon coast along **U.S. 101** is dedicated as a scenic byway, from Astoria in the north near Washington, and following 363 miles (584 kilometers) down to Brookings near California.

MOUNT BACHELOR FROM THE CASCADE LAKES HIGHWAY

# SCENIC BYWAYS IN EASTERN OREGON

Eastern Oregon is road-trip country, and several routes in this region are designated National Scenic Byways.

- The **Wallowa Mountain Loop Road** (closed in winter) is a 54-mile (86-kilometer) drive through Hells Canyon Country, beginning with the Joseph-Imnaha Highway. Turn south on Wallowa Mountain Loop Road to the Imnaha River, then ascend into alpine forests along Dry Creek Road to Halfway to come out on the south flank of the Wallowas. Turn east for a shoreline view of the Snake River and Hells Canyon.

- Explore the high country by driving the 106-mile (170-kilometer) **Elkhorn Drive National Scenic Byway,** which runs northwest from Sumpter—a cross between ghost town and tourist town, with 150 residents—through gold-mining territory to the ghost town of Granite, across the north fork of the John Day, and past Anthony Lake to Baker City. The Elkhorn Byway climbs higher than any other paved road in Oregon (7,392 feet/2,253 meters) after passing North Fork John Day Campground and the junction with Blue Mountains Scenic Byway. Portions are closed by snow early November-June or early July.

than half a dozen lakes in the shadow of the snowcapped Cascades. From Bend, drive south on Franklin Avenue, which becomes Galveston Avenue, about a mile (1.6 kilometers) to the traffic circle at 14th Street. Take the exit for Century Drive. The route is well marked, and the road climbs in elevation for a significant portion of the drive. Although there are many places to stop and explore along the highway, the stretch between **Mount Bachelor** (541/382-1709; www.mtbachelor.com), the Pacific Northwest's largest and most complete ski area, and **Crane Prairie Reservoir** is the most spectacular.

# BEST PARKS AND RECREATION AREAS

## MOUNT HOOD

Oregon's highest peak, Mount Hood (or Wy'east, as the region's Native Americans knew it), rises 11,249 feet (3,428 meters) above sea level less than an hour's drive from Portland and dominates the city's eastern horizon. Hood is a composite volcano (or stratovolcano), a steep-sided conical mountain built up of layers of lava and ash over millennia. Today, the mountain is the breathtaking centerpiece of the **Mount Hood National Forest**. Hikes in the **Zigzag Ranger District** (70220 E. U.S. 26, Zigzag; 541/666-0704 or 503/622-3191) are an excellent introduction to the wealth of recreation options in the area. The **Ramona Falls Trail,** a 4.5-mile (7.2-kilometer) loop to a stunning waterfall, is one of the most popular on Mount Hood. Other activities on the mountain include **climbing** and **mountain biking.**

The mountain is also home to five downhill ski resorts, including **Mount Hood Meadows** (503/537-2222; www.skihood.com), the largest and most varied ski area, and **Timberline Ski Area** (503/272-3158, snow report 503/222-2211; www.timberlinelodge.com), known for its nearly year-round season and **Timberline Lodge.** For an easy trip up the mountain, the **Magic Mile Chair Lift** at Timberline is open to the 7,000-foot (2,133-meter) level for sightseers as well as skiers.

## SILVER FALLS STATE PARK

26 miles (41 kilometers) east of Salem, 22024 Silver Falls Hwy., Sublimity; 503/873-8681, ext. 31; www.oregonstateparks.org

With 10 major waterfalls, nearly 30 miles (48 kilometers) of trails, and over

9,000 acres (3,642 hectares) of woodlands (much of it temperate rainforest), Silver Falls State Park was considered for national park status in the 1920s, but was rejected because parts of the land had been clear-cut. Much of the park's infrastructure was created by the Civilian Conservation Corps (CCC) during the 1930s using the rustic stone and log construction typical of national parks. The highlight of the park is the **Trail of Ten Falls,** a 7-mile (11-kilometer) loop that links all the falls.

## OSWALD WEST STATE PARK

Off U.S. 101; 800/551-6949; www.oregonstateparks.org

Most of Neahkahnie Mountain and the prominent headlands of Cape Falcon are encompassed within the 2,500-acre (1,011-hectare) the extraordinary natural beauty of Oswald West State Park. Several hiking trails weave through the park. A 0.5-mile (0.8-kilometer) trail follows Short Sands Creek to **Short Sands Beach,** where rainforests crowd the secluded boulder-strewn shoreline. It's also possible to hike to **Neahkahnie Mountain** (4 miles/6.4 kilometers) one-way) with some stiff climbing. The summit view south to Cape Meares and east to the Nehalem Valley ranks as one of the finest on the coast.

## OREGON DUNES NATIONAL RECREATION AREA

885 U.S. 101, Reedsport; 541/271-6100; www.fs.usda.gov/siuslaw

The dunes, located on Oregon's central coast, are a fantastic landscape of dazzling white-sand mountains and jewel lakes stretched along nearly 50 miles (80 kilometers) of shoreline. The best way to appreciate the dunes is on foot on numerous designated hiking trails, ranging from easy 0.5-mile (0.8-kilometer) loops to 6-mile (9.6-kilometer) round-trips. The soundtrack is provided by over 200 species of birds—along with your heartbeat—as you scale these elephantine promontories of sand. A favorite trail is the **John Dellenback Trail:** After you emerge

OREGON DUNES NATIONAL RECREATION AREA

from a 0.5-mile (0.8-kilometer) hike through coastal evergreen forest, you'll be greeted by dunes 300-400 feet (91-121 meters) high. The trail, marked by blue-banded wooden posts, continues another 2.5 miles (4 kilometers) to the beach.

## ROGUE RIVER

The most popular way to take in the mighty Rogue is on a jet-boat ride from **Gold Beach.** It's an exciting and interesting look at the varied flora and fauna along the estuary as well as the changing moods of the river. Most of the estimated 50,000 people per year who "do" the Rogue in this way take a 64-mile (102 kilometers) round-trip cruise, although longer trips are also offered. Bears, otters, seals, and beavers may be sighted en route, and anglers may hold up a big catch to show off. Ospreys, snowy egrets, eagles, mergansers, and kingfishers are also seen with regularity in this stopover for migratory waterfowl.

## OREGON CAVES NATIONAL MONUMENT

Hwy. 46; 541/592-3400; www.nps.gov/orca

In the southwest corner of the state, you'll find the Oregon Caves National Monument. The cave itself—there is really only one, which opens onto successive caverns—features impressive formations such as stalactites, stalagmites, and columns. Other cave sculptures you'll see include helicites, formations that twist and turn in crazy directions; draperies, looking just like their household namesakes but cast in stone instead of cloth; and soda straws, stalactites that are hollow in the center like a straw, carrying mineral-rich drops of moisture to their tips.

## JOHN DAY FOSSIL BEDS NATIONAL MONUMENT

32651 Hwy. 19, Kimberly; 541/987-2333; www.nps.gov/joda

The 14,000-acre (5,665-hectare) John Day Fossil Beds National Monument is the richest concentration of prehistoric early mammal and plant fossils in the world. The days of 50-ton apatosaurus and 50-foot (15-meter) crocodiles, as well as delicate ferns and flowers, are captured in the rock formations of the fossil beds. The park is divided into three areas: the **Sheep Rock Unit,** with the monument's excellent interpretive center; the **Painted Hills Unit,** with highly photogenic red, yellow, green, ocher, gray, and black layers; and the **Clarno Unit,** whose petrified mudslide preserves ancient plants.

## HELLS CANYON NATIONAL RECREATION AREA

Oxbow; 541/785-3395; www.fs.usda.gov

SHEEP ROCK UNIT, JOHN DAY FOSSIL BEDS NATIONAL MONUMENT

The Hells Canyon National Recreation Area straddles a 71-mile (114-kilometer) portion of the Snake River and encompasses the 215,223-acre (87,097-hectare) Hells Canyon Wilderness. The remote Hells Canyon is the deepest river gorge in North America. For a distance of 106 miles (170 kilometers) no bridge crosses the river, and few paved roads even come near the canyon. At its deepest point, the gorge walls rise nearly 8,000 feet (2,438 meters). Most of the canyon's terrain is precipitous rock walls and steep, slot-like side valleys, which means that just about the only way to experience this epic landscape is on foot, horseback, or—most accessibly—by boat.

# FESTIVALS AND EVENTS

## OREGON SHAKESPEARE FESTIVAL

15 S. Pioneer St., Ashland; 541/482-4331 or 800/219-8161; www.osfashland.org; mid.-Feb.-late Oct./early Nov.

Few towns are as closely identified with theater as Ashland, and Shakespeare is the soul of this community. The Oregon Shakespeare Festival is one of the world's great theater festivals, and tickets often sell out months in advance. Performances run mid-Feb.-late Oct. or early Nov. across three theaters. The famed outdoor **Elizabethan Theatre** (open summer only), modeled after the Fortune Theatre of London circa 1600, is the largest of the festival's venues. The 600-seat **Angus Bowmer** is an indoor complex with excellent acoustics, digital sound and lighting, and nary a bad seat in the house, and the 150-seat **Thomas Theatre** is where modern works and experimental productions are the norm. Free **Green Shows** on the plaza outside the Elizabethan Theatre feature live music, lectures, performance, storytelling, and other entertainment.

## CINCO DE MAYO FIESTA

Portland; www.cincodemayo.org; May

The Cinco de Mayo Fiesta celebrates Latino heritage at Portland's Tom McCall Waterfront Park the first weekend

# BEST SOUVENIRS

- For many visitors, **Powell's City of Books** (1005 W. Burnside St., Portland; 503/228-0540 or 800/878-7323; www.powells.com) is one of Portland's primary attractions. Pick up new or used book to read on your trip, or grab a bookmark, tote bag, or mug with the store's logo.
- Portland has quite the coffee culture, and perhaps its best-known brand is **Stumptown Coffee Roasters** (855/711-3385; www.stumptowncoffee.com), with a few locations around town. Stop by the original coffee shop in Southeast Portland where it all began (4525 SE Division, Portland) for a cup of java and a bag of beans to bring home with you.
- Ask any Oregonian and they'll tell you that **Tillamook** makes the best cheddar around. Head to their **creamery** (4175 U.S. 101 N., Tillamook; 503/815-1300; www.tillamook.com) in—you guessed it—Tillamook to watch the workers making cheese and grab some samples. The large gift shop has a selection of cheese that goes way beyond what's shipped to grocery stores, plus apparel and other merch

(Thurs.-Sun.) in May. This has become one of the largest celebrations of its kind in the country. Mariachis, folk dance exhibitions, a large selection of Mexican food, and fireworks displays are included in the festivities.

## PORTLAND ROSE FESTIVAL

Portland; 503/227-2681; www.rosefestival.org; June

The Portland Rose Festival has been the city's major summer event for over a century. The Rose Queen and her court (chosen from among local high school entrants), navy sailors, and floats from several parades clog Portland's traffic arteries during this 18-day citywide celebration each June. Two of the more colorful events of the June fete are the **Grand Floral Parade** and the **Festival of Flowers** at Pioneer Courthouse Square. In the latter, all manner of colorful blossoms fill the square to overflowing during the first week of the festival. The Grand Floral Parade, which usually begins the Saturday following the opening of the festival, is the second-largest all-floral parade in the United States.

## OREGON COUNTRY FAIR

Near Veneta on Hwy. 126; 541/343-4298; www.oregoncountryfair.org, July

Don't expect to see livestock displays and prize-winning jelly. This is a place where body paint, feathers, man kilts, tie-dye, and good-natured frivolity rule. The Oregon Country Fair is like a giant street fair, with artisans, food, and music in a beautiful wooded setting along the Long Tom River about 13 miles (20 kilometers) west of Eugene. The crafts are high quality, and there's no better place to shop for a tie-dyed T-shirt. Don't miss the Fighting Instruments of Karma Marching Chamber Band-Orchestra; various permutations of the band have been rocking the joint with everything from Sousa marches to Bollywood dance tunes for over 40 years.

# BEST FOOD AND DRINK

## PACIFIC NORTHWEST CUISINE

Pacific Northwest cuisine is defined by the exceptional quality of raw ingredients. Fresh fish and seafood are the cuisine's cornerstone, most notably salmon, Dungeness crab, and oysters. Small farms in the Willamette Valley produce vegetables and berries of superlative quality. Oregon is also one of the world's largest producers of nuts, and hazelnuts in particular find their way into many dishes. Foragers head deep into forests to find wild greens and mushrooms. This close-to-the-earth vitality is what makes the food here so memorable.

To feast on Pacific Northwest cuisine, check out these restaurants:

- **Higgins** (1239 SW Broadway, Portland; 503/222-9070; www.higginsportland. com): One of Portland's first farm-to-table restaurants is still one of the best, with lots of dishes focused on local vegetables and fish.

- **Celilo Restaurant and Bar** (16 Oak St., Hood River; 541/386-5710; www.celilorestaurant.com): Up-to-the-moment food trends meet the freshest of local ingredients in a comfortable, lodge-like dining room.

- **Local Ocean Seafoods** (213 SE Bay Blvd., Newport; 541/574-7959; http://localocean.net): This is as much a fish market as a restaurant, but you'll have a chance to sample the day's freshest catch, simply prepared, just steps from the town's busy harbor.

## CRAFT BREWS

**Portland,** also known as Beervana, is the epicenter of the craft brewing revival in North America, boasting more breweries than any other city in the world. The rest of the state has followed Portland's example, and you'll find craft brewpubs all around Oregon. In **Bend,** the microbrewery scene is the fastest-growing in the state, and the central Oregon city has its own **Bend Ale Trail.**

Here are some top picks around the state to get you started.

- **Hopworks Urban Brewery** (2944 SE Powell Blvd., Portland; 503/232-4647; http://hopworksbeer.com): HUB is as Portland as it gets, with a commitment to good beer, bikes, and sustainability.

- **Rogue Farms Hopyard** (3590 Wigrich Rd., Independence; 503/838-9813; www.rogue.com): See hops growing at this riverside farm. Visit around fall harvest time to drink fresh-hopped brew.

- **Deschutes Brewery and Public House** (1044 NW Bond St., Bend; 541/382-9242; www.deschutesbrewery.com): The Mirror Pond pale ale is an Oregonian staple.

## OREGON WINES

Although there are wine regions in southern Oregon and the Columbia Gorge, the state's most noted wine production area is in the hills of the northern Willamette Valley, southwest of Portland, particularly in Yamhill and southern Washington Counties. In summer, Oregon's northern latitude makes for long, sunny days without excessive heat, while slow-cooling fall days allow grapes to produce a complexity of flavor by inhibiting high sugar concentrations while maintaining the acidity of the grape. Willamette Valley wines, particularly pinot noir and chardonnay, are world-class, and there are over 700 wineries in the state, of which many are small family operations. **Willamette Valley Wineries** (503/646-2985; http://willamettewines.com) maintains an excellent website of wineries in the area.

# MAJOR AIRPORTS

- **Portland International Airport:** PDX; 877/739-4636; www.flypdx.com

# MORE INFORMATION

## TRAVEL AND TOURISM INFORMATION

- **Travel Oregon:** www.traveloregon. com

- **Oregon State Parks:** www.oregonstateparks.org

## NEWSPAPERS

- *The Oregonian:* www.oregonlive.com

# CALIFORNIA

Diverse, wacky, and unforgetta-ble, California is larger than life. The boisterous cities seem bigger, redwood forests and snow-capped mountains loom taller, and sandy coastlines stretch longer than anywhere else. California is on the tra-ditional lands of nearly 200 Indigenous tribes, from Tolowa, Shasta, Karok, and Modoc lands in the north to Kumeyaay lands in the south.

**AREA:** 163,696 square miles / 423,970 square kilometers (3rd)

**POPULATION:** 39,368,078 (1st)

**STATEHOOD DATE:** September 9, 1850 (31st)

**STATE CAPITAL:** Sacramento

The pace of life is as diverse as everything else in the state. Fast moving and fast living are hallmarks of the Los Angeles basin, yet the quiet frenzy of the San Francisco Bay Area sometimes seems just as fast. Outside the major urban areas, things move more slowly. California's numerous wine regions invite visitors to relax. Beyond the farms and vineyards, an even more venerable and variable pace emerges—that of nature. The gushing waterfalls of Yosemite, towering red-woods of Humboldt County, bone-dry deserts of Death Valley, delicate native wild-flowers along the coast... even the imperceptible crawl and occasional sudden jolt of the land itself all make up the unique rhythm of California.

OCEAN VIEW NEAR BIXBY BRIDGE IN BIG SUR

# *Major* CITIES

**LOS ANGELES:** California's most populous city, Los Angeles is a massive mix of Southern California beach town, Hollywood dream factory, and 21st-century metropolis. Unmissable attractions include world-class art, a beach scene that begs for some time in the sand and surf, and an amusement park devoted to a cartoon mouse.

**SAN DIEGO:** Maritime museums ring the downtown harbor, while across the bay in Coronado, the vibrant and historic Hotel del Coronado creates a centerpiece for visitors to the city. Gorgeous beaches stretch from Point Loma north to La Jolla and the North County coast, begging surfers, swimmers, strollers, and sunbathers to ply their sands.

**SAN FRANCISCO:** The politics, the culture, the food—they all make San Francisco world famous. Dine on cutting-edge cuisine at high-end restaurants and offbeat food trucks, tour classical and avant-garde museums, bike through Golden Gate Park and explore its hidden treasures, and stroll along Fisherman's Wharf, where barking sea lions and frenetic street performers compete for attention.

**SAN JOSE:** Sprawled across the south end of Silicon Valley, San Jose proudly claims the title of biggest city in the Bay Area. It is the workhorse of the valley's high-tech industry and is home to eBay, Cisco, Adobe, and many others.

## ORIENTATION

California is divided into the coast to the west and mountains or desert to the east, with the great breadbasket of the **Central Valley** in between. Coastal Southern California is the California of the imagination, with the beaches and surf of **San Diego, Orange County,** and **Los Angeles.** The central coast stretches from **Santa Barbara,** through the dramatic **Big Sur** coast, up to the **Monterey Bay. San Francisco** is the gateway to northern California, with its wine country and redwoods. **Sacramento,** the state capital, sits inland from San Francisco, at the northern end of the Central Valley. In the east, **Yosemite,** the jewel of the **Sierra** mountain range, is near the middle of the state. North of Yosemite, **Lake Tahoe** sits on the California-Nevada border, and east of the southern Sierras lies **Death Valley.** Whereas mountains define the eastern part of central and northern California, desert is the dominant terrain in the south, with such arid landscapes as the **Mojave Desert** and **Joshua Tree National Park.**

## WHEN TO GO

California's best feature is its all-season appeal. The crowds are smaller in **spring,** and the weather starts to get warmer, especially in southern California. In **summer,** unsuspecting visitors are frequently surprised by the wind and fog that blow through San Francisco June-Aug. Regardless, summer remains California's travel season; expect crowds at popular attractions, beaches, wineries, national parks, and campgrounds. **Fall** is a wonderful time to visit, as the summer crowds have left, but winter rain and snow have not yet closed areas in the eastern mountains. In **winter,** ski destinations like Tahoe draw crowds, but this is a quieter season for much of the state.

# HIGHLIGHTS

## ALCATRAZ

Tours depart from Pier 33, San Francisco; www.nps.gov/alcatraz

The isolation of the island in the bay, the frigid waters, and the nasty currents surrounding "The Rock" made it a perfect spot to keep prisoners contained, with little hope of escape and near-certain death if the attempt were ever made.

The fortress became a Civil War prison in the 19th century, and in 1934, construction began to turn Alcatraz into a new style of prison ready to house a new style of prisoner: Depression-era gangsters. A few of the honored guests of this maximum-security penitentiary were Al Capone, George "Machine Gun" Kelly, and Robert Stroud, "the Birdman of Alcatraz." The prison closed in 1963, and in 1964 and 1969 occupations were staged by Indians of All Tribes, an exercise that eventually led to the privilege of self-determination for North America's original inhabitants.

Today Alcatraz is a hugely popular attraction for locals and tourists. Visitors take a ferry ride to the island prison and tour the cells with a recorded audio guide. But the views of San Francisco from Alcatraz might be the highlight of the trip.

## CABLE CARS

San Francisco; www.sfmta.com/getting-around/muni/cable-cars

Perhaps the most recognizable symbol of San Francisco is the cable car, originally conceived as a safe way to travel the city's steep hills. The cable cars ran as regular mass transit from 1873 into the 1940s, when buses and electric streetcars took over. Today there are only three lines, but cable cars have become a rolling national landmark.

The California cable car line goes up Nob Hill from near the Ferry Building, and two lines, the Powell-Mason and the Powell-Hyde, travel from Union Square through Chinatown and out to Fisherman's Wharf. Take a seat, or grab one of the exterior poles and hang on!

To learn more, make a stop at the sweet little **Cable Car Museum** (1201 Mason St.; 415/474-1887; www.cable-carmuseum.org), where exhibits depict the life and times of the cable cars and an elevated platform overlooks the engines, winding wheels, and thick steel cable that keeps the cars humming.

## SAN FRANCISCO CHINATOWN

www.sanfranciscochinatown.com

The massive Chinese migration to California began almost as soon as news of gold in the mountain streams made it to East Asia. In San Francisco, Chinese immigrants carved out a thriving community at the border of **Portsmouth Square,** then center of the young city, which eventually became known as Chinatown. Along with much of San Francisco, the neighborhood was destroyed in the 1906 earthquake and fire.

Today visitors see the post-1906 visitor-friendly Chinatown that was built after the quake, particularly if they enter through the **Chinatown Gate** (Grant Ave. and Bush St.) at the edge of Union Square. In this historic neighborhood—the largest Chinatown outside of Asia—beautiful Asian architecture mixes with blocky city buildings to create a unique skyline. Small alleyways wend between the commercial corridors, creating an intimate atmosphere. During the **Chinese New Year Parade** (www.chineseparade.com; Feb.), the neighborhood celebrates the lunar new year with a parade of costumed dancers, floats, firecrackers, and the Golden Dragon. Year-round, don't miss out on dim sum: **Great Eastern** (649 Jackson St; 415/986-2500; www.greateasternsf.com) is one of many great places to get it.

CALE CAR WITH ALCATRAZ IN THE BACKGROUND

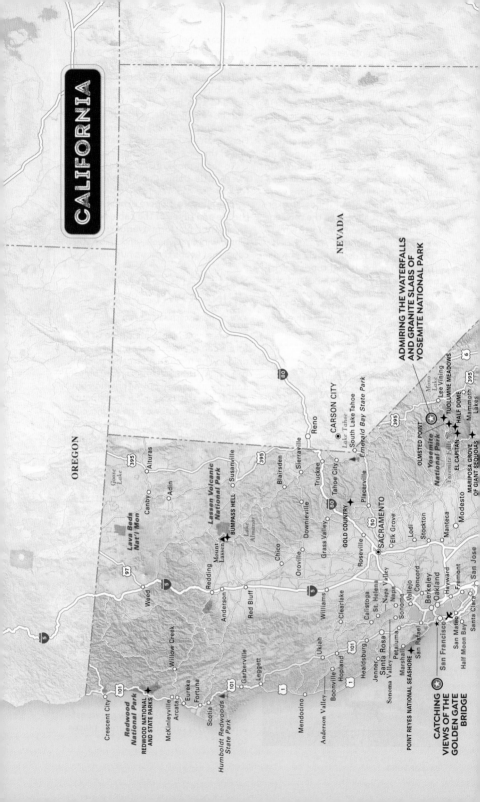

# CALIFORNIA

OREGON

NEVADA

Crescent City

*Redwood National Park*
REDWOOD NATIONAL AND STATE PARKS

McKinleyville
Arcata
Eureka
Fortuna
Scotia

*Humboldt Redwoods State Park*

Willow Creek

Weed

Anderson

Redding

Red Bluff

*Lava Beds Nat'l Mon*

Canby

Adin

Alturas

*Goose Lake*

395

97

5

*Lessen Volcanic National Park*
BUMPASS HELL

Mount Lassen

Susanville

Chico

Oroville

*Lake Almanor*

Downieville

Grass Valley

Blairsden

Sierraville

Truckee

Reno

80

CARSON CITY

*Lake Tahoe*

South Lake Tahoe

*Emerald Bay State Park*

395

Placerville

GOLD COUNTRY

50

80

Roseville

SACRAMENTO

Elk Grove

Lodi

Stockton

Manteca

Modesto

Mariposa Grove OF GIANT SEQUOIAS

El Capitan

HALF DOME

*Yosemite National Park*

OLMSTED POINT

TUOLUMNE MEADOWS

Lee Vining

*Mono Lake*

Mammoth Lakes

395

6

ADMIRING THE WATERFALLS AND GRANITE SLABS OF YOSEMITE NATIONAL PARK

Garberville

Leggett

Mendocino

Anderson Valley

Boonville

Hopland

Ukiah

Healdsburg

Santa Rosa

Jenner

Sonoma Valley

Petaluma

Marshall

POINT REYES NATIONAL SEASHORE

San Rafael

CATCHING VIEWS OF THE GOLDEN GATE BRIDGE

San Francisco

San Mateo

Half Moon Bay

Santa Clara

San Jose

Fremont

Hayward

Oakland

Berkeley

Concord

Vallejo

Sonoma

Napa

Napa Valley

St. Helena

Calistoga

Clearlake

Williams

101

1

11

5

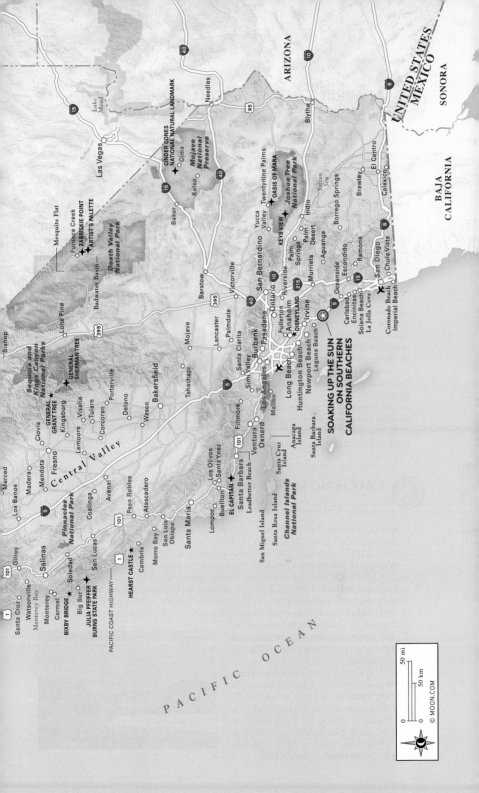

# TOP

## 1 ADMIRING THE WATERFALLS AND GRANITE SLABS OF YOSEMITE NATIONAL PARK

www.nps.gov/yose

Of all the natural wonders that California has to offer, Yosemite may be the most iconic. If this is your first visit, prepare to be overwhelmed.

The first place most people go is **Yosemite Valley,** the most visited region in the park, filled with sights, hikes, and services. This is where you'll find **Half Dome,** the park's most famous sight. (You'll need a permit if you want to climb to the top.) The other star of Yosemite Valley is **El Capitan,** a massive hunk of granite that is accessible two ways—a long hike from Upper Yosemite Fall or **rock-climbing** the face—but most visitors just gaze up adoringly from the El Capitan picnic area. Other top sights here include **Bridalveil Fall** and **Yosemite Falls,** and don't miss a hike on the **Mist Trail to Vernal and Nevada Falls.**

Other areas of the park beckon, too. Often referred to as "the grandest view in all the West," **Glacier Point** is a 7,214-foot (2,199-meter) overlook with a vista of Yosemite Valley, Half Dome, and all its granite neighbors. For more amazing views, hike the trail to **Sentinel Dome,** or try the difficult **Panorama Trail.** In the **Mariposa Grove of Giant Sequoias,** you can see the largest living trees on earth by volume. A drive along **Tioga Pass Road** offers more giant wonders: Two giant sequoia groves—the **Merced** and **Tuolumne Groves**—wait to be explored, as does **Tuolumne Meadows,** the largest subalpine meadow in the Sierra Nevada.

YOSEMITE NATIONAL PARK

## 2 CATCHING VIEWS OF THE GOLDEN GATE BRIDGE

U.S. 101/CA-1 at Lincoln Blvd., San Francisco; 415/921-5858; www.goldengatebridge.org

People come from the world over to gaze at the Golden Gate Bridge. A marvel of human engineering constructed in 1936 and 1937, the suspension bridge spans the narrow "gate" from which the Pacific Ocean enters the San Francisco Bay.

**Walking** or **biking** the 1.7-mile (2.7-kilometer) bridge is a popular way to experience it. On a clear day, the whole bay, Marin Headlands, and city skyline are visible. Pedestrians and wheelchair users are allowed on the **east sidewalk;** cyclists are allowed on both sidewalks (check the website for the schedule). While crossing via the sidewalks is free in either direction, a vehicle toll (www.bayareafastrak.org) is charged by license plate recognition if you're crossing the bridge into San Francisco by car. (There's no toll leaving San Francisco.)

On the bridge's northern end, **Vista Point** is a great perch for photos, as is **Battery Spencer,** which is accessed via the Alexander Avenue exit from U.S. 101. If you're looking for great views or photo ops of the Golden Gate Bridge while exploring the city, head to **Baker Beach, Crissy Field,** or **Lands End.**

GOLDEN GATE BRIDGE FROM BAKER BEACH

# ③ SOAKING UP THE SUN ON SOUTHERN CALIFORNIA BEACHES

Whether you want to surf, swim, play some beach volleyball, or just lie out on the sand, Southern California offers up a seemingly endless stretch of public beaches along the Pacific Ocean.

## LOS ANGELES

The sun shines over the sands of **Santa Monica State Beach** (Pacific Coast Hwy.; 310/458-8300; www.smgov.net) more than 300 days each year. The nearby **Santa Monica Pier** (Ocean Ave. at Colorado Ave., Santa Monica; 310/458-8901; www.santamonicapier.org), dotted with an amazing array of carnival-style food stands, an arcade, and a small amusement park, offers the ultimate in SoCal beach kitsch.

For even more chaos and kitsch, head on down to the **Venice Boardwalk** (Ocean Front Walk at Venice Blvd., Venice; 310/396-6764; www.venicebeach.com), where you'll pass an astonishing array of tacky souvenir stores, tattoo and piercing parlors, and plenty of L.A.'s colorful characters. The beach side includes the famous **Muscle Beach** (two blocks north of Venice Blvd., Venice; www.musclebeach.net).

To get away from the chaos—and to surf some of the best waves around—head north to **Malibu,** where you'll find **Malibu Lagoon State Beach** (23200 Pacific Coast Hwy., Malibu; 310/457-8143; www.parks.ca.gov) and **Zuma Beach** (30000 Pacific Coast Hwy., Malibu; 19 miles/30 kilometers north of Santa Monica, surf report 310/457-9701; http://beaches.lacounty.gov).

## SANTA BARBARA

Superb meetings of sand and sea abound in Santa Barbara. Many consider **Leadbetter Beach** (Shoreline Dr. and Loma Alta Dr., Santa Barbara) the best beach in town; it's an ideal spot for swimming.

LEADBETTER BEACH IN SANTA BARBARA

## ORANGE COUNTY

Located in Surf City USA, **Huntington City Beach** (Pacific Coast Hwy. from Beach Blvd. to Seapoint St., Huntington Beach; 714/536-5281; www.huntingtonbeachca.gov) has that casual California vibe, with good surf, volleyball courts, and a bike path.

**Newport Beach** (www.visitnewportbeach.com) is popular for fishing, swimming, surfing, and other ocean activities. On the east end of Balboa Peninsula, **The Wedge** is the world's most famous bodysurfing spot.

The town of **Laguna Beach** offers many great sandy spots to choose from. It has a tidepool-pocked coastline and clear ocean water that beckons snorkelers and divers.

## SAN DIEGO

A top pick here is **La Jolla Cove** (1100 Coast Blvd., La Jolla), a popular beach for swimming and snorkeling.

**Coronado Beach** (Ocean Blvd. from Hotel del Coronado to North Island Naval Air Station, Coronado; 619/522-7346; www.coronado.ca.us) is routinely listed among the best beaches in the United States.

# *Best* ROAD TRIP

**DAY 1** Fly into **San Francisco** and rent a car. Spend the day in **Golden Gate Park,** indulging your artistic side at the **de Young Museum.** Unwind with a walk through the park's **Japanese Tea Garden.** Then, make your way to the **Golden Gate Bridge,** one of the world's most famous photo-ops. End your day with a meal at one of the city's culinary hot spots—or grab an authentic burrito at a local taqueria.

**DAY 2** Start you day in **Wine Country** in downtown **Napa.** Get your bearings at the **Oxbow Public Market** (610 1st St., Napa; 707/226-6529; https://oxbowpublic-market.com), where you can shop, nibble pastries, and sip a cup of coffee. Drive north on the **Silverado Trail** to **Robert Sinskey Vineyards,** a great place to try pinot noir, followed by some cabernet at **Stag's Leap.** Head north to **St. Helena** to dine at one of the town's many farm-to-table restaurants.

**DAY 3** Leave the Bay Area in the morning to reach **Yosemite** by midday. The drive to the **Big Oak Flat entrance** takes at least four hours; however, traffic can make it much longer. Spend the afternoon touring around **Yosemite Valley,** seeing **Half Dome, El Capitan,** and **Yosemite Falls.** Spend the night under the stars at

THE JAPANESE TEA GARDEN IN SAN FRANCISCO

one of the park's campgrounds or at the classic **Ahwahnee Hotel** (just be sure to make reservations well in advance).

**DAY 4** Continue your adventure in Yosemite National Park today. If you want to break a sweat, hike the 5.4-mile (8.6-kilometer) round-trip **Mist Trail.** Drive up to **Glacier Point** for incredible views of Half Dome, Clouds Rest, Liberty Cap, and Vernal and Nevada Falls. Walk through the **Mariposa Grove of Giant Sequoias** to be awed by magnificent trees. Exit the park via its southern entrance; it's time for the 5-hour drive to **Los Angeles.**

VINEYARD IN NAPA VALLEY

EL CAPITAN, YOSEMITE NATIONAL PARK

**DAY 5** It's time for the beach! Experience the best of Southern California beach culture at the chaotic but entertaining **Venice Boardwalk** or the **Santa Monica Pier.** If time allows, head inland a few miles to stroll **Griffith Park** and look out upon the City of Angels from the observatory.

**DAY 6** Get an early start and head to **Disneyland** for a full day at the Happiest Place on Earth. If that's not your cup of tea, drive 2 hours south to **San Diego.** You can relax on the beach, visit **Balboa Park** and its many museums, or see the pandas at the **San Diego Zoo.** Whatever you do, don't leave town without eating some **tacos.** Return to L.A. to spend the night.

**DAY 7** To get back to Northern California, take the scenic route along **Pacific Coast Highway.** You can make this 500-mile (804-kilometer), 9-10-hour drive in one long day if you make only a few stops (such as getting lunch midway in San Luis Obispo), but it's better to break it up over two days and enjoy the coast. On the first day, stop in **Santa Barbara** for lunch at one of the great restaurants off **State Street.** Continue on to **San Luis Obispo** to spend the night.

**DAY 8** On this day, take your time driving up PCH through **Big Sur.** Popular stops include the Depression-era **Bixby Bridge** and **McWay Falls** in Julia Pfeiffer Burns State Park. Stop in **Monterey** or **Carmel** (or both) before heading back to San Francisco.

VENICE BOARDWALK

## MONTEREY BAY AQUARIUM

886 Cannery Row, Monterey; 831/648-4800; www.montereybayaquarium.org

The first aquarium of its kind in the country, the Monterey Bay Aquarium centers its mission around conservation. Many of the animals in the aquarium's tanks were rescued, and those that survive may eventually be returned to the wild. All the exhibits you'll see in this mammoth complex contain only local sea life. The living, breathing **Kelp Forest** is just like the kelp beds outside in the bay, except this one is 28 feet (8.5 meters) tall. Inside the deep-water tank of the **Open Sea** exhibit, hammerhead sharks and an enormous odd-looking sunfish coexist. The **Sea Otters** exhibit gives visitors a personal view of the adorable, furry marine mammals. Another of the aquarium's most popular exhibits is its **Jellies** display, which illuminates delicate crystal jellies and the comet-like lion's mane jellyfish.

## SANTA BARBARA

It's been called the American Riviera, with sun-drenched beaches reminiscent of the Mediterranean coast. In truth, Santa Barbara is all California. It's one of the state's most picturesque cities, famous for its Spanish colonial revival architecture. After a 1925 earthquake, the city rebuilt itself in the style of the **Santa Barbara Mission** (2201 Laguna St.; 805/682-4149; www.santabarbaramission.org), arguably the most beautiful of California's 21 missions, with white stucco surfaces, red-tiled roofs, arches, and courtyards. Down by the water, warm sandy beaches invite lingering, and a paved path traces the coastline, alongside grassy areas with palm trees gently swaying in the breeze.

## HOLLYWOOD WALK OF FAME

Hollywood Blvd. from La Brea Ave. to Vine St., Los Angeles; 323/469-8311; www.walkoffame.com

One of the most recognizable facets of Hollywood is its star-studded Walk of Fame. This area contains more than 2,500 five-pointed stars honoring both real people and fictional characters that have contributed significantly to the entertainment industry and the Hollywood legend. Each pink star is set in a charcoal-colored square and has its honoree's name in bronze. At the edges of the Walk of Fame, you'll find blank stars waiting to be filled by up-and-comers making their mark on Tinseltown. Along the Walk of Fame, you can't miss the **TCL Chinese Theatre** (6925 Hollywood Blvd.; 323/461-3331; www.tclchinesetheatres.com), perhaps the most visited and recognizable movie theater in the world.

SANTA BARBARA MISSION

## GRIFFITH PARK

**Los Feliz Blvd., Zoo Dr., or Griffith Park Blvd., Los Angeles; 323/913-4688; www.laparks.org**

Griffith Park is the country's largest municipal park with an urban wilderness area. In addition to hiking trails and picnic areas, the park is also home to the **L.A. Zoo and Botanical Gardens** (5333 Zoo Dr.; 323/644-4200; www.lazoo.org) and **The Autry National Center of the American West** (4700 Western Heritage Way; 323/667-2000; www.theautry.org), which showcases artifacts of the American West. Kids love riding the trains of the operating miniature railroad at both the **Travel Town Railroad** (5200 Zoo Dr.; 323/662-9678; www.griffithparktrainrides.com) and the **Griffith Park & Southern Railroad** (4730 Crystal Springs Rd.; www.griffithparktrainrides.com).

A visit to the **Griffith Observatory** (2800 E. Observatory Rd.; 213/473-0800; www.griffithobservatory.org) is a Los Angeles must. It's not just for lovers of the night sky—though free telescopes are available and experienced demonstrators help visitors gaze at the stars. The art deco building is gorgeous, and the views are incredible.

The **Hollywood Sign** sits on Mount Lee, which is part of the park and indelibly part of the mystique of Hollywood. A strenuous 5-mile (8-kilometer) hike will lead you to an overlook just above and behind the sign. To get there, drive to the top of Beachwood Drive, park, and follow the Hollyridge Trail.

## THE GETTY CENTER

**1200 Getty Center Drive., Los Angeles; 310/440-7300; www.getty.edu**

The Getty Center is a famed institution of art and culture. Donated by the family of J. Paul Getty to the people of Los Angeles, this museum features European art, sculpture, manuscripts, and European and American photos. Rivalling the collections are the modern Richard Meier-designed buildings of the fabulous museum campus. On a clear day, the views from The Getty, which sweep from downtown L.A. west to the Pacific, are remarkable. There is also a central garden to stroll through and a cactus garden perched on a south-facing

GRIFFITH OBSERVATORY, LOS ANGELES

promontory with a view of the city below.

## LOS ANGELES COUNTY MUSEUM OF ART

**5905 Wilshire Blvd., Los Angeles; 323/857-6000; www.lacma.org**

The Los Angeles County Museum of Art, better known as LACMA, is the largest art museum in the western United States. Its most recognizable spot for a photo op is the "Urban Light" exhibit out front, made up of rows of restored streetlamps from the 1920s and '30s. This museum complex prides itself on a diverse array of collections and exhibitions of art from around the world, from ancient to modern. There are nine full-size buildings filled with galleries, so don't expect to get through the whole thing in an hour, or even a full day. Specialties of LACMA include Japanese art and artifacts in the beautifully designed Pavilion for Japanese Art and the costumes and textiles of the Doris Stein Research Center.

## DISNEYLAND

**1313 N. Harbor Blvd., Anaheim; 714/781-4623; http://disneyland.disney.go.com**

The "Happiest Place on Earth" lures millions of visitors of all ages each year with promises of fun and fantasy. During high seasons (whenever school is out), massive waves of humanity flow through Disneyland, moving slowly from land to land and ride to ride. Even the most cynical and jaded resident Californians can't quite keep their cantankerous scowls once they're here—it really *is* a happy place. Can't-miss rides include Pirates of the Caribbean and the Haunted Mansion in New Orleans Square, Indiana Jones Adventure in Adventureland, and "It's a Small World" and the Matterhorn Bobsleds in Fantasyland. For the biggest thrill in the park, head to Tomorrowland and ride Space Mountain.

Adjacent to Disneyland, you'll find **Disney California Adventure Park** (http://disneyland.disney.go.com), which celebrates much of what makes California special. Rides here include high-tech roller coaster California Screamin', located in the Santa Monica-esque Paradise Pier; Grizzly River Run, a white-water raft ride through a landscape inspired by the Sierra Nevada foothills; and Radiator Springs Racers, based on the movie *Cars*.

## BALBOA PARK

San Diego; www.balboapark.org

Balboa Park houses a number of museums, theaters, and gardens, but its central promenade, known as **El Prado** (El Prado between Cabrillo Bridge and Park Ave.), serves as a sight in itself. Locals regularly stroll the 0.5-mile-long (0.8-kilometer) Prado just for the pleasure of wandering its fountains, plazas, and ponds, and appreciating the Spanish Revival architecture throughout the park. Smack in the middle of Balboa Park, you'll find the **San Diego Zoo** (2920 Zoo Dr.; 619/231-1515; www.sandiegozoo. org), home to more than 600 species and covering 100 acres (40 hectares). Popular beasts include polar bears, tigers, elephants, and more, but the zoo's pride and joy is its family of pandas.

# BEST SCENIC DRIVES

## PACIFIC COAST HIGHWAY

Hwy. 1

The Pacific Coast Highway is one of the world's best drives. The route itself is sometimes a highway, sometimes a city street, and often a slow, winding roadway. Synonymous with Hwy. 1, the route hugs the California coast, with the stretch between Los Angeles and San Francisco the most exalted. North of L.A., **Ventura** and **Santa Barbara** are two coastal cities that enjoy the near-perfect Southern California climate without the sprawl of nearby Los Angeles. Following the coastline's contours up past Point Conception, the roadway is

BALBOA PARK IN SAN DIEGO

BIXBY BRIDGE AND PACIFIC COAST HIGHWAY AT SUNSET

dotted with the communities of **San Luis Obispo, Morro Bay,** and **Cambria.** These unassuming towns make ideal stops for road-trippers, especially those who want to explore some of the state's best beaches. And nearby is one of California's most popular attractions: opulent **Hearst Castle** (San Simeon; 800/444-4445; www.hearstcastle.org).

**Big Sur** is the standout section of the drive along PCH. The roadway perches between steep coastal mountains and the Pacific, with big views seemingly around every turn. For that classic photo of **McWay Falls** flowing down to a deserted beach, stop at **Julia Pfeiffer Burns State Park.** North of Big Sur, you'll cross **Bixby Bridge,** one of the most photographed bridges in the nation. On the Monterey Peninsula, you'll find **Carmel,** with its stunning white-sand beach, and the cannery town turned tourist magnet **Monterey.** The north end of the Monterey Bay is the location of the quirky surf town **Santa Cruz.**

The final leg up the coast from Santa Cruz to San Francisco has plenty of wide-open space. Its coastal terraces are punctuated by surprisingly undeveloped towns like **Half Moon Bay.** These are ideal places to indulge in some hiking, surfing, or kayaking before returning to the urban atmosphere of **San Francisco.**

## TIOGA PASS ROAD

Hwy. 120

Yosemite National Park's Tioga Pass Road starts at Crane Flat and winds through red fir and lodgepole pine forest, past meadows, lakes, and granite domes and spires, leaving the park at its Eastern Entrance near Tioga Pass. Along the way, be sure to pull over at **Olmsted Point** for a unique side view of Half Dome, plus stunning views of Clouds Rest and Tenaya Canyon. You'll also pass **Tenaya Lake,** with deep-blue waters and white sands that make it hard to resist pulling over for a picnic. The grassy expanse of **Tuolumne Meadows,** the largest subalpine meadow in the Sierra Nevada, sits near the eastern end of the road. For a thrilling view of the high country, take the 2.8-mile (4.5-kilometer) round-trip hike up **Lembert Dome.**

## AVENUE OF THE GIANTS

Hwy. 254, between Weott and Myers Flat

The most famous stretch of redwood trees in **Humboldt Redwoods State Park,** located 3-4 hours north of San Francisco, is the Avenue of the Giants. It parallels U.S. 101 and the Eel River for 32 miles (51 kilometers) between Garberville and Scotia (look for signs on U.S. 101). Visitors come from all over the world to drive this two-lane road and gaze in wonder at the sky-high old-growth redwoods along the way. Campgrounds and hiking trails sprout among the trees off the road. Park your car at various points at any of the eight stops along the way to walk among the giants. If you're just looking for the big trees, jump on at Myers Flat and continue through Pepperwood.

## MOJAVE SCENIC DRIVE
I-15

The **Mojave National Preserve** (between I-15 and I-40; 760/928-2572; www.nps.gov/moja) offers a less-crowded way to explore California's vast Mojave region. If you've only got one day, the best (and easiest) introduction is the Mojave Scenic Drive from the northern edge of the park along the smooth, well-kept pavement of I-15.

From the town of **Baker,** turn south off I-15 onto **Kelbaker Road** for the 35-mile (56-kilometer) drive to Kelso. You'll traverse an alien landscape composed of volcanic activity, part of the **Cinder Cones National Natural Landmark.** Stop in Kelso to explore the Spanish Revival facade of the **Kelso Depot Visitor Center** (Kelbaker Rd., Kelso; 760/252-6108), which once held the railroad depot that supported the many desert mining camps. From there, turn onto **Kelso-Cima Road.** The road follows the Union Pacific rail line along the edge of the Providence Mountains to the town of **Cima,** where you'll find snacks and drinks (but no gas). Take the right fork, **Morning Star Mine Road,** for a turnoff to the abandoned mine that gives the road its name. From the mine, turn left onto Ivanpah Road and continue to Nipton Road to return to the freeway.

This drive takes about 90 minutes without stops, but consider hiking the many desert trails or spending the night at one of the two campgrounds.

ZABRISKIE POINT, DEATH VALLEY NATIONAL PARK

# BEST PARKS AND RECREATION AREAS

## DEATH VALLEY NATIONAL PARK
760/786-3200; www.nps.gov/deva

Famed for its uncompromising climate, Death Valley National Park epitomizes the stark beauty and mystery of the desert. The smooth, shifting sand dunes of **Mesquite Flat** are mesmerizing, while the salt flats at **Badwater Basin,** the point with the lowest elevation in the Western Hemisphere (281 ft/85 meters below sea level) have a by turns serene or eerie stillness. The main visitors center is at **Furnace Creek,** and nearby, a stunning view of the crinkled badlands awaits at **Zabriskie Point.** South of Furnace Creek, the "painted" hills of **Artist's Palette** along Artists Drive show off brilliant colors resulting from a random conglomeration of different minerals. If you are very lucky and arrive during an early spring super bloom (about once a decade), you'll see the desert floor covered in wildflowers.

## JOSHUA TREE NATIONAL PARK
760/367-5500; www.nps.gov/jotr

Joshua Tree National Park sprawls across a desert landscape, featuring the strange shapes of the plant that is its namesake. The northern, more popular, half of the park sits in the high-altitude Mojave Desert, and as the park's lands stretch south, they also dip down into the lower-set Colorado Desert. The park is a great place for hiking and rock-climbing.

One of the best views in all of Joshua Tree is the **Keys View** (end of Keys View Rd., bear south off Park Blvd. past Cap Rock). On a clear day, this view redefines the concept of "panoramic"—travelers will gaze upon Palm Springs and the Coachella Valley, spy the notorious San Andreas Fault, and maybe even see the Salton Sea to the southeast. Another highlight is the **Oasis of Mara** (Hwy. 62 and Utah Trail), home to a number of small springs that provide life-giving water that supports a large

# CALIFORNIA'S NATIONAL PARKS

California is home to nine national parks—more than any other state. Yosemite, Joshua Tree, and Death Valley are the most visited in the state, but the other six offer natural wonders with fewer crowds.

- **Sequoia and Kings Canyon National Parks** (559/565-3341; www.nps.gov/seki): South of Yosemite, Sequoia and Kings Canyon National Parks hold some of the tallest and oldest trees on earth. The **General Sherman Tree,** in Sequoia, is the world's largest tree by volume, and the **General Grant Tree,** in Kings Canyon, a 1,700-year-old giant sequoia, is the second largest.

- **Lassen Volcanic National Park** (530/595-4480; www.nps.gov/lavo): One of the more remote and rugged of California's national parks, Lassen is also one of its most beautiful. A paved road (closed in winter) runs through Lassen, making for an easy tour of the park's highlights, such as **Bumpass Hell** and its boiling mud pots and steaming springs. **Mount Lassen** itself is an active volcano with a long recorded history of eruptions, the last of which took place in 1914-1917; a difficult 5-mile (8-kilometer) hike reaches its highest point.

- **Redwood National and State Parks** (www.nps.gov/redw): This complex of state and national parkland encompasses most of California's northern redwood forests. For a gorgeous scenic road through the redwoods, **Newton B. Drury Scenic Parkway,** off U.S. 101 about halfway between Orick and Klamath, features old-growth trees and a grove or trailhead every hundred yards or so.

- **Channel Islands National Park** (1901 Spinnaker Dr., Ventura; 805/658-5730; www.nps.gov/chis): Only accessible by boat or plane, Channel Islands National Park covers a group of five islands. **Santa Cruz,** California's largest island at 24 miles (38 kilometers) long and up to 6 miles (9.5 kilometers) wide, and **Anacapa** are the closest and most frequented. **Santa Rosa** and **Santa Barbara** are farther out, while **San Miguel** is accessible by permit only. Kayaking and whale-watching are popular activities.

- **Pinnacles National Park** (5000 Hwy. 146, Paicines; 831/389-4486; www.nps.gov/pinn): True to its name, this 26,000-acre (10,521-hectare) park is studded with huge rock formations jutting up into the sky. Accessed from the eastern entrance, **Bear Gulch Cave** is a talus cave that you can climb through.

and lush ecosystem. You'll see the palm trees, hardy grasses, and huge boulders that characterize the region.

## LAKE TAHOE

Sparkling blue Lake Tahoe and its surrounding mountains, lakes, ski resorts, hiking trails, hot springs, charming mountain towns, casinos, and varied wilderness areas say "vacation" to just about anyone. The Tahoe area has an international reputation as a **skiing** paradise, with some of the finest ski resorts in the nation and many opportunities for skiers, snowboarders, cross-country skiers, and snowshoers. Tahoe is slightly less crowded in the summer months than during ski season, and the weather is gorgeous every day.

One of the best ways to soak up every view of sparkling Lake Tahoe is to drive around its entire perimeter. Perhaps one of the most gorgeous stretches of the 72-mile (115-kilometer) route is the part that passes through **Emerald Bay State Park.** Even if you don't have plans to visit the park, pull over at one of the several scenic overlooks, such as **Inspiration Point**.

## POINT REYES NATIONAL SEASHORE

1 Bear Valley Rd.; 415/464-5100; www.nps.gov/pore

The Point Reyes area boasts acres of unspoiled grassland, forest, and beach. Cool weather presides even in the

POINT REYES NATIONAL SEASHORE

summer, but the result is lustrous green foliage and spectacular scenery. Point Reyes National Seashore stretches between Tomales Bay and the Pacific, north from Stinson Beach to the tip of the land at the end of the bay.

Dedicated **hikers** can trek from the bay to the ocean, or from the beach to land's end. Numerous other hikes cross the area, and it's also a great place for **road biking** and **kayaking.** In the marshes and lagoons, a wide variety of birds—including three different species of pelicans—make their nests. The pine forests shade shy deer and larger elk. Oyster lovers will want to add a stop in **Marshall,** on the mainland side of Tomales Bay, for a dozen or so fresh or barbecued bivalves.

# FESTIVALS AND EVENTS

## PASADENA TOURNAMENT OF ROSES PARADE

Pasadena, 626/449-4100; www.tournamentofroses.com; New Year's Day

You've probably seen it on TV: The Pasadena Tournament of Roses Parade is one of the nation's most popular New Year's Day events. The parade of flower-covered floats has been occurring since 1890. To see the floats up close and without the crowds, you can purchase tickets to view the floats as they are being decorated. And after the parade ends, the floats are on display, too.

## COACHELLA VALLEY MUSIC FESTIVAL

Empire Polo Field, 81-800 Ave. 51, Indio; 888/833-1031; www.coachella.com; usually Apr.

A perennial favorite for music lovers is the Coachella Valley Music Festival, where concertgoers immerse themselves in live music from sunup to sundown. The festival runs two long weekends each spring and includes art installations and plenty of pop-up restaurants. The fun rarely stops after the music ends, so many choose to camp at the festival.

## SAN FRANCISCO LGBT PRIDE CELEBRATION AND PARADE

Market St., San Francisco; www.sfpride.org; June

One of San Francisco's biggest parades is the San Francisco LGBT Pride Parade and Celebration. Hundreds of thousands of people of all orientations take to the streets for this quintessentially San Franciscan party-cum-social justice movement.

## COMIC CON

111 W. Harbor Dr., San Diego; www.comic-con.org; July

Year after year, Comic Con is the biggest event at the Downtown San Diego Convention Center. More than 125,000 people descend on San Diego to attend 600 staged events and 1,500 exhibitor booths. Take note when Comic Con takes place. It sells out far in advance, as do most of the hotels anywhere near downtown at triple their normal rates.

## MONTEREY JAZZ FESTIVAL

2004 Fairground Rd., Monterey; 831/373-3366; www.montereyjazzfestival.org; Sept.

As the site of the longest-running jazz festival on earth, Monterey attracts top performers from around the world. Held each September—the best month for beautiful weather on Monterey Bay—this long weekend of amazing music can leave you happy for the whole year.

## SPECTATOR SPORTS

California has a wealth of professional sports teams—not to mention universities with top-tier athletic programs, such as UCLA and USC. You'll be sure to find a game to attend anywhere in the state, any time of year.

California is home to several **Major League Baseball** teams: the San Francisco Giants, Oakland A's, Los Angeles Angels (who play in Anaheim), Los Angeles Dodgers, and San Diego Padres. The rivalry between Giants and Dodgers fans is particularly fierce.

As for **football** teams, in the NFL, you'll find the Los Angeles Chargers, Los Angeles Rams, and San Francisco

49ers (who play in Santa Clara). California's **NBA** teams are the Los Angeles Lakers, Los Angeles Clippers, Golden State Warriors (who play in San Francisco), and the Sacramento Kings.

# BEST FOOD AND DRINK

## CALIFORNIA CUISINE

California cuisine was defined by famous restaurants **The French Laundry** (6640 Washington St., Napa; 707/944-2380; www.frenchlaundry.com) and **Chez Panisse** (1517 Shattuck Ave., Berkeley; 510/548-5525; www.chezpanisse.com). To learn their preparation secrets, sign up for a class at the **Culinary Institute of America** (CIA, 2555 Main St., Napa; 707/967-1100; www.ciachef.edu).

## WINE

The beautiful grapevines of **Napa and Sonoma Valleys** north of San Francisco are renowned worldwide for producing top-quality vintages and economical table wines. Other top California wine regions include the **Anderson Valley** in the northern county of Mendocino, **Gold Country** in the Sierra Foothills, **Monterey and Carmel** on the Central Coast, **Paso Robles** in Central California, and **Santa Barbara.** California produces more than 100 types of grapes;

SAN FRANCISCO PRIDE PARADE

# BEST SOUVENIRS

- Don't leave California without a bottle of **wine.** Most wineries will waive their tasting fee if you buy a bottle for yourself.

- Celebrate the state's history and proximity to Mexico with a piece of **Mexican folk art.** You'll find crafts, jewelry, decorative wares, and Talavera tiles around Southern California, especially in San Diego.

- Embrace California's counterculture with a visit to San Francisco's legendary **City Lights bookstore** (261 Columbus Ave., 415/362-8193, www.citylights. com). Or, for music lovers, peruse the massive selection at **Amoeba Records** (www.amoeba.com). There are locations in San Francisco, Berkeley, and Hollywood.

- Embrace California's green lifestyle with **ecofriendly gifts.** Reusable water bottles, reusable straws, and tote bags are a good place to start.

here are a few of the most notable varietals and the best places to try them.

## Chardonnay

Most of the white wine made and sold in California is chardonnay. Most California chardonnays taste smooth and buttery and a bit like fruit, and they often take on the oak flavor of the barrels in which they are aged.

- **Grgich Hills Winery:** 1829 St. Helena Hwy., Rutherford; 707/963-2784; www. grgich.com

## Pinot Noir

Pinot noir grapes do best in a cool coastal climate with limited exposure to high heat. The Anderson Valley and the Monterey coastal growing regions tend to specialize in pinot noir, though many Napa and Sonoma wineries buy grapes from the coast to make their own versions. California vintners make up single-varietal pinot noir wines that taste of cherries, strawberries, and smoke.

- **Robert Sinskey Vineyards:** 6320 Silverado Tr., Napa; 707/944-9090; www.robertsinskey.com
- **Hop Kiln:** 6050 Westside Rd., Healdsburg; 707/433-6491; www.hopkilnwinery.com

## Zinfandel

A true zinfandel is a hearty, deep red wine that boasts the flavors and smells of blackberry jam and the dusky hues

of venous blood. Zinfandel often tastes wonderful on its own, but it's also good with beef, buffalo, and even venison.

- **Ravenswood Winery:** 18701 Gehricke Rd., Sonoma; 707/933-2332 or 888/669-4679; www.ravenswood-winery.com

## Cabernet Sauvignon

Cabernet sauvignon, a grape from the Bordeaux region of France, creates a deep, dark, strong red wine. In California, especially in Napa, winemakers use cabernet sauvignon on its own to brew some of the most intense single-grape wines in the world. A good dry cab might taste of leather, tobacco, and bing cherries.

- **Stag's Leap Wine Cellars:** 5766 Silverado Tr., Napa; 866/422-7523; www.cask23.com

## MEXICAN FOOD

In San Francisco, the Mission District neighborhood is known for its abundant taquerias, and specifically a local invention: the **Mission burrito**—essentially an incredibly large burrito (one can usually feed two people). Try them at popular spots like **El Farolito** (2779 Mission St., San Francisco; 415/824-7877) or James Beard-recognized **La Taqueria** (2889 Mission St., San Francisco; 415/285-7117).

However, eating tacos must be done in San Diego. There are a number of places that serve them, whether authentic Baja street tacos or some traditional local take on fried fish. **South Beach Bar & Grille** (5059 Newport Ave., Ocean Beach; 619/226-4577; www.southbeachob.com) is the fish taco destination for locals and out-of-town guests. Another good pick, **Puesto** (1026 Wall St., San Diego; 858/454-1260; www.eatpuesto.com) offers a wide variety of taco fillers boasting authentic flavors and made with local and sustainable ingredients.

## FRESH PRODUCE

California is an agricultural powerhouse, so it only makes sense that the state has some of the best fresh fruits and veggies around. The lush fields portrayed in Steinbeck's novels still supply much of the world with crops of almost all kinds, from grapefruit to grass-fed beef. Along the fertile **Central Valley** you'll find everything from rice to corn to tomatoes. Elsewhere, orchards of nut and fruit trees, and fields of sweet strawberries and spiky artichokes, fill the landscape. The town of **Gilroy,** near Monterey, is famous for its **garlic** and hosts a popular festival (https://gilroygarlicfestival.com; July) to celebrate the pungent bulb.

No matter what part of the state you're in, you're sure to find an excellent farmers market. Top farmers market locations include the **Ferry Building** in San Francisco and the **Original Farmers Market** (6333 W. 3rd St.; https://farmersmarketla.com) in Los Angeles. The town of **San Luis Obispo** on the central coast has one of the largest farmers markets in the state; the weekly gathering offers the goods of 70 farmers and lots of live music.

## MAJOR AIRPORTS

- **Los Angeles International Airport:** LAX; 1 World Way, Los Angeles; 855/463-5252; www.lawa.org

- **San Francisco International Airport:** SFO; U.S. 101, Millbrae; 800/435-9736; www.flysfo.com

- **San Diego International Airport:** SAN; 619/400-2404; www.san.org

## MORE INFORMATION

### TRAVEL AND TOURISM INFORMATION

- **Visit California:** www.visitcalifornia.com

- **California State Parks:** www.parks.ca.gov

### NEWSPAPERS

- *Los Angeles Times:* www.latimes.com

- *San Francisco Chronicle:* www.sfchronicle.com.

BAJA-STYLE FISH TACOS

# SOUTHWEST

◀ MONUMENT VALLEY, ARIZONA

# THE SOUTHWEST
## *State by State*

### NEVADA

**Why Go:** Las Vegas attends to worldly pursuits, while ghost towns and the Extraterrestrial Highway offer the otherworldly.

### ARIZONA

**Why Go:** The vistas associated with the West—mesas rising out of the desert, swirling red slot canyons, anthropomorphic saguaro, and the mind-blowing Grand Canyon—are all here.

### UTAH

**Why Go:** Utah's five national parks showcase nature's architecture: sheer cliffs, fanciful rock formations, craggy spires, and graceful arches.

### NEW MEXICO

**Why Go:** The distinctive Pueblo culture continues in the 19 Pueblos located across the state, including the oldest continually inhabited communities in the United States, while dazzling white-sand deserts provide a setting for contemplative isolation.

### TEXAS

**Why Go:** The country's second-largest state (in size and in population) encompasses everything from the longhorns of the Fort Worth Stockyards to the remote undulations of the Rio Grande's Big Bend, and from the Space Center in Houston to the artistic compound in Marfa, not to mention the barbecue, Tex-Mex, and global cuisine.

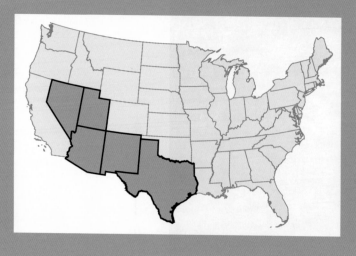

# Southwest ROAD TRIP

You can see a huge swath of the southwest by driving in a loop of roughly 2,000 miles (3,200 kilometers). This road trip ticks off many places on your U.S. bucket list: Utah's five national parks, Route 66, the Grand Canyon, and more. Consider getting an annual National Parks Pass at your first park—it'll pay for itself on this trip.

## UTAH

**Utah's National Parks: 4 Days / 575 miles (925 kilometers)**
From Las Vegas, Utah's **Zion National Park** is about a 3-hour drive without traffic. Explore iconic attractions like **Court of the Patriarchs** and the **Emerald Pools**. The next day, head to **Bryce Canyon National Park** (1.5 hours away), and see the hoodoos. Don't miss watching the sun go down from **Sunset Point**. On the third day, you'll hit your third national park, **Capital Reef.** Spend the day

making the scenic 120-mile (193-kilometer) trip from Bryce Canyon and the **scenic drive** within the park. Make the 2.5-hour drive to **Moab** to spend the night. In the morning, head to **Arches National Park,** then **Canyonlands,** or vice-versa (they are an hour apart), to get your fill of beautiful natural arches and other rock formations.

## NEW MEXICO

**Taos, Santa Fe, Albuquerque, Route 66: 4-5 Days / 800 miles (1,290 kilometers)**
From Moab, detour into Arizona for a tour of **Monument Valley Navajo Tribal Park,** 3 hours away. In the morning, drive out to the **Four Corners Monument** (2 hours) to step foot in New Mexico—and Utah and Arizona and Colorado. Then make the 5-hour drive to **Taos.** Spend the rest of the day and next morning in the high-elevation

ARCHES NATIONAL PARK, UTAH

TRADITIONAL WHITE LADDERS IN ACOMA PUEBLO, NEW MEXICO

town. Take one of the two scenic routes to **Santa Fe** (2-3 hours), and spend the night (or two—you've done a lot of driving, and Santa Fe is a great place to relax). Head an hour south to **Albuquerque** for a ride on the **Sandia Peak Tramway,** then start your journey on **Historic Route 66** with a 2-hour drive out to **Gallup.**

## ARIZONA

**Route 66, Grand Canyon: 3 days / 470 miles (755 kilometers)**
From Gallup, drive I-40/Route 66 west into Arizona, stopping at **Petrified Forest National Park** after an hour or so. Make it an early the night in **Flagstaff** (2 hours away), so you can set out early for the **Grand Canyon** the next day. Take in the views from the **Rim Trail** or descend into the canyon on the **Bright Angel Trail.** The next day, head out to **Ash Fork** (2 hours from Grand Canyon Village) for more Route 66: The longest remaining stretch of the road starts here. Take it west to **Kingman** (2 hours from Ash Fork), where you can spend the night in a neon-signed motor inn.

## NEVADA

**Hoover Dam, Las Vegas: 1 day / 145 miles (230 kilometers)**
From Kingman, head to **Hoover Dam** (1.5 hours), which straddles the Arizona-Nevada border. Take a tour to admire the engineering marvel and then set your sights on **Las Vegas,** where you'll arrive in an hour or so. Spend the rest of the day at the pool, in a spa, or at any of the thousands of diversions the city has to offer.

## ADDING TEXAS

**Guadalupe Mountains National Park, Marfa, and Big Bend National Park: 3 days / 615-660 miles (990-1,060 kilometers) one-way**
Getting to Texas takes a lot of driving, often through very remote areas. Given that it's the largest state in the Lower 48, it could certainly justify its own trip. If you want to add Texas as part of this Southwest road trip, you could head down to **Big Bend National Park** over three days (one way) from Santa Fe or Albuquerque. On the first day, stop in Roswell and **Carlsbad Caverns National Park** on the New Mexico side, 5-6 hours of driving, depending on where you start. On the second day, you'll hit **Guadalupe Mountains National Park,** which is just across the Texas border, then head south on Highway 54, which is very scenic, and U.S. 90 to **Marfa,** 2 hours away. On the third day, you'll make it to **Big Bend,** about 2.5 hours southeast of Marfa.

COWBOY BOOTS FOR SALE IN TEXAS

# NEVADA

The independent spirit of Native Americans' respect for the land, pioneers' sense of adventure, prospectors' optimism, and Basque immigrants' industriousness still abides here. Located on Hualapai, Northern Paiute, Southern Paiute, Shoshone, and Washoe land, the state is full of incongruities: the urbanity of Las Vegas balanced by agrarian idylls; the forbidding barrenness of the desert contrasted by fruit trees and grapevines. While cowboy conservatism is prevalent in much of the state, Nevada remains the only place in the U.S. where not only gambling but also rural prostitution and recreational marijuana are both legal and vital to the economy.

There's plenty of opportunity for vice and consumption in Nevada, but there's more to this state than bright lights and unchecked hedonism. Far from the neon jungle, you can plunge deep into the hot springs and otherworldly landscapes of Nevada's backcountry. Though the Vegas Strip, Reno, and Lake Tahoe shine like nuggets in a gold pan, Nevada's real treasures lie just below the surface.

AREA: 110,577 square miles / 286,393 kilometers (7th)

POPULATION: 3,080,156 (32nd)

STATEHOOD DATE: October 31, 1864 (36th)

STATE CAPITAL: Carson City

RHYOLITE GHOST TOWN

## ORIENTATION

**Las Vegas** is located near the pointy southern corner of this trapezoidal state, and farther north, **Lake Tahoe, Carson City,** and **Reno** sit in the bend of California. In between, the **Great Basin** stretches across central and southern Nevada, crossed by The Loneliest Road (U.S. 50). The remote landscapes of the Great Basin also hold **Area 51.** The **Humboldt River Valley** covers northern Nevada, where the **Black Rock Desert** hosts Burning Man and the **Ruby Mountains** stand.

## WHEN TO GO

Nevada makes a great **winter** escape, whether you want to shred the manicured slopes around Lake Tahoe or enjoy sunny mild temperatures in Las Vegas. In **summer,** these big destinations still draw plenty of visitors, despite temperatures that push 100°F (37°C) in the desert. If you're headed to Nevada to enjoy outdoor recreation, **spring** and **fall** are perhaps the best times to visit. The spring sun is bright but not too hot and showers bring out desert wildflowers. Fall sees the baking heat abate in time for picnics, outdoor events, and camping trips.

# HIGHLIGHTS

## HOOVER DAM

After a great flood in 1905, federal overseers decided that the Colorado River had to be tamed. An architectural and engineering marvel, Hoover Dam was completed in 1935. By 1938, **Lake Mead**—measuring 110 miles (177 kilometers) long and 500 feet (152 meters) deep and containing 28.5 million acre-feet (3.5 hectare meters) of water (just over 9 trillion gallons/34 trillion litres)—was the largest artificial lake in the West. The reservoir irrigates 2.25 million acres (910,542 hectares) of land in the United States and Mexico and supplies water for more than 14 million people. Nine million people use Lake Mead each year as a recreational resource.

The **Lake Mead visitors center** (702/494-2517; www.usbr.gov/lc/hooverdam) has exhibits, a movie, and elevators into the dam. Two guided tours of the dam are offered; on each, visitors walk through tunnels, access viewing platforms, and feel the shaking of water rushing through pipes.

VIEW FROM HOOVER DAM OVER THE COLORADO RIVER

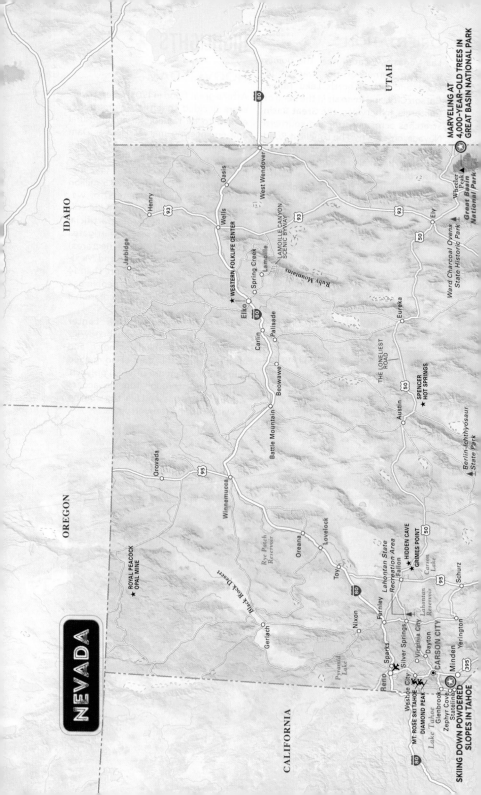

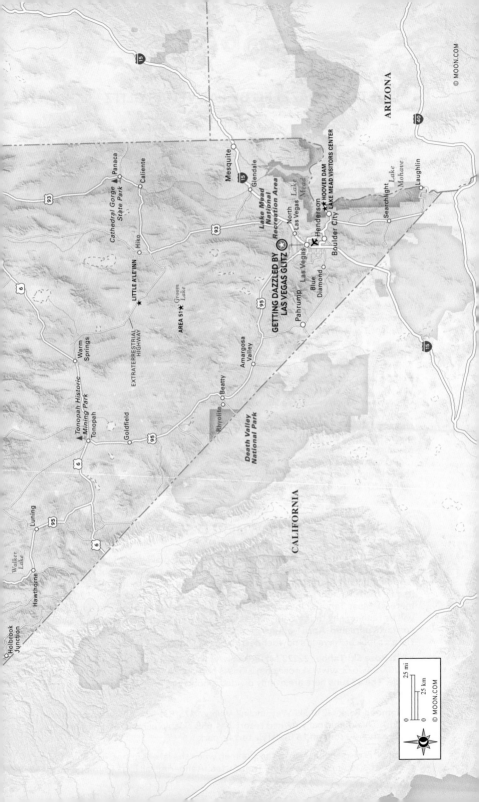

# TOP  3

## ① GETTING DAZZLED BY LAS VEGAS GLITZ

Flashing neon, luxury resorts, and over-the-top shows—it doesn't get any glitzier than Vegas. The city has a way of winning people over. Even nongamblers horrified at the thought of throwing away hard-earned cash might slide $20 into a slot machine—hey, you never know, right?

For the iconic Las Vegas experience, head straight to the center of **the Strip,** aka Las Vegas Boulevard South. Between Harmon Avenue and Spring Mountain Road, the casinos are packed tight, and all the temptations are within walking distance. At the **Venetian** (3355 Las Vegas Blvd. S.; 702/607-3982; www. venetian.com), pass beneath quaint bridges and idyllic sidewalk cafés in one of their gondolas. **Caesars Palace** (3570 Las Vegas Blvd. S.; 866/227-5938; www. caesars.com) has all of ancient Rome's decadence with a few thousand slot machines. For classic Las Vegas, the **Lower Strip** is a living city timeline, starting with the **"Welcome to Fabulous Las Vegas" sign** and the **Tropicana** (3801 Las Vegas Blvd. S.; 702/739-2222; www.

THE LAS VEGAS STRIP AFTER DARK

troplv.com), which provides a link to the mobbed-up city of the 1960s and 1970s.

Beyond the casino floor, most resorts are full of other diversions—restaurants, shops, pools, spas, nightclubs—so there's hardly a reason to leave, unless there's a particular show you want to see. Although Las Vegas made the feathered showgirl famous, the popular shows these days, such as the Mirage's Beatles-inspired *Love* (3400 Las Vegas Blvd. S.; 866/983-4279, www.cirquedusoleil.com/beatles-love) or the Bellagio's watery *O* (3600 Las Vegas Blvd. S.; 866/983-4279; www.cirqueduso-leil.com/O) feature Cirque du Soleil or well-known headliners.

## ② SKIING DOWN POWDERED SLOPES IN TAHOE

Surrounded by majestic peaks, this bluest of lakes makes the ideal setting for hiking, camping, and of course, skiing. Although most of Lake Tahoe and its recreational opportunities are across the state border in California, Nevada boasts its fair share. Annual snowfall averages 40 feet, with snowpack around 20 feet (6 meters). Most Tahoe slopes open around **Thanksgiving,** but you can bet the lifts will be running any time a cold front dumps a foot or so of the white stuff. Ski season lasts until **mid-April**—or until temperatures rise enough for the snow to melt. Here's a look at Nevada's powder destinations in Tahoe.

- **Mt. Rose Ski Tahoe** (22222 Mt. Rose Hwy., New Washoe City; 775/849-0704 or 800/754-7673; www.skirose.com): This is perhaps the best resort on the Nevada side. The 43 runs here are evenly divided among beginner, intermediate, and expert.

- **Diamond Peak** (1210 Ski Way, Incline Village; 775/831-3211; www.diamondpeak. com): This municipally owned resort has 655 skiable acres (265 hectares) and more than 30 runs and a freestyle terrain park.

Tahoe is also enchanting in the summer, when the lake is impossibly blue. Walk part of the 165-mile **Tahoe Rim Trail** (https://tahoerimtrail.org) from one of the

MT. ROSE SKI TAHOE RESORT

three Nevada-side trailheads: Tahoe Meadows to Spooner Summit, Spooner Summit, and Kingsbury.

 ## MARVELING AT 4,000-YEAR-OLD TREES IN GREAT BASIN NATIONAL PARK

Baker; www.nps.gov/grba

The air is fresh, the views are grand, and the vibe is reverent in this hallowed temple of the wilderness. Great Basin National Park was created to preserve and showcase a preeminent example of the vast ecosystem that covers 20 percent of the lower 48 states, including almost all of Nevada. The **Snake Range** packs a more diverse ecology into a discrete mountain range than any of the other 250 ranges in this vast western desert. All five Great Basin biological zones occur in the roughly 8,000 feet (2,438 meters) from the valley to **Wheeler Peak,** the second-highest point in Nevada. The range contains the only permanent glacier-like ice in the state. It also boasts a large forest of 4,000-plus-year-old **bristlecone pines,** the oldest living organisms on the planet. Within the quartzite limestone are corridors of **caverns** that have been carved by water over millions of years. To see both the glacier and the pines on Wheeler Peak, hike the 4.6-mile (7.4-kilometer) **Bristlecone and Glacier Trail,** which starts out with an easy stroll around the ancient trees and then climbs over steep and rocky terrain to the glacial cirque.

BRISTLECONE PINE, GREAT BASIN NATIONAL PARK

# *Best* ROAD TRIP

**DAY 1** In **Las Vegas,** partake in the glitzy pleasures of **the Strip,** from the **Venetian's** gondolas to an extravagantly produced show.

**DAY 2** Leave Las Vegas for a brief trip southeast to the roaring **Hoover Dam** before heading northwest to the "ghost city" of **Rhyolite.** After exploring landmarks like the **Bottle House,** where the walls are covered in thousands of empty bottles, head to **Mel's Diner** in nearby Beatty to refuel.

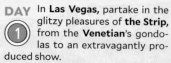

THE VENETIAN, LAS VEGAS

**DAY 3** It's a long drive to capital **Carson City,** but there are some great stops along the way, from a meal at nostalgic **Dinky Diner,** to learning about Nevada's history at **Tonopah Historic Mining Park,** to wildlife viewing at **Lahontan State Recreation Area.**

**DAY 4** If it's ski season or you want a great hike, make a detour west to **Lake Tahoe;** otherwise, head back east on **the Loneliest Road,** stopping at **Grimes Point** and **Hidden Cave** for views into Nevada's Indigenous history, ending up in **Spencer Hot Springs** for a soothing soak.

LAKE TAHOE

**DAY 5** Head for **Great Basin National Park** to marvel at limestone **caves,** ancient **bristlecone pines,** and maybe summit **Wheeler Peak.**

**DAY 6** Driving south, linger over the view of the otherworldly pillars of **Cathedral Gorge.** From here, you're not far from the kitschy mysteries of the **Extraterrestrial Highway,** which skirts the buffer zone of **Area 51** and ends up at the **Little A'Le'Inn** restaurant and motel. It's a 2-hour drive back to Las Vegas the next day.

CATHEDRAL GORGE

# Major CITIES

**LAS VEGAS:** Today, Sin City is known for its fine restaurants, entertainment, and people-watching as much as for its slot machines and craps tables.

**RENO:** Beyond the slot machines and access to Lake Tahoe, Reno offers the Truckee Riverwalk and an emerging art scene.

**CARSON CITY:** A Gold Rush-era town, Nevada's political capital successfully combines outdoor recreation with rich dining and historic sights, such as the **Kit Carson Trail,** a walking path connecting 60 Victorian-style homes, museums, and churches.

## GHOST TOWNS

Following the lure of a big strike, miners, gamblers, and entrepreneurs have long bet big on Nevada. More than 100 ghost towns testify to the Silver State's booms and busts. **Rhyolite,** near Beatty and Death Valley, at one time boasted a population of more than 10,000. In addition to the famous **Bottle House,** with 10,000 barroom empties encrusting the walls, the ruins of several other buildings befitting a metropolis still stand. In the state's remote northeast corner, **Jarbidge** is the site of one of America's last gold rushes (1929) and last stagecoach robbery (1916). Miners' cabins still line Main Street, and former brothels are tucked away off side streets.

## VIRGINIA CITY

Virginia City was Nevada's first boomtown, thanks to the Comstock Lode, still one of the largest silver strikes in the world. Today, the town's attractions are as authentic and as close as you're likely to come to imagining yourself a miner on payday, eager to soak up all the entertainment, culture, and whiskey your money can buy. To get a feel for those heady Comstock days, get under the ground to see what the miners saw, visit a silver baron's home, and stay in one of the town's many old-timey hotels. The **Chollar Mine** (615 S. F St.; 775/847-0155; www.chollarminetours.com) offers tours, while the **Mackay Mansion** (129 S. D St.; 775/847-0373; www.uniquitiesmackaymansion.com) reigns as the best way to see how the other half lived during the Comstock's heyday.

## GRIMES POINT AND HIDDEN CAVE

Take U.S. 50 west out of Fallon and south around the naval air station for 10 miles (16 kilometers) to Grimes Point, one of Nevada's largest and most accessible prehistoric rock art sites. With about 150 basalt boulders covered in petroglyphs, the site can be toured via a 1-mile (1.6-kilometer) trail. A mile (1.6 kilometers) northeast of Grimes Point, Hidden Cave is a grotto where a trove of Native American artifacts, including leatherwear, basketry, carved wooden and stone tools, and stored food were excavated. The Hidden Cave interpretive loop includes petroglyphs, tufa, and obsidian. The cave itself is only accessible via tours by the **Churchill County Museum** (1050 S. Maine, Fallon; 775/423-3677; www.ccmuseum.org).

## WARD CHARCOAL OVENS STATE HISTORIC PARK

775/867-3001 or 775/289-1693; http://parks.nv.gov

The main attraction of this state park south of Ely in eastern Nevada is the view of the beehive-shaped ovens lined up in the desert, hemmed in by a broken ridgeline. These six charcoal ovens, the largest in the state, were built in 1876 and were only used for three years to supply smelters with superhot burning fuel to refine the complex lead-silver-copper ore mined in the surrounding Ward Mining District. Each oven is 30 feet (9 meters) high and 27 feet (8 meters) wide at the base, with a door, window, and chimney hole; after they fell into disuse, they sheltered travelers—sometimes even stagecoach bandits.

# BEST SCENIC DRIVES

## THE LONELIEST ROAD

### U.S. 50

The Loneliest Road in America, aka U.S. 50, starts in **Carson City,** heading toward **Lahontan State Recreation Area** (16799 Lahontan Dam Rd., Fallon; 775/867-3500; http://parks.nv.gov/parks/lahontan), where you can commune with wild horses, foxes, herons, and Nevada's only nesting bald eagles. It's a little over halfway to **Fallon,** not far from **Grimes Point** and **Hidden Cave.** Next, head toward **Berlin-Ichthyosaur State Park** (Austin, http://parks.nv.gov/parks/berlin-ichthyosaur), where you can spend a few hours strolling among well-preserved mining town relics and ichthyosaur fossil beds. Continue to **Spencer Hot Springs,** one of the most visitor-friendly hot springs in Nevada. From here, you can retrace your route back to **Reno** or continue eastward to **Great Basin National Park.** Better yet, jump on **NV 305** north and take **I-80** back to Reno through the small towns of **Winnemucca** and **Lovelock.**

## LAMOILLE CANYON SCENIC BYWAY

### National Forest Road 660

This 12-mile (19-kilometer) byway takes visitors deep into the Lamoille Canyon, a microcosm of the entire Ruby Mountain range, which are called the Alps of Nevada. This deep canyon features high peaks dusted with snow year-round and crystal-clear waterfalls created by spring runoff. Access the scenic byway by taking NV 227 (Lamoille Highway) south from **Elko** for 19 miles (30 kilometers). Turn right onto the byway a mile (1.6 kilometers) outside the hamlet of Lamoille; look for the sign. Along the scenic byway are wonderful trails, such as the easy 4-mile (6.4-kilometer) **Thomas Canyon Trail** from Thomas Canyon Campground, offering lake and ridge views, and diverse animal and plant life. The road ends at a turnaround with more trails; it's also the northern terminus of the 37-mile (59.5-kilometer) **Ruby Crest National Scenic Trail.**

## EXTRATERRESTRIAL HIGHWAY

### NV 375

An otherwise nondescript section of blacktop, the 100-mile (160-kilometer) stretch of NV 375 skirts the top-secret Air Force installation known as Area 51. While the federal government has insisted—when compelled by Freedom of Information Act requests—that the area is used for research and testing experimental aircraft, self-styled ufologists, conspiracy theorists, and aviation buffs beg to differ.

Begin your extraterrestrial journey just south of **Hiko,** where you can stop for a photo op at the junction of U.S. 93 and NV 318 under the official **"Extraterrestrial Highway" road sign.** Previous visitors have covered it with stickers, nearly obliterating the sign's text and artwork. A mile (1.6 kilometers) of U.S. 318 connects you to the ET Highway itself. After 40 miles (64 kilometers) or so, turn right onto a dirt road that leads 12 miles (19 kilometers) to the buffer zone that protects the entrance to **Area 51,** the rumored secret location where the U.S. government hides its secret intelligence on extraterrestrial life. You'll be nowhere close to anything sensitive or unearthly, but you wouldn't know it by the warning signs on the fence. Then, hightail it to the **Little A'Le'Inn** (9631 Old Mill Rd., Rachel;

## SOUVENIRS AND COLLECTIBLES

- **Opals:** Head to the shops in thriving small towns like **Winnemucca** or pay-to-dig opal mines like **Royal Peacock Opal Mine** (10 Virgin Valley Rd., Denio; 775/941-0374; www.royalpeacock.com) in search of these light-refracting gems.

- **Area 51 merch:** No trip on the Extraterrestrial Highway is complete without a T-shirt or some alien memorabilia from a kitschy gift shop.

775/729-2515; http://littlealeinn.com), where Alien Burgers are on the menu and the selection of alien merchandise is extensive and varied.

# BEST PARKS AND RECREATION AREAS

## CATHEDRAL GORGE STATE PARK

Panaca; 775/728-4460; http://parks.nv.gov/parks/cathedral-gorge

Park at the pullout at Cathedral Gorge, and give the reins to your imagination. A horizontal line runs along the formation; the darker rock on top is compacted clay hardened by lime from decomposing limestone, while the light greenish rock below is siltstone. The clay protects the siltstone from accelerated erosion, which is believed to have already worn away roughly 1,000 feet (304 meters) of deposits. A **visitors center** at the entrance has interpretive exhibits and park information.

From here, hikes disappear into areas where the canyon walls narrow down so much that they almost create natural bridges. The **Moon Caves** formation (the "Rabbit Hole" to locals) squeezes you through a narrow opening on your belly, where you emerge Alice-like in a room surrounded on all sides by towering pillars. The best time for pictures is in the evening, as the cliffs face west.

## TONOPAH HISTORIC MINING PARK

110 Burro St., Tonopah; 775/482-9274; www.tonopahminingpark.com

The highlight of the 70-acre (28-hectare) Tonopah Historic Mining Park is poking around the former **Silver Top** and **Mizpah** mines, sorting rooms, hoists, and railroad trestles. The tour's centerpiece is the **Burro Tunnel Underground Adventure;** you'll have a bird's-eye view of a 500-foot (152-meter) stope as you enter the viewing cage suspended above. Spare parts and cases of core samples sit gathering dust in buildings along the tour route, unchanged since the mines shut down. You'll walk across an exposed 2-foot-wide (0.6-meter) vein of silver ore, and peer into the 100-foot-deep (30-meter) **Glory Hole,** site of a 1922 cave-in caused by mining too near the surface.

# FESTIVALS AND EVENTS

## BURNING MAN

Black Rock Desert; https://burningman.org, late Aug.-early Sept.

Growing every year since Larry Harvey burned a human effigy in San Francisco

BURNING MAN

in 1986, Burning Man has become a $10 million, 50,000-person annual festival. A city is built and taken down in the middle of the desert for this week-long event that is part art show, part rebellion against commercialism, part self-actualization. Huge art installations, ornate costumes, all-night music parties, lights everywhere, and, of course, lots and lots of fire are the hallmarks of the party. So are nudity, alcohol, and drugs. The climax is the burning of the Man, a towering sculpture of a person.

## GREAT RENO BALLOON RACE

www.renoballoon.com; Sept.

More than 100 colorful hot-air balloons of all shapes dot the skies north of Reno, starting very early in the morning. A craft and souvenir show, food, balloon rides, and a student tissue-paper balloon launch add to the excitement.

## NATIONAL COWBOY POETRY GATHERING

Elko; www.nationalcowboypoetrygathering. org; Jan.

Hosted by the **Western Folklife Center** (510 Railroad St., Elko; 775/738-7508; www.westernfolklife.org), this week-long celebration of the rural West features poetry and music performances, as well as dance, crafts, and cooking workshops.

# BEST FOOD

## RETRO DINERS

With plenty of nostalgic charm and backroads made for road trips, Nevada boasts countless diners serving old-fashioned American favorites.

- **Gold 'n Silver Inn:** 790 W. 4th St., Reno; 775/323-2696; www.goldnsilverreno. com
- **Mel's Diner:** 600 U.S. 95., Beatty; 775/553-9003
- **Dinky Diner:** 323 Crook St., Goldfield; 775/485-3231

## BASQUE FOOD

Many Basque people migrated to Argentina from Europe and made their way north in the 1850s to the California gold rush. Following the silver exodus east to Nevada, they mined and then turned to sheepherding, a familiar skill from the old country. Outside the herding season, herders drifted into town

GREAT RENO BALLOON RACE

GOLD 'N SILVER INN, RENO

to hotels run by fellow Basques. These boardinghouses became the center of Basque culture in Nevada, and today the legacy that endures: No traveler to Nevada should leave without experiencing a meal at a Basque hotel.

These meals are never taken lightly, with courses served family-style: soup, salad, beans or pasta, french fries, and usually an entrée of chicken, beef, or lamb. Make sure to try a Picon punch, made with Amer Picon (a liqueur), grenadine, and a shot of brandy.

- **Martin Hotel:** 94 W. Railroad St., Winnemucca; 775/623-3197; http://themartinhotel.com

- **Star Hotel:** 246 Silver St., Elko; 775/738-9925 or 775/753-8696; www.elkostarhotel.com

## MAJOR AIRPORTS

- **McCarran International Airport:** LAS; 5757 Wayne Newton Blvd., Las Vegas; 702/261-5211; www.mccarran.com

- **Reno-Tahoe International Airport:** RNO; 2001 E. Plumb Ln., Reno; 775/328-6400; www.renoairport.com

## MORE INFORMATION

### TRAVEL AND TOURISM INFORMATION

- **Nevada Commission on Tourism:** www.travelnevada.com

- **Nevada State Parks:** http://parks.nv.gov

### NEWSPAPERS AND MAGAZINES

- *Nevada Magazine:* www.nevadamagazine.com

- *Las Vegas Review Journal:* www.reviewjournal.com

- *Reno Gazette-Journal:* www.rgj.com

# ARIZONA

Arizona is hot, rugged, and beautiful. All of its institutions, its attractions, and even its mythologies were forged through hard experience, trial, and error. The state is on Mojave, Hualapai, Havasupai, Pueblo, Paiute, Hopi, Navajo, Yavapai Apache, Akimel O'odham, Maricopa, Pascua Yaqui, O'odham Jewed, Tohono O'odham, San Carlos Apache, Western Apache, Quechan, Cocopah, and Zuni land, and that land was built by the movement and explosion of the earth—canyons ripped open and mountains kicked up over millennia of shaking and oozing. This roiling has provided a wonderland of diversity, building—all at once—hot and verdant desert scrublands, cool evergreen mountain forests, dry sweeping grasslands, and red-rock, river-carved, fairy-tale canyons.

In many a traveler's imagination, this place is the home to rattlesnakes, tumbleweeds, and vast tracts of arid wilderness. Luckily, Arizona still has all of these; there are still trackless spaces to explore. But the youngest state in the lower 48 is also one of the fastest-growing regions in the nation. It is never boring here. There is always something, or someone, being created anew, changing, and blooming.

AREA: 113,990 square miles / 295,232 square kilometers (6th)

POPULATION: 7,278,717 (14th)

STATEHOOD DATE: February 14, 1912 (48th)

STATE CAPITAL: Phoenix

SOUTH RIM OF GRAND CANYON NATIONAL PARK

## ORIENTATION

In northern Arizona, the **Colorado River** curves through the **Grand Canyon,** while Route 66/I-40 cuts across the state a little south of there, with **Flagstaff** the largest city in that region. **Phoenix** sits in the south-central portion of the state, surrounded by towns like Scottsdale and Mesa that form the **Valley of the Sun. Tucson** is farther south, closer to the border with Mexico. Between Phoenix and Flagstaff are the **Verde Valley** and **Sedona. Hopi Tribal Lands** and the **Navajo Nation** are located on the high-desert northeastern plateaus.

## WHEN TO GO

**Spring,** February-May, is high season for Arizona's lowland deserts, including Phoenix and Tucson. The weather is gorgeous, often in the high 70s and 80s. It's also the season for Cactus League spring training baseball games throughout March.

It typically stays triple-digit hot on Arizona's deserts from **summer** deep into **October**; nonetheless summer is the **busy tourist season** in the northern regions of the state that include the Grand Canyon, North-Central Arizona, and Indian Country. By November the weather cools off, and from December into February a kind of **winter** comes to the desert, drawing snowbirds from colder climates, crowding the areas around Tucson and the Valley of the Sun.

# HIGHLIGHTS

### HEARD MUSEUM

2301 N. Central Ave., Phoenix; 602/252-8848; www.heard.org

It is possible for the observant visitor to the Heard Museum to come away with a rather deep knowledge of the cultures, religions, and histories of the state's Indigenous peoples. The museum has 10 galleries featuring the art, artifacts, and historical narratives of each of the state's tribes. The large display on the Hopi is particularly comprehensive and includes Barry Goldwater's kachina collection. It's not all static history, though. Several galleries feature contemporary art by Native Americans and others. Sculptures dot the grounds while artists demonstrate their methods to onlookers. If you're in the market for Native American art (or if you just like looking at it), especially that produced by Hopi and Navajo artists, don't miss the museum's store.

### ARIZONA-SONORA DESERT MUSEUM

2021 N. Kinney Rd., Tucson; 520/883-2702; www.desertmuseum.org

OVERLOOK AT THE ARIZONA-SONORA DESERT MUSEUM IN TUCSON

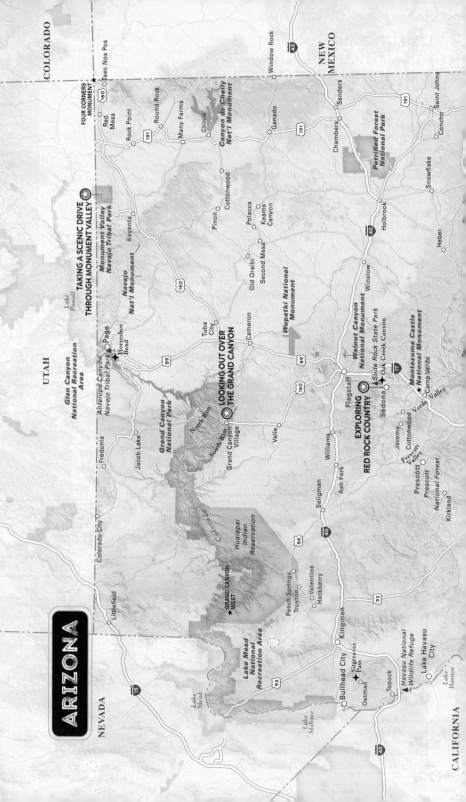

# TOP  3

## 1 LOOKING OUT OVER THE GRAND CANYON

928/638-7888; www.nps.gov/grca

The Grand Canyon must simply be seen to be believed. Most visitors observe it from one of the South Rim's easily accessible **lookouts.** Staring into the canyon brings up all kinds of existential questions; its brash vastness can't be taken in without conjuring some big ideas and questions about life and humanity.

BRIGHT ANGEL TRAILHEAD, GRAND CANYON

For the single best way to see all of the South Rim, walk along the easy, accessible **Rim Trail,** past historical buildings, famous lodges—and the most breathtaking views in the world. Another must-do is a hike down the popular **Bright Angel Trail** to get a feeling of what it's like to be below the rim. The more adventurous can make reservations, obtain a permit, and enter the desert depths of the canyon by taking a hike, or even a **mule ride,** to the Colorado River or spending a weekend trekking rim to rim with an overnight at the famous **Phantom Ranch** (888/297-2757; www.grandcanyonlodges.com), deep in the canyon's inner gorge. The really brave can hire a guide and take a once-in-a-lifetime **rafting trip** down the great river, camping on its serene beaches.

A ride on the park's free **shuttle** along **Hermit Road** (7 miles/11 kilometers) also offers views of the South Rim. The shuttle stops at eight viewpoints on the drive from **Grand Canyon Village** to Southwestern architect Mary Colter's **Hermit's Rest.** And don't miss a climb up to the deck of **Desert View Watchtower.** This rock tower standing tall on the edge of the canyon is Colter's artful homage to smaller Ancestral Puebloan-built towers found at Hovenweep National Monument in Utah and elsewhere in the Four Corners region.

Although the South Rim is the main stop for visitors to the Grand Canyon, there are other places to appreciate it. You can go to the less-visited, forested, and often snowy **North Rim,** a five-hour drive from the South Rim. Located on the Hualapai Indian Reservation, **Grand Canyon West** (www.grandcanyonwest.com), with its glass-bottom platform, combines a thrilling view of the canyon with a visit to one of Arizona's most remote locales.

## 2 EXPLORING RED ROCK COUNTRY

Famed Red Rock Country is one of the world's most celebrated landscapes, with the posh city of **Sedona** at the center. Red Rock Country's towering natural monuments were once a part of the Colorado Plateau, the connection eaten away by erosion over millions of years. High concentrations of iron oxide, or rust, in the sediment layers stain the rock statues many shades of red. The result is one of the most beautiful and sought-after landscapes on earth.

Many of the red-rock buttes, spires, and monuments around Sedona have been given names over the years. Some of the more famous rocks—**Chimney Rock, Coffee Pot Rock,** and **Snoopy Rock,** for example—can be seen from the road at designated pull-offs, and most of them have relatively easy trails around them if you want to get closer. Arguably the most beautiful drive in the state is the twisty, streamside drive north out of Sedona on State Highway 89A through **Oak Creek Canyon** and back up to the plateau. You'll see towering red rocks, topped with white caps, and greenery peppered throughout. Stop for a hike or to splash around in the water at **Slide Rock State Park** (6871 N. Hwy. 89A; 928/282-3034; http://azstateparks.com), where you can try out an 80-foot (24-meter) natural red-rock slide.

The landscape's famous rusty buttes, red slickrock, mystical slot canyons, and lush and shady creek sides reward the traveler who takes to the rocky **trails.** Many of the trails around Sedona are open to **hikers, equestrians,** and **mountain bikers.** A top hike in the area is along the **West Fork of Oak Creek Trail**

SEDONA

(north of Sedona; 6.5 miles/10.4 kilometers round-trip; 2-3 hours), where dark green evergreens mingle with red rocks and trickling water to create an exotic Southwestern Eden.

# 3  TAKING A SCENIC DRIVE THROUGH MONUMENT VALLEY

https://navajonationparks.org/tribal-parks/monument-valley

The scenic drive 22 miles (35 kilometers) north from **Kayenta** along **U.S. 163** to **Monument Valley Navajo Tribal Park** is almost as dramatic as the destination itself. About a third of the way along the paved route you'll see the aptly named **Owl Rock** to the west and the hulking, jagged **Agathla Peak** (also known as El Capitan) to the east, which tribal lore says marks the center of the world.

It was the director John Ford who made this remote place a symbol of the West's dueling freedom and danger, most memorably in *The Searchers.* Now, to drive around the park is to enter a thousand car commercials, magazine layouts, road films, and Westerns; it's a landscape that's comfortably, beautifully familiar even if you're seeing it for the first time.

The Navajo have not overdeveloped this sacred place, so the only way to see the park without a Navajo guide is to drive the 17-mile (27-kilometer) unpaved **Valley Drive** with 11 pullouts for views of some of the more famous mesas, buttes, and spires. This is one of the most scenic, inspirational, and absolutely essential drives in the Southwest. Upon entering the park you'll get a map of the drive with the name of each "Monument"—names like

VALLEY DRIVE THROUGH MONUMENT VALLEY

Wetherill Mesa, John Ford's Point, and The Thumb. If you can, it's worth arriving about an hour or so before sundown to see sunset over the valley—you'll wonder how you got here, and you'll stay until the lights go out. Be warned, though, that with the constant stream of cars driving the dry, dirt road, the air tends to get dusty. For more access to the Monument Valley's wondrous landscapes, hire a Navajo guide at the visitor center or ahead of your visit. The **Navajo Parks and Recreation Department** (www.navajonationparks.org) offers a list of reputable Navajo-owned guide companies.

# *Best* ROAD TRIP

**DAY 1** Arrive at **Sky Harbor International Airport** in Phoenix and spend a few hours getting to know Phoenix, touring the **Heard Museum,** the **Phoenix Art Museum** (1625 N. Central Ave., Phoenix; 602/257-1222; www.phxart.org), or Frank Lloyd Wright house **Taliesin West** (12621 Frank Lloyd Wright Blvd., Scottsdale; 480/860-2700; www.franllloydwright.org). Feast on **Mexican food** for dinner.

**DAY 2** Drive 2 hours (116 miles/186 kilometers) north to **Sedona.** Spend the day shopping, hiking, sightseeing, and exploring Sedona and the **Verde Valley.** Check out **Montezuma Castle National Monument,** about 26 miles (41 kilometers) from town, or hike into red-rock country.

**DAY 3** Eat breakfast in Sedona, and then head north on Highway 89A through scenic **Oak Creek Canyon.** Continue north to **Flagstaff,** about an hour's drive (30 miles/48 kilometers) from Sedona. Check into one of the historic hotels downtown. Stroll and shop downtown before dinner.

**DAY 4** Drive 1 hour 45 minutes (116 miles/186 kilometers) to **Petrified Forest National Park,** where the slickrock remains of a swampy forest are now a parched land strewn with reminders of the earth's unfathomable age. Then take I-40 to Highway 191 north to **Chinle** on the Navajo Reservation, a distance of 170 miles (273 kilometers), about 3 hours. Stay at the **Thunderbird Lodge** (928/671-5841; http://thunderbirdlodge.com) near **Canyon de Chelly.**

THE RED ROCK COUNTRY OF SEDONA

PETRIFIED FOREST NATIONAL PARK

GRAND CANYON NATIONAL PARK

**DAY 5** Spend the morning hiking into **Canyon de Chelly** to the **White House Ruin** and driving the scenic rim roads, or hire a Navajo guide and go deeper into the canyon. After lunch head to **Kayenta,** a distance of about 75 miles (120 kilometers) or about 1.5 hours. Get a hotel room in Kayenta, drive through **Monument Valley** late in the afternoon, and watch the sun set. Monument Valley is 50 miles (80 kilometers) from Kayenta, a drive that takes about an hour.

**DAY 6** Eat breakfast in Kayenta and then drive 2 hours (130 miles/209 kilometers) to **Grand Canyon National Park** and make your way to the east entrance. Check out the **Desert View** sights, then drive on into **Grand Canyon Village.** Spend the remainder of the day looking around the rim and staring into the majestic canyon, and spend the night here.

**DAY 7** In the morning, hike down one of the **South Rim trails** for as far as you feel like going. If you're not a hiker, you can take a **mule ride** to the river and back. In the afternoon, make the 3.5-hour drive (230 miles/370 kilometers) back to **Phoenix.** If you have more time to spare, you can head 1.5 hours (100 miles/160 kilometers) south to **Saguaro National Park** and **Tucson.**

SAGUARO NATIONAL PARK

Easy trails wind through this beautiful 21-acre (8.5-hectare) preserve, passing exhibits of semidesert grasslands and mountain woodlands similar to those surrounding and growing on the Sonoran Desert's high mountain ranges. There's a desert garden exhibit, a cactus and succulent garden, and a butterfly and wildflower display. There are also displays on desert fish and dunes, and a walk-in aviary that holds dozens of native birds.

## SAN XAVIER DEL BAC

1950 W. San Xavier Rd., Tucson; 520/294-2624; www.sanxaviermission.org

Founded in 1692 by Father Eusebio Francisco Kino and then built slowly over decades by others, the mission San Xavier del Bac sits pure white against the perpetually blue sky about 9 miles (14 kilometers) south of Tucson on the Tohono O'odham's San Xavier Indian Reservation. It is considered by many to be the foremost example of Mission architecture remaining in the United States, blending elements of Moorish, Byzantine, and late Mexican Renaissance architecture. Few Arizona architectural landmarks have received as much worldwide attention as the "White Dove of the Desert," which has been called America's answer to the Sistine Chapel. Mass is still celebrated daily in the church, but non-Catholic visitors are encouraged and welcomed.

## BISBEE

The most charming town in Cochise County began life in the 1880s as a copper mining camp. Eventually several billion pounds of the useful ore would be taken out of the ground here, and by 1910 Bisbee was said to be the biggest city between the Midwest and West Coast. But in the 1970s, with the mines long-closed, the town, with its labyrinthine staircases and cozy little bungalows built precariously on the slopes of the Mule Mountains, was nearly moribund when it was revived by hippies, artists, and artisans into what it is today. **Old Town Bisbee,** centered around Main Street and Brewery Gulch, is stuffed full of shops, galleries, restaurants, historic landmarks, and some of the best old hotels in the West. Perhaps

# *Major* CITIES

**PHOENIX:** Phoenix is the transportation, government, and cultural hub of the state. The city anchors a loose affiliation of cities and suburbs spreading to the wild northern Sonoran Desert known as the Valley of the Sun, one of the largest metro areas in the nation, boasting world-class hotels, restaurants, museums, theaters, sports, and shopping.

**TUCSON:** This characterful and historic city anchors a region of saguaro forests, sweeping grasslands, and quirky desert outposts. Tucsonans have tried to hold on to a semblance of the small, funky city character that once dominated the Old Pueblo, and the area serves as a reminder that this land was considered the northern end of Mexico not too long ago.

**FLAGSTAFF:** Flagstaff isn't the biggest of Arizona's cities, but it's a thriving tourism hub in northern Arizona and a gateway to the Grand Canyon.

the most fun to be had in Bisbee comes from just walking around, climbing the scores of off-kilter steps, and exploring its back alleys and narrow streets.

## HORSESHOE BEND

**U.S. 89, milepost 545**

As you drive into Page from the south along U.S. 89, look for milepost 545, where you can walk 0.75 mile (1.2 kilometers) one-way to a viewpoint above the famous, much-photographed Horseshoe Bend, where the Colorado River curves like a horseshoe around a lonely pink butte far below. You'll likely know you're there by the crowds. In recent years this barrier-free roadside lookout has become very popular. It's of course incredibly beautiful—the green

river meanders in a tight curve around red rock—but it's also thrilling because there's nothing between you and the river far, far below.

## FOUR CORNERS MONUMENT

About 70 miles (113 kilometers) east on Highway 160 from Kayenta is the Four Corners Monument, where a concrete slab marks the only spot in the United States where four states meet.

# BEST SCENIC DRIVES

## HISTORIC ROUTE 66

The longest remaining stretch of Route 66 runs through the dry grasslands, cholla forests, and barren rocky mountains of northwestern Arizona, about 165 miles (265 kilometers) between Ash Fork to the east and Topock on the Colorado River to the west.

From **Ash Fork,** which sits just off I-40, head west to the Colorado River, following the Route 66 signs. Or, you can start from **Topock,** near the Havasu National Wildlife Refuge, and drive east, ending at Ash Fork. Either way, you'll pass through sleepy **Peach Springs,** capital of the Hualapai Indian Reservation, and the nearly abandoned **Truxton** and **Valentine,** a few buildings dating from the 1930s to the 1950s moldering along the road. You'll pass **Hackberry,** with its famous and much-photographed Hackberry

HORSESHOE BEND

## HIGHWAY 89A FROM PRESCOTT TO JEROME

The best way to start a tour of the ancient oasis of the **Verde Valley** is to drive up and over the mountain that watches over it from the west, 7,743-foot (2,360-meter) **Mingus Mountain,** part of the Black Hills range and Prescott National Forest. Take **Highway 89A** from the mountain's base—either from the Verde Valley on the east side or Prescott Valley on the west—and slowly negotiate the switchbacks along the two-lane road, towered over by cliffs and overlooking deep, pine-swept draws. It's a scenic drive, one of the region's most stunning, usually taking about an hour to go the 30 miles (48 kilometers) or so over the mountain, through the old mining metropolis of **Jerome** and down the other side. The drive is understandably popular with motorcycle enthusiasts and sports car pilots, so you might have to pull over and let some of them pass.

HISTORIC ROUTE 66

General Store, and **Kingman,** with its neon-signed motels. Then climb up over **Sitgreaves Pass** and down the other side of the mountain to **Oatman,** home of the wild burros of Route 66, each descended from the beasts of burden that helped prospectors fight these desert hills more than a century ago.

## U.S. 60 TO THE SALT RIVER CANYON

Take a detour north on Route 77 (which doubles as U.S. 60 for this stretch) from old mining town **Globe** along the edge of the **Apache Mountains** for about 40 miles (64 kilometers) to spectacular **Salt River Canyon,** one of the more impressive roadside natural wonders in a state chock-full of them. Once used as a hideout by the Apache during the Indian wars, this 2,000-foot-deep (609-meter) jagged desert gorge is where the Salt River runs free and wild. There's a parking area before the bridge where you can learn about the canyon and take pictures, and easy paved trails lead down to the flowing river. If you've got a 4WD vehicle, you can head off on a riverside Jeep trail and explore the canyon in more depth.

# BEST PARKS AND RECREATION AREAS

## PETRIFIED FOREST NATIONAL PARK

1 Park Rd., Petrified Forest; 928/524-6228; www.nps.gov/pefo

What once was a swampy forest frequented by ancient oversize reptiles is now Petrified Forest National Park, a blasted scrubland strewn with multicolored, quartz-wrapped logs some 225 million years old, each one possessing a smooth, multicolored splotch or swirl seemingly unique from the rest. You can walk among the logs on several easy, paved **trails** and view a small ruin and petroglyph-covered rocks. Then, while driving through the pastel-hued badlands of the **Painted Desert,** which, seen from a promontory along the park's 28-mile (45-kilometer) scenic drive, will take your breath away, stop at the **Painted Desert Inn Museum.** The Pueblo Revival-style structure, originally a rustic, out-of-the-way hotel and taproom, was redesigned by Mary Colter, the great genius of Southwestern

# WINDOWS TO THE PAST

Arizona and the Southwest are home to many native cultures that are no longer around to tell their stories and legends. Luckily, the ruins of the Hohokam, Ancestral Puebloans, Salado, Sinagua, and others are protected throughout the state by federal law. You could make a whole trip out of visiting these structures, learning about the cultures that lived on these lands.

## THE HOHOKAM AND SALADO

Use Phoenix and the Valley of the Sun as your base as you discover ruins left behind by the Hohokam and Salado tribes.

- **Pueblo Grande Museum and Archaeological Park** (4619 E. Washington St., Phoenix; 602/495-0900; www.pueblogrande.org): Discover how the Hohokam coaxed an empire out of the Salt River Valley here at the ruin and museum in the middle of the city, near the ruins of the canals the Hohokam built to irrigate the desert.

- **Tonto National Monument** (26260 N. AZ Hwy 188 Lost 2, Roosevelt; 928/467-2241; www.nps.gov/tont): Take the backcountry route called the **Apache Trail,** east of Phoenix, and witness a well-preserved cliff dwelling once inhabited by the Salado tribe rising above slopes crowded with saguaros.

- **Casa Grande Ruins National Monument** (1100 W. Ruins Dr., Coolidge; 520/723-3172; www.nps.gov/cagr): Located between Phoenix and Tucson, the huge molded-dirt apartment building called Casa Grande is the largest example of Hohokam architecture left.

## THE SINAGUA

Use Sedona or Flagstaff as your base for visiting the awesome ruins of the Sinagua, who flourished in the Flagstaff and Verde Valley regions from around AD 500 to 1425.

- **Wupatki National Monument** (25137 N. Wupatki Loop Rd., Flagstaff; 928/679-2365; www.nps.gov/wupa): Just north of Flagstaff, this monument preserves the ruins of several awesome red-sandstone great houses.

- **Montezuma Castle National Monument** (I-17 Exit 289, Camp Verde; 928/567-3322; www.nps.gov/moca): This Verde Valley cliff dwelling features a cliff-wall castle molded out of limestone and is one of the best preserved in the Southwest.

## THE ANCESTRAL PUEBLOANS

In addition to **Canyon de Chelly,** other abandoned cliff cities of the Ancestral Puebloans can be seen in the Navajo Nation.

- **Navajo National Monument** (Hwy. 564, Shonto; 928/672-2700; www.nps.gov/nava): While visiting Tsegi Canyon, you can spot the ruin called **Betatakin** from the rim, nestled in a rock alcove above a bottomland forest. You can also sign up for a 17-mile (27-kilometer) round-trip hike below the rim of Tsegi Canyon to spend the night near the spectacularly preserved **Keet Seel** ruin hidden deep in the canyon.

style and elegance. There's a gift shop and bookstore at the inn now, and you can walk through it and gaze at the evocative, mysterious murals, full of Hopi mythology and symbolism, painted by Fred Kabotie, the great Hopi artist whom Colter commissioned to decorate the inn's walls.

## SAGUARO NATIONAL PARK

www.nps.gov/sagu

The icon of arid America, the saguaro (pronounced sa-WAH-ro) is so supremely adapted to the arid environment, in which the rains come but twice a year, that it anchors an entire busy community of desert creatures, be they cactus wrens, coyotes, or screech owls. The split Saguaro National Park has a **western section** (2700 N. Kinney Rd., Tucson) at the base of the Tucson Mountains and a larger **eastern section** (3693 S. Old Spanish Trail, Tucson; 520/733-5153) at the base of the Rincon Mountains. Together they protect about 91,300 acres (36,947 hectares) of magnificent Sonoran Desert landscape, including large and crowded saguaro forests surrounded by a thick underbrush of ocotillo, prickly pear, cholla, mesquite, and paloverde.

The easiest way to see the eastern section of the park—the section to visit if you only have time for one—is to stroll, bike, or drive very slowly along the paved **Cactus Forest Drive,** an 8-mile (12-kilometer) one-way road that begins at the visitors center and winds up and across the flatland. The desert here is gorgeous, especially after a rainstorm or early in the morning during the bloom months.

## GLEN CANYON NATIONAL RECREATION AREA

928/608-6200; www.nps.gov/glca

Sprawling over the Arizona-Utah border and some 1.25 million acres (505,857 hectares), Glen Canyon National Recreation Area is a popular boating, fishing, and hiking area centered on **Lake Powell,** which has more than a thousand miles (1,609 kilometers) of meandering desert shoreline. Its waters run through a red-rock maze of narrow side canyons, like canals around an ornate sandstone city, now abandoned. During the spring and summer months the lake is crowded with Jet Skiers, water-skiers, and houseboat residents.

## ANTELOPE CANYON NAVAJO TRIBAL PARK

928/698-2808

A color-swirled, water-worn slot in a mesa on Navajoland, Antelope Canyon Navajo Tribal Park is a popular crevice of twisting and twirling slickrock. Exploring the canyon requires a **Navajo guide** (https://navajonationparks.org/guided-tour-operators/antelope-canyon-tour-operators), but it's easy to find one. You pile into a big 4WD vehicle and ride several bumpy miles down a sandy wash to the slit in the rocks rising up out of the ground—the entrance to a **slot canyon** wonderland. It's an easy walk along a sandy bottomland, with the canyon walls rising 130 feet (39 meters) and impossibly narrow in some stretches. The slot canyon's unique undulations and warm reds and pinks, especially in the summer with the sun high in the sky and shining in laser-like shafts through small gashes high above, make it one of the most

ANTELOPE CANYON

photographed in the canyonlands, if not the world.

## CANYON DE CHELLY NATIONAL MONUMENT

928/674-5500; www.nps.gov/cach

The most visually impressive wind- and water-worn canyon in Arizona save for the one they call Grand, Canyon de Chelly (pronounced "de Shay"; the name is a Spanish approximation of the Navajo word for canyon, *tsegi*), is a labyrinth of eroded sandstone mesas, buttes, and spires, washed in pink and red and varnished with black and purple. The canyon's fertile bottomlands and safe, hidden alcoves have drawn people here for some 4,000 years. Ancestral Puebloans built several hanging villages against the red-rock cliffs, the remains of which are still slowly crumbling in their shady alcoves. The highlight here is seeing Ancestral Puebloan ruins up close at the **White House Ruin** via a slickrock hike along the White House Ruin Trail.

The federal monument comprises about 84,000 acres (33,993 hectares) of the canyon; however, nearly all of the canyon is off-limits without a hired **Navajo guide** (https://navajonationparks.org/guided-tour-operators/canyon-de-chelly-tour-operators).

CANYON DE CHELLY

# FESTIVALS AND EVENTS

## CACTUS LEAGUE SPRING TRAINING

late Feb.-early Mar.

The Valley of the Sun's Cactus League offers baseball fans a unique opportunity to watch their favorite Major League Baseball teams prepare for the coming season in intimate and family-friendly ballparks scattered around greater Phoenix. Fifteen big-league teams play in the Cactus League:

- **Salt River Fields** (7555 N. Pima Rd., Talking Stick Resort; 480/270-5000): Arizona Diamondbacks and Colorado Rockies
- **Hohokam Stadium** (1235 Center St., Mesa; 480/644-4451): Oakland Athletics
- **Sloan Park** (2330 W. Rio Salado Pkwy., Mesa; 480/668-0500): Chicago Cubs
- **Camelback Ranch Stadium** (10710 W. Camelback Rd., Glendale; 623/302-5000): Los Angeles Dodgers and Chicago White Sox
- **Goodyear Ball Park** (1933 S. Ball Park Way, Goodyear; 623/882-3120): Cleveland Indians and Cincinnati Reds
- **Surprise Stadium** (15850 N. Bullard Ave., Surprise; 623/222-2222): Kansas City Royals and Texas Rangers
- **Maryvale Baseball Park** (3600 N. 51st Ave., Phoenix; 623/245-5555): Milwaukee Brewers
- **Peoria Sports Complex** (16101 N. 83rd Ave., Peoria; 623/773-5700): San Diego Padres and Seattle Mariners
- **Tempe Diablo Stadium** (2200 W. Alameda Dr., Tempe; 480/350-5205): Los Angeles Angels of Anaheim
- **Scottsdale Stadium** (7408 E. Osborn Rd., Scottsdale; 480/312-2580): San Francisco Giants

Tickets for most of the teams are relatively abundant and affordable, and many of the ballparks offer package deals that include opportunities to take batting practice and work out with the team. Most of the teams' workouts are open to the public, and if you arrive about 30 minutes before the games, there are usually opportunities to get player autographs.

# BEST SOUVENIRS

- **Southwestern Indian arts and crafts:** There are hundreds of Native American artists living in Arizona, and many sell their work at markets and fairs held throughout the year in Phoenix, Tucson, Flagstaff, and elsewhere. Silverwork, carvings, pottery, rugs, and paintings of the Hopi, Navajo, and others are among the pieces on display and for sale.

- **Kachina dolls:** A particularly popular Native American piece is the Hopi kachina doll, carved out of cottonwood root. You'll find these at shops, galleries, and markets around the state.

- **Day of the Dead goods:** In the Arizona borderlands these days it's difficult to find a boutique, gift shop, or gallery that doesn't sell *calavera* (skeletons doing human things) statues, paintings, T-shirts, and all manner of other consumer goods featuring the Day of the Dead aesthetic. Generally, these art objects re-create the spirit of the work of Posada, a late-19th-century and early-20th-century Mexican printmaker and illustrator whose broadsides and newspaper illustrations employed the *calavera* and Day of the Dead traditions in social commentary.

## NAVAJO NATION FAIR

Window Rock; http://navajopeople.org; Sept.

The population of Window Rock swells every year in early September as the Navajo Nation Fair brings Navajos and others to one of the largest Native American cultural fairs anywhere. The weeklong event features a rodeo, horticulture contests, pageants (for babies, teens, and Miss Navajo), a parade, a midway and carnival, native foods, arts and crafts, drumming, dancing, and myriad other events. Don't count on getting a hotel room in town, or even in nearby Gallup, New Mexico, unless you book far ahead of the fair.

## DAY OF THE DEAD

Nov.

The Day of the Dead, El Día de los Muertos, falls on November 2, but the celebrations begin on November 1 or even before that. The Day of the Dead reminds us that death and the dead have a profound influence on the living. Celebrations vary but generally they include feasts in graveyards with a dead relative's favorite dishes prepared and set aside. There are also parades and marches, candles and altars, sugar skulls, and sweet breads shaped like skulls and skeletons. In Tucson, the **All Souls Procession** (www.allsoulsprocession.org), held the first weekend in November, culminates in a colorful and rather spooky nighttime parade through the downtown streets, featuring ghouls, ghosts, skeletons, big-headed puppets, and lots of other walking works of art.

# BEST FOOD

## MEXICAN FOOD

In Arizona, Mexican food reigns supreme, and **Tucson** and **Nogales** are the best places in the state to eat it. In Tucson you'll find dozens of restaurants featuring a variety of regional Mexican

ALL SOULS PROCESSION IN TUCSON

foods, but the most prevalent is the style of northern Mexico, "El Norte."

A ranching frontier, northern Mexico (specifically the states of Sonora and Chihuahua) has a cuisine based on beef, beans, cheese, and chilies. You are more likely to find flour tortillas in northern Mexico, as the desert and semidesert land is harder on corn than on wheat. A popular ranchland delicacy is *machaca*, also called *carne seca*—dried, shredded beef that is available at nearly every restaurant as a filling for burritos and tacos or on its own. Many Tucson restaurants are famous for their **carne asada**, or grilled meat—thin strips of beef spiced and grilled and then stuffed in tacos or burritos or served on their own with rice and beans. Another popular northern dish is **menudo**, available around Tucson and Phoenix. It's a kind of soup made with tripe, hominy, and cow's foot that's said to cure hangovers—it is often offered only on the weekends.

Originating in Hermosillo, the capital of the Mexican border state of Sonora, the so-called **Sonoran hot dog** is a decadent variation of the great American street food. You can find them all over Tucson and Phoenix at restaurants and from vendors on street corners. The classic version is a grilled hot dog wrapped in bacon and then couched in a fluffy Mexican-style bun (**bolillo**), and topped with beans, salsa, tomatoes, onions, creamy mayonnaise, and mustard.

## NATIVE CUISINE

Head to either the Navajo or Hopi Reservation, and you can sample the native cuisine, centered mainly around mutton and corn and a kind of Mexican-Native American amalgam called the **Navajo taco** (or Hopi taco)—a delicious hunk of fry bread piled high with meat and beans. Check out these restaurants to give the cuisine a try:

▪ One of the best restaurants on Navajoland, the **Blue Coffee Pot Restaurant** (0.25 mile/0.4 kilometer east of U.S. 160 and 163 junction, Kayenta; 928/697-3396) serves outstanding home-style Navajo, American, and Mexican food. The Navajo taco here is simply terrific, as are the beef ribs.

▪ **Painted Desert Diner** (Petrified Forest National Park; 928/524-3756) serves delicious fried chicken, Navajo tacos, burgers, and other road-food favorites in a cool Route 66 retro dining room.

▪ The independently operated **Turquoise Room** (303 E. 2nd St., Winslow; 928/289-2888; www.theturquoiseroom.net), in La Posada hotel, serves Southwestern- and Native American-inspired dishes. In a nod to the Hopi people who live on the mesas just north of Winslow, Sharpe serves piki bread, a traditional Hopi staple, made by a Hopi baker from Second Mesa.

## MAJOR AIRPORTS

▪ **Phoenix Sky Harbor International Airport:** PHX; 3400 E. Sky Harbor Blvd., Phoenix; 602/273-3300; www.skyharbor.com

▪ **Tucson International Airport:** TUS; 7250 S. Tucson Blvd., Tucson; 520/573-8100; www.flytucson.com

## MORE INFORMATION

### TRAVEL AND TOURISM INFORMATION

▪ **Arizona Office of Tourism:** www.visitarizona.com

▪ **Discover Navajo:** www.discovernavajo.com

▪ **Arizona State Parks Department:** http://azstateparks.com

### NEWSPAPERS

▪ *Arizona Republic:* www.azcentral.com

# UTAH

Few places on earth combine such spectacular terrain and unusual history as is present in Utah. The state is on Shoshone, Ute, Goshute, Paiute, and Pueblo land, and it hosts the majestic splendor of the Wasatch Range, the colorful canyon lands of the Colorado Plateau, and the remote deserts and arid mountain ranges of the Great Basin. This region beckoned as the "Promised Land" to members of the struggling Church of Jesus Christ of Latter-day Saints in the 1840s—a place where those faithful to the Book of Mormon could survive and prosper in a land of their own.

AREA: 84,899 square miles / 219,887 square kilometers (13th)

POPULATION: 3,206,000 (30th)

STATEHOOD DATE: January 4, 1896 (45th)

STATE CAPITAL: Salt Lake City

Today, this once insular state has put out the welcome mat and its extravagant scenery and superlative recreational opportunities lure sightseers, mountain bikers, hikers, and skiers from around the world. Outside of a few large cities in the sprawling Wasatch Front metropolitan area, most of the state is utterly vacant—and dramatically beautiful. If you're intrigued by impressive canyons, remote and rugged mountain ranges, glistening salt flats, ancient rock art and cliff dwellings, fossilized dinosaur footprints, and old mining towns, Utah is the place for you.

▲ ZION NATIONAL PARK

# TOP 3

## 1 TAKING IN THE VIEWS AT ARCHES AND CANYONLANDS NATIONAL PARKS

Intricate mazes of canyons, delicate arches, and massive rock monoliths make southeastern Utah seem primordial at times and lunar at others. Two neighboring national parks—Arches and Canyonlands—preserve some of the most astounding of these landscapes. The postcard-perfect vistas of Delicate Arch in Arches, framing distant canyons and mountains, and Mesa Arch in Canyonlands, poised on a dramatic cliff-top, make for stunning pictures and lasting memories.

DELICATE ARCH, ARCHES NATIONAL PARK

In **Arches National Park** (435/719-2299; www.nps.gov/arch), paved roads and short hiking trails provide easy access to some of the more than 1,500 arches in the park. If you're short on time, a drive to the **Windows Section** (23.5 miles/38 kilometers round-trip) affords a look at some of the largest and most spectacular arches. For those who are able, the hike to the base of **Delicate Arch** (3 miles/4.8 kilometers round-trip), which stands in a magnificent setting atop gracefully curving slickrock, is one of the park's highlights. The classic photo of Delicate Arch is taken late in the afternoon when the sandstone glows with golden hues.

The canyon country puts on its supreme performance in the vast **Canyonlands National Park** (2282 SW Resource Blvd., Moab; 435/719-2313; www.nps.gov/cany), which spreads across 527 square miles (1,364 square kilometers). The park is divided into four districts and a separate noncontiguous unit: The Colorado and Green Rivers form the River District; the Island in the Sky District is north, between the rivers, and is the best choice for those short on time; the Maze District is to the west; and Needles District is to the east. The small Horseshoe Canyon Unit, farther to the west, preserves a canyon on Barrier Creek, a tributary of the Green River, in which astounding petroglyphs and ancient rock paintings are protected. Located in the Island in the Sky District, an easy trail (0.5 miles/0.8 kilometers round-trip) leads to the dramatic **Mesa Arch** that rises on the rim of a sheer 800-foot (243-meter) cliff.

## 2 HIKING AMONG THE HOODOOS AT BRYCE CANYON NATIONAL PARK

435/834-5322; www.nps.gov/brca

In Bryce Canyon National Park, a geologic fairyland of rock spires rises beneath the high cliffs of the Paunsaugunt Plateau. Bryce Canyon isn't a canyon at all, but the largest of a series of massive amphitheaters cut into the Pink Cliffs. This intricate maze, eroded from a soft limestone, now glows with warm shades of reds, oranges, pinks, yellows, and creams. A 17-mile (27-kilometer) **scenic drive** traces the length of the park and passes many overlooks and trailheads.

The spectacular Pink Cliffs contain the famous erosional features known as hoodoos. Variations in hardness of the rock layers result in these strange features, which seem almost alive. Water flows through cracks, wearing away softer rock around hard erosion-resistant caps. Finally, a cap becomes so undercut that the overhang allows water to drip down, leaving a "neck" of rock below the harder cap. Traces of iron and manganese provide the distinctive coloring. Bryce Canyon's pink and gold hoodoos are magnificent viewed from a distance, but you can also explore the pillars up-close.

**Bryce Point** is a good spot for a huge panoramic view filled with hoodoos. To pack the most hoodoos into a short visit, hike the 1-mile (1.6-kilometer) section of the **Rim Trail** between **Sunrise and Sunset Points.** This area of the Bryce Amphitheatre has the highest concentration of hoodoos and offers the most up-close and personal views,

HIKING IN BRYCE CANYON

and the two points are spectacular at their namesake times of day. A short walk down either the **Queen's Garden Trail** (1.8 miles/2.9 kilometers round-trip) or the **Navajo Loop Trail** (1.5 miles/2.4 kilometers) from Sunset Point (or connect the two to form a loop) will bring you close to Bryce's hoodoos and provide a totally different experience from what you get atop the rim.

# ROAMING DINOSAUR COUNTRY AT DINOSAUR NATIONAL MONUMENT

Hwy. 149; 435/781-7700; www.nps.gov/dino

Utah is littered with dinosaur fossils and tracks. Straddling the Utah-Colorado border, Dinosaur National Monument owes its name and fame to one of the world's most productive sites for dinosaur bones. The quarry here was discovered in the early 1900s and has produced more complete skeletons, skulls, and juvenile specimens than any other site in the world. Some bones were shipped off to museums around the world, but most were left in the soil as they were found. At the monument's **Quarry Exhibit Hall,** approximately 1,500 bones of 11 different dinosaur species cover a rock face now sheltered by a striking building a short drive from the **visitors center.** This is one of the few museums where visitors are actually allowed to touch the dinosaur bones. In addition, the exhibit hall houses reconstructions of dinosaurs whose bones were found scattered in the quarry.

Beyond the exhibit hall and visitors center, **Cub Creek Road** is a 10-mile (16-kilometer) drive through the southwestern corner of the monument that goes past the quarry turnoff to a historic ranch, passing sites of Fremont rock art on the way. The scenic road offers wide vistas of the landscape that once was the stomping grounds of dinosaurs.

If you can't make it to the far eastern reaches of the state, the **Utah Museum of Natural History** (301 Wakara Way, Salt Lake City; 801/581-6927; http://nhmu.utah.edu) in Salt Lake City, has great exhibits, including the skeleton of a recently discovered new dinosaur species.

QUARRY EXHIBIT HALL, DINOSAUR NATIONAL MONUMENT

Utah's top sights form a ring within the state, making it easy to take a 10-day loop road trip that connects the state's most alluring attractions.

**DAY 1** Arrive in **Salt Lake City.** Take in the Mormon historic sites at **Temple Square,** and wander through the historic neighborhoods along South Temple Street. Or spend the afternoon at **Antelope Island State Park,** which juts out into the **Great Salt Lake.**

PARK CITY

**DAY 2** Leave Salt Lake City, and head east on I-80 to **Park City,** Utah's top ski resort and film festival center. Ride the Town Lift of the **Park City Mountain Resort** for a mountain hike, then wander along Main Street for window shopping and dinner. For real fun, head to **High West,** a distillery with good food and a Western vibe, before turning in for the night.

**DAY 3** Today, you'll put quite a few miles on the car. Drive from Park City to **Provo** on U.S. 189, through the very scenic **Provo Canyon.** Continue south on I-15 all the way to **Springdale,** just outside Zion National Park.

ZION NATIONAL PARK

**DAY 4** Two national parks in one day? No problem! Head into **Zion,** where you'll drop off the car and ride the park shuttle, hopping on and off to take short hikes in the mighty **Zion Canyon.** Stop for lunch at the **Zion Park Lodge,** then drive the beautiful **Zion-Mount Carmel Highway.** Head north on U.S. 89 and turn onto Highway 12 for **Bryce Canyon.** Check into the **Lodge at Bryce Canyon** (435/834-8700 or 877/386-4383; www.brycecanyonforever.com), then hop on a free afternoon shuttle along the parkway. Be sure to catch the sunset over the park's mysterious pink and orange hoodoos.

LOWER CALF CREEK FALLS, GRAND STAIRCASE-ESCALANTE NATIONAL MONUMENT

**DAY 5** Get an early start leaving Bryce Canyon, going east along Highway 12 to **Escalante.** Spend the rest of the morning hiking the easy, mostly level hike to **Lower Calf Creek Falls.** Up next is a scenic drive with cliffs, rock spires, and views along **Highway 12** and across **Capitol Reef National Park** on Highway 24—**Moab** is your destination, which you'll reach in about 4 hours, if you don't stop. (But you'll want to stop.)

**DAY 6** Moab is your jumping-off point for your last two Utah national parks. Start by driving 50 miles (80 kilometers) south of town to **Newspaper Rock Historical Monument** to see amazing petroglyphs on smooth sandstone. Then, head back north, passing Moab, to reach the **Island in the Sky District** of **Canyonlands National Park** where you can make the short hike to **Mesa Arch.** Before heading back to Moab, stop in **Arches National Park**—the late afternoon is the time to take the classic photo of **Delicate Arch.**

**DAY 7** **Salt Lake City** is about a 4-hour drive from Moab, so you could spend the morning trying out one of the area's mountain biking trails before heading back to the big city.

CANYONLANDS NATIONAL PARK

## ORIENTATION

**Salt Lake City,** Park City, and the Wasatch Range are located in northern Utah, and southern Utah boasts the state's five **national parks** and Grand Staircase-Escalante National Monument. In between is **Provo** in the central part of the state. The northeastern corner of Utah, with Wyoming to the north and Colorado to the east, is **dinosaur country.**

## WHEN TO GO

**Spring** (Apr.-early June) and **fall** (Sept.-Oct.) are the most pleasant times to visit, but the same spring showers that make the desert country shine with wildflowers can also dampen trails and turn dirt roads to absolute muck. Arm yourself with insect repellent late spring-midsummer. Except in the mountains, **summer** heat can easily top 100°F and rapidly drain your energy. Travel doesn't let up in **winter**—the ski areas here are some of the nation's best, and they are very easy to get to from Salt Lake City or Ogden.

# HIGHLIGHTS

### TEMPLE SQUARE

Between North Temple St. and South Temple St., Salt Lake City; www.templesquare.com

Easily Salt Lake City's most famous attraction, Temple Square has a special meaning for Mormons. Brigham Young chose this site for Temple Square in July 1847, just four days after arriving in the valley. The tabernacle, visitors centers, museums, and a host of other buildings that play a role in LDS church administration also line the streets around Temple Square. You're welcome to visit most of these buildings, which provide an excellent introduction to the LDS religion and Utah's early history. Enthusiastic **guides** offer several tours of Temple Square, which covers an entire block in the heart of the city. Points of interest, which you can also visit on your own, include the Seagull Monument, commemorating the seagulls that devoured the cricket plague in 1848, and a meridian marker (outside the walls

# *Major* CITIES

**SALT LAKE CITY:** Utah's state capital enjoys a physical setting of great visual drama, located between the Great Salt Lake to the northwest and the Wasatch Range to the east. It is also the seat of the Mormon faith, the Church of Jesus Christ of Latter-day Saints.

**PROVO:** Best known as the home of Brigham Young University, Provo is a good base for exploring the dramatic Wasatch peaks that rise directly behind it.

**OGDEN:** Located 35 miles (56 kilometers) north of Salt Lake City, Ogden was one of the West's most important rail hubs at the beginning of the 20th century. Today, it serves as a major administrative, manufacturing, and livestock center for the intermountain West.

TEMPLE SQUARE

at Main St. and South Temple St.) from which surveyors mapped out Utah.

## GOLDEN SPIKE NATIONAL HISTORIC SITE

32 miles/52 kilometers west of Brigham City; 435/471-2209; www.nps.gov/gosp

At 12:47pm on May 10, 1869, railroad tracks from the East Coast and the West Coast met for the first time. The joining of rails at this 4,905-foot-high (1,495-meter) windswept pass in Utah's Promontory Mountains marked a new chapter in the growth of the United States. A transcontinental railroad at last linked both sides of the nation. The Golden Spike National Historic Site, authorized by Congress in 1965, re-creates this momentous episode of railroad history. The **Golden Spike Visitor Center** offers exhibits and programs that illustrate the difficulties of building the railroad and portrays the officials and workers who made it possible. Reenactments of the Golden Spike ceremony are held at 11am and 1:30pm on Saturdays and holidays between May 1 and Labor Day at the same location where the original ceremony was held more. The annual **Last Spike Ceremony** (May 10) reenacts the original celebration with great fanfare.

## TOPAZ MUSEUM AND CAMP

11000 W 4500 N, Delta

About 9,000 Japanese Americans—most of them U.S. citizens—were brought from the West Coast to this desolate desert plain in central Utah in 1942 for relocation to an internment camp. Topaz sprang up in just a few months and included barracks, schools, churches, and other service buildings. Barbed wire and watchtowers with armed guards surrounded the small city, which was actually Utah's fifth-largest community for a time. All internees were released at war's end in 1945, and today, little more than the streets and piles of rubble remain. You can still walk or drive along the streets of the vast camp, which had 42 neatly laid-out blocks. A concrete memorial stands at the northwest corner of the site.

Even if you don't drive out to the camp, which is about 15 miles (24 kilometers) west of the town of Delta, visit the excellent **Topaz Museum** (55 W. Main St., Delta; 435/864-2514; www.topazmuseum.org). A couple of short films (including one taken by an interned man with camera smuggled into him by a camp official) set the stage for a tour of the artifacts and photos from the camp, reconstructed living quarters, and video displays.

## NEWSPAPER ROCK HISTORICAL MONUMENT

Hwy. 211, 15 miles (24 kilometers) north of Monticello

Located just outside the Needles District of Canyonlands National Park, Newspaper Rock is the site of a profusion of petroglyphs depicting human figures, animals, birds, and abstract designs. These represent 2,000 years of human history during which archaic Native Americans as well as Ancestral Puebloan, Fremont, Paiute, Navajo, and Anglo travelers passed through Indian Creek Canyon. The patterns on the smooth sandstone rock face stand out clearly, thanks to a coating of dark desert varnish. A short nature trail introduces you to the area's desert and riparian vegetation.

PETROGLYPHS AT NEWSPAPER ROCK HISTORICAL MONUMENT

## HOVENWEEP NATIONAL MONUMENT

South of Blanding; 970/562-4283; www.nps.gov/hove

Hovenweep National Monument protects six groups of villages left behind by the Ancestral Puebloans, who built many impressive masonry buildings during the early-mid-1200s, near the end of their 1,300-year stay in the area. The sites are near the Colorado border southeast of Blanding. The Ute word *hovenweep* means "deserted valley," an appropriate name for the lonely high desert country left behind. The **Square Tower Ruins Unit,** where the **visitors center** is, has the greatest number of ruins and the most varied architecture. In fact, you can find all of the Hovenweep architectural styles here. Obtain a trail guide booklet of the area from the visitors center. You'll see towers (D-shaped, square, oval, and round), cliff dwellings, surface dwellings, storehouses, kivas, and rock art. Take care not to disturb the fragile ruins, which remain essentially unexcavated, awaiting the attention of future archaeologists.

## NATURAL BRIDGES NATIONAL MONUMENT

end of Hwy. 275, west of Blanding off Hwy. 95; www.nps.gov/nabr

Natural Bridges preserves some of the finest examples of natural stone architecture in the southwest. Streams in White Canyon and its tributaries cut deep canyons, and then floodwaters sculpted the bridges by gouging tunnels between closely spaced loops in the meandering canyons. You can distinguish a natural bridge from an arch because the bridge spans a streambed and was initially carved out of the rock by flowing water. In the monument, these bridges illustrate three different stages of development, from the massive, relatively newly formed **Kachina Bridge** to the middle-age **Sipapu Bridge** to the delicate and fragile span of **Owachomo.** All three natural bridges will continue to widen and eventually collapse under their own weight. **Bridge View Drive,** a 9-mile (14.5-kilometer) scenic drive around the park, has overlooks of the picturesque bridges, Ancestral Puebloan ruins, and the twisting canyons. You can follow short trails down from the rim to the base of each bridge or hike through all three bridges on a 9-mile (14.5-kilometer) trail loop.

## ANASAZI STATE PARK MUSEUM

Hwy. 12, 1 mile/1.6 kilometer north of Boulder; 435/335-7308; https://stateparks.utah.gov/parks/anasazi

At the excellent Anasazi State Park Museum, indoor exhibits and an outdoor excavated village site and pueblo replica provide a look into the life of these ancient people. The Ancestral Puebloans stayed here for 50-75 years sometime between AD 1050 and 1200. The village population peaked at about 200, with an estimated 40-50 dwellings. You can view pottery, ax heads, arrow points, and other tools found at the site in the museum, along with delicate items like sandals and basketry that came from more protected sites elsewhere. At the ruins behind the museum, you'll see a whole range of Ancestral Puebloan building styles—a pit house, masonry walls, jacal walls (mud reinforced by sticks), and combinations of masonry and jacal.

# BEST SCENIC DRIVES

## ALPINE LOOP SCENIC DRIVE

Hwy. 92

From its start at the mouth of American Fork east of Highland, Highway 92 climbs through a stunning canyon past **Timpanogos Cave National Monument** (801/75-5239; www.nps.gov/tica). Stop for a cave tour if you have most of the day to make this drive. It then climbs to an 8,000-foot (2,438-meter) summit with views of **Mount Timpanogos.** The road continues through a grove of aspen trees, passes **Sundance Resort** (8841 N. Alpine Loop Rd., Sundance; 866/259-7468; www.sundanceresort.com) and descends to **Provo Canyon** at the junction

of U.S. 189. This route takes 1-3 hours; booths at either end of the 20-mile (32-kilometer) drive sell the required $6 admission ticket. Don't aim for a winter drive here; snow usually closes the road from late October until late May.

## HIGHWAY 12

This "All-American Road" from U.S. 89 near Panguitch to Highway 24 in Torrey (123 miles/198 kilometers) packs in more parks, monuments, and geology than just about any other road in the country. Pass through red rock arches in **Red Canyon,** skirt the edge of **Bryce Canyon National Park,** get within easy striking range of the sand pipe rock pillars of **Kodachrome Basin State Park** (south of Cannonville; https://stateparks.utah.gov/parks/kodachrome-basin), and continue east through the northern edge of **Grand Staircase-Escalante National Monument** across the **Hells Backbone** bridge and the narrow Hogsback to **Boulder** and **Hell's Backbone Grill** (Hwy. 12, Boulder; 435/335-7464; http://hellsbackbonegrill.com), one of Utah's best restaurants. The road turns north to cross over **Boulder Mountain** and practically lands in the lap of **Capitol Reef National Park.** You'll pass cliffs, rock spires, petroglyphs, and views of the Grand Staircase and much of the Colorado Plateau. Driving straight through takes about 4 hours, but you could spend a week exploring all the stops along the road.

## ZION-MOUNT CARMEL HIGHWAY

Hwy. 9

Starting at the Zion National Park visitor center in **Zion Canyon,** this 24.5-mile (39-kilometer) road climbs through a series of switchbacks, passes through a crazy long tunnel, and provides access to the canyons and high plateaus to the east. The drive is about 2 hours between Zion and Mount Carmel Junction, the end point. Along the way, take the easy 1-mile (1.6-kilometer) round-trip **Canyon Overlook** trail to peer down at the huge **Great Arch of Zion,** and stop to admire **Checkerboard Mesa,** a huge lump of hatch-marked sandstone right at the road's edge.

ZION-MOUNT CARMEL HIGHWAY

Zion-Mount Carmel Highway is part of the route that links Zion to Bryce Canyon National Park—from Mount Carmel Junction, head north on U.S. 89 to go the rest of the way.

## NOTOM-BULLFROG ROAD

The views of the eastern edge of the **Waterpocket Fold** are a highlight of this fair-weather, partially paved road from the eastern edge of Capitol Reef (turnoff from Highway 24) to **Bullfrog Marina,** on **Lake Powell.** The 70-mile (113-kilometer) drive is long and slow but beautiful; consider taking the whole day to hikes into relatively uncrowded dry washes and slot canyons. From Bullfrog, take a ferry across the lake to **Halls Landing** and an easy route to **Natural Bridges National Monument,** or head back north on a paved road to Hanksville and **Goblin Valley State Park** and its rock formations that look like the faces of goblins.

## MIRROR LAKE HIGHWAY

### Hwy. 150

Starting in **Kamas,** head up Highway 150 into the forested **Uinta Mountains,** a rare east-west range, with near-mandatory stops at **Provo River Falls,** 10,687-foot (3,257-meter) **Bald Mountain Pass,** and pretty **Mirror Lake.** The Utah-side portion of the drive ends at the Wyoming state line, 55 miles (88.5 kilometers) away from Kamas and takes 2-3 hours. A good supply of scenic viewpoints, hiking trails, and campgrounds

make it possible to extend your stay (though the road does close in winter!). Buy a $6 pass at the kiosk near the start of the drive.

# BEST PARKS AND RECREATION AREAS

## THE GREAT SALT LAKE

The Great Salt Lake is North America's largest salt-water lake and is the second-saltiest lake in the world. Only the Dead Sea has a higher salt content. Linked by a causeway to the mainland, **Antelope Island State Park,** near Ogden in northern Utah, is the best place to experience the lake. Its rocky slopes, rolling grasslands, marshes, sand dunes, and lake views instill a sense of remoteness and rugged beauty. Campsites are available, and park trails are open to hiking, bicycling, and horseback riding. There's also a swimming area in the northwest corner of the island and a marina for sailboats and kayaks. Antelope Island is also home to more than 600 bison as well as deer, bighorn sheep, pronghorn, and other wildlife.

## WASATCH RANGE SKI RESORTS

Immediately east of Salt Lake City, the Wasatch Range soars to over 11,000 feet (3,352 meters). Its steep canyons

ALTA SKI RESORT

# STARGAZING

Given its vast, remote stretches and concentrated urban populations, Utah is a great place to stargaze. In fact, four out of its five national parks (Zion is the exception) and many of its state parks have been designated as International Dark Sky Parks. Here are a few of the best places to watch the night sky:

- **Natural Bridges National Monument** (the first park designated as an International Dark Sky Park)

- **Cedar Breaks National Monument**

- **Hovenweep National Monument**

- **Bryce Canyon National Park**

and abundant snowfall make for legendary skiing. Near Salt Lake City, ski resorts are in three adjacent areas. **Big Cottonwood Canyon**, home to the **Solitude** (801/534-1400 or 800/748-4754; http://solitudemountain.com) and **Brighton** (801/532-4731; www.brightonresort.com) ski and snowboard areas, is just southeast of the city; the next canyon south, **Little Cottonwood**, has **Snowbird** (801/933-2122 or 800/232-9542; www.snowbird.com) and **Alta** (801/359-1078, snow report 801/572-3939; www.alta.com), two world-class resorts. When the snow melts, the hiking is every bit as great as the skiing and boarding, and many of the resorts have summer operations with lift-assisted mountain biking being the most popular activity.

About 45 minutes east of Salt Lake via I-80, **Park City** is home to two ski areas: **Deer Valley** (435/649-1000 or 800/424-3337; www.deervalley.com), the crème de la crème of Utah ski areas, and the **Park City Mountain Resort** (435/649-8111; www.parkcitymountain. com), which, with 7,300 skiable acres (2,954 hectares), is the largest ski and snowboard resort in the United States.

## FLAMING GORGE NATIONAL RECREATION AREA

The **Flaming Gorge Dam** impounds the Green River just south of the Wyoming border, backing up a reservoir through 91 miles (148 kilometers) of gentle valleys and fiery red canyons. The rugged land displays spectacular

scenery where the Green River cuts into the Uinta Mountains—cliffs rising as high as 1,500 feet (457 meters), twisted rock formations, and sweeping panoramas. Although much of the lake is in Wyoming, most of the campgrounds and other visitor facilities, as well as the best scenery, are in Utah. The **Red Canyon Visitor Center** (1475 Red Canyon Rd., Dutch John; 435/889-3713) has what may be Utah's best picture window onto sheer cliffs dropping 1,360 feet (414 meters) to the lake below. Nearby viewpoints, connected by a trail along the canyon rim, offer splendid panoramas up and down the canyon and to the lofty Uinta Mountains in the distance. The **Canyon Rim Trail** is a popular 4.2-mile (6.8-kilometer) each way hike or mountain bike ride with trailheads at Red Canyon Visitor Center.

## CEDAR BREAKS NATIONAL MONUMENT

4730 South Hwy. 148, Brian Head; www.nps. gov/cebr

Cedar Breaks is much like Bryce Canyon, but it's on a different high plateau and lacks the crowds that flock to the national park. Here, on the west edge of the Markagunt Plateau, a giant amphitheater 2,500 feet (762 meters) deep and more than 3 miles (4.8 kilometers) across has been eroded into the stone. Ridges and pinnacles extend like buttresses from the steep cliffs. Traces of iron, manganese, and other minerals have tinted the normally white limestone a rainbow of warm hues. A 5-mile

(8-kilometer) **scenic drive** leads past four spectacular overlooks, each with a different perspective. **Spectra Point-Wasatch Rampart Trail** (4 miles/6.5 kilometers) begins at the visitors center, then follows the rim along the south edge of the amphitheater to an overlook.

## ZION NATIONAL PARK

1 Zion Park Blvd., Springdale; 435/772-3256; www.nps.gov/zion

Among the top five most-visited national parks, Zion is a magnificent park with stunning, soaring scenery. The first thing to catch your attention will be the sheer cliffs and great monoliths of **Zion Canyon** reaching high into the heavens. Energetic streams and other forces of erosion created this land of finely sculptured rock. **Zion Canyon Scenic Drive** winds along the canyon floor along the North Fork of the Virgin River past some of the most spectacular scenery in the park. (From mid-February through Thanksgiving, a **shuttle bus** ferries visitors along this route.) Hiking trails branch off to lofty viewpoints and narrow side canyons. For a relatively easy hike, do the **Upper Emerald Pool Trail** (3 miles/4.8 kilometers round-trip) from the Grotto Picnic Area to the truly green pool, where towering

cliffs rise above a white-sand beach. The strenuous **West Rim Trail** to **Angel's Landing,** the famous sheer-walled monolith with a breathtaking panorama at the top, also starts at the Grotto Picnic Area (5.4 miles/8.7 kilometers round-trip). For adventurous souls, hiking the eerie depths of the Virgin River **Narrows** in upper Zion Canyon is an experience of a lifetime.

## CAPITOL REEF NATIONAL PARK

52 W. Headquarters Dr., Torrey; 435/425-3791; www.nps.gov/care

Wonderfully sculpted rock layers in a rainbow of colors put on a fine show at Capitol Reef. About 70 million years ago, gigantic forces within the earth began to uplift, squeeze, and fold more than a dozen rock formations into the central feature of the park today—the **Waterpocket Fold,** so named for the many small pools of water trapped by the tilted strata. Erosion has since carved spires, graceful curves, canyons, and arches. You'll also see remnants of the area's long human history—petroglyphs and storage bins of the prehistoric Fremont people, a schoolhouse and other structures built by Mormon pioneers, and several small uranium mines from the 20th century.

A drive on **Highway 24** passes through an impressive cross section of Capitol Reef cut by the Fremont River—be sure to stop at **Sunset Point**, where you can enjoy panoramic views of the Fremont River Gorge and the Capitol Reef Cliffs via an easy 0.3-mile (0.5-kilometer) trail. You can see more of the park on the **Scenic Drive,** a narrow paved road (21 miles/34 kilometers round-trip) that heads south from the visitors center. The drive passes beneath spectacular cliffs of the reef and enters **Grand Wash** and **Capitol Gorge Canyons.**

## GRAND STAIRCASE-ESCALANTE NATIONAL MONUMENT

435/644-4600; www.blm.gov

Grand Staircase-Escalante contains a vast and wonderfully scenic collection

HIKING THE NARROWS, ZION NATIONAL PARK

of slickrock canyon lands and desert, prehistoric village sites, Old West ranch land, arid plateaus, and miles of back roads linking stone arches, mesas, and abstract rock formations. It is the largest public land grouping designated as a national monument in the Lower 48 states. Grand Staircase-Escalante includes three units. On the eastern third are the narrow wilderness canyons of the **Escalante River** and its tributaries, which make up the **Escalante Canyons** unit. In the center of the monument is a vast swath of arid rangeland and canyons of the **Kaiparowits Plateau**. The western third of the monument edges up against the Gray, White, and Pink Cliffs of the **Grand Staircase** unit.

The monuments of Grand Staircase-Escalante preserve some of the best long-distance hiking trails in the southwest, but it also has shorter trails for travelers who want to sample the wonderful slot canyons and backcountry without venturing too far afield. Hiking the **Escalante River Canyon** is recognized worldwide as one of the great wilderness treks; most people devote 4-6 days to exploring these slickrock canyons. Hikers without a week to spare can sample the landscape along the **Dry Fork Coyote Gulch Trail** (about 3.5 miles/5.6 kilometers), which links two fascinating and beautifully constricted slot canyons. The trail at the stunning and accessible **Calf Creek Recreation Area** (Hwy. 12, 15 miles/24 kilometers east of Escalante) leads through a magical landscape to 126-foot (38-meter) **Lower Calf Creek Falls** (6 miles/9.7 kilometers round-trip).

## MOAB BIKE TRAILS

Moab has become the West's most noted mountain biking destination. The famed and challenging slickrock trails wind through astonishing desert landscapes. Beware: The most famous trails are not for beginners. The undulating slickrock of the well-known **Slickrock Bike Trail** in the **Sand Flats Recreation Area** just east of Moab challenges even the best mountain bike riders. This "trail" consists only of painted white lines, and the main loop is 10.5 miles (16.9 kilometers) round-trip. Other trails are better matched to the skills of

MOAB'S SLICKROCK TRAIL

novices. The loops and spur trails of the **Moab Brand Trails** (8 miles/12.9 kilometers north of town on U.S. 191) form a trail system with several options that are especially good for beginners or riders who are new to slickrock. Try **Circle O** (no motor vehicles) for a good 3-mile (4.8-kilometer) initiation to slickrock riding.

# FESTIVALS AND EVENTS

## SUNDANCE FILM FESTIVAL

Park City; 435/658-3456; www.sundance.org; Jan.

Robert Redford began this noted festival in 1981 as a venue for independent films that otherwise had a difficult time reaching the screen or a mass audience. Since then, the Sundance Film Festival has become the nation's foremost venue for new and innovative cinema. Tickets to the screenings can be hard to come by, especially for films with advance buzz or big stars; if you can't get tickets, put your name on waiting lists or join the lines at the theaters for canceled tickets. However, tickets to less well-known films are usually available at the last minute. If you are coming to Park City expressly to see the films, inquire about package tours that include tickets.

## PIONEER DAY

### June 24

Throughout Utah, the year's biggest summer event is Pioneer Day on July 24, with parades and fireworks in almost every Utah community. It commemorates the day in 1847 when Brigham Young first saw the Salt Lake Valley and declared "This is the place."

## SPEED WEEK

### Bonneville Salt Flats International Speedway; Aug.

A brilliant white layer of salt left behind by prehistoric Lake Bonneville covers more than 44,000 acres (17,806 hectares) of the Great Salt Lake Desert. For much of the year, a shallow layer of water sits atop the salt flats. The hot sun usually dries out the flats enough for speed runs in summer and autumn. For six days in August, the Bonneville Salt Flats are the site of Speed Week, when vehicles come to "shoot the salt." Vehicles of an amazing variety of styles—ranging from motorcycles to diesel trucks—and ages take off individually to set new records in their classes.

# BEST FOOD AND DRINK

## HIGH WEST WHISKEY

Although Utah is known for restrictive liquor laws (until 2010, there was a "private club" requirement where you had to purchase a membership in order to have a drink in a bar), the state boasts a highly regarded whiskey distillery. Located just outside Park City, **High West Distillery** (27649 Old Lincoln Hwy., Wanship; 435/649-8300; www.highwest.com) offers tours of the facility with an optional tasting flight (fee charged). The affiliated **High West Saloon** (703 Park Ave., Park City; 435/649-8300; www.highwest.com) is one of the best bars in Park City.

## CROWN BURGERS

www.crown-burgers.com

In and around Salt Lake City, the local fast food purveyor Crown Burgers is the favorite for char-grilled burgers and good fries. For that special Utah touch, ask for **fry sauce** with your french fries—it's a local condiment that's remarkably like Thousand Island dressing without relish.

## AGGIE ICE CREAM

750 N. 1200 E., Logan; 435/797-2112; https://aggieicecream.usu.edu

The Utah State University dairy department is justifiably proud of its milk, cheese, and ice cream. Get a double scoop at the shop in Logan.

# MAJOR AIRPORTS

- **Salt Lake City International Airport:** SLC; 776 N. Terminal Dr.; 801/575-2400; https://slcairport.com

# MORE INFORMATION

## TRAVEL AND TOURISM INFORMATION

- **Utah Travel Council:** www.utah.com
- **Utah State Parks:** https://stateparks.utah.gov

## NEWSPAPERS

- *Salt Lake Tribune:* www.sltrib.com

A WHISKEY FLIGHT AT HIGH WEST DISTILLERY

# NEW MEXICO

The Land of Enchantment, on Apache, Comanche, Jocome, Jano, Pueblo, Navajo, Ute, and Zuni land, entrances all the senses. Green chiles roast at farmer's markets and fragrant piñon crackles in kiva fireplaces. Coyotes howl at night, and the deep boom of drums and jingle of bells resound at pueblo ceremonies. Then there are the austere mesas, sandstone canyons, and snowcapped mountain peaks, all below a turquoise sky—just like the locally crafted jewelry.

AREA: 121,590 square miles / 314,916 square kilometers (5th)

POPULATION: 2,096,829 (36th)

STATEHOOD DATE: January 6, 1912 (47th)

STATE CAPITAL: Santa Fe

New Mexico is a sort of alternate world. The state is home to some of the country's oldest settlements and to the world's first spaceport for tourists. Hike along mountainsides thick with yellow-leafed aspens or on surreal gypsum dunes, or bunk down under a buzzing neon motel sign along Route 66. At the end of the day, you can always pull yourself back into the present with a cold margarita and *carne adovada* with a kick—but there's no guarantee you'll shake off New Mexico's spell.

BANDELIER NATIONAL MONUMENT

## ORIENTATION

**Albuquerque, Santa Fe,** and **Taos** sit along an invisible diagonal line pointing through north-central New Mexico, and **Route 66** goes through Albuquerque along a not-quite-straight line across the state. The **Navajo Nation** is located in the northeast. In the southwest is the mesmerizing Chihuahuan Desert, while the southeast holds the state's two **national parks.**

## WHEN TO GO

**Summer,** June-September, is high season in northern New Mexico. It's also the only time to hike at higher elevations, as snow finally melts, but lower elevations are baking. Be prepared for a temperature drop from the 90s to the 60s after sunset. **Fall** is beautiful, with crisp temperatures and brilliant leaves in the mountains. **Winter** is busy (and pricey) in ski towns like Taos, but many sights have limited hours. Towns at lower elevations remain balmy, but be prepared for freezing temperatures even in southern desert areas. **Spring** is perhaps the harshest time, switching from snowfall and mud to dry, hot winds.

# HIGHLIGHTS

## SANDIA PEAK TRAMWAY

30 Tramway Rd., Albuquerque; 505/856-7325; www.sandiapeak.com

The longest single-cable tram in the world, the Sandia Peak Tramway whisks passengers 2.7 miles (4.3 kilometers) and 4,000 feet (1,219 meters) up, along a continuous line of Swiss-made cables. The ride from Albuquerque's northeast foothills to the crest takes about 15 minutes; the view of the cityscape and beyond along the way can be breathtaking.

## SANTA FE ART GALLERIES

**Canyon Road** is ground zero for Santa Fe's art market. The intersection of Paseo de Peralta and Canyon Road is the beginning of a 0.5-mile (0.8-kilometer) strip that contains more than 80 galleries. In the summer, the street is a solid mass of strolling art lovers—pro collectors and amateurs alike. It's especially thronged on summer Fridays, when most galleries have an open house or an exhibition opening. Here are a few spots to seek out.

- **Nüart Gallery** (670 Canyon Rd.; 505/988-3888) showcases a variety

SANDIA PEAK TRAMWAY

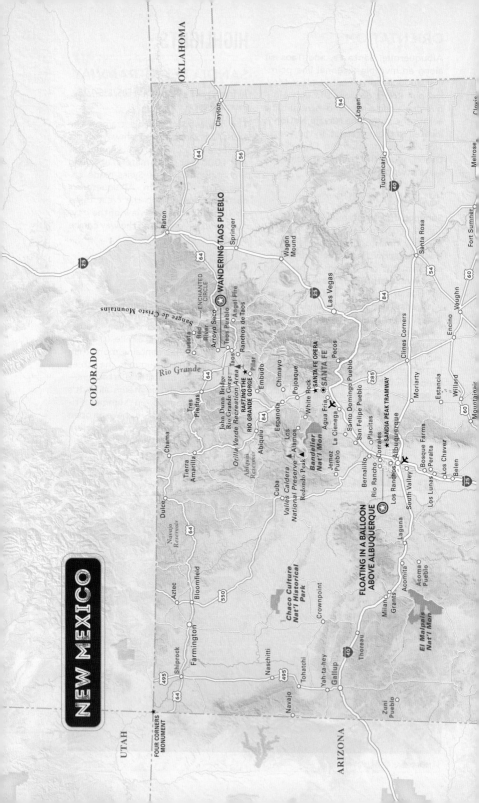

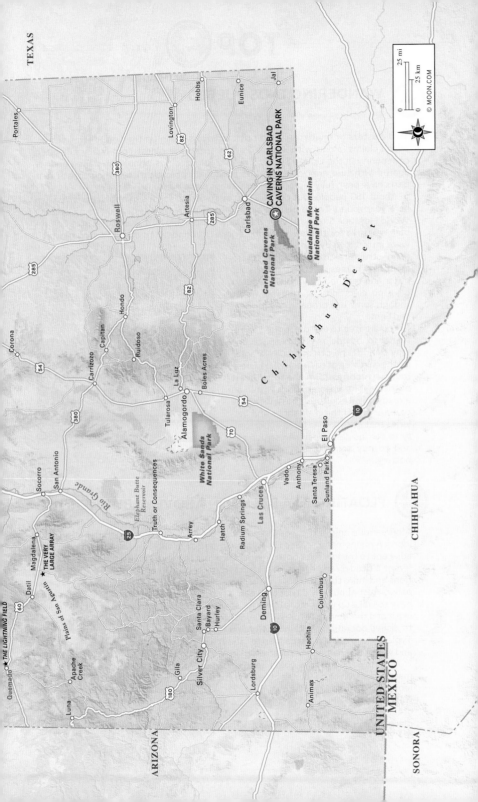

**TOP 3**

# WANDERING TAOS PUEBLO

575/758-1028; www.taospueblo.com

Two clusters of multistory mud-brick buildings make up the core of this village, which claims, along with Acoma Pueblo, to be the oldest continually inhabited community in the United States. The current buildings, annually repaired and re-coated with mud, are from the 1200s, though it's possible that all their constituent parts have been fully replaced several times since then.

About 150 people (out of the 1,900 or so total Taos reservation residents) live here year-round. These people, along with the town's designation as a UNESCO World Heritage Site, have kept the place remarkably as it was in the pre- Columbian era, save for the use of adobe bricks (as opposed to clay and stone), which

were introduced by the Spanish, as the main structural material. The apart-ment-like homes, stacked upon each other and reached by wooden ladders, have no electricity or running water, though some use propane gas for heat and light.

ANCIENT DWELLINGS AT TAOS PUEBLO

You are free to explore, but be mind-ful not to intrude on private space, and stay clear of the ceremonial kiva areas on the east side of each complex. These round structures form the ritual heart of the pueblo, a secret space within an already private culture. You're welcome to enter any of the craft shops and gal-leries that are open—a good opportuni-ty to see inside the earthen structures and to buy some of distinctive Taos pottery.

# FLOATING IN A BALLOON ABOVE ALBUQUERQUE

Albuquerque enjoys the world's most perfect weather for navigating hot-air bal-loons. A phenomenon called the Albuquerque Box, created by the steep mountains adjacent to the low river bottom, enables pilots to move at different speeds at dif-ferent altitudes, and even to backtrack, if necessary. Thanks to these ideal condi-tions and more than 300 days of sunshine per year, you can go up, up, and away in a balloon just about any day of the year. A trip is admittedly an investment (and you have to wake up well before dawn for sunrise trips), but there's no other ride quite like it and the views can forever change how you see the city. One of the longest es-tablished operations is **Rainbow Ryders** (505/823-1111; www.rainbowryders.com). Typically, you're up in the balloon for about an hour, depending on wind conditions, and you get a champagne toast when you're back on solid ground.

An experience to rival going up in one yourself is witnessing an early morning mass ascension of balloons at the **Albuquerque International Balloon Fiesta** (Bal-loon Fiesta Park, Albuquerque; 505/821-1000; www.balloonfiesta.com). You can watch as the balloons glow against the dark sky, then lift silently into the air in a great wave. Started in 1972, the fiesta is the city's biggest annual event and takes place over nine days in October at a dedicated park on the north side of town, west of I-25.

HOT-AIR BALLOONS AT THE ALBUQUERQUE INTERNATIONAL BALLOON FIESTA

## ③ CAVING IN CARLSBAD CAVERNS NATIONAL PARK

727 Carlsbad Caverns Hwy., Carlsbad; 575/785-3137; www.nps.gov/cave

One of the country's most awesome natural wonders, Carlsbad Caverns is mesmerizing. You could easily spend days here, visiting ever more obscure underground worlds. Aboveground, the **Chihuahuan Desert** is especially scenic here, studded with spiky plants; you may also want to make time for a bit of a drive through the terrain.

The basic entrance ticket gives you access to two major parts of the cave: the **Natural Entrance Trail,** which descends about 800 feet (243 meters) in the course of a mile (1.6 kilometers), on a paved trail dense with switchbacks, and **The Big Room,** the largest cave in the Carlsbad complex. Lit in tasteful white lights like a natural cathedral, the Big Room soars up into the dark, and the space is 1.25 miles (2 kilometers) long.

In the summer months, allow an extra hour of waiting time at the **visitors center.** Probably the best time to go is in winter, because you'll have the whole place to yourself. Still, there are two reasons to consider a spring or summer visit: Hundreds of thousands of bats fly out every evening, and the 56°F temperature underground is a relief.

THE NATURAL ENTRANCE TRAIL AT CARLSBAD CAVERNS NATIONAL PARK

# *Best* ROAD TRIP

**DAY 1** You'll likely start in **Albu-querque**, where you'll make a beeline to **Mary & Tito's Café** for a great introduction to New Mexican cuisine. Learn about New Mexico's native communities at the **Indian Pueblo Cultural Center** before driving 2.5 hours northeast to **Taos**.

**DAY 2** Start the morning at awesome, ancient, and living **Taos Pueblo,** before taking the **Enchanted Circle** drive around **Wheeler Peak**, stopping for a hike near **Red River**. If it's spring or early summer, you can also raft or float the **Rio Grande Gorge.**

THE ENCHANTED CIRCLE SCENIC BYWAY

**DAY 3** Backtrack southwest to Santa Fe, stopping at **Sugar's** en route for a green chile cheeseburger. In Santa Fe, browse the art galleries on **Canyon Road**. You have your pick of museums, such as the **Museum of Contemporary Native Arts,** or head out for a hike in nearby **Valles Caldera National Preserve.**

**DAY 4** Today it's a 4.5-hour drive south to **White Sands National Park.** Cruise the 16-mile (25-kilometer) **Dunes Drive,** marveling at the shimmering gypsum, stopping to hike some of the trails or for a ranger-led tour.

CARLSBAD CAVERNS NATIONAL PARK

**DAY 5** It's another long, but worthwhile, desert drive of 3.5 hours to **Carlsbad Caverns National Park.** Hike the **Natural Entrance Trail,** descending into the truly massive **Big Room.**

**DAY 6** Drive the 4.5 hours northwest back to **Albuquerque** today, stopping in **Roswell** to visit the **UFO Museum & Research Center.**

WHITE SANDS NATIONAL PARK

of international artists, focusing on magical realism.

- **Robert Nichols Gallery** (419 Canyon Rd.; 505/982-2145) specializes in Native American pottery, including some with whimsical, boundary-pushing sensibilities.

- Near Canyon Road, **Gerald Peters Gallery** (1011 Paseo de Peralta; 505/954-5700) and **Nedra Matteucci Galleries** (1075 Paseo de Peralta; 505/982-4631) are the biggies when it comes to Taos Society of Artists and other Western art.

## BANDELIER NATIONAL MONUMENT

15 Entrance Rd., Los Alamos; www.nps.gov/band

One of New Mexico's most entrancing ancient sites, Bandelier National Monument comprises 23,000 acres (9,307 hectares) of wilderness, including the remarkable Frijoles Canyon, lined on either side with *cavates*—rooms carved by the Ancestral Puebloans that served as their homes—while the remnants of a massive settlement from the 16th century occupy the valley floor. It is these dwellings and the foundations of kivas that were central to Ancestral Puebloan society that the park is most known for today. Several of the *cavates* are just a short walk from the **visitors center**—it's possible to climb inside some of them—and there's a network of much longer trails that wend deeper into the canyon, the mesa and the backcountry.

## ROSWELL

Launched into national notoriety in 1947 by an alleged UFO crash (and subsequent government cover-up) northwest of town, Roswell has become a pilgrimage site for true believers and kitsch seekers alike. The city seal sports an alien, the green streetlamps have eyes, and the McDonald's resembles a spaceship about to lift off. Most visitors make a beeline to the **International UFO Museum & Research Center** (114 N. Main St.; 800/822-3545; www.roswellufomuseum.com), where the events of the July 1947 are dissected with obsessive care.

## *THE LIGHTNING FIELD*

505/898-3335; www.lightningfield.org

Installed in 1977 by sculptor Walter de Maria, *The Lightning Field i*s an elaborate work of land art: 400 stainless-steel poles stand in a grid measuring 1 mile by 1 kilometer. The light glints off the poles, and summer storms create a field of crackling, brilliant electricity across their pointed tips. De Maria envisioned an immersive experience, in which the viewer, in pure isolation, watches the light shift over the course of the day. To this end, casual visitors are not allowed; you must make reservations for an overnight stay and leave your car in Quemado, a tiny town on U.S. 50 in remote western New Mexico. This ranks as one of the state's most remarkable places to spend the night, not to mention one of the great places to meditate on New Mexico's phenomenal landscape.

If you've made it out to *The Lightning Field,* you could head an hour east of Quemado on U.S. 50 to **The Very Large Array** (Highway 52; www.vla.nrao.edu), an installation of 27 deep space radio telescopes jutting out of the Plains of San Agustín.

BANDELIER NATIONAL MONUMENT

# NATIVE NEW MEXICO TODAY

Visitors to New Mexico can learn about the culture that developed before the arrival of the Spanish in the 16th century across the state in pueblos and in excellent museums that hold some of the state's finest treasures.

- In Albuquerque, the **Indian Pueblo Cultural Center** (2401 12th St. NW; 505/843-7270; www.indianpueblo.org) should be your first stop, for its information on all the American Indian settlements.

- West of Albuquerque, the dramatic **Acoma Pueblo** (I-40, exit 102, Acoma; 800/747-0181; www.acomaskycity.org), aptly known as Sky City due to its position atop a mesa, is accessible only by guided tour. At the base is an excellent cultural museum, which displays delicate white pottery painted with fine black lines.

- **Zuni Pueblo** (1239 State Hwy 53, Zuni; 505/782-7238; www.zunitourism. com) is the only pueblo where you can stay overnight; it's also the source of beautiful jewelry. Take a walking tour of the mission church, with its resplendent kachina murals, and check out the **A:shíwi A:wan Museum** (2 E. Ojo Caliente Rd., Zuni; 505/782-4403; www.ashiwi-museum.org).

- In Santa Fe, stop by the **Museum of Contemporary Native Arts** (108 Cathedral Pl., Santa Fe; 505/983-8900; www.iaia.edu), the showcase for students, professors, and alumni of the prestigious **Institute of American Indian Arts.**

# BEST SCENIC DRIVES

## HISTORIC ROUTE 66

Though officially decommissioned, Route 66 (now traced by I-40) is still alive in New Mexico in the form of neon signs and cruising culture. Dedicated drivers can hop off the interstate and cruise a remote—sometimes winding—two-lane stretch of old Route 66, resurfacing at **Laguna** and then cruising parallel to I-40 almost to **Gallup**. Outside **Albuquerque**, take exit 126, heading south on Highway 6. Then turn right (southwest) on old Route 66. This road eventually meets, then crosses I-40, winding a bit, settling in as the frontage road up to exit 47, west of **Thoreau.**

## ENCHANTED CIRCLE

The Enchanted Circle, the loop formed by **U.S. 64, Highway 38,** and **Highway 522,** is named for its breathtaking views of the Sangre de Cristo Mountains, including **Wheeler Peak.** The main towns on the route—**Angel Fire** and **Red River**—are ski resorts. As the scenery is really the thing, you can drive the 84-mile (135-kilometer) route in a short day, with time out for a quick hike around Red River or a detour along the **Wild Rivers scenic byway.**

Driving counterclockwise around the loop gives you the arresting descent into the Taos Valley from **Questa**—not to be missed, if you can manage it. To do this, start by heading east out of **Taos** on Kit Carson Road, which

HISTORIC BLUE SWALLOW MOTEL ON ROUTE 66

turns into U.S. 64, winding along next to the Taos River. At Palo Flechado Pass, the road descends into the high Moreno Valley, a gorgeous green expanse in early spring and a vast tundra in winter.

# BEST PARKS AND RECREATION AREAS

## WHITE SANDS NATIONAL PARK

U.S. 70 between Alamogordo and Las Cruces; 575/479-6124; www.nps.gov/whsa

At White Sands, 275 square miles (712 square kilometers) of blinding, shimmery gypsum, the sand looks like no desert you've ever seen: your brain can't stop thinking snow and ice. In the summer, temperatures exceed 100°F, so you'll probably want to visit either early or late in the day—but there is also something undeniably overwhelming about this featureless landscape at high noon. A number of nature trails, including the 5-mile (8-kilometer) **Alkali Flat Trail** into the **Heart of the Sands,** lead off the 16-mile-long (25-kilometer) **Dunes Drive.** Stop in at the pleasant **visitors center** at the main gate for the schedule of ranger tours.

## VALLES CALDERA NATIONAL PRESERVE

575/829-4100; www.nps.gov/vall

Spreading out for 89,000 acres (36,017 hectares) to the north of Highway 4, Valles Caldera National Preserve is a series of vast green valleys, rimmed by the edges of a volcano that collapsed into a massive bowl millennia ago. At the center is rounded Redondo Peak (11,254 feet/3,430 meters). The surrounding meadows are home to herds of elk. To get oriented, drive in 2 miles (3.2 kilometers) to the **Valle Grande Contact Station,** where you can get a hiking map and the latest trail conditions. A full roster of guided activities is available in winter and summer, including group day hikes, elk sightseeing, and full-moon snowshoeing in winter.

## RAFTING THE RIO GRANDE GORGE

The **Taos Box,** the 16-mile 25-kilometer) stretch of the Rio Grande between the John Dunn Bridge and Pilar, provides the most exhilarating rafting in New Mexico, with Class III and Class IV rapids with ominous names like Boat Reamer and Screaming Left-Hand Turn. The river mellows out south of the Taos

VALLES CALDERA NATIONAL PRESERVE

# *Major* CITIES

**ALBUQUERQUE:** Founded three centuries ago, New Mexico's largest city is fun, down-to-earth, and affordable. It was named for a Spanish nobleman (hence its nickname, the Duke City).

**LAS CRUCES:** Located in southwest New Mexico, the state's second-largest city is a proud farm town where the influence of Mexico is strongly felt in a cross-border culture that's distinct from the Hispanic communities in the northern part of the state.

**SANTA FE:** Founded over 400 years ago as a remote Spanish outpost, state capital Santa Fe has a larger proportion of writers and artists than any other community in the United States.

Box, then leads into a shorter Class III section called the **Racecourse**—the most popular run, usually done as a half-day trip. Beyond this, in the **Orilla Verde Recreation Area** around Pilar, the water is wide and flat, a place for a relaxing float in an inner tube. For guided trips, try **Los Rios River Runners** (575/776-8854; www.losriosriverrunners.com) or **Far Flung Adventures** (575/758-2628; www.farflung.com). Both offer excursions from Pilar. The best time of year to be on the river is late May-late June, when the water is high from mountain runoff.

# FESTIVALS AND EVENTS

The **Albuquerque International Balloon Fiesta** in October is one of New Mexico's most famous events, but other celebrations and events happen throughout the year.

## PUEBLO DANCES AND FEAST-DAY CELEBRATIONS

Visiting a pueblo for a ceremonial dance or feast-day celebration is one of the most memorable parts of a trip to New Mexico. There will usually be a main, seasonal dance—such as the corn dance at the summer solstice—followed by several others. A pueblo dance is a ceremony and a religious ritual, not a performance—visitors are guests, not part of an audience. Applause is not appropriate, nor is conversation during the dance. Queries about the meaning of the dances are generally not appreciated. Never walk in the dance area, and try not to block the view of pueblo residents. The kivas, as holy spaces, are always off-limits to outsiders. Photography is strictly forbidden at dances.

Ceremonial dances take place throughout the year at pueblos around the state. **Indian Pueblo Cultural Center** (2401 12th St. NW, Albuquerque; 505/843-7270; www.indianpueblo.org) is a good resource to find out specific events and dates.

## SANTA FE OPERA

301 Opera Dr., Santa Fe; 505/986-5900; www.santafeopera.org; July-Aug.

The Santa Fe Opera is not the night at the opera of Edith Wharton novels. Half the fun is arriving early to "tailgate" in the parking lot, which involves gourmet goodies and lots of champagne. The show itself features the country's best singers, who treat this as their "summer camp," as the season runs July-August and takes place in an elegant 2,000-plus-seat open amphitheater that is beautiful at sunset; pack blankets to ward off the chill later on.

# BEST FOOD

## NEW MEXICO CUISINE

The state cuisine is a distinctive culinary tradition that shouldn't be confused with Tex-Mex, Californian Mex, or south-of-the-border Mexican. The **New Mexico chile pepper** is the cuisine's distinguishing element. "Red or

# BEST SOUVENIRS

- If you're serious about purchasing native-made art and jewelry, you may want to time your visit with the **Santa Fe Indian Market** (121 Sandoval St., Santa Fe; 505/983-5220, https://swaia.org) which takes place every August and showcases more than 1,100 artisans.

- **Taos pottery:** Lightly decorated but glimmering with mica from the clay of the area, these pots are also renowned for cooking tender beans. You can buy them from the source in Taos Pueblo.

- **Navajo rugs:** A small Navajo community hosts the Crownpoint Rug Auction (State highway 371, 30 minutes north of I-40, Thoreau, exit #53; 505/736-2130; https://crownpointrugauction.com), which has been connecting buyers and sellers from all around the region since 1968. Even if you have no interest in buying, it's a great cultural experience, and an opportunity to see some beautiful work up close.

green?" is the official state question, the dilemma diners face when choosing either an earthy red-chile sauce (produced from chiles that have been left to ripen) or a chunky, vegetal green one (from chiles picked green). Hint: Choose "Christmas" if you can't decide.

- **Best traditional New Mexican: Mary & Tito's Café** (2711 4th St. NW, Albuquerque; 505/344-6266) is an Albuquerque institution, named a James Beard American Classic in 2009.

- **Best Green Chile Cheeseburger:** If you're taking the low road to Taos, don't miss out on a juicy green-chile cheeseburger at **Sugar's** (1799 Hwy. 68, Embudo; 505/852-0604), a beloved roadside trailer.

## FRY BREAD

One major element of American Indian cuisine is fry bread, a round of deep-fried dough served with honey or topped with ground meat, cheese, and lettuce to make an "Indian taco"; a "Navajo taco" often uses shredded lamb or mutton in place of ground beef. Try it at flea markets, such as the ones in **Albuquerque** (weekends at the fairgrounds) or **Shiprock** (daily, intersection of U.S. 491 and U.S. 64), or at **AshKii's Navajo Grill** (123 W. Broadway, Farmington; 505/326-3804).

# MAJOR AIRPORTS

- **Albuquerque International Sunport:** ABQ; 2200 Sunport Blvd., Albuquerque; 505/244-7700; www.cabq.gov/airport

- **Santa Fe Municipal Airport:** SAF; 121 Aviation Dr., Santa Fe; 505/955-2900; www.santafenm.gov/airport

# MORE INFORMATION

## TRAVEL AND TOURISM INFORMATION

- **New Mexico Board of Tourism:** www.newmexico.org

- **New Mexico State Parks:** www.emnrd.state.nm.us/SPD

## NEWSPAPERS

- *Albuquerque Journal:* www.abqjournal.com

- *Santa Fe New Mexican:* www.santafenewmexican.com

- *Taos News:* www.taosnews.com

# TEXAS

You can't talk about Texas without mentioning size. It's enormous. And it's not just flat and dry—Texas is geographically diverse, with mountains, tropics, pine forests, beaches, and prairies within its borders. On Apache, Bidai, Coahuiltecan, Caddo, Comanche, Jumano, Karankawa, Kiowa, Kitsai, Tawakoni, Tonkawa, and Wichita land, the state is racially diverse, too—now the U.S.'s second-most diverse state and growing. Texas also offers a thriving international food scene in Houston and vibrant Tejano culture. Toss in barbecue, quirky Austin, and real-life cowboys and you'll find a rich experience representative of Texas's distinct character.

Texas has an unmatched independent spirit. Its people, like its landscapes, are rugged, captivating, and endearing. The one element that ropes them all together is an immense Texas pride.

**AREA:** 268,596 square miles / 695,660 square kilometers (2nd)

**POPULATION:** 29,360,759 (2nd)

**STATEHOOD DATE:** December 29, 1845 (28th)

**STATE CAPITAL:** Austin

RIO GRANDE, BIG BEND NATIONAL PARK

## ORIENTATION

North Texas is dominated by the **Metroplex** of Dallas, Fort Worth, and Arlington, the state's largest metropolitan area. **Houston** anchors East Texas, which has a distinct Southern bayou influence, given its proximity to neighboring Louisiana. The **Gulf Coast,** along the Gulf of Mexico, stretches southwest from **Galveston,** down to **Corpus Christi** and **South Padre Island.** Inland, occupying the southern point of a triangle with Dallas and Houston, **San Antonio** is the big city in South Texas, despite its northerly neighbor, **Austin,** getting much of the attention. Beyond the big cities, **West Texas,** with El Paso and the state's two national parks, is a rugged, more isolated landscape. And finally, Route 66 cuts across the **Panhandle** in the northwestern part of the state.

## WHEN TO GO

Texans like to joke about their two seasons: hot and less hot. **Summer** can be brutal, with long stretches at 100°F-plus (38°C), and humidity usually also a factor. Many Texans take summer vacations at the Gulf Coast, but travelers prefer **spring,** an optimal time to visit Texas parks. **Fall** can be variable—it often reaches 90°F (32°C) as late as November—and **winter** surprisingly chilly, with ice storms and snow in the Panhandle and northern plains, though the Rio Grande Valley remains comparatively balmy.

# HIGHLIGHTS

## NASA SPACE CENTER

1601 NASA Pkwy., Houston; 281/244-2100; www.spacecenter.org

The NASA Space Center is about as big as it gets for Houston attractions, the hub of American spaceflight for the past six tumultuous decades. Established in 1961 as the Manned Spacecraft Center and renamed the Lyndon B. Johnson Space Center in 1973, it will forever be associated with its early Gemini and Apollo missions.

Most of the facility features educational exhibits, including **Starship Gallery,** containing impressive space-related artifacts such as the Apollo 17 command module, the Gemini 5 capsule, lunar rovers, and even a moon rock. On the open-air tram tour, you'll peer into the remarkably restored **Mission Control Center,** see real astronauts in action at the **Space Vehicle Mockup Facility,** and visit the enormous structure housing the immense **Saturn V rocket,** an awe-inspiring sight that must be seen to be believed.

NASA SPACE CENTER

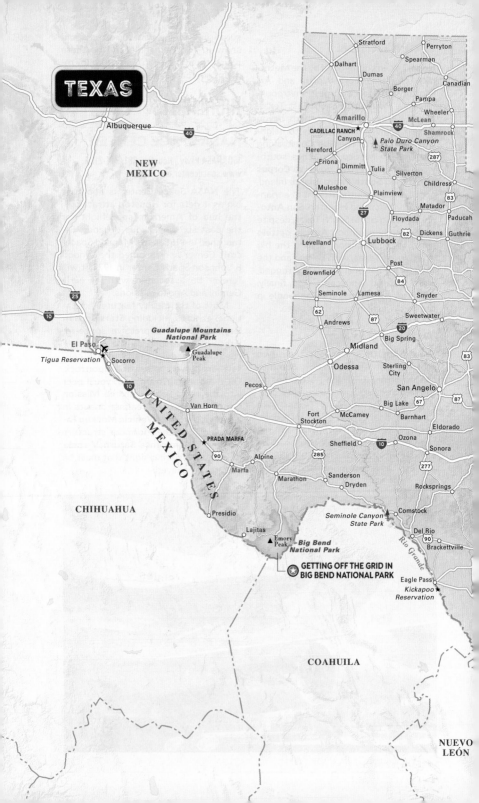

# TOP 3

## 1 JAMMING IN AUSTIN, THE "LIVE MUSIC CAPITAL OF THE WORLD"

Musicians have been drawn to Austin for decades to take advantage of the city's abundant stages, open-minded atmosphere, and (formerly) cheap rent. Several notable artists persevered beyond free meals and tip-jar paychecks, including Janis Joplin and Stevie Ray Vaughan, and, more recently, acts such as Spoon and Gary Clark Jr. have seen their names ascend from the bottoms of flyers to the tops of marquees. Drop by any of the 100-plus venues in town that host live music, and you just might be lucky enough to discover the next Black Angels or Black Pumas.

LIVE MUSIC ON 6TH STREET IN AUSTIN

For the most part, the "Live Music Capital of the World" lives up to its billing. On any given night you can catch blues, reggae, country, and punk. **Red River Street** has a core of steady live-music venues, **6th Street** retains its distinction as a mini Bourbon Street, the **Warehouse District** offers folks in their 30s a place to gather without screaming to be heard, and **East Austin** is the hipster hot spot.

- The coolest spot to catch a show is the comfy **White Horse Tavern** (500 Comal St.; 512/553-6756; www.thewhitehorseaustin.com). The two best words to describe the vibe here are "honky-tonk" and "hipster," both in the most accommodating way.

- For a true Austin experience, head to **Cheer Up Charlie's** (900 Red River St.; 512/431-2133; www.cheerupcharlies.com), a welcoming spot with an amazing outdoor stage and patio for live indie rock, lounging, and dancing.

- ACL Live at the **Moody Theater** (310 W. Willie Nelson Blvd.; 512/225-7999; www. acl-live.com) has become the city's favorite place to see a show, with its impeccable, professionally designed acoustics.

- **Antone's** (305 E. 5th St.; 512/814-0361; www.antonesnightclub.com) has been a fixture on the music scene for nearly three decades, staging legendary artists like B. B. King along with local blues and roots rock acts.

## 2 GETTING OFF THE GRID IN BIG BEND NATIONAL PARK

www.nps.gov/bibe

The namesake bend in the Rio Grande isn't the only enormous thing around here—this colossal park encompasses more than 800,000 acres (323,748 hectares) of spectacular canyons, mesmerizing Chihuahuan Desert, awe-inspiring Chisos Mountains, and unexpectedly temperate woodlands. It's the kind of place that words can't quite describe, and photos can't do justice. Its remote location, though inconvenient to get to, makes the park wonderfully isolated and peaceful. Once you've experienced its many unique charms, you'll be able to justify the long drive for many future visits to this unrivaled natural masterpiece.

There's no shortage of activities in Big Bend National Park (www.nps.gov/bibe), from raft trips to scenic drives to day hikes. For unbelievably dramatic mountain scenery, it's imperative to make the drive to **Chisos Mountains Lodge.** Your ears will pop and your jaw will drop as you ascend the road into the mountain range, with the famous formations of

SANTA ELENA CANYON, BIG BEND NATIONAL PARK

**Casa Grande** and **Emory Peak** acting as a beacon to the basin. Or you can see the canyon walls from the source—by boat along the Rio Grande. One of the most popular options is **Santa Elena Canyon** (downstream from Lajitas), a 13-mile (20-kilometer) adventure featuring easy desert paddling and severe rapid navigating.

Big Bend also offers more than 200 miles (321 kilometers) of hiking trails ranging from short, easy nature walks to primitive mountain trails for experienced hikers. Considered one of the ultimate Big Bend hikes, **Lost Mine Trail** (4.8 miles/7.7 kilometers round-trip, roughly 4 hours) offers an ideal combination of moderate grades, a wide range of vegetation, and extraordinary vantage points.

## ③ BROWSING SAN ANTONIO'S MARKET SQUARE

514 W. Commerce St., San Antonio; 210/207-8600; www.marketsquaresa.com

San Antonio is one of the oldest continuously inhabited places in Texas, a place where Mexico, the old Wild West, and the New World genuinely and successfully collaborate to create a unique culture and relaxed lifestyle that can't be found anywhere else. A quick walk west from the city's famous River Walk (www.thesanantonioriverwalk.com), Market Square, referred to as El Mercado by locals, is the largest Mexican marketplace outside of Mexico, a bustling pedestrian area filled with roaming mariachis and street vendors selling pottery,

HISTORIC MARKET SQUARE, SAN ANTONIO

blankets, handmade crafts, and authentic Mexican food.

Stop by **Mi Tierra Cafe & Bakery** (218 Produce Row; 210/225-1262; www.mitierracafe.com) for famous pan dulce or a hearty meal. Next door is welcoming craft shop **Little Mexico Imports** (202 Produce Row; 210/226-7765), packed with colorful clothing and folk art. For something unique, drop by **Old Mexico Imports** (888/522-8434), which specializes in talavera goods, white-glazed ceramic plates, bowls, tiles, and furnishings with simple or colorfully decorated designs.

# *Best* ROAD TRIP

Since Texas is such an enormous state, a week-long trip barely scratches the surface. This trip focuses on the areas around major cities Houston, San Antonio, and Dallas and Fort Worth; to head out to West Texas, it's at least an 8-hour detour.

PELICANS AT PADRE ISLAND NATIONAL SEASHORE

**DAY 1** Start your journey in **Houston,** with a side trip to the moon at the **NASA Space Center,** followed by a detour around the world with a meal at one of the city's many **international restaurants,** from Vietnamese to Chinese to Pakistani.

**DAY 2** Drive southwest along the Gulf Coast with a stop at the massive **King Ranch,** a living embodiment of Texas's cattle-driving past, finishing at **Padre Island National Seashore,** the longest remaining undeveloped stretch of barrier island in the world.

**DAY 3** Head north to **San Antonio,** where you can make a Texan pilgrimage to **the Alamo** and to the lively stalls of historic **Market Square.** Be sure to sample some of the state's best **Tex-Mex** food while you're there.

GERMAN-STYLE MAYPOLE IN FREDERICKSBURG

**DAY 4** Take a pleasant drive through the **Hill Country,** stopping by quaint **Fredericksburg** for some fudge and German heritage, before visiting the **Lyndon B. Johnson National Historical Park.** You'll get to **Austin** in time to bar-hop the Live Music Capital's best concert venues.

**DAY 5** Head north to **Fort Worth,** and see the **Stockyards,** a district entirely dedicated to cattle. If it's the weekend, you may want to stick around for the **Championship Rodeo** in the evening. An hour east in **Dallas,** spend a few hours in the fascinating **Sixth Floor Museum,** dedicated to the life, death, and legacy of President John F. Kennedy. To complete the loop, the drive back to Houston is 4-5 hours.

COWBOY AND LONGHORNS IN THE FORT WORTH STOCKYARDS

## KING RANCH

2205 Hwy. 141 W., Kingsville; 361/592-8055; www.king-ranch.com

At King's Ranch, longhorn cattle, vast ranchlands, and genuine cowboys evoke a sense of mystique and grandeur. America's ranching legacy was revolutionized by Richard King, who left New York City in 1835 as a pre-teen stowaway on a cargo ship. He went on to become a steamboat baron along the Rio Grande before overseeing his ranching empire. Today, King Ranch sprawls across 825,000 acres (333,865 hectares), larger than the state of Rhode Island.

The **King Ranch Visitor Center** offers daily guided tours past majestic **longhorns** with the iconic running-W brand on their hindquarters. A couple of miles down the road is the **King Ranch Museum** (405 N. 6th St., Kingsville; 361/595-1881). Housed in a historic downtown ice plant, the museum contains stunning 1940s photos of the ranch, fancy saddles and firearms, antique coaches and carriages, and other historic ranch items. Another must-see is the restored 1909 Ragland Mercantile Building that now houses the leather-filled **King Ranch Saddle Shop** (201 E. Kleberg Ave., Houston; 877/282-5777; www.krsaddleshop.com), which offers leather goods and clothing to the world.

## PRESIDENTIAL LEGACIES

Texas has played witness to some significant moments in U.S. presidential history, including the JFK assassination and the humble Hill Country roots of Lyndon B. Johnson.

Among the most-visited attractions in North Texas is the **Sixth Floor Museum** (411 Elm St., Dallas; 214/747-6660; www.jfk.org), dedicated to the life, death, and legacy of John F. Kennedy, the 35th president of the United States. The museum's exhibits, artifacts, and films provide a slice of American life in the early 1960s and the subsequent impact of JFK's assassination. The most intense and sobering area of the museum is the spot near the 6th-floor window where the fatal shots were allegedly fired.

Lyndon B. Johnson remains a larger-than-life figure who brought acclaim (and electricity) to the Hill Country. Be sure to set aside a few hours to tour the remarkable **Lyndon B. Johnson National Historical Park**, (830/868-7128; www.nps.gov/lyjo), with two sites in the Hill Country. The **Johnson City District** (100 Lady Bird Lane, Johnson City) comprises his boyhood home and his grandparents' log cabin home. The **LBJ Ranch** (Hwy. 290, near Stonewall), a.k.a. the Texas White House, is 14 miles (23 kilometers) west. Here, you can view the president's office, living room, dining room, and the Johnsons' bedroom suites. For more on the 36th president, visit the **Lyndon Baines Johnson Library and Museum** (2313 Red River St., Austin; 512/721-0200) on the University of Texas campus.

## THE ALAMO

300 Alamo Plaza, San Antonio; 210/225-1391; www.thealamo.org

Established in 1718 as a mission to spread Catholicism and protect Spain's colonial interests, the site of the Alamo had subsequent incarnations as a hospital and cavalry post. In 1835, the formation of the Mexican Republic meant increased immigration and tariff enforcement that, in turn, incited immigrants in the border region between Mexico and Texas, largely from the United States, to revolt. Texan soldiers

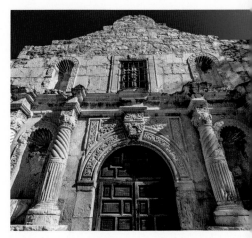

ENTRANCE TO THE ALAMO

# *Major* CITIES

**HOUSTON:** The fourth-largest city in the United States, Bayou City is notorious for its urban sprawl and unbearably hot summers, but it's not without its charm, with world-class cultural facilities and its international population contributing to a truly cosmopolitan setting.

**SAN ANTONIO:** San Antonio is a legendary city whose beginnings predate the founding of the United States. The Alamo is its cultural icon, and with the city's welcoming lack of pretense, it's no surprise that San Antonio regularly appears on Top 10 lists of favorite travel destinations.

**DALLAS:** Often remembered as the site of John F. Kennedy's assassination or for the prime-time soap opera that bore its name, Dallas, with Fort Worth and Arlington, is part of a diverse Metroplex that is Texas's largest metropolitan area.

eventually captured the Alamo Mission, but by March 1836 thousands of Mexican troops had descended on San Antonio, raising a red flag of "no quarter." Over a 13-day siege, some 200 badly outnumbered Texans and Tejanos fought to the death to defend the Alamo, making it an enduring symbol of Texas's struggle for independence.

Referred to as the "Shrine of Texas Liberty," visitors to the Alamo are asked to remove their hats and refrain from taking photos out of respect. In addition to the famous mission building, the grounds include the Long Barrack Museum, a lush courtyard with a well dating to the mission era (1724-1793), and an informative timeline displayed on large outdoor panels.

## MARFA

The small West Texas railroad stop of Marfa (population 1,772) has become an unlikely cultural hotbed for artists and visitors from across the world. Contemporary artist Donald Judd arrived in Marfa from New York City in the early 1970s and purchased several buildings in and around Marfa that ultimately became the **Chinati Foundation** (1 Cavalry Row, Marfa; 432/729-4362; www.chinati.org). Art lovers and artists from around the world come to this West Texas outpost for its amazing array of artwork, from Judd's largescale pieces—most notably, a mammoth artillery shed containing stark metal boxes of varying size—to patterned

fluorescent light sculptures, as well as sketches and paintings.

Another popular attraction in the area is **Prada Marfa** (about 37 miles/57 kilometers west of Marfa on the south side of U.S. Hwy. 90), a permanent art installation mimicking a small Prada retail store. It's well worth the half-hour drive for the photo op (even Beyonce has done it).

# BEST SCENIC DRIVES

## HILL COUNTRY JOURNEY

A pleasant drive through the bucolic Hill Country provides visitors with sweeping views of rolling hills and sheer canyon walls lining the rivers that carve through limestone bluffs. Start the Hill Country journey (66 miles/106 kilometers, allow at least 2 hours) in **Bandera**, a.k.a. the "Cowboy Capital of the World," with gentle pastures and scenic ranches. Head west on Highway 16 and FM 337, where you'll be treated to inviting scenery along the lazy **Medina River.** Things start to change as you get farther west and closer to the **Frio River,** which runs north-south along Highway 83. Take a few hours to check out a swimming hole on the Frio, or spend the night at a classic Hill Country cabin in a charming river community like **Leakey** or **Concan.**

## ROUTE 66

Travelers can get their kicks along Texas's entire stretch of Route 66, along I-40 in the Panhandle between Oklahoma and New Mexico (95 miles/153 kilometers, allow over 2 hours), but the best collection of roadside attractions is between **Amarillo** and **Shamrock,** from art deco motor courts and service stations to diners. Amarillo is home to the famous **Cadillac Ranch,** (about 10 miles/16 kilometers west of downtown Amarillo between exits 60 and 62—exit Arnot Rd. on the south side of I-40) one of the premier photo ops in Texas, a permanent art installation of 10 Cadillacs buried nose-down in a field.

An hour or so east, tiny **McLean** is home of the **Texas Old Route 66 and Devil's Rope Museums** (100 Kingsley St., McLean; 806/779-2225; www.barbwiremuseum.com). Though the barbed wire (aka "devil's rope") portion of the building is intriguing, the Texas Old Route 66 Museum offers a fascinating glimpse into the not-too-distant past, with vintage road signs, artwork from tourist traps, and hundreds of mementos and souvenirs from the golden age of automobile travel. A little farther east in Shamrock, the **U-Drop Inn and Conoco Station** (1242 N. Main St., Shamrock; 806/256-2516) is a remarkable 1936 art deco landmark with a steeple-like spire that advertised food, gas, and lodging—three essential elements for Route 66 travelers.

# BEST PARKS AND RECREATION AREAS

Many of Texas's state and national parks offer a glimpse into its complicated Indigenous history, which unfortunately in many cases ended with native tribes being driven away in the U.S.'s unceasing conquest west. As a result, only three reservations currently exist in Texas today. They are the Alabama-Coushatta near Houston, the Tigua east of El Paso, and the Kickapoo along the Rio Grande between Del Rio and Laredo. To learn more about contemporary Indigenous culture in Texas, visit https://indigenouscultures.org.

## PADRE ISLAND NATIONAL SEASHORE

3829 Park Rd. 22, Corpus Christi; 361/949-8068; www.nps.gov/pais

Padre Island National Seashore is a lowkey, nature-oriented, protected shoreline not to be confused with the commercial-minded party atmosphere of South Padre Island, a 3-hour drive south. Padre Island National Seashore is the longest remaining undeveloped stretch of barrier island in the world and appeals to naturalists who delight in its birding and fishing opportunities. In the fall and spring migration seasons, thousands of birds drop by, including sandhill cranes, hawks, and songbirds.

The park is also considered the most important nesting beach for the most endangered sea turtle, the Kemp's ridley. Park officials incubate sea turtle eggs found along the coast and release the hatchlings into the gulf during summer. You can watch this fascinating event—for release dates and directions to the site, call the **Hatchling Hotline** (361/949-7163). Other popular activities at the park include swimming, fishing, windsurfing, and beachcombing.

## PALO DURO CANYON STATE PARK

11450 Park Rd. 5, Canyon; 806/488-2227; www.tpwd.state.tx.us

America's second-largest canyon is an absolute must. Palo Duro (Spanish for "hard wood"; namely, the abundant

PALO DURO CANYON STATE PARK

mesquite and juniper trees) features a vast expanse of colorful soil and spectacular geographic formations. The stratified colors are particularly intriguing, with sheer cliffs, rock towers, and canyon walls displaying muted hues of red, yellow, and orange exposed by erosion from a tributary of the Red River and the ubiquitous High Plains winds.

People have inhabited Palo Duro Canyon for nearly 12,000 years, including the Folsom and Clovis groups who hunted mammoth and giant bison. Later, the Apache, Comanche, and Kiowa sought out the water and animals that gathered at its watering holes. It wasn't until 1852 that a U.S. settler first saw its colorful walls. Two decades later, the canyon was a battle site during the Red River War with Native American tribes.

Visitors can experience Palo Duro's topographic splendor by foot, bike, car, or horse year-round. The park's 18,000 acres (7,284 hectares) offer a topographical getaway unlike any other in the Lone Star State. In addition to hiking and biking, Palo Duro visitors enjoy picnicking and camping, wagon rides, and campfire breakfasts, along with the park's souvenir shop, interpretive center, and amphitheater.

## GUADALUPE MOUNTAINS NATIONAL PARK

400 Pine Canyon, Salt Flat; 915/828-3251; www.nps.gov/gumo

GUADALUPE MOUNTAINS NATIONAL PARK

The Guadalupe Mountains are an underappreciated natural wonder straddling the Texas-New Mexico border, more than 86,000 acres (34,802 hectares) with elevations ranging 3,650-8,749 feet (1,112-2,666 meters), including the summit of **Guadalupe Peak,** the highest point in Texas. Travelers who make the effort to visit this remarkably rugged and remote park are rewarded with deep canyons, the world's finest example of a fossilized reef, a rare mixture of plant and animal life, and West Texas's only legally designated wilderness.

Historically, this was the land of the Mescalero Apache before white settlers arrived in the mid-1800s. By the late 1800s, ranchers and the military had established a presence in the mountains, driving away the Mescalero Apaches for good. In the early 1920s, geologist Wallace Pratt with the then-tiny Humble Oil and Refining Company (now enormous Exxon) became captivated with the area while scouting for oil in the nearby Permian Basin. In subsequent decades, he bought a significant amount of property in the McKittrick Canyon and eventually donated nearly 6,000 acres (2,428 hectares) that became the nucleus for the park. It remains a compelling destination for hikers, backpackers, and campers who appreciate its solitude and challenging terrain.

## SEMINOLE CANYON STATE PARK

U.S. 90, Comstock; 432/292-4464; https://tpwd.texas.gov/state-parks/seminole-canyon

Ancient Native American artwork is the focal point of Seminole Canyon State Park. The park's main attraction, **Fate Bell Shelter,** contains a mesmerizing array of ancient pictographs, including shamanic figures, animal images, and soul-stirring handprints. Made with rust-colored paint derived from animal oils and plant materials, the paintings depict many of these animals, along with shamanic figures. Volunteers with the nonprofit **Rock Art Foundation** (888/762-5278; www.rockart.org) conduct tours. The park also includes an insightful and well-researched interpretive center, 8 miles

# SOUVENIRS AND COLLECTIBLES

## FREDERICKSBURG FUDGE

218 E. Main St., Fredericksburg; 830/997-0533; www.fbgfudge.com

The small Hill Country town of Fredericksburg is a favorite weekend destination for Texans, with the community's German heritage being the major draw. A stroll down Main Street would be incomplete without stopping by Fredericksburg Fudge, a traditional candy shop that has been doling out thick chunks of rich, sweet, made-from-scratch fudge for decades.

## BOOTS AND WESTERN WEAR

**El Paso** is one of the best places in Texas to find authentic Western wear. Boots and hats are required apparel in this sunbaked, windswept region.

- Ranching families and their workers have been outfitting themselves at **Starr Western Wear** (two locations—112 E. Overland Ave.; 915/533-0113; and 11751 Gateway Blvd.; 915/594-0113; www.starrwesternwear.com) for nearly 50 years.

- For boots, there's no excuse not to drop by one of the legendary **Tony Lama Factory Stores** (particularly 7156 Gateway E.; 915/772-4327; www.tonylamabootshop.com), one of the most recognized names on the Western wear scene.

(12.9 kilometers) of multi-use trails for hiking and mountain biking, and nature and interpretive trails.

# FESTIVALS AND EVENTS

## STOCKYARDS CHAMPIONSHIP RODEO

Fort Worth; year-round

The Stockyards, a district 2 miles (3.2 kilometers) north of downtown Fort Worth, are a place of genuine cowboy stuff—livestock pens, saloons, a rodeo arena, and dozens of other historic structures tell the stories of the cattle drives and the rugged trail hands that followed their trampled tracks 100-plus years ago. The understated grandeur of the **1908 Cowtown Coliseum** (121 E. Exchange Ave., Fort Worth; 817/625-1025; www.cowtowncoliseum.com) is a perfect backdrop for one of the world's oldest indoor rodeo arenas. It's still home to the Stockyards Championship Rodeo (Fri.-Sat. 8pm) and occasionally **Pawnee Bill's Wild West Show** (Sat. afternoon), featuring trick roping, shooting, and riding as well as cowboy songs

and entertainment. Daily, the Stockyards' **cattle drives** (11:30am and 4pm) showcase a dozen magnificent longhorn cattle sauntering and clip-clopping down the main drag accompanied by period-costumed drivers.

## SOUTH BY SOUTHWEST

Austin; 512/467-7979; www.sxsw.com; Mar.

Each March, thousands of musicians and their critics, businesspeople, and groupies flock to Austin for South by Southwest for the ideal weather, beer, barbecue, Tex-Mex, and every kind of music under the sun. During 10 days, Austin becomes the epicenter of the music industry, complete with international media coverage and plenty of black leather. The original concept was to expose bands and sign contracts for up-and-coming artists, but SXSW has evolved into an enormous showcase hosting big names and reunion gigs for the publicity factor.

JUNETEENTH PARADE

## AUSTIN CITY LIMITS

www.aclfest.com; Sept.-Oct.

Literally one of the country's hottest festivals takes place during the inferno of Austin's early fall. The **Austin City Limits Music Festival** takes place over two weekends, featuring artists ranging from rock legends like Paul McCartney and David Byrne to big names like Lizzo, Kanye West, and Wilco. Despite the sweltering conditions, 70,000 fans snap up tickets each year.

## JUNETEENTH

Galveston is the birthplace of the now nationwide Juneteenth celebration, commemorating news of the Emancipation Proclamation reaching Texas, more than two years late. Though the Proclamation was signed on January 1, 1863, news of freedom didn't come to Texas's 250,000 enslaved African Americans until June 19, 1865. Today, huge celebrations are held throughout the state, including in Fort Worth and Houston, featuring parades, hundreds of vendors lining the streets, plenty of good eats and revelry, and national gospel, blues, and jazz acts taking the stage.

# BEST FOOD

## BARBECUE

Barbecue is an art form and a lifestyle in Texas, a calculated effort of smoking specific meats with the right kind of wood for the optimal amount of time. Several different styles of barbecue are said to be the most authentic, depending on where you are. Why not try all of them and decide for yourself?

- Purists insist the ideal experience is at **Kreuz Market** (619 N. Colorado St., Lockhart; 512/398-2361; www.kreuzmarket.com), where the meat, particularly the pork chop, is so perfectly smoked, it would be insulting to slather it with sauce.

- Several joints in Austin and around are nationally known for venerable and authentic 'cue. At **Franklin Barbecue** (900 E. 11th, Austin; 512/653-1187; https://franklinbbq.com), diners regularly wait at least 3 hours to experience the succulent beef brisket, tender pork ribs, and flavorful sausage.

- West Texas's open-pit cowboy-style barbecue is also worth sampling. At **Jack Jordan's Bar-B-Q** (1501 John Ben Shepperd Pkwy., Odessa; 432/362-7890; www.jackjordansbbq.com), the beef ribs reign supreme and there's an ample supply of jalapeños and Tabasco.

## TEX-MEX

In Texas, Mexican food can mean many things—cuisine from the interior of Mexico with savory sauces and meats, or border-inspired Tex-Mex with thick cheese, seasoned beef, and tortillas. Tex-Mex dishes like enchiladas, tacos, and tamales prevail in the Lone Star State, with rice, beans, guacamole, lettuce, and tomato as typical side accompaniments. Try it at San Antonio's **Casa Rio** (430 E. Commerce St., San Antonio; 210/225-6718; www.casa-rio.com). Interior Mexican cuisine is distinguished by more complex ingredients, especially the chilies (ancho, poblano), cheeses (queso fresco, queso panela), sauces (moles with nuts, chilies, and chocolate), and meat (duck, seafood, venison). Chile relleno is a prime example of interior Mexican food. **Rosario's Mexican Café** (910 S. Alamo St., San Antonio; 210/223-1806; www.rosariossa.com), also in San Antonio, is a great place to try it.

## SOUTHERN

Texas is in a geographically undefined region—it isn't really the South, and it doesn't quite qualify as the Southwest. Although Southern cooking is on the menu in most Texas cities, it's especially prevalent in East Texas, with geographical proximity to the South. Like everything else, Texas puts its own spin on down-home country cuisine.

- **Chicken-fried steak** is a thin cut of steak that's tenderized, breaded in a seasoned flour mixture or egg batter, pan fried, and served with peppered cream gravy. Try it at **Dolli's Diner** (116 S. Pecan St., Nacogdoches; 936/305-5007).

- Chefs near the Gulf Coast take a Cajun approach to **catfish,** dipping the fillet in hot sauce and milk and a traditional blend of cornmeal, paprika, and cayenne. Try it at **Vautrot's Cajun Cuisine** (13350 Hwy. 105, Beaumont; 409/753-2015)

- **Fried okra** starts with egg and buttermilk and cornmeal, flour, brown sugar, salt, and peppers, before frying. Try it at **Courthouse Whistlestop Café** (318 N. Washington Ave., Livingston; 936/327-3222).

## INTERNATIONAL FOOD IN HOUSTON

Houston's humongous growth (population 2,325,502) has it closing in on Chicago as the third-largest city in the country, and it was recently named the nation's most diverse metropolis. Its international food scene has benefitted from all this diversity. There's not only Cajun, barbecue, and Tex-Mex, but also Vietnamese, Chinese, and Pakistani cuisine.

- Go to **Lua Viet Kitchen** (1540 W. Alabama St., 346/227-7047, www.luavietkitchen.com) for modern, fresh Vietnamese.

- **Mala Sichuan** (9348 Bellaire Blvd.; 713/995-1889) serves dishes featuring the trademark, numbing Sichuan peppercorn.

- Try **Khyber Restaurant** (2410 Richmond Ave.; 713/942-9424) for cult-classic, no-fuss Pakistani meals.

# MAJOR AIRPORTS

- **George Bush Intercontinental Airport:** IAH; 2800 N. Terminal Rd., Houston; www.fly2houston.com

- **Dallas/Fort Worth International Airport:** DFW; 2400 Aviation Dr., DFW Airport; www.dfwairport.com

- **Austin-Bergstrom International Airport:** AUS; 3600 Presidential Blvd., Austin; www.austintexas.gov/airport

- **San Antonio International Airport:** SAT; 9800 Airport Blvd., San Antonio; www.flysanantonio.com

- **El Paso International Airport:** ELP; 6701 Convair Rd., El Paso; www.elpasointernationalairport.com

# MORE INFORMATION

## TRAVEL AND TOURISM INFORMATION

- **Travel Texas:** www.traveltexas.com
- **Texas Parks and Wildlife Department:** www.tpwd.texas.gov

## NEWSPAPERS AND MAGAZINES

- *Texas Monthly:* www.texasmonthly.com
- *The Dallas Morning News:* www.dallasnews.com
- *Houston Chronicle:* www.chron.com

# ROCKY MOUNTAINS

GARDEN OF THE GODS, COLORADO

# THE ROCKY MOUNTAINS
## State by State

### IDAHO

**Why Go:** Outdoor recreation in the Sawtooth Mountains and elsewhere in the state is making Idaho a popular destination.

### MONTANA

**Why Go:** Under Montana's big sky, you can have a Western dude ranch vacation, learn about Blackfeet culture, and hike to an actual glacier.

### WYOMING

**Why Go:** Yellowstone and Grand Teton National Parks are two of the most spectacular parks in the national parks system.

### COLORADO

**Why Go:** Get a combination of city (Denver) and mountains (the Rockies), along with a hint of the southwest (Mesa Verde).

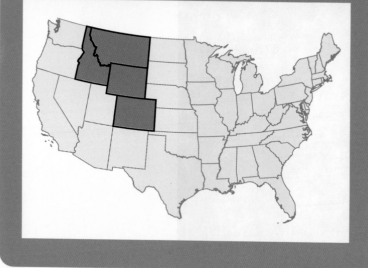

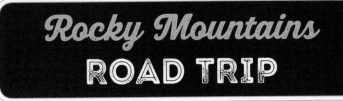

# Rocky Mountains
## ROAD TRIP

In two weeks, you can string together the four national parks that highlight different parts of the Rocky Mountain region. This epic trip climbs roads carved into the sides of mountains, passes rushing waterfalls and spouting geysers, and stops for views of glaciers. Be sure to make reservations far in advance for in-park accommodations, like Jackson Lake Lodge and the Old Faithful Inn.

## COLORADO

**Denver and Rocky Mountains National Park: 2 Days / 112 miles (180 kilometers)**
Start with a city day in **Denver,** enjoying the shops, restaurants, and excellent craft brews. The next day, head out to **Estes Park** and the start of **Trail** **Ridge Road** in **Rocky Mountain National Park.** Spend the day winding through the park and stopping for hikes. Spend the night in **Grand Lake,** at the west end of the road.

## WYOMING

**Yellowstone and Grand Teton National Parks: 5 Days / 786 miles (1,265 kilometers)**
From Grand Lake, head into Wyoming, stopping in **Laramie** and ending up in **Casper.** Spend the next day getting from Casper to Moran, and get your first taste of **Grand Teton National Park** as you drive from Moran to **Jackson** for the night. Take a day to drive **Teton Park Road** from Jackson to Jackson Lake Lodge, stopping at pullouts to admire the views.

DOWNTOWN DENVER

DEVIL'S TOWER, WYOMING

From Jackson Lake Lodge, drive to **Yellowstone National Park**. Hit West Thumb Geyser Basin on the way to **Old Faithful**. From Old Faithful, follow a reverse S through the park, stopping at **Grand Prismatic Spring** and **Grand Canyon of the Yellowstone**, passing through **Lamar Valley** to spot bison, ending the day at **Mammoth Hot Springs**.

## MONTANA

**Glacier National Park: 3 days / 480 miles (775 kilometers)**
From Mammoth Hot Springs, power through a day-long drive to **St. Mary**, Montana, just outside **Glacier National Park**. Then have a minimal driving day to explore the **Many Glacier** area of the park, including a hike to Grinnell Glacier. Get up early the next morning to drive the epic **Going-to-the-Sun Road** through the park. You'll end the day in Whitefish, a resort town west of Glacier.

## GETTING BACK TO DENVER

**16 hours**
The trip from Whitefish to Denver is about 1,000 miles (1,609 kilometers) and takes a minimum of 16 hours. You can break it up over two days, spending the night in **Billings**, Montana. Or you can make more stops in cities and towns like **Butte**, Montana, and **Sheridan** and **Cheyenne** in Wyoming.

## ADDING IDAHO

**Coeur d'Alene, Boise, Craters of the Moon: 6-7 days / 1,465-1,510 miles (2,360-2,430 kilometers)**
To add a swing through Idaho, head west from Whitefish to **Coeur d'Alene**, about 4 hours away. Stay a day at the lakeside getaway, then spend a day driving south to Boise, which takes about 7 hours. Tool around **Boise** and the nearby **Snake River Valley** for a day. The next day, wake up early to head back east to **Jackson**, Wyoming, about 6.5 hours away, and you'll want to stop midway to explore **Craters of the Moon National Monument**. From Jackson, you can make the 8-hour drive back to **Denver** in one day. Or, you can retrace your drive through Grand Teton National Park out to Casper, then back to Denver, over two days.

MANY GLACIER, GLACIER NATIONAL PARK

# IDAHO

daho is often misunderstood. When this rugged northwestern state is not being confused with Iowa, it's usually the brunt of some bad potato joke. True, farmers here do grow more spuds than any other state in the country, but Idaho goes beyond russet potatoes.

It's hard to fathom the varied landscapes of this beautiful state on Nimiipu (Nez Perce), Shoshone-Paiute, Shohone-Bannock, Salish Kootenai (Flathead), and Schitsu'umsh (Coeur d'Alene) land. As you snowshoe across a frozen lake in the Sawtooths, you'll be reminded of the intense volcanic activity and major floods that helped to shape the land. The basalt-hemmed cliffs along the Snake River Canyon seem like a different planet than the cedar-ringed glacial lakes in the northern Panhandle. Juxtaposed with Idaho's remote wilderness are thriving urban areas. Boise, the state capital, has a surprisingly mellow vibe for a city with the third-largest metropolitan population in the Northwest. The people of Idaho are as varied as the land itself, yet their adoration for the remarkable landscape that surrounds them is the only common thread they need.

> **AREA:** 83,569 square miles / 216,442 kilometers (14th)
>
> **POPULATION:** 1,787,065 (39th)
>
> **STATEHOOD DATE:** July 3, 1890 (43rd)
>
> **STATE CAPITAL:** Boise

FLY-FISHING ON THE COEUR D'ALENE RIVER

## ORIENTATION

**Boise,** the capital city, is located in southwestern Idaho. Between Boise and the Oregon border lies the **Snake River Valley** wine country. The **Snake River** stretches across the wide southern part of the state. The largest potato farms are located in southeastern Idaho. **Sun Valley** and the **Sawtooths,** Idaho's central Rockies, sit in the middle of the state, east of Boise. The narrow **Panhandle** at the tip-top of Idaho is home to the state's largest lakes, including **Coeur d'Alene Lake.**

## WHEN TO GO

**Summer** is peak season in most of the state, including Coeur d'Alene, the Sawtooths, and Island Park in southeast Idaho. **Wintertime** brings tons of snow to the mountains, making Idaho's mountain resorts like Sun Valley, McCall, and Kellogg, popular destinations for skiers and snowboarders. **Spring** and **fall** are also good times to visit the mountain resort towns for biking, fishing, and hiking: The streets are less crowded, and room rates are lower.

# HIGHLIGHTS

## THE BASQUE BLOCK

600 block of Grove Street, Boise

Basques began settling here in significant numbers in the late 1890s, and today, Boise's Basque culture is a colorful part of the city's identity. One highlight of this enclave is the **Basque Center** (601 W. Grove St., Boise; 208/342-9983; www.basquecenter.com), which serves as a center for Basque culture and a social center for older Basques who play cards and converse in their native tongue. It has a bar that is open to the public—a great spot to soak in the culture while enjoying a glass of Rioja.

The **Basque Museum and Cultural Center** (611 Grove St., Boise; 208/343-2671; www.basquemuseum.com) is two doors down, home to exhibits on musical instruments, crafts, and other items unique to the Basques. On the end of

THE BASQUE CENTER

the block is **Bar Gernika** (202 S. Capitol Blvd., Boise; 208/344-2175; www.bargernika.com), one of Boise's classic pubs. It's a great place to get a taste of Basque cuisine and culture intertwined with a hip modern scene.

## OLD IDAHO PENITENTIARY

2445 Old Penitentiary Rd., Boise; 208/334-2844

The Old Idaho Penitentiary is one of only four U.S. territorial prisons still standing. It was built in 1870 and remained in use for more than a century. Among its famous tenants: Harry Orchard, convicted for the 1905 assassination of Governor Frank Steunenberg; and Lyda "Lady Bluebeard" Southard, convicted of killing her fourth husband for insurance money and suspected of doing away with the first three as well.

The Old Pen looks like something from another time—part Wild West military fortification, part medieval castle. You can tour this State Historic Site, which boasts a beautiful rose garden that juxtaposes the original prison gallows, where numerous unfortunate convicts were dispatched to their final resting places.

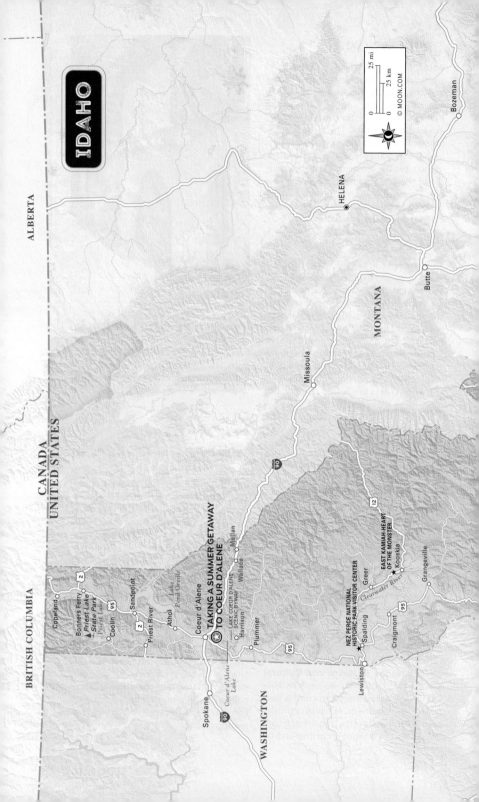

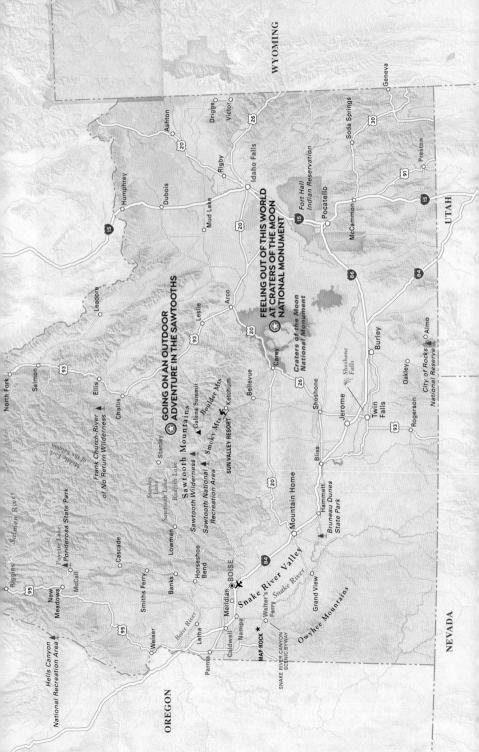

# TOP 3

## 1 FEELING OUT OF THIS WORLD AT CRATERS OF THE MOON NATIONAL MONUMENT

1266 Craters Loop Rd., Arco; 208/527-1300; www.nps.gov/crmo

Craters of the Moon National Monument is an eerie, otherworldly landscape that has been pocked, cracked, contorted, and charred by lava flows and eruptions occurring at various times over thousands of years. Lava fields cover much of southeastern Idaho, but what makes this area unique is the concentration of different volcanic features. Craters of the Moon lies along the Great Rift, a 60-mile-long (96-kilometer) perforation in the earth's crust along which eruptions have occurred as recently as about 110 BC. Scientists say the area is due for another eruption any day now, sometime in the next 1,000 years.

CRATERS OF THE MOON NATIONAL MONUMENT

Hop in the car to drive the 7-mile (11-kilometer) road that loops south into the heart of the monument. Among the highlights: the **Devil's Orchard,** where a short, wheelchair-accessible interpretive trail loops through some bizarre formations; **Inferno Cone Viewpoint,** where you can hike up to the top of Inferno Cone for sweeping views across the lava flows and the Snake River Plain; the **Tree Molds** area, where a short hike leads to some prime examples of that phenomenon; and the **Cave Area,** where a trail leads to numerous lava tube "caves," most of which require a flashlight to explore. There's also a **visitors center** (208/527-1335), where exhibits and videos explain the geology, flora and fauna, and history of the area.

## 2 TAKING A SUMMER GETAWAY TO COEUR D'ALENE

Coeur d'Alene—French for "heart like an awl" and pronounced "Cortalane"—ranks as one of Idaho's top summer resort towns. The city, which is centered near the scenic beach areas of the eponymous lake, teems with recreational activity during the warmer months, when droves of people show up for boating, swimming, and a healthy dose of beachside relaxation at **City Beach.** One of the city's highlights, the beautiful **Tubbs Hill,** a 120-acre (48-hectare) wooded preserve, juts out into the lake right next to **The Coeur d'Alene Resort** (115 S. 2nd St., Coeur d'Alene; 208/765-4000; www.cdaresort.com), arguably the grandest hotel in Idaho. Trails loop around the peninsula through groves of Douglas fir and century-old ponderosa pine. Some paths climb up the hill for panoramic views, while others drop down to hidden coves and beaches. At night, **Sherman Avenue** in town comes alive with a profusion of restaurants, bars, and ice-cream shops.

To see more of the lake, take I-90 and go south on Highway 97, which is state's designated **Lake Coeur d'Alene Scenic Byway.** Keep your eyes peeled for ospreys; this area has the largest concentration of them in the western United States. to see the east shore of the lake. The route passes **Arrow Point,** a finger of land jutting into the lake; crosses the Coeur d'Alene River; and heads into the town of **Harrison,** a recreation hub on the southeast shore. At the junction with Highway 3 south of Harrison, turn north (left) to drive up the South Fork Coeur d'Alene River past 10 lakes, until you get back to I-90.

SHORES OF LAKE COEUR D'ALENE

## ③ GOING ON AN OUTDOOR ADVENTURE IN THE SAWTOOTHS

Driving on Highway 75 around the center of the state, you don't need a sign to tell you when you've entered the 765,000-acre (309,584-hectare) Sawtooth National Recreation Area (NRA). The houses suddenly disappear, and the grandeur of the mountains and the tranquility of the wooded river valley return.

The NRA encompasses parts of four different mountain ranges. From the head-quarters in the Wood River Valley, the Smoky Mountains are visible to the west, and the Boulder Mountains to the east. Across Galena Summit to the north, the famous Sawtooth Mountains dominate the western skyline with a string of jagged summits, while the eastern horizon is shaped by the inscrutable White Cloud Peaks. More than 50 summits in the NRA stand over 10,000 feet (3,048 meters).

Among these mountains are 300-plus alpine lakes, all suitable for **fishing,** some even big enough for **boating** and **sailing.** Gorgeous **Redfish Lake** is the largest and most popular, attracting crowds of swimmers and sunbathers in summer, and also home so several hiking trails. And four major Idaho rivers, namely the Salmon, South Fork Payette, Boise, and Big Wood, start within the boundaries of the NRA.

Although the entire NRA is spectacular and wild, the centerpiece of the area is the 217,000-acre (87,816-hect-

PACKING HORSE IN THE SAWTOOTH WILDERNESS

are) **Sawtooth Wilderness,** an alpine realm closed to motor vehicles and even mountain bikes. **Hikers** and **horse-packers** here can enjoy some of the country's most magnificent scenery. Unlike most mountain ranges, the Sawtooths rise suddenly. They're not particularly tall, as far as peaks go (the tallest is just under 11,000 feet/3,352 meters), but their steep relief and abundant granite walls and spires are a mountaineer's paradise. **Birders** can watch for many of the 214 bird species found here either year-round or part-time.

**DAY 1** Upon arrival in **Boise,** stretch your legs with a stroll or a bike ride along the **Boise River,** before heading to the **State Capitol** (700 W. Jefferson St.) and **Basque Block** for a few local history lessons. After checking out the city, enjoy some wine and Basque pub fare before having a cocktail and calling it a night.

**DAY 2** After breakfast in Boise, get in the car and drive 35 miles (56 kilometers) west to the **Sunny Slope** area of Caldwell. This is the beating heart of Idaho's wine country, the **Snake River Valley,** where you will find about a dozen wineries with tasting rooms. Head back to Boise for dinner and to spend the night.

BIKE PATH OVER THE BOISE RIVER

**DAY 3** From Boise, head north along Highway 55 for 2.5 hours until you reach **Ponderosa State Park.** Check into your reserved cabin and spend the rest of the day **hiking** and **biking** around the wooded park that juts out on a 1,000-acre (404-hectare) peninsula into Payette Lake.

**DAY 4** Get up early and drive 1 hour (48 miles/77 kilometers) to **Riggins** for a day of **rafting** on the **Salmon River,** world-famous for its wild rapids. Expect to get a little wet along the way, but the river professionals who work this stretch of the river are good at keeping the rafts upright. Or you could book a trip on a **wooden dory** with **Wapiti River Guides.** After shooting the tube all day, head to a restaurant in Riggins for dinner (an elk burger, perhaps?) and a few microbrews.

WINERY IN THE SNAKE RIVER VALLEY

PONDEROSA STATE PARK

**DAY**  After breakfast, travel north on U.S. 95, until you come to the Clearwater River near Lewiston, about 2 hours and 110 miles (177 kilometers) from Riggins. Here you'll find the interpretive center for the **Nez Perce National Historic Park,** an excellent spot for a picnic and to soak in some of Idaho's Native American history. Next, continue heading north on U.S. 95 for 2 hours (116 miles/186 kilometers) until you reach the shores of **Coeur d'Alene Lake,** where you'll be spending the night.

**DAY 6** Spend the day in **Coeur d'Alene** frolicking in the lake and relaxing on a lawn chair at **City Beach.** Nearby, Sherman Avenue has a multitude of cool shops and art galleries to peruse, with a few strategically placed ice cream shops along the way. Watch the fiery sunset on **Tubbs Hill,** a nature preserve with scenic hiking trails next to Coeur d'Alene Resort. Your drive back to **Boise** the next day will take 7 hours (380 miles/611 kilometers).

LAKE COEUR D'ALENE

## SUN VALLEY RESORT

1 Sun Valley Rd., Sun Valley; 208/622-4111 or 800/786-8259; www.sunvalley.com

The landmark accommodation of the Wood River Valley, Sun Valley Resort opened in 1936. Old-world elegance is the lodge's hallmark, and a patina of history graces these venerable halls. The ghost of Ernest Hemingway still haunts Room 206, where the author holed up while working on *For Whom the Bell Tolls.*

Known as the country's first bona fide **ski resort,** this charming mountain getaway has been a popular destination for powder fanatics since it opened. The resort is spread over two mountains, Bald and Dollar Mountains, and is home to 18 lifts and more than 100 runs for all abilities.

Amenities at the lodge include a year-round glass-enclosed heated pool, an indoor and an outdoor ice-skating rink, and four restaurants. The bowling alley, golf course, stables, tennis courts, and a trapshooting range are open to resort guests and nonguests alike.

## SHOSHONE FALLS

East of the town of Twin Falls, Shoshone Falls has been called the "Niagara of the West." At 1,000 feet (304 meters) wide and 212 feet (64 meters) high, the horseshoe-shaped waterfall is 52 feet (15 meters) higher than Niagara. The falls are often a mere trickle, since much of the water is diverted to the region's irrigation system; spring is usually the best time to see a torrent of water going over the big boulders. Fortunately, there's more to do if the falls aren't falling. Trails provide some nice hiking opportunities, and **Dierkes Lake** is a favorite haunt for fishing, swimming, paddling, and rock climbing.

## WALLACE

Of all the towns in the Panhandle's Silver Valley, Wallace feels most like the quintessential mining town. In the small downtown, you'll find a multitude of well-preserved 19th-century buildings. As a matter of fact, the entire town is listed on the National Register of Historic Places. This colorful downtown corridor is packed with antique shops,

# *Major* CITIES

**BOISE:** The third-largest city in the Northwest, behind Seattle and Portland, is a hotspot in the region for entertainment, shopping, and dining with kayaking, mountain biking, skiing, and hiking nearby in the Boise Foothills and Owyhee Canyonlands. The City of Trees is also home to the largest Basque population in the United States.

**NAMPA:** The suburb of Nampa has come a long way since its humble days as an Oregon Short Line rail stop—though it's still a busy railroad hub. Today, its downtown boasts a thriving historic neighborhood where you can nosh on inventive cuisine and shop for used books and antiques in the century-old Belle District.

**IDAHO FALLS:** Since Idaho Falls owes a great deal of its economy to the Idaho National Laboratory, the U.S. Department of Energy's top nuclear research facility, the eastern Idaho city is home to an interesting mix of farmers and nuclear scientists. It serves as a gateway to the state's wild backcountry, and you can't miss the town's large Mormon Temple.

old saloons, restaurants, and weird museums, making it a great place to get lost in time. Wallace is home to several museums that commemorate its history and industries, and you can take the **Sierra Silver Mine Tour** (420 5th St., Wallace; 208/752-5151; www.silverminetour.org) to explore a once-operating silver mine.

# BEST SCENIC DRIVES

## SNAKE RIVER CANYON SCENIC BYWAY

The Snake River Canyon Scenic Byway winds its way through 53 miles (85 kilometers) of bountiful agricultural land, ranging from near the Oregon border to Walter's Ferry in the Owyhee hinterlands. **Parma** is the western starting point for the byway. From this spot, the route meanders southeast along the Snake River on a series of well-marked rural roads, passing by family-run farms, fruit orchards, and vineyards. You'll go through the winery district of **Sunny Slope** before ascending onto a sagebrush-dotted bench that skirts the river canyon, where **Map Rock** near Walter's Ferry shows ancient petroglyphs. Up here, dormant cinder cones punctuate the landscape, and the deep-canyon rim—long ago carved out by the Bonneville Flood—offers dramatic views of

the **Owyhee Mountains.** Besides cattle, bison, and sheep, also expect to see abundant wildlife, like deer, coyotes, badgers, and red-tailed hawks, along this spectacular drive.

## PONDEROSA PINE SCENIC BYWAY

Hwy. 21

Spectacular mountain vistas and vast meadows awash in wildflowers combine to make this stretch of pavement, along Highway 21 east of Boise to **Sawtooth** and **Stanley Lakes,** one of the most beautiful drives in Idaho. Several

PONDEROSA PINE SCENIC BYWAY

angler access roads branch off the highway and lead down to meandering Valley Creek, while other spur roads lead south off the highway to campgrounds at the foot of the Sawtooths.

# BEST PARKS AND RECREATION AREAS

## BRUNEAU DUNES STATE PARK

27608 Sand Dunes Rd., Mountain Home; 208/366-7919

One of the state's larger parks, Bruneau Dunes State Park encompasses some 4,800 acres (1,942 hectares) of southwestern Idaho desert. Two enormous interconnecting sand dunes—the tallest nearly 500 feet (152 meters) high—rise from the center of the park. Unlike most sand dunes, these don't shift much, thanks to prevailing winds that blow in opposite directions for roughly equal amounts of time. The pristine dunes are closed to motor vehicles, but you can hike right up to the top, where you'll find an interesting crater that the two dunes seem to spiral out of, along with great views across the Snake River Plain. Various hiking trails lead around the base of the dunes, past a couple of lakes that attract both wildlife and anglers. Another feature of the park is an observatory with a 25-inch (63-centimeter) telescope and several smaller scopes.

## CITY OF ROCKS NATIONAL RESERVE

Almo; 208/824-5901; www.nps.gov/ciro

Castles of eroded granite, some over 600 feet (182 meters) tall, create a mythic fairy-tale landscape at the out-of-the-way City of Rocks National Reserve, located in south-central Idaho near the Utah border. They also make this natural landmark one of the country's top **rock-climbing** destinations. Rock jocks have put up more than 600 routes that range in difficulty. Among the most impressive rock formations at City of Rocks is **Twin Sisters,** on the west side of the preserve. The elder sister is composed of 2.5-billion-year-old

CITY OF ROCKS

granite, while the younger one was formed just 25-30 million years ago.

The 14,300-acre (5,787-hectare) preserve also lies at a major intersection of pioneer trails. Today the signatures of these California-bound settlers and miners can still be seen on the rock, between the preserve and Almo. Another bit of history here concerns a famous heist. In 1878, bandits held up the Overland Stage near Almo. Supposedly they buried their loot somewhere out in the City of Rocks, but the granite towers remain silent as to its whereabouts.

## PONDEROSA STATE PARK

Considered by many to be the crown jewel of Idaho's state park system, Ponderosa State Park occupies a 1,000-acre (404-hectare) peninsula jutting into **Payette Lake,** 2 miles northeast of downtown McCall. The peninsula was never logged in the early days, so the old-growth ponderosa pines (some up to 400 years old and 150 feet/45 meters tall) are big and abundant. Lodgepole pine, Douglas fir, and grand fir tower over the park, and wildflowers brighten the meadows and forest floor. Besides conifer forest, marshes and arid sagebrush flats provide a habitat for a wide variety of species, including woodpeckers, muskrats, ducks, foxes, ospreys,

# NEZ PERCE NATIONAL HISTORIC PARK

The Nez Perce homeland spans from eastern Oregon all the way across Idaho into Montana. The Nez Perce National Historic Park is a concept park made up of 38 separate historic sites in Idaho, Washington, Oregon, and Montana. Taken together, the sites tell the story of 11,000 years of Nez Perce culture, from their pre-Lewis and Clark days to the present. To visit them all entails a 400-mile (643-kilometer) drive. Of the 38 sites, 29 are located in Idaho; here are a few to visit.

- **Visitors Center** (39063 U.S. 95, Lapwai; 208/843-7001; www.nps.gov/nepe): The park's visitors center near Lewiston, Idaho, is the nerve center of the collection of sites and contains exhibits on Nez Perce history.

- **Weis Rockshelter:** Located off U.S. 95, about 8 miles (12 kilometers) south of Cottonwood, this habitation site was used by Indigenous people for more than 8,000 years.

- **East Kamiah-Heart of the Monster** (U.S. 12, mile marker 68): According to their legend, the Nez Perce people originated at the site. Before human beings inhabited the earth, a monster was devouring all the creatures in his path. The hero Iceye'ye (Coyote) kills the monster and cut it into little pieces. Each piece became a different Native American tribe. Coyote then wrung the blood from the monster's heart, and the Nez Perce people sprang from the drops. What was left of the monster's heart is said to be a rock formation here.

- **Looking Glass's 1877 Campsite** (U.S. 12, mile point 75.9): Looking Glass was a Nez Perce war chief who tried to remain neutral in the conflict between the U.S. Army and the nontreaty Nez Perce but was drawn in when the Army destroyed his village. This site is the location of a battle during the Nez Perce Flight of 1877.

and in summer, big hungry mosquitoes. Summer visitors can **hike** or **bike** through the park, or head for the park's beaches to play in the waters of Payette Lake. In winter, the park becomes especially quiet and serene under a blanket of snow. Cross-country ski trails lead to views overlooking frosty Payette Lake and the mountains beyond.

## HELLS CANYON NATIONAL RECREATION AREA

This 652,488-acre (264,052-hectare) preserve straddles the Snake River in Idaho and Oregon. For some 71 wild and scenic miles (114 kilometers), the Snake carves its way northward through Hells Canyon, the deepest river gorge in North America. A few roads lead down to it in places, but none dare run through it.

Below Hells Canyon Dam, the Snake River's raging rapids and placid pools make for a recreational haven for **rafters** and **jet boaters. Hikers** can follow trails along the water's edge, beneath towering walls of crumbling black basalt, or climb out of the canyon to explore the high country along its rim (most notably the **Seven Devils Mountains**). This range of high peaks has some of the state's most magnificent alpine scenery and offers great views of the canyon floor more than a vertical mile (1.6 kilometers) below.

## RIGGINS

Riggins is considered by many to be the best place for white water in Idaho. The **Salmon River** flows right through town on the last legs of its run down from Redfish Lake. The Little Salmon River joins it here, and the Salmon flows another 60 miles (96 kilometers) through

RAFTING TRIP IN THE MIDDLE FORK OF THE SALMON RIVER

Lower Salmon Gorge to the Snake River. Several guide services offer float trips on either or both the main Salmon run above town and the Salmon River Gorge stretch downstream. Among the many are **Exodus Wilderness Adventures** (208/628-3586; www.exoduswildernessadventures.com) and **Wapiti River Guides** (208/628-3523; www.doryfun.com), which uses wooden dories on its trips.

## FRANK CHURCH–RIVER OF NO RETURN WILDERNESS

The various forks of the wild and scenic **Salmon River** vein the craggy, batholithic core of the state, which comprises a majority of central Idaho. The Salmon River is known for its world-class **white-water rafting.** Thrill seekers show up every summer for the never-ending churning rapids, which slice through some of the most beautiful high country in the United States. Find an outfitter in around the town of **Salmon** through the Idaho Outfitters and Guides Association (www.ioga.org).

The **Middle Fork of the Salmon** is one of the world's greatest and most popular white-water trips, drawing rafters and kayakers from around the globe. From the put-in at Boundary Creek, northwest of Stanley, the river flows 100 wet and wild miles (160 kilometers) through a wilderness little tarnished by human activity. Bighorn sheep, black bears, mountain goats, salmon and steelhead, bald eagles, and even wolves inhabit the area.

## PRIEST LAKE

Lakes don't get much more scenic than they do in Idaho's Panhandle, especially remote Priest Lake near the Canadian border. Snow-tipped peaks loom over this cedar-ringed lake (pocked out by widespread glaciers that once covered this part of North America) as it shines like a jewel down below. Two units of **Priest Lake State Park** are situated right on the shores, and there's a string of small islands with remote campgrounds. The lake is a favorite of **anglers,** who fish for lunker mackinaw in forest-shaded coves along the lake's edge. **Trails** through cool, dense forest lead between the lower and upper lakes to campgrounds reached only by boat or on foot. You won't be able to get the beauty of this place out of your head.

# FESTIVALS AND EVENTS

## IDAHO SHAKESPEARE FESTIVAL

5657 Warm Springs Ave., Boise; 208/336-9221; https://idahoshakespeare.org; mid-June-Sept.

Boise's bard-based Idaho Shakespeare Festival troupe ranks among the city's shiniest cultural gems. Shakespeare's works and other dramatic delights come alive in an **outdoor amphitheater** along the river east of downtown. The festival grounds are a wonderful place to picnic before the show.

## NATIONAL OLDTIME FIDDLERS' CONTEST AND FESTIVAL

2235 Paddock Ave., Weiser; 208/414-0255; www.fiddlecontest.org; June

Each year during the third full week of June, thousands of fiddle fans converge on this otherwise sleepy town in southwest Idaho for one of the most prestigious fiddle contests in the United States. The competition itself is staged in the air-conditioned gymnasium at **Weiser High School** (W. 7th St. and Indianhead Rd., Weiser), but some of the best music at this event happens in the sprawling, makeshift campground behind the high school, aptly called Fiddle Town, where you will hear impromptu jamming day and night. Free live musical performances get scheduled throughout the week at the **City Park Bluegrass Village Stage** in downtown Weiser. More food vendors and hawkers of arts and crafts relating to bluegrass and old-timey fiddle music can be found at this venue.

## SHOSHONE-BANNOCK INDIAN FESTIVAL AND RODEO

Fort Hall Indian Reservation; www.sbtribes.com/festival; Aug.

The spectacular Shoshone-Bannock Indian Festival and Rodeo draws Native Americans from all over the United States and Canada. Traditional Indian dancing takes center stage, and multitudes of dancers and drummers come

NATIONAL OLDTIME FIDDLERS' CONTEST AND FESTIVAL

attired in intricate dress and face paint. In addition, the event features a rodeo, an arts and crafts show, and a softball tourney. It all takes place the second week of August at the Fort Hall rodeo grounds.

## SNAKE RIVER STAMPEDE

Nampa; 208/466-8497; www.snakeriverstampede.com; July

This professional rodeo bucks into the Ford Idaho Center every year around the third week of July. The Professional Rodeo Cowboys Association-sanctioned stampede is one of the country's top 25 rodeos, attracting some 500 world-champion pros competing in bareback and saddle bronc riding, bull riding, steer wrestling, individual and team roping, and barrel racing. The week kicks off with one of the West's largest horse parades and a buckaroo breakfast.

# BEST FOOD AND DRINK

Idaho is a meat-and-potatoes state. Cowboy cooking is dear to the heart of many Idahoans; Dutch-oven cookouts and grilled steaks are the prime offerings of many tourist resorts and excursion providers. Chefs in mountain resort towns make good use of hand-foraged foodstuffs such as morel mushrooms and huckleberries as well as farm-raised elk and trout.

## SNAKE RIVER VALLEY WINES

The Snake River Valley west of Boise is an official American Viticultural Area, and the state now has more than 50 wineries.

In sheer size, the Snake River Valley AVA is one of the largest in the nation, an astonishing 5.27 million acres (2.1 million hectares), nearly the size of New Jersey. The **Sunny Slope** area, south of downtown Caldwell, is the epicenter of the wine country. The Snake River Valley's high-desert terrain, with its long, hot days and cool nights, makes for exceptional fruit, resulting in fruit-forward wines with pronounced tannins and well-balanced acidity. Hearty Rhône varietals such as **syrah** and **viognier** thrive, but this area has a long-standing tradition of growing

# BEST SOUVENIRS

- Everyone knows Idaho is famous for its **potatoes.** You'll find potato fudge, potato hand lotion, and other potato products at gift shops around the state.

- **Native American crafts** (primarily beadwork and leatherwork) are also widely available across the state. Visitors to the big **Shoshone-Bannock Indian Festival and Rodeo,** at Fort Hall the second week in August, will be faced with an enormous array of craftworks.

- The town of Preston, in the southeast corner of the state, is famous for being the filming location of independent hit film *Napoleon Dynamite.* Fans of the movie should head to the **Preston Chamber of Commerce** (49 N. State St., Preston; 208/852-2403; www.prestonidaho.org) gift shop, which sells *Napoleon Dynamite* paraphernalia, including tote bags, postcards, hats, and T-shirts.

Bordeaux-style varietals like **cabernet sauvignon, merlot,** and **cabernet franc. Riesling** and **chardonnay** grapes have also been grown in the Snake River Valley for more than 30 years.

## IDAHO POTATO VODKA

The Gem State's prized potato crop gets turned into a multitude of products, like potato chips, french fries, instant mashed potatoes, potato soup, and even potato-based skin lotion. But did you know that potato vodka is also produced in Idaho? **Silver Creek Distillers** (134 N. 3300 E., Rigby; 208/754-0042) uses local russets to produce **Teton Glacier Vodka.** Over on the west side of the Snake River Plain, in the heart of Idaho's wine country at Sunny Slope, **Koenig Distillery** (20928 Grape Ln., Caldwell; 208/455-8386) makes exceptionally smooth potato vodka in ornate copper-pot stills. These vodkas can be purchased at Idaho state liquor stores and at liquor stores throughout the country.

## MOREL MUSHROOMS

Soon after the snow melts away in Idaho's mountains, morels pop up on the forest floor. These coveted edible mushrooms are a tasty harbinger that summer is on its way. They have a deliciously nutty, creamy taste with a meaty texture. Morels grow in great numbers in the **McCall** area, about 2 hours north of Boise. It's permissible to forage for morels on Forest Service land, unless you're doing it for commercial purposes.

Most locals aren't willing to give up their prized morel spots, but they will generally offer you some advice at the pub, especially if you buy them a pint. If you don't feel like combing the forest on your hands and knees, just head to **Rupert's** (Hotel McCall, 1101 N. 3rd St., McCall; 208/634-8108; www.rupertsathotelmccall.com) or **The Narrows** (501 W. Lake St., McCall; 800/657-6464), two restaurants in McCall that use morels in creative ways in the spring and summer months.

## MAJOR AIRPORTS

- **Boise Airport:** BOI; 3201 Airport Way, Boise; 208/383-3110; www.iflyboise.com

## MORE INFORMATION

### TRAVEL AND TOURISM INFORMATION

- **Idaho State Travel Planner:** www.visitidaho.org
- **Idaho State Parks and Recreation:** www.parksandrecreation.idaho.gov

### NEWSPAPERS

- *Idaho Statesman:* www.idahostatesman.com

# MONTANA

Montana is as vast as the big sky that blankets it, rich with natural resources—fertile soil, rivers, gold, forests, wind—and overflowing with beauty. The state is on Blackfeet, Crow, Salish, Kootenai, Assiniboine (or Nakoda), Gros Ventre, Sioux, Northern Cheyenne, Chippewa, and Cree land. The dramatic landscape has been carved over eons by water, wind, fire, and ice. Blue-ribbon trout streams, tumbling and falling, etch themselves ever deeper into green valleys. From Glacier National Park to the Little Bighorn, its sites are enchanting… and sometimes haunting.

The populations are perpetually shifting too, bringing new ideas, new conflicts, and an evolving culture. Montana today is defined by the continuing growth in the western United States, but it's those little dots on the map that remind us of its almost magical timelessness. Ultimately, it's the forces of nature that make this state so captivating.

**AREA:** 147,040 square miles / 380,831 square kilometers (4th)

**POPULATION:** 1,068,778 (43rd)

**STATEHOOD DATE:**
November 8, 1889 (41st)

**STATE CAPITAL:** Helena

HORSES STAMPEDE BY MONTANA FOOTHILLS

## ORIENTATION

**Glacier National Park** is tucked into northwestern Montana, right at the border with Canada. It's surrounded by the **Flathead Valley** to the west and vast plains and soaring peaks of the **Rocky Mountain Front** to the east. Farther east is **Billings**, Montana's largest city, and four of the state's seven Native American reservations. **Missoula, Helena,** and **Butte** form a sort of triangle in the central-southwestern part of the state, while **Bozeman** leads into the towns that serve as gateways to **Yellowstone**—three of Yellowstone's entrances are located in Montana, but the bulk of the park is just over the state border in Wyoming.

## WHEN TO GO

**Summer** is a great time to visit Montana, when the front- and backcountry roads are at their busiest and easiest to drive. Be sure to make advance reservations, particularly for hotels and campgrounds, during this season. Winter brings lower rates for accommodations and more available rooms, except around ski areas, but **winter road travel** can be challenging because of the inevitable storms and possible closures. The **spring** and **fall** shoulder seasons can be a delightful time to travel. **Glacier National Park** is heavenly and much less crowded in autumn, but keep in mind that winter comes very early at high elevations.

# HIGHLIGHTS

## CAROUSEL FOR MISSOULA

101 Carousel Dr., Missoula; 406/549-8382; www.carouselformissoula.com

Aside from being a beautiful hand-carved carousel, one of the first built in the United States since the Great Depression, what makes the Carousel for Missoula so sweet is the way in which it came to be. Local cabinetmaker Chuck Kaparich vowed to the city of Missoula in 1991 that if they would "give it a home and promise no one will ever take it apart," he would build a carousel by hand. For four years, he carved ponies, taught others to carve, and worked to restore and piece together the more than 16,000 pieces of an antique carousel frame he had purchased. The town raised funds and collectively contributed more than 100,000 volunteer hours. In May 1995 the carousel opened with 38 ponies, 3 replacement ponies, 2 chariots, 14 gargoyles, and the largest band organ in continuous use in the United States.

## BIG HOLE NATIONAL BATTLEFIELD

16425 Hwy. 43, 10 miles/16.1 kilometers west of Wisdom; 406/689-3155; www.nps.gov/biho

BIG HOLE NATIONAL BATTLEFIELD

# MONTANA

ALBERTA

BRITISH
COLUMBIA

Eureka
Fortine
93

Glacier
National Park
Babb

Blackfeet
Indian Reservation
St. Mary

**HIKING IN
GLACIER NATIONAL PARK**

**LEARNING ABOUT
BLACKFEET CULTURE IN BROWNING**

**WHITEFISH MOUNTAIN RESORT**

Libby

Whitefish

Columbia Falls

GOING-TO-THE-SUN
ROAD

Browning

Cut Bank

Shelby

Chester

Joplin

Gildford

Kalispell

Evergreen

Lake
McDonald

2

**MUSEUM OF THE
PLAINS INDIAN**

2

Heron

Noxon

Somers

Bigfork

Heart
Butte

Conrad

Power

87

2

Lakeside

Dayton

Rollins

**TAKING A
RANCH VACATION**

89

15

Loma

Fort Benton

Trout Creek

Niarada

Elmo

Flathead
Lake

Choteau

Carter

87

Lonepine

Polson

Pablo

Augusta

Fort
Shaw

Great Falls

Paradise

93

Dixon

Ravalli

89

Saint Regis

90

Arlee

Evaro

Frenchtown

Missoula

White
Sulfur
Springs

Lolo

Clinton

Avon

Elliston

HELENA

Canyon
Ferry
Lake

Harlowton

Florence

Garrison

Jefferson
City

Clancy

Corvallis

Hamilton

Philipsburg

Basin

Boulder

89

191

93

Butte

15

**LEWIS AND CLARK
CAVERNS**

Belgrade

Bozeman

Livingston

*Big Hole River*

Cardwell

Harrison

90

Big Hole
National Battlefield

Wisdom

Norris

Emigrant

**CHICO
HOT SPRINGS
RESORT**

Maverick
Mountain

Ennis

Big Sky

Alder

Cameron

89

Cooke
City

IDAHO

Dillon

287

191

Gardiner

West
Yellowstone

*Yellowstone
National Park*

15

*Grand Teton
National Park*

Idaho Falls

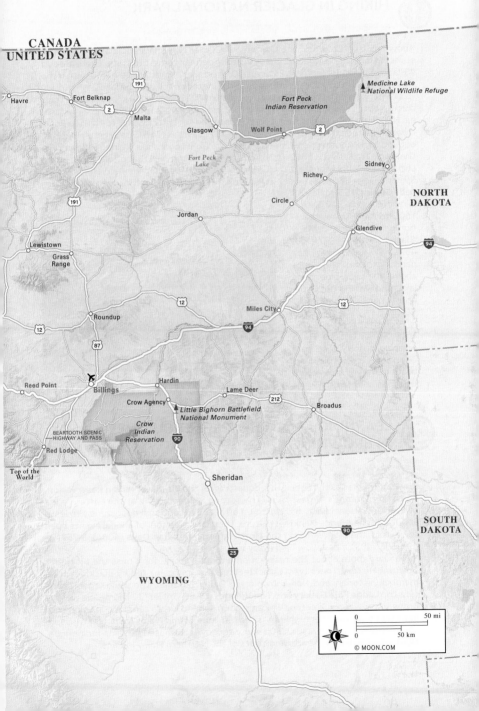

# TOP 3

## 1  HIKING IN GLACIER NATIONAL PARK

64 Grinnell Dr., West Glacier; 406/888-7800; www.nps.gov/glac

Known as the "Crown of the Continent," Glacier National Park is an amalgam of stunning landscapes that, for many visitors, defines the entire state. There are still 25 "active" glaciers (at least 25 acres/10.1 hectares in area) to be found within the park, along with countless waterfalls and hundreds of crystalline lakes.

The park is a hiker's paradise, with more than 745.6 miles (1,210 kilometers) of trails throughout the park. Certainly among the best-loved trails is the breathtakingly scenic **Highline Trail.** Leaving from Logan Pass at the summit of Going-to-the-Sun Road, the high-altitude trail to Granite Park Chalet is 15.2 miles (24.5 kilometers) round-trip, out and back. Another popular and scenic hike from Logan Pass is along **Hidden Lake Overlook Trail.** It's a 2.7-mile (4.3-kilometer) round-trip hike that offers views of the striking Clements Mountain, the Garden Wall, and Mount Oberlin, and on clear days, Sperry Glacier in the distance. To hike to an actual glacier, opt for the trail to **Grinnell Glacier** (5.5 miles/8.9 kilometers one-way with a 1,600-foot/488-meter elevation gain). It starts at **Many Glacier Hotel** (855/753-4522; www.glaciernational-parklodges.com) and climbs above impossibly blue alpine lakes and within sight of the aptly named Salamander Glacier.

HIDDEN LAKE OVERLOOK TRAIL

Hiking isn't the only way to enjoy Glacier National Park's stunning scenery. The park also offers excellent **bicycling, boating, fishing, cross-country skiing,** and more.

## 2  LEARNING ABOUT BLACKFEET CULTURE IN BROWNING

www.blackfeetnation.com

Browning serves as the agency headquarters for the **Blackfeet Indian Reservation,** home to Montana's largest tribe. The setting is spectacular, at the eastern edge of Glacier National Park, and the town offers an exceptional opportunity to learn about and experience Blackfeet culture. There are a number of annual events open to visitors, the biggest being the **North American Indian Days** (406/338-7521 or 406/338-7103), a powwow held every July.

To learn more about the reservation and its history, don't miss the **Blackfeet Cultural History Tours** (www.blackfeetculturecamp.com), led by Blackfeet tribe member, historian, and well-known artist Darryl Norman. The same organization runs the **Lodge Pole Gallery and Tipi Village** (U.S. 89, 2 miles/3.2 kilometers west of Browning; www.blackfeetculturecamp.com), where guests can camp in traditional Blackfeet tipis. Another highlight is the **Museum of the Plains Indian** (19 Museum Loop, Browning; 406/338-2230; www.doi.gov/iacb/museum-plains-indian-location), which exhibits the arts and crafts of the Northern Plains Indians.

LODGE POLE GALLERY AND TIPI VILLAGE

# ③ TAKING A RANCH VACATION

Southwest Montana is a natural destination for ranch vacations, with an age-old ranching history, wide-open spaces, and spectacular mountain scenery. Indeed, the challenge is choosing among the dozens of wonderful and welcoming ranches in the region.

Options range from **working ranches,** where you'll immerse yourself in ranch life and cowboy style, helping with daily chores like rounding up cattle; **dude ranches,** where you can more casually play rancher for a week; and **ranch resorts,** where you'll find some serious luxury with a little bit of Western flavor tossed in for good measure. Some ranches offer other activities, too, such as fishing, golf, activities for kids, and sightseeing day trips. Accommodations can range from lodge rooms to individual cabins, and amenities vary dramatically, from no cell service or TV to full-on wireless Internet, massages, and luxury accommodations.

HORSES AT A MONTANA RANCH

To pick your perfect ranch vacation, check out the **Montana Dude Ranchers' Association** (888/284-4133; www.montanadra.com). Here are a couple standouts:

▪ **Averill's Flathead Lake Lodge** (150 Flathead Lodge Rd., Bigfork; 406/837-4391; www.flatheadlakelodge.com) is a historic family ranch set right on the water. From sailing to horseback riding, fly-fishing to mountain biking, this ranch is exceptional.

▪ Set on 10,000 acres (4,047 hectares) of mountains and forests, **Mountain Sky Guest Ranch** (480 National Forest Development Rd. 132, Emigrant; 406/333-4911; www.mountainsky.com) offers impeccable service, gourmet dining, charming log cabins, and fantastic activity possibilities, including endless alpine trails for horseback riding and hiking, swimming, and even a spa.

**DAY 1** Arrive in **Missoula;** check out the shops on **Higgins Avenue** and the hip **Missoula Art Museum** (335 N. Pattee St.; 406/728-0447; www.missoulaartmuseum.org), and walk along the lovely riverfront trails. Next, head north toward Glacier country and the east shore of **Flathead Lake** to the waterfront village of **Bigfork.** Stop along the way to gorge yourself on seasonal **Flathead cherries** or just to stretch your legs and dip your toes in the lake.

FLATHEAD LAKE CHERRY STAND

**DAY 2** Try **kayaking** on the lake with the **Flathead Raft Company,** or rent your own craft at **Bigfork Outdoor Rentals.** Then head north to **Whitefish:** Consider a hike or bike ride at **Whitefish Mountain Resort,** perhaps hiking the **Danny On Trail,** just 3.8 miles (6.1 kilometers) to the summit, and then taking a **gondola** ride down. Settle in early for the night.

**DAY 3** Get up early and have a hearty breakfast before heading into **Glacier National Park.** Stop at **Lake McDonald** to soak in the majestic beauty, and prepare yourself for the vistas still ahead on **Going-to-the-Sun Road.** Stop at Logan Pass for the views and a hike—the **Hidden Lake Overlook Trail** is a stunner. Continue east out of the park through **St. Mary** and **Babb,** before heading back into the phenomenal **Many Glacier** region of the park to camp or stay at the historic **Many Glacier Hotel** (855-733-4522; www.glacier-nationalparklodges.com).

MANY GLACIER HOTEL IN GLACIER NATIONAL PARK

**DAY 4** Spend the day adventuring around Many Glacier. The hike to **Grinnell Glacier** is a classic. Afterward, make the 1-hour drive to the **Lodgepole Gallery and Tipi Village,** where you'll spend the night in a traditional Blackfeet tipi.

GRINNELL GLACIER

**DAY 5** Be sure to view the Native American art at Lodgepole Gallery, and take a half-day **Blackfeet Cultural History Tour.** Then, head south to **Boulder Hot Springs,** 3 hours away, for a relaxing night at a hot springs spa.

**DAY 6** In the morning, drive out to **Lewis and Clark Caverns** for a tour of the limestone cave the explorers missed on their journey. Turn west toward **Butte** for lunch, where you can try one of their specialties, Cornish pasties. In the afternoon, drive out to **Big Hole National Battlefield,** the site of the ambush by the U.S. Army on a Nez Perce group resisting relocation to a reservation. From there, it's a 2-hour drive back to **Missoula.**

LEWIS AND CLARK CAVERNS

Among the most moving historic sites in the state, the Big Hole National Battlefield is an important stop for visitors interested in the state's Native American history and, more specifically, the flight of the Nez Perce. The site is haunted by the ghosts of the battle on August 9, 1877, between Chief Joseph's band of Nez Perce. Often referred to as the "Nontreaty Nez Perce," they were fleeing the U.S. Army and their own homeland in Wallowa Valley in Oregon, rather than be sent to a reservation, as ordered by the U.S. government. The battlefield is as serene and beautiful today as it is stirring. The National Park Service has done an extraordinary job of presenting information about the Nez Perce War and this battle in particular. Because so little has changed in this region—from the actual landscape to the overall view—visitors can easily imagine the events that gave this spot its bloody legacy.

## MUSEUM OF THE ROCKIES

600 W. Kagy Blvd., Bozeman; 406/994-2251; www.museumoftherockies.org

Best known for its paleontology exhibit curated by dinosaur guru Jack Horner, Museum of the Rockies is a fantastic resource for the entire state. The museum tackles 500 million years of history—no small feat—with permanent exhibits that reflect Native American culture and 19th- to 20th-century regional history; there's also an outdoor living history farm (open only in summer), and a planetarium, and, of course, the dinosaurs.

## LEWIS AND CLARK NATIONAL HISTORIC TRAIL INTERPRETIVE CENTER

4201 Giant Springs Rd., Great Falls; 406/727-8733; www.fs.usda.gov

Beautifully built into a bluff overlooking the Missouri River, the Lewis and Clark National Historic Trail Interpretive Center provides visitors with a hands-on interpretation of the explorers' cross-country journey. With a two-story diorama of the portage at

# *Major* CITIES

**BILLINGS:** The hub for much of eastern Montana, Billings is a center for industry, including oil refineries and stockyards, and attracts visitors from around the state for practical and entertainment purposes. The rimrocks around the city offer a great network of hiking and biking trails, and Billings's lively food and drink culture will sate any appetite.

**MISSOULA:** Given its location at the hub of five river valleys and about half-way between Yellowstone and Glacier National Parks, Missoula has long been an important trade center and a natural stopping point for visitors to the region. Missoula is also home to the University of Montana, which keeps the city young, vibrant, and relatively liberal.

**GREAT FALLS:** With the falls long since dammed to create power—Great Falls is known as the "Electric City" for all its dams and power plants—the city has worked to capitalize on the beauty of the Missouri River. But it's is still a rough-and-tumble Montana town, with cowboy culture, military culture, and a little bit of an edge.

the Missouri River's five great falls, impressive videos by Ken Burns and others, and ranger-led programs, the center does an excellent job of portraying the importance of Native Americans to the journey along with a comprehensive natural history exhibit. There is also a nice outdoor component to the center with a network of self-guided trails, one of which leads you to the nearby Giant Springs Heritage State Park.

## GRIZZLY AND WOLF DISCOVERY CENTER

201 S. Canyon St., West Yellowstone; 406/646-7001 or 800/257-2570; www.grizzlydiscoveryctr.org

If you have your heart set on seeing a grizzly or a wolf in Yellowstone National Park in adjacent Wyoming, get it out of the way before you even go into the park. The Grizzly and Wolf Discovery Center is a nonprofit organization that acts something like an orphanage, giving homes to problem, injured, or abandoned animals that have nowhere else to go. Although there is something melancholy about watching these incredible beasts confined to any sort of enclosure, particularly on the perimeter of a chunk of wilderness as massive as Yellowstone, there is also something remarkable about seeing them close enough to count their whiskers.

Watching a wolf pack interact from a comfy bench behind floor-to-ceiling windows in the warming hut is a worthwhile way to spend an afternoon. The naturalists on staff are excellent at engaging with visitors of all ages and have plenty to teach everyone.

## SOAKING IN HOT SPRINGS

Thanks to geothermal and hydrothermal activity, most of Montana's hot springs can be enjoyed year-round. Options range from middle-of-nowhere holes in the ground to well-known natural features and developed pools in resort-like settings. Here are a few to seek out:

BOILING RIVER

- **Boulder Hot Springs** (31 Hot Springs Rd., Boulder; 406/225-4339; www.boulderhotsprings.com): Set in the middle of nowhere about halfway between Helena and Butte, Boulder Hot Springs has both indoor and outdoor pools of varying temperatures and mineral content. The on-site hotel offers simple rooms and great food.

- **Chico Hot Springs Resort** (163 Chico Rd., Pray; 406/333-4933; www.chicohotsprings.com): Just up the road from Yellowstone, Chico Hot Springs Resort is a classic, known for its wonderful outdoor pools, cozy accommodations, fabulous dining room, and lively tavern.

- **Boiling River** (3 miles/4.8 kilometers south of Yellowstone North Entrance): This river—which is not, in fact, boiling—is a small stretch of the Gardner River where thermally heated water from nearby Mammoth Hot Springs in Yellowstone flows into the icy waters of the river, mixing to make perfect a swimming temperature any time of year. The snowcapped peaks and great plumes of steam coming off the water make winter an especially unforgettable time to swim here.

## LITTLE BIGHORN BATTLEFIELD NATIONAL MONUMENT

65 miles/105 kilometers southeast of Billings, 15 miles/24 kilometers southeast of Hardin, 1 mile/1.6 kilometers east of I-90 on U.S. 212; 406/638-2621; www.nps.gov/libi

This historic site is a moving tribute to one of the last armed battles in which Native Americans fought to preserve their land and way of life. It's is a desolate, somber, and terribly meaningful place, commemorating a tragic battle with no true victors, only bloodshed marking the end of an era. The actual monument on **Last Stand Hill** is on a paved trail within walking distance of the visitors center. The granite memorial on Last Stand Hill was built in July 1881, and in 1890 marble markers replaced stakes that stood where each soldier had fallen. Starting in 1999, red granite markers were placed to honor the Native Americans who died in the battle, including Cheyenne warriors Lame White Man and Noisy Walking, and Lakota warriors Long Road and Dog's Back Bone. Another monument, titled "Peace Through Unity," was dedicated in 2003 to honor the Native Americans who fought and died in the Battle of the Little Bighorn.

## MEDICINE LAKE NATIONAL WILDLIFE REFUGE

223 North Shore Rd., Medicine Lake; 406/789-2305; www.fws.gov/refuge/medicine_lake

The Medicine Lake National Wildlife Refuge is a wetland oasis in a sea of prairie. Established in 1935, the area provides a much-used breeding and stopover habitat for an enormous range of migratory birds, including ducks, geese, swans, cranes, white pelicans, and grebes. It is a startlingly beautiful place on a breezy afternoon when the grasses sway in watery waves or on a stormy night when lightning flashes across the sky, illuminating clouds that are 15 shades of blue, pink, and purple—or any time, really; it's just that beautiful. And like so much of eastern Montana, it is not what you might expect to see in a state known for its mountains.

# BEST SCENIC DRIVES

## GOING-TO-THE-SUN ROAD

Glacier National Park; www.nps.gov/glac

Completed in 1932, the famed Going-to-the-Sun Road is a marvel of modern

WATERFALL VIEW FROM GOING-TO-THE-SUN ROAD

engineering. Spanning 50 miles (81 kilometers) from West Glacier to St. Mary, the road snakes up and around mountains that include its namesake, **Going-to-the-Sun Mountain,** giving viewers some of the most dramatic vistas in the country. The road, which crosses the **Continental Divide,** climbs more than 3,000 feet (914 meters) with only a single switchback, known as **The Loop.** Going-to-the-Sun is an architectural accomplishment as well: All of the bridges, retaining walls, and guardrails are built of native materials, so the road blends seamlessly into its majestic alpine setting. In addition to being an experience all on its own, Going-to-the-Sun is also the primary access road to Glacier National Park and the only way to get to some of the park's best-known highlights: the visitors center at **Logan Pass,** the **Highline Trail, Lake McDonald,** and an array of hiking trails.

## BEARTOOTH SCENIC HIGHWAY AND PASS

Considered one of the most beautiful roadways in the country, the Beartooth Scenic Highway begins in **Red Lodge,** climbs and twists its way west through 60-million-year-old mountains, and ends 65 miles (105 kilometers) later in **Cooke City** at the Northeast Entrance to **Yellowstone National Park.** This drive lasts about 3 hours without stops. The scenic road has numerous switchbacks and steep grades that,

VIEW FROM THE BEARTOOTH SCENIC HIGHWAY

once you're driving on it, clearly demonstrate why it is closed during winter. As you ascend, you come upon magnificent vistas of the Beartooth Plateau, Glacier Lake, and the canyons forged by the Clarks Fork River. After about 30 miles (48 kilometers), you reach the mountain summit at 10,947 feet (3,337 meters). Here you will encounter the aptly named **Top of the World** rest area, which provides the only services on the route. Keep an eye out for a herd of mountain goats that frequents the area.

# BEST PARKS AND RECREATION AREAS

### FLATHEAD LAKE

The largest freshwater lake in the western United States, Flathead Lake has endless recreational opportunities, including hiking, boating, and unbeatable swimming. Go on a kayaking trip with the **Flathead Raft Company** (50362 U.S. 93 N., Polson; 406/883-5838 or 800/654-4359; www.flatheadraft-co.com), or rent your own craft at **Bigfork Outdoor Rentals** (110 Swan River Rd., Bigfork; 406/837-2498; www.bigforkoutdoorrentals.com). The area around the lake has a vacation culture all its own, with luxe lodges and sprawling lakeside manses. The busiest town is **Polson,** on the south side of the lake; arguably the most beautiful is **Bigfork** at the lake's northeast corner.

### SKIING IN WHITEFISH MOUNTAIN RESORT

3840 Big Mountain Rd., Whitefish; 406/862-2900; www.skiwhitefish.com

When it comes to skiing in Montana, it doesn't get much better than skiing at the Whitefish Mountain Resort, which offers 94 trails, 11 lifts, 2,353 feet (717 meters) of vertical drop, and a 3.3-mile (5.3-kilometer) run. When the snow conditions are just right, the trees all across the top of the mountain look like enormous snow monsters. It's magical—or terrifying, depending upon your point of view. This is a big mountain, with serious skiing and family fun

WHITEFISH MOUNTAIN RESORT

at its best. The mountain stays open year-round for hiking, mountain biking, zipline tours, and an alpine slide, among other activities. In addition to offering regular daytime lift hours, it's also one of the few mountains in Montana that offers lighted night skiing.

## SKIING ON MAVERICK MOUNTAIN

1600 Maverick Mountain Rd., Polaris; 406/834-3454; www.skimaverick.com

A well-kept secret, Maverick Mountain boasts 24 trails, 450 skiable acres (182 hectares), and just over 2,000 feet (610 meters) of vertical drop. There are two lifts, one of which is a rope tow, and a nice breakdown of beginner runs (30 percent), intermediate (40 percent), and expert runs (30 percent). The area receives an average of 200 inches (508 centimeters) of the white stuff annually. An antidote to ski areas like Aspen and Sun Valley, the real charm of Maverick is its total lack of pretense: Skiing at Maverick is a little bit like skiing somewhere small but fantastic in about 1968, with no lift lines and wide-open skiing. It is as family-friendly as a ski hill gets, and the terrain is excellent.

## FISHING THE BIG HOLE

South of Butte, the Big Hole is a region defined by fishing and hunting. For generations, the land and rivers here have provided pristine habitat for an abundance of wildlife and terrific access for anglers and hunters. The 155-mile-long

(250-kilometer) **Big Hole River** is spectacularly beautiful and offers a diversity of terrain, from its origin high in the Bitterroot Range through the wide flats of the Big Hole Valley. It is known for early-season salmonfly hatches and then a golden stone hatch in late June-early July. It is also considered the last river where an angler can catch all five species of trout.

## LEWIS AND CLARK CAVERNS

25 Lewis and Clark Caverns Rd., 17 miles/27 kilometers east of Whitehall off Hwy. 2; 406/287-3541; https://fwp.mt.gov/state-parks/lewis-and-clark-caverns

Among the sights Lewis and Clark missed on their travels through the region is the Lewis and Clark Caverns, a phenomenal limestone cave several hundred yards above the Jefferson River on which the explorers traveled. The caverns are among the largest in the Northwest and were Montana's first state park. Filled with several rooms and lined with stalactites, stalagmites, columns, and helictites, the temperature in these colorful caverns stays at around 50°F (10°C) year-round, making them the perfect spot to escape the rare blisteringly hot days in southwest Montana. The caves can only be accessed on a 2-hour guided tour that includes a roughly 2-mile (3.2-kilometer) hike up to and down from the caverns.

## BIG SKY

In the shadow of Lone Peak, tucked in the winding and rugged beauty of Gallatin Canyon, the resort town of Big Sky actually has three resorts, **Big Sky Resort** (50 Big Sky Resort Rd.; 800/548-4468; https://bigskyresort.com), **Moonlight Basin** (66 Mountain Loop Rd.; 800/506-6650; www.moonlightbasin.com), and the entirely private Yellowstone Club. The town and resorts are clearly geographically blessed with mountains for skiing, hiking, climbing, and biking; rivers for fishing and floating; and trails aplenty for horses, hiking, cross-country skiing, and mountain biking. The area can also be used as a launching point for **Yellowstone National Park** (51 miles/82 kilometers south).

# FESTIVALS AND EVENTS

## CROW FAIR

Powwow grounds in Crow Agency; 406/638-3708 or 406/679-2108; www.crow-nsn.gov; Aug.

Crow Fair is an annual powwow held on the Crow Indian Reservation the third week in August to celebrate the past, present, and future of the Crow people. The event is one of the best times to visit the reservation; it's called the "tipi capital of the world" for the more than 1,000 tipis that are erected at the site. Considered the largest outdoor powwow in the world, Crow Fair is a major event not only for the Crow but also for Native Americans across North America, who come to participate in the competitive dancing and drumming and the rodeo.

## LITTLE BIG HORN DAYS

Hardin; 406/665-1672 or 888/450-3577, www.hardinmt.com; June

Little Big Horn Days entails four days of celebrations close to the June 25 anniversary of the famous battle—some festive, others sober—commemorating

CROW INDIAN RESERVATION

the region's history and, in particular, its proximity to the Battle of the Little Bighorn. The festivities include a quilt show, a book fair, and a historical dance—the 1876 Grand Ball—as well as arts and crafts sales, a symposium, and a parade, all culminating in the dramatic and well-attended **Battle of the Little Bighorn Reenactment** (E. Frontage Rd. between Crow Agency and Garryowen, Hardin; www.littlebighorn-reenactment.com). The reenactment requires more than 200 actors and is performed from the Indian perspective in a script written by historian Joe Medicine Crow.

## RED ANTS PANTS MUSIC FESTIVAL

Jackson Ln., 3 miles/4.8 kilometers northeast of White Sulphur Springs; 406/209-8135; www.redantspantsmusicfestival.com; July

Voted the Best Event of the Year for the State of Montana in 2018, Red Ants Pants Music Festival is held in late July. It's a family-friendly, three-day weekend of music, food, and camping for those who don't mind the dust. Past headliners have included Dwight Yoakum, Shooter Jennings, Lucinda Williams, Lyle Lovett, and the Wailing Jennies. There's a kids' tent, a beer garden, hayrides, great food vendors, and room to dance. This is a wholesome place to listen to great music.

## GREAT MONTANA SHEEP DRIVE

Reed Point; 406/322-4505; www.stillwater-countychamber.com; Labor Day weekend

It's not exactly Pamplona's Running of the Bulls, but Reed Point's Great Montana Sheep Drive, also known as "Running of the Sheep," is a Montana classic. On the Sunday of Labor Day weekend, roughly 2,000 sheep make their way down Main Street of this small central Montana town, sandwiched between thousands of spectators and more than 70 food vendors. The annual event also includes a mutton cook-off, a parade, a car show, a street dance, a kids' carnival and petting zoo, local crafts sales, and a variety of entertainment.

## BEST SOUVENIRS

- You'll find plenty of excellent **antiques** shopping in Montana—in addition to small businesses that are antiques themselves, founded in the days of the Wild West and still owned by the same families today. The southwest Montana city of **Butte** has plenty of antique shops in its historic uptown.

- You'll find **Native American crafts, art,** and other items, including beads, face paint, animal hides, dance bells, and even Crow and Sioux tipis.

- Stop by any small-town **gallery** to peruse and buy art by local Montana artists.

## SMALL TOWN RODEOS

With more than 100 annual events on the calendar between May and November, it's hard to drive through Montana without running into rodeo action somewhere. Some of the best rodeos are the smaller ones, often called "ranch rodeos," that feature real cowboys and cowgirls from area ranches competing against each other in real-life ranch activities. Many rodeos offer events for kids, such as greased-pig contests or wild-sheep riding.

- **Miles City Bucking Horse Sale** (third full weekend in May): Since 1914, the country's best bucking stock—and the most ambitious cowboys—have been showcased at this world-famous event in the eastern Montana town of Miles City. The party atmosphere follows the crowds from the rodeo into town and every bar throughout the long weekend for concerts, street dances, and a good old small-town parade. For horses, bulls, and riders, this is the place to get noticed.

- **Augusta American Legion Rodeo and Parade** (last Sunday in June): Held in the hamlet of Augusta, at the edge of the spectacular Rocky Mountain Front, this is the largest and oldest one-day rodeo in the state. The town throws its biggest party of the year with rodeo action, a barbecue, a street dance, and even an art show.

- **Wolf Point Wild Horse Stampede** (second weekend in July): Montana's oldest rodeo, on the Fort Peck Indian Reservation, is a three-day event that includes professional rodeo, daily parades and a carnival, the famous wild horse race, street dances, and a kids' stick-horse rodeo.

# BEST FOOD AND DRINK

## FLATHEAD CHERRIES

Picking fresh, sweet Flathead cherries, or just eating them, is an idyllic way to spend an afternoon in Montana. Several orchards dot the east side of Flathead Lake between Polson and Bigfork, so don't be shy about stopping at roadside stands to do a little taste-testing. The primary harvest is late July-mid-August. The average season lasts just 7-10 days. Try **Bowman Orchards** (19944 East Shore Rd./Hwy. 35, 10 miles/16.1 kilometers south of Bigfork at mile marker 21.5 on the east shore of Flathead; 406/982-3246), a family-owned business since 1921 that grows a variety of cherries. **Hockaday Orchards** (45 Hockaday Ln., Lakeside; 406/844-3547; www.hockadayorchards.com) lets cherry lovers climb up the ladders to harvest their own crop. Bring your own bucket or box, as the cherries will get crushed in a bag.

## HUCKLEBERRIES

You'll see this small fruit covering the landscape of Glacier National Park in summer, and you'll find it served up in an infinite number of dishes throughout the state—pastries, cake, pancakes, cocktails, milk shakes, pie, and on and on. **Huckleberry Days Art Festival** (Depot Park, Whitefish; 406/862-3501; www.whitefishchamber.org), held over three days in mid-August, celebrates the juicy purple berry with music, entertainment, an art fair, and lots of family fun.

## PASTIES

For a unique Montana meal, try traditional Cornish meat pies, called pasties (PASS-tees), long favored for their hearty taste and convenience by Montana miners. You can get yours filled with everything from eggs, cheese, onions, and potatoes to beef tenderloin and mushrooms. It's a specialty in Butte. Try one in **Gamer's Café** (15 W. Park St., Butte; 406/723-5453) or **Doe Brothers Restaurant** (120 E. Broadway, Philipsburg; 406/859-6676) in the hidden-gem town of Philipsburg.

## MONTANA WINES

Since 1984, when Tom Campbell Jr. and his father first started experimenting with growing grapes along the shores of Flathead Lake, in prime Montana cherry territory, several other wineries have sprouted up across the state, primarily in the western region. Though many vintners buy grapes from out of state, there are several growers among them, including a few that opt for unconventional but delicious base fruits like cherries, huckleberries, chokecherries, apples, pears, currants, and rhubarb.

- **Glacier Sun Winery & Tasting Room** (3250 U.S. 2 E., Kalispell; 406/257-8886; www.glaciersunwinery.com) grew out of the idea of a small, roadside fruit and veggie stand. Today the winery still sells fruits, veggies, and prepared foods, but also produces 18 varietals from locally grown fruits and regionally grown grapes.
- **Mission Mountain Winery** (82420 U.S. 93, Dayton; 406/849-5524; www.missionmountainwinery.com) is the state's first bonded winery and produces more than 6,500 cases annually of more than 10 different award-winning varietals. Its vineyards grow the grapes for its highly regarded pinot noir and pinot gris.
- **Tongue River Winery** (99 Morning Star Ln., Miles City; 406/853-1028; www.tongueriverwinery.com) is the only winery in southeastern Montana. It offers an expansive list of award-winning wines, and tours of both the vineyard and winery can be arranged.

# MAJOR AIRPORTS

- **Bozeman Yellowstone International Airport:** BZN; 850 Gallatin Field Rd., Belgrade; www.bozemanairport.com
- **Billings Logan International Airport:** BIL; 1901 Terminal Cir., Billings; www.flybillings.com
- **Missoula International Airport:** MSO; 5225 U.S. 10 W, Missoula; www.flymissoula.com
- **Glacier Park International Airport:** FCA; 4170 U.S. 2, Kalispell; www.iflyglacier.com
- **Great Falls International Airport:** GTF; 2800 Terminal Dr., Great Falls; www.flygtf.com

# MORE INFORMATION

## TRAVEL AND TOURISM INFORMATION

- **Montana Office of Tourism:** www.visitmt.com
- **Montana Fish, Wildlife & Parks:** www.fwp.mt.gov

## MAGAZINES

- *Big Sky Journal:* www.bigskyjournal.com
- *Montana Quarterly:* www.themontanaquarterly.com.

# WYOMING

Embodied by the bucking bronco on its license plates, Wyoming is a child's Western fantasy come to life, with rodeos aplenty and dude ranches where even city slickers can try their hand at riding and roping. But what strikes people most about Wyoming is its authenticity. The harsh climate and isolation that make Wyoming the least populated state in the union result in an uncommon grace in its residents. There is glitz here too, in places like Jackson Hole and Cody, but it doesn't distract from the essence of Wyoming. Those towns are but a flash of silver, the shiny buckle on a well-worn belt.

On Crow, Cheyenne, Eastern Shoshone, Arapaho, Mandan, Hidatsa, and Arikara land, the state's landscape—from soaring mountains and narrow valleys to sweeping plains—were carved over eons by water, wind, fire, and ice. The culture was also shaped by conflict: between those who were from here and those who were not; those who valued the land itself and those who sought its riches. Its distinct histories—both natural and cultural—are evident everywhere, not just tucked away in dusty museums, as the state continues to redefine itself.

**AREA:** 97,914 square miles / 253,596 square kilometers (10th)

**POPULATION:** 578,759 (50th)

**STATEHOOD DATE:** July 10, 1890 (44th)

**STATE CAPITAL:** Cheyenne

BULL BISON IN YELLOWSTONE NATIONAL PARK

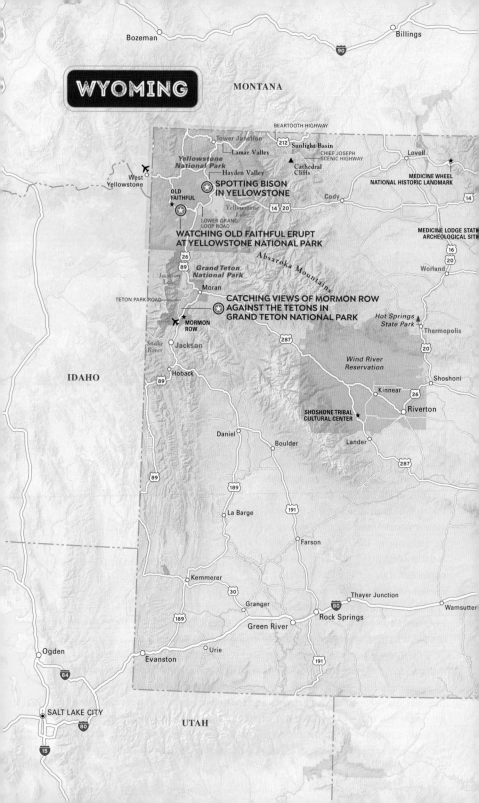

**WYOMING**

MONTANA

Bozeman

Billings

90

BEARTOOTH HIGHWAY

Tower Junction

212   Sunlight Basin

Lamar Valley

CHIEF JOSEPH
SCENIC HIGHWAY

Lovell

*Yellowstone
National Park*

Hayden Valley

Cathedral
Cliffs

MEDICINE WHEEL
NATIONAL HISTORIC LANDMARK

West
Yellowstone

**SPOTTING BISON
IN YELLOWSTONE**

OLD
FAITHFUL

Cody

14   20

14

*Yellowstone
Lake*

LOWER GRAND
LOOP ROAD

MEDICINE LODGE STATE
ARCHEOLOGICAL SITE

**WATCHING OLD FAITHFUL ERUPT
AT YELLOWSTONE NATIONAL PARK**

16

20

26

89

*Grand Teton
National Park*

Absaroka Mountains

Worland

*Jackson
Lake*

Moran

TETON PARK ROAD

**CATCHING VIEWS OF MORMON ROW
AGAINST THE TETONS IN
GRAND TETON NATIONAL PARK**

Hot Springs
State Park

Thermopolis

MORMON
ROW

*Snake
River*

Jackson

287

20

*Wind River
Reservation*

Shoshoni

IDAHO

Hoback

89

Kinnear

26

Riverton

SHOSHONE TRIBAL
CULTURAL CENTER

Lander

Daniel

Boulder

287

189

La Barge

191

Farson

89

Kemmerer

30

Thayer Junction

Granger

80

Wamsutter

189

Rock Springs

Green River

Ogden

84

Urie

Evanston

191

SALT LAKE CITY

80

15

UTAH

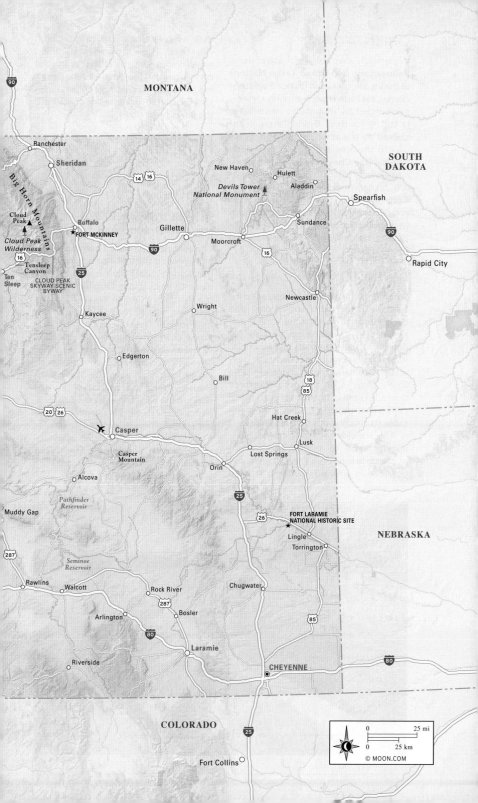

## ORIENTATION

Wyoming's two biggest attractions, **Yellowstone** and **Grand Teton National Parks,** are tucked in its northwestern corner. **Jackson Hole,** the valley entirely surrounded by mountains immediately to the south of Grand Teton, is anchored by the town of **Jackson,** gateway to the area and the national park. The capital, **Cheyenne,** is at the opposite end of the state, in the southeastern corner, near the Colorado border. **Cody** and **Sheridan** are in the northern part of the state, with the **Bighorn Mountains** in between. In the northeast corner is **Devil's Tower National Monument.**

## WHEN TO GO

**Summer** is the easiest and busiest time to travel the roads, both front- and backcountry. Thoughtful planning and advance reservations, particularly for hotels and campgrounds, are essential. Rates for accommodations are generally lower and rooms more available when snow is on the ground, except around ski areas, but **winter** road travel can be challenging because of the inevitable storms and possible closures.

The **shoulder seasons** can be a delightful time to travel. The national parks are heavenly and much less crowded in **autumn,** but keep in mind that winter comes very early at high elevations. There are also little-known ways to enjoy the parks by bicycle in the **spring,** before they open to cars. Opening and closing times for the parks can vary by year, so make sure to check with the parks before travel.

## HIGHLIGHTS

### HOT SPRINGS STATE PARK

538 N. Park St., Thermopolis; 307/864-2176; http://wyoparks.state.wy.us

The entire town of **Thermopolis** is built around natural hot springs, and Hot Springs State Park is a wonderful place to enjoy them. Originally part of the Wind River Indian Reservation, the area was sold to the U.S. Government in 1896 with the stipulation from Shoshone chief Washakie that the waters would always be freely available so that anyone could benefit from their healing properties. Today, the **State Bath House** offers the only free thermal pools in the park. there are several commercial facilities inside the park, including **Hellie's Tepee Spa** (144 Tepee St., Thermopolis; 307/864-9250; www.tepeepools.com) and **Star Plunge** (115 Big Springs Dr., Thermopolis; 307/864-3771; www.starplunge.com).

HOT SPRINGS STATE PARK

# Major CITIES

**CHEYENNE:** Wyoming's capital and most populous city is synonymous with its legendary **Frontier Days** rodeo. Located near the Colorado border at the intersection of I-80 and I-25, Cheyenne has been an important crossroads since it first sprang up as a settlement in 1867 in advance of the Union Pacific Railroad's arrival.

**CASPER:** This sprawling onetime frontier town is experiencing a renaissance as a hub for outdoor adventure. Make Casper your home base for fishing on the North Platte River and recreational activities in the nearby Laramie Mountains, Medicine Bow National Forest, and Casper Mountain.

**LARAMIE:** Located in southeastern Wyoming, Laramie is a charming combination of sophisticated university town and Old West frontier town—all with immediate proximity to the natural rocky playground that envelops the city.

## WIND RIVER RESERVATION

The Wind River Reservation sits on 2.2 million acres (890,308 hectares) and is home to more than 8,600 Northern Arapaho (www.northernarapaho.com) and 3,900 Eastern Shoshone (www.easternshoshone.org) tribal members. It surrounds the city of Riverton, with the towns of Lander, Shoshoni, and Thermopolis close to its borders. Although the reservation struggles with poverty and unemployment, it is also home to an incredibly rich history, important traditions, and pristine wilderness.

A drive through the reservation affords visitors magnificent views of Wyoming's undeveloped natural beauty and the majestic Wind River Mountains. In Fort Washakie, you'll find the **Shoshone Tribal Cultural Center** (90 Ethete Rd., Fort Washakie; 307/332-3515) and the gravesites of the two most prominent Shoshone, **Chief Washakie** (it was his hometown) and Lewis and Clark's fearless guide **Sacagawea.** The biggest draw to the reservation is the **powwows** held throughout the summer season by both the Shoshone and Arapaho.

## MEDICINE WHEEL NATIONAL HISTORIC LANDMARK

Bighorn National Forest

High in the Big Horns on a narrow ridge is this mysterious, Stonehenge-esque feature thought to be 500-800 years old. Medicine Wheel National Historic Landmark is an 82-foot-wide (25-meter) stone circle with 28 interior spokes connecting the exterior with an interior circular mound. Made of limestone slabs and boulders, the Medicine Wheel is a mysterious landmark that has spiritual but unexplained significance to many Native American groups. The star alignments suggest the medicine wheel could have been constructed as early as the 13th century, and the solstice alignments are accurate even today. There are tepee rings around the site and worn travois trails to the site, suggesting heavy usage. Stone markers in the shape of arrows point to a number of nearby medicine wheels, including those in

MEDICINE WHEEL NATIONAL HISTORIC LANDMARK

# TOP 3

## 1 WATCHING OLD FAITHFUL ERUPT AT YELLOWSTONE NATIONAL PARK

www.nps.gov/yell

If you can see just one thing in Yellowstone National Park, make it this world-famous geyser. When Old Faithful erupts, it shoots up to 8,400 gallons (31,707 litres) of hot water as high as 185 feet (56 meters). It's one of the most regular geysers in the park, erupting about every 90 minutes for 1.5-5 minutes. Though often crowded, the Old Faithful complex brings together so many of the phenomena—both natural and human-made—that make Yellowstone special: the landmark geyser and the incredible assortment of geothermal features surrounding it, the wildlife, the grand old park architecture of the **Old Faithful Inn,** and even the mass of people from around the world who come to witness the famous geyser.

SUNSET ERUPTION OF OLD FAITHFUL

Beyond Old Faithful, Yellowstone's geothermal features draw visitors throughout the park. Here are some of the other highlights:

- The travertine formations at **Mammoth Hot Springs Terraces** look like an enormous cream-colored confection.

- **Grand Prismatic Spring** is the largest hot spring in Yellowstone and the third largest in the world. Fiery arms of orange, gold, and brown thermophiles radiate in a full circle from the yellow-rimmed, blue hot pool.

- On the western edge of Yellowstone Lake is the eerie **West Thumb Geyser Basin,** a collection of hot springs, geysers, mud pots, and fumaroles. The striking turquoise and emerald **Abyss Pool** here may be one of the deepest in the park.

## 2 SPOTTING BISON IN YELLOWSTONE

307/344-7381; www.nps.gov/yell

Yellowstone is the only place in the continental United States where bison have existed since prehistoric times. Two herds fluctuating from 2,300 to 5,500 bison roam within the borders of Yellowstone National Park, a far cry from the millions that once lived throughout central North America from Canada to Mexico. Bison can commonly be seen almost any time of the year in Yellowstone, often causing traffic jams as they stand on the road.

The Lamar Valley and Hayden Valley are prime places to see bison in Yellowstone. Immense herds feed along the Lamar River, which flows through the sagebrush **Lamar Valley,** accessed from Northeast Entrance Road. Similarly, thundering herds of bison occupy **Hayden Valley;** driving on Lower Grand Loop Road through the valley during the bison rut and migration in late summer is one of the most scenic experiences in the park.

Bison aren't the only wildlife to be seen in Yellowstone. Park guides often refer to the Lamar Valley as "America's Serengeti," where you can see pronghorn, bighorn sheep, elk, bears, coyote, and wolves. In fall, listen for bighorn sheep butting horns

BISON HERD IN YELLOWSTONE NATIONAL PARK

or elk bugling as displays of dominance. In addition, Hayden Valley is also home to moose, raptors, grizzly bears, trumpeter swans, and hordes of Canada geese.

## ③ CATCHING VIEWS OF MORMON ROW AGAINST THE TETONS IN GRAND TETON NATIONAL PARK

Moose; 307/739-3399; www.nps.gov/grte

In Grand Teton National Park, sawtooth spires claw the sky in one of the youngest mountain ranges in the Rockies. Towering thousands of feet culminating in the Grand Teton itself, these peaks command attention from almost every location in the park. **Mormon Row,** a cluster of buildings from an 1890s Mormon ranch settlement, is set against the spectacular backdrop of the Teton Mountains. This view is iconic and makes for an impressive image, even for amateur photographers. You'll find other top views in the park at:

- **Signal Mountain:** Its position as the lone peak above the valley of Jackson Hole makes for big views of islands in Jackson Lake and the Teton Mountains.

- **Teton Park Road:** From Jackson Lake Junction in the north to Moose in the south, the Teton Park Road (open May-Oct.), called the Inside Road by locals, gives up-close views of the Teton Mountains.

- **Mural Room at Jackson Lake Lodge:** Dining in the Mural Room is an experience for the panoramic views of the Tetons outside and the murals depicting western Native American and Wyoming trapper life inside.

MORMON ROW

The beautiful surroundings also make Grand Teton a paradise for outdoors enthusiasts. Top hiking trails include the **Taggart Lake-Bradley Lake Loop** and **Hidden Falls Trail.** Boating on **Jenny Lake** is a quiet, idyllic experience, and paddlers can find fun cubbyholes to explore on **Jackson Lake.** In winter, some roads in the national park close to vehicles and become cross-country ski and snowshoe routes.

# *Best* ROAD TRIP

**DAY 1** Fly into **Casper** and if you want to get a hike in before your drive, head to Casper Mountain. Otherwise, drive out to **Thermopolis** (134 miles/216 kilometers, 2 hours) and its **Hot Springs State Park.** Have a soak either in the free **State Bath House** or one of the commercial properties in the park.

**DAY 2** In the morning, head to **Cody** (82 miles/132 kilometers, 1.5 hours) for a stop at the **Buffalo Bill Center of the West.** Then take the **Chief Joseph Scenic Highway** and the **Beartooth Highway** to the Northeast Entrance of **Yellowstone National Park** (75 miles/120 kilometers, 2 hours). It's another hour to **Tower Junction** and the classic **Roosevelt Lodge Cabins** (307/344-7311; www.yellowstonenationalparklodges.com), where you can spend the night, if you have reservations.

**DAY 3** A sunrise drive through the famed **Lamar Valley** offers amazing opportunities to spot wildlife, including bison, wolves, and bears. Then turn south to the **Grand Canyon of the Yellowstone** for its rushing waterfalls. If you have time, loop around to **Mammoth Hot Springs Terraces,** where you can amble around the colorful geothermal features.

**DAY 4** Make it another early morning to get to **Old Faithful** to try to beat the crowds. After marveling at its eruption, head down to **West Thumb Geyser Basin,** an incredible selection of geothermal features on **Yellowstone Lake.** From there, continue south to **Grand Teton National Park.** Stop for views at **Signal Mountain** (46 miles/74 kilometers, 1 hour), then take **Teton Park Road** to Moose (20 miles/32 kilometers, 1 hour) for the iconic photo of **Mormon Row** against the Tetons. Head to nearby **Jackson** for the night.

HOT SPRINGS STATE PARK

YELLOWSTONE NATIONAL PARK

WEST THUMB GEYSER BASIN

Meeteetse and Steamboat Mountain in southwest Wyoming near Rock Springs.

**DAY (5)** White-water enthusiasts will have no shortage of options on the **Snake River** near Jackson. While you're in the area, make sure to take the fabulous **gondola** at **Jackson Hole Mountain Resort.**

**DAY (6)** After breakfast, head north back through Grand Teton National Park. Stop at **Jenny Lake** for a hike on the **Hidden Falls Trail** or a boat ride. Leave the park through the Moran Entrance, and head back toward **Casper** (250 miles/400 kilometers, 4 hours), driving through **Wind River Reservation.**

RAFTING THE SNAKE RIVER

JENNY LAKE

## BUFFALO BILL CENTER OF THE WEST

720 Sheridan Ave., Cody; 307/587-4771; www.centerofthewest.org

The West's version of the Smithsonian, the Buffalo Bill Center of the West is a collection of five extraordinary museums plus a research library. The **Buffalo Bill Museum** celebrates the private and public life of town father W. F. "Buffalo Bill" Cody. The **Whitney Gallery of Western Art** reflects the diverse history of art of the American West from the early 19th century to today. The **Plains Indian Museum** examines the culture and history of the Arapaho, Crow, Cheyenne, Blackfeet, Sioux, Shoshone, and others through a collection of Native American art and artifacts. The **Cody Firearms Museum** is home to the world's largest assemblage of American arms. The **Draper Museum of Natural History** offers exhibits that interpret the Greater Yellowstone Ecosystem from human and natural science perspectives. Finally, the **Harold McCracken Research Library** is an extraordinary resource for studies of the American West. This complex is indeed the grande dame of Western history and art.

## WYOMING TERRITORIAL PRISON STATE HISTORIC SITE

975 Snowy Range Rd., Laramie; 307/745-3733; http://wyoparks.state.wy.us

Built in 1872 to deal with the ruffians in lawless Laramie, the Wyoming Territorial Prison was restored in 1989 and made into a 190-acre (76.9-hectare) state historic site. The prison was in use 1872-1903; Butch Cassidy was among the most famous residents. The historic site is home to an entirely re-created frontier town; there are a number of buildings in various stages of restoration, including the broom factory where many of the prisoners worked on a variety of different jobs, authentic pioneer cabins, a schoolhouse, and agricultural buildings where kids can stick their arms into a simulated (and gooey!) cow's belly. Still, the prison is the main attraction. There are also numerous volunteers throughout the property, dressed as late 19th-century prisoners, who answer questions and tell fascinating stories.

## FORT LARAMIE NATIONAL HISTORIC SITE

965 Gray Rocks Rd., Fort Laramie; 307/837-2221; www.nps.gov/fola

An indelible part of Wyoming's history, Fort Laramie sits at the confluence of the Laramie and North Platte Rivers. It was a major trading center, a military garrison, and the site where the infamous Treaty of 1868 between the U.S. government and the Plains Indians was signed. People from all walks of life, including Native Americans, trappers, missionaries, and homesteaders, passed through the fort during its almost 50 years of existence. Today there are 22 original structures on the 830 acres (335.9 hectares) of this National Historic Site. While at the fort, visit the cavalry barracks, which give a clear sense of the cramped living quarters of the soldiers, and Old Bedlam, initially the fort headquarters and later used as officers' quarters.

# BEST SCENIC DRIVES

## LOWER GRAND LOOP ROAD

If you only do one drive in Yellowstone, make it Lower Grand Loop Road (96 miles/154 kilometers round-trip; 4 hours round-trip without stops). This route links **Old Faithful, Grand Prismatic Spring,** and **West Thumb Geyser Basin** and takes in loads of wildlife-watching, plus **Grand Canyon of the Yellowstone,** a colorful, swath of sheer cliffs with dramatic waterfalls cut by the **Yellowstone River.**

## CHIEF JOSEPH SCENIC HIGHWAY

Hwy. 296

Linking **Cody** with the Northeast Entrance to **Yellowstone National Park** is the seasonally open 47-mile (76-kilometer) Chief Joseph Scenic Highway. It is a winding and at times hair-raising drive that cuts through mountainous country, providing views of spectacular waterfalls and mountain vistas of the **Absarokas, Cathedral Cliffs,** the mouth of **Sunlight Basin,** and occasionally a glimpse of **wildlife.** Interpretive signs along the way tell the story of the

FORT LARAMIE NATIONAL HISTORIC SITE

Nez Perce's 1877 flight from the U.S. Army under the leadership of Chief Joseph, for whom the highway is named. For adventurers, the highway gives unparalleled access to some incredible hiking trails.

## CLOUD PEAK SKYWAY SCENIC BYWAY

### U.S. 16

Traveling from **Buffalo** on U.S. 16 over the southern portion of the **Big Horn Mountains** toward **Ten Sleep** and **Worland,** the 45-mile (72-kilometer) paved Cloud Peak Skyway Scenic Byway offers breathtaking scenery of the **Cloud Peak Wilderness** and the only view of **Cloud Peak** itself, the highest mountain in the Big Horns. This remarkable stretch of road is the southernmost route across the Big Horns. The summit is at 9,666 feet (2,946 meters), and the road also winds through the spectacular **Tensleep Canyon.** Multiple turnouts are along the way for travelers to stretch their legs and enjoy the view; the road also passes **Fort McKinney** and runs just 20 miles (32 kilometers) south of **Medicine Lodge State Archeological Site,** known for its ancient petroglyphs, pictographs, and idyllic campgrounds. There is also ample access to hiking trails in the Bighorn National Forest.

# BEST PARKS AND RECREATION AREAS

Wyoming's two spectacular national parks, **Yellowstone** and **Grand Teton,** are the top recreational spots in the state, with hundreds of miles of hiking trails, boating and paddling, and cross-country skiing.

## SNAKE RIVER

One of the greatest attractions for summertime visitors to Jackson is rafting the Snake River. There are close to two dozen rafting companies to choose from in the area, offering options from a tranquil day float through Grand Teton National Park or white-water adventure a little farther south in the canyon. **Barker-Ewing** (307/733-1000 or 800/448-4202; www.barker-ewing.com) is a family-operated business that has been running small trips for more than 50 years.

## SKIING IN JACKSON

Jackson's reputation among the West's premier ski towns is not hard to explain. **Snow King Mountain** (400 E. Snow King Ave., Jackson; 307/201-5464; www.snowkingmountain.com) soars skyward just six blocks from Town Square. The area boasts 1,571 feet (479 meters) of vertical drop over 400 acres (161.9 hectares) with two double chairlifts, one triple lift, a surface tow, and the ever-popular Snow Tubing Park.

The ski area at **Jackson Hole Mountain Resort** (Teton Village; 307/733-2292 or 888/DEEP-SNOW; www.jacksonhole.com) is in fact two mountains, Apres Vous and Rendezvous, which together offer skiers 2,500 skiable acres (1,012 hectares), a vertical drop of 4,139 feet (1,262 meters), and open access to more than 3,000 acres (1,214 hectares) of backcountry terrain. This is the mountain to ski and be seen. The **aerial tram** (307/733-2292), known as Big Red or the Red Heli, takes hikers, bikers, paragliders, backcountry skiers, and the like up to the summit of Rendezvous Peak.

Although you need to go through Idaho to get there, **Grand Targhee Resort** (3300 Ski Hill Rd., Alta; 307/353-2300; www.grandtarghee.com), is a

JACKSON HOLE MOUNTAIN RESORT

destination in itself. The skiing in winter is out of this world, with huge dumps of powder and expansive terrain.

## DEVILS TOWER NATIONAL MONUMENT

Rising 1,267 feet (386 meters) above the Belle Fourche River, Devils Tower is an iconic rocky sentinel that was formed some 50-60 million years ago and has fascinated people for generations. The country's first national monument, Devils Tower is both a sacred site to many Native Americans and a climbing mecca for rock hounds from around the globe. The two groups have managed a hard-won, if somewhat delicate, respect for each other through a voluntary climbing closure in June every year, the month traditionally known for the greatest number of Native American ceremonies.

The entire tower offers more than 200 climbing routes with varying technical difficulties, with **Durrance Route** being the most common. For nonclimbers, there are some 8 miles (12.9 kilometers) of hiking trails that circle the tower and wind through the nearby forests and meadows.

# FESTIVALS AND EVENTS

## FRONTIER DAYS

www.cfdrodeo.com; July

The biggest event in Cheyenne—and the biggest in Wyoming—is Frontier Days, an affair that has been defining

FRONTIER DAYS

Wyoming's capital city since 1897. This 10-day event, spanning two weekends, draws more than 250,000 people who show up to attend events that include parades, major rock and country music concerts, free pancake breakfasts, a carnival, dances, and nine days of PRCA rodeo. This event has clearly earned its nickname, "the daddy of 'em all."

## SMALL TOWN RODEOS

It's hard to drive through Wyoming without running into rodeo action somewhere. Stop. Buy a ticket. The bleachers are fine. These small-town rodeos offer a unique window into life here. Sitting on a sunbaked wooden bench, cold beer in one hand and a bag of popcorn in the other, is the best first date in small towns. Locals wear their Sunday best, and no one seems to mind the dust.

- **Thermopolis Cowboy Rendezvous** (weekend after Father's Day): From tailgate parties and a Western dance to a pancake breakfast and parade, the small-town rodeo in Thermopolis ushers in the pro rodeo circuit for the Big Horn Basin with plenty of action and family fun.

- **Cody Stampede Rodeo** (July 1-4): With all the showmanship one would expect from a town named after Buffalo Bill Cody, this professional rodeo lets the town shine with all the classic events including bareback riding, roping, steer wrestling, barrel racing, and saddle bronc and bull riding. The rest of the summer, visitors can get a true sense of small-town rodeo at the **Cody Nite Rodeo.**

- **Ten Sleep Fourth of July Rodeo** (two days over Fourth of July): With a rodeo history that dates back to 1908 and includes some of the biggest names in the sport, Ten Sleep boasts rodeo action throughout the summer. Special events at the annual Fourth of July shindig include a Pony Express Ride from nearby Hyattville, a Main Street parade, an old-fashioned rodeo, fireworks, and a sometimes-bloody wild horse race.

- **Sheridan WYO Rodeo** (usually the second week in July): This is the biggest week of the year for Sheridan. There is a golf tournament, art show, rodeo royalty pageant, carnival,

# BEST SOUVENIRS

- Get decked out in **Western duds,** including cowboy boots, hats, buckles, ropes, saddles, and other accessories.
- Bring home a taste of the state with made-in-Wyoming smoked elk and bison jerky or summer sausage, barbecue sauces, jams, spices, and other **local specialties.**
- Shop for **jewelry** handmade in the state out of local rocks and gemstones, including vintage Native American pieces.

Indian relay races, parade, and street dance on top of four nights of pro-rodeo action.

## WIND RIVER RESERVATION POWWOWS

The biggest draw to the Wind River Reservation, located near Lander and home to Northern Arapaho and Eastern Shoshone, is the powwows held throughout the summer season. These large cultural celebrations usually take place over a three-day weekend and include dancing, singing, parades, and traditional games. The largest Shoshone powwow is the **Eastern Shoshone Indian Days Powwow and Rodeo** (307/332-9106 or 307/349-7089), an all-Indian rodeo usually held the fourth weekend in June. The event hosts more than 700 dancers and 15 professional drumming groups. The largest Arapaho powwow is the **Ethete Celebration** (307/223-6430 or 307/438-3706) in late July.

## BEST FOOD

### BEEF, BISON, AND WILD GAME

One thing is certain: This is meat-and-potatoes country, which can be great for those craving a good steak, as you can find one in almost every town. Locally raised beef can be found on the menus of many restaurants, and bison is becoming increasingly popular

as well. If you haven't had it, it's highly recommended, and beef lovers will generally enjoy bison. A good bison burger or tenderloin is hard to beat, but if you are asked how you like it cooked, never ask for anything more than medium. Wild-game dishes, mostly elk and venison, are also found at finer establishments, with pheasant and other regional game occasionally on the menu. If you enjoy trying new fare, this can be an exciting option.

## MAJOR AIRPORTS

- **Jackson Hole Airport:** JAC; 1250 E. Airport Rd., Jackson; www.jacksonholeairport.com
- **Casper/Natrona County International Airport:** CPR; 8500 Airport Pkwy., Casper; www.iflycasper.com
- **Yellowstone Airport:** WYS; 607 Airport Rd., West Yellowstone; www.yellowstoneairport.org

## MORE INFORMATION

### TRAVEL AND TOURISM INFORMATION

- **Wyoming Travel and Tourism:** www.travelwyoming.com
- **Wyoming State Parks, Historic Sites, and Trails:** https://wyoparks.wyo.gov

### MAGAZINES

- *Wyoming Magazine:* www.wyomingmagazine.com

# COLORADO

Colorado is an environment for exploration and adventure. The state is on the traditional lands of the Pueblo, Ute, Navajo, Cheyenne, Sioux, Shoshone, and Arapaho peoples. The Rocky Mountains are much more than a backdrop; they are the pulse that sets the rhythm of life, dictating a relaxed pace and weekend escapes, creating famously variable weather, and underpinning much of the economy.

**AREA:** 104,185 square miles / 269,837 square kilometers (8th)

**POPULATION:** 5,758,736 (21st)

**STATEHOOD DATE:** August 1, 1876 (38th)

**STATE CAPITAL:** Denver

In Colorado, you can relax in unspoiled nature and its primeval rhythms. Gaze at forever views of craggy, snowcapped peaks. Get goose bumps listening to the bugling of a bull elk drift through the crisp morning air. You'll want to actively experience Colorado's knee-deep powder, plunge down its frothing white-water rapids, and soak away in steaming hot springs. Delve into its unparalleled history—from the ancients who constructed Mesa Verde's pueblos to the hardy souls who pioneered its creaking ghost towns. At the end of each adventure-filled day, savor the fresh flavors at a farm-to-table restaurant, sample some of the state's sudsy microbrews, and then slumber in a luxurious lodge or camp beneath a dark sky teeming with brilliant stars.

▲ ROCKY MOUNTAIN NATIONAL PARK

## ORIENTATION

The **Rocky Mountains** stand as a veritable north-south wall on much of the western side of the state, with Rocky Mountain National Park toward the northern end and ski towns like **Vail** and **Aspen** near the center. Southeast of Rocky Mountain National Park, **Denver** is situated slightly north of the center of the state, with **Fort Collins** almost due north and **Colorado Springs** almost due south. East of this string of cities, the state resembles the Great Plains, and to the west of the Rockies, the state looks more like the southwest, with **Dinosaur National Monument** spilling into Utah and **Mesa Verde National Park** tucked near the Four Corners.

## WHEN TO GO

Colorado is a year-round destination with seasonal activities that typically influence the best times to visit. The majority of guests arrive either during **ski season,** which runs from Thanksgiving through early April, or during the **summer. Spring** is also a wonderful time to visit, with warm, sunny days—though the weather is notoriously fickle. **Autumn,** when the mountains are carpeted with golden aspen trees, is also a beautiful season in Colorado.

# HIGHLIGHTS

## RED ROCKS AMPHITHEATRE

18300 W. Alameda Pkwy., Morrison; 720/865-2494; www.redrocksonline.com

**Red Rocks Park** hosts the famous Red Rocks Amphitheatre, Colorado's iconic outdoor concert venue that regularly attracts top music stars from around the world. The nearly 900-acre (364-hectare) park has a **visitors center** with displays about the venue's musical history and the amazing geologic events that created this remarkable amphitheater. You can see the fossilized fragments of a 40-foot-long (12-meter) sea serpent and flying reptiles, view dinosaur tracks, and get up-close looks at the amphitheater's two main rock slabs, Ship Rock and Creation Rock, which are both about 300 feet (91 meters) tall.

## DINOSAUR RIDGE

16831 W. Alameda Pkwy., Morrison; 303/697-3466; www.dinoridge.org

Atop the first ridge of the foothills west of Denver, Dinosaur Ridge is one of the world's most famous fossil localities. Some of the best-known giants were first discovered here, including

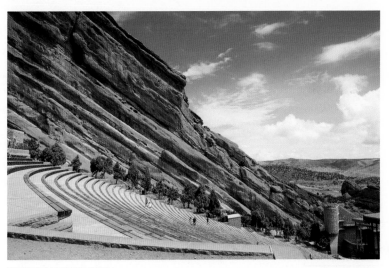

RED ROCKS AMPHITHEATRE

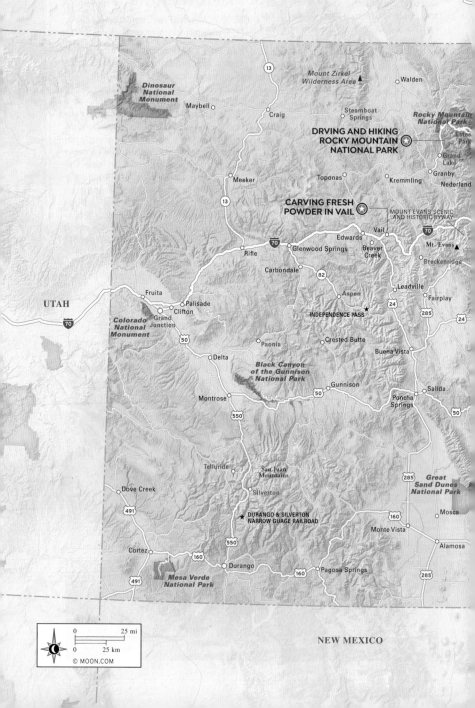

WYOMING

Dinosaur
National
Monument

Maybell

Craig

Mount Zirkel
Wilderness Area

Walden

Steamboat
Springs

Rocky Mountain
National Park

**DRVING AND HIKING
ROCKY MOUNTAIN
NATIONAL PARK**

Estes
Park

Meeker

Toponas

Kremmling

Grand
Lake

Granby

Nederland

**CARVING FRESH
POWDER IN VAIL**

Vail

MOUNT EVANS SCENIC
AND HISTORIC BYWAY

Edwards

Mt. Evans

Rifle

Glenwood Springs

Beaver
Creek

Breckenridge

Carbondale

82

Leadville

Fairplay

Fruita

Palisade

Clifton

Aspen

24

285

24

**INDEPENDENCE PASS**

Colorado
National
Monument

Grand
Junction

UTAH

70

50

Delta

Paonia

Crested Butte

Buena Vista

Black Canyon
of the Gunnison
National Park

Montrose

550

Gunnison

50

Poncha
Springs

Salida

50

Telluride

San Juan
Mountains

Great
Sand Dunes
National Park

285

Dove Creek

Silverton

Mosca

**DURANGO & SILVERTON
NARROW GUAGE RAILROAD**

160

Monte Vista

550

491

Cortez

160

Durango

Mesa Verde
National Park

160

Pagosa Springs

Alamosa

285

491

0        25 mi

0        25 km

© MOON.COM

**NEW MEXICO**

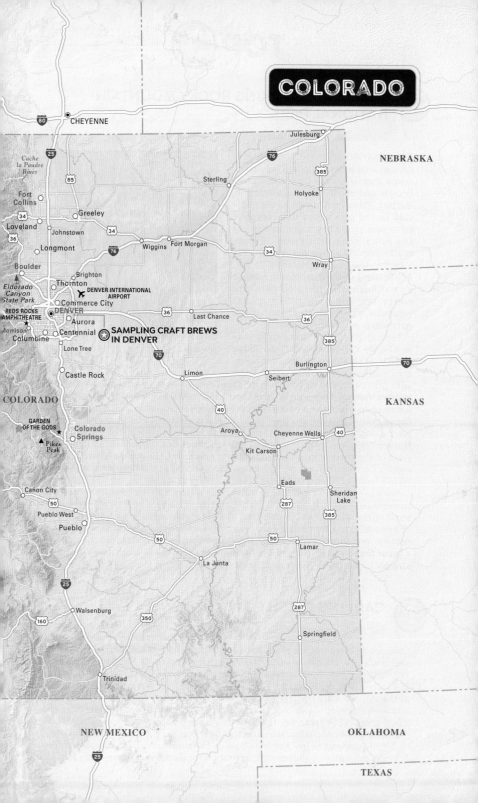

# TOP 3

## 1 DRIVING AND HIKING ROCKY MOUNTAIN NATIONAL PARK

970/586-1206; www.nps.gov/romo

This 265,000-acre (107,242-hectare) park guards a dramatic and wild landscape that is by far Colorado's best-known and most popular attraction. Bustling **Estes Park** serves as the gateway to the park's east side, which is open year-round and home to most of the park's iconic attractions. In town, don't miss **The Stanley Hotel** (333 Wonderview Ave., Estes Park; 970/577-4040; www.stanleyhotel.com), famous as the inspiration for Stephen King's horror tale *The Shining*. The quieter west side of the park is just north of the gateway town of **Grand Lake.**

BEAR LAKE

Linking Estes Park and Grand Lake is 48-mile (77-kilometer) **Trail Ridge Road** (U.S. 34, May-mid-Oct.), the country's highest continuous paved road, with great views all along the route. From east to west, great viewpoints include **Hidden Valley,** where you can often spot chipmunks, **Many Parks Curve,** the highest point to which the eastern side of Trail Ridge is plowed in winter, and **Rainbow Curve,** where you can see the flat Great Plains stretching far to the east. Farther west along the road, you can learn more about the tundra at the **Tundra World Nature Trail,** an easy half-hour walk from the **Rock Cut.** Two miles (3.2 kilometers) west of the road's highest point, which is unmarked, the **Alpine Visitors Center** awaits. Continuing west on Trail Ridge Road, you cross the **Continental Divide** at 10,758-foot (3,279-meter) **Milner Pass.**

Hiking—whether a quick leg-stretcher or a long butt-kicker—is the best way to experience the park. See the glistening, turquoise-blue beauty of **Bear Lake** by strolling the undulating, 0.5-mile-long (0.8-kilometer) walking path around it. Keep an eye out for the dramatic line of rocky cliffs known as **Lumpy Ridge,** a well-known destination for hiking and technical rock climbing as no roads cross the ridge. For a great first summit hike, try **Deer Mountain** (3 miles/4.8 kilometers one-way), a straightforward trail on the park's east side.

## 2 CARVING FRESH POWDER IN VAIL

970/754-0015; www.vail.com

Colorado's ski resorts are synonymous with plentiful powder, long runs, extended seasons, and expansive resorts. The state's largest ski area, Vail Mountain, boasts 195 trails on nearly 5,300 acres (2,145 hectares) of varied terrain and an average of 354 inches (899 centimeters)—29.5 feet (9 meters)—of snow per year. Highlights of the mountain are the legendary **Back Bowls,** seven wide-open, ungroomed basins with stunning views on the back of Vail Mountain. Covering little more than 3,000 acres (1,214 hectares), the Back Bowls are great places for experienced skiers, many of whom challenge themselves by trying to ski all seven in a single day.

Off the slopes, the **town of Vail,** built as the mountain's base village in the early 1960s, perpetuates the resort's reputation for glitz and glamour, with exclusive

VAIL'S SNOW-COVERED SLOPES

clubs, luxury amenities, fine art galleries, and scores of award-winning restaurants. In **summer,** Vail and the surrounding Central Rockies are a paradise for warm weather recreation, from hiking and cycling to golf, rafting, and sailing.

## SAMPLING CRAFT BREWS IN DENVER

Colorado is one of the nation's hottest spots for craft brews. With 125 breweries and taprooms, it's hard to go anywhere in Denver without finding the perfect spot for a pint of craft beer. Denver's bars and brewpubs are clustered in several hot spots, especially the neighborhoods of LoDo, the Highlands, and Cherry Creek. Here are some of the best spots in the city to kick back with a brew.

- **Wynkoop Brewing Company** (1634 18th St.; 303/297-2700; www.wynkoop.com) was Colorado's first brewpub. It was started in the 1980s by four guys, including John Hickenlooper, who later went on to become Denver's mayor, then the governor of Colorado. They built a brewery and a couple of bars in an old mercantile building in what at the time was a much sketchier LoDo. Today, Wynkoop is one of the state's largest breweries and still known for its innovative brews.

- **Great Divide Brewing Company** (2201 Arapahoe St.; 303/296-9460; https://greatdivide.com) has been brewing beer since 1994. Enjoy a brew on the patio or a take tour at their downtown brewery and taproom location.

CRAFT BEER IN DENVER

- **TRVE** (227 Broadway #101; 303/351-1021; www.trvebrewing.com) is a heavy-metal themed brewpub serving up creative brews.

Outside Denver, **Fort Collins,** which was dry until 1969, has 20 breweries, including the industry-leading **New Belgium Brewing** (www.newbelgium.com) and **Odell Brewing Company** (www.odellbrewing.com), the state's second-oldest brewery. Colorado Springs, Boulder, Breckenridge, and Aspen also offer excellent brewpubs and craft breweries.

# *Best* ROAD TRIP

**DAY 1** Start in **Denver,** where you can stroll through the **Denver Botanic Gardens** (1007 York St., Denver; 720/865-3500; www.botanicgardens.org) or shop in bustling **Larimer Square** (www.larimersquare.com), the city's oldest block, before enjoying a cold craft beer and a farm-to-table dinner.

**DAY 2** Head to **Rocky Mountain National Park,** 1.5-2 hours away, and choose an east-side hike to get a taste of the scenery. Then drive the winding hairpins along **Trail Ridge Road,** one of Colorado's most spectacular drives, to make your way to the town of Grand Lake, where you'll spend the night.

**DAY 3** Head 2 hours northwest to Colorado's cowboy corner, anchored by the ranching-turned-recreation town of **Steamboat Springs.** Spend the afternoon hiking or horseback riding through the **Mount Zirkel Wilderness Area** or zip-lining near Rabbit Ears Pass.

**DAY 4** Drive 3.5 hours to the sandstone towers and hidden crannies of **Colorado National Monument.** View the fossil treasures at the **Dinosaur Journey Museum** (550 Jurassic Ct., Fruita; 970/858-7282; www.museumofwesternco.com) before spending the night in or near **Grand Junction.**

**DAY 5** Up next, **Telluride** is 2.5 hours away. Enjoy a leisurely lunch in the historic downtown and soak up the scenery by riding the free, year-round gondola up to the mountain village or hiking to beautiful Bridal Veil Falls.

LARIMER SQUARE, DOWNTOWN DENVER

DENVER BOTANIC GARDENS

COLORADO NATIONAL MONUMENT

**DAY 6** To get to **Mesa Verde National Park,** it's a 2-hour drive through the stunning San Juan Mountains. Arrive early at the visitor center to snag tickets to Balcony House or Cliff Palace, then head to Chapin Mesa to tour the archaeological museum and drive the scenic Mesa Top Loop Road.

**DAY 7** It's a 6.5-hour drive back to **Denver** via U.S. 160 and U.S. 285.

the bus-size, armored stegosaurus, the Colorado state fossil; the huge carnivorous allosaurus; and the long-necked, plant-eating apatosaurus (formerly called brontosaurus), which at 33-38 tons (29-34 metric tons) was one of the largest land animals that ever lived.

The highlight of any visit is walking the paved **Dinosaur Ridge Trail** (1.5 mile/2.4 kilometers one way) between the two visitors centers. From the west-side Discovery Center, interpretive signs point out many interesting natural features, such as the **Dinosaur Bone Quarry,** where a jumble of dark-brown dinosaur bones are encased in a block of buff-colored sandstone, and the **Jurassic Time Bronto Bulges,** an impressive set of tracks left by a 30-ton (27-tonne), long-necked dinosaur.

## BOULDER

Bohemian Boulder, home of the **University of Colorado** and several federal research labs, thrives on its reputation as the brainiest, fittest, and foodiest city in the state. Its eye-popping backdrop of pointed rock fins and snowcapped summits attracts a liberal, affluent, and environmentally conscious crowd of people who enthusiastically embrace all the town has to offer—organic food at the local farmers market, farm-to-table restaurants, Buddhist meditation centers, distinguished lectures, and a vibrant performing arts scene.

Boulder's social hub is the **Pearl Street Mall** (Pearl St. between 11th and 15th Sts.; www.boulderdowntown. com). You'll find visitors and locals wandering the four brick-paved pedestrian blocks, browsing bookstores, and popping into art galleries. Another Boulder highlight is the historic complex of the **Colorado Chautauqua,** a National Historic Landmark where the nonprofit **Colorado Chautauqua Association** (303/442-3282; www.chautauqua.com) offers artistic performances, scholarly lectures, and films here. On the complex's western edge is the jewel of Boulder's extensive open-space system, gorgeous **Chautauqua Park** (900 Baseline Rd.; www. https://bouldercolorado.gov/parks-rec/chautauqua-park), where grassy meadows dotted with spring wildflowers rise to meet the serrated Flatirons.

TRAIL RIDGE ROAD

CLIFF PALACE IN MESA VERDE NATIONAL PARK

# *Biggest* CITIES

**DENVER:** The Mile High City is Colorado's lively cosmopolitan core, home to colorful art galleries, bustling bars, and neighborhood eateries. Above it all, to the west, is what truly sets Denver apart: the stunning backdrop of jagged, snow-covered peaks.

**COLORADO SPRINGS:** The Springs, as Colorado's second-largest city is often called, is a rapidly growing metropolis. Located at the base of Pike's Peak, the city has a wealth of attractions, including the rocky fins of the Garden of the Gods, the U.S. Olympic Training Center, and the mineral waters in artsy Manitou Springs.

**FORT COLLINS:** Artsy Fort Collins is an active college town, home to Colorado State University. Its charming Old Town Square hops with microbreweries and art deco buildings housing trendy boutiques, cafés, and confectioneries.

## TELLURIDE

Nestled in the bottom of a glacial valley so steep that it's called a box canyon, the town of Telluride is stunningly beautiful and offers exceptional year-round recreation. Once a relaxed hippie hangout far off the beaten path, the town has turned into an increasingly expensive festival and skiing destination for the rich and famous. The town is considered one of the most important locations associated with American mining history and is designated a National Historic Landmark District; to learn more, visit the **Telluride Historical Museum** (201 W. Gregory Ave.; 970/728-3344; www.telluridemuseum.org). The region is also well known for intermediate to advanced downhill skiing at the **Telluride Ski Resort** (565 Mountain Village Blvd.; 877/935-5021; www.tellurideskiresort.com). Telluride also has more than a dozen festivals during the summer, including the **Telluride Bluegrass Festival.**

## DURANGO & SILVERTON NARROW GAUGE RAILROAD

479 Main Ave., Durango; 877/872-4607; www.durangotrain.com

If you visit Colorado's southwestern corner, try to set aside a day for an unforgettable trip on the Durango & Silverton Narrow Gauge Railroad. The train follows the historic 45-mile-long (72-kilometer), 3-foot-wide (0.9-meter) track originally laid along the sparkling Animas River in 1882. The track connected the railroad hub of Durango with the rich mines in Silverton, a picturesque Victorian mining town in the heart of the rugged **San Juan Mountains.**

From the painstakingly restored depot on the south side of Durango's bustling downtown, the coal-fired steam locomotive pulls a series of vintage railroad cars through a roadless wilderness of soaring peaks and steep river valleys. After 3.5 hours of chugging through some of the San Juans' incredible scenery, the train reaches tiny **Silverton,** where (on most trips) you have a couple of hours to stretch your legs, grab a bite to eat, and explore the quaint shops along the main street before reboarding for the return trip. The round-trip journey takes about 9 hours, so it's a full-day adventure.

# BEST SCENIC DRIVES

## MOUNT EVANS SCENIC AND HISTORIC BYWAY

Hwy. 5; www.fs.usda.gov

One of the highlights of any summer visit to the Denver foothills is driving or biking the Mount Evans Scenic and Historic Byway, the highest paved road in North America. From its start at about 7,500 feet (2,286 meters) elevation near Idaho Springs, this "road to the sky" climbs nearly 7,000 vertical feet (2,133 meters) in just 28 miles (45 kilometers), passing large stands of aspen, dense evergreen forest, and treeless, windblown tundra bursting with wildflowers.

Highlights along the road include beautiful **Echo Lake; Mount Goliath Natural Area,** home to beautiful bristlecone pines that range 700-1,600 years old; glistening **Summit Lake Park,** the byway's most accessible alpine lake, and the summit of **Mount Evans,** where you'll find some of the best views in the state.

## INDEPENDENCE PASS

One of the highest passes in the state and the highest paved crossing of the Continental Divide is 12,095-foot-high (3,686-meter) Independence Pass. With its snaking switchbacks, narrow pavement, and slow-moving vehicles, Independence Pass is an adventure to drive (or cycle), but the spectacular scenery is well worth the effort.

Begin your drive in **Aspen,** and as the road climbs, you'll pass a number of campgrounds and trailheads before arriving at **the Grottos,** a popular picnic area where you can take a short walk to look down on an **ice cave,** a photogenic slot canyon whose shady interior harbors ice long into summer.

Next, you'll arrive at the ghost town of **Independence,** where you can stroll past more than a dozen wooden buildings constructed by miners trying to eke out a living in the harsh environment at almost 10,100 feet (3,078 meters). From Independence, it's another 4 miles (6.4 kilometers) up the impressively steep and winding road to the pass, where you can easily pull over to snap photos and enjoy close-up views of the hardy alpine tundra, and fantastic 360-degree vistas of the Sawatch and Elk mountain ranges.

# BEST PARKS AND RECREATION AREAS

## CACHE LA POUDRE RIVER

Fort Collins

This river is best known for having Colorado's only Wild and Scenic River designation for its unspoiled beauty and abundant recreation. The sparkling stream is a favorite fishing spot for trout and a destination for white-water rafting and kayaking. The Cache La Poudre has a good variety of runs, ranging from intermediate (Class III) to expert (Class V) rapids.

## SKI RESORTS

Beyond **Vail,** Colorado boasts other top skiing and snowboarding destinations. **Breckenridge Ski Resort** (1599 Ski Hill Rd.; 800/453-5000; www.breckenridge.com) has 2,908 skiable acres (1,176 hectares) and up to 3,398 feet (1,035 meters) of vertical drop. With a high base area at 9,600 feet (2,926 meters) elevation and peaks topping out at nearly 13,000 feet (3,962 meters), "Breckenfridge," as it's sometimes jokingly called, is typically colder and often windier than other Colorado ski areas. Another top area, **Aspen** has four ski resorts, all owned and operated by the **Aspen Skiing Company** (800/525-6200 or 970/923-1227; www.aspensnowmass.com). The towns themselves have charming, walkable streets lined with shops and restaurants. Colorado's ski areas don't lose their appeal in the summer, when the mountains become hiking and biking spots.

BRECKENRIDGE SKI RESORT

# DINOSAUR NATIONAL MONUMENT

435/781-7700; www.nps.gov/dino

Dinosaur National Monument is a long drive from anywhere, stretching over portions of both Utah and Colorado, and this isolation, along with its diverse scenery and amazing fossil display, is a huge part of its appeal. The famous **Dinosaur Quarry** is located on the Utah side of the border, about a 20-minute drive from tiny Dinosaur, Colorado's westernmost town. The larger and quieter Colorado side of the monument features **Echo Park,** the gorgeous valley where the Green and Yampa Rivers meet, one of the top spots in the state for thrilling white-water rafting. Not far to the south, the peaceful **Canyon Pintado** preserves dozens of pictograph sites, where you can gaze at handprints, painted animals, and masonry walls made by people of the Fremont culture 2,000 years ago.

# MOUNT ZIRKEL WILDERNESS AREA

Medicine Bow-Routt National Forest; 307/745-2300; www.fs.usda.gov

Tucked into the heart of Routt National Forest in the northwest area of Colorado are 160,308 untrammeled acres (64,874 hectares) of azure alpine lakes, lofty snowcapped peaks, and pristine pine and spruce woodlands. The Mount Zirkel Wilderness Area straddles the Continental Divide and encompasses some of Colorado's highest and most rugged country, with 15 peaks exceeding 12,000 feet (3,657 meters) in elevation, as well as 70 alpine lakes. A network of more than 150 miles (241 kilometers) of trails lace through this remote and rugged landscape. A standout hike is the **Gilpin Lake Trail** (5.7 miles/9.1 kilometers one way), a gorgeous hike through dense conifer forest to the cobalt-blue lake.

# COLORADO NATIONAL MONUMENT

Fruita; 970/858-3617; www.nps.gov

Colorado National Monument is a 20,500-acre (8,296-hectare) wonderland of quintessential Western high-desert scenery. Here, Mother Nature has chipped away at the relatively soft rock, carving 11 deep canyons through the colorful sandstone. Bike, hike, or drive through this pristine wilderness of twisting canyons, sloping slickrock, and sandstone towers looming above piñon- and juniper-dotted slopes.

# BLACK CANYON OF THE GUNNISON NATIONAL PARK

Hwy. 347; 970/641-2337; www.nps.gov/blca

Carved by the powerful Gunnison River, the Black Canyon of the Gunnison is so deep and sheer that its walls are higher than Chicago's Willis Tower, and its inner gorge so narrow that it receives only minutes of sunlight each day. These deep shadows, plus the rocks' dark hue, gave rise to its unusual name. The main recreational activities at this quiet, uncrowded national park are hiking on one of the park's seven trails (or, in winter, cross-country skiing on the four South Rim trails) and cycling along the rim roads.

BLACK CANYON OF THE GUNNISON NATIONAL PARK

## MESA VERDE NATIONAL PARK

U.S. 160; 970/529-4465; www.nps.gov/meve

Beautiful Mesa Verde National Park protects nearly 5,000 archaeological sites spread across a large and beautiful mesa. The park's main draw is its remarkable cliff dwellings. The most spectacular of these are Cliff Palace, Balcony House, and Long House, which can only be visited on ranger-guided tours. Sadly, Spruce Tree House, the park's best-preserved dwelling, remains closed due to danger from rock falls.

After living on the mesa top for nearly 600 years, the Ancestral Puebloans began building pueblos beneath the area's impressive overhanging cliffs. The largest of these structures is **Cliff Palace** (tours late May-mid-Sept.), with more than 150 rooms and 20 circular kivas, distinctive pits likely used for performing cultural rituals. With just 40 rooms, nearby **Balcony House** (tours late Apr.-Oct.) is an intermediate-size complex, where villagers used hand- and footholds carved into the sandstone, as well as tall, wooden ladders to access their mesa-top gardens; this tour involves climbing up ladders and staircases and through a tunnel.

**Long House** is the park's second-largest cliff dwelling. (Purchase tickets for the 2-hour tour in advance of driving out here.) Archaeologists believe that 150-175 people once lived beneath the shadow of its 300-foot-long (91.4-meter) alcove. Of special note is a well-preserved, triangular tower rising four stories from floor-to-ceiling at the western end of the alcove.

## GARDEN OF THE GODS

1805 N. 30th St., Colorado Springs; 719/634-6666; www.gardenofgods.com

Garden of the Gods is a 1,300-acre (526.1-ha) park with rows of radically tilted, 300-foot-high (91.4-m) red and white rock fins that form a stunning foreground for Pikes Peak's dramatic slopes and lofty summit. Explore these dramatic fins via horseback, hiking, climbing, or a gorgeous scenic drive.

## PIKES PEAK

www.pikespeak.us.com or www.pikes-peak.com

Pikes Peak is a magnificent mountain that soars 8,000 feet (2,438 meters) above the Great Plains. Unlike most of Colorado's Front Range peaks, Pikes has no shroud of foothills to obscure it. Today, more than 600,000 people ascend Pikes Peak each year, making it the most-ascended mountain in the United States.

## GREAT SAND DUNES NATIONAL PARK AND PRESERVE

11999 Hwy. 150, Mosca; 719/378-6399; www.nps.gov/grsa

Along the eastern edge of Colorado's San Luis Valley is a vast, high-elevation basin almost as large as the state of New Jersey. The Great Sand Dunes National Park and Preserve hosts a remarkable dune field with mounds of sand up to 750 feet (228 meters) high—the tallest dunes in North America. There are no trails cross the ever-shifting dune field, but visitors can explore via **sandboard** or **sand sled,** equipment specifically made for sliding down sand.

# FESTIVALS AND EVENTS

## NATIONAL WESTERN STOCK SHOW

Denver; www.nationalwestern.com; Jan.

GREAT SAND DUNES NATIONAL PARK

## BEST SOUVENIRS

- You'll find apparel shops around the state where you can get decked out in **Western wear.** Think snap-button shirts, boots, buckles, belts, and more. **Rockmount Ranchwear** (1626 Wazee St., Denver; 800/776-2566; www.rockmount.com) is a third-generation family business that sells all the apparel you'll need, or, if you're in Steamboat Springs, check out fifth-generation family business **F. M. Light & Sons** (830 Lincoln Ave., Steamboat Springs; 970/879-1822; http://fmlight.com).

- Founded by three friends from Boulder, **Crocs** have become an international sensation. Head to the store in the quirky rubber shoes' hometown (1129 Pearl St., Boulder; 303/442-4261; www.crocs.com).

The world's largest stock show features livestock, horse and trade shows, plus a professional rodeo.

## FROZEN DEAD GUY DAYS

Nederland; http://frozendeadguydays.org; Mar.

Held in early March each year in the mountain community of Nederland, Frozen Dead Guy Days is a fun tribute to Grandpa Bredo Morstoel, a native Norwegian who lies cryogenically frozen in a Tuff shed on the edge of town. After a few turns of events, Grandpa Bredo's body ended up in Nederland with relatives and then put in the care of local Bo Shaffer, whose job is to pack Bredo's shed with dry ice once every month to keep him at a cool -60°F (-51.1°C).

This unique tale is the inspiration for the festival that celebrates the end of

THE POPULAR COFFIN RACES DURING FROZEN DEAD GUY DAYS

winter. For three days, most of the town closes down and people from near and far join in zany contests like coffin races, frozen T-shirt contests, and the frozen salmon toss. Thirty bands play live music in heated tents, the beer flows fast, and local breweries, distilleries, and food vendors peddle everything from bacon to Frozen Dead Guy ice cream, a custom **Glacier Ice Cream** blend of blue ice cream with crushed cookies and gummy worms.

## HOT AIR BALLOON RODEO

Bald Eagle Lake, 35565 S. U.S. 40; mid-July

The long-standing Hot Air Balloon Rodeo is a colorful mix of hot air balloon launches and unique balloon rodeo events.

## TELLURIDE BLUEGRASS FESTIVAL

Telluride; www.bluegrass.com; mid-June

The biggest and best-known event in Telluride is the Telluride Bluegrass Festival, encompassing four days of musical festivities and concerts by big names like Sam Bush, Mumford & Sons, and the Counting Crows.

## SPECTATOR SPORTS

Denver is a football town, and people across the state tend to wear orange and blue whenever the **Denver Broncos** (www.denverbroncos.com) play. Denver has six other professional sports teams, including the **Colorado Rockies** (www.mlb.com/rockies) baseball team. Opening day for the Rockies is celebrated by the painting of a purple stripe down the center of Blake Street near Coors Field.

# BEST FOOD

The state's variety of microclimates, abundant sunshine, fertile soil, and a commitment to sustainable farming practices create a uniquely Colorado cuisine. Specialties include juicy Western Slope peaches, Southwestern green chiles, the state's famous trout, and grass-fed beef, bison, and lamb. Summer **farmers markets** in Boulder, Fort Collins, Colorado Springs, and Denver are ideal places to shop for local produce and handmade products.

## FARM-TO-TABLE

Colorado is a growing center for the farm-to-table movement, which is based on the concept of cooking with locally grown and sourced foods and beverages as much as possible. In the Gunnison River's beautiful North Fork Valley, the tiny town of **Paonia** has the greatest concentration of sustainable organic growers and is a center of fresh farm-to-table food and drink, including the fabulous **Living Farm Café** (120 Grand Ave.; 970/527-3779; http://thelivingfarmcafe.com). In downtown Denver, a delicious farm-to-table option is **The Kitchen Denver** (1560 Wazee St., Denver; 303/623-3127; http://thekitchen.com).

## WILDERNESS RESTAURANTS

Colorado's several wilderness restaurants combine a love of outdoor recreation with great food. Accessible only on foot, skis, or sleigh, these quintessential experiences handsomely reward the extra effort to get there. A couple standouts include **Starlight Dinners by Sleigh** (www.breckstables.com) in Breckenridge and **Beano's Cabin** (www.beanoscabinbeavercreek.com), a cozy hut at Beaver Creek that's only accessible on horseback or via a snowcat-pulled open sleigh.

## WESTERN CUISINE

To try Western Cuisine—think buffalo meat—head to **The Fort** (19192 Hwy. 8, Morrison; 303/697-4771; http://thefort.com), one of the state's most unique dining experiences. The restaurant specializes in the food and drink of the early West, including dishes that the early pioneers, Spanish traders, and native tribes ate. The restaurant's signature dishes are meat—buffalo, quail, elk, and choice cuts of Colorado-raised beef. The Fort also serves authentic cocktails whose recipes date back to the 1840s.

# MAJOR AIRPORTS

- **Denver International Airport:** DEN; 8500 Peña Blvd., Denver; www.flydenver.com

# MORE INFORMATION

## TRAVEL AND TOURIST INFORMATION

- **Colorado Tourism:** www.colorado.com
- **Colorado Parks & Wildlife:** https://cpw.state.co.us/placestogo/parks
- **Colorado Ski Country USA:** www.coloradoski.com

## NEWSPAPERS

- *The Denver Post:* www.denverpost.com

# GREAT PLAINS

◄ BISON IN KANSAS

# THE GREAT PLAINS
## State by State

## NORTH DAKOTA

**Why Go:** Wide-open spaces make a perfect setting for roadside art against a big blue sky.

## SOUTH DAKOTA

**Why Go:** The Black Hills and Badlands have beauty and views for miles.

## NEBRASKA

**Why Go:** Come find out what the sandhill cranes, who flock here in spring and fall, seem to know: Nebraska has great ways to relax and some beautiful natural areas.

## KANSAS

**Why Go:** The natural wonders of Kansas include a park of preserved tallgrass prairie and outcroppings that were once at the bottom of a vast inland sea.

## OKLAHOMA

**Why Go:** Oklahoma has the largest population of Indigenous people in the country, and a wide range of sights present the history and culture of the 39 tribal nations in the state.

## IOWA

**Why Go:** Unique geography, ancient animal-shaped mounds, and a dynamic capital city that hosts a signature state fair make Iowa a destination for everyone, not just presidential hopefuls.

## MISSOURI

**Why Go:** Kansas City's barbecue is reason enough, but St. Louis also has a great musical legacy.

# Great Plains
# ROAD TRIP

The Great Plains are vast, so seeing them involves a lot of driving, often with few services between stops. The big openness of the landscape can itself be an attraction. This road trip takes nearly 2 full weeks to visit 5 states and involves some driving on unpaved roads.

## MISSOURI

**Kansas City to Springfield: 1 day / 165 miles (265 kilometers)**
Start in Kansas City. Head to the **Negro Leagues Baseball Museum,** and have some of the famous **barbecue** before driving south 3 hours to **Springfield,** the birthplace of Route 66, for the night.

## OKLAHOMA

**Tulsa, Oklahoma City, and Route 66: 3 days / 630 miles (400 kilometers)**
From Springfield, drive **Route 66** through Carthage, Joplin, a few miles in Kansas, and into Oklahoma. When you

get to **Tulsa** (about a 3-hour drive from Springfield), spend the rest of the day visiting the Greenwood Cultural Center and touring the art deco buildings downtown. In the morning, take a day trip on the **Cherokee Hills Byway,** returning to Tulsa at the end of the day. The next morning, head to Sulphur to visit the **Chickasaw Cultural Center.** Afterward, drive north to **Oklahoma City** for the night.

## KANSAS

**Tallgrass Prairie, Wichita, and Western Kansas: 3 days / 775 miles (1,250 kilometers)**
From Oklahoma City, make the 3.5-hour drive north to **Tallgrass Prairie National Preserve.** After walking around the grasslands that once covered the Great Plains, head to **Wichita,** 1.5 hours away, for the night. In the morning, check out Wichita's murals before pointing your car to **Dodge City,** the old western town, to spend the night. From Dodge

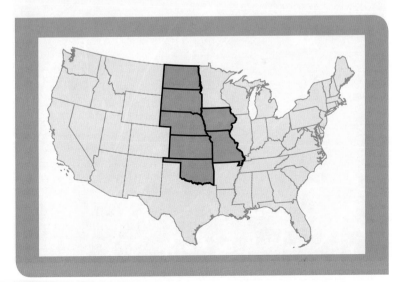

TANKING DOWN THE NORTH PLATTE RIVER, NEBRASKA

City, it's a 2-hour drive to the amazing rock formations in **Little Jerusalem Badlands State Park** and **Monument Rocks Natural Area.** Afterward, head north 3 hours to spend the night in North Platte, Nebraska.

## NEBRASKA

**North Platte: 2 days / 280 miles (450 kilometers)**
Relax in **North Platte** for a day, making sure you've scheduled a tanking trip down the river. The next day, make the 4-hour trip east to **Omaha.** Along the way, you can stretch your legs in **Fort Kearny State Park** and explore the city of **Lincoln.**

## IOWA

**Loess Hills, Des Moines, and Effigy Mounds: 2 days / 435 miles (700 kilometers)**
From Omaha, Iowa is just across the Missouri River. Get a view of the unique geography of the **Loess Hills** at Hitchcock Nature Center before heading to **Des Moines,** 2 hours away. Be sure to see the **Pappajohn Sculpture Park** while you're in the Iowa capital. In the morning, make the 3.5-hour drive east to see the animal-shaped prehistoric mounds at **Effigy Mounds National Monument.** Spend the night in **Dubuque.**

## MISSOURI

**St. Louis and back to Kansas City: 2 days / 165 miles (265 kilometers)**
Spend one day making the 6-hour drive from Dubuque to **St. Louis.** Spend part of the next day seeing the sights in St. Louis before driving 4 hours west back to Kansas City.

## ADDING NORTH AND SOUTH DAKOTA

**Badlands and Theodore Roosevelt National Parks: 4-5 days / 1,285-1,320 miles (2,215-2,070 kilometers)**
To add the Dakotas to the trip, you could head north from North Platte, Nebraska, to South Dakota's **Badlands National Park,** about 4 hours away. Spend the night in **Wall,** and then drive 4.5 hours up to **Medora,** North Dakota, which is just outside **Theodore Roosevelt National Park.** From Medora, it's about a 10-11 hour drive to Omaha. You could break up the drive by spending a night in **Fargo** (4.5 hours east of Medora and 6 hours north of Omaha).

MERAMEC CAVERNS, MISSOURI

# NORTH DAKOTA

Although it's at the northern border of the lower 48 states, North Dakota sits near the geographic center of North America, on Mandan, Hidatsa, Arikara, Yanktonia, Sisseton, Wahpeton, Hunkpapa, Lakota, Dakota, Nakota, Pembina Chippewa, Cree, and Metis land. At certain spots in the state, with the plains stretching in all directions, it can feel like you're in the middle of an endless land. With its open spaces and low population density, North Dakota offers a range of adventures that may be under the national radar, but delight those who experience them. One-of-a-kind roadside attractions, beautiful badlands, and rolling prairies all await under the big sky of the Peace Garden State.

AREA: 70,762 square miles / 183,273 square kilometers (19th)

POPULATION: 762,062 (47th)

STATEHOOD DATE: November 2, 1889 (39th/40th—North Dakota and South Dakota became states simultaneously, making the two the 39th and 40th states in the U.S.)

STATE CAPITAL: Bismarck

▲ THE LITTLE MISSOURI RIVER AT THEODORE ROOSEVELT NATIONAL PARK

## ORIENTATION

**Bismarck** is located near the center of the state, on I-94, North Dakota's main east-west corridor. Many attractions are in the western part of the state, including **Theodore Roosevelt National Park.** The first and third biggest cities, **Fargo** and **Grand Forks,** sit on the North Dakota's eastern border with Minnesota.

## WHEN TO GO

North Dakota is perhaps most associated with harsh **winters,** which can be bitingly cold and windy. **Spring** is a transition period with changeable weather. **Summer** (May-Sept.), when temperatures warm up to the high 70s or hotter, is the best season to visit, though sudden thunderstorms can bring downpours. **Fall** is also a pleasant time with lingering warm temperatures, though nights can get very chilly.

# HIGHLIGHTS

## KNIFE RIVER INDIAN VILLAGES NATIONAL HISTORIC SITE

564 County Rd. 37, Stanton; 701/745-3300; www.nps.gov/knri

A reconstructed earthen lodge is the centerpiece of this park that re-creates the villages of the Hidatsa and Mandan people. Also on the site is a museum with artifacts from villages that were located in the area. Trails connect village sites and also lead to views of the Missouri River.

## LEWIS AND CLARK INTERPRETIVE CENTER

2576 8th St. SW, Washburn; 701/462-8435; www.parkrec.nd.gov/lewis-clark-interpretive-center

The Lewis and Clark National Historic Trail follows the route of the expedition charged with surveying the lands west of the Mississippi River to the Pacific Ocean, much of which ostensibly became United States territory through the Louisiana Purchase. The trail stretches across the United States from Pittsburgh, Pennsylvania, to Astoria, Oregon, and is dotted with numerous interpretive centers that contain exhibits on the journey, the Indigenous cultures inhabiting the lands being explored, and the explorers' activities in the area. This center in Washburn is located near **Fort Mandan,** a re-creation of the spot where the expedition spent the winter of 1804-1805.

## TURTLE MOUNTAIN CHIPPEWA HERITAGE CENTER

3959 SkyDancer Way NE, Belcourt; 701/244-5530; www.chippewaheritage.com

Learn more about the Turtle Mountain Band of Chippewa at this museum,

KNIFE RIVER INDIAN VILLAGES NATIONAL HISTORIC SITE

# NORTH DAKOTA

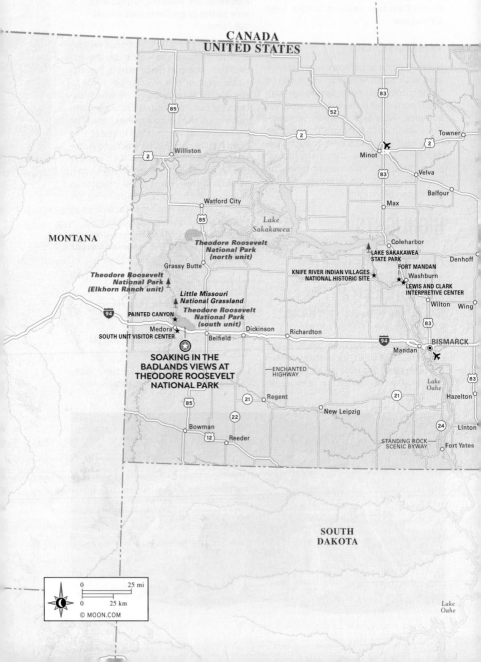

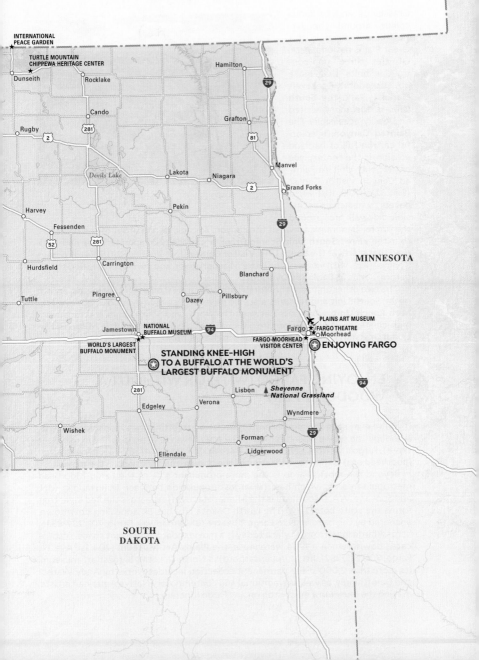

MANITOBA

INTERNATIONAL
PEACE GARDEN

TURTLE MOUNTAIN
CHIPPEWA HERITAGE CENTER

Hamilton

Dunseith          Rocklake

Cando

Grafton

Rugby          281                81

2

Manvel

Lakota          Niagara

Devils Lake                              Grand Forks

2

Harvey          Pekin

Fessenden                                              MINNESOTA

52    281

Hurdsfield          Carrington                Blanchard

Tuttle          Pingree          Dazey    Pillsbury

PLAINS ART MUSEUM

Jamestown    NATIONAL          94        Fargo    FARGO THEATRE
BUFFALO MUSEUM                              Moorhead
FARGO-MOORHEAD
WORLD'S LARGEST                              VISITOR CENTER    ENJOYING FARGO
BUFFALO MONUMENT
STANDING KNEE-HIGH
TO A BUFFALO AT THE WORLD'S
LARGEST BUFFALO MONUMENT

Lisbon    Sheyenne
281                              National Grassland
94

Edgeley          Verona
Wyndmere

Wishek                              29
Forman

Ellendale          Lidgerwood

SOUTH
DAKOTA

# TOP 3

## 1 SOAKING IN THE BADLANDS VIEWS AT THEODORE ROOSEVELT NATIONAL PARK

315 Second Ave., Medora; 701/623-4466; www.nps.gov/thro

Grasslands and badlands collide around the Little Missouri River in this Great Plains national park. Of the three non-contiguous units that make up Theodore Roosevelt National Park, the **South Unit** is the most visited and easily accessible. The **Painted Canyon,** a colorful canyon full of badland erosion, is the centerpiece of the South Unit. At Painted Canyon Visitor Center (Exit 32 off U.S. 10/I-94), a paved wheelchair-accessible sidewalk arcs around

PAINTED CANYON

the rim for panoramic views of the canyon. For an extended tour of the badlands, tour the paved **South Unit Scenic Drive,** a 48-mile (77-kilometer) out-and-back road that starts at the **South Unit Visitor Center** (Exit 27 off U.S. 10/I-94). It passes Skyline Vista, with views of the Little Missouri River, and several prairie dog towns before it ends at **Badlands Overlook.**

The two other units are the **North Unit,** which is 70 miles (113 kilometers) north of the South Unit and features a scenic drive with several overlooks, and the **Elkhorn Ranch Unit,** which sits between the North and South Units and requires a high-clearance vehicle. The entire national park sits within the **Little Missouri National Grassland,** the largest grassland in the country.

## 2 ENJOYING FARGO (WITH OR WITHOUT A WOODCHIPPER)

If you've ever seen the movie *Fargo,* there's no forgetting the woodchipper scene. Although the movie wasn't filmed in the town it made famous (or even really set there), Fargo's **visitors center** (2001 44th St. S., Fargo; 701/282-3653; www.fargomoorhead.org) is the proud location of the original machine used in the movie.

Beyond the movie, Fargo is the more prominent side of the Fargo-Moorhead metropolitan area, which has the largest population between Minneapolis, MN, and Spokane, WA. (Moorhead is the Minnesota town just across the Red River that forms the state boundary.) The North Dakota city has an appealing downtown, anchored by the historic 1926 **Fargo Theatre** (314 Broadway, Fargo; 701/239-8385; https://fargotheatre.org), which today is a movie theater and event space. Also located downtown in a 1904 warehouse, the **Plains Art Museum** (704 1st Ave. N., Fargo; 701/232-3821; https://plainsart.org) is North Dakota's biggest art museum. Its more than 2,000-piece permanent collection includes works by Andy Warhol and Dale Chihuly, as well as traditional and contemporary Native American artists, making the museum a must-stop on any Fargo itinerary.

FARGO THEATRE AT DUSK

## 3 STANDING KNEE-HIGH TO A BUFFALO AT THE WORLD'S LARGEST BUFFALO MONUMENT

404 17th St. SE, Jamestown

Nothing says "road trip" like stopping at a random, giant rendering of...anything, really, and this 26-foot-tall (7.9-meter) concrete sculpture of the West's iconic animal is classic roadside Americana. Named Dakota Thunder, the sculpture is located in Jamestown, a town on the I-94 corridor between Bismarck and Fargo that has dedicated itself to celebrating bison. The main activity here is gazing upon and taking photos of and with the World's Largest Buffalo. (Of course, you should never stand this close to actual bison, which may not be 26 feet/7.9 meters tall but are still plenty large and can do serious bodily injury.) You can also wander next door to the small **National Buffalo Museum** (500 17th St. SE, Jamestown; 701/252-8648; www.buffalomuseum.com), where displays include a taxidermic rare white bison. There's also a live herd of bison, viewable from the back of the museum.

DAKOTA THUNDER, THE WORLD'S LARGEST BUFFALO, DESIGNED BY ELMER PETERSEN

# *Best* ROAD TRIP

**DAY 1** Start by spending the day in **Fargo**, North Dakota's biggest city, making sure to stroll the **downtown** area and visit the **Plains Art Museum.**

**DAY 2** Prepare for a day of roadside attractions. Take I-94 west for 1.5 hours to Jamestown, home of the **World's Largest Buffalo Monument.** Peek into the **National Buffalo Museum** before hopping back into the car for another 1.5 hours to **Bismarck.** Have lunch in the capital city, and then head out west on I-94 for 1.5 hours again, keeping an eye out for Exit 72. Spend the rest of the afternoon driving the **Enchanted Highway** to see its whimsical oversize sculptures. Afterward, head to **Dickinson,** the biggest town near Theodore Roosevelt National Park, for the night.

**DAY 3** Start your exploration of **Theodore Roosevelt National Park** at **Painted Canyon,** then head to Medora for the **South Unit Scenic Drive.** Then, head up to the scenic drive in the **North Unit.** Spend the night back in Dickinson.

**DAY 4** In the morning, drive to **Knife River Indian Villages National Historic Site** to learn more about the Indigenous cultures who lived there. Spend the early afternoon at nearby **Lake Sakakawea State Park,** on a trail, on the water, or just relaxing. Stay overnight nearby or back in Bismarck. Head back to Fargo in the morning.

DOWNTOWN FARGO

SCULPTURE BY GARY GREFF ALONG THE ENCHANTED HIGHWAY

THEODORE ROOSEVELT NATIONAL PARK

# *Major* CITIES

**FARGO:** Paired with Minnesota's Moorhead across the state line to form the Fargo-Moorhead metro area, North Dakota's largest city is perhaps most recognizable as the name of a memorable movie directed by Joel and Ethan Coen. Laidback Fargo embraces that legacy: The visitors center displays the most memorable prop used in the movie.

**BISMARCK:** Like its sibling in South Dakota, North Dakota's state capital sits on the banks of the Missouri River. Its location in the center-west of the state puts it within reach of many attractions.

**GRAND FORKS:** Like Fargo, the state's third-largest city shares a metro area with Minnesota across the Red River. It's also the home of the University of North Dakota, the state's largest university.

located within the Turtle Mountain Reservation. Displays include leather-work, jewelry, tools, carvings, and other art and artifacts that convey and pre-serve the history, culture, and language of the community.

## INTERNATIONAL PEACE GARDEN

10939 Hwy. 281, Dunseith; 701/263-4390; https://peacegarden.com

Look at a North Dakota license plate, and you'll notice the state's moniker, "Peace Garden State," in the lower left corner. The nickname comes from this 2,400-acre (971-hectare) park that straddles the U.S.-Canada border. The main attraction is the colorful formal gardens that boast more than 80,000 plants with various monuments to peace, such as the Peace Poles from Japan and 9/11 Memorial Site, erect-ed around them. Visitors need to pass through customs and border control on the way out of the garden, so bring a passport.

# BEST SCENIC DRIVES

## ENCHANTED HIGHWAY

I-94, Exit 72 to Regent

The open expanses of North Dako-ta's backroads and seemingly endless blue sky are an ideal canvas for larger-than-life roadside sculptures, and the Enchanted Highway, the brainchild of Gary Greff, takes full advantage with seven whimsical artworks spread over

32 miles (51 kilometers), starting off I-94 near Gladstone and ending in the town of Regent, where there is a small gift shop. From north to south, the piec-es are "Geese in Flight," "Deer Crossing," "Grasshoppers," "Fisherman's Dream," "Pheasants on the Prairie," "Teddy Roo-sevelt Rides Again," and "Tin Family."

## STANDING ROCK SCENIC BYWAY

Hwy. 1806 and Hwy. 24, Standing Rock Sioux Nation; www.standingrock.org

Starting at the Cannon Ball River and extending to the South Dakota border, this 35-mile-long (56-kilometer) route traces the Missouri River through the Standing Rock Sioux Nation. This land came into the spotlight in 2016 for the protests against the Dakota Access Pipeline, which, if built, would threaten

"TEDDY ROOSEVELT RIDES AGAIN," ENCHANTED HIGHWAY

LAKE SAKAKAWEA

the Standing Rock Sioux Nation's water source. In between views of this important waterway are a number of sights related to the Standing Rock Sioux Tribe. The **Prairie Knights Casino and Lodge** (7932 Highway 24, Fort Yates; 800/425-8277; https://prairieknights.com) is owned by the tribe, and its grounds feature a marina and scenic nature trails. Outside the nation's agency office in Fort Yates, the **Standing Rock Monument** (Standing Rock Ave., Fort Yates) preserves a sacred stone said to be a woman and child. Nearby is the **original burial site of Sitting Bull,** the Hunkpapa Sioux leader who defeated General George Custer.

# BEST PARKS AND RECREATION AREAS

## LAKE SAKAKAWEA

720 Park Ave., Pick City; 701/487-3315; www.parkrec.nd.gov/lake-sakakawea-state-park

Created by the construction of Garrison Dam on the Missouri River, this lake named for the Shoshone woman who guided the Lewis & Clark Expedition is the largest lake in North Dakota. A playground for fishing, watersports, and hiking, the state park on the south shore also features summer cabins for camping. Lake Sakakawea is also the western end of the **North Country National Scenic Trail** (the eastern end is in Crown Point, New York).

## DEVILS LAKE

www.devilslakend.com

Devils Lake is the largest natural lake in North Dakota. The lake and the town of the same name serve as a summer getaway for watersports, fishing, and other outdoor activities. The unique environment of wetlands and grasslands around the lake draws a number of bird species, and it's also on a migration route in the fall, making it a great spot for bird-watching.

## SHEYENNE NATIONAL GRASSLAND

www.fs.usda.gov/dpg

Part of the Dakota Prairie Grasslands, this park preserves the only national grassland in the tall-grass prairie region of the United States. Recreational opportunities here include hiking, biking, camping, and wildlife-watching. A section of the **North Country National Scenic Trail**—a multistate hiking trail that starts in Crown Point, New York, and ends at North Dakota's Lake Sakakawea—passes through the grasslands, and walking a portion of it is a great way to appreciate the natural features of the park.

## BEST SOUVENIRS

- **North Dakota Mill** (www.ndmill.com) is the only state-owned mill in the United States. Pick up a bag of flour or pancake mix for a unique souvenir.
- Much in North Dakota is named for Theodore Roosevelt, who built two ranches in the Dakota Territory near Medora. Although the famed bear incident took place in Colorado, the **Theodore Roosevelt teddy bear** is a common item in North Dakota souvenir shops.

# FESTIVALS AND EVENTS

## NORTH DAKOTA STATE FAIR

Minot; https://ndstatefair.com; July

With concerts, contests, a carnival, rodeo and motocross events, and of course fair food, North Dakota's state fair takes place over the course of nine days in late July.

# BEST FOOD

## CHOKECHERRIES AND JUNEBERRIES

A tart berry in the same family as the blueberry, the chokecherry is North Dakota's state fruit, thanks to a petition drive by sixth graders from the town of **Williston** in 2007. You'll find the berry served as jams, jellies, and syrups around the state, and Williston

celebrates its accomplishment with an annual **Chokecherry Festival** in August.

Juneberries are also similar to blueberries but are less fickle about growing conditions and sweeter than chokecherries. Find them in jams and jellies, as well as pies and cobblers. Juneberry pie is a specialty at **Lund's Landing Restaurant** (11350 Highway 1804, Ray; 701/568-3474; www.lundslanding.com) on the north side of Lake Sakakawea.

# MAJOR AIRPORTS

- **Fargo-Hector International Airport:** FAR; 2801 32nd Ave. NW, Fargo; 701/241-8668; https://fargoairport.com
- **Bismarck Municipal Airport:** BIS; 2301 University Dr., Bismarck; 701/355-1808; www.bismarckairport.com
- **Minot International Airport:** MOT; 305 Airport Rd., Minot; 701/857-4724; www.motairport.com

# MORE INFORMATION

## TRAVEL AND TOURISM INFORMATION

- **North Dakota Tourism:** www.nd-tourism.com
- **North Dakota Parks and Recreation:** www.parkrec.nd.gov

CHOKECHERRIES

# SOUTH DAKOTA

On the land of the Oceti Sakowin, whom French fur trappers and traders called the Sioux, South Dakota has a rugged beauty that has persisted through wars, gold and mining booms, droughts, and even a plague of grasshoppers. Today, much of the state is still rural—28 percent of the population lives in the two biggest cities, Sioux Falls and Rapid City—and entwined with agriculture, ranching, and tourism.

The Black Hills are frequently referred to as an "Island in the Plains," and the description is an apt one. The vast Great Plains cover much of the state, while the Black Hills and the Badlands, tucked in the southwest corner, occupy an outsized place in the popular imagination of South Dakota. A scenic drive through Custer State Park, a viewpoint in the Badlands, or a bridge over the Missouri River all give a different perspective on the South Dakota landscape—and afford opportunities to appreciate its enduring appeal.

**AREA:** 77,184 square miles / 199,730 square kilometers (17th)

**POPULATION:** 884,659 (46th)

**STATEHOOD DATE:** November 2, 1889 (39th/40th—North Dakota and South Dakota became states simultaneously, making the two the 39th and 40th states in the U.S.)

**STATE CAPITAL:** Pierre

▲ BIGHORN SHEEP IN BADLANDS NATIONAL PARK

## ORIENTATION

The hub of tourism in the state is in its southwestern corner, where **Mount Rushmore** is etched into the **Black Hills.** The **Missouri River** runs through the middle of the state, dividing it neatly into eastern and western halves. In between the Black Hills and the Missouri River lie the otherworldly **Badlands.** The state capital of **Pierre** sits on the banks of the Missouri, at the center of the state. South Dakota's biggest city, **Sioux Falls,** is at the far eastern side of the state, near the border with Iowa and Minnesota.

## WHEN TO GO

High season for tourism is generally between **Memorial Day** and **Labor Day,** although during the **late spring** and **early fall,** most attractions are open and there is still plenty to do. National monuments and national parks (including Mount Rushmore) are open year-round; however, **winter** is the slowest time, when hours of operation are reduced and fewer programs are offered.

The Great Plains have the reputation for harsh winters with frequent blizzards and scorching **summers,** and that also applies to the Badlands. However, weather in the Black Hills is much less dramatic. The hills are semi-arid, and they see an average of 275 days of sunshine per year.

# HIGHLIGHTS

## THE JOURNEY MUSEUM AND LEARNING CENTER

222 New York St., Rapid City; 605/394-6923; www.journeymuseum.org

The Journey Museum and Learning Center is a great resource for visitors interested in the cultural, historical, and environmental aspects of South Dakota's Black Hills. Collections include a museum of geology, with exhibits provided by the South Dakota School of Mines and Technology; an archaeology research center that explores the lives of Black Hills inhabitants from ice-age hunters through 19th-century miners; a paleontology display outlining the dinosaur history of the area; and a Native American museum that provides visitors with an introduction to the culture and artworks of the various Sioux tribes that lived in the region. Both traditional and contemporary art are on display, and a pioneer museum is dedicated to exploring the lives of mountain men, military expeditions, and miners.

## MOUNT RUSHMORE NATIONAL MONUMENT

13000 Hwy. 244, Keystone; 605/574-2523; www.nps.gov/moru

Located in the Black Hills of South Dakota, Mount Rushmore is a mark of the

MOUNT RUSHMORE NATIONAL MONUMENT

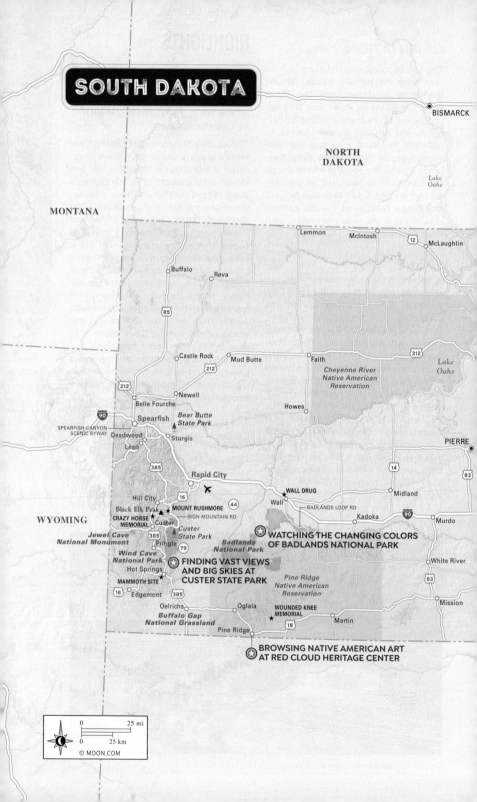

# SOUTH DAKOTA

BISMARCK

NORTH DAKOTA

MONTANA

Lake Oahe

Lemmon
McIntosh
12
McLaughlin

Buffalo
Reva

85

Castle Rock
Mud Butte
Faith
212
Lake Oahe
212
Newell

Belle Fourche
*Bear Butte State Park*
Howes

Cheyenne River Native American Reservation

90
SPEARFISH CANYON SCENIC BYWAY
Spearfish
Deadwood
Lead
Sturgis

PIERRE

385
Rapid City
14
83

Hill City
WALL DRUG
Midland

Black Elk Peak
16 MOUNT RUSHMORE
44
Wall
BADLANDS LOOP RD
WYOMING
CRAZY HORSE MEMORIAL
Custer
IRON MOUNTAIN RD
Kadoka
90
Murdo

*Jewel Cave National Monument*
385
*Custer State Park*
*Badlands National Park*
⭐ WATCHING THE CHANGING COLORS OF BADLANDS NATIONAL PARK

*Wind Cave National Park*
79
Pringle
White River

Hot Springs
*Pine Ridge Native American Reservation*
83

MAMMOTH SITE
18
Edgemont
385
⭐ FINDING VAST VIEWS AND BIG SKIES AT CUSTER STATE PARK
Mission

Oelrichs
Oglala
WOUNDED KNEE MEMORIAL
Martin

*Buffalo Gap National Grassland*
Pine Ridge
18

⭐ BROWSING NATIVE AMERICAN ART AT RED CLOUD HERITAGE CENTER

0    25 mi
0    25 km
© MOON.COM

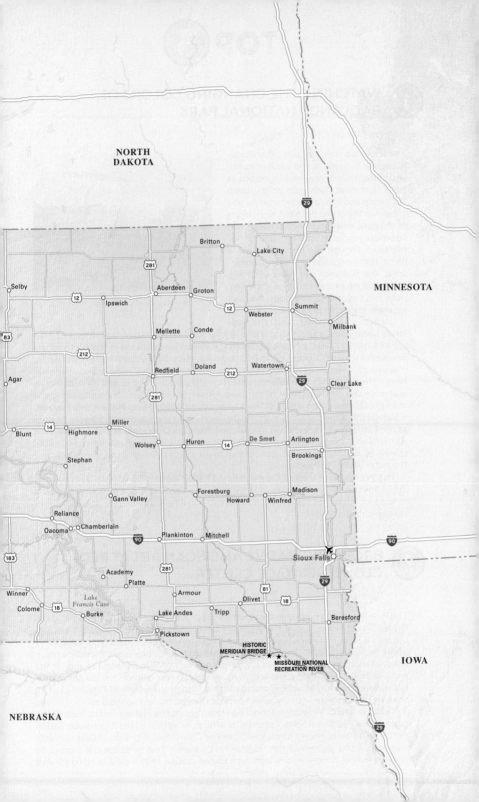

# TOP 3

## 1 WATCHING THE CHANGING COLORS OF BADLANDS NATIONAL PARK

www.nps.gov/badl

The Badlands are a place of otherworldly beauty. In daylight, the twisted spires and pinnacles look gray and faded, but at early light or at dusk, pale yellow, deep burgundy, and light pinks emerge. As you gaze over the plains from the high ridges of the park, miles and miles of open plain lie before you, with little evidence of humankind. Though the dusty gray guise gives the landscape a barren appearance, the Badlands are filled with life, hosting bison, pronghorn, bighorn sheep, deer, fox, coyotes, prairie dogs, burrowing owls, and other prairie animals.

SUNRISE IN BADLANDS NATIONAL PARK

Located in the North Unit, the **Badlands Loop Road** is the only paved road through the National Park. It is a 23-mile (37-kilometer) road that runs between the **Pinnacles Entrance** in the north to the **Ben Reifel Visitor Center** (25216 Ben Reifel Rd.; Hwy. 240; 605/433-5361), the park's main visitors center, in the southeast. The drive takes about an hour and winds between the ridges of the **Badlands Wall,** literally a wall of spires and pinnacles that was once the northern bank of the White River. Several scenic turnouts along the road provide dramatic vistas of the Badlands and **Buffalo Gap National Grassland,** which borders the park. From the north, heading to the southeast, be sure to stop at the **Pinnacles Overlook** and the **Ancient Hunters Overlook.** The easy **Door Trail** (0.75 mile/1.2 kilometers; 30 minutes), which starts at the Ben Reifel Visitor Center, travels to a "door" in the Badlands Wall to give great views of the grasslands and the outer wall of the Badlands.

The **White River Visitor Center** (Hwy. 27, Pine Ridge; 605/455-2878) is located in the **South Unit,** or Stronghold District, within the Pine Ridge Reservation. It is a remote location that serves people interested in Pine Ridge and serious backcountry camping and hiking.

## 2 BROWSING NATIVE AMERICAN ART AT RED CLOUD HERITAGE CENTER

100 Mission Dr., Pine Ridge; 605/867-5491; www.redcloudschool.org

The Pine Ridge Reservation in the southwest corner of South Dakota is home to the Oglala Sioux Nation. One of the largest reservations in the United States, it encompasses 3,468 square miles (8,982 square kilometers) of land, including the South Unit of the Badlands. Life for the Oglala Sioux (Lakota) has not been easy. Forced to move onto reservation land at the end of the Indian Wars of 1876, stripped of their lands and livelihood, their language, and, in many cases, their culture, the Lakota people still have a long road of healing ahead of them. Today, the people of Pine Ridge work to share their culture with the world outside the reservation boundaries.

Visit the Red Cloud Indian School and learn about the history and culture of the Lakota. The Red Cloud School started its affiliation with the Pine Ridge Reservation as the Jesuit Holy Rosary Mission—Chief Red Cloud, one of the great Lakota chiefs and one of the signers of the original Fort Laramie Treaty, chose the Jesuits to provide Native American children with the education they would need to survive in both the outside and tribal worlds. On the grounds of the Red Cloud School, the Red Cloud Heritage Center is housed in the old mission building where children had been taught. The museum's fine arts collection has over 10,000 pieces, including paintings, drawings, and sculptures. The tribal arts collection focuses on artifacts reflecting Oglala culture and history. Every summer, June-August, the Heritage Center hosts the **Red Cloud Indian Art Show,** which brings together the work of artists from Indigenous tribes across the United States and Canada. The **gift shop** adjacent to the museum sells the works of local Lakota artists.

WOUNDED KNEE MEMORIAL

Just to the left of the Heritage Center building, you will see a path that heads up a small hill and ends at the **cemetery.** It is in this cemetery that **Chief Red Cloud** lies buried. Also be sure to visit the **Holy Rosary Church** on the school property. The building contains beautiful Lakota-designed stained-glass windows.

Nearby, on a dusty hilltop overlooking the grassy plains of the Pine Ridge Reservation, the **Wounded Knee Memorial** is a small fenced-in cemetery, within which a tall stone stands as quiet testimony, covered with the names of some of the many Lakota who were killed by the U.S. cavalry at the Wounded Knee Massacre of 1890. It sits at the junction of BIA 27 and BIA 28 just south of the community of Porcupine.

## ③ FINDING VAST VIEWS AND BIG SKIES AT CUSTER STATE PARK

13329 U.S. 16A; headquarters 605/255-4515; www.custerstatepark.com

Encompassing 71,000 acres (28,732 hectares), Custer State Park is one of the largest state parks in the United States, and there's no better place for scenic beauty, wildlife viewing, and outdoor activity. In the southernmost areas of the park, the landscape is all soft rolling hills, with fields of prairie grasses and small stands of ponderosa pine scattered throughout. It is here that grassland wildlife abounds. Bison, pronghorn, deer, and prairie dog populations are common sights. Traveling north, the elevation rises, and the rolling low hills turn into craggy peaks with steep canyon walls and sheer granite outcroppings. Four in-park lodges (reservations 888/875-0001; www.custerresorts.com) allow leisurely exploration.

The best drive in the park—and perhaps the entire state—is the **Needles Highway** (Highway 87, closed in winter) from south to north. Begin at the junction of U.S. 16A and Highway 87. The 14-mile (22.5-kilometer) road slowly climbs in elevation as it winds through narrow tunnels and weaves its way past towering granite spires, which are the needles for which the road is named, and ponderosa pine forests. Several turnouts along the way allow viewing some spectacular formations: **Cathedral Spires** is a collection of massive granite towers, and the **Eye of the Needle** is a narrow spire over 30 feet (9 meters) tall with a 3-foot-wide (0.9-meter) slit at the top.

The Needles Highway ends at **Sylvan Lake,** the most northern and western spur of the park. It is a small lake but the prettiest in the park, with wonderful views of the surrounding granite formations and an easy, 1-mile (1.6-kilometer) walking trail that meanders around the water. The hike to **Black Elk Peak** from the Sylvan Lake trailhead (Trail #9) is one of the best in the park. Moderate in difficulty, it is a 6-mile (9.6-kilometer) round-trip walk that provides spectacular views of both the plains and the hills. At 7,242 feet (2,207 meters), Black Elk Peak is the highest point in South Dakota.

# *Best* ROAD TRIP

**DAY 1** Start out in **Rapid City,** and head east on I-90 and take exit 110 at the town of Wall and the famous **Wall Drug.** Then drive south to the main entrance of **Badlands National Park.** Meander the **Badlands Loop Road,** take in the views, and stop at the **Ben Reifel Visitor Center** at the southern end of the park. Stretch your legs along the easy **Door Trail.** Spend the night back in Rapid City.

**DAY 2** The next morning, drive down to **Wind Cave** to see another national park, this time underground. After taking a cave tour and exploring the trails above ground, head up to **Custer State Park** and check in at one of the lodges (make reservations ahead of time). Drive the **Wildlife Loop** around dusk for the best wildlife-watching.

**DAY 3** Keep exploring Custer State Park. Drive the **Needles Highway** to **Sylvan Lake** and tackle the hike up to **Black Elk Peak,** the highest point in South Dakota. Afterward, stop by the **Crazy Horse Memorial.** In the evening, experience a chuckwagon dinner, a South Dakota classic, at **Blue Bell Lodge.**

**DAY 4** Leave Custer State Park, and head out to **Mount Rushmore** on **Iron Mountain Road,** the best way to approach the monument. Watch out for the view of the presidents' faces framed by the three tunnels along the way. Explore the monument, take a short hike, and learn about Lakota, Nakota, and Dakota culture at the **Heritage Village.** From there, make the hourlong drive to **Deadwood** for an escape to the Wild West.

BADLANDS LOOP ROAD

GEOLOGICAL FORMATION OF ROCKS, WIND CAVE NATIONAL PARK

CUSTER STATE PARK

**DAY 5** After breakfast, head to **Lead,** 3 miles (4.8 kilometers) away, where you can get onto U.S. 14A, otherwise known as the **Spearfish Canyon Scenic Byway.** Stop at the **76 Trail** for a hike up to the top of the rim of Spearfish Canyon. Stop in **Spearfish** at the other end of the byway for a bite to eat, then make the 1-hour drive back to **Rapid City.** Be sure to stop by **Prairie Edge Trading Company and Galleries** to browse the various arts and crafts by local artists.

IRON MOUNTAIN ROAD

SPEARFISH CANYON SCENIC BYWAY

country's expansion. Started in 1927 and completed in 1941, these faces of four presidents—George Washington, Thomas Jefferson, Abraham Lincoln, and Theodore Roosevelt—were carved into the hard granite mountain, and the monument is controversial for its presence on land that the Lakota people consider sacred.

As you enter the park, a flag-lined pedestrian walkway, called the **Avenue of the Flags,** forms a colorful frame for the presidential faces straight ahead. Fifty-six flags are on display, one for each state, district, commonwealth, and territory of the United States. The Avenue of Flags terminates at the **Grand View Terrace,** one of the most popular locations in the park for photographs. Other highlights include the **Presidential Trail,** a pleasant half-mile (0.8-kilometer) loop that starts from the Grand View Terrace and brings visitors to the closest viewing points for the monument, and the **Lakota, Nakota, and Dakota Heritage Village,** where volunteer interpreters give talks about the traditional lifestyle and customs of Indigenous people before the arrival of Europeans.

## CRAZY HORSE MEMORIAL

12151 Avenue of the Chiefs, Crazy Horse; 605/673-4681; www.crazyhorsememorial.org

Started in 1948, the Crazy Horse Memorial is the only ongoing mountain carving in the world; when completed, the carving—envisioned as Crazy Horse on horseback, pointing to the Black Hills, his homeland—will be 641 feet long by 563 feet (195x171 meters) high. There is no estimated finish date on the memorial. The face, 87 feet (26.5 meters) high, is virtually complete, and much work has been accomplished on the horse's head. During the summer months, a **laser light show** is presented nightly.

In addition to the mountain carving, the grounds of the Crazy Horse Memorial include the **Welcome Center;** the **Native American Museum,** which is filled with Native American artwork and artifacts; and the **Native American Educational and Cultural Center,** where visitors are encouraged to participate in Lakota games and listen to

# *Major* CITIES

**SIOUX FALLS:** With more than twice the population of South Dakota's next-largest city, Sioux Falls is located on the southeastern edge of South Dakota. See the city's namesake Falls of the Big Sioux River at Falls Park, within walking distance of downtown.

**RAPID CITY:** The state's second most populous city serves as a gateway and base for Mount Rushmore National Monument.

staff and Native American vendors discuss Lakota history and culture.

## JEWEL CAVE NATIONAL MONUMENT

11149 U.S. Hwy. 16; 605/673-8300; www.nps.gov/jeca

Named for the glittering calcite crystals that line the walls, Jewel Cave National Monument is one of the prettiest caves in South Dakota and the third-longest cave in the world. Currently measuring over 196 miles (315 kilometers) in length, Jewel Cave is honeycombed under just 3 square miles (7.7 square kilometers) of land. The largest room in the cave is over 570 feet (173 meters) long, 180 feet (54 meters) at its widest, and 30 feet (9 meters) tall. In addition to the sparkling calcite crystals that gave the cave its name, it also features popcorn (small round clusters of calcium carbonate that looks like popcorn), stalactites, and stalagmites. Popular cave tours take you below the surface; arrive at the visitors center before late morning to get a spot. Advance reservations are available for some tours.

## MAMMOTH SITE

1800 Hwy. 18; Hot Springs; 605/745-6017; www.mammothsite.com

The first mammoth tusk discovered at the fascinating Mammoth Site was overturned by accident. Early in 1974, a bulldozer, working to level out the hill for a planned real estate development, exposed the item. Since then, the skeletal remains of 61 mammoths have been found and are displayed where they were uncovered. In addition to the mammoths, 85 other species of animals and plants, and several unidentified insects dating back 26,000 years to the Pleistocene era have been archived. A guided tour of the **Sink Hole and Dig Site** includes a 30-minute guided walk of the bone bed. After the tour is complete, visitors are free to wander the site as long as they please and to explore the **Ice Age Exhibit Hall** adjacent to the dig site. The hall features replicas of many of the animals found at the dig, a mammoth bone hut, and a collection of some of the oldest North American arrowheads. Skeletons of now-extinct carnivores are on display, including the short-faced bear and the American lion.

JEWEL CAVE NATIONAL MONUMENT

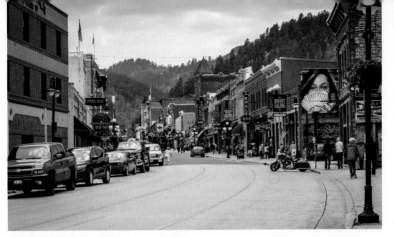
DEADWOOD

## DEADWOOD

www.cityofdeadwood.com

Gold was first discovered in the Black Hills in the city of Custer in 1874. As prospectors flocked to the region, claims were paying off all over the hills, but the richest claims and longest-running mines were to be found in Deadwood and its sister city of Lead, just 3 miles (4.8 kilometers) away. Life was wild in all the gold camps, but Deadwood managed to attract the most colorful characters, including James Butler "Wild Bill" Hickok and Calamity Jane, both of whom are interred in the town's **Mount Moriah Cemetery.**

To this day, Deadwood remains one of the edgiest and most dynamic towns in South Dakota's Black Hills. Deadwood Gulch is a fairly narrow canyon, and most of the town is squeezed in along just a few main streets. The historic district of the town looks much as it did after 1879, when it was rebuilt in the wake of a destructive fire. You can learn more about Deadwood's history at the **Adams Museum** (www.deadwoodhistory.com) or venture into an old gold mine at the **Broken Boot Gold Mine** (www.brokenbootgoldmine. com). To immerse yourself in Old West ambiance, head to **Saloon No. 10** (www.saloon10.com), which is at once a museum, restaurant, bar, and gambling hall. It also holds reenactments of Wild Bill Hickock's death several times a day.

## WALL DRUG

510 Main St., Wall; 605/279-2175; www.walldrug.com

Famous for its signs advertising free ice water, Wall Drug is the ultimate roadside attraction. Occupying over 76,000 square feet (7,060 square meters), Wall Drug sells all the tourist paraphernalia your heart could desire, and the backyard is home to unlimited photo opportunities, including a giant jackalope saddled up and ready to ride and a roaring, smoke-spewing T. rex. Inside, the complex is divided into several small shops. A fine art gallery sells paintings, art prints, pottery, and bronze sculptures, and there is a great little bookstore with a fine collection of regional books. Look for Western clothing, leather goods, a rock shop, camping supplies, a jewelry store, a doughnut shop, an espresso bar, and a restaurant. And, there is a drugstore. Coffee is still five cents (though better coffee is available for a bit more), and ice water is still free.

# BEST SCENIC DRIVES

In addition to the **Needles Highway,** other routes showcase the state's scenery.

## IRON MOUNTAIN ROAD

U.S. 16A

Iron Mountain Road (17 miles/27 kilometers) connects Custer State Park to

Mount Rushmore, and with three tunnels that frame the presidential faces as you drive through them, this drive makes for the most dramatic approach to the monument. Head south on Highway 79 and take a right on Highway 40, just past Hermosa. About 13 miles (20 kilometers) in, take a left on Playhouse Road. Four miles (6.4 kilometers) later, take a right and head north on Iron Mountain Road. Wind through the hills, and enjoy the gorgeous views, the pigtail bridges, and the narrow tunnels on the way to the Mount Rushmore.

## WILDLIFE LOOP

Custer State Park

On the north side of Custer State Park, the Wildlife Loop (18 miles/29 kilometers) begins just east of the **State Game Lodge** off U.S. 16A. The southwestern entrance to the loop is off Highway 87, just about 1 mile (0.6 kilometer) south of the **Blue Bell Lodge** area. It doesn't matter which end of the loop you start from, but what does matter is the time of day. Wildlife is most active and visible early in the morning or near dusk. Pronghorn, bison, white-tailed deer, mule deer, and prairie dogs are common along the route. On lucky occasions, the elusive elk herd will make an appearance. The park's small herd of burros is usually found somewhere along the way, too. Turnouts along the route to allow for photographs and wildlife-viewing. Expect "traffic jams" when bison herds decide to cross the road. For your safety and theirs, keep your distance from the animals.

BURROS ON THE WILDLIFE LOOP, CUSTER STATE PARK

## SPEARFISH CANYON SCENIC BYWAY

U.S. 14A

Spearfish Canyon Scenic Byway is a state and national forest scenic byway that winds for about 20 miles (32 kilometers) along Spearfish Creek between the communities of **Spearfish** and **Lead.** All the views are straight up the canyon walls to heights of over 1,000 feet (304 meters), but don't forget to keep an eye on the road, as many bicyclists and hikers may be riding or walking along the shoulders. There are several beautiful hiking, biking, and horseback riding trails along the byway. The **76 Trail** (across the road from Spearfish Canyon Lodge; 1.5 miles/2.4 kilometers round-trip, 1.5-2 hours) is the only formal hiking trail to climb to the top of the rim of Spearfish Canyon. The trail is short, but it rises more than 1,000 feet (304 meters) from start to finish. The panoramic view from the ridge at the top of the canyon makes the effort well worthwhile. Be careful and attentive while hiking as many spots are slippery with pine needles and loose soil.

# BEST PARKS AND RECREATION AREAS

## WIND CAVE NATIONAL PARK

26611 U.S. 385; 605/745-4600; www.nps.gov/wica

On the surface, Wind Cave National Park, at more than 33,000 acres (13,354 hectares), boasts over 30 miles (48 kilometers) of hiking trails. The mixed-grass prairie ecosystem supports abundant wildlife, including bison, mule deer, white-tailed deer, prairie dogs, pronghorn, wild turkeys, and elk. It is a place where east meets west, where the Great Plains prairie meets the ponderosa pine forest. It's a wonderful area to watch the not infrequent summer thunderstorms cross the plains.

Below the surface, under just 1 square mile (2.5 square kilometers) of the park, lie over 148 miles (238 kilometers) of explored cave passages. Wind

## BEST SOUVENIRS

- No visit to Wall is complete without a piece of **Wall Drug memorabilia,** like a magnet, bumper sticker, or mug.

- **Prairie Edge Trading Company and Galleries** (606 Main St., Rapid City; 605/342-3086 or 800/541-2388; www.prairieedge.com) presents the best in traditional and contemporary Native American art, as well as work by local and regional artists who are not native to the land. It is not to be missed. From drums to dresses and artifacts to jewelry, beadwork, glassware, pottery, quilts, fine art, clothing, art supplies, and unique gift items, this store has it all.

Cave is the third-longest cave in the United States and the seventh-longest cave in the world. Unlike other well-known caves, Wind Cave is not filled with stalactites and stalagmites but rather is famous for its boxwork, an unusual type of speleothem (cave formation) that is made of thin slices of calcite projecting from the cave walls and intersecting with each other in a honeycomb-like fashion. The pattern looks like a collection of diamond and rectangular boxes protruding from the walls and ceilings. Five **cave tours** give you a chance to head into the cool depths of the cave to see these formations.

### BEAR BUTTE STATE PARK

20250 Hwy. 79, Sturgis; 605/347-5240; https://gfp.sd.gov/parks/detail/bear-butte-state-park

Located about 6 miles (9 kilometers) northeast of Stugis off Highway 79, this butte is Mato Paha or "Bear Mountain," a place of prayer for the Lakota people. Hiking, boating, and horseback riding are available in the surrounding state park, but be respectful to the land and the people who hold it sacred. The **Centennial Trail,** Trail #89, is a 111-mile (178-kilometers) trail that starts in the prairies just south of Bear Butte and leads down to **Wind Cave National Park** in the south.

### MISSOURI NATIONAL RECREATIONAL RIVER

508 E. 2nd St., Yankton; 605/665-0209; www.nps.gov/mnrr

In the southeastern corner of South Dakota, the Missouri River forms the state border with Nebraska. Two natural stretches of North America's longest river are preserved as national parkland, separated by **Lewis and Clark Lake.** The **59-Mile District** is located southeast from Yankton and includes the **Historic Meridian Bridge** that crosses from South Dakota to Nebraska. The **39-Mile District** is to the west of Lewis and Clark Lake. Both stretches have access points for paddlers. There are also more than 40 miles (64 kilometers) of trails in and around the city of Yankton, including along the riverfront.

# FESTIVALS AND EVENTS

## STURGIS MOTORCYCLE RALLY

Sturgis; www.sturgismotorcyclerally.com; Aug.

The Sturgis Motorcycle Rally is the biggest event in South Dakota, doubling

STURGIS MOTORCYCLE RALLY

the population of the state for the first full week of August (the first Saturday of the month and the subsequent week). There are races and poker runs and daily rides into the hills. Every motorcycle manufacturer in the world is there, from the smallest custom bike creator to Harley-Davidson. At night, there are world-class concerts.

## OGLALA NATION WACIPI RODEO AND FAIR

Powwow Grounds, Pine Ridge Reservation; 605/455-2685; Aug.

The Oglala Nation Wacipi Rodeo and Fair is held the first weekend in August and includes powwows and the rodeo. The powwow is a community celebration and dance competition. Be sure to be on time for the grand entry, which is the opening ceremony for the powwow. It is a swirl of color and movement as contestants from each dance category enter the powwow grounds. The dances are performed to drums, and the dancers are judged on their poise, footwork, demeanor, and showmanship. The powwow is held outside, and chairs are not provided, so bring something to sit on.

## LAURA INGALLS WILDER PAGEANT

De Smet; www.desmetpageant.org; July

Fans of Laura Ingalls Wilder's *Little House* books will remember De Smet

as the *Little Town on the Prairie* where Almanzo Wilder courted Laura. Since 1971, the town has celebrated its connection to Wilder with an annual outdoor performance of a story from one of her books.

# BEST FOOD

## CHUCKWAGON DINNERS

A decidedly Western phenomenon, the chuckwagon dinner and show generally features music, corny jokes, and food served as diners walk through a line, plates in hand. Traditional chuckwagon food includes sliced barbecue beef or baked chicken with potatoes, beans, and biscuits and honey. In Custer State Park, chuckwagon dinners and hayrides are offered nightly at **Blue Bell Lodge** (25453 Hwy. 87; 605/255-4531 or 888/875-0001; www.custerresorts. com).

# MAJOR AIRPORTS

- **Rapid City Regional Airport:** RAP; 4550 Terminal Rd., Rapid City; 605/394-4195; www.rapairport.com
- **Sioux Falls Regional Airport:** 2801 Jaycee Lane, Sioux Falls; 605/336-0762; www.sfairport.com

# MORE INFORMATION

## TRAVEL AND TOURISM INFORMATION

- **South Dakota Department of Tourism:** www.travelsd.com
- **South Dakota Department of Game, Fish and Parks:** https://gfp.sd.gov

## MAGAZINES

- *South Dakota Magazine:* www. southdakotamagazine.com

OGLALA NATION WACIPI RODEO AND FAIR

# NEBRASKA

The wide, slow Platte River defines much of Nebraska, with its main artery of I-80 following it through a good portion of the state. This land of the Pawnee, Cheyenne, Oglala, Sicangu, Oceti Sakowin, Oohenumpa, Jiwere, Yankton, and Omaha people provided water and grass for westward settlers in the 1800s, with many homesteaders calling it their own.

Today, vibrant cities have added to the natural landscapes that have always made Nebraska a beautiful place to visit. Omaha offers many cultural institutions and a lively restaurant and nightlife scene, while Lincoln is a lively and multicultural college town. But as the sandhill cranes that flock here every spring seem to know, the natural setting—with more miles of river than any other state and parks preserving rock formations and natural history—makes Nebraska a special place. It won't take visitors long to see why the state motto is "The Good Life."

AREA: 77,421 square miles / 200,519 square kilometers (16th)

POPULATION: 1,934,408 (37th)

STATEHOOD DATE: March 1, 1867 (37th)

STATE CAPITAL: Lincoln

RESTORED WAGONS ON THE OLD OREGON TRAIL AT SCOTTS BLUFF NATIONAL MONUMENT

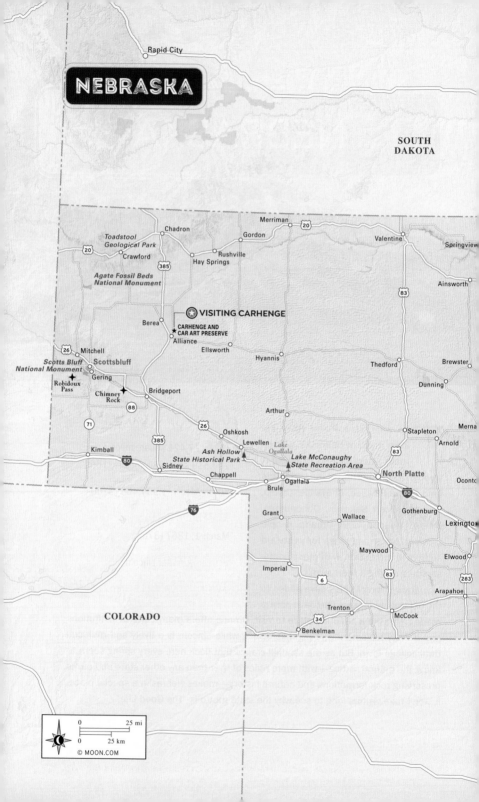

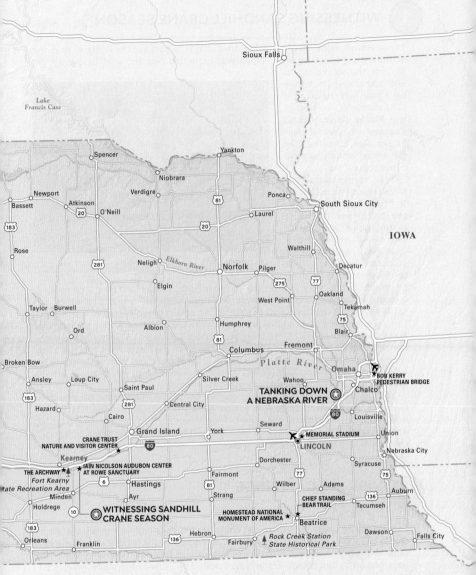

# TOP 3

## 1   WITNESSING SANDHILL CRANE SEASON

The seasonal migration of sandhill cranes along the banks of the Platte River is one of the most popular sights in Nebraska, attracting bird and wildlife lovers from all over the world. Up to 500,000 cranes flock here each year, and the 80-mile (130-kilometer) section of the **Platte River** around **Kearney** in central Nebraska sees 80 percent of the entire world's sandhill crane population.

SANDHILL CRANES

Every spring and fall, the birds migrate from Canada to Mexico and back, using the Platte River as a major resting point. Spring (late Feb.-early Apr.) is the biggest event, as the cranes stop for weeks at a time to feed before pushing on; mid-March is the prime season. In fall (mid-Oct.-late Nov.) they stop for only a night or two. Morning and evening, you can catch them flocking together, and some days you'll see thousands of them flying, sheets of white specks in the sky.

To see the birds, you can take a tour with the **Iain Nicolson Audubon Center at Rowe Sanctuary** (44450 Elm Island Rd., Gibbon; 308/468-5282; http://rowe.audubon.org), which is located on a beautiful stretch of the Platte River and has some nice walking trails to explore, or the **Crane Trust Nature and Visitor Center** (9325 S. Alda Rd., Wood River; 308/382-1820; http://cranetrust.org), which also hosts virtual tours for people who'd rather watch from home.

You can also check out the cranes on your own by heading to the northeastern corner of **Fort Kearny State Recreation Area.** The bridge over the Platte River makes a perfect spot to spy the cranes. If you time it correctly for the early morning or evening, you'll be able to watch them take off from their night's rest, or fly right over you and gracefully land in the water.

## 2   VISITING CARHENGE

Hwy. 87; 308/762-3569; www.carhenge.com

Out in remote western Nebraska, a circle of cars rises high in the sky like a surrealistic Paleolithic monument. This is Carhenge, 39 vehicles placed in the exact dimensions of the original Stonehenge in southern England. This remote site was dreamed up by Jim Reinders, who was inspired by Stonehenge while living in England. It's a strange experience to wander around the gray cars on the prairie, but around 60,000 visitors come each year. Nearby, the **Car Art Preserve** outdoor gallery holds additional car sculptures, like a Conestoga wagon and a spawning salmon. The **Pit Stop Gift Shop** offers plenty of postcards and other souvenirs.

CARHENGE

## TANKING DOWN A NEBRASKA RIVER

The unique Nebraska activity of tanking is floating down a river with your friends and family in a giant stock feed tank. Yes, that's right: Sitting inside a circular buoyant livestock watering tank, with benches for seating and room in the middle for a cooler, has become a favorite local way to float alongside the plains. Each tank holds 3-8 people, and you get a paddle to help with steering. This affords a slow, calm ride, great for all ages. With the most river miles in the United States, Nebraska has plenty of places to float. Here are a few of the various companies around the state.

LIVESTOCK WATERING TANKS FLOATING DOWN A NEBRASKA RIVER

- **Dusty Trails** (2617 N. Buffalo Bill Ave., North Platte; 308/530-0048; www.dustytrails.biz) arranges trips on the North Platte River.

- **Tank Down the Elkhorn** (www.tank-down.com) offers trips just outside Omaha.

- In north-central Nebraska, **Calamus Outfitters** (www.calamusoutfitters.com) runs trips on the Calamus River.

# *Best* ROAD TRIP

**DAY 1** Spend the day exploring **Omaha's** downtown and riverfront and popping into one or two of its excellent museums. Have a meal at the **Old Market** district before turning in for the night.

**DAY 2** Nebraska's next biggest city, **Lincoln,** is an hour away. Explore the **Historic Haymarket District,** then drive an hour south of town to the **Homestead National Monument of America** to learn about the country's complicated history with the land. Then hike nearby along the wagon ruts at **Rock Creek Station State Historical Park.** From here, wind through Nebraska farmland on rural highways for about 3 hours to reach **Kearney,** where you'll spend the night.

**DAY 3** If it's spring, get up early to see the sandhill cranes at **Fort Kearny State Recreation Area,** which is a good place to stroll any time of year. Otherwise, head 2 hours away to **North Platte** to spend a few lazy hours tanking down the **North Platte River.** Stay overnight in North Platte.

**DAY 4** Continue west on I-80 to U.S. 26 to **Ash Hollow State Historical Park,** where you can check out deep wagon ruts on **Windlass Hill.** From there, head to the only-in-Nebraska roadside attraction, **Carhenge.** Afterward, make your way back to I-80 so you don't miss viewing the iconic Oregon Trail landmark, **Chimney Rock.** From there, head to **Scottsbluff** for the evening, making sure to try a *runza,* Nebraska's signature sandwich, at **Gering Bakery.**

**DAY 5** In the morning, drive to **Scotts Bluff National Monument** to hike on the actual Oregon Trail. Later, drive 1 hour north to see **Agate Fossil Beds National Monument.** Spend another night in Scottsbluff or start heading east back to **Omaha,** a 7-hour drive.

OMAHA'S OLD MARKET

BARN AT ROCK CREEK STATION

SCOTTS BLUFF NATIONAL MONUMENT

## ORIENTATION

Nebraska's two biggest cities are located in the eastern part of the state: **Omaha** sits on the Missouri River, which forms the state boundary with Iowa, and **Lincoln** is an hour southwest. The main road corridor of **I-80** crosses the vast plains, following the Platte River through much of the state.

## WHEN TO GO

Nebraska, like most of the Great Plains, has extreme climates: It's cold in **winter,** averaging 35°F (2°C) and prone to blizzards, and humid and hot in the high season of **summer,** with an average temperature of 85°F (29°C). **Spring** and **fall** are likely to have comfortable temperatures, but you'll always run the risk of an early or late snowstorm. Summers see big thunderstorms—a memorable sight across the expansive prairie—and occasional tornadoes. Bird-watchers will want to come in spring, when **sandhill cranes** stop in Nebraska during their annual migration.

# HIGHLIGHTS

## OMAHA MUSEUMS

Among Omaha's many attractions, its museums rank near the top. The **Durham Museum** (801 S. 10th St.; 402/444-5071; https://durhammuseum.org) showcases the history of the region in Union Station, a gorgeous art deco former railway station that alone is worth a visit. The **Great Plains Black History Museum** (2221 N. 24th St.; 402/932-7077; https://gpblackhistorymuseum.org) is dedicated to the history of Black Americans in the region. The **Joslyn Art Museum** (2200 Dodge St.; 402/342-3300; www.joslyn.org) is a fine arts museum with wide holdings spanning Greek pottery, Impressionist works, modern and contemporary art, and an excellent collection of American art that includes the art of the American West.

Although not strictly a museum per se, Omaha's **Henry Doorly Zoo and Aquarium** (3701 S. 10th St.; 402/733-8400; www.omahazoo.com) also offers chances to learn, with exhibits showcasing the ecosystems of the world, most notably the world's largest indoor desert. The headquarters and main visitor center for the **Lewis & Clark National Historic Trail** (601 Riverfront Dr.; 402/661-1804; www.nps.gov/lecl), which winds through the Great Plains and is ubiquitous in the region's tourism, is also located in Omaha, right next to the Missouri River that the expedition followed. If you need to stretch your legs after visiting all these

JOSLYN ART MUSEUM

**OMAHA:** Located on the banks of the Missouri River, Nebraska's largest city boasts a vibrant downtown and riverfront area, a world-class zoo, and a diverse array of museums.

**LINCOLN:** Nebraska's capital is the home of the University of Nebraska and a multicultural population, drawn by its reputation as a refugee-friendly city.

museums, try strolling across the **Bob Kerry Pedestrian Bridge** next to the visitor center or getting a bite to eat at the **Old Market** (1100 Howard St.; 402/916-1769; https://oldmarket.com), a historic entertainment district near the Durham Museum.

## HISTORIC HAYMARKET DISTRICT

Lincoln; https://lincolnhaymarket.org

Like Omaha's Old Market, the **Historic Haymarket District** is where history is given new lease in the form of restaurants, shops, nightlife, and galleries. The district is named for the original market square that sprang up here in 1867 to sell wagons, tools, and hay to local farmers. Spend an afternoon or evening strolling the repurposed warehouses for great dining and shopping options. The district's center is at **Bill Harris Iron Horse Park** (7th St. and Q St.), where visitors can see a

LINCOLN'S HISTORIC HAYMARKET DISTRICT

three-dimensional brick mural of a locomotive train chugging along; it rises up from the brick wall like a relief, creating the illusion that the train is emerging from the wall. The depicted train is from 1870, the first into Lincoln on Independence Day. The small brick-laid park also has an 1890s water tower, now a fountain, and actual trains in back—see a restored Chicago, Burlington and Quincy Railroad (CB&Q) steam engine beside the old Burlington Northern Railroad depot.

## SPEEDWAY MOTORS MUSEUM OF AMERICAN SPEED

599 Oakcreek Dr., Lincoln; 402/323-3166; www.museumofamericanspeed.com

Dedicated to all things racing, this museum is for car lovers. See galleries dedicated to racecars old and new, engines, historic figures in racing, and even toy cars in this 150,000-square-foot (13,935-square-meter) space.

## HOMESTEAD NATIONAL MONUMENT OF AMERICA

8523 W. Hwy. 4, Beatrice; 402/223-3514; www.nps.gov/home

This national monument is dedicated to the history of homesteading, which, spurred by the Homestead Act of 1862, drew many from the U.S. east coast to head west—including newly arrived immigrants, women, and formerly enslaved people. In offering "free" land, the act had far-reaching consequences for the nation, changing the face of the country. People such as George Washington Carver, Laura Ingalls Wilder, and

COVERED WAGONS AT ROCK CREEK STATION STATE HISTORICAL PARK

Nebraska's beloved author Willa Cather were all homesteaders. The act remained in effect until 1976—the last claim was filed in 1974 in Alaska.

The monument is spread out over 150 acres (60 hectares), encompassing prairie grass and woodlands. Start at the **Homestead Heritage Center,** which has exhibits on the impacts of homesteading. The uniquely shaped building is meant to look like a plow cutting through the thick sod, and it points west across the prairie, offering visitors beautiful views of the restored tallgrass ecosystem out of its big glass windows. Don't skip the thoughtful and award-winning film *Land of Dreams— Homesteading America,* which gives voice to Native American nations who were displaced by the act and discusses the continuing reverberations.

## ROCK CREEK STATION STATE HISTORICAL PARK

57426 710th Rd., Fairbury; 402/729-5777; www. outdoornebraska.gov/rockcreekstation

Built in 1857, this barn and cabin served as a **Pony Express station** during the 18 months the service ran in 1860-1861. These old buildings likely would've fallen into the past if it weren't for a shootout that occurred here in the spring of 1859 between the owner, David McCanles, and one James Butler Hickok, who soon became known as "Wild Bill" Hickok. The event left McCanles dead and spurred Hickok's career as a legendary gunfighter— though the fight may not have been fair, as McCanles was likely unarmed.

Today the site is the Rock Creek Station State Historical Park, where you can see reconstructed buildings that include the Pony Express station, a barn, a bunkhouse, and a few cabins. Get a map for a self-guided tour from the **visitors center,** then hike your way up the hill to wander past the buildings and some covered wagons, and along ruts from wagons plying the Oregon Trail.

## ASH HOLLOW STATE HISTORICAL PARK

4055 U.S. 26, Lewellen; www.outdoornebraska. gov/ashhollow

This park is split into two sections. At the **Windlass Hill** site, you'll find a sod house (a common shelter used by homesteaders built from the main material available in the area, sod), a giant metal wagon with informational kiosks, and a paved trail that takes you up the hill to see ruts. The 0.5-mile (0.8-kilometer) loop takes 30 minutes to hike and offers excellent views of the hilly terrain that wagons conquered on their way down into the valley—deep ruts and gorges are visible along the trail, and a stone monument at the top marks where the **Oregon Trail** passes.

The rest of the Ash Hollow site is 2.5 miles (4 kilometers) north of Windlass Hill on U.S. 26. Turn right into the gate to find the **visitors center** at the top of the hill. From the center, a short walk takes you to a prehistoric cave and archaeological dig site; the "cave" is more of a rocky overhang, but is worth a visit to see the dig site and prehistoric tools displayed there, proof of early Americans as long ago as 9,000 years.

## CHIMNEY ROCK

### U.S. 26

The spire of Chimney Rock, at a height of 325 feet (99 meters) from its base, stands tall over the prairie. A remnant of volcanic ash and clay left from ancient floods and weathering, it's the most mentioned landmark of the Oregon, California, and Mormon Trails, capturing the imagination of pioneer traveling west year after year and recorded in hundreds of diaries. For westward travelers during the days of U.S. expansion, the rock and the spring at its base offered a nice spot to camp, and emigrants made sure to mark their names here. Today, you can only see Chimney Rock from a distance; in order to preserve it, there is no access or trail to it. Road-trippers can easily identify it from the highway, but for a better look go to the **Chimney Rock Visitor Center** (9822 County Rd. 75; www.nps. gov/places/000/chimney-rock-national-historic-site.htm), which has telescopes pointed right at the rock.

## AGATE FOSSIL BEDS NATIONAL MONUMENT

### 308/665-4113; www.nps.gov/agfo

FOSSILS IN THE MUSEUM AT AGATE FOSSIL BEDS NATIONAL MONUMENT

One of the most remote national park sites is in the Panhandle of eastern Nebraska. Agate Fossil Beds National Monument is small but packs a big punch for those interested in fossils, prehistoric mammals, or big prairie views. This site, encompassing massive deathbeds of prehistoric creatures, was a rich land for fossil hunters of the 1880s, when the study of paleontology was booming. Many of the larger fossil specimens are now preserved at institutions such as Harvard University and the Smithsonian. A small but excellent museum is at the national monument, and two interpretive trails allow you to see fossils in situ and enjoy beautiful views.

# BEST SCENIC DRIVES

## ROBIDOUX PASS

Until Mitchell Pass opened in 1851, westward settlers used Robidoux Pass to get through the hills around what's now Scotts Bluff National Monument. Robidoux's route was named for a Frenchman who opened a trading post along the way; many emigrant diaries mention the post and the blacksmith services offered there. Today, you can drive out to Robidoux's Trading Post. It's a beautiful scenic drive; you'll leave the plains and enter the foothills, with grassy bluffs flecked by pine trees surrounding you.

Starting at **Scotts Bluff National Monument,** head toward Gering on K Road, the Old Oregon Trail. In 1 mile (1.6 kilometers), turn right onto Five Rocks Road. Follow this road, which becomes County Road 21 and then Highway 71, for 2.5 miles (4 kilometers). Turn right onto Carter Canyon Road, continuing away from town and into hills for 8 miles (12.9 kilometers)—you'll see the **trading post** on your right. There isn't much to do at the post, but you'll find some trail ruts with historical markers, reconstructions of the trade buildings, and possibly some rattlesnakes. The last 2 miles (3.2 kilometers) of the route are on dirt roads, which can get muddy and treacherous after a rainstorm, so use caution. The drive takes about 20 minutes one-way.

# BEST PARKS AND RECREATION AREAS

## CHIEF STANDING BEAR TRAIL

Trailhead at 577 Perkins St., Beatrice

Chief Standing Bear Trail is a rails-to-trails line that runs 22.9 miles (37 kilometers) south of Beatrice to the Nebraska-Kansas state line, where it connects to the Blue River Rail Trail, which runs another 12 miles (19 kilometers) south to Marysville, Kansas. Leaving Beatrice, the trail is a well-maintained path that rolls over farmland, under the shade of trees, over bridges, and through prairie grasses. A rest area with picnic shelters, water, and restrooms is located at Holmesville, about 7 miles (11.3 kilometers) down the trail. While there aren't any bike rental options in Beatrice, you can easily walk or run the trail.

The trail is named for Chief Standing Bear of the Ponca Tribe, which owns it today. In 1877 the U.S. Cavalry evicted the Ponca people from their home in northern Nebraska near the Niobrara River. They were forced to walk 200 miles (320 kilometers) to a reservation in Oklahoma, only to find unsuitable conditions when they arrived. One-third of the group died within 18 months from sickness, cold, and poor nutrition. Historical signs and interpretive panels are posted along the trail, allowing visitors to dig deeper into the history of Chief Standing Bear and the Ponca Tribe.

## FORT KEARNY STATE RECREATION AREA

1020 V. Rd., Kearney; 308/865-5305; http://outdoornebraska.gov/fortkearnysra

Adjoining the Fort Kearny State Historical Park and jointly administered, Fort Kearny State Recreation Area offers a bevy of outdoor recreation options. It has seven artificial groundwater lakes with sandy shores. Find swimming and a sandy beach at **Lake 7,** which has restrooms and a picnic shelter. The Fort Kearny hike-bike trail begins here and heads north over the **Platte River** for 1.8 miles (2.8 kilometers). It follows an old portion of the Burlington and Missouri River Railroad. A nice destination from here is **The Archway,** which spans I-80, about 4 miles (6.4 kilometers) away. The recreation area is also popular for viewing sandhill cranes during the spring migration season; the cranes spend the night on the shallow Platte River.

## LAKE MCCONAUGHY STATE RECREATION AREA

1475 Hwy. 61 N.; 308/284-8800; www.outdoornebraska.gov/lakemcconaughy

You may not think of white-sand beaches when you think of Nebraska, but the

KITEBOARDING LAKE MCCONAUGHY

state's largest reservoir, Lake McConaughy—called "Big Mac"—has miles of them. At 22 miles (35 kilometers) long and 4 miles (6.5 kilometers) wide, the lake stretches across 30,500 surface acres (12,342 hectares) with over 100 miles (160 kilometers) of shoreline. Fish grow to trophy sizes, with many state records won on these shores. Just east and adjacent to Lake McConaughy is **Lake Ogallala**, a smaller recreational area with about 5 miles (8 kilometers) of shoreline and great fishing. The **visitors center** has exhibits on the Platte River, the local watershed, and Kingsley Dam. Public restrooms, fishing licenses, and camping information are here as well.

## SCOTTS BLUFF NATIONAL MONUMENT

190276 Old Oregon Trail, Gering; 308/436-9700; www.nps.gov/scbl

Settlers traveling west encountered Scotts Bluff after making it through the flat valley around the North Platte River, forcing them to find a route through the rocky formations. Early travelers found one via Robidoux Pass, a few miles south, but by the 1850s pioneers created an easier road through Mitchell Pass. Scotts Bluff National Monument encompasses Scotts Bluff and South Bluff, bisected by **Mitchell Pass.** The road through the monument takes you through Mitchell Pass, following the path of the Oregon Trail. This is a fantastic place to enjoy some history, hikes, and great views.

TOADSTOOL GEOLOGICAL PARK

Just outside the **visitors center** are wagons that look ready to roll away to Oregon—these restored beauties are on the old Oregon Trail itself. From here you can take a short 1-mile (1.6-kilometer) round-trip walk that takes about 30 minutes. Once the paved path transitions to dirt, you're hiking on the actual Oregon Trail. There are big swales where the roadbed can be seen. Wagons would travel single file through the bluffs at this point, where it was called Mitchell Pass. Soon you'll be back on asphalt, and the old trail will be marked by wooden posts.

## TOADSTOOL GEOLOGICAL PARK

FS Road 902 near Crawford

This remote park in the northwest corner of Nebraska features unique geological features. Among hills reminiscent of the Badlands are wrinkled rock formations with caps like mushrooms that give the park its name. Three trails ranging in length from 1 to 6 miles round-trip allow appreciation of these natural sculptures of clay and sandstone. There's also a primitive campground but no water.

# FESTIVALS AND EVENTS

## NEBRASKALAND DAYS

Wild West Arena, North Platte; 308/532-7939; www.nebraskalanddays.com; June

The state's biggest celebration, NEBRASKAland Days is held during the third week of June for four nights of rodeo fun, live country music featuring top performers, and parades. The **Buffalo Bill Rodeo** is the main event; started in 1882 by the man himself, it's the oldest spectator rodeo in the country.

## CORNHUSKERS FOOTBALL

Memorial Stadium, 1 Memorial Stadium Dr., Lincoln; 402/472-3111; www.huskers.com; Sept.-Nov.

Each fall, the city of Lincoln turns red in support of Cornhuskers Football. The University of Nebraska's football team

# BEST SOUVENIRS

In Nebraska, souvenir shopping is often less about what you buy and more about where you buy them.

- From its Western-style facade and boardwalk to the Nebraska T-shirts and souvenirs for sale, **Stagecoach** (310 3rd Ave., Kearney; 308/234-3313; https://stagecoachgifts.biz) is deliciously kitschy. Find a fantastic selection of jewelry handcrafted by Native American artists with beautiful and complicated inlaid patterns. Look for the unique Sonoran Gold turquoise, which has a deep-green color with gold accents.

- The **Grain Bin Antique Town** (10641 S. Old Hwy. 82 Rd., North Platte; 308/539-7401; www.grainbinantiquetown.com) has 13 repurposed circular grain bins and one giant red barn, all holding unknown antique treasures. Each bin is roughly themed so you know where to look for teacups or vintage signs, while the barn has high-quality vintage crystal, furniture, and stone crockery.

hosts a series of home games each year that turn Memorial Stadium into the state's third-largest city with 90,000 attendees—all, inevitably, wearing red. Every game is usually sold out; check for tickets a month or two ahead of time.

# BEST FOOD

Steak and barbecue are common in Nebraska, as they are in the west and Great Plains, but the state lays claim to a sandwich all its own.

## RUNZA

A beloved sandwich that only Nebraskans have heard of, the *runza* is a legacy of German-Russian immigrants in the 18th century. It's a hoagie-shaped sandwich made of fluffy yeast dough filled with spiced beef, cabbage, and onions. In Kansas it's known as a *bierock* and comes in a bun shape rather than the longer *runza*.

Today, the sandwich owes its popularity to a Lincoln-based fast-food chain, also called **Runza** (in fact, the company trademarked the name). The chain, perhaps the only one to popularize cabbage, makes their sandwiches fresh every day from bread baked in-store, seasoned beef, and freshly chopped kraut. For a different version, try the **Gering Bakery** (1446 10th St., Gering; 308/436-5500; www.geringbakery.com), on the west side of the state, where it goes by the name "cabbage burger."

## MAJOR AIRPORTS

- **Eppley Airfield:** OMA; 4501 Abbott Dr., Omaha; 402/661-8017; www.flyomaha.com

- **Lincoln Airport:** LNK; 2400 W. Adams St., Lincoln; 402/458-2480; www.lincolnairport.com

## MORE INFORMATION

### TRAVEL AND TOURISM INFORMATION

- **Visit Nebraska:** www.visitnebraska.com

- **Nebraska Game and Parks:** http://outdoornebraska.gov

# KANSAS

On the land of a number of Indigenous nations, including the Pawnee, Osage, Kansa, Arapaho, Cheyenne, Comanche, Kiowa, Shawnee, and Wichita, Kansas sits at the heart of the heartland, with the halfway point between New York and San Francisco in Kinsley, Kansas. Broken treaties, an adamantly free state stance, and a landmark civil rights case are all part of the history of this state.

**AREA:** 82,277 square miles / 213,096 square kilometers (15th)

**POPULATION:** 2,913,314 (35th)

**STATEHOOD DATE:**
January 29, 1861 (35th)

**STATE CAPITAL:** Topeka

Today, Kansas encompasses tallgrass prairie, landforms of an ancient seabed, wetlands, and vibrant cities. Its gentle plains invite closer examination, and you may be surprised at what you see: a fossil embedded in a rock formation, a mural painted in a doorway, a field bursting with sunflowers.

SUNFLOWER FIELD AT SUNSET

## ORIENTATION

The main metro areas of Kansas—**Wichita, Kansas City,** and **Topeka**—are all in the eastern part of the state. **Dodge City** and the Niobara chalk outcroppings at **Little Jerusalem Badlands State Park** are located in rural and arid western Kansas.

## WHEN TO GO

**Late spring-early fall** is the most popular season to travel in Kansas, avoiding the state's brutal winters, when temperatures can get below 20°F (-7°C).

# HIGHLIGHTS

## WICHITA MURALS

Wichita boasts more than 100 murals and public art installations throughout the city. Most are concentrated in the 3-mile-long (4.8-kilometer) **Douglas Design District** (E. Douglas Ave. between Washington and Oliver St.), where you can find art deco-y *Strength through the Spirit of Growth* (E. Douglas Ave. and Washington St.); a mural that depicts **Gene Simmons, Frankenstein, and Joey Ramone** (E. Douglas Ave. and S. Laura St.); and a colorful rendition of a *Welcome to Wichita* postcard (E. Douglas Ave. between N. Hillside and N. Rutan St). Beyond the

Douglas Design District, the **Beachner Grain Elevator Mural** (519 E. 20th St. N.) holds records for its size and showcases the city's diversity. **Visit Wichita** (www.visitwichita.com) maintains an online map of the city's murals so you can design your own self-guided mural tour.

## EVEL KNIEVEL MUSEUM

2047 SW Topeka Blvd., Topeka; 785/215-6205; www.evelknievelmuseum.com

Topeka's ode to the daredevil motorcycle stuntman is appropriately located next door to a Harley-Davidson dealership. Inside is an incredible collection of dented helmets, costumes, motorcycles, X-rays of broken bones, videos of jumps, and an 18-wheeler. Even those who might not proclaim themselves rabid Evel fans will enjoy the exhibits on his exploits, as well as a virtual reality motorcycle experience.

## MASSACHUSETTS STREET

Lawrence

Abolitionists from Massachusetts founded the city of Lawrence, and the name of its main downtown street attests to that beginning. While many visitors may be drawn to cheer on the University of Kansas Jayhawks, the stretch of Mass Street from U.S. 40 to

MASSACHUSETTS STREET, LAWRENCE

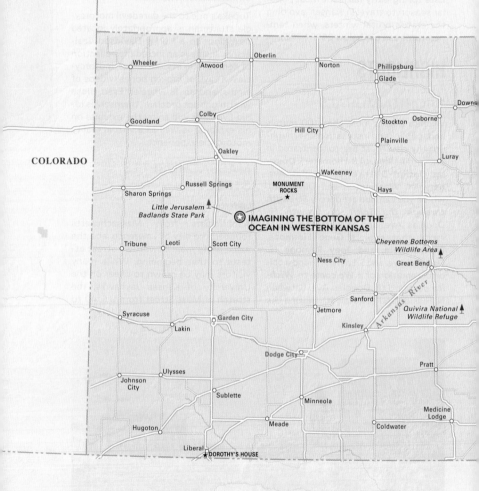

NEBRASKA

Wheeler  Atwood  Oberlin  Norton  Phillipsburg  Glade  Downs

COLORADO

Goodland  Colby  Hill City  Stockton  Osborne

Oakley  Plainville  Luray

WaKeeney

Sharon Springs  Russell Springs  Hays

*Little Jerusalem Badlands State Park*

MONUMENT ROCKS ★

★ **IMAGINING THE BOTTOM OF THE OCEAN IN WESTERN KANSAS**

Tribune  Leoti  Scott City  Ness City

*Cheyenne Bottoms Wildlife Area*

Great Bend

Sanford  *Arkansas River*

Syracuse  Lakin  Garden City  Jetmore  Kinsley  *Quivira National Wildlife Refuge*

Dodge City  Pratt

Ulysses

Johnson City  Sublette  Minneola

Hugoton  Meade  Coldwater  Medicine Lodge

Liberal ★ **DOROTHY'S HOUSE**

0    25 mi
0    25 km
© MOON.COM

TEXAS

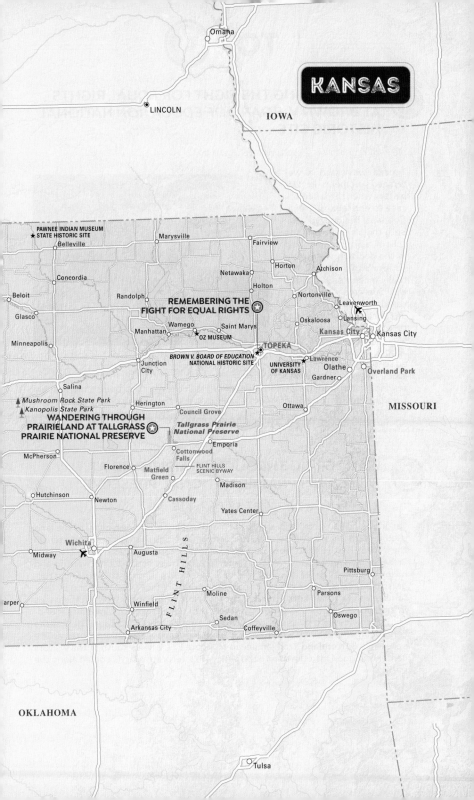

**KANSAS**

Omaha

LINCOLN

IOWA

★ PAWNEE INDIAN MUSEUM
STATE HISTORIC SITE

Belleville          Marysville          Fairview

Concordia                        Netawaka          Horton      Atchison

Holton                  Nortonville      Leavenworth

Beloit      Randolph          **REMEMBERING THE**          Oskaloosa      Lansing
                              **FIGHT FOR EQUAL RIGHTS**
Glasco                                                      Kansas City      Kansas City
                    Wamego      Saint Marys
Minneapolis      Manhattan          OZ MUSEUM                **TOPEKA**

                Junction      *BROWN V. BOARD OF EDUCATION*      Lawrence      Olathe
                City          *NATIONAL HISTORIC SITE*      UNIVERSITY
                                                          OF KANSAS      Gardner      Overland Park
Salina
▲ *Mushroom Rock State Park*          Herington      Council Grove      Ottawa      **MISSOURI**
▲ *Kanopolis State Park*
**WANDERING THROUGH**                *Tallgrass Prairie*
**PRAIRIELAND AT TALLGRASS**          *National Preserve*
**PRAIRIE NATIONAL PRESERVE**
                                    Emporia
McPherson                          Cottonwood
                                    Falls
            Florence      Matfield      *FLINT HILLS*
                        Green      *SCENIC BYWAY*
Hutchinson      Newton          Madison

                    Cassoday      Yates Center

Wichita
Midway              Augusta

                                F
                                L
                                I
                                N
                                T          Pittsburg
Harper                          Moline          Parsons
                                H
                        Winfield      I      Oswego
                                L
                            Sedan      L
                    Arkansas City      S      Coffeyville

**OKLAHOMA**

Tulsa

# TOP 3

## REMEMBERING THE FIGHT FOR EQUAL RIGHTS AT *BROWN V. BOARD OF EDUCATION* NATIONAL HISTORIC SITE

1515 SE Monroe St., Topeka; www.nps.gov/brvb

Topeka witnessed a watershed moment in U.S. history when the landmark case to end legal segregation was decided in 1954. Both the plaintiffs and the school systems involved in the decision were from Topeka, and the case eventually made its way to the U.S. Supreme Court. You can visit the *Brown v. Board of Education* National Historic Site, located in the old Monroe Elementary School, the once-segregated school that the plaintiff, student Linda Brown, at-

*BROWN V. BOARD OF EDUCATION* NATIONAL HISTORIC SITE

tended. Visitors will find galleries and exhibits in the old classrooms that examine the court decision, the Civil Rights Movement, and the history of segregation and education. The kindergarten room reflects its 1954 segregated appearance, and a 30-minute video plays in the old auditorium.

## WANDERING THROUGH PRAIRIELAND AT TALLGRASS PRAIRIE NATIONAL PRESERVE

2480B K-177, Strong City; 620/273-8494; www.nps.gov/tapr

Tallgrass once covered large swaths of North America, but with much of the land used for farming, now only a small fraction remains. See this delicate ecosystem in the Kansas Flint Hills at the 11,000-acre (4,451-hectare) Tallgrass Prairie National Preserve, located between Wichita and Topeka. Trails dedicated to walking and hiking (no bikes, horses, or motorized vehicles) weave through the remaining tallgrass prairieland, where the stalks can grow up to 4-7 feet (1.2-2.1 meters) by September and October. Keep your eye out for bison, who wander freely in the park's **Windmill Pasture** on the **Scenic Overlook Trail** (6.4 miles/10.2 kilometers round-trip). Historic ranch buildings can be viewed on a self-guided tour. The visitors center contains exhibits where you can learn more about the tallgrass prairie. The accessible **Bottomland Trail** (trailhead on Route 227, 2 miles south of the visitors center) is a good introduction to the park with interpretive signs posted along the path.

TALLGRASS PRAIRIE NATIONAL PRESERVE

## ③ IMAGINING THE BOTTOM OF THE OCEAN IN WESTERN KANSAS

Located in western Kansas, **Little Jerusalem Badlands State Park** (off U.S. 83 between Oakley and Scott City; 620/872-2061; https://ksoutdoors.com/State-Parks/Locations/Little-Jerusalem-Badlands) features outcroppings of Niobara chalk in fantastic formations, which are remnants from an ancient inland sea that once covered this area—and much of North America. Impressive from afar, the formations also contain fossils of sea creatures, which are visible in some places. Do not take any that you see—fossil collecting is prohibited, as is climbing on the rocks, in order to preserve this precious natural area. Two hiking trails (0.5-2.5 miles/0.8-4 kilometers) leading to scenic overlooks start from the parking area. Off-trail guided tours are available and require advance reservations.

Nearby, across U.S. 83, another group of chalk outcroppings can be seen at **Monument Rocks Natural Area** (U.S. 83, 20 miles/32 kilometers south of Oakley), where you would be forgiven for thinking that you've been transported to Dover in southern England or Étretat on the Normandy Coast of France. These Chalk Pyramids, another name for Monument Rocks, stand up to 70 feet (21 meters) tall. Although designated as a National Natural Landmark, Monument Rocks is on private property, and reaching them requires driving on unpaved roads, which may become impassable when muddy. Visitors are

MONUMENT ROCKS NATURAL AREA

allowed during the day only and must heed the posted rules—such as prohibitions on climbing the rocks, camping, and collecting fossils.

These two areas are in a remote part of the state, a more than 4-hour drive from Wichita. For accommodations and other services, the town of **Oakley** is about 20 miles north (32 kilometers, 30 minutes), while the larger **Garden City** is 65 miles south (104 kilometers, around 1 hour).

# *Best* ROAD TRIP

**DAY 1**
Start in **Wichita** and spend the day exploring the city, making sure to check out the murals in the **Douglas Design District.**

**DAY 2**
Drive northeast out of the city to **K-177** at Cassoday. Drive through the **Flint Hills,** and walk a trail in the **Tallgrass Prairie National Preserve.** Afterward, head up to **Council Grove**—if you're hungry, stop by **Hays House** (112 W. Main St.; 620/767-5911; www.hayshouse.com), the oldest restaurant west of the Mississippi. **Topeka** is your destination at the end of the day.

TALLGRASS PRAIRIE NATIONAL PRESERVE

**DAY 3**
Split your time today between the capital city and neighboring **Lawrence,** the home of the University of Kansas. Make stops at the *Brown v. Board of Education* National Historic Site and **G's Frozen Custard** in Topeka, and **Mass Street** in Lawrence.

**DAY 4**
This is a driving day. From Topeka, head west to **Dodge City,** a 4.5-hour drive. Just before you reach Dodge City, stop in **Kinsley** to mark the fact that you're halfway between New York and San Francisco.

MONUMENT ROCKS CHALK OUTCROPPINGS

**DAY 5**
From Dodge City, drive out 2 hours to **Little Jerusalem Badlands State Park** and **Monument Rocks,** two sets of scenic and fascinating chalk outcroppings in the middle of the plains. Spend the night in **Garden City.**

**DAY 6**
Head east toward **Wichita,** a 4-hour drive from Garden City. Birders and nature lovers will want to detour to **Cheyenne Bottoms Wildlife Area** or **Quivira National Wildlife Refuge** or both before going back to the city.

QUIVIRA NATIONAL WILDLIFE REFUGE

# *Major* CITIES

**WICHITA:** The Arkansas River flows through Wichita, with the Little and Big Arkansas converging in Midtown, where the town's famous *Keeper of the Plains* statue stands. The biggest city in Kansas blends history with food, entertainment, and a healthy mural scene.

**KANSAS CITY:** The confusing thing about Kansas City, Kansas, is that it shares a name with the much bigger city across the river in Missouri. Nonetheless, it's the third-biggest city in Kansas (after neighboring **Overland Park** in the same metro area), with sights like the Kansas Speedway and Quindaro Townsite, which was a stop on the Underground Railroad.

**TOPEKA:** Once part of the rolling tallgrass prairie that supported herds of bison, the Kansas capital was known for its free-state stance against enslavement in the years leading up to the Civil War, while later its board of education was the defendant in the famous *Brown* case that resulted in the ruling that segregation was illegal. This history is showcased in its museums, while the beautiful parks offer visitors a green look at today's Kansas.

14th Street, with its shops, restaurants, and bars, is the best place to get a feel of the city.

## KINSLEY

Also known as Midway USA, Kinsley sits equidistant (1,561 miles/2,512 kilometers, to be exact) from New York City and San Francisco. Here, you're smack-dab in the middle of the country! A big sign—perfect for a photo—indicates this fact on the grounds of the **Edwards County Historical Society Museum** (U.S.-50/U.S.-56; 620/659-2420; www.edwardscountymuseum.com).

## DODGE CITY

This frontier town in southwest Kansas—the "Dodge" of the adage "get out of Dodge"—was once home to notorious gunfights, cattle drives, and Wyatt Earp. Known as "Hell on the Plains" during its 1800s heyday, Dodge City is now a law-abiding place. You can't see the original Boot Hill Cemetery, where gunslingers were said to be buried, having "died with their boots on"—there's a distillery there now—but you can spend a fun hour or two at **Boot Hill Museum** (500 W. Wyatt Earp Blvd., Dodge City; 620/227-8188; www.boothill.org). It's a re-created Old West town with interactive displays, artifacts, live shows, staged gunfights, building replicas, and a nice souvenir shop.

## PAWNEE INDIAN MUSEUM STATE HISTORIC SITE

**480 Pawnee Trail; 785/361-2255**

The only museum of its kind in Kansas or Nebraska, Pawnee Indian Museum State Historic Site offers a glimpse into day-to-day Pawnee life. In the 19th century, the Pawnee people lived throughout Kansas and Nebraska in villages of dome-shaped earth lodges. In 1875, the Pawnee people ceded their territory in Kansas and Nebraska to the United

PAWNEE INDIAN MUSEUM STATE HISTORIC SITE

# THE WIZARD OF OZ

"We're not in Kansas anymore" is the oft repeated line from the classic film *The Wizard of Oz*. Given that Dorothy and Toto blew away to Oz from a farm in Kansas, it's no surprise that there are Oz-themed sights in the state. For a collection of memorabilia related not only to the film, but also to the L. Frank Baum book and other renditions of the story, such as *The Wiz*, head to the **OZ Museum** (511 Lincoln, Wamego; 866/458-TOTO; https://ozmuseum.com), located about an hour outside Topeka. In the town of Liberal, near the Oklahoma border, a self-styled **Dorothy's House** (567 E. Cedar St., Liberal; www.dorothys-house.com) is a lookalike of Dorothy's Kansas home, and the neighboring **Land of Oz** sets scenes from the movie along a painted yellow brick road.

States, which moved them to reservations in Oklahoma. Today the Pawnee Nation of Oklahoma is a federally recognized government and numbers over 3,200 people who take great pride in their ancestral heritage of rich myths and religious rites, supporting yearly dances and intertribal meetings.

Located in northern Kansas, this site preserves a rare example of an earth lodge from the Kitkahaki band of the Pawnee, who lived in the area. Visitors can step inside the excavated lodge—the museum was built directly over the excavation site, allowing artifacts to be left where they were found. Other items on display include Pawnee star charts, a robe made of bison, and the special not-to-be-photographed Sacred Bundle, which contains ceremonial items wrapped in bison hide, that was passed down through families and donated by a member of the Pawnee Nation. Outside, a nature trail guides you past depressions in the earth where other lodges were located in the village.

## SUNFLOWERS

One of the state's nicknames is the Sunflower State, and taking photos surrounded by blooming sunflowers has become a popular Kansas activity, albeit one that can only be done within a short window of time in late summer. Blooms last about 10-14 days, roughly around the two weeks before and after Labor Day. Located between Kansas City and Topeka, **Grinter's Sunflower Farm** (24154 Stillwell Rd., Lawrence) is the most well-known sunflower field, to the point of causing major traffic

over Labor Day weekend. Western Kansas—Sherman County, in particular—is actually the top sunflower-producing region of the state, though it's a quite a distance from the main population centers in the state.

# BEST SCENIC DRIVES

## FLINT HILLS SCENIC BYWAY

K-177; www.fhwa.dot.gov/byways/byways/2095

This 48-mile (77-kilometer) stretch of K-177 traverses the beautiful Flint Hills, named for the flint that's eroded from the bedrock near the earth's surface. Starting in **Council Grove,** a former frontier stop where travelers made final repairs on their covered wagons before continuing west on the Santa Fe Trail, the drive south passes the **Tallgrass Prairie National Preserve** and small ranching towns like **Cottonwood Falls** and **Matfield Green** before reaching **Cassoday,** the southern end of the scenic byway.

## WETLANDS AND WILDLIFE SCENIC BYWAY

www.fhwa.dot.gov/byways/byways/59011

This drive northwest of Wichita weaves through small country roads to join **Quivira National Wildlife Refuge** (www.fws.gov/refuge/quivira) and **Cheyenne Bottoms Wildlife Area** (56

MUSHROOM ROCK STATE PARK

NE 40 Rd., Great Bend; 620/793-7730; www.ksoutdoors.com) two major wetlands for migratory birds, such as sandhill and whooping cranes.

# BEST PARKS AND RECREATION AREAS

## KANOPOLIS STATE PARK

200 Horsethief Rd., Marquette; 785/546-2565; www.ksoutdoors.com/kanopolis-state-park

Set on the northeast shore of Kanopolis Reservoir, the first state park in Kansas offers nearly 30 miles (48 kilometers) of trails through canyons and prairieland. The nearby **Mushroom Rock State Park,** under the same management, features a formation shaped like its eponymous fungus.

# FESTIVALS AND EVENTS

## AMERICAN ROYAL WORLD SERIES OF BARBECUE

Kansas City; www.americanroyal.com/bbq; Sept./Oct.

Kansas City, Missouri, may get a big share of the attention around Kansas City barbecue, but it's Kansas City, Kansas, that hosts an epic barbecue competition. Held in the fall at the **Kansas Speedway** (400 Speedway Blvd.; www.

kansasspeedway.com), the American Royal World Series of Barbecue draws contestants from all over the country in a celebration of this smoke-filled culinary artform.

## UNIVERSITY OF KANSAS SPORTS

Lawrence; https://kuathletics.com

The sports teams at the University of Kansas, known as the Jayhawks, are a huge draw for the college town of Lawrence. Fans crowd the city whenever there's a home game during the fall football season. Basketball is also big. Plan ahead if you want to see a game.

STADIUM ON THE CAMPUS OF THE UNIVERSITY OF KANSAS

## SOUVENIRS AND COLLECTIBLES

Topeka is an antiques lover's paradise, with dozens of stores offering hidden treasures. Here are a few good spots:

- **Washburn View Antique Mall:** 1507 SW 21st St.; 785/233-3733; www.washburnviewantiquemall.com
- **Brickhouse Antiques:** 3711 SW Burlingame Rd.; 785/266-6000; www.brickhouseantiquestopeka.com
- **Wheatland Antique Mall:** 2905 SW 29th St., Suite A; 785/272-4222

# BEST FOOD

### BROWN BREAD FROZEN CUSTARD

Brown Bread frozen custard at **G's Frozen Custard** (1301 SW 6th Ave., Topeka; 785/234-3480; https://gsfrozencustard.com) is a local Topeka tradition that harks back to the Victorian era. While you're there, the other homemade flavors are delicious, too.

### *BIEROCKS*

The Kansas cousin to Nebraska's *runza,* the *bierock* is a sandwich filled with savory meats served on a bun. Try one at

**Josey Baking Co.** (3119 SW Huntoon St., Topeka; 785/408-1552).

### PIZZA HUT

www.pizzahut.com

The first location of the nation-wide Pizza Hut chain was located in Wichita. That building is now a **museum** (www.wichita.edu/museums/pizzahutmuseum) on the Wichita State University campus. Although you can't get Pizza Hut pizza at the museum, there are several locations in Wichita, including at the campus student center.

# MAJOR AIRPORTS

- **Wichita Dwight D. Eisenhower National Airport:** ICT; 2277 Eisenhower Airport Parkway, Wichita; www.flywichita.com
- **Kansas City International Airport:** KCI; 1 International Square, Kansas City, MO; www.flykci.com

# MORE INFORMATION

### TRAVEL AND TOURISM INFORMATION

- **Kansas Tourism:** www.travelks.com
- **Kansas Wildlife, Parks & Tourism:** https://ksoutdoors.com

BIEROCKS

# OKLAHOMA

From 1828 to 1887, the U.S. government began a series of forced migrations that took Indigenous people off their traditional lands and onto the Trail of Tears to walk to the "Indian Territory"—what eventually became the state of Oklahoma. These resulted in relocating 67 tribes to Oklahoma; today, 39 nations are within Oklahoma's borders. In 1887, the federal government passed the Dawes Act, opening up nearly 2 million acres (809,370 hectares) of land to white settlement.

During the Great Depression, the Dust Bowl saw more than 200,000 survivors use Route 66 to escape poverty.

This history can be seen throughout the state, in museums and cultural centers and along the state's preserved sections of Route 66. And history continues to be made here. In 2020, the Supreme Court ruled that almost half of the state was within a Native American reservation—in a different trajectory from what had taken place for much of U.S. history, the court upheld treaties that promised lands to the Five Tribes, which are the Cherokee, Chickasaw, Choctaw, Muscogee (Creek), and Seminole people.

AREA: 69,898 square miles / 181,034 kilometers (20th)

POPULATION: 3,956,971 (28th)

STATEHOOD DATE: November 16, 1907 (46th)

STATE CAPITAL: Oklahoma City

BISON IN THE WICHITA MOUNTAINS

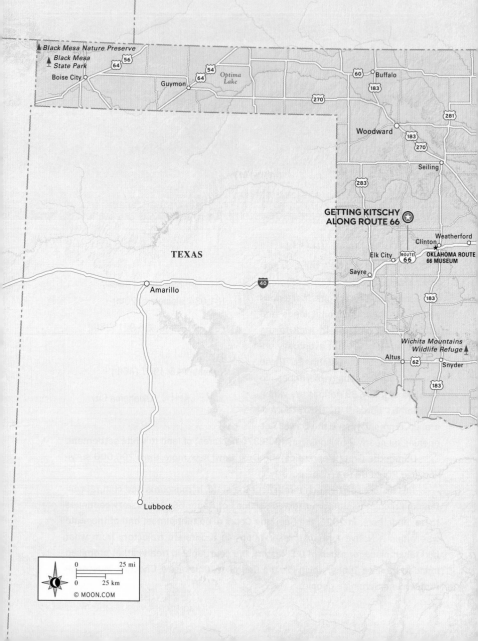

# OKLAHOMA

COLORADO

KANSAS

▲ Black Mesa Nature Preserve
   ▲ Black Mesa
      State Park
Boise City ○          56
                 64
              54
          64      Optima
                   Lake            60    Buffalo
      Guymon                              183
                         270
                                    281

                              Woodward    183
                                          270

                                     Seiling

                              283

                    **GETTING KITSCHY
                    ALONG ROUTE 66** ✪
                                        Weatherford
                                    Clinton ★
TEXAS                          Elk City  ROUTE  **OKLAHOMA ROUTE
                                         66      66 MUSEUM**
                              Sayre
                    40
Amarillo

                                   *Wichita Mountains
                                   Wildlife Refuge* ▲
                              Altus   62
                                         Snyder  183

                                          183

○ Lubbock

0          25 mi
0          25 km
© MOON.COM

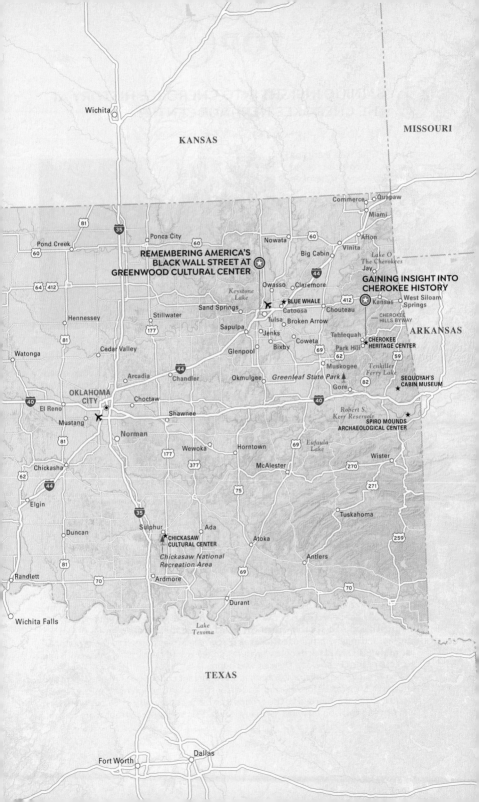

## 1 GAINING INSIGHT INTO CHEROKEE HISTORY AT THE CHEROKEE HERITAGE CENTER

21192 S. Keeler Dr., Park Hill; 918/456-6007; www.cherokeeheritage.org

At the Cherokee Heritage Center, two re-created villages show Cherokee life at different historical periods. The centerpiece is **Diligwa,** a reproduction of an early 18th-century Cherokee village, where guides describe the traditions and daily lives of the Cherokee people from that time. **Adams Corner Rural Village** illustrates life in the 1890s with dwellings, such as a log cabin, and town buildings, including a general store and a church. Inside the **Trail of Tears**

CHEROKEE HERITAGE CENTER

**Exhibit,** six galleries trace the history of the forced removal of the Cherokee people from Tennessee, Georgia, and Alabama in the 1830s. In addition to these interpretive exhibits, the center holds an archive Cherokee historical documents and artifacts, and the Cherokee Family Research Center, where people with Cherokee ancestry can research their genealogy.

## 2 REMEMBERING AMERICA'S BLACK WALL STREET AT GREENWOOD CULTURAL CENTER

322 N. Greenwood Ave., Tulsa; 918/596-1020; www.greenwoodculturalcenter.com

Booker T. Washington referred to Tulsa's **Greenwood District** as America's "Black Wall Street." The 35-block area was once a vibrant community with the wealthiest Black neighborhoods in the South. Not only was it a hotbed of jazz and blues in the 1920s, but it also housed more than 300 Black-owned businesses, from theaters and restaurants to hotels and law offices.

The Greenwood District was thrust in the national spotlight in June 1921, when one of the nation's worst acts of racial violence broke out. The **Tulsa Race Riot** was instigated by a rumor that a Black man had assaulted a white woman. No one knew what really happened, but as the story spread through the town, an angry white mob gathered and set the Greenwood District on fire. After 16 hours of rioting, looting, and mayhem, hundreds died as Black Wall Street burned to the ground. An estimated 10,000 Black people were left homeless, and nearly all of the wealth and success of the Greenwood District was gone.

The Greenwood Cultural Center has an important collection of memorabilia and photos of the area before, during, and after the riot. Although most of the Greenwood District was burned to the ground, the Black community of Tulsa persevered and opened thriving businesses, many located just down the street from the cultural center.

SIGN LISTING BLACK-OWNED BUSINESSES THAT ONCE STOOD IN TULSA'S GREENWOOD DISTRICT

## ③ GETTING KITSCHY ALONG ROUTE 66

Oklahoma has more drivable miles of Route 66 than any other state. The original alignment of Route 66 entered the state at the Kansas border and continued through Quapaw, Commerce, and Miami, a stretch of Route 66 primarily labeled U.S. 69. Once you hit Afton, the road becomes U.S. 60/69 into Vinita, then is mostly labeled Route 66 into Tulsa, Oklahoma City, and beyond. Running between **Miami** and **Afton,** the 1922 **Sidewalk Highway** is one of the oldest still drivable roadbeds on Route 66. In **Catoosa,** you can check out an oddball roadside attraction, the **Blue Whale** (2680 N. SR-66, Catoosa; www.travelok.com/listings/view.profile/id.653). Spend a few hours in **Tulsa** soaking up the **art deco architecture.** In **Arcadia,** you can browse the selection of 600 sodas at **Pop's** (660 SR-66, Arcadia; 405/928-7677; www.pops66.com), and see an honest-to-goodness **Round Barn** (107 SR-66, Arcadia; 405/396-0824; www.arcadiaroundbarn.org). One of the most popular Route 66 museums along the entire Chicago-to-Santa Monica drive is the **Oklahoma Route 66 Museum** (2229 W. Gary Blvd., Clinton; 580/323-7866; www.route66.org).

BLUE WHALE OF CATOOSA ALONG HISTORIC ROUTE 66

# *Best* ROAD TRIP

**DAY 1** Start your trip in **Oklahoma City.** Get a sense of the state at the **Oklahoma History Center,** then visit the **Oklahoma City National Memorial and Museum.** Be sure to have a meal at a Vietnamese restaurant—Oklahoma City has some of the best **Vietnamese food** in the country.

**DAY 2** Today, you'll get a taste of the Mother Road. Head out east on **Route 66,** but don't be in a hurry. Right outside OKC, stop in **Arcadia** for two classic Route 66 stops: Pop's and the Round Barn. When you hit **Chandler,** you can pick up some Mother Road memorabilia. **Tulsa** is your destination for the night.

**DAY 3** Spend the day in Tulsa, which is full of history. Don't miss the **Greenwood Cultural Center,** which tells the story of the prosperous Black neighborhood burned down in the 1921 Tulsa Race Riot. Then, check out the **art deco landmarks** around downtown Tulsa. Spend another night in Tulsa.

**DAY 4** On the way out of Tulsa, squeeze in another Route 66 sight by stopping in Catoosa, home of the **Blue Whale.** Then, head west to the town of **Kansas** to pick up the **Cherokee Hills Byway.** Wend your way to **Park Hill** to visit the **Cherokee Heritage Center.** Afterward, keep heading south along the byway until you reach the end in **Gore.** If you have reservations to stay at one of the WPA-built cabins in **Greenleaf State Park,** head there from Gore, or go up to **Muskogee** to spend the night.

OKLAHOMA HISTORY CENTER

ROUTE 66 THROUGH ARCADIA

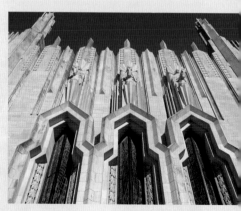

ART DECO ARCHITECTURE ON TULSA'S BOSTON AVENUE

**DAY 5** From Greenleaf State Park or Muskogee, it's about a 3-hour drive to the **Chickasaw Cultural Center.** Give yourself time to see the art and exhibits and also stroll the grounds. Afterward, head to the nearby **Chickasaw National Recreation Area** for a short hike or even a swim. From there, make the 1.5-hour drive back to **Oklahoma City** to complete the loop. If you haven't had an onion burger yet, make the 30-minute jaunt west from OKC to **El Reno** for this classic Oklahoma food.

CHEROKEE HERITAGE CENTER

CHICKASAW CULTURAL CENTER

## ORIENTATION

**Oklahoma City** is located near the center of the state, near the transition between the more forested eastern part of the state and the drier prairie in the west. **Tulsa** is in eastern Oklahoma, and the sights related to Indigenous history and culture are concentrated in the eastern part of the state, where the **Cherokee, Muscogee (Creek), Choctaw, Seminole, Chickasaw,** and **Osage Nations** are located.

## WHEN TO GO

Oklahoma weather can be intense and unpredictable; in November, Oklahoma can be colder and windier than Chicago. Ice storms are also a concern in the **winter. Late spring** to **early summer** and **early autumn** are generally the best times to visit Oklahoma, as the weather is usually temperate. Avoid **late summer** when the weather can get hot and oppressively muggy.

# HIGHLIGHTS

### SPIRO MOUNDS ARCHAEOLOGICAL CENTER

18154 1st St., Spiro; 918/962-2062; www.okhistory.org/sites/spiromounds

Located along the Arkansas River in eastern Oklahoma, this mound site covered ancient villages of the Indigenous Caddoan Mississippian culture. Though looted by White residents in the 1930s, the mounds still contained one of the most important troves of ancient Indigenous artifacts in the United States, which illuminated the trading activity among the Mississippians that extended far beyond what is now Oklahoma. The museum displays tools, sculptures, conch shells, and other artifacts found at the site, and interpretive trails around the center tell more of the Spiro story.

### SEQUOYAH'S CABIN MUSEUM

470288 Hwy. 1010, Sallisaw; 877/779-6997

# *Major* CITIES

**OKLAHOMA CITY:** Developed as a result of the Land Rush after the Dawes Act of 1887, the state capital, often shortened to OKC, boasts pedestrian-friendly streets, public art, bike lanes, a canal and waterfront area, as well as some of the most authentic Vietnamese food in the country.

**TULSA:** A small frontier settlement turned oil boomtown, Tulsa is home to one of the largest concentrations of art deco structures in the United States.

**NORMAN:** Oklahoma's third-largest city is home of the University of Oklahoma.

A blacksmith by trade, Sequoyah was the creator of the system for writing Cherokee, assigning a symbol for each sound in the language. Born in Tennessee, he came to eastern Oklahoma and built this single-room log cabin in 1829, where he lived for about 15 years. Today, the cabin is preserved in an enclosure, and you can see the dwelling and other related displays.

## WILL ROGERS MEMORIAL MUSEUM

1720 W. Will Rogers Blvd., Claremore; 800/324-9455; www.willrogers.com

Most people know Will Rogers (1879-1935) as a movie star, but he was also a writer, speaker, philosopher, and comedian. His father was a Cherokee senator and judge who helped write the Oklahoma constitution, and his mother descended from a Cherokee chief. This museum delves into his early years and

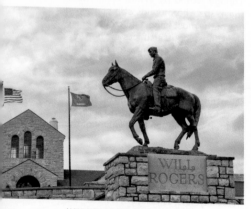

WILL ROGERS MEMORIAL MUSEUM

explores his legacy as a newspaper columnist and radio, film, and vaudeville star. Although Rogers is gone, his aphorisms live on. One still rings true for die-hard road-trip fans: "You would be surprised what there is to see in this great country within 200 miles (320 kilometers) of where any of us live. I don't care what state or what town."

## TULSA ART DECO MUSEUM

511 S. Boston Ave., Tulsa; 918/804-2669; www.tulsaartdecomuseum.com

This small but informative museum about the design and era of art deco holds a collection of artifacts such as jewelry, advertising artwork, silverware, and clothing. The museum is located in the lobby of the gorgeous Philcade Building, located in downtown Tulsa, which offers up one of the most extensive collections of art deco architecture in the United States. After visiting the museum, embark on a self-guided art deco tour of the city—a few places to see include the Philtower building, Tulsa Club, Atlas Life building, Oklahoma Natural Gas Building, and the Boston Avenue Methodist Church. For a list of nearly 40 art deco buildings throughout Tulsa, visit the **Tulsa Preservation Commission** (www.tulsapreservationcommission.org). The **Tulsa Historical Society** (2445 S. Peoria Ave.; 918/712-9484; www.tulsahistory.org) provides art deco walking tours.

## GILCREASE MUSEUM

1400 N. Gilcrease Museum Rd., Tulsa; 888/655-2278; www.gilcrease.utulsa.edu

The Gilcrease Museum sits on 460 acres (186 hectares) with 23 gardens and features more than 10,000 paintings, prints, drawings, and sculptures by 400 artists from past and present. The museum also has an unparalleled collection of American Indian artifacts, historical manuscripts, and art.

## OKLAHOMA HISTORY CENTER

800 Nazih Zuhdi Dr., Oklahoma City; 405/522-0765; www.okhistory.org/historycenter

A Smithsonian affiliate, this 215,000-square-foot (19,974-square-meter), 18-acre (7.3-hectare) site explores everything from aviation, transportation, and commerce to heritage and geology. There are five state-of-the-art permanent galleries, an outdoor oil-field exhibit with drilling derricks, and more than 200 interactive exhibits that not only educate but also entertain.

## OKLAHOMA CITY NATIONAL MEMORIAL AND MUSEUM

620 N. Harvey Ave., Oklahoma City; 405/235-3313; http://oklahomacitynationalmemorial.org

In 1995, a terrorist bombing at Alfred P. Murrah Federal Building by Timothy McVeigh catapulted Oklahoma City into tragic infamy. About 800 people were maimed, and 149 men and women and 19 children were killed. The Oklahoma City National Memorial and Museum honors those who lost their lives in the attack. With interactive exhibits and powerful oral histories, videos, and bomb-damaged artifacts, the museum walks you through the day of the attack, and the days, weeks, and years following, to help you understand how this event forever shaped the city. The memorial park contains a survivor tree and a field filled with 168 chairs engraved with the name of each person who died.

## CHICKASAW CULTURAL CENTER

867 Cooper Memorial Dr., Sulphur; 580/622-7130; www.chickasawculturalcenter.com

This extensive facility recounts the history and cultural traditions of the Chickasaw people through permanent and temporary exhibits of fine art and artifacts, a re-creation of a traditional village, and interpretive programs. In addition to the indoor displays, the 109-acre (44-hectare) grounds feature gardens, sculptures, and an elevated viewing platform that looks over the traditional village.

# BEST SCENIC DRIVES

## CHEROKEE HILLS BYWAY

Starting in the town of **West Siloam Springs** on the Arkansas border and ending in **Gore,** this 84-mile (135-kilometer) route winds through the Ozark foothills in eastern Oklahoma, tracing the history of the Cherokee people along the way. From West Siloam Springs, take **U.S. 59** to the town of **Kansas,** where the route turns south on **Highway 10,** following the **Illinois River.** At the junction with **U.S. 62,** turn west, which brings you to the Cherokee Nation capital of **Tahlequah** and nearby Park Hill, where the **Cherokee Heritage Center** and other significant Cherokee Nation sights are located. From Park Hill, keep traveling south on U.S. 62, then southeast on **Highways 82** and **100,** passing **Tenkiller Ferry Lake,** to the town of Gore. From Tahlequah to Gore, the byway intersects with the

OKLAHOMA CITY NATIONAL MEMORIAL AND MUSEUM

WICHITA MOUNTAINS WILDLIFE REFUGE

**Trail of Tears National Historic Trail** (www.nps.gov/trte), which preserves the route of the forcible removal of the Cherokee people from Tennessee, Georgia, and Alabama to Oklahoma.

# BEST PARKS AND RECREATION AREAS

## CHICKASAW NATIONAL RECREATION AREA

901 W. 1st St., Sulphur; 580/622-7234; www.nps.gov/chic

Situated around Lake of the Arbuckles, Veterans Lake, and Travertine Creek, this park has campgrounds and more than 20 miles (32 kilometers) of hiking trails, along which you may see wildlife like bison and armadillos, but the most popular activities involve the water. Travertine Creek is often crowded on warm weekends with swimmers, waders, and people just enjoying the scenery. The recreation area includes the grounds that were once designated as Platt National Park, which protected the springs around Travertine and Rock Creeks.

## GREENLEAF STATE PARK

12022 Greenleaf Rd., Braggs; 918/487-5622; www.travelok.com/state-parks/greenleaf-state-park

The eponymous lake is the centerpiece of this state park, but it's the 16 WPA-built cabins that make Greenleaf stand out. Up to four guests can stay in most of these original stone cabins that resulted from the massive federal employment program in the 1930s—one cabin only sleeps two, while another can accommodate eight. Minimum stays may be required during peak season.

## WICHITA MOUNTAINS WILDLIFE REFUGE

32 Refuge Headquarters, Indiahoma; 580/429-3222; www.fws.gov/refuge/Wichita_Mountains

Established in 1901 with almost 60,000 acres (24,281 hectares) of wilderness, the refuge is home to more than 250 animal species, including bald eagles, whooping cranes, and black-tail

CHICKASAW NATIONAL RECREATION AREA

# BEST SOUVENIRS

## INDIGENOUS ART AND GIFTS

In addition to the **Cherokee Heritage Center** and the **Chickasaw Cultural Center,** the museums of other Native American nations have gift shops with items made by Indigenous artists and craftspeople.

- **Seminole Nation Museum:** 524 S. Wewoka Ave., Wewoka; 405/257-5580; www.seminolenationmuseum.org

- **Five Civilized Tribes Museum:** 1101 Honor Heights Dr., Muskogee; 918/683-1701; www.fivetribes.org

- **Choctaw Nation of Oklahoma Capitol Museum:** 163665 N. 4355 Rd., Tuskahoma; 918/569-4465; www.choctawnation.com/tribal-services/cultural-services/museum

## ROUTE 66 MEMORABILIA

- The gift shop at the **Route 66 Interpretive Center** (400 E. 1st St., Chandler; 405/258-1300; www.route66interpretivecenter.org) sells plenty of Route 66-themed gifts as well as the handiwork of local artisans.

- Also in Chandler, **McJerry's Route 66 Gallery** (306 Manvel Ave.; 405/240-7659; www.mcjerry66.com) houses artist and painter Jerry McClanahan's paintings, postcards, and prints, which capture special moments from his travels along Route 66. You can even commission him to record your own road-trip experience on canvas.

---

prairie dogs. In 1907, 15 bison were brought here from the New York Bronx Zoo; today, there are 650. There are also about 700 elk and 300 longhorns. You can hike, rock climb, bike, fish, and camp throughout this wild and rugged landscape.

## BLACK MESA STATE PARK AND NATURE PRESERVE

County Rd. 325, Kenton; 580/426-2222; www.travelok.com/state-parks/black-mesa-state-park-nature-preserve

At 4,973 tall, Black Mesa, so named for the dark lava rock that covers it, is the highest point in Oklahoma. Located in the remote western panhandle, the park is divided into two, non-contiguous sections: the state park, which is centered around Lake Carl Etting, and the preserve, which is about 15 miles (24 kilometers) northwest. Black Mesa is in the preserve, and the highest point is accessible via an 8.5-mile (13.6-kilometer) round-trip hike along

an exposed trail that can get very hot in the summer.

# FESTIVALS AND EVENTS

## RED EARTH FESTIVAL

Oklahoma City; 405/427-5228; www.redearth.org; June

Held in OKC's Grand Casino, this annual festival brings together more than 100 Indigenous tribes from across the United States. The art show exhibits Indigenous artists' work, such as baskets, pottery, and paintings, much of which can be purchased. The highlight of the festival is the Dance Showcase, an elite competition featuring dancers from various tribes.

## WEWOKA SORGHUM FESTIVAL

Wewoka; www.sorghumfestivalok.org; Oct.

Since 1976, this annual festival has celebrated sorghum, a plant that's used as a sweetener, and all its forms. A parade, food vendors, and interpretive demonstrations take place all over downtown Wewoka, with the **Seminole Nation Museum** (524 S. Wewoka Ave., Wewoka; 405/257-5580; www.seminolenationmuseum.org) being the main center of activity.

# BEST FOOD

## ONION BURGER

For a truly authentic Oklahoma gastronomical experience, try an onion burger. The onion burger was born out of economic necessity during the Great Depression. Since meat was scarce at that time, cooks grilled thin ribbons of onion, then added them to ground beef to bolster the size of the patty. A happy accident occurred: As the onions caramelized, they formed a savory crust on the patty. Thus, the cost-saving measure boosted the flavor and texture of the burger. Try them at **Sid's Diner** (300 S. Choctaw Ave., El Reno; 405/262-7757; www.sidsdinerelreno.com), with its red and black booths lining the walls and historic pictures.

## VIETNAMESE FOOD IN OKLAHOMA CITY

In the 1970s, Vietnamese immigrants flocked to Oklahoma City, and today there are a number of authentic restaurants, mostly located around 23rd Street and Classen Boulevard. Try **Lido Restaurant** (2518 N. Military Ave.; 405/521-1902; www.lidorestaurantokc.com), which blends Vietnamese and colonial French dishes, or **Pho Lien Hoa** (901 NW 23rd St.; 405/521-8087) with the best pho in the state.

# MAJOR AIRPORTS

- **Will Rogers World Airport:** OKC; 7100 Terminal Dr., Oklahoma City; 405/316-3200; www.flyokc.com
- **Tulsa International Airport:** TUL; 7777 E. Apache St., Tulsa; 918/838-5000; www.tulsaairports.com

# MORE INFORMATION

## TRAVEL AND TOURISM INFORMATION

- **Oklahoma Tourism and Recreation Department:** www.travelok.com
- **Oklahoma State Parks:** www.travelok.com/state-parks

## NEWSPAPERS AND MAGAZINES

- *The Oklahoman:* www.oklahoman.com
- *Oklahoma Today:* www.oklahomatoday.com

# IOWA

On land of the Oceti Sakowin, Iowa, Sauk, Meskwaki, Kickapoo, Jiwere, and Yankton people, Iowa exerts a pull on the entire United States from its location in the middle of the country. The politically minded explain this influence as a result of the Iowa Caucuses, which kick off the presidential nominating contests every four years. The interests of Iowans, the rationale goes, are of outsized concern to politicians who want their support in the caucuses, where a win could give a candidate the needed boost toward the nomination. That may be why corn prices and soybean exports, two of Iowa's top agricultural products, are hot policy topics.

Iowa shows up as the setting for quotidian life as well. From the *American Gothic* house to the *Field of Dreams* to the *Bridges of Madison County*, Iowa has served as the backdrop of Americana. Perhaps it's the country's vision of itself as rolling green valleys, wide tracts of farmland, blazing fall foliage, and wholesome family fun that makes Iowa seem like the everystate. But that's not to say that you don't have to visit Iowa to know it—there are definitely corners that will fascinate and surprise.

**AREA:** 56,272 square miles / 145,743 square kilometers (26th)

**POPULATION:** 3,155,070 (31th)

**STATEHOOD DATE:** December 28, 1846 (29th)

**STATE CAPITAL:** Des Moines

CORN FIELD, RURAL IOWA

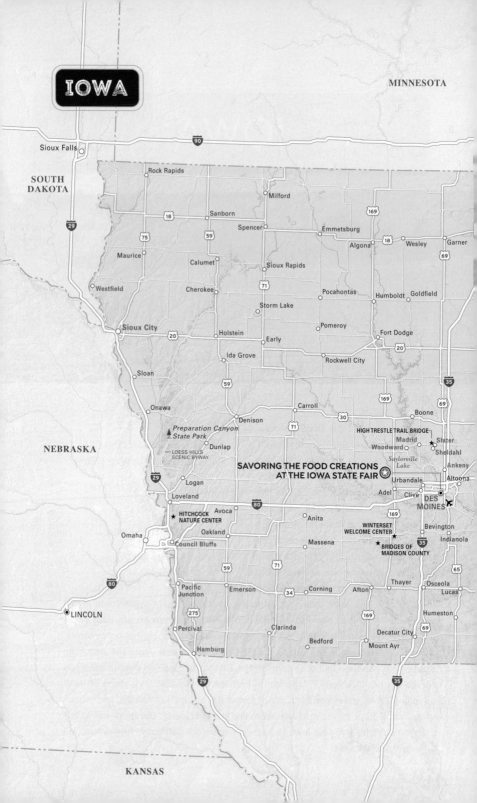

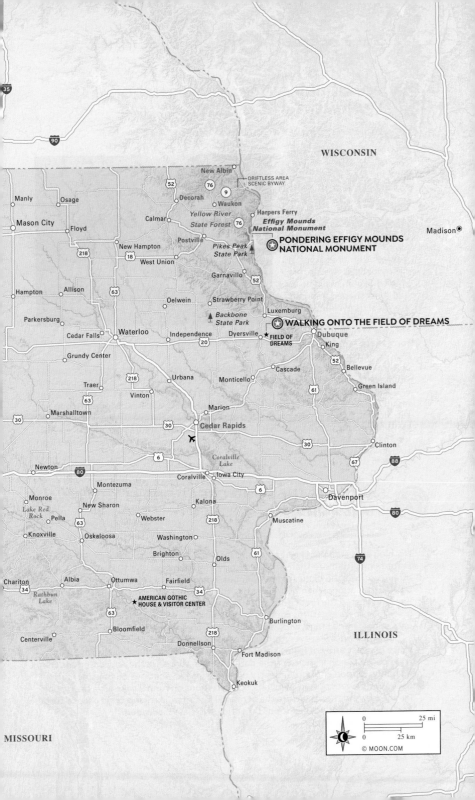

# TOP 3

## ① PONDERING EFFIGY MOUNDS NATIONAL MONUMENT

151 Highway 76, Harpers Ferry; 563/873-3491, ext. 123; www.nps.gov/efmo

The largest known concentration of mounds in the country, Effigy Mounds National Monument protects 191 prehistoric mound sites set along the Mississippi River in eastern Iowa. In addition to conical burial mounds seen at other sites, some of the mounds at this site are shaped like animals; bear- and bird-shaped mounds are most prevalent. Their meaning and use are not entirely known, but these formations are sacred to the 20 Indigenous tribes culturally associated with Effigy Mounds and should be viewed with care.

MARCHING BEAR GROUP OF PREHISTORIC MOUNDS

The park encompassing the mounds is split into a North Unit and a South Unit, and the visitors center is located in the North Unit. Trails lead to the different mound groups. The **Little Bear Mound Group** and **Great Bear Mound Group** are the closest to the visitor center and can be viewed along a 3-mile (4-kilometer) trail. In the South Unit, parking is available at a day use area, and from there, viewing the **Marching Bear Group** requires a 4-mile (6-kilometer) hike. Trails also lead to overlooks with views of the Mississippi River.

## ② SAVORING THE FOOD CREATIONS AT THE IOWA STATE FAIR

3000 E. Grand Ave. Des Moines; 800/545-FAIR; www.iowastatefair.org; Aug.

Nothing says summer like a state fair, and the Iowa State Fair is the quintessential state fair. With more than 1 million attendees each year, the 10-day, mid-August affair is one of the biggest, most famous events of its kind, especially in the run-up to an election, when politicians try to win some supporters in the state that has long hosted the first contest of the presidential nominating season. Like other state fairs, Iowa's features carnival rides, a parade, evening concerts with headliner acts at the Grand Stand, and various livestock and amateur cooking contests.

But overshadowing everything is the food. For the practical, multitasking eaters, there is a vast array of **items served on a stick,** from the salad on a stick to deep-fried pecan pie on a stick. For the daring eaters, there are the new creations that imaginative food entrepreneurs try out at the fair—variations on **poutine,** such as decadently sweet or spicy versions, and variations on **funnel cake** have been popular entries. And then there are the perennial favorites, like **deep-fried cheese curds** and the granddaddy of fair foods on a stick, the classic **corndog.**

CANDY APPLES AT THE IOWA STATE FAIR

 ## WALKING ONTO THE FIELD OF DREAMS

28995 Lansing Rd., Dyersville; 563/875-8404; www.fieldofdreamsmoviesite.com

You may remember the line from the 1989 film *Field of Dreams*: "Hey Dad, you wanna have a catch?" It's hard for a passionate baseball fan not to tear up when hearing that line. You can relive the emotion of that moment, and the joy of a simple catch, by visiting the actual *Field of Dreams,* which was constructed on two farms specifically for the movie. The field really is set amid nothing but Iowa farmland—meaning lots of corn. You can walk the green on your own, but the better option is to schedule a tour, which includes the family farm house that's set to look like a late-1980s residence.

If you're visiting with a group, you can rent out the field to play a ball game. You can also rent out the farmhouse for overnight stays.

FIELD OF DREAMS

# *Best* ROAD TRIP

**DAY 1** Start in the capital city of **Des Moines,** and get in a bit of contemporary art at the **Des Moines Art Center** and its nearby Pappajohn Sculpture Park. After lunch, hop in the car for the 3.5-hour drive east to **Dubuque.** On the way, stop in Dyersville to see the **Field of Dreams.**

**DAY 2** From Dubuque, head an hour north, mostly along the Mississippi River, to **Pikes Peak State Park,** where you can take short walk to see a waterfall and a prehistoric mound. Then go a few miles north to **Effigy Mounds National Monument** where you can see more clusters of mounds over the two units of the park. From there, drive up to **Harpers Ferry** to start the first half of the **Driftless Area Scenic Byway** to **Decorah,** an hour away.

**DAY 3** From Decorah, finish the rest of Driftless Area Scenic Byway, admiring the geography on the way to **New Albin** and back down to Harpers Ferry. From there, make a detour to **Yellow River State Forest,** which has some of the best views in the area, before heading back to Des Moines.

**DAY 4** If you have an extra day, do a day trip out to see the **Bridges of Madison County,** southwest of Des Moines, or go for a bike ride on the **High Trestle Trail,** north of the city.

DES MOINES ART CENTER

PIKES PEAK STATE PARK

COVERED BRIDGE IN MADISON COUNTY

# Major CITIES

**DES MOINES:** Iowa's state capital and largest city not only harbors a local paper working with one of the best political pollsters, but also has a noted contemporary art museum and a fast-growing population.

**CEDAR RAPIDS:** The state's second-largest city prides itself on its livability, offering its residents the worldly trappings of a metropolitan area without the crowds and traffic.

## ORIENTATION

**Des Moines,** the state capital, sits a little south of the center of the state, while **Cedar Rapids** is located in eastern Iowa. **Dubuque, Effigy Mounds National Monument,** and the **Driftless Area** are all in the far east of the state, along the Mississippi River. The **Loess Hills** sit in the western Iowa, near the Missouri River, which forms the state's western border.

## WHEN TO GO

Iowa has cold, freezing temperatures in **winter,** and hot, muggy, rainy **summers.** **Spring** weather varies with milder temperatures, but also thunderstorms. The state is arguably at its best in **fall,** when the foliage turns bright colors and the weather is warm, but less humid.

# HIGHLIGHTS

## PAPPAJOHN SCULPTURE PARK

1330 Grand Ave., Des Moines; www.desmoinesartcenter.org/visit/pappajohn-sculpture-park

This park in downtown Des Moines is the setting for 31 contemporary art sculptures, including works by Louise Bourgeois, Ugo Rondinone, Yoshitomo Nara, and 22 others. It's part of the **Des Moines Art Center** (4700 Grand Ave.; 515/277-4405; www.desmoinesartcenter.org), which is an excellent modern and contemporary art museum located 2.5 miles (4 kilometers) west of the park on Grand Avenue.

## BRIDGES OF MADISON COUNTY

www.madisoncounty.com/the-covered-bridges

The 1995 Clint Eastwood and Meryl Streep movie, *The Bridges of Madison County,* put a spotlight on this bucolic county southwest of Des Moines, where there are six historic covered bridges still standing. It's possible to visit all six, although only three—Imes Bridge, Cutler-Donahoe Bridge, and Cedar Bridge—can be reached by paved roads. The others—Holliwell Bridge, Hogback Bridge, and Roseman Bridge—require driving on 2-4.3 miles (3.2-7 kilometers) of unpaved roads, depending on the bridge and the direction of your approach. Cedar Bridge, reopened in 2019 after a fire, is the only bridge that can be driven through; the others can be entered on foot. Pick up a map of the bridges at the **Winterset Welcome Center** (73 Jefferson St., Winterset;

PAPPAJOHN SCULPTURE PARK; SCULPTURE BY MARK DI SUVERO

515/462-1185; www.madisoncounty. com).

## AMERICAN GOTHIC HOUSE & VISITOR CENTER

300 American Gothic St., Eldon; 641/652-3352; https://americangothichouse.org

The house in the background of Grant Wood's iconic painting, *American Gothic,* still stands in a small community in southeastern Iowa. Although the house itself is only open for tours one Saturday a month between April and October, there is an adjacent visitors center with a small exhibit about the house and the painting. The most popular activity here is taking a photo in the style of the couple depicted in the painting, and the visitors center has a selection of costumes and props—including pitchforks, of course—available to borrow.

## NATIONAL MISSISSIPPI RIVER MUSEUM

350 E. 3rd St., Port of Dubuque; 563/557-9545; www.rivermuseum.com

Although the Mississippi River, which forms Iowa's eastern boundary) isn't the longest river in the United States (that's the Missouri River, which is the state's western boundary), it has a defining place in the country's imagination. This museum explores the role of

AMERICAN GOTHIC HOUSE

the river and other waterways through various displays, including a section devoted to the Indigenous peoples living along the river, an aquarium with species from the Gulf of Mexico, and an actual dredge boat. Afterward, stop by the **Fenelon Place Elevator Company** (512 Fenelon Pl., Dubuque; www. fenelonplaceelevator.com), about 5 minutes away by car, to ride what's billed as "the world's shortest, steepest scenic railway."

# BEST SCENIC DRIVES

## DRIFTLESS AREA SCENIC BYWAY

Intersecting at points with the Great River Road, which follows the Mississippi River through multiple states, the Driftless Area Scenic Byway winds through the northeastern corner of Iowa that, unlike other parts of the state, were not subject to glacial movement, or drift. This left a scenic, rolling landscape still dotted with bluffs and hills, forests and streams. The roughly 100-mile (160-kilometer) drive has a couple options for routes. The most extensive route starts in **Postville** and makes a wide S-shape through the region, hitting the Mississippi River at **Harpers Ferry,** turning west toward **Waukon** and **Decorah,** then heading back east toward the Mississippi. At **New Albin,** near the Minnesota state line, the route turns south, back toward Harpers Ferry. Some of the best views are just outside Harpers Ferry, at **Yellow River State Forest** (729 State Forest Rd.). A map of the route, marked with sections that travel unpaved roads and many points of interest, is available at www.traveliowa.com/trails/ driftless-area-scenic-byway/3.

## LOESS HILLS SCENIC BYWAY

www.visitloesshills.org

Wind-blown silt is called loess, and the Loess Hills in western Iowa are the world's highest accumulation of it outside the Yellow River Valley in China. This 220-mile (354-kilometer) drive, designated a National Scenic Byway,

VIEW FROM THE DRIFTLESS AREA SCENIC BYWAY

offers views of this unique natural feature as it tracks a north-south route—from **Westfield** in the north through **Sioux City** and **Council Bluffs** to **Hamburg** in the south—along roads and highways east of I-25. Parks and preserves with trails and camping, like **Hitchcock Nature Center** and **Preparation Canyon State Park,** are located along and a short distance off the route.

# BEST PARKS AND RECREATION AREAS

## HIGH TRESTLE TRAIL

www.inhf.org/what-we-do/protection/high-trestle-trail

This 25-mile (40-kilometer) rails-to-trails bike path is a flat, paved ride connecting the towns of Ankeny, Slater, Sheldahl, Madrid, and Woodward. The highlight of the route is the **High Trestle Trail Bridge** over the Des Moines river west of Madrid, which shows its magic upon walking or biking through it. The angular steel forms over the bridge don't look dramatic from afar, but they become a visual spiral when you're on the bridge itself.

## PIKES PEAK STATE PARK

32264 Pikes Peak Rd., McGregor; 563/873-2341; www.iowadnr.gov/Places-to-Go/State-Parks/Iowa-State-Parks/Pikes-Peak-State-Park

Not to be confused with the Pikes Peak in Colorado, this state park is one of the best in Iowa. Set along the Mississippi River south of Effigy Mounds National Monument, this park also contains a mound, viewable along the 0.5-mile (0.8-kilometer) boardwalk that also leads to Bridal Veil Falls. Other hikes among the 11 miles (17 kilometers) of trails bring you to scenic overlooks with wide views of the river and the surrounding area.

## BACKBONE STATE PARK

1347 129th St., Dundee; 563/924-2527; www.iowadnr.gov/Places-to-Go/State-Parks/Iowa-State-Parks/Backbone-State-Park

Named for the high ridge within its bounds, Backbone is Iowa's oldest

HIGH TRESTLE TRAIL BRIDGE

PIKES PEAK STATE PARK

state park and offers a range of activities from hiking, biking, and rock climbing to water-based recreation on Backbone Lake and cross-country skiing in the winter.

# FESTIVALS AND EVENTS

The **Iowa State Fair** is the biggest event in Iowa.

## TULIP TIME

Pella; www.visitpella.com; May

This three-day festival celebrates the southeastern Iowa town of Pella's Dutch roots. There are various festivities like a parade and performances, but the focal point is the blooming tulips that are planted around town. The main plots are in Central Park (720 Franklin St.) and Scholte House Gardens (728 Washington St.).

# BEST FOOD

Although 99 percent of the **corn** produced in Iowa isn't of the sweet variety we eat off the cob, it seems wrong to visit the state and not sample its signature agricultural product, especially in the summer. Like its other Great Plains neighbors, the state also has a form of spiced ground beef sandwich, this one popularized by the **Maid-Rite** (http://maid-rite.com) chain of diners, with 21 locations around Iowa.

# MAJOR AIRPORTS

- **Des Moines International Airport:** DSM; 5800 Fleur Dr., Des Moines; 515/256-5050; www.flydsm.com
- **Eastern Iowa Airport:** CID; 2121 Arthur Collins Pkwy. SW, Cedar Rapids; 319/362-8336; https://flycid.com

# MORE INFORMATION

## TRAVEL AND TOURISM INFORMATION

- **Travel Iowa:** www.traveliowa.com
- **Iowa State Parks:** www.iowadnr.gov/Places-to-Go/State-Parks

## NEWSPAPERS

- *Des Moines Register:* www.des-moinesregister.com

# MISSOURI

Missouri is on Oceti Sakowin, Osage, Kickapoo, Kaskaskia, Sauk, Meskwaki, O-ga-xpa land, and a number of important pathways, routes, and trails have roots in the state: Osage migratory paths, a patchwork of rutted back roads, farm-to-market routes, Route 66. Lewis and Clark started their explorations of the Louisiana Purchase lands from St. Louis, Gateway to the West. By 1830 the frontier had moved farther west, to towns like Independence, Missouri—the official start of the Oregon Trail, which launched emigrants from all over the nation out toward the west coast.

Even with all these routes traveling through Missouri, there are many reasons to stop for a while, whether it's the sights and flavors of the two biggest cities, Kansas City and St. Louis, the relaxation of Lake of the Ozarks, or the rollicking fun of Branson. Missouri may be known for its Gateway to the West, but it's also the Show-Me State—the origins of that nickname may be hazy, but finding out what the state has to show is half the fun.

**AREA:** 69,704 square miles / 180,532 square kilometers (21st)

**POPULATION:** 6,137,428 (18th)

**STATEHOOD DATE:** August 10, 1821 (24th)

**STATE CAPITAL:** Jefferson City

▲ VIEW OF THE OZARKS IN HA HA TONKA STATE PARK

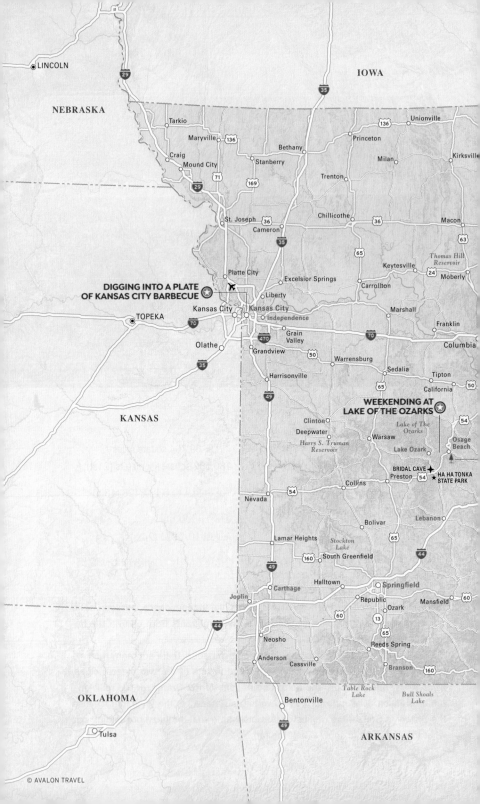

# TOP 3

## 1 DIGGING INTO A PLATE OF KANSAS CITY BARBECUE

Kansas City is known for its barbecue. This rich tradition harks back to the first outdoor pits of Henry Perry, "The Father of Kansas City Barbecue," in the early 1900s. So what makes KC's so popular? One answer is the burnt ends, a traditional part of the city's barbecue scene. They're made from the end points of brisket slabs and are exactly what they sound like. A crusty, fatty, juicy vehicle for sauce, they're served as a main dish, side dish, in sandwiches, and sometimes as a topping. Kansas City barbecue traditionally calls for slowly smoked meat (beef, pork, chicken, even fish) slathered in a tomato-based sauce. Usually sweet as well as spicy, Kansas City barbecue sauce typically features a well-balanced flavor profile, though each restaurant has its own secret recipe. Over 100 places in the Kansas City area serve barbecue, and the saying goes that if you ask two locals about their favorite place, you'll get three answers. Here are a couple of the best places in town.

BARBECUED BRISKET, KANSAS CITY STYLE

- **Arthur Bryant's Barbeque** (1727 Brooklyn Ave.; 816/231-1123; www.arthurbryantsbbq.com) is the legacy of one of the most popular pit masters in history. Try the secret recipe sauce (original or rich and spicy) slathered over any number of slow-roasted meats.

- **Gates** (3205 Main St., Kansas City; 816/753-0828; https://gatesbbq.com), a sometime rival of Arthur Bryant's, serves up all the meats—brisket, ribs, chicken, sausage, mutton, etc.—as entrees and offers a mixed plate for variety.

## 2 RIDING TO THE TOP OF GATEWAY ARCH

11 N. 4th St., St. Louis; 314/655-1600; www.gatewayarch.com and www.nps.gov/jeff

Rather than a park of natural wonders, Gateway Arch National Park is a historical landmark in an urban setting. The 630-foot (192-meter) silver arch on the west bank of the Mississippi River commemorates one of the main routes for westward expansion during the 19th century. From Missouri, Lewis and Clark launched their Corps of Discovery upriver, opening the gateway for the riverboats, pioneers, and homesteaders who followed them west into the frontier. The park, formerly known as the Jefferson National Expansion Memorial, is also a memorial to Thomas Jefferson, who initiated the Corps of Discovery.

The only way to go up into the Arch is via the **Arch Tram** (877/982-1410; www.gatewayarch.com). Futuristic five-person pods—not for the claustrophobic—zoom you to the top of the Gateway Arch in 4 minutes, where views of the city through the small windows can stretch as far as 30 miles (48 kilometers) on a clear day. The trams are a popular attraction, and tickets sell out quickly.

To access the tram, you'll walk through the **Museum at the Gateway Arch.** The museum contains six large exhibit rooms that look at St. Louis and the role it played in the United States' westward push. Some exhibits examine the problematic aspects of the concept of Manifest Destiny, the expansionist belief, popular in the 19th century, that the United States had a God-given right to stretch across the continent and spread its own values and way of life. Viewpoints from the perspective of Native Americans and free and enslaved African Americans, as well as Mexico, which also had a large historical stake in the West, are represented.

The park grounds also include the **Old Courthouse,** where in 1846 husband-and-wife Dred and Harriet Scott filed petitions for their freedom. The case went all the way to the Supreme Court, which infamously ruled that the Scotts and, by extension, all African Americans, were not citizens, and had no rights or privileges.

VIEW OF ST. LOUIS FROM THE GATEWAY ARCH

## ③ WEEKENDING AT LAKE OF THE OZARKS

A weekend at the Lake of the Ozarks means different things to different people. Some have fond memories of childhood summers spent on the lake's sandy shores. Others think of it as a business conference destination. Still others will wink knowingly at a mention of Lake of the Ozarks—they're undoubtedly thinking of the secluded area called Party Cove (formally known as Anderson Hollow Cove), which *The New York Times* dubbed a "floating bacchanal."

The reasons for going to Lake of the Ozarks are varied, but the fact is that people flock there in droves. The body of water itself—one of the largest artificially constructed lakes in the nation—is great for boaters and water-skiers. (Swimmers, on the other hand, should be advised that this isn't exactly the cleanest place around.) The glittering lake and hilly topography make the region a truly lovely place, particularly once you get away from the bars and tchotchke shops of the main tourist drag, **Bagnell Dam Boulevard** in Lake Ozark, which turns into **Osage Beach Parkway** in Osage Beach.

At 17,626 acres (7,132 hectares), the beautiful **Lake of the Ozarks State Park** (304 Hwy. 134, Kaiser; 573/348-2694; www.mostateparks.com/park/lake-ozarks-state-park) is the largest park in Missouri. This is a great place to escape the touristy noise of the lake's bars and resorts, as the emphasis here is truly on nature. Hikers and bicyclists can take advantage of the park's 12 trails, which wind along 85 miles (136 kilometers) of shoreline and through old-growth hickory forests. The park's two public beaches are prime spots for fishing, swimming, and boating.

LAKE OF THE OZARKS

Another popular sight, **Bridal Cave** (526 Bridal Cave Rd., Camdenton; 573/346-2676; www.bridalcave.com) is full of veil-like stalactites and contains more onyx formations than any other cavern. It was once the site of Osage Indian marriage ceremonies and remains a popular wedding location. Nearby to the south, at **Ha Ha Tonka State Park** (1491 State Rte. D, Camdenton; 573/346-2986; https://mo-stateparks.com/park/ha-ha-tonka-state-park), you can see the stone ruins of an early-20th-century castle overlooking the lake.

# Best ROAD TRIP

**DAY 1**
Start in **Kansas City,** and spend the day at one of its fascinating museums. Be sure to try Kansas City's famous **barbecue** for at least one of your meals.

**DAY 2**
Make the 4-hour drive east across the state to **St. Louis.** Stretch your legs with a walk across **Chain of Rocks Bridge.** In the evening, head to **Blueberry Hill,** the legendary music club—check out the **Walk of Fame** on your way in.

OSAGE BEACH AREA, LAKE OF THE OZARKS

**DAY 3**
Make your way to **Lake of the Ozarks** on this day, 3 hours west of St. Louis. It's a pretty drive, if you take the route going on I-44 West to Highway 68 to Highway 63 then along Highway 42, which is also known as West 5th Street. End up in **Osage Beach,** in the heart of Lake of the Ozarks.

**DAY 4**
Spend the day doing what people do at Lake of the Ozarks—take out a boat, hike in the state park, or sightsee at **Bridal Cave** or **Ha Ha Tonka State Park.**

HA HA TONKA STATE PARK

**DAY 5**
In the morning, make the 1-hour drive southeast to **Devil's Elbow** for a jaunt on **Route 66.** Admire the scenery, and stop in **Springfield** for lunch. From here, you can make the 3-hour drive back to **Kansas City.** Or, you can complete Missouri's stretch of Route 66 by going all the way west to **Joplin,** another 1.5 hours, and return to Kansas City from there (about 2.5 hours north).

ROUTE 66

## ORIENTATION

Missouri's two biggest cities, Kansas City and St. Louis, sit at opposite ends of the state. **Kansas City** is in the far west, on the Kansas state line, while **St. Louis** is in the far east, on the Illinois state line. The capital, **Jefferson City,** is west of St. Louis in central Missouri. The summer destination **Lake of the Ozarks** is in the middle of the state, and entertainment destination **Branson** is located in the southwest part of the state, near the Arkansas border.

## WHEN TO GO

**Late spring-early fall** is the most popular season to travel in Missouri, avoiding the brutal **winters,** when temperatures can sink below 20°F (-7°C). **Summers** can be hot and muggy.

# HIGHLIGHTS

## ANHEUSER-BUSCH BREWERY

12th St. and Lynch St., St. Louis; 314/577-2626; www.budweisertours.com

Even though today Anheuser-Busch Brewery is a behemoth corporation (notably as the maker of Budweiser),

when it opened in 1852, it was a small-batch brewery. It was the first company to bottle and market pasteurized beer, and to transport it in refrigerated railroad cars across the country. The St. Louis location is the original and also the largest, and as such, offers several tours and tasting options. The 45-minute complimentary tour takes visitors to the Clydesdale stables and demonstrates the entire seven-step brewing process. You could also just grab a pint from the on-site Biergarten.

## BLUEBERRY HILL

6504 Delmar Blvd., St. Louis; 314/727-4444; http://blueberryhill.com

Legendary concert venue Blueberry Hill opened in 1972 with a jukebox spinning cool tunes and soon built a stage for live music acts. The father of rock and roll Chuck Berry himself performed here regularly in the 1990s, and these days, several nights a week, the venue still hosts top performers on multiple stages. Outside, the **St. Louis Walk of Fame** (6504 Delmar Blvd.; 314/727-7827; www.stlouiswalkoffame.org) has over 150 brass stars dedicated to famous city folks including Maya Angelou, Miles Davis, Scott Joplin, and Harry Caray. Also look for the bronze **Chuck Berry sculpture** (6555 Delmar Blvd.) with his guitar.

BLUEBERRY HILL

# Major CITIES

**KANSAS CITY:** The biggest city in the state is diverse and metropolitan—rooted in Midwestern hospitality, and known far and wide for its barbecue.

**ST. LOUIS:** The Gateway to the West, as the city is known, was once a jumping-off point for traders and fur trappers heading west. In addition to that history, St. Louis is also known for live music and claims Chuck Berry and Miles Davis as hometown legends.

**SPRINGFIELD:** Located in southwestern Missouri, Springfield is known as the birthplace of Route 66 and, appropriately, has a few kitschy attractions, like the World's Largest Fork and Fantastic Caverns, a tram ride through a cave.

## CHAIN OF ROCKS BRIDGE

Chain of Rocks Rd. near Schillinger Rd., St. Louis; 314/416-9930

This steel truss bridge stands 60 feet (18 meters) above the Mississippi River and sports an unusual 30-degree kink in the middle. It's named after a 17-mile (27-kilometer) granite rocky outcrop that formed treacherous rapids in the river and caused huge problems for boaters. The bridge was originally designed to be straight, but boaters protested because the placement of the bridge was going to make river travel even more difficult. The only solution was to incorporate a bend in the middle of the bridge. The designer assured officials that the turn wouldn't be a problem, but it caused endless bottlenecks. As cars got longer and bigger, and the interstate systems called for wider roads, a new Chain of Rocks

Bridge opened less than 2,000 feet (610 meters) upstream in 1967, and the bent bridge closed in 1968. It sat abandoned until a nonprofit organization converted it into a bicycle and pedestrian bridge in 1989, which is how it's still used today. Spared from the wrecking ball, this is one of the best-preserved remnants of large-scale bridge construction from the 1920s.

## MERAMEC CAVERNS

1135 Hwy. W, Sullivan; 573/468-2283; www.americascave.com

Under the verdant rolling hills of Missouri lie networks of deep caverns. In fact, Missouri is home to more than 6,000 surveyed caves. One of the most popular is Meramec Caverns, a 4.6-mile (7.4-kilometer) system of caverns, rumored to have been used as a hideout by outlaw Jesse James. Discovered in 1720 and developed during the Civil War (when the natural saltpeter was mined for manufacturing gunpowder), the limestone cave drips with stalactites and stalagmites in astonishing natural colors. Though not huge in terms of size, the caves, which can be visited on guided tours, are some of the most sculpturally delicate in the country. The interior temperature of Meramec Caverns is a constant chilly 58°F (14°C); bring a jacket and wear sturdy shoes.

## ARABIA STEAMBOAT MUSEUM

400 Grand Blvd., Kansas City; 816/471-1856; www.1856.com

CHAIN OF ROCKS BRIDGE

# THREE TRAILS

The hometown of President Harry S. Truman, **Independence** was the jumping-off point for three historic trails. Each followed the same route out of town and split off at later points.

- **Santa Fe Trail (1821-1880):** The original trail west, the Santa Fe Trail was a commercial venture, busy with merchant traffic. It headed from Missouri across the Southwest to Santa Fe, where merchants could meet up with others who came north from Mexico. Traffic transporting goods went in both directions on the trail.

- **Oregon Trail (1843-1869):** The Oregon Trail was the main route that led thousands of emigrants from Missouri to Oregon City, 2,000 miles (3,200 kilometers) west. Unlike the Santa Fe Trail and earlier routes used by trappers and explorers, the Oregon Trail was mostly used by families: men, women, and children who uprooted their lives to move west in hopes of a better life.

- **California Trail (1841-1869):** The California Trail stretches a little farther than the Oregon Trail, at about 3,000 miles (4,800 kilometers). After gold was discovered in the state in 1848, miners rushed the trail over the next year to strike it rich. Known as the 49ers, they stayed on the path with their Oregon-bound cohorts until eastern Idaho, where they dipped southwest into Nevada to cross the Sierra Nevada mountain range into California.

The **SantaCaliGon Days Festival** (Independence Square; www.santacaligon.com) attracts over 300,000 people each year during Labor Day weekend in early September to celebrate the beginning of these three trails.

This museum houses the rescued cargo from a steamboat that went down in the Missouri River in 1856. Not only is the story of the group of men who located and excavated the boat a fascinating modern treasure hunt—it was found underground in the middle of a farmer's field, due to the changing course of the river—but also the cargo unearthed is the biggest collection of pre-Civil War items ever discovered. The ship was supplying the frontier, and the *Arabia*'s cargo included everything a new town might need: boots, fine china, blacksmith tools, hats, awls, jewelry, buttons, weapons, and more. Visits start with a guided tour and an introductory video, and then you're allowed to tour the display rooms freely.

## NEGRO LEAGUES BASEBALL MUSEUM

1616 E. 18th St., Kansas City; 816/221-1920; www.nlbm.com

The Negro Leagues Baseball Museum tells the story of organized baseball played by African Americans and other people of color, who were denied the opportunity to play in Major League Baseball for decades. Take a self-guided tour and find artifacts like a Kansas City Monarchs jersey worn by star hitter Newt Allen and a glove worn by the leagues' greatest ambassador, Buck O'Neil, during his days managing the Kansas City Monarchs, plus a pretty remarkable non-baseball piece: iconic pitcher Satchel Paige's original gravestone. Located in Kansas City's 18th and Vine district—also known as the Historic Jazz district, a community where Black culture has thrived—the museum shares its building with the **American Jazz Museum** (1616 E. 18th St.; 816/474-8463; www.americanjazzmuseum.org), which displays items like a saxophone played in 1953 by Charlie Parker.

## BRANSON

The town of Branson, in southwest Missouri, is Las Vegas in the Ozarks, complete with its own Strip, the **Highway 76 Strip,** that is. This 5-mile (8-kilometer) stretch of Highway 76, also known as 76 Country Boulevard, is lined with more than 50 neon-lit theaters that stage live shows. Going for more than 50 years, one of the original shows is the **Presleys' Country Jubilee** (2920 W. 76 Country Blvd. Branson; 800/335-4874; www.presleys.com), featuring a family of performers (who are distantly related to The King). **Dolly Parton's Stampede** (1525 W. 76 Country Blvd., Branson; 417/336-3000; https://dp-stampede.com) brings horses into the mix with a riding show. For a different experience, the **Titanic Museum Attraction** (3235 76 Country Blvd., Branson; 800/381-7670 or 417/334-9500; https://titanicbranson.com) re-creates the doomed ship for self-guided tours. Off the Strip, the **Silver Dollar City** (399 Silver Dollar City Pkwy., Branson; 417/336-7100; www.silverdollarcity.com) theme park is one of Missouri's top attractions.

# BEST SCENIC DRIVES

## ROUTE 66

The nearly 300-mile (482-kilometer) stretch of Route 66 through Missouri gives you a glimpse of Ozark country—tree-covered hills that gently rise and dip, and lush valleys that spread before you. Starting in **St. Louis,** the route heads west across the state, exiting into Kansas just past **Joplin.** Along the way, stop in **Laumeier Sculpture Park** (12580 Rott Rd., Sappington; 314/615-5278; www.laumeiersculpturepark.org) just outside St. Louis for its 60 large-scale outdoor sculptures, and admire the view between **Devil's Elbow** and **Lebanon,** where there are dramatic 200-foot (61-meter) rock bluffs, deep and verdant valleys, and rivers snaking through limestone rock. When you hit **Springfield,** you'll be in the official birthplace of Route 66. The drive from there to **Carthage** is especially scenic with its hilly contours and leafy trees. **Joplin,** where Bonnie and Clyde went on a robbery spree and killed two police officers, is the last city in Missouri before hitting the Kansas state line.

# BEST PARKS AND RECREATION AREAS

## FOREST PARK

5595 Grand Dr., St. Louis; 314/367-7275; www.forestparkforever.org

Stretching 500 green acres (202 hectares) larger than New York's Central Park, Forest Park is one of the largest urban parks in the United States—and one of the prettiest. Running and walking trails circle sparkling ponds, pass under leafy trees, and wind past grassy meadows. At 1,300 acres (526 hectares), the park has an entire ecosystem of forests, lakes, and streams, as well as plenty of room to house five cultural centers: **St. Louis Art Museum, St. Louis Science Center, St. Louis Zoo, The Muny,** and the **Missouri History Museum.** Whatever you do in Forest Park, don't miss the **Jewel Box** (Wells and McKinley Dr.; 314/531-0080). This art deco greenhouse boasts 50-foot (15-meter) glass walls and 17 acres (6.9 hectares) of tropical trees, brightly colored flowers, and exotic plants, plus a fountain and water feature.

## KATY TRAIL STATE PARK

Machens to Clinton; 573/449-7402; https://mostateparks.com/park/katy-trail-state-park

The centerpiece of this park is the 225-mile (362-kilometer) recreational trail that it's named after. Built on the bed of a former railroad track and one of the longest of its kind in the nation, the Katy Trail is hugs the Missouri River and leads hikers and cyclists through

CYCLISTS ON THE KATY TRAIL

some of the state's most beautiful rural corners. The trail's outstanding website (www.bikekatytrail.com) offers downloadable maps, trail FAQs, and links to several Katy Trail trip-planning services.

# FESTIVALS AND EVENTS

## KANSAS CITY PRIDEFEST

Kansas City; www.kcpridefest.org; last weekend in May

Situated in the conservative Midwest, Kansas City is a hot spot of LGBTQ pride year-round, but the biggest celebration is Kansas City PrideFest, named by *The Advocate* as one of the top 10 festivals in the nation. The family-friendly event offers a weekend full of fun at Berkeley Riverfront Park, with performances by national headliners, drag queens, and men's choruses.

## SPECTATOR SPORTS

Kansas City ranks as one of the best in the Midwest for spectator sports, and fans are passionate—the football stadium is in the Guinness Book of World Records as the loudest in the world! The **Kansas City Royals** baseball team play at "The K," or **Kauffman Stadium** (1 Royal Way; 800/676-9257; www.mlb.com/royals; Mar.-Sept.). Possibly the biggest game in town is found at **Arrowhead Stadium** (1 Arrowhead Dr.; 816/920-9300; Sept.-Jan.), home to NFL football's **Kansas City Chiefs.** Don't miss out on the ultimate fan experience—tailgating. It's a cultural experience unto itself, with thousands of fans cooking food, playing music, and partying before the game.

# BEST FOOD

Of course, there's Kansas City barbecue, but that's not the only culinary specialty in the state.

## CONCRETE

To non-Missourians, it's custard. To locals, it's called a concrete. Concretes are ice-cream custard treats so thick and dense they have the consistency of concrete. Order one at **Ted Drewes** (6726 Chippewa, St. Louis; 314/481-2652; www.teddrewes.com), a local institution.

## CASHEW CHICKEN

In Springfield, David Leong's cashew chicken took the city by storm in the 1970s. Leong came to the United States from China in 1940, and he opened Leong's Tea House in 1963. Once he saw how much the locals worshipped fried chicken, he modified the already-established cashew chicken dish from a stir-fried version to a deep-fried remix. He slathered it with oyster sauce and sprinkled it with green onions. It was a hit. Although the original Leong's Tea House closed in 1997, **Leong's Asian Diner** (1540 W. Republic Rd., Springfield; 417/887-7500) still serves that famous dish. You can also find Springfield-style cashew chicken throughout the city.

# MAJOR AIRPORTS

- **Kansas City International Airport:** MCI; 1 International Square, Kansas City; 816/243-5237; www.flykci.com

- **St. Louis Lambert International Airport:** STL; 10701 Lambert International, St. Louis; 314/426-8000, www.flystl.com

# MORE INFORMATION

## TRAVEL AND TOURISM INFORMATION

- **Visit Missouri:** www.visitmo.com
- **Missouri State Parks:** https://mostateparks.com

## NEWSPAPERS AND MAGAZINES

- *St. Louis Post-Dispatch:* www.stltoday.com
- *Kansas City Star:* www.kansascity.com
- *Missouri Life:* https://missourilife.com

# GREAT LAKES

◄ MILWAUKEE PIERHEAD LIGHT, WISCONSIN

# THE GREAT LAKES
## State by State

### MINNESOTA

**Why Go:** The beautiful landscapes in Minnesota encompass boreal forests, tallgrass prairie, and thousands of lakes.

### WISCONSIN

**Why Go:** Shaped by glaciers, Wisconsin is dotted with lakes and lined with rivers that beckon paddlers and hikers alike.

### ILLINOIS

**Why Go:** The diverse metropolis of Chicago, with its skyscrapers, jazz and blues, and museums, is the center of gravity in the region.

### INDIANA

**Why Go:** Picturesque small towns, sand dunes, and a slice of creamy Hoosier pie are some of Indiana's highlights.

### MICHIGAN

**Why Go:** Michigan may be the best place to appreciate the grandeur of the Great Lakes, being surrounded by four of them.

### OHIO

**Why Go:** Ohio combines its trio of major cities that all start with C with the rolling landscapes of the Appalachian foothills.

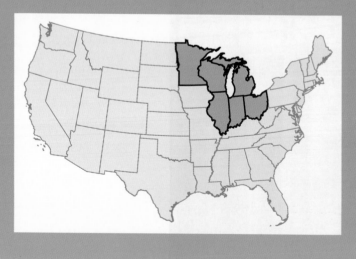

# Great Lakes ROAD TRIP

This road trip takes in four Great Lakes in eight days. If you have more time, add Minnesota or linger longer at one of these stops. You could easily spend twice the time on this trip with all the vibrant cities and beautiful natural landscapes you'll encounter.

## ILLINOIS

### Chicago: 1 day

Start in Chicago, spending the day among its great buildings, admiring the vastness of **Lake Michigan,** and going out for live jazz or blues in the evening.

## INDIANA

### Indiana Dunes National Park: 1 day / 250 miles (400 kilometers)

From Chicago, make the hour-long drive to Indiana Dunes National Park, where you can climb over mounds of sand in a windy, lunar landscape.

Afterward, point east into Ohio, where you'll end up in Toledo (3.5 hours away) for the night.

## OHIO

### Toledo and Kelleys Island or Cedar Point: 1 day / 130 miles (210 kilometers)

From Toledo, make a day trip to Kelleys Island, one of Ohio's four **Lake Erie** islands, hopping on a ferry at Marblehead, an hour away. Or, head to Cedar Point, also about an hour, to experience the best amusement park in the country.

## MICHIGAN

### Detroit, Mackinac Island, and Pictured Rocks: 3 days / 670 miles (1,080 kilometers)

Head up to Detroit (1 hour from Toledo), and dedicate the rest of the day

CHICAGO'S SKYLINE, ILLINOIS

COLORFUL FOLIAGE DURING AUTUMN, OHIO

to cruising Motor City and learning about its Black history and culture. The next day, make the 4-hour drive up to St. Ignace, where you'll hop on a ferry to Mackinac Island, a car-free island in **Lake Huron.** The next day, drive 2 hours from St. Ignace to Pictured Rocks National Lakeshore, on the north side of Michigan's Upper Peninsula. Take a cruise on **Lake Superior** to fully appreciate this natural wonder. Afterward, head south to Wisconsin's Green Bay, 3.5 hours away.

## WISCONSIN

**Green Bay, Door County, and Milwaukee: 2 days / 240 miles (385 kilometers)**
Set out from Green Bay for a day in magnificent Door County, a peninsula jutting into Lake Michigan. Visit one or more of the state parks, and spend the night in Fish Creek. In the morning, make the 3-hour drive to Milwaukee and relax with a beer when you get there. It's a 2-hour drive from Milwaukee to Chicago, to complete the loop.

## ADDING MINNESOTA

**Duluth, North Shore, and Minneapolis: 4 days / 750 miles (1,207 kilometers)**
To add Minnesota to the trip, you could spend a day making the 6-hour drive from Pictured Rocks to Duluth. From Duluth, take one day to explore the North Shore of Lake Superior. It's 2.5 hours from Duluth to Minneapolis, where you can spend another day. From Minneapolis to Green Bay is about 4.5 hours.

LAKE MICHIGAN SHORELINE AT INDIANA DUNES, INDIANA

# MINNESOTA

**W**ith everything from sod houses to skyscrapers, from steamboat towns on the Mississippi and St. Croix Rivers to farm country in the west, and from Minneapolis's world-class arts scene to a record-setting ball of twine, this state will likely leave even seasoned travelers impressed.

On Dakota and Ojibwe land, Minnesota is known to be some beautiful country. The boreal forests of the northeast fade into the tallgrass prairie of the southwest, and in between are the lakes—far more than the sloganized 10,000. It's difficult to find any place more beautiful than the Boundary Waters: thousands of lakes rimmed by ancient bedrock and littered with islands. Just next door, the rocky Lake Superior shore, lined with cliffs and waterfalls, is as lovely a coast as you'll ever see. With all this, it's not surprising that Minnesota regularly tops nationwide rankings in quality of life. Don't be surprised if, after your visit, you just can't bring yourself to leave: Every year thousands of people arrive as visitors and return as residents.

**AREA:** 86,935 square miles / 225,162 square kilometers (12th)

**POPULATION:** 5,639,632 (22nd)

**STATEHOOD DATE:** May 11, 1858 (32nd)

**STATE CAPITAL:** St. Paul

▲ BOUNDARY WATERS CANOE AREA

## ORIENTATION

The Twin Cities of **Minneapolis** and **St. Paul** lie in the southeast quadrant of the state. The **Boundary Waters Canoe Area** is in the far northern reaches of the state, along the eastern part of the border with Canada. Also in the northeast part of the state, **Duluth**, the jumping off point for the **North Shore** of Lake Superior, sits in the notch where the Great Lake presses into Minnesota.

## WHEN TO GO

Minnesota's glorious **summers**, with long, lingering evenings and temperatures in the 80s, are the most popular with tourists, but visitors shouldn't write off **winter**, when locals make the most of the snow with outdoor activities and festivals.

**Spring** comes in like a lion and races through like a cheetah, lasting as little as a couple of weeks. Few visitors come at this time, but a profusion of wildflowers and the cheapest lodging of the year are bonuses for those who do. With mild, sunny, dry weather, beautiful foliage, and off-season discounts, **fall** is the best time to visit.

# HIGHLIGHTS

## LOCAL THEATER IN THE TWIN CITIES

On any given weekend night during the theater season—and even in the summer—somebody with an urge to see a play will have more than 40 shows to choose from in Minneapolis and St. Paul. The Twin Cities metro area, in fact, is second only to New York City in per capita attendance at theater and arts events. Which means you'll find high-quality productions and enthusiastic audiences as well as just plain variety. Don't expect safe old chestnuts to dominate the playbills, either, with some theaters well known for presenting original scripts or regularly premiering works by internationally known playwrights. Here are some good places to start exploring the Twin Cities' theater scene:

- **Guthrie Theater** (818 2nd St. S., Minneapolis; 612/377-2224; www.guthrietheater.org): This is the crème de la crème of Minnesota theater, with top national performers in classics and contemporary favorites.

- **Mixed Blood Theatre** (1501 4th St. S., Minneapolis; 612/338-6131; www.mixedblood.com): Mixed Blood expands the boundaries of the theatrical canon, with plays by and about marginalized people, from immigrants to the elderly.

- **Penumbra Theatre** (270 Kent St. N., St. Paul; 651/224-3180; www.penumbratheatre.org): The nation's largest African American theater launched the career of August Wilson, and it continues to lead the way.

## MALL OF AMERICA

60 Broadway E., Bloomington; 952/883-8800; www.mallofamerica.com

GUTHRIE THEATER

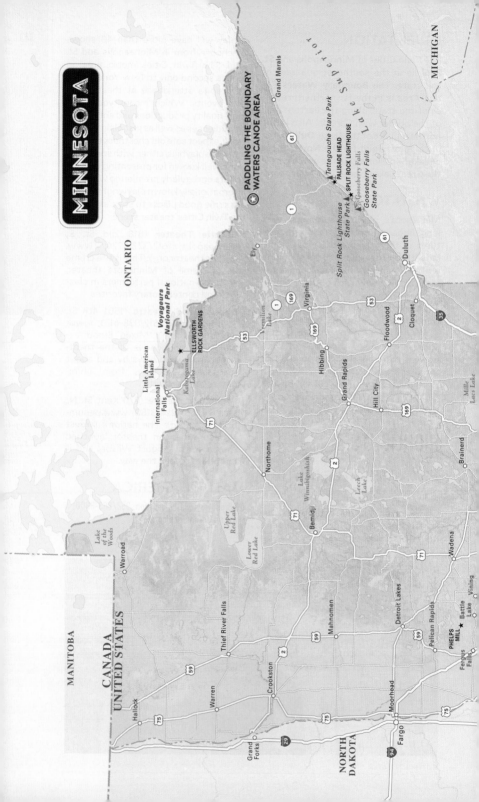

MINNESOTA

MANITOBA

CANADA
UNITED STATES

Hallock

Warroad

Lake
of the
Woods

ONTARIO

Thief River Falls

Warren

Crookston

Grand Forks

NORTH
DAKOTA

Moorhead

Fargo

Detroit Lakes

Mahnomen

Upper
Red Lake

Lower
Red Lake

Bemidji

Northome

Lake
Winnibigoshish

Leech
Lake

Pelican Rapids

PHELPS
MILL
Battle
Lake
Vining
Wadena

Fergus Falls

Brainerd

Mille
Lacs Lake

Voyageurs
National Park

Little American
Island

International
Falls

ELLSWORTH
ROCK GARDENS

Kabetogama
Lake

Ely

Vermilion
Lake

Virginia

Hibbing

Grand Rapids

Hill City

Floodwood

Cloquet

Duluth

PADDLING THE BOUNDARY
WATERS CANOE AREA

Grand Marais

Lake Superior

Tettegouche State Park
PALISADE HEAD
SPLIT ROCK LIGHTHOUSE
Gooseberry Falls
State Park

Split Rock Lighthouse
State Park

MICHIGAN

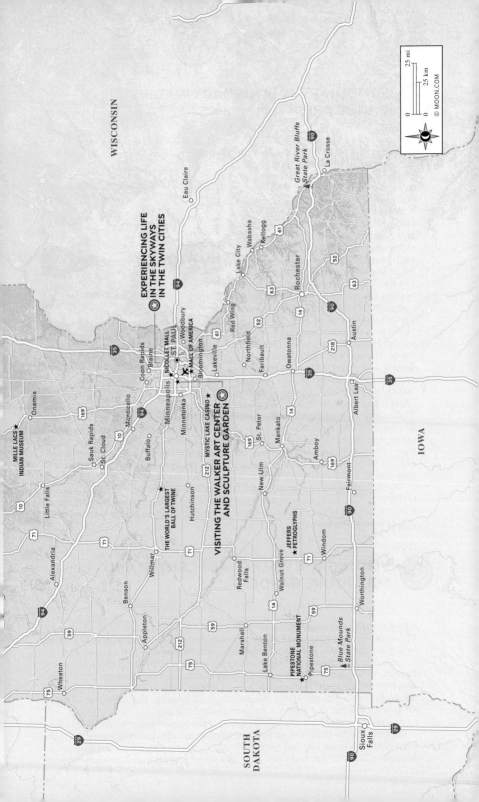

# TOP 3

## ① PADDLING THE BOUNDARY WATERS CANOE AREA

With over 1 million acres (404,685 hectares) and nearly 1,200 lakes set aside for silent sports, this is one of the best canoeing destinations—not to mention one of the most beautiful places—in the world.

Stretching 150 miles (241 kilometers) along the Canadian border, the Superior National Forest's Boundary Waters Canoe Area Wilderness (BWCAW) is the largest wilderness east of the Rockies, and padding here is an unforgettable experience. With over 200,000 visitors each year, this paddlers' paradise is the most heavily used wilderness area in the country; however, a strict permit system protects the beauty, solitude, and wildlife, and ensures a quality wilderness experience.

CANOEING ONE OF 1,200 LAKES IN THE BOUNDARY WATERS

Streams and portages connect the myriad lakes, allowing unlimited canoe travel. There are 56 entry points to the waters and 1,200 miles (1931 kilometers) of canoe routes, and trips might include seeing the northern lights, spotting a moose, or casting for trout. The nearby town of **Ely** has many outfitters waiting to set you up with everything you need for a Boundary Waters canoe trip. The **Ely Chamber of Commerce** (www.ely.org/outfitters/boundary-waters-outfitters) maintains a list of member outfitters, including **Piragis Northwoods Company** (105 Central Ave. N., Ely; 218/365-6745 or 800/223-6565; www.piragis.com) and **Voyageur North Outfitters** (1829 Sheridan St. E., Ely; 218/365-3251 or 800/848-5530; www.vnorth.com).

The Boundary Waters isn't just for boating, either. There are also many **hiking trails,** including short, easy trails on the edge of the wilderness and long-distance treks through its heart. During winter, a number of **cross-country skiing** trails cross through the area.

## ② VISITING THE WALKER ART CENTER AND SCULPTURE GARDEN

1750 Hennepin Ave., Minneapolis; 612/375-7600; www.walkerart.org

Like a giant tinfoil marshmallow floating on the southeast corner of downtown Minneapolis, the Walker Art Center makes an impression. It's known as one of the best places to experience multidisciplinary contemporary art in the country. When it opened in 1927, it was the first public gallery of art in the Upper Midwest, and it has now grown into one of the world's most lauded modern art centers. The Walker is best known for its major exhibitions of cutting-edge 20th-century art. It holds works by Pablo Picasso, Henry Moore, Claes Oldenburg, Roy Lichtenstein, Yoko Ono, Andy Warhol, and others in its permanent collection.

Across the street from the Walker is one of the largest urban sculpture gardens in the country, the 11-acre (4.45-hectare) **Minneapolis Sculpture Garden.** The highlight of the park and beloved symbol of Minneapolis is Oldenburg and Coosje van Bruggen's *Spoonbridge and Cherry,* but the park contains over 40 mostly massive

THE WALKER ART CENTER IN MINNEAPOLIS

sculptures. Another highlight is Katharina Fritsch's joyful *Hahn/Cock,* a cobalt blue rooster standing proudly over the other pieces.

 ## EXPERIENCING LIFE IN THE SKYWAYS IN THE TWIN CITIES

In the 1960s, the business leaders of downtown Minneapolis realized they needed to compete with the expanding parking lots and indoor amenities of the suburbs (Southdale, the nation's first enclosed shopping mall, opened in Edina, Minnesota, in 1956). Their solution has become one of the Twin Cities' most recognizable traits: the skyway system. In Minneapolis, second-floor glass-enclosed walkways total 9.5 miles (15 kilometers) and connect more than 80 blocks—nearly every building in downtown's central business district, including 4,000 hotel rooms. It's the nation's first and most extensive system of its kind. St. Paul's smaller system totals about 5 miles (8 kilometers).

Detractors say moving people up to the skyways kills street-level businesses. Others argue that you have to redefine "street-level." About 200,000 pedestrians walk the skyways in Minneapolis every day, patronizing small shops, restaurants, and businesses of all kinds.

SKYWAY IN DOWNTOWN MINNEAPOLIS

The skyway-level restaurants are a great place to people-watch, and the passageways also offer fun windows onto street life below; find a skyway crossing **Nicollet Mall** for the prettiest street views. Skyway maps are posted throughout each system.

# Best ROAD TRIP

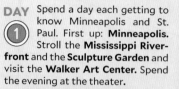

**DAY 1** Spend a day each getting to know Minneapolis and St. Paul. First up: **Minneapolis.** Stroll the **Mississippi Riverfront** and the **Sculpture Garden** and visit the **Walker Art Center.** Spend the evening at the theater.

**DAY 2** **St. Paul's** must-see is **Summit Avenue.** Afterward, visit the **Mall of America.**

DOWNTOWN MINNEAPOLIS

**DAY 3** Drive 2.5 hours (150 miles/241 kilometers) north to **Duluth** to watch ships slip under the **Aerial Lift Bridge** and visit the many museums in and around **Canal Park,** including the **Lake Superior Maritime Visitor Center** (600 Lake Ave. S.; 217/727-2479; www.lsmma. com) and the **S.S. *William A. Irvin* Museum** (350 Harbor Dr.; 218/722-7876; www.decc.org). If you can get a reservation, spend the night in the **Two Harbors Lighthouse** (1 Lighthouse Point Dr.; www.lighthousebb.org).

**DAY 4** Follow Highway 61 as it hugs the North Shore of **Lake Superior** for just 150 miles (241 kilometers), passing eight state parks, each more impressive than the last. You'll have to pick just one or two. **Gooseberry Falls** is the most visited state park for good reason; **Split Rock Lighthouse** is a Minnesota icon; and **Tettegouche** has some of the most impressive shoreline on the whole lake. Spend the night in charming **Grand Marais,** where there is good food, interesting art, and fun shopping.

SPLIT ROCK LIGHTHOUSE

**DAY 5** Head northwest to **Ely** (a 2-hour drive, 107 miles/172 kilometers from Grand Marais), gateway to the glorious **Boundary Waters Canoe Area Wilderness,** and enjoy paddling one of the world's most beautiful and wildlife-rich wildernesses. You can paddle for a day or enjoy a weeklong canoe and camping trip. From Ely, it's a 4-hour (254-mile/408-kilometer) drive back to the Twin Cities.

BOUNDARY WATERS CANOE AREA

Visitors come to the Mall of America to gawk, to say they've seen the largest mall in the United States, and, yes, to shop. The sheer density of stores makes the mall a shopper's mecca.

In addition to the shops, the **Nickelodeon Universe** theme park (952/883-8800; www.nickelodeonuniverse.com) occupies the center, with a full-size Ferris wheel, roller coaster, and log chute. Other thrilling experiences in the mall include **Flyover America** (5120 Center Court; www.flyover-america.com), a virtual aerial tour of the country's landmarks; and the **Crayola Experience** (S300; www.crayolaexperience.com), where you can play with colors in myriad ways. **Sea Life** (952/883-0202; www.visitsealife.com/minnesota) is a full-size aquarium located under the mall. There are also two hotels, **Radisson Blu** and **JW Marriott,** attached to the mall.

## PALISADE HEAD

Arguably the most beautiful site in the state, Palisade Head's ruddy cliff climbs 350 feet (106 meters) straight out of Lake Superior. A slim road at mile marker 57 snakes to the top, where you can walk along as much of the rim as your fear lets you—needless to say, be careful. Even severe acrophobes should make the trip just to take in the wonderful scenery in the distance. Shovel Point, another rhyolite lava headland, crawls out of the lake to the north, and Wisconsin's Apostle Islands are visible on the horizon. Palisade Head is a part of **Tettegouche State Park** (5702 Hwy. 61; 218/226-6365).

## MILLE LACS INDIAN MUSEUM

43411 Oodena Dr., Onamia; 320/532-3632; www.mnhs.org/millelacs

The Ojibwe tell their own story at the Mille Lacs Indian Museum, the best Native American museum in the state. The museum traces Ojibwe history, and displays let you learn about fantastic beadwork, the significance of what you'll see at a powwow, and modern sovereignty issues. The heart of the center is the Four Seasons Room, where life-sized dioramas show what life was like here 200 years ago. Cooking, craft

## MINNESOTA'S INDIGENOUS POPULATION

Since the time the first Europeans came in search of furs, the Native Americans residing in Minnesota have been almost exclusively the **Dakota** and **Ojibwe.** The Dakota have four reservations, all under 2,000 acres (809 hectares), while the Ojibwe, by far the larger of the two, have seven reservations, none smaller than 48,000 acres (19,424 hectares). The Dakota lands are so small because following the Dakota Conflict they were expelled from the state and only a few later returned, at which time the government gave them new land.

Minnesota, with about 53,000 Native American residents, has the 14th-largest Native population in the United States. Only about a third actually live on the reservations, while nearly 40 percent live in the Twin Cities metro area.

demonstrations, and other cultural programs are offered regularly. You can shop for authentic Native American crafts at the restored 1930s **Trading Post** next door.

## JEFFERS PETROGLYPHS

507/628-5591; www.jefferspetroglyphs.com

The 80-acre (32-hectare) Jeffers Petroglyphs Historic Site protects over 2,000 ancient petroglyphs. Many of the buffalo, deer, elk, turtles, thunderbirds, humans, weapons, and other similar subjects were cut by Native Americans in the exposed shelf of bedrock as far back as 3,000 BC. Others, it appears, are as recent as the 1750s. The glyphs likely served a ceremonial purpose, and this remains sacred ground for many tribes—religious ceremonies are still held here on occasion.

Even if there weren't a single carving this would be a worthwhile trip; the small islands of pink quartzite

# *Major* CITIES

**MINNEAPOLIS AND ST. PAUL:** With four internationally known art museums, three Tony Award-winning theaters, and a full slate of festivals year-round, Minneapolis is one of the country's most cultured cities. The second half of the Twin Cities is quieter St. Paul, which is compact and pretty, and offers plenty in the way of sights and classic neighborhood bars.

**ROCHESTER:** In the heart of Bluff County in the southeast corner of the state, Rochester is best known as the home of the Mayo Clinic. The clinic has brought gleaming skyscrapers and some cosmopolitan flair to this city of 86,000.

**DULUTH:** Located in the northeast corner of the state on Lake Superior, Duluth is the biggest port city on the Great Lakes. It blends this gritty industrial side with small-town charm and a wild side, as the resident bears and wandering moose will affirm.

surrounded by the sea of prairie make this one of the most beautiful spots in Minnesota. It is also a great place to see the subtleties of prairie ecology since each of the three main prairie types—wet, mesic, and dry—are represented, and together they contain well over 100 species of flower and forb.

## WALNUT GROVE

Laura Ingalls Wilder, author of the "Little House" series of books that inspired the TV show *Little House on the Prairie,* arrived as a seven-year-old girl and lived in this small prairie town in southwestern Minnesota for about five years (1874-1876 and 1877-1879). She described life here in her book *On the Banks of Plum Creek.*

The real story of Laura and her family, both in Walnut Grove and elsewhere, is told at the **Laura Ingalls Wilder Museum** (330 8th St.; 507/859-2358 or 888/528-7298; www.walnutgrove.org). The collection includes many family photos and mementos, such as Laura's sewing basket and quilt. People at the museum can direct you to other Wilder sites in town, such the original **Ingalls Dugout** and places where Laura worked and went to school.

## PIPESTONE NATIONAL MONUMENT

36 Reservation Ave., Pipestone; 507/825-5464; www.nps.gov/pipe

For many Native Americans, the Pipestone National Monument is one of the most sacred places in North America. Pipestone is so named because it is carved primarily into ceremonial pipe bowls (peace pipe is a common misnomer), and the finished pipes are highly revered. Native Americans are still the only ones allowed to quarry here, and today quarriers from across the United States and Canada still dig through some 10 feet (3 meters) of solid quartzite by hand to reach the 1- to 3-inch-thick (2.5- to 7.6-cm) layer of pipestone. During late summer and fall you will probably see people working one of the many pits. The **visitors center** not only explains the entire process of making a pipe, but April-October you can watch local Dakota artists carving them. The

PIPESTONE NATIONAL MONUMENT

finished products, along with other Native crafts, are for sale in the **gift shop.**

Although the stone is the main focus, there is much more to see in this 282-acre (114-hectare) park. The 0.75-mile (1.2-kilometer) **Circle Trail** leads along a beautiful ridge of quartzite with a waterfall and many interesting rock formations. On your way in or out of the park, take a look at the **Three Maidens,** six large granite boulders, named in honor of legendary women who live inside them.

## THE WORLD'S LARGEST BALL OF TWINE

Make the trip to tiny Darwin (pop. 296), just over an hour from Minneapolis, to experience the one-of-a-kind genius of Francis A. Johnson. Johnson gave the tiny village its one claim to fame: the world's largest ball of twine made by just one man. This "magnificent sphere" is 11 feet (3.3 meters) tall and 12 feet, 9 inches (3.8 meters) wide, and weighs nearly 9 tons (8 metric tons)—it used to weigh 11 tons (9.97 metric tons), but all the water has finally evaporated. He rolled his first strand of baler twine in March 1950 and didn't stop until 1979. There are other giant twine balls out there, some even a bit bigger, but they are just imitations—all were collective efforts inspired by Johnson's creation. The whole town celebrates **Twine Ball Days** on the second Saturday in August.

## SPLIT ROCK LIGHTHOUSE STATE PARK

3755 Split Rock Lighthouse Road, Two Harbors; 218/595-7625; www.dnr.state.mn.us/ state_parks

On November 28, 1905, a great gale whipped Lake Superior into such a rage that half a dozen ships were wrecked within 12 miles (19 kilometers) of the Split Rock River. In response, the **Split Rock Lighthouse** (3713 Split Rock Lighthouse Rd., Two Harbors; 218/226-6372) was built atop this magnificent 130-foot (39-meter) cliff; it began operations in 1910. The gorgeous facility has been restored to its pre-1924 appearance, and when you tour the lighthouse,

SPLIT ROCK LIGHTHOUSE

fog-signal building, and keeper's home, costumed interpreters share their tales.

# BEST SCENIC DRIVES

## OTTER TRAIL SCENIC BYWAY

A Minnesota microcosm, this lovely circular 150-mile (241-kilometer) scenic drive zigs and zags past a variety of small towns, historic sites, oversized statuary, and natural areas. Even more appealing than the sights themselves is driving between them. Get an early start and you can cover it all in a day, but that would be seriously rushing things. This is rural Americana at its best.

The first—and best—stop along the byway, if traveling clockwise from Fergus Falls, is the impressive **Phelps Mill** (29024 County Hwy. 45, Underwood; 218/826-6159). Not only is it a beautiful sight from the outside, but the original equipment is still in place. The route then passes through the towns of Pelican Rapids, Battle Lake, and Vining.

## GREAT RIVER ROAD

Below its confluence with the St. Croix River, the Mississippi River quickly expands, spanning up to 5 miles (8

THE MISSISSIPPI RIVER AS SEEN FROM AN OVERLOOK AT GREAT RIVER BLUFFS STATE PARK

kilometers) across, while towering half-dome bluffs hedge it in along the rest of its Minnesota journey. U.S. Highway 61 hits the bluffs as it approaches **Red Wing** and meets the river at **Lake City,** and from this point on you'll have unrivaled scenery. There is ample opportunity to turn inland and climb the mountain-like terrain for glorious valley views. Though you are never far from one of the historic river towns, the floodplain and impossibly steep hills thwart development, allowing moments where you can imagine yourself deep in a lost wilderness. Wildlife, best enjoyed from a canoe in the river's backwaters, but quite often seen from behind the wheel, abounds all year long. Each fall, waterfowl, shorebirds, and raptors follow the valley south to warmer wintering grounds. For bald eagles the river is their winter residence—well over a thousand of them fish in these open waters. Follow the **Great River Road** north alongside the Mississippi, shopping and sightseeing in the historic river towns of **Wabasha** and **Red Wing,** and keeping your eyes out for resident eagles and migrating birds. Along the way, stop at some of the bluff-top parks, such as **Great River Bluffs State Park** (43605 Kipp Dr., Winona; 507/643-6849), for spectacular valley views.

# BEST PARKS AND RECREATION AREAS

## VOYAGEURS NATIONAL PARK

360 Hwy 11 East, International Falls; 218/283-6600; www.nps.gov/voya

Befitting the Land of 10,000 Lakes, Voyageurs National Park is dominated and defined by water. The park is centered on four large lakes—Rainy, Kabetogama (cab-eh-to-ga-ma), Namakan, and Sand Point—and water covers nearly 40 percent of its 218,200 acres (88,302 hectares). Minnesota's only national park brings hundreds of thousands of visitors to these remote forests and waters, but it's one of the least visited national parks—so it is still easy to commune with nature in peace.

Water isn't just part of the scenery, it's the primary means of transportation. Except for those leading up to the four entry points, there are no roads in the park. To witness the hundreds of lopsided islands and slender bays or explore the rugged 75,000-acre (30,351-hectare) Kabetogama Peninsula at the heart of the park, you'll have to travel by boat. Most park visitors get around in a motorboat of some kind, though there is some excellent paddling here, too. And although Voyageurs is all about the water, there are several hiking trails.

A highlight in the park is the red-and-white **Kettle Falls Hotel** (12977 Chippewa Tr., Kabetogama; 218/240-1724; www.kettlefallshotel.com), and people come from all corners of the park to stroll the grounds, have a meal or a drink in the Lumberjack Saloon, or just relax on the endless veranda. Just a short walk from the hotel is the **Dam Tender's Cabin,** a restored 1912 log home. On **Little American Island,** you'll learn the story of the Rainy Lake Gold Rush along the short trail, which takes you past a mineshaft, tailings piles, and other mining remnants. **Ellsworth Rock Gardens,** on the north shore of Kabetogama Lake, features 52 terraced flower beds and over 150 geometric and animal-themed sculptures assembled out of the local granite. This singular spot makes an ideal picnic ground.

# GRAND ROUNDS NATIONAL SCENIC BYWAY

The Twin Cities have a well-deserved reputation for a vibrant cycling culture and a strong infrastructure for two-wheeled transportation. St. Paul maintains 101 miles (162 kilometers) of paved off-street trails, 24 miles (38 kilometers) of dirt trails, and 30 miles (48 kilometers) of dedicated bike lanes. Minneapolis has 81 miles (130 kilometers) of on-street bikeways and 85 miles (136 kilometers) of off-street bikeways. One of the most beautiful and accessible rides—and a good way to see Minneapolis's leafy, green residential neighborhoods—is the Grand Rounds National Scenic Byway, a 50-mile (80-kilometer) ring of interconnected bike trails. It loops around the outer edges of the city, taking in Theodore Wirth Park, the Chain of Lakes (four interconnected bodies of water: Cedar Lake, Lake of the Isles, Bde Maka Ska, and Lake Harriet) in southwest Minneapolis, about 10 miles (16 kilometers) of riverfront on the Mississippi, downtown Minneapolis, and the parkways of North Minneapolis. The Grand Rounds is the only urban trail system designated as a National Scenic Byway.

ICE SKATING IN WINTER

# ICE SKATING

In hockey-mad Minnesota, skating is a way of life, with outdoor ice rinks all over the state. Generally speaking, these are no-amenities spots: just a rink with some sideboards and overhead lights and a warming house if you're lucky, and pretty much everyone brings their own skates. Some rinks are divided into designated areas for **hockey** and for **figure skating**. Be courteous—and safe—by staying out of the hockey players' way. If you see teams of people out on the ice chasing a ball with sticks that look like giant Q-tips, that's **broomball.** Similar to hockey but played without pads, it's a quintessentially Minnesotan thing and a good way to get some really nice bruises to take home as a souvenir.

# GOOSEBERRY FALLS STATE PARK

3206 Hwy 61 E., Twin Harbors; 218/834-3855; www.dnr.state.mn.us/state_parks

With your first glimpse of Gooseberry Falls you'll quickly understand why this is Minnesota's most popular state park. The swift Gooseberry River shoots around a narrow bend, drops over Upper Falls into a rocky gorge, blankets the 100-foot-wide (30-meter) rock wall forming Middle Falls, and plunges over the split Lower Falls before calmly marching on to Lake Superior. Though nearly 600,000 people gaze upon these scenes each year—the whole 90-foot drop sits just a short stroll down a wheelchair-accessible trail—a relatively small number of them venture through the rest of the 1,675-acre (677-hectare) park.

A pair of excellent hiking trails follows the river down to Lake Superior: the **River View Trail** and the **Gitchi-Gami Trail. Fifth Falls Trail** (part of the North Shore-length **Superior Hiking Trail**) hugs the river as it climbs to its namesake cascade. Another 12 miles (19 kilometers) of trails, most of them open to **mountain bikes,** wind through the park's hills. Come winter most of the trails are groomed for **cross-country skiing,** while the Gitchi-Gami and Fifth Falls Trails are available for winter

MINNESOTA STATE FAIR

hiking. There is also a **kayak** site on Lake Superior.

## BLUE MOUNDS STATE PARK

1410 161st St., Luverne; 507/283-1307; www.dnr.state.mn.us/state_parks

Although it receives far fewer visitors than most of Minnesota's state parks, in many ways Blue Mounds State Park is one of the best. The namesake mound at the heart of the park, which appeared blue to the earliest settlers passing by in the distance, is a massive outcrop of Sioux quartzite bedrock rising gradually from the west and ending in a spectacular 1.5-mile-long cliff. This ridge, nearly 100 feet (30 meters) tall in many places, is one of the best **rock-climbing** sites in the state.

The **hiking** here is arguably the best in southwest Minnesota, and all 13 miles (20 kilometers) of trails crossing the prairie are beautiful. **Bird-watchers** seeking western species could have a field day along these trails. The Blue Mound and most of the 1,826-acre (738-hectare) park is topped by original tallgrass prairie, and bison graze on the prairie once again as they did through the early 19th century.

# FESTIVALS AND EVENTS

## POWWOWS AND *WACIPIS*

Minnesota's Indigenous communities hold dozens of gatherings every year, known often as powwows, but more commonly by the Dakota word *wacipi*. They are held throughout the summer, but Memorial Day, the Fourth of July, and Labor Day are popular times. The public is generally welcome at these events. The centerpiece of every wacipi is the grand entry honoring veterans, then dancers in regalia perform and compete, and drum circles gather.

One of the biggest is the annual wacipi of the **Shakopee Mdewakanton Sioux Community** (www.shakopeedakota.org) in late August on their wacipi grounds to the north of the Mystic Lake Casino. Other popular events include the Memorial Day Powwow at the **Mille Lacs Indian Museum** near Onamia, and the **Mahkato Wacipi** (www.mahkatowacipi.org) in Mankato in September.

## MINNESOTA STATE FAIR

State Fairgrounds, 1265 Snelling Ave. N., St. Paul; 651/288-4400; www.mnstatefair.org; late Aug.-early Sept.

If you are anywhere near St. Paul during the 12 days leading up to Labor Day, the Minnesota State Fair is not to be missed. The 320-acre (129-hectare) fairgrounds

## BEST SOUVENIRS

- In the tiny town of Kellogg, you'll find **LARK Toys** (63604 170th Ave.; 507/767-3387; www.larktoys.com), the largest independent toy store in North America. On offer are board games, chemistry sets, Russian nesting dolls, wind-up toys, and more plus the handmade wooden toys that started it all.

- **Native American arts** are found throughout the state. Beadwork and silver jewelry are most common, though the least Minnesotan. Baskets made of birch bark can be true works of art, while other birch-bark items, such as toy canoes, make good mementos. Though sold across the nation, **pipestone carvings** come from Minnesota.

- Also common at craft fairs and in gift shops are **Scandinavian folk arts,** like rosemaling—a decorative painting characterized by flowers and flowing scrolls—and chip carving. Most large and mid-sized cities have Scandinavian gift shops.

becomes the third-largest city in Minnesota, with more than 100,000 visitors each day. What began as an agricultural fair in 1855 has evolved to include more than 100 musical acts, a massive midway, butter carving, daily marching band parades, and nightly fireworks. Fuel up with a gut-bedeviling array of foods, including more than 60 served on a stick. In Minnesota, you know summer is over when you have eaten your last deep-fried cheese curd.

### WINTER CARNIVAL

Rice Park, St. Paul; 651/223-4700; www.wintercarnival.com; Jan.

Since 1886, St. Paulites have spent much of the month of January thoroughly enjoying the winter weather with its Winter Carnival, which draws about 350,000 visitors a year. While the Ice Palace is the biggest draw, it isn't built every year, for economic and weather reasons. The entire city of St. Paul bustles with ice skating, ice-carving contests, and a 5K run and half marathon (yes, outside). Warm up in the Hotdish Tent with Minnesotans' favorite comfort food, hot dish (that's casserole to the rest of the country).

## BEST FOOD

While many Minnesotans regard the **hot dish** (local vernacular for a casserole) as a gourmet meal, Midwestern cuisine should not be dismissed out of hand. Featured prominently are locally grown ingredients such as cranberries, raspberries, morel mushrooms, pumpkin, wild rice, fresh fish, and wild game such as venison and elk. **Walleye,** the most prevalent Minnesota specialty (though it almost always come from Canada), is usually served batter-fried, and menus will often have multiple variations of it.

### SCANDINAVIAN CUISINE

Though you won't find it on too many menus, the state's most distinctive cuisine is Scandinavian. Swedish meatballs are well known throughout the country, but it's the three Ls, lutefisk, lefse, and lingonberries, that most intrigue visitors. These and other Scandinavian staples are largely reserved for church and lodge suppers and family get-togethers, but you'll find them on the occasional restaurant menu.

**Lefse** comes in many varieties, but the most common combines potato (occasionally rice), flour, butter, and salt. The mix is rolled flat and baked on a griddle, producing a bread that resembles a thick tortilla. Traditionally lefse was wrapped around meat or fish—today it is mostly eaten on the side with butter and a sprinkling of sugar, brown sugar, or cinnamon, or with a spread of jam. **Lingonberries** are similar to cranberries, and are sometimes called mountain cranberries.

A much greater culinary adventure is **lutefisk**—dried North Atlantic cod reconstituted in water for three days, soaked in lye for another three, and then put back into water for up to a week. Traditionally Norwegians top it with butter and Swedes with a cream sauce, while a mustard sauce helps many non-fans get it down year after year. Minnesotans consume several tons of it annually, mostly between October and December.

A few churches also host communal **Lapskaus** (a traditional Norwegian beef stew) dinners, which might include a side course of sing-along. If you want to sample some of this ethnic cuisine, you can always pick some up at Scandinavian gift shops and many grocery stores. Microwaveable lutefisk dinners are a new option.

## HMONG FOOD

The Twin Cities' large Hmong population's cooking traditions have started to come out of home kitchens and into the public. Start your exploration of Hmong cuisine at one of two massive marketplaces. **Hmong Village** (1001 Johnson Pkwy., St. Paul) is a complex of small stores selling everything from clothes to kitchenware, along with about two dozen restaurant stalls in an industrial area of St. Paul. **Hmongtown Marketplace** (217 Como Ave., St. Paul; 651/487-3700; www.hmongtown-marketplace.com) is even bigger, with more than 200 stalls, indoors and out.

Look for rich barbecue, stuffed chicken wings, fruity bubble teas, fried noodles, papaya salads, *laab* (meat salads, some raw, some cooked), and chicken feet. The cooking is 100 percent authentic and cooked to please a Hmong eater, with one exception: The real heat is often toned down, with chili sauce served on the side.

## MAJOR AIRPORTS

- **Minneapolis-St. Paul International Airport:** MSP; Terminal 1 4300 Glumack Dr., St. Paul; Terminal 2 7150 Humphrey Dr., St. Paul; 612/726-5555; www.mspairport.com

## MORE INFORMATION

### TRAVEL AND TOURISM INFORMATION

- **Explore Minnesota Tourism:** www.exploreminnesota.com
- **Minnesota Department of Natural Resources:** www.dnr.state.mn.us

### NEWSPAPERS AND MAGAZINES

- *Minneapolis Star Tribune:* www.startribune.com
- *Minnesota Monthly:* www.minnesotamonthly.com

# WISCONSIN

For generations, bumper stickers proclaimed "Escape to Wisconsin." The Department of Tourism later shelved this for other PR slogans, but the people were so opposed that the state resurrected it. It's succinctly Wisconsin: a retreat, a sojourn, a mental breather—a genuine escape.

On the land of the Ojibwa, Menominee, Potawatomi, Stockbridge-Munsee, Oneida, Ho-Chunk, Illinois, Fox, Sauk, Miami, Kickapoo, Satee, Ottawa, and Mascouten people, Wisconsin is generally content to remain in the middle on most things—except such important issues as livability quotients, at which it tends to excel. It's also the Midwest's overall most popular travel destination, boasting the planet's most diverse glacial topography, amazing cataracts, and an immense North Woods region. Even onetime University of Wisconsin Badger John Muir had it figured out in the 19th century when he proclaimed, "Oh, that glorious Wisconsin wilderness!" That still holds true today for the hordes coming into the state pulling boats, bikes, kayaks, and canoes, all for that chance of bucolic splendor.

AREA: 65,498 square miles / 169,639 kilometers (23rd)

POPULATION: 5,822,434 (20th)

STATEHOOD DATE: May 29, 1848 (30th)

STATE CAPITAL: Madison

ANGLERS AT SUNSET

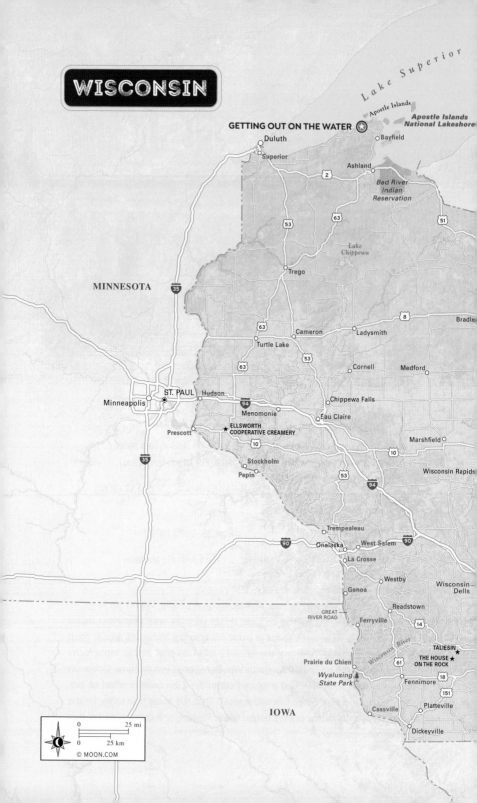

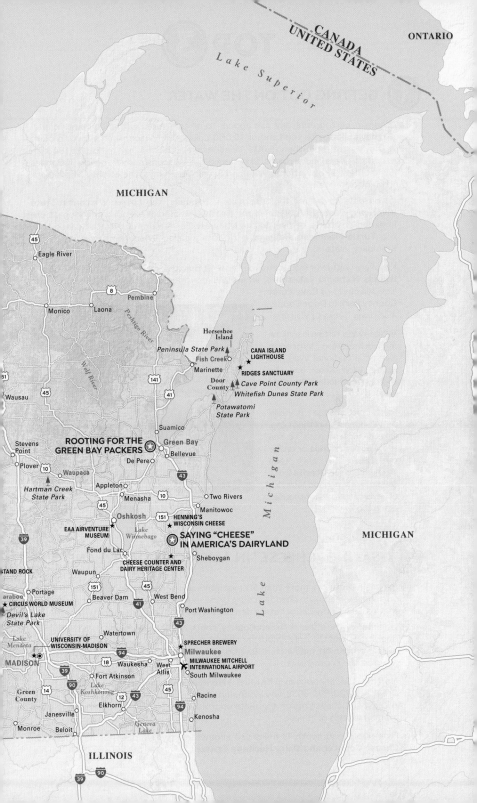

CANADA
UNITED STATES
ONTARIO

*Lake Superior*

MICHIGAN

45 Eagle River

8 Pembine
Monico    Laona
*Peshtigo River*

Horseshoe
Island
*Peninsula State Park*
Fish Creek          CANA ISLAND
141          Marinette          LIGHTHOUSE
*Wolf River*
51          Door          RIDGES SANCTUARY
Wausau    41    County    Cave Point County Park
45                    Whitefish Dunes State Park
*Potawatomi*
*State Park*
Suamico

**ROOTING FOR THE**
**GREEN BAY PACKERS**    Green Bay
Stevens          De Pere    Bellevue
Point
Plover    10    Waupaca          43
*Hartman Creek*          Appleton
*State Park*          Menasha    10    Two Rivers
39          Oshkosh          Manitowoc
EAA AIRVENTURE          151    HENNING'S
MUSEUM    *Lake*          WISCONSIN CHEESE
*Winnebago*          **SAYING "CHEESE"**
Fond du Lac          **IN AMERICA'S DAIRYLAND**          MICHIGAN
STAND ROCK          CHEESE COUNTER AND    Sheboygan
Waupun          DAIRY HERITAGE CENTER
araboo    151    Beaver Dam    45    West Bend
*Devil's Lake*    Portage          41
*State Park*    *Lake*                    Port Washington
*Mendota*          Watertown    43
UNIVERSITY OF                    SPRECHER BREWERY
WISCONSIN-MADISON          94    **Milwaukee**
MADISON    18    Waukesha    West    MILWAUKEE MITCHELL
39          Allis    INTERNATIONAL AIRPORT
Green    14    Fort Atkinson          South Milwaukee
County    90    *Lake*
*Koshkonong*    12    43    Racine
Janesville    Elkhorn          94    Kenosha
Monroe    Beloit    *Geneva Lake*

**ILLINOIS**

39    90

## TOP 3

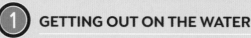

### 1. GETTING OUT ON THE WATER

Wisconsin, cartographically, can appear to be splattered with blue paint. Minnesota may claim to be the Land of 10,000 Lakes, but Wisconsinites love to point out they've got more than 15,000. Wisconsin also has 84,000 miles (135,184 kilometers) of rivers and streams. Experience the Wisconsin River; nearly 300 miles (482 kilometers) of National Wild and Scenic Riverways; the Mighty Mississippi; and many other gems.

- If you only have time for one, make it canoeing the **Lower Wisconsin State Riverway,** west of Madison, in the Driftless Region. It's among the longest unimpeded stretches of river in the Midwest. For a more underrated canoe trail, the **Turtle-Flambeau Flowage** is rightfully called Wisconsin's version of the Boundary Waters.

- Kayakers will never forget an experience at the otherworldly sea caves of **Apostle Islands National Lakeshore,** where Wisconsin runs up against Lake Superior. The sea caves of **Cave Point County Park** in Door County also draw flocks of visitors.

- White-water rafting is sublime in Northeastern Wisconsin along the National Wild and Scenic **Wolf River** and the slightly more sedate **Peshtigo River.**

- From picturesque Bayfield on Wisconsin's northern cap, take a sunset cruise to see the **Apostle Islands** or cruise out Green Bay onto Lake Michigan to see **Death's Door** (along with a good number of eye-catching lighthouses along the way).

KAYAKING THE APOSTLE ISLANDS SEA CAVES

### 2. SAYING "CHEESE" IN AMERICA'S DAIRYLAND

Wisconsin produces more than 500 varieties and more than one-third of the nation's cheese, leading in cheddar, colby, brick, muenster, limburger, and many Italian varieties. Learn why Badger State denizens wear foam cheese heads with pride.

- One star of the show is **Green County,** south of Madison, home to a number of operations and the only limburger cheese maker in the country. And try the limburger and onion sandwich at **Baumgartner's** (1023 16th Ave.; 608/325-6157) in Monroe, the county seat.

- Northwest of Sheboygan in tiny Kiel is **Henning's Wisconsin Cheese** (20201 Point Creek Rd.; 920/894-3032; www.henningscheese.com), notable for possibly being the last U.S. cheese maker to create enormous (up to 12,000 pounds/5,442 kilograms!) wheels of cheese.

- From Kiel, head south 13 miles (20 kilometers) to Plymouth for its wondrous **Cheese Counter and Dairy Heritage Center** (133 E. Mill St.; 920/892-2012). This little town is responsible for producing, storing, or shipping a significant percentage of U.S. cheese, and this place tells you about it.

- Wisconsinites are addicted to cheese curds. Officially declared Wisconsin's "Cheese Curd Capital," **Ellsworth Cooperative Creamery** (232 N. Wallace St., Ellsworth; 715/273-4311) along the Great River Road makes 160,000 pounds (72,574 kilograms) of fresh curds daily.

TRADITIONAL CHEESE CURDS

## 3 ROOTING FOR THE GREEN BAY PACKERS

920/569-7500; www.packers.com

One of the oldest professional football teams in the United States and the only community-owned team in professional sports is the Green Bay Packers. If there are any awards for professional sports fandoms, the Green Bay Packers football team and its beloved legions win hands-down. One grizzled sportswriter wrote, "The Dallas Cowboys were only another football team; the Packers were a practicing religion." But you don't need to bleed green and gold to get swept up in the Green Bay Packers fandom.

Don't miss a tour of renovated but still classic **Lambeau Field;** perhaps no stadium mixes tradition with modernity more than this national treasure. Myriad tours exist, and the more expensive the tour, the more things you see. Visitors can explore the press box, the visitors' locker room, the skyboxes, and even the field itself. If nothing else, check out the stadium from the outside. The number-one Packer destination is the Lambeau Field Atrium—its restaurants and shops are open to the public almost every day of the year—which is home to the **Green Bay Packers Hall of Fame** (920/569-7512).

People often crowd the free twice-a-day practices during the Packers' late-summer **training camp,** held at the practice facility along Oneida Street across from Lambeau Field. Sometimes practices are held indoors in the team's state-of-the-art Hutson Practice Facility. Practices begin in mid-July and run until preseason games begin in late August. In mid-July is the **Packer Hall of Fame Induction Ceremony,** a very big deal to Packers fans.

It's virtually impossible to get face-value tickets to regular season Packers games; preseason games are another matter. Check www.packers.com for ticket information.

GREEN BAY PACKERS TRAINING CAMP AND PRACTICE

**DAY 1** After arriving in Milwaukee, spending time on the **lakefront** is a must. Tour **Miller Brewing** or the **Harley-Davidson Museum** and step into the unparalleled **Milwaukee Public Museum** (814 W. Wisconsin Ave.; 414/286-3000). Stay overnight downtown in the historic **Pfister** or at **Brewhouse Suites** in the renovated **Pabst Brewery** just northwest of downtown.

MILWAUKEE'S WATERFRONT

**DAY 2** Drive 1 hour 20 minutes (80 miles/128 kilometers) to **Madison,** and tour an architectural gem: Frank Lloyd Wright's **Monona Terrace.** Stroll the pedestrian-friendly State Street area to the **University of Wisconsin-Madison campus.**

**DAY 3** See the real **Dells** of the Wisconsin River (1 hour, 54 miles/86 kilometers from Madison) on a World War II-era duck boat tour. If you've had your fill of water, **Devil's Lake State Park** down the road offers superb hiking and, next door, fetching **Baraboo** is small-town quaint and has a grand circus museum, replete with outdoor shows.

MONONA TERRACE

**DAY 4** Continue your outdoor adventure with a trip to **Door County;** base yourself in **Fish Creek** (3.5 hours, 200 miles/321 kilometers from the Dells). Must-sees are hiking or kayaking at **Whitefish Dunes State Park** or **The Ridges Sanctuary**, and visiting the nation's densest county concentration of lighthouses.

**DAY 5** Your return drive to **Milwaukee** will take 3 hours (170 miles/273 kilometers).

DEVIL'S LAKE STATE PARK

## ORIENTATION

The largest city of **Milwaukee** sits against **Lake Michigan** in southeastern Wisconsin, while due west is **Madison,** the state capital. **Door County,** the peninsula stretching into Lake Michigan with **Green Bay** at its base, is north of Milwaukee, while the **Wisconsin Dells** lie northwest of Madison. The **Mississippi River** flows along the western border until it enters Minnesota, where the **St. Croix River** takes over as the state line.

## WHEN TO GO

Wisconsin is a four-season destination with something for everyone in any season. High season is **summer,** between Memorial Day and Labor Day. Another peak season is **fall,** from late September through late October, when throngs arrive to witness autumn's splendorous colors. **Winter** in general sees fewer visitors except for snowmobilers and skiers. Few people come in March and early April, as these months are gray, muddy, and windy.

# HIGHLIGHTS

## FOLLOWING FRANK LLOYD WRIGHT

The famed architect Frank Lloyd Wright, a native Badger, melded the natural world into his architecture. In 1938, *Time* magazine called him "the greatest architect of the twentieth century." In 2019, two of his Wisconsin works—Taliesin in Spring Green and a private home in Madison—were added to UNESCO's World Heritage Sites.

Highlights of Wright's work in Wisconsin include:

- Wright's Madison masterwork, the **Monona Terrace Community and Convention Center** (1 John Nolen Dr., Madison; 608/261-4000; www.mononaterrace.com), has a view so sublime that even his detractors will be in awe. Also in Madison, the privately owned **Herbert and Katherine Jacobs House** was named a UNESCO World Heritage Site in 2019.

- In the Wisconsin Dells, you can sleep in one of the only Frank Lloyd Wright-designed buildings available for rent—

the **Seth Peterson Cottage** (608/254-6551; www.sethpeterson.org).

- Along the Wisconsin River is the pilgrimage to Spring Green, home to **Taliesin,** Wright's home and studio and a UNESCO World Heritage Site. Have lunch at the Riverview Terrace Restaurant in the **Frank Lloyd Wright Visitor Center** (5607 County Rd. C, Spring Green; 877/588-7900; www.taliesinpreservation.org or www.wrightinwisconsin.org), the only Wright-designed eatery anywhere. Driving through the area, you'll see "Wright-inspired" everything.

The state also has the **Frank Lloyd Wright Trail** (https://wrightinwisconsin.org) marked along I-94 from Racine in Southeastern Wisconsin to Richland Center in south-central Wisconsin. The brown signs will lead you to highlights of his work.

## HARLEY-DAVIDSON MUSEUM

Canal St. and S. 6th St., Milwaukee; 877/436-8738

Harley-Davidson has created hog heaven in the 100,000-square-foot (9,290-square-meter) Harley-Davidson Museum. This $30 million project features an interactive museum and exhibits on the history, culture, and lifestyle engendered by the company and its devoted riders. Rooms are full of vintage vehicles; not surprisingly, Elvis's bike probably gets the most attention.

## THE DELLS

These lovely rock formations, oddballs with names such as Devil's Elbow, Fat Man's Misery, Witches Gulch, and Cold

WISCONSIN DELLS BOAT TOUR

# *Major* CITIES

**MILWAUKEE:** The low-key residents are proud of their cultural, educational, and architectural gems along Milwaukee's fabulous lakefront. And don't forget the names that made Milwaukee famous: the gargantuan Miller Brewing and Harley-Davidson.

**MADISON:** The Mad City, also known as Madtown, is a vibrant city among a quartet of jewellike lakes. It's home to the State Capitol and the University of Wisconsin. But most residents are nature lovers; you'll find native state flora at the UW's Arboretum and the Olbrich Botanical Gardens.

**GREEN BAY:** This city on the edge of its namesake Lake Michigan bay is best-known for its beloved Green Bay Packers football team. It's also home to some notable museums and an amusement park.

Water Canyon, make for one of the nicest boat tours in the state. They can be found along 15 miles (24 kilometers) of upper and lower dells, and everywhere you see craggy palisades and soft-hued sandstone. The trademark of the Wisconsin Dells is **Stand Rock,** a mushroom-shaped sandstone protuberance made famous in 19th-century first-of-its-kind stop-action photography.

To see the Dells, hop onboard a tour with the **Original Wisconsin Ducks** (608/254-8751; www.wisconsinducktours.com), where you'll ride in green-and-white, 14,000-pound (6,350-kilogram) amphibious World War II landing craft. They slowly roar along the main drag of the Dells, picking up passengers for a 1-hour, 8-mile (12-kilometer) trip that includes jaunts through restored prairie lands and access to wilderness trails. The **Dells Boat Tours** (608/254-8555; www.dellsboats.com) uses modern cabin cruisers and offers separate Upper Dells tours; this is the only boat tour that offers a stop at the Dells trademark Stand Rock.

## CIRCUS WORLD MUSEUM

426 Water St., Baraboo; 608/356-8341; www.circusworldbaraboo.org

The site of the Circus World Museum was the original headquarters of the Ringling Brothers circus in an attractive setting along the Baraboo River. Summer is the best time to visit, when the 51-acre (20-hectare) grounds are open and the three-ring circus and sideshows reappear. Under the big top is a dazzling, frenetic, fun mélange of jugglers, aerialists, clowns, bands, magic, circus nuts and bolts, steam-driven calliope concerts, and animal shows. Another hall has memorabilia and displays from long-gone U.S. circuses and an exhaustive historical rundown of the Ringlings. Also in the hall is the world's most complete collection of circus vehicles (214 and counting) and circus posters (8,000 and counting). It is so comprehensive that Disney designers consulted here for the 2019 movie *Dumbo.*

## EAA AIRVENTURE MUSEUM

3000 Poberezny Rd., Oshkosh; 920/426-4818; www.airventuremuseum.org

Wisconsin has officially decreed the Experimental Aircraft Association (EAA) AirVenture Museum a state treasure. In

EAA AIRVENTURE MUSEUM

one of the largest museums of its kind in the world, more than 250 airplanes of every possible type are displayed—aerobatic planes, home-built, racers, and more. Five theaters, numerous display galleries, and tons of multimedia exhibits make this well worth the admission price. The newest and most popular is an interactive F-22 simulator. Be there when flights are offered in old-timey planes, complete with the leather hat, goggles, and wind-blown hair. The museum owes much of its popularity to the 800,000 or so visitors who converge on Oshkosh each summer for the annual **fly-in.**

## THE HOUSE ON THE ROCK

Hwy. 23, south of Spring Green; 608/935-3639; www.thehouseontherock.com

The House on the Rock defies description. Back in the 1940s, Alex Jordan stumbled over a 60-foot (18-meter) candle-like outcropping in the Wyoming Valley. Intending to construct a weekend retreat and artists haven, Jordan somehow wrestled the original structure into completion atop the chimney. Today, the original house sits atop the rock, plus several other mind-blowing rooms and add-ons, all stuffed with the detritus that Jordan accumulated through a lifetime. Included are the Largest Carousel (20,000 lights and 275 handcrafted wooden animals, not one of which is a horse), the Organ Room (with three of the world's largest), and more. The best is the loopy Infinity Room, a glassed-in room that spikes 218 feet (66 meters) over the valley floor.

# BEST SCENIC DRIVES

## GREAT RIVER ROAD

This famed route stretches from the source of the Mississippi River in Lake Itasca, Minnesota, and parallels the Mississippi all the way to New Orleans. Wisconsin's mileage is road-trip eye candy. This includes the best-known stretch, the 85 miles (136 kilometers) north from La Crosse; the southern half seems at times to be absolutely untouched.

## WISCONSIN'S INDIGENOUS POPULATION

Wisconsin is home to six sovereign Native American nations on 11 reservations, not all of which are demarcated by boundaries. In addition to the six nations, Wisconsin is on the land of the Illinois, Fox, Sauk, Miami, Kickapoo, Satee, Ottawa, and Mascouten people. The total Native American population is around 40,000, or 1 percent of the population. The **Great Lakes Intertribal Council** (www.glitc. org) is a good resource for information.

The largest Indigenous group is the **Ojibwa,** also rendered historically as Chippewa and now Ojibway, Ojibwe, and Ojibwa. Wisconsin has five Ojibwa communities. The Ojibwa inhabited the northern woodlands of the upper Great Lakes, especially along Lakes Huron and Superior. The **Bad River** group today lives on a 123,000-acre (49,776-hectare) reservation along Lake Superior in Ashland County. It's the largest reservation in the state and is famed for its wild rice beds on the Kakagon Sloughs.

Wisconsin is also home to the Algonquian **Menominee,** who have been in Wisconsin longer than any other people; the Forest County **Potawatomi,** also Algonquians; Wisconsin's only Mohicans, the **Stockbridge-Munsee** people; the **Oneida,** who belonged to the Iroquois Five Nations Confederacy; and the Winnebago Nation, which reverted to its original name, **Ho Chunk.**

If you're coming from the Indianhead region, you'll start in **Prescott,** 10 minutes southeast of Minneapolis. Drive slowly and find some art, antiques, or coffee in the tiny town of **Stockholm,** and visit Laura Ingalls Wilder's birthplace in **Pepin** before dining at everyone else's favorite pit stop, **Trempealeau,** famous for its anachronistic hotel-restaurant. In **La Crosse,** get a snapshot of the sunset from Granddad's Bluff and spend the night.

Heading toward Iowa, do some barge fishing in **Genoa,** or at least visit its fascinating fish hatchery, before picking up some snacks at Ferryville Cheese in **Ferryville.** Next stop is **Prairie du Chien** and its historically perfect Villa Louis, an examination of early Wisconsin. Picnic with some of that cheese high above the confluence of the Wisconsin and Mississippi Rivers at **Wyalusing State Park** before heading south to **Cassville,** keeping an eye out for eagles. After arriving, you can take an awesome ferry across the Mississippi.

## RUSTIC ROAD-TRIPPING

Travel media writers have consistently voted Wisconsin one of the United States' greatest road-touring states, in part because many rural roads, originally farm-to-market routes, seem to have changed little in a century and a half.

Wisconsin's Department of Transportation (www.wisconsindot.gov) has highlighted 120 of the state's best backroads trips with its **Rustic Roads designation.** Every Rustic Road in the state is guaranteed to offer an amazing palette of colors **mid-September–late October.**

- Heading for East-Central Waters? From Waupaca, go southwest on Highway 22 to the Yankee village of Rural, possibly the state's quaintest original. From here, **Rustic Roads 23 and 24** (3 miles/4.8 kilometers total) form a V shape around Hartman Creek State Park and take you three times over the Crystal River atop stone bridges, then past a spring-fed trout stream.

- In Northeastern Wisconsin, the Peshtigo River Parkway **(Rustic Road 32)** cannot be beat for river beauty and waterfalls. To get here, head to little Pembine at the junction of U.S. 141 and U.S. 8. Head west on U.S. 8 approximately 9 miles (14 kilometers) to signs leading you south. This is a big one, 37 miles (59 kilometers) long, but you'll have plenty of places to stop and rest at state and county parks.

- In Southwestern Wisconsin, **Rustic Road 31** starts in West Salem northeast of La Crosse at the exit off I-90 at Highway C, running to Highway 16. Head north on Highway 16 to Highway 108 and the **Mindoro Cut,** 20 miles (32 kilometers) of some of the loveliest roller-coaster driving imaginable.

## BAYFIELD TO SUPERIOR
### Hwy. 13

Here's where the windshield vistas become worthy of Ansel Adams—the modest Bayfield County mosaic of orchards, multihued patches of crops, enormous rolls of hay, dilapidated one-eyed shotgun shacks weathering by the side of the road, even an abandoned truck rusting in the cattails. Highway 13 from Bayfield hugs the coastline, coming out almost as far west as Superior—about 80 miles (128 kilometers) and totally worth the effort. These parts were settled predominantly by Finnish and other Scandinavian immigrants pushing west out of Michigan's Upper Peninsula around the middle of the 19th century. They would eventually spread through the ore docks and shipyards of Superior and into the mines of the Mesabi and Vermilion Iron Ranges in Minnesota. A number of their homesteads can still be seen poking through the weeds along the route.

ONE OF WISCONSIN'S MANY SCENIC RURAL ROADS

# BEST PARKS AND RECREATION AREAS

## GENEVA LAKE

Geneva Lake, one of the larger lakes in southern Wisconsin, is a tranquil resort area. One can't help but love its loopy mix of restored Victorian and low-key resort structures, natural splendor, and, most of all, its accessibility to the public. The 26-mile-long (41-kilometer) **footpath** that circles the lake via linked ancient Native American trails is one of the loveliest lakeside strolls anywhere.

The easiest and most popular way to experience the lake is on a tour in either a replica Mississippi paddle wheeler or lake steamer. You can also get out on the water on a ski boat or sailboat; the Geneva Lake region has more marinas than you can imagine. And for a more unique activity? Lake Geneva residents still get their mail delivered by boat, just as in the 1930s, and visitors can also hop on the mail boat, the *Walworth II* (Riviera Docks; 262/248-6206 or 800/558-5911; www.cruiselakegeneva.com), to come along for the ride.

## DOOR COUNTY

www.doorcounty.com

Door County is often called the "Cape Cod of the Midwest," or "California of the North," although in spots the area seems just as much like chilled, stony Norwegian fjords. Bays in all the colors of an artist's palette are surrounded by variegated shoreline: 250 miles/402 kilometers (more than any other U.S. county) of alternately rocky beaches, craggy bluffs, blossom-choked orchards, bucolic heath, and meadows. A great touring base is the town of **Fish Creek,** the "soul of Door County," home to historic buildings and a local winery.

One of the stars of the show here is picturesque and popular **Peninsula State Park** (920/868-3258; https://dnr.wisconsin.gov/topic/parks/peninsula). More than 20 miles (32 kilometers) of hiking trails lace the park and the shores of the bays, and there are 15 miles (24 kilometers) of road and off-road bike trails. The most popular is the **Sunset Trail,** which is open to pedestrians, wheelchair traffic, and bikes. And you won't forget a kayak or canoe trip to **Horseshoe Island.**

Other highlights here include **Potawatomi State Park** (920/746-2890; https://dnr.wisconsin.gov/topic/parks/potawatomi), where you can hike the first miles of Wisconsin's epic 1,200-mile (1,931-kilometer) Ice Age Trail, and **Whitefish Dunes State Park** (https://dnr.wisconsin.gov/topic/parks/whitefish) and **Cave Point County Park** (920/823-2400; www.doorcounty.com/experience/cave-point-county-park), where you can hike to the beach, check out dunes and wildlife, and visit Cave Point's eponymous caves. Visit the beloved **Ridges Sanctuary** (Ridges Rd.; 920/839-2802; www.ridgessanctuary.org), a must for birders and wildlife lovers, which leads to the grand, brilliantly white **Cana Island Lighthouse.**

## DEVIL'S LAKE STATE PARK

The diamond-hard, 1.5-billion-year-old quartzite bluffs of the Baraboo Range tower above a primeval icy lake. Wisconsin's number-one state park, the lake reflects the earthy rainbow colors of the rises—steel gray and blood red—and mixes them with its own obsidian for dramatic results.

The hiking here cannot be beat; nearly 30 miles (48 kilometers) encompass both the east and west bluffs. On the east bluff, the best trails are the **Grottos Trail** and the **Potholes Trail.** Many of these trails are used in winter for

PADDLEBOAT ON GENEVA LAKE

cross-country skiing, and 8 miles (12.8 kilometers) are also available for mountain biking. The hard quartzite bluffs of the park are ready-made for excellent rock climbing, and you can even plumb the depths of Devil's Lake with a scuba-diving outfitter.

## SNOWMOBILING

Snowmobiling is a big deal here. In some communities, snowmobiling accounts for more business than fishing. In total, the state maintains 25,000 miles (40,233 kilometers) of interconnected trails, so well linked that you can travel on them continuously from Kenosha in Southeastern Wisconsin all the way to Lake Superior in the northwest. Nearly half of the 42 state recreation trails permit snowmobiling; so do 15 state parks and forests, and the national forests are wide open.

# FESTIVALS AND EVENTS

## WORLD CHAMPIONSHIP SNOWMOBILE DERBY

Eagle River; 715/479-4424; www.derbycomplex.com; Jan.

Every January, throngs of aficionados of Wisconsin's de facto pastime—snowmobiling—descend on Eagle River for a weekend of cacophonic, boisterous revelry, an Indy 500 of supercharged sleds. Held at the "Best Little Racetrack in the World," it's the most important snowmobile championship race in the world, with 400 racers in 20 classes. Getting a pit-side seat is truly a dramatic experience.

The Thursday-night qualifier has become a smash hit with the crowds, as have vintage racing and the fact that fans can pay to roar around the track. The weekend sees dozens of manufacturers, tour operators, and sponsors bringing in state-of-the-art equipment for demonstrations and some hands-on opportunities.

## SUMMERFEST

Milwuakee; www.summerfest.com; June

Summerfest is the granddaddy of all Midwestern festivals and the largest music festival in the world (says *Guinness World Records*). For 11 days in late June, top national musical acts as well as unknown college-radio mainstays perform on innumerable stages along the lakefront, drawing millions of music lovers and partiers.

## OSHKOSH FLY-IN

Oshkosh; www.airventure.org; July/Aug.

The gathering known as the **EAA AirVenture Oshkosh,** often referred to as the Oshkosh Fly-In or Airshow, is a legendary jaw-dropping display of airplanes that draws hundreds of thousands of people from around the world. It's a spectacle. The skies are filled with planes and pilots with an appetite for aviation the way it used to be

OSHKOSH FLY-IN

# BEST SOUVENIRS

- **Hmong crafts** can be found at craft fairs and farmers markets throughout the state. Keep an eye out for story cloths, which recount narratives visually, and exquisite decorative *paj ntaub*, a 2,000-year-old hybrid of needlework and appliqué, usually featuring geometric designs and often animals. These quilts and wall hangings require more than 100 hours of work.

- Pick up some famous Wisconsin **cheese** as a souvenir—the requisite items are cheddar cheese foam-wedge hats and cheese-and-bratwurst gift packs. Or bring home some Door County **cherries** in the form of jam, pie filling, or other cherry-themed souvenirs.

done—strictly by the seat of the pants. Handmade and antique aircraft are the highlights, but lots of contemporary military aircraft are also on show. Thrilling air shows go on nonstop. In all, almost 12,000 aircraft and more than 750,000 people are on hand.

# BEST FOOD AND DRINK

Wisconsin's best cooking is a thoughtful mélange of ethnicities, stemming from the diverse populace and prairie-cooking fare that reflects a heritage of living off the land. Midwest regional cuisine is a blend of originally wild food such as cranberries, wild rice, pumpkins, blueberries, whitefish livers, catfish cheeks, and morel mushrooms incorporated into standard old-country recipes. Added to the mix are game animals such as deer, pheasant, and goose.

## FRIDAY FISH FRIES

Cuisine experience number one in Wisconsin is a Friday-night fish fry. On the menu is deep-fried perch or one of the other species variants—haddock, walleye pike, or cod. Fish fries are generally set up as smorgasbords, where the fish is served with slathered-on homemade tartar sauce and a relish tray or salad bar. Sometimes you'll find platefuls of chicken, too.

- For an only-in-Wisconsin fish-fry experience, the **American Serbian Hall** (5101 W. Oklahoma Ave., Milwaukee; 414/545-6030; www.americanserbmemorialhall.com) serves 2,500 people at a drive-through with a line down the street.

- For an overall experience, try the fish fry on offer at the **Beer Hall** at Lakefront Brewery (1872 N. Commerce St., Milwaukee; 414/372-8800; www.lakefrontbrewery.com) with live polka music and real-deal potato pancakes. The brewery, which offers tours, is also the best all-around experience in Wisconsin for beer lovers.

## DOOR COUNTY CHERRIES

Wisconsin's cherry trees blossom in May, and harvest season runs from mid-July to early August. Strolling through an orchard to pick your own cherries is a top Door County experience—the fragrance of the place is equally astonishing. Here are a couple places to get you started:

- **Lautenbach's Orchard Country Winery & Market** (9197 Hwy. 42 S., Fish Creek; 866/946-3263; www.orchardcountry.com) is a winery with award-winning county fruit wines, pick-your-own fruits, sleigh rides, and more. They hold a summer cherry festival at the end of July.

- At **Seaquist Orchards Farm Market** (11482 Hwy. 42, Sister Bay; 920/854-4199), you can explore the farm to take in all of the cherry trees. They also sell cherry pies as well as cherry jams, pie filling, salsa, vinaigrette, and more.

## MILWAUKEE BEER

Milwaukee has been known as the Brew City (or Brew Town) for some 160 years. Even the major league baseball team is named the Brewers, after all! Here's where to go to experience the city's beer culture.

- Industry leviathan **Miller Brewing** (4251 W. State St., Milwaukee; 414/931-2337; www.millercoors.com) is the megabrewer that most people associate with Milwaukee today. Its enormous city-state-size complex showcases original 19th-century beer caves through up-to-the-minute brewing technology.

- The former offices and interiors of the original Pabst Brewery have been rejuvenated into the **Best Place at the Historic Pabst Brewery** (901 W. Juneau Ave., Milwaukee; 414/630-1609; http://bestplacemilwaukee.com).

- **Sprecher Brewery** (701 W. Glendale Ave., Glendale; 414/964-2739; www.sprecherbrewery.com) is known for being a leader of Milwaukee's craft-brewing renaissance beginning in the 1980s.

# MAJOR AIRPORTS

- **Milwaukee Mitchell International Airport:** MKE; 5300 S Howell Ave, Milwaukee; 414-747-5300; www.mitchellairport.com

# MORE INFORMATION

## TRAVEL AND TOURISM INFORMATION

- **Travel Wisconsin:** www.travelwisconsin.com

- **Wisconsin Association of Convention and Visitors Bureaus (WACVB):** www.escapetowisconsin.com

- **Wisconsin Department of Natural Resources:** https://dnr.wi.gov

## NEWSPAPERS

- *Milwaukee Journal Sentinel:* www.jsonline.com

- *Star Tribune:* www.startribune.com

# ILLINOIS

Many who come to Illinois envision images of Al Capone's Chicago and Michael Jordan's United Center, a place where winds whip off the lakeshore and beyond the city stretch endless corn and soybean fields. And of course they've heard about Abe Lincoln.

But dig deeper and you'll often find yourself saying, "Wow, I didn't know Illinois had this." Illinois is on Chickasaw, Dakota, Ho-Chunk, Illini, Miami, and Shawnee land. It's home to the remains of pre-Columbian civilizations, cypress swamps, lush forests, and river canyons. There's beauty in the sun setting over a cornfield, or a red-winged blackbird among the waving big bluestem grass.

So ride to the top of a Chicago skyscraper and take in the view, head downstairs to the photography exhibits at the Art Institute, jam to up-and-comers and household names at music festivals, and jazz and blues clubs. But don't forget there's more than corn and soybeans outside the big city. Roll down the car window, slow down, and rumble down Route 66—you're bound to be surprised.

AREA: 57,914 square miles / 149,997 square meters (25th)

POPULATION: 12,671,821 (6th)

STATEHOOD DATE: December 3, 1818 (21st)

STATE CAPITAL: Springfield

▲ CHICAGO

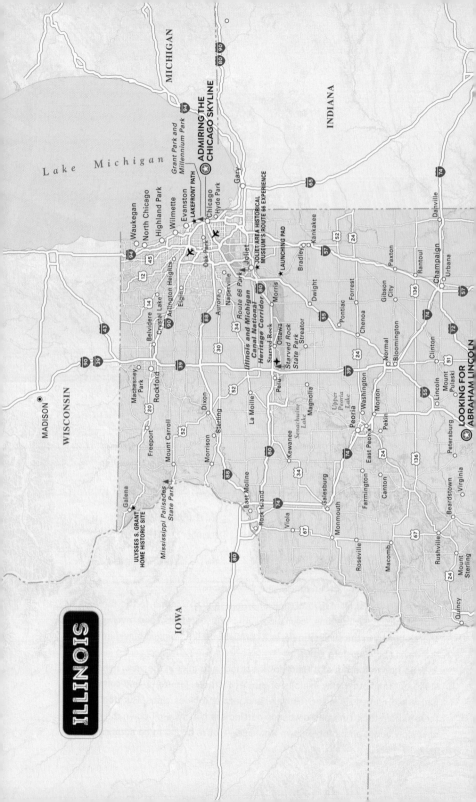

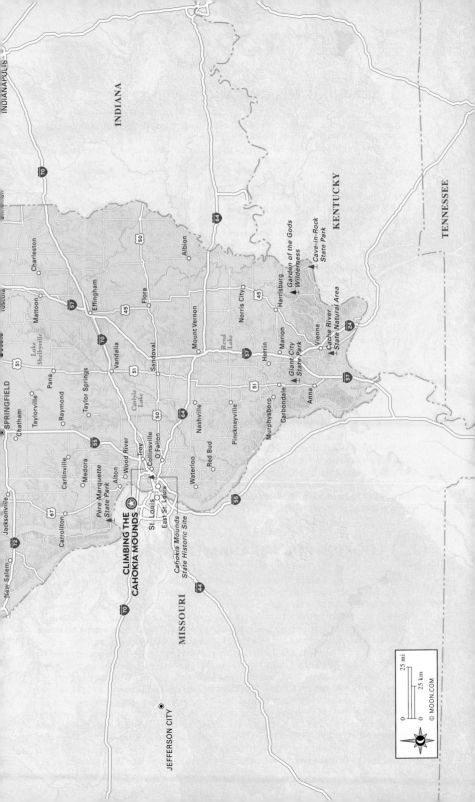

CLIMBING THE
CAHOKIA MOUNDS

## 1 ADMIRING THE CHICAGO SKYLINE

Approaching Chicago, the Loop rises before you, the birthplace of the skyscraper where steel and glass pierce the clouds. After the devastating Chicago Fire of 1871, architects such as Daniel Burnham, Louis Sullivan, Jens Jensen, and Frank Lloyd Wright, helped the city rebuild in grand style.

Landmarks from the early days include the **Rookery** (181 feet/55 meters; 209 S. LaSalle St.), built in 1888 and later renovated inside by Frank Lloyd Wright, and the art deco **Chicago Board of Trade** (605 feet/184 meters; 141 W. Jackson Blvd.), built in 1930. The **John Hancock Building** (1,127 feet/343 meters; 875 N. Michigan Ave., was built in 1969, and not long after, another tower would change the Chicago skyline. The **Willis Tower** (1,450 feet/442 meters; 233 S. Wacker Dr.), still stubbornly referred to by its former name, the Sears Tower, by locals, was built in the early 1970s, and held its claim to fame as the world's tallest building until 1998. It was the tallest building in the U.S. until

CHICAGO'S SKYLINE AS SEEN FROM THE CHICAGO RIVER

the completion of New York City's One World Trade Center in 2014.

The Hancock Building's **360 Chicago Observation Deck** (https://360chicago.com) and the Willis Tower's **Skydeck** (https://theskydeck.com) are excellent ways to see the city's concrete jungle from above. Boat tours on the Chicago River given by the **Chicago Architecture Center** (224 S. Michigan Ave.; 312/922-3432; www.architecture.org) are an absolute must; they also offer bus and walking tours as well as rotating exhibits on architecture. Other great vantage points to see the skyline include driving **Lakeshore Drive,** walking or biking the **Lakefront Trail,** or taking newer urban pathways like the **606** (www.the606.org) or the **Chicago Riverwalk** (www.chicagoriverwalk.us).

## 2 LOOKING FOR ABRAHAM LINCOLN

Abraham Lincoln lived in Illinois from 1831-1861. Before practicing law, he worked as a general store clerk (and various other jobs) in **New Salem** (Hwy. 97, 2 miles (3.2 kilometers) south of Petersburg; 217/632-4000; www.lincolnsnewsalem.com), a pioneer town where he went to make a living for himself at the age of 22. But **Springfield** is where he matured as a politician and orator. The **Lincoln Home National Historic Site** (426 S. 7th St.; 217/492-42141; www.nps.gov/liho/index.htm) is best place to start your visit; you'll listen to an interpreter share a little background on Lincoln's life and activities in Springfield, and in the historic district that surrounds it, you can amble down the street on plank sidewalks just like Abe used to do.

Nearby, the **Abraham Lincoln Presidential Library and Museum** (212 N. 6th St.; 217/558-8844; www.alplm.org) encompasses several city blocks and contains exhibits that chronicle Lincoln's life and politics, and the state of the nation while he was president. And as far as tombs and monuments go, the **Lincoln Tomb State Historic Site** (Oak Ridge Cemetery, North Grand. Ave. to Monument Ave.) is pretty magnificent. The rest of this fun, friendly town is dotted with other Lincoln sites, including the **Lincoln-Herndon Law Offices State Historic Site** (6th and Adams St.;

LINCOLN HOME NATIONAL HISTORIC SITE

217/785-7960 or 217/785-7289) and the **First Presbyterian Church** (321 S. 7th St.; 217/528-4311; www.first-pres-church.org), where the Lincolns had a pew reserved.

 ## CLIMBING THE CAHOKIA MOUNDS

Collinsville Rd. and Ramey St., Collinsville; 618/346-5160; www.cahokiamounds.org

Even if it's a hot summer day, tough it out and climb to the top of **Monks Mound,** a 100-foot-tall (30.5-meter) earthen mound east of the Mississippi River. With dozens of mounds rising from the land, the Cahokia Mounds are an impressive sight.

The area is called Cahokia after an Illinois Indian tribe that lived in the same region in the 1600s, but we don't know the real name of the 10,000-20,000 Indians who lived here from about AD 700-1400, when it was a bustling city that stretched 6 square miles (15.5 square meters). Originally there were about 120 mounds of various sizes, built with dirt dug from nearby pits; today 69 mounds have been documented in the 2,200-acre (9-square kilometer) park. You can easily spend several hours here, starting at the **interpretive center,** walking the grounds, climbing Monks Mound, and checking out **Woodhenge,** a calendar made of wooden posts. Researchers believe Cahokia was a trade center; no one is quite sure what happened to the city after about AD 1200 or 1400, but many believe the city may have deteriorated or been abandoned because of overpopulation, overuse of natural resources, disease, or war.

CAHOKIA MOUNDS

As you can imagine, the landscape has changed drastically since Cahokia was inhabited by Native American tribes. You can still find cornfields in this fertile area, but the residential and commercial districts directly surrounding the mounds are not exactly picturesque. Nevertheless, this is one of the rarest finds in North America, a state and National Historic Landmark as well as a UNESCO World Heritage Site, and well worth a visit.

# *Best* ROAD TRIP

**DAY 1** Begin your trip in **Chicago,** where you'll admire paintings and sculptures at the **Art Institute of Chicago** and get lost in other great museums downtown, such as the **Field Museum** or **Shedd Aquarium.** Take in an architectural boat tour or wander through **Millennium Park** and the **lakefront,** followed by a live blues or jazz show.

**DAY 2** Spend the morning visiting the historic museums of **Hyde Park,** followed by a trip to **Oak Park** and its many sites related to Hemingway and Frank Lloyd Wright. Be sure to grab iconic Chicago-style pizza or hot dogs for dinner.

CHICAGO WATERFRONT

**DAY 3** Drive just under 3 hours on U.S. 20 West from Chicago toward the former mining town of **Galena,** where you can browse charming art galleries and visit the **Ulysses S. Grant Home Historic Site.**

**DAY 4** Head south along the Great River Road, with views of the mighty Mississippi accompanying you on the way. Drop in for a quick hike at **Mississippi Palisades State Park** after 40 minutes, before high-tailing it the rest of the way to **Springfield,** another 3 hours and 30 minutes on I-74 E. Grab a horseshoe sandwich to refuel after all that driving.

DOWNTOWN GALENA

**DAY 5** Spend the morning following in the footsteps of Abraham Lincoln at the **Lincoln Home National Historic Site and Presidential Library and Museum,** followed by a 1 hour and 30 minute drive on I-55 South to the majestic **Cahokia Mounds State Historic Site,** returning to your hotel in Springfield for the night.

**DAY 6** Having sampled much of what Illinois has to offer, make the 4-hour drive northwest via I-55 North and I-39 N back to Chicago, stopping en route for another hike in **Starved Rock State Park.**

STARVED ROCK STATE PARK

## ORIENTATION

**Chicago** is located on the shores of Lake Michigan, and its suburbs, which include **Oak Park,** cover the northeastern corner of the state. The rest of the state is fairly rural, with farmland covering about 75 percent of the land. **Springfield,** land of Abraham Lincoln, is in the middle of the state between Chicago and St. Louis, Missouri. The **Mississippi River** forms Illinois's western border.

## WHEN TO GO

The best time to visit Illinois is **mid-spring–mid-fall.** Things don't shut down November–March, but the landscape becomes, quite frankly, dull. The **festival season** kicks in around June and continues through the fall. If you're sensitive to **humidity,** stick to the northern part of the state in July and August and leave the south to the spring or fall. You can visit **Chicago** anytime; the city never shuts down, and **December** is magical, dazzled in white lights and outdoor markets.

# HIGHLIGHTS

## HYDE PARK

### Chicago

On the city's south side, the historic neighborhood of Hyde Park is home to the Victorian and Collegiate Gothic **University of Chicago** campus and several sites relating to the 1893 World's Columbian Exhibition. The **Museum of Science and Industry** (57th and Lake Shore Dr.; 773/684-1414; www.msichicago.org), for example, offers hands-on exhibits including the Aurora 7 Mercury spacecraft and a German U-505 submarine. Hyde Park is also home to a few sites that are great introductions to Chicago's rich Black history.

The **DuSable Museum of African-American History** (740 E. 56th Pl.; 773/947-0600; www.dusablemuseum. org), founded in 1961, was the nation's first independent museum dedicated to the history and culture of African Americans. It features exhibits on Harold Washington, the city's first Black mayor; the Tuskegee Airmen; and the Civil Rights Movement. Black-owned businesses line major thoroughfares like 53rd Street; just to the north, historic Kenwood is an upper-class Black neighborhood, and until recently was home to Barack Obama. The neighborhood is full of sights related to the first Black president, who was a professor of law at U of C before turning to politics. A local greasy spoon cafeteria, **Valois** (www.valoisrestaurant.com), proudly displays a list of Obama's favorites, and is the future site of the Barack Obama Presidential Library, with construction set to begin in 2021.

## OAK PARK

The Chicago suburb of Oak Park, a picturesque old town lined with mature trees, boasts the largest collection of Frank Lloyd Wright designed homes, plus sites related to Ernest Hemingway, who was born here in 1905. Let's start with Papa Hemingway, adored by Oak Park residents. The **Ernest Hemingway Birthplace** (339 N. Oak Park Ave.; 708/848-2222; www.ehfop.org) and nearby **Hemingway Museum** (200 N. Oak Park Ave.) are decorated with period furniture, toys and family pieces, lots of photos and letters, and various editions of Hemingway's books. The writer graduated from nearby Oak Park and River Forest High School. He famously dismissed the city of "broad lawns and

ERNEST HEMINGWAY BIRTHPLACE

# *Major* CITIES

**CHICAGO:** The Windy City is home to iconic skyscrapers, the Cubbies, world-class museums and architecture, and deep-dish pizza, and that's only scratching the surface.

**JOLIET:** A working-man and woman's town, Joliet is home to a few nostalgic Route 66 sights and was formerly an important outpost for the steel and stone industries.

**SPRINGFIELD:** Justly proud of its connection to Abraham Lincoln, the Illinois state capital has a historic feel to it, with brick-lined streets and restored Victorian architecture.

narrow minds," though that quote may be apocryphal.

About five blocks from Hemingway's birthplace is the **Frank Lloyd Wright Home and Studio** (951 Chicago Ave., Oak Park; 708-848-1976; www. wrightplus.org), where Wright crafted his trademark Prairie-style architecture. After arriving in Chicago seeking employment in 1887, Wright built and settled in this house with his family in 1889. Visitors have a couple different tour options, including guided interior tours to see the family's home and architecture studio, and self-guided audio exterior tours. Thirteen more Wright-designed homes can be found in the surrounding area.

## GALENA

In northwestern Illinois is perhaps the state's most picturesque town, with white church steeples visible among tall oak trees, a Main Street lined with historic and beautifully preserved brick

buildings, and the hills above the Galena River dotted with steamboat captains' Italianate mansions that have been turned into bed-and-breakfasts. Galena can thank two industries for its growth in the early to mid-1800s: river travel and lead mining. Today it's a popular weekend destination. Visitors can tour the **Ulysses S. Grant Home State Historic Site** (500 Bouthillier St.; 815/777-3310; www.granthome.com), where the Grants lived before the future president went off to fight in the Civil War, is open to the public.

Potters, painters, weavers, and other artists have shops in and around Main Street, selling landscape paintings, jewelry, ceramics, and more; good stops include the **Old Market House Square,** on the 100 block of Commerce Street, and **Stone House Pottery & Gallery** (418 Spring St./Hwy. 20; 815/777-0354; www.stonehousepotterygalena.com).

## CHICAGO SPORTS

Even if sports aren't your thing, a trip to see the **Cubs** play at **Wrigley Field** (1060 W. Addison St.; 800/843-2827; www.cubs.com), aka the Friendly Confines, or watching the **Bulls** (www.nba.com/bulls) or **Blackhawks** (www.chicagoblackhawks.com) play at the **United Center** (1901 W. Madison St.; 312/455-4000) is one of the best ways to understand what makes Chicago tick. The **Bears** play at **Soldier Field** (3425 E. McFetridge Dr.; 312/559-1212; www.chicagobears.com) in the shadow of the Loop's skyscrapers, and farther south the **White Sox** play at **U.S. Cellular Field** (333 W. 35th St.; 312/831-1769; www.mlb.com/whitesox) and engage

FRANK LLOYD WRIGHT HOME AND STUDIO

in a healthy rivalry with the other baseball team to the north.

## LIVE MUSIC

Chicago was one of the main destinations of the 20th-century Great Migration of African Americans from south to north, and Black Americans brought southern blues with them, beginning a long legacy of roots music in the city. Chicago is still home to many of the best blues clubs in the country. Top choices include **Kingston Mines** (2548 N. Halsted St.; 773/477-4646; www. kingstonmines.com) or **Buddy Guy's Legends** (754 S. Wabash Ave.; 312/427-0333; www/buddyguy.com). The intimate **Green Mill** (4802 N. Broadway; 312/878-5552; www.greenmilljazz. com) is a great spot for late-night jazz music.

# BEST SCENIC DRIVES

With seemingly endless wide-open spaces, Illinois is definitely a road trip-friendly state.

## LAKE MICHIGAN CIRCLE TOUR

www.lakemichigancircletour.com

The Circle Tour loops all the way around the Great Lake, and the Illinois section passes several breathtaking sights and landmarks. Much of it follows Chicago's famous **Lake Shore Drive,** with views of the Chicago skyline, the Loop's museums and parks, and Navy Pier. Farther north, you'll turn onto **Sheridan Road,** with of its elite mansions and well-manicured lawns.

## ROUTE 66

www.illinoisroute66.org

The mother of all two-lane highways begins at Chicago's lakefront and winds down southwest toward St. Louis, mostly along I-55. The historic route is dotted with all manner of quirky, nostalgic roadside attractions, from the **Joliet Area Historical Museum's Route 66 Experience** (204 Ottawa St.; 815/723-5201; www.jolietmuseum.org) and **Route 66 Park** (920 N. Broadway

# ILLINOIS'S BEST BEACHES

This isn't Santa Monica, but Chicago has plenty of beaches along the Lake Michigan shoreline. If you're not here in summer or lounging isn't your thing, a walk, jog, or cycle along the 18.5-mile (30-kilometer) **Lakefront Path** will give you a good sense of how integral the lake is to life in the city.

- On Chicago's far north side, the family-friendly **Montrose Avenue Beach** has sandy beaches, picnic areas, soccer fields, a bathhouse, nature trail, and fishing pier.

- That blue-and-white ocean liner on **North Avenue Beach** is actually a beach house where you can change into your swimsuit, buy ice-cream cones, rent volleyballs, or talk to the lifeguards.

- Less than a mile (1.6 kilometers) south is the upscale **Oak Street Beach,** a popular stretch of sand near the fancy Gold Coast neighborhood.

St., Joliet) to drive-ins like the **Launching Pad** (810 E. Baltimore, Wilmington; 815/476-8535).

## GREAT RIVER ROAD

www.greatriverroad-illinois.org

The great Mississippi River gives the western side of Illinois its distinctive shape, and played an indelible role in its history. On **Highway 84,** the Great River Road, south of Galena, the landscape becomes more dramatic the closer you get to the Mississippi. Parks like the **Mississippi Palisades State Park** (16327 Hwy. 84, Savanna; 815/273-2731; www2. illinois.gov/dnr/Parks/Pages/MississippiPalisades) and **Père Marquette State Park** (Hwy. 100, Grafton; 618/786-3323; www2.illinois.gov/dnr/Parks/About/Pages/PereMarquette) allow you to get closer to the bluffs and shores of this mighty river.

CLOUD GATE, AKA "THE BEAN," IN MILLENNIUM PARK

# BEST PARKS AND RECREATION AREAS

## GRANT PARK AND MILLENNIUM PARK

Chicago

East of Chicago's downtown, which is known as the Loop, a collar of green spaces and amazing museums line the harbors and piers of the lakefront. Massive Grant Park, known as the city's front yard, is the site of concerts, festivals, impromptu soccer games, picnics, and the iconic beaux-arts style **Buckingham Fountain.** It melds with newer **Millennium Park** (www.millenniumpark.org), with the Frank Gehry-designed **Jay Pritzker Pavillion,** gardens, fountains, and sculptures, including the famous stainless steel *Cloud Gate,* better known as "the bean." Chicago's famous skyline can be viewed from both Grant and Millennium Parks. In between and around, you'll find some of the city's best museums, including the **Field Museum** (1400 S. Lake Shore Dr.; 312/922-9410; www.fieldmuseum.org), **Adler Planetarium** (1300 S. Lake Shore Dr.; 312/922-7827; www.adlerplanetarium.org), **Shedd Aquarium** (1200 S. Lake Shore Dr.; 312/939-2438; www.sheddaquarium.org), and **Art Institute of Chicago** (111 S. Michigan Ave.; 312/443-3600; www.artic.edu).

## STARVED ROCK

Hwy. 178, Utica; 815/667-4726; www2.illinois.gov/dnr/Parks/Pages/StarvedRock.aspx

On the south side of the Illinois River near the town of Utica stands a 125-foot-tall (38-meter) sandstone bluff, after which Starved Rock State Park is named. It is the scene of a tragic event in local Native American history. The story goes that after the leader of an Ottawa Indian tribe, Pontiac, was killed in 1769 by a member of another tribe, the Illiniwek, a war broke out between the two tribes. Allies of the Ottawa Indians, the Potawatomi reportedly drove a group of Illiniwek Indians to the bluff, where the Illiniwek stayed until they died of starvation.

Today, hiking is the thing to do at Starved Rock State Park. All in all there are about 13 miles (20 kilometers) of trails, ranging in length from the 0.3-mile (0.5-kilometer) **Starved Rock Trail** to the 4.7-mile (7.5-kilometer) **Illinois Canyon Trail.**

# FESTIVALS AND EVENTS

## MUSIC FESTIVALS

Chicago hosts some of the country's most popular music festivals, including **Lollapalooza** (www.lollapalooza.com) and **Pitchfork Music Festival** (https://pitchforkmusicfestival.com).

## PUMPKIN FESTIVAL AND PUNKIN' CHUNKIN'

Morton; 309/263-2491; www.mortonpumpkinfestival.org; Sept.-Oct.

Illinois's famously fertile soil means tons of delicious produce, from corn

# THE PARKS OF SOUTHERN ILLINOIS

The southern tip of Illinois escaped the glaciers' advances, and as a result the land is rugged and gorgeous.

- **Giant City State Park:** This popular 4,000-acre (16-square-kilometer) park south of Carbondale is loaded with outdoor adventure possibilities, such as climbing or rappelling off sandstone bluffs, hiking through ravines, and horseback riding through hardwood forests and prairie.

- **Cache River State Natural Area** (930 Sunflower Ln., Belknap; 618/634-9678; www2.illinois.gov/ dnr/Parks/Pages/CacheRiver. aspx): Visitors can explore this 13,000-acre nature preserve by walking on a floating boardwalk over cypress swamps or canoeing along a quiet river.

- **Garden of the Gods Wilderness:** (www.fs.usda.gov/recarea/ shawnee/recarea/?recid=82129) Millions of years of wind and rain have eroded the land to create startling rock formations that can be visited on foot or on horseback.

- **Cave-in-Rock State Park** (1 New State Park Rd., Cave-in-Rock; 618/289-4325; www2.illinois.gov/ dnr/Parks/Pages/CaveInRock. aspx): A 19th-century a hide-out for thieves, the cave within this state park right on the Ohio River is now a tourist-friendly destination with walking trails and picnic tables.

how far they can shoot pumpkins using slingshot-type contraptions and heavy-duty air cannons. You'll find various other ways to celebrate the orange gourd throughout Illinois, including **The Great Pumpkin Patch** (Springfield Rd., west of County Rd. 1800E, southwest of Arthur; www.the200acres.com).

# BEST FOOD

Illinois likes its pizza thick and its meat topped with fries and cheese, so take a break from counting calories and don't forget napkins.

## CHICAGO–STYLE PIZZA

Chicago-style pizza is a thick, cheesy pie in which the top layer is chunky tomato sauce, not mozzarella (the cheese is packed on top of the dough). Early purveyors of this dish, **Pizzeria Uno** (29 E. Ohio St.; 312/321-1000) and **Pizzeria Due** (619 N. Wabash Ave.; 312/943-2400), in the tourist-driven River North neighborhood, still serve up good pies.

## CHICAGO–STYLE HOT DOGS

Chicago-style hot dogs are all-beef wieners topped with green relish, chopped onions, sliced tomatoes, serrano peppers, yellow mustard, and celery salt in a poppy-seed bun. Head to classic joints **Superdawg** (6363 N. Milwaukee Ave.; 773/763-0660) and **The Wiener's Circle** (2622 N. Clark St.; 773/477-7444),

to peaches, but in one crop the Land of Lincoln reigns supreme: pumpkins. Morton, Illinois calls itself the pumpkin capital of the world because 85 percent of the world's pumpkins are processed here; at its early September Pumpkin Festival and hilarious Punkin Chuckin' at the end of October, participants see

CHICAGO-STYLE PIZZA

## BEST SOUVENIRS

- **Popcorn:** Enjoy a snack direct from the miles and miles of cornfields growing around the state. You'll find popcorn for sale in Chicago storefronts or roadside stands.

- **Galena arts and crafts:** This picturesque river town is home to many of Illinois's best artists and craftspeople.

or stop for a dog anywhere you see the Vienna Beef sign.

## MEXICAN FOOD

Chicago is home to the largest Mexican-American population outside of the southwestern U.S., and the taquerias, carnicerias, and panaderias are appropriately top-notch. Head straight to the **Pilsen neighborhood,** southwest of the Loop, to get your taco fix.

## HORSESHOE SANDWICH

The horseshoe sandwich is open-faced, layered with toast, meat (hamburger, ham steak, turkey, or corned beef), French fries, and melted cheese, often found in and around Springfield. Try **Norb Andy's Tabarin** (518 E. Capitol Ave., Springfield; 217/523-7777).

## BURGOO AND BARBECUE

With its rolling green hills and southern drawl, southern Illinois may remind you of Kentucky in more ways than one. This also applies to the food: burgoo, a meat stew cooked over an open flame, and barbecue can be found throughout the region. The famous local favorite is **17th Street Bar and Grill** (32 N. 17th St., Murphysboro; 618/684-3722; https://17bbq.com).

# MAJOR AIRPORTS

- **O'Hare International Airport:** ORD; 10000 W. O'Hare Ave., Chicago; www.flychicago.com/ohare

- **Midway International Airport:** MDW; 5700 S. Cicero Ave., Chicago; www.flychicago.com/midway

# MORE INFORMATION

## TRAVEL AND TOURISM INFORMATION

- **Illinois Bureau of Tourism:** 800/226-6632; www.enjoyillinois.com

- **Illinois Department of Natural Resources:** www2.illinois.gov/dnr/parks

## NEWSPAPERS AND MAGAZINES

- *Chicago Tribune:* www.chicagotribune.com

- *Chicago Sun-Times:* https://chicago.suntimes.com

- *Chicago:* www.chicagomag.com

# INDIANA

ndiana's motto, "The Crossroads of America," seems fitting for a state that many people think of as a place to drive through without stopping. But there's plenty in the Hoosier state to make you get out of your car and want to learn more.

On Illini, Miami, and Shawnee land, Indiana is a state where, the more time you spend in it, the more you realize it's not just a flat expanse of corn and soybean fields (though the state does produce a lot of corn and soybeans). It's the majestic Indiana Dunes hugging Lake Michigan to the north and the forested hills and lowlands rolling to the Ohio River to the south. It's the growing city of Indianapolis, regularly named one of the best places to live in the Midwest, and picturesque, historic small towns. It's home to pioneering innovators who visualized utopian societies and modern architectural marvels. So don't just cross through: find yourself a slice of Hoosier pie and stay awhile.

**AREA:** 36,418 square miles / 94,322 square kilometers (38th)

**POPULATION:** 6,732,219 (17th)

**STATEHOOD DATE:**
December 11, 1816 (19th)

**STATE CAPITAL:** Indianapolis

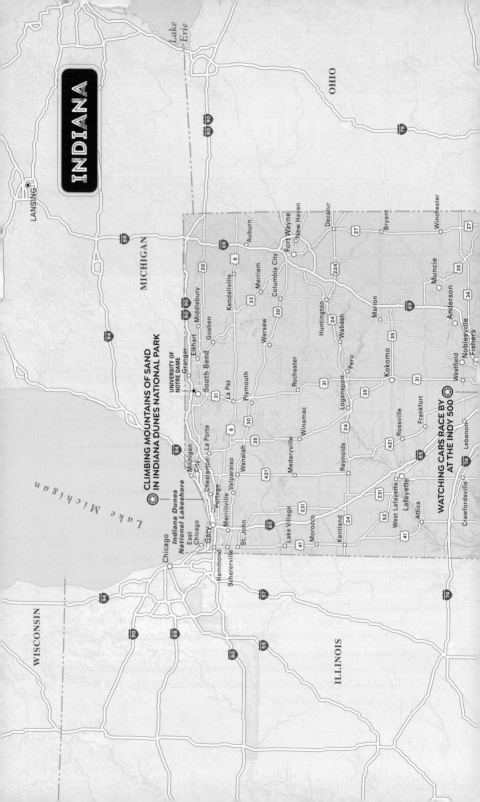

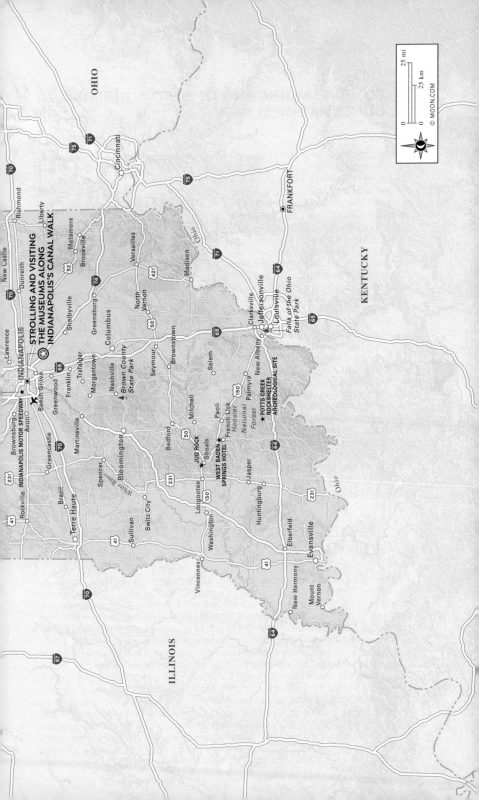

**TOP 3**

## 1 CLIMBING MOUNTAINS OF SAND IN INDIANA DUNES NATIONAL PARK

www.nps.gov/indu

Covering 15,000 acres (6,070 hectares) along the southern shores of Lake Michigan, the Indiana Dunes became the U.S.'s 61st national park in 2019. This 15-mile (24-kilometer) stretch of coastline is a glimpse into the region's glacial past: As the glaciers that once covered this part of the Midwest began to retreat northward some 20,000 years ago, the shoreline of Lake Michigan was formed, and wind has been carrying sand here ever since. The dunes are still very much "living," with the most active, **Mount Baldy** (126 feet/38 meters), moving as much as 20 feet (6 meters) a year, and areas called "blowouts" where layers of sand have eroded away, revealing "skeleton forests" of dead trees buried long ago. See this windy, lunar landscape up close on a hike, like the 1.5-mile (2.4-kilometer) **3 Dune Challenge** (taking in the park's highest dunes, Mount Holden, Mount Jackson, and Mount Tom, topping off at 192 feet/58 meters) or the 3.4-mile (5.4-kilometer) West **Beach 3-Loop Trail.**

INDIANA DUNES NATIONAL PARK

The sight of these massive, ever-shifting dunes is mesmerizing, but that's not all the park has to offer: It's also full of protected wetlands, marshes, and groves of rare trees, habitats for almost 400 bird species, making this the 7th-most biodiverse national park in the U.S. Start at the **Indiana Dunes Visitor Center** (1215 N. State Rd., Porter; 219/926-2255; www.nps.gov/indu) to learn more about this landscape and plan your visit.

## 2 STROLLING AND VISITING THE MUSEUMS ALONG INDIANAPOLIS'S CANAL WALK

The fact Indianapolis has a canal at all is something of an accident. Originally, the Indiana Central Canal was meant to extend some 300 miles (482 kilometers) through the state, part of a massive 19th-century infrastructure plan that eventually bankrupted the state, after only 8 miles (12 kilometers) of the canal had been completed. Those 8 miles (12 kilometers) played an outsize role in Indianapolis history, though, bringing workers to the city and providing a power source for purification plants and pumping stations. The canal was donated to the city in the 1980s, when Indianapolis began the project of restoring the downtown section into a park. Today, the 3-mile (4.8-kilometer) Canal Walk is a great place to stroll, cycle, rollerblade, or even rent a kayak, all in view of the Indianapolis skyline.

This vibrant pedestrian haven also provides access to public art, great restaurants, and some of the capital's best museums. The **Indiana State Museum** (650 W. Washington St.; 317/232-1637; www.indianamuseum.com) is beloved by kids and history buffs, covering Indiana from prehistoric times to the present, from geology and dinosaur fossils to famous Hoosiers and local artists. Nearby, the **Eiteljorg Museum** (500 W. Washington St.; 317/636-9378; www.eiteljorg.org) was founded

INDIANA STATE MUSEUM AND THE CANAL WALK

by businessman Harrison Eiteljorg in 1989 to "inspire an appreciation and understanding of the art, history, and cultures of the American West and the Indigenous peoples of North America"; it's the only museum of its kind in the Midwest. Spending an afternoon people-watching, popping into museums, and grabbing a riverside drink is a great way to get to know this growing city with a small-town feel.

## ③ WATCHING CARS RACE BY AT THE INDY 500

For some people, the word "Indianapolis" only brings one thing to mind: the Indianapolis 500, the annual 500-mile (804-kilometer) race in which 33 cars zoom 200 times around a 2.5-mile (4-kilometer) track, reaching speeds of over 200 miles (321 kilometers) per hour. Since the inaugural race held in 1911, this event has grown to the most highly attended single-day sporting event in the world, with the **Indianapolis Motor Speedway** (4790 W. 16th St.; www.indianapolismotorspeedway.com) seating 250,000. Beloved race day traditions include the singing of "Back Home Again in Indiana" and the winner celebrating with a bottle of milk.

Excitement for the big race starts building up in May, with practice races being held in preparation for the main event, which takes place on Labor Day weekend. If you're not in town at this festive time of year, you can always visit the **Indianapolis Motor Speedway Museum** (4750 W. 16th St., Indianapolis; 317/492-6784; https://imsmuseum.org), which includes the Indianapolis Motor Speedway Hall of Fame as well as general exhibits on automotive history, and even the option to add a lap around the famous Brickyard track to your tour.

INDIANAPOLIS 500 AT INDIANAPOLIS MOTOR SPEEDWAY

# *Best* ROAD TRIP

**DAY 1** Start your trip in the northwest corner of the state at the **Indiana Dunes National Park.** (If you've flown into Chicago Midway, it's about a 2-hour drive to the park.) Once you've hiked, bird-watched, and dune-climbed to your heart's delight, stop by **3 Floyds Brewpub** for a well-deserved craft beer. Make the 2.5-hour drive southeast to capital city **Indianapolis** for the night.

**DAY 2** In Indy, stroll the **Canal Walk,** spend a few hours in the **Eiteljorg Museum,** devoted to Indigenous Americans, and make a reservation at the famous **St. Elmo Steak House.**

**DAY 3** Before leaving the capital, make a pilgrimage to the **Indianapolis Motor Speedway Museum,** not far from where the spectacle that is the Indy 500 takes place every year. Then drive 50 minutes south to **Columbus** to take in a world-class collection of mid-century modern architecture.

**DAY 4** Drive west through **Brown County State Park,** Indiana's largest state park and a great place for a hike. Stop in small town **Nashville** (not to be confused with its famous Tennessee cousin to the south) to check out a few art galleries, then spend the rest of the day in **Bloomington,** exploring **Indiana University**'s beautiful campus.

**DAY 5** Heading south, be sure to drive on scenic **State Road 450,** with views of the White River and a notable geological stop at the 50-foot (15-meter) tall **Jug Rock** formation. You'll end up at beautiful, historic **West Baden Springs Hotel,** where you can relax with a spa treatment or round of golf.

INDIANA DUNES NATIONAL PARK

DEER SCULPTURES OUTSIDE THE EITELJORG MUSEUM

INDIANAPOLIS MOTOR SPEEDWAY MUSEUM

**DAY 6** After a relaxed morning at your hotel, grab lunch at **German Café** in nearby French Lick: Be sure to try a famous pork tenderloin sandwich. You'll drive south through **Hoosier National Forest** to **Falls of the Ohio State Park,** which features exposed Devonian fossil beds. From here, it's 2.5 hours back to Indianapolis or 5 hours back to Chicago.

BROWN COUNTY STATE PARK

THE ENTRANCE TO WEST BADEN SPRINGS HOTEL

## ORIENTATION

The capital city of **Indianapolis** is located right in the middle of the state, with the university town of **Bloomington** to its southwest. **South Bend,** where Notre Dame is located, is almost due north of Indianapolis near the Michigan state line, while **Indiana Dunes National Park** is in the northwest corner of the state, which briefly borders on Lake Michigan.

## WHEN TO GO

Indiana is subject to the typical Midwestern weather extremes: a hot, humid **summer** and a frigidly cold **winter.** The Indianapolis 500, which takes place in late May, is the kickoff to the summer festival season, the busiest time in the state. The **spring** is more temperate and a great time to visit Indiana, as is **autumn,** when the bounties of the state's rich farmland are being harvested and the trees turn pretty shades of red, orange, and yellow.

# HIGHLIGHTS

## MAIN STREETS

Dotting the lush farmland of the countryside, Indiana is home to many picturesque small towns, whose well-preserved main streets will make you feel like you're stepping into the past.

- **Madison** boasts one of the country's largest national historic districts, as well as a burgeoning small-town food scene.

- For a tiny town, **Nashville** has an incredible arts scene, the legacy of an art colony formed here in the early 20th century.

- Though not technically a main street, the small town of **Metamora** is home to the Whitewater Canal Historic Site, which provides a view into a 19th-century canal town, a place for people traveling by boat to find food and lodging.

## NEW HARMONY

In 1814, a group of separatists from the German Lutheran Church came from Pennsylvania to found their "Neu Harmonie," where over the next

# *Major* CITIES

**INDIANAPOLIS:** Indiana's capital is growing and surprisingly cosmopolitan, with a great museum and dining scene.

**BLOOMINGTON:** Home to Indiana University, this beautiful college town has enough athletics and culture to keep students, townies, and visitors busy.

**SOUTH BEND:** South Bend is northern Indiana's unofficial hub and the home of the University of Notre Dame and the famous Fighting Irish.

10 years—while waiting for Christ to come—they built over 180 buildings (many of which are still standing) and a thriving economy, producing textiles, rope barrels, and large quantities of whiskey and beer, among other products. One of the most fascinating remnants of the Harmonists is the **New Harmony Labyrinth** (309 North St.), with only one path to the center. In 1825, Robert Owen, an industrialist, and William Maclure, known as the founder of American geology, bought the town from the Harmonists and sought to establish a utopia of their own. Their utopian vision of equal education and social status for all never came to fruition, but over a century later, Jane Blaffer Owen (wife of a descendent of Robert Owen), renewed the idea of utopia in New Harmony, commissioning beautiful modern architecture, including the **Roofless Church** (420 North St.; 812/682-3050; www.robertleeblafferfoundation.org).

## COLUMBUS

This once unremarkable town has become a mecca for lovers of modernist architecture, all thanks to the inspiration of one man. J. Irwin Miller headed the Columbus-based Cummins Engine Co. in the mid-20th century and envisioned his town filled with buildings designed by the greatest architects of the time: I.M. Pei, Kevin Roche, Cesar Pelli, and more. His plan succeeded, so much so that the American Institute of Architects ranked Columbus sixth among cities in the U.S. for architectural innovation and design. Tour the **Miller House,** designed by Eero Saarinen, for a glimpse into one of Columbus' most treasured buildings, or visit the town's

website (https://columbus.in.us) for a full list of tour options.

## WEST BADEN SPRINGS HOTEL

8538 West Baden Ave., Baden Springs; 888/936-9360; www.frenchlick.com

A grand, turn-of-the-19th-century hotel inspired by the spa resorts of Europe is still one of the best places in Indiana to go for rest and relaxation. The preponderance of mineral springs in the area have made it a popular health resort since the mid-19th century, but it was in the early 20th century, after a fire burned down existing buildings, that the resort really came into its own as a luxury spa destination. The owner at the time, Lee Wiley Sinclair, worked with an architect to design a magnificent, 200-foot (60-meter) dome that is now the hotel's center atrium. Though the Great Depression forced the hotel to close, careful restoration efforts beginning in the 1990s allowed it to reopen in 2007. Today, the West Baden Springs Hotel is a unique getaway for a spa treatment, round of golf, or even just a tour of the impressive Queen Anne architecture.

# BEST SCENIC DRIVES

## STATE ROAD 450

This 28-mile (45-kilometer) route between **Bedford** and **Shoals** snakes along the northern side of the **White River,** with views of the water that might just tempt you to stop and for a swim, if the weather's warm enough. In Shoals, don't miss **Jug Rock** (722 Albright Ln., Shoals; 317/232-4052; http://

SCENIC VINCENNES CITY

20 miles (32 kilometers) of treelined roads and scenic overlooks of fiery autumn forest, Brown County State Park is often referred to as Indiana's version of the Great Smoky Mountains. Far enough south that the glaciers never reached it, the land here is characterized by rolling slopes, gullies, and ridges. A playground for outdoor enthusiasts in Bloomington, the largest nearby city, this is Indiana's largest state park, with 9 miles (14.4 kilometers) of hiking trails, 25 miles (40 kilometers) of mountain bike trails, two manmade lakes for fishing and swimming, and a nature center.

jug-rock-nature.edan.io), the biggest free-standing table rock formation east of the Mississippi River, a 50-foot (15-meter) tall stone pillar with a massive boulder perched improbably on top of it. About midway through, you'll see a picturesque, red-walled **covered bridge,** near the town of Williams.

## INDIANA'S HISTORIC PATHWAYS—SOUTH SPUR

U.S. 150; www.indianashistoricpathways.org

This scenic 135-mile (217-kilometer) drive, mostly on U.S. 150, starts in **Vincennes,** a charming small town, then cuts through southern Indiana and **Hoosier National Forest** (www.fs.usda.gov/hoosier). You'll pass the **Potts Creek Rockshelter Archeological Site,** where evidence of Paleo-Indian camps has been found, and **New Albany,** with a historic downtown and specialty shops and boutiques to browse. You'll end up on the banks of the **Ohio River,** on the doorstep of **Louisville,** Kentucky.

# BEST PARKS AND RECREATION AREAS

## BROWN COUNTY STATE PARK

1801 Indiana 46 East, Nashville; www.in.gov/dnr/parklake/2988.htm

One of the most spectacular places in the state to visit in the fall, with over

## FALLS OF THE OHIO STATE PARK

201 W. Riverside Dr., Clarksville; 812/280-9970; www.fallsoftheohio.org

This 165-acre (66-hectare) park on the shores of the Ohio River, across from Louisville, Kentucky, boasts more than just water and skyline views: Over millennia, the river has eroded the limestone to reveal a massive, 390-million-year-old fossil bed, a treasure trove of ancient sea creatures that can be explored on foot. An excellent interpretive center provides background on the history of the park, both ancient and modern. In addition to fossil-viewing,

BROWN COUNTY STATE PARK

## BEST SOUVENIRS

- Hoosiers love their **popcorn,** producing more of it than other state besides Nebraska. A tin of gourmet popcorn from a local company like **Pop Around the Clock** (www.poparoundtheclock.net) or **Concannon's** (www.concannonsbakery.com) makes a great souvenir.

- Wayne County has put together two interlocking loop trails they call **Indiana's Antique Alley** (www.visitrichmond.org) to help you find the perfect vintage treasure during your time in the Hoosier state.

people come here to hike, fish, bird watch, and picnic.

## FESTIVALS AND EVENTS

In addition to the Indy 500, a few other sporting events draw crowds each year, to two of the most famous schools in the state: **Indiana University-Bloomington,** and the **University of Notre Dame.** If you can't make it to IU's big bike race or to see the Fighting Irish during football season, try taking a tour of the campuses, both of which are replete with green spaces and 19th-century buildings, and regularly voted among the most beautiful college campuses in the country.

### LITTLE 500

https://iusf.indiana.edu/little500; Apr.

A tradition at Indiana University-Bloomington for more than 70 years, the Little 500 (familiarly known as the Little 5) is a bike race modeled off that big car race that takes place in Indianapolis each year. This relay race for teams of 4, many of them coming from some of IU's many fraternities (or sororities for the women's Little 5, which has been taking place since 1988). The cyclists take turns riding 200 times around a quarter-mile (0.4-kilometer) track, typically in the third week of April at the **Bill Armstrong Stadium** (1606 N. Fee Ln., Bloomington; 866/487-7678) on IU's campus. Billed as "The World's Greatest College Weekend," it's typically attended by 25,000 fans.

## NOTRE DAME FOOTBALL

Football is a big deal in South Bend, Indiana, adjacent to the University of Notre Dame, home of the Fighting Irish. Faithful supporters like to roll out the statistics: the second-highest winning percentage in NCAA Division I football history, the second-most wins in the NCAA, most players drafted in to the NFL... the list goes on. Since their first game, played in 1887, Notre Dame has built a truly legendary football program, one with rabid fans across the country ready to chew you out if you even mention the University of Michigan or the University of Southern California, two of their biggest rivals.

The avid fanbase can make it hard to get tickets, but there are plenty of ways to enjoy a game day weekend: visit the **Guglielmino Athletics Complex,** or "the Gug," the team's primary practice facilities; tour the **Notre Dame Stadium** (2010 Moose Krause Cir., Notre Dame; 574/631-5036; http://nd.edu), attend a pep rally or a marching band performance, or tailgate on one of the campus parking lots.

## BEST FOOD

Indiana food is humble and hearty, best washed down with a bottle of **3 Floyds Zombie Dust Pale Ale** (9750 Indiana Pkwy., Munster; 219/922-3565; www.3floyds.com) or **Triple XXX Root Beer** (2 N. Salisbury, West Lafayette; 765/743-5373; www.triplexxxfamilyrestaurant.com), the last remaining outpost of a chain that once had 100 roadside stations throughout the country.

It's rare that it's easy to name a state's most famous restaurant, but in Indiana it just might be possible: Indianapolis's **St. Elmo Steak House** (127 Illinois St.; 317/635-0636; stelmos.com), known for its legendary shrimp cocktail, is about as famous as it gets.

## BREADED PORK TENDERLOIN SANDWICH

Indiana's quintessential sandwich is a flat, lean cut of pork, breaded, fried, and stuck between two buns. It seems like almost every restaurant has a version of this sandwich on the menu, but here are a few of the best places to try it.

- **Steer-In:** 5130 E 10th St, Indianapolis; 317/356-0996; www.steerin.net
- **Nick's Kitchen:** 506 N Jefferson St, Huntington; 260/356-6618; www.nicksdowntown.com
- **German Café:** 452 S Maple St, French Lick; 812/936-1111; www.germancafe-frenchlick.com

## HOOSIER PIE

Also known as sugar cream pie, the official Indiana State Pie has humble roots in Amish and Shaker communities, who whipped up this creamy, satisfying dessert made of nothing much more than sugar, butter, and cream when no other ingredients were available.

- **Locally Grown Gardens:** 1050 E 54th St., Indianapolis; 317/255-8555
- **Mrs. Wick's Pies:** 100 Cherry St., Winchester; 765/584-7437; www.wickspies.com
- **Das Dutchman Essenhaus:** 240 U.S. 20, Middlebury; 574/825-9471; www.essenhaus.com

TRADITIONAL HOOSIER PIE

## MAJOR AIRPORTS

- **Indianapolis International Airport:** IND; 800 Col. H. Weir Cook Memorial Dr., Indianapolis; 317/487-9594; www.indianapolisairport.com

## MORE INFORMATION

### TRAVEL AND TOURISM INFORMATION

- **Visit Indiana:** www.visitindiana.com
- **Indiana State Parks:** www.in.gov/dnr/parklake

### NEWSPAPERS

- *The Indianapolis Star:* www.indystar.com

# MICHIGAN

The name "Michigan" comes from the Algonquian Indian word for "big lake"—fittingly, since it's surrounded by four of the five Great Lakes, bodies of water so massive that scientists classify them as inland seas. Beyond the constancy of these majestic shorelines, the Great Lakes State offers a great deal of diversity. The mitten-shaped Lower Peninsula boasts a wealth of rural areas, nostalgic villages, resort towns, bevies of art galleries, wineries and breweries, and urban centers like Detroit, the comeback city with the highest African American population in the country. North of the Mackinac Bridge is the Upper Peninsula and its uncrowded forests, beaches, mountains, and waterfalls.

Michigan is on Fox, Kickapoo, Menominee, Miami, Ojibwe, Potawatomi, and Sauk land. The four seasons in all their splendor make themselves known throughout the landscape: Most tourists visit in spring and summer, yet the snowy winters have grown popular too, for adventures like riding snowmobiles through glistening forests. Autumn invites drives along winding country roads, flanked by apple orchards and crimson maple trees.

**AREA:** 96,714 square miles / 250,488 square kilometers (11th)

**POPULATION:** 9,986,857 (10th)

**STATEHOOD DATE:** January 26, 1837 (26th)

**STATE CAPITAL:** Lansing

▲ SLEEPING BEAR DUNES NATIONAL LAKESHORE

## ORIENTATION

On the mitten that is Michigan's Lower Peninsula, **Detroit** and neighboring **Ann Arbor** sit at the base of the thumb in the southeast of the state. **Traverse City** is in the opposite corner, near the pinky (if this mitten also had a pinky) that is the **Leelanau Peninsula,** in the northwest. The **Mackinac Bridge** connects the tip of the Lower Peninsula to Michigan's **Upper Peninsula** (the UP), which is the strip of land extending out from Wisconsin between Lakes Michigan and Huron to the south and Lake Superior to the north. **Pictured Rocks** is on the Lake Superior side of the UP.

## WHEN TO GO

The most popular time to visit Michigan is **Summer** (June-Aug.), when people flock here for beaches and festivals, but **autumn** (Sept.-Oct.) may be the best time to visit, when days are cool and fall colors are outstanding. **Winter** usually descends in December in the Upper Peninsula and in January in the Lower Peninsula, and can linger through March. Peak snow is usually in January and February. **Spring** emerges in southern Michigan in early May, working its way northward, and bringing moderate temperatures and blossoming trees.

# HIGHLIGHTS

## MACKINAC BRIDGE

Linking Lakes Huron and Michigan, the Straits of Mackinac (MAK-i-naw) have been a crossroads of the Great Lakes for hundreds of years. The 5-mile-long (8-kilometer) drive across the Mackinac Bridge from the Lower to the Upper Peninsula can feel like a journey between two disparate countries. Although there are several ways to reach the UP, most travelers utilize the "Mighty Mac" bridge, the only vehicular link. Opened in 1957, it's the third-longest suspension bridge in the world. On the UP side, make a quick stop at lovely **Bridge View Park,** where you can snap pictures of this modern engineering marvel. You've now crossed through the gateway to the enormous, sparsely populated Upper Peninsula with its rushing rivers, thunderous cascades, dramatic cliffs, deserted beaches, and vast tracts of forested terrain.

## MACKINAC ISLAND

On Mackinac Island, the Victorian era has been beautifully preserved, from the exquisite 1887 **Grand Hotel** (286 Grand Ave.; 906/847-3331 or 800/334-7263; www.grandhotel.com) to the clopping of the horse-drawn carriages down the car-free streets. A full 80

MACKINAC ISLAND

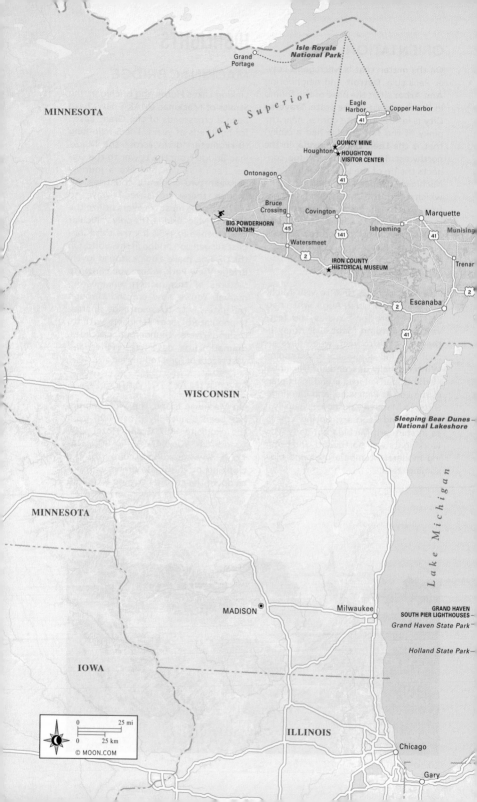

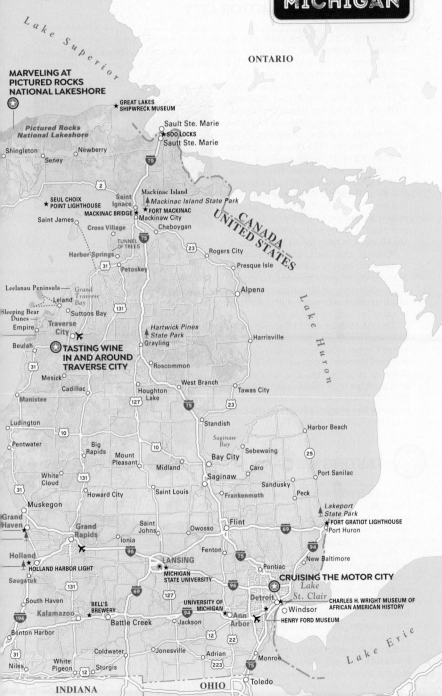

# MICHIGAN

ONTARIO

Lake Superior

## MARVELING AT PICTURED ROCKS NATIONAL LAKESHORE

GREAT LAKES
★ SHIPWRECK MUSEUM

Pictured Rocks
National Lakeshore

Sault Ste. Marie
★ SOO LOCKS
Sault Ste. Marie

Shingleton        Newberry
Seney

75

2

Mackinac Island
Saint            ★ Mackinac Island State Park
SEUL CHOIX        Ignace
★ POINT LIGHTHOUSE  ★ FORT MACKINAC
MACKINAC BRIDGE ★   Mackinaw City

Saint James       Cross Village        Cheboygan

Harbor Springs    TUNNEL
OF TREES

31     Petoskey          23     Rogers City

Presque Isle

Leelanau Peninsula   Grand
Leland    Traverse   Alpena
Sleeping Bear  Bay
Dunes    Suttons Bay
131
Empire
Traverse
City
Beulah   ● TASTING WINE        Harrisville
IN AND AROUND        Hartwick Pines
TRAVERSE CITY        ★ State Park
31   Grayling
Mesick
Cadillac    Roscommon
127
West Branch
Houghton
Lake        Tawas City
Manistee          75    23
Ludington          Standish
10
Pentwater               Saginaw        Harbor Beach
Bay
Big
Rapids    Mount            Sebewaing
Pleasant   Bay City    25
White   131    Midland
Cloud           Caro
Saginaw   Port Sanilac
Muskegon   Howard City   Saint Louis
Frankenmuth   Sandusky
Peck
Saint
31   Johns    Owosso   Flint   Lakeport
Grand   Grand            ★ State Park
Haven   Rapids        69    ★ FORT GRATIOT LIGHTHOUSE
Ionia            Fenton        Port Huron
Holland   96         75   Pontiac   94
HOLLAND HARBOR LIGHT                New Baltimore
Saugatuck               LANSING            CRUISING THE MOTOR CITY
131   MICHIGAN            Lake
South Haven   69   STATE UNIVERSITY   96        St. Clair
BELL'S   127         Detroit   CHARLES H. WRIGHT MUSEUM OF
Kalamazoo   BREWERY   94   UNIVERSITY OF   Windsor   AFRICAN AMERICAN HISTORY
Battle Creek   MICHIGAN   Ann   HENRY FORD MUSEUM
Benton Harbor        Jackson   Arbor
196   12
31   Coldwater   22   Monroe
White   Jonesville   Adrian   75
Niles   Pigeon   223
12   Sturgis   Toledo
INDIANA      OHIO   Lake Erie

CANADA
UNITED STATES

Lake Huron

Lake St. Clair

# TOP 3

## 1 CRUISING THE MOTOR CITY

In the early 20th century, Henry Ford's refinement of the assembly line changed the face of Detroit, and the country, seemingly overnight. Evidence of the Detroit auto industry's rise (and fall) is visible everywhere you look, from its broad boulevards in a spoke and hub layout to facilitate vehicle traffic, to grand, art deco skyscrapers like the **Fisher Building** (3011 W. Grand Blvd.; free tours provided by www.puredetroit.com), financed by the sale of Fisher Body Works to General Motors. (The remains of **Fisher Body Plant 21**, in disuse since 1984, can be seen a 5-minute drive to the east, at 6051 Hastings St.) In between, the **Ford Piquette Avenue Plant** (461 Piquette St.; 313/827-8759; www.fordpiquetteplant.org), Ford's first purpose-built factory and the birthplace of the Model T, is open for visits and tours.

HENRY FORD MUSEUM

Perhaps the best place to learn about auto history is the **Henry Ford Museum** (20900 Oakwood Blvd., Dearborn; 313/982-6001; www.thehenryford.org), in the suburb of Dearborn, a 20-minute drive southwest of downtown. It's an impressive and enormous colonial-style museum housing one vast collection after another, including an encyclopedic assemblage of historic American autos.

Though today most of Detroit's auto industry has moved to the suburbs, some of its more modern incarnations include the soaring and fortress-like **GM Renaissance Center** (100 Renaissance Center; 313/567-3126; free tours provided by www.puredetroit.com), opened in 1977 and proposed by Henry Ford II in the hopes of drawing suburbanites and catalyzing development downtown (it didn't work); and, perhaps improbably, the old **Michigan Central Train Depot** (2001 15th St.), a beautiful beaux-arts station that hasn't seen a train since 1988. Ford's 2018 purchase of the property to house its autonomous vehicle division caused much fanfare throughout the city.

## 2 TASTING WINE IN AND AROUND TRAVERSE CITY

In recent years, Michigan has gained a reputation for crafting award-winning wines. The winter months' lake-effect snow protects the vines and extends the growing season for up to a month.

The area surrounding Traverse City is the epicenter of Michigan wineries, where you'll find the greatest density of established wineries, vineyards and tasting rooms. The **Old Mission Peninsula** (www.wineriesofoldmission.com) pierces the waters north from Traverse City; across the West Arm of Grand Traverse Bay is the **Leelanau Peninsula** (www.lpwines.com). These ragged lands of hills, lakes, and scrib-

VINEYARD ON THE OLD MISSION PENINSULA OVERLOOKING GRAND TRAVERSE BAY

bled shoreline straggling northward provide surprisingly conducive climates for growing wine grapes. Altogether, the peninsulas now boast more than 30 wineries; below are just a few of the highlights. Most are open for tastings and wine shopping 7 days a week, with no appointments necessary.

- **Chateau Grand Traverse** (12239 Center Rd., Traverse City; 231/223-7355 or 800/283-0247; www.cgtwines.com): This pioneer in bringing European viniferous wines to the Midwest has a spacious tasting room offering understated elegance.

- **Bowers Harbor Vineyards** (2896 Bowers Harbor Rd., Traverse City; 231/223-7615 or 800/616/7615; www.bowersharbor.com): At this small, friendly, family-run winery, dogs are welcome on the patio.

- **L. Mawby Vineyards** (4519 S. Elm Valley Rd., Suttons Bay; 231/271-3522; www.lmawby.com): One of the region's smallest wineries, Mawby has a big reputation, especially for its sparkling whites.

## ③ MARVELING AT PICTURED ROCKS NATIONAL LAKESHORE

906/387-2607; www.nps.gov/piro

Lake Superior takes center stage at the Pictured Rocks National Lakeshore, which is just 3 miles (4.8 kilometers) wide by more than 40 miles (64 kilometers) long, located along the magnificent lake. The National Park Service property on the north side of the Upper Peninsula derives its name from the sandstone bluffs that rise 200 feet (60 meters) directly from the water's surface. The bluffs are washed in shades of pink, red, and green due to the mineral-rich water that seeps from the rock, and sculpts them into caves, arches, and castle-like turrets, including **Miners Castle**, a nine-story-high rock formation.

You'll also find lakes, forest trails, waterfalls, a lighthouse, and other historic attractions, but the optimal way to experience the grandeur of this shoreline is from a boat. **Pictured Rocks Cruises** (100 City Park Dr., Munising) has three exciting cruise options: the classic daytime cruise, the sunset cruise, and the Spray Falls cruise, which offers an up-close view of the **Spray Falls**—a 70-foot (21-meter) drop of cascading water flowing into the lake.

Sea kayakers consider this one of the finest paddles on all the Great Lakes. That said, the importance of safety cannot be overemphasized: Only experienced paddlers should venture out on their own, and only in a closed cockpit after scrupulously monitoring weather conditions. **Great Northern Adventures** (906/225-8687; www.greatnorthernadventures.com) offers guided paddling trips.

PICTURED ROCKS NATIONAL LAKESHORE

# *Best* ROAD TRIP

**DAY 1** Spend the day cruising **Detroit,** learning about its automotive and cultural history at institutions like the **Henry Ford Museum** and the **Charles H. Wright Museum of African American History.**

**DAY 2** From the Motor City, a 2.5-hour drive on I-96 West will have you sipping **craft beer** in thriving downtown **Grand Rapids,** with stops in between at the **cafés** and **art galleries** of **Ann Arbor,** and **Kalamazoo,** with its own lively craft beer scene.

**DAY 3** Make your way 40 minutes southwest on I-196 West to **Saugatuck,** known for its concentration of art galleries. Begin a scenic drive on U.S. 31 North along Lake Michigan's eastern coast, passing **lighthouses** and gorgeous **beaches** along the way in cities like **Holland** and **Grand Haven.** You'll end up in bustling **Traverse City,** a drive of just over 3 hours in total.

**DAY 4** In the morning, head 40 minutes on M-72 West to **Sleeping Bear Dunes,** aiming to get there early to have them all to yourself. Then, you're in for a treat driving the **M-22** around the **Leelanau Peninsula;** be sure to stop at one of the area's excellent **wineries** en route. Rounding Grand Traverse Bay, you'll head farther north on U.S. 31 N, passing charming lakeside towns like **Petoskey** and driving the **Tunnel of Trees** before finally making it to the **Mackinac Bridge,** a drive of just over 4 hours in total. It's a long day of travel, but it will be worth it if you make it to the bridge in time to drive over it at sunset; bed down in **St. Ignace,** just on the other side of the bridge, for the next few nights.

DETROIT

HOLLAND, MICHIGAN

SLEEPING BEAR DUNES

**DAY 5** It's a 2-hour drive to beautiful **Pictured Rocks National Lakeshore** via U.S. 2 West, where you can spend much of the day **hiking** and **kayaking**. Back in St. Ignace, take a late afternoon ferry to **Mackinac Island** for dinner and charming, car-free strolling.

**DAY 6** From St. Ignace, it's a 4-hour drive back to **Detroit** on I-75 South. Luckily, you'll have beautiful memories to keep you company and a stop in **Hartwick Pines State Park,** covered in majestic old growth forest, to stretch your legs.

PETOSKEY

KAYAKING PICTURED ROCKS NATIONAL LAKESHORE

percent of the island is protected by **Mackinac Island State Park** (906/847-3328; www.mackinacparks.com), encompassing whitewashed **Fort Mackinac** (231/436-4100), struggled over by the British and Americans for nearly 40 years and worth a visit for the views over the charming downtown, marina, and Lake Huron. Getting to this wonderful place to retreat from the outside world is easy: two ferry services, **Shepler's Mackinac Island Ferry** (231/436-5023, 906/643-9440, or 800/828-6157; www.sheplersferry.com) and **Star Line** (800/638-9892; www.mackinacferry.com), can shuttle you across the Straits of Mackinac in less than 20 minutes from both Mackinaw City (in the Lower Peninsula) and St. Ignace (in the UP).

## MINING HISTORY

In the Upper Peninsula, many town names highlight mining: Copper Harbor, Ironwood, Iron Mountain, and Mineral Hills. For the UP, the economic heyday was the latter half of the 19th century, known as the Copper Rush, which yielded an astonishing 10 times the mineral wealth of California's better-known gold rush. Thousands of eager immigrants flocked to the area, resulting in the creation of cities virtually overnight. Following a decline in the 20th century, only remnants of this mineral-rich past remain—enormous mansions, abandoned mines, ghost towns, and occasional cave-ins beneath homes and streets.

Just north in the town of Hancock, in the middle of the rugged Keweenaw Peninsula, the mammoth shaft house of the **Quincy Mine** (49750 U.S. 41, Hancock; 906/482-3101; www.quincymine.com) dominates the skyline. The Quincy mine was once among the world's richest copper mines, and a few of its buildings still stand. A glass-enclosed tram descends a few thousand feet (about 900 meters) into shafts that stretched more than 1.5 miles (2.4 kilometers) deep—an amazing 92 levels—and 2 miles (3.2 kilometers) wide. At the rambling, funky, homegrown **Iron County Historical Museum** (100 Brady Ave., off M-189, Caspian; 906/265-2617; www.ironcountyhistoricalmuseum.org), on the site of the productive Caspian iron mine, you'll find an eclectic

## *Major* CITIES

**DETROIT:** Now is a great time to visit the Motor City, increasingly also called the "Renaissance City." It's a tenacious town, Michigan's largest, known for its Motown music as well as its resiliency, always managing to reinvent itself through mind-crushing lows and soaring highs.

**GRAND RAPIDS:** The state's second-largest city, once a cornerstone of the furniture industry and birthplace of President Gerald R. Ford, is today a thriving showcase for the arts, local history, and business, especially craft beer.

**ANN ARBOR:** Home of the University of Michigan, Ann Arbor has a unique blend of big-city energy and college-town friendliness.

**LANSING:** Michigan's capital boasts a beautifully restored state capitol, excellent museums, and a full plate of university events thanks to Michigan State University, based in neighboring East Lansing.

blend of local history, including a mechanized iron mine and train model.

A vestige of mining history that's still fresh and warm is the **pasty** (PASS-tee), a hand pie filled with meat and vegetables. The rush to the copper mines brought English immigrants, who favored the pasty because it's simple, portable, and filling. Later, Finnish immigrants adopted the dish very much as their own, and today you'll see dozens of pasty shops as you drive around the UP.

## SHIPWRECKS AND LIGHTHOUSES

A staple bar ballad in Michigan, especially the further north you go, "The

Wreck of the Edmund Fitzgerald" by Gordon Lightfoot refers to the real-life 1975 wreck of a 729-foot (222-meter) lake carrier, lost off Whitefish Point, the very tip of the UP, in the notorious November gales of Lake Superior. The lasting popularity of this song is a tribute to the importance of the shipping and fishing industries to Michigan's economy, and the heroism, endurance, and ingenuity of the people that work in them.

The dangerous waters off Whitefish Point are known as the "Graveyard of the Great Lakes"; to commemorate the many ships that failed to round this point of safety, the **Great Lakes Shipwreck Museum** (18335 Whitefish Point Rd., Paradise; 888/492-3747; www.shipwreckmuseum.com) traces the history of Great Lakes commerce and the disasters that sometimes accompanied it. In safer waters to the southeast, the **Soo Locks** of Sault Ste. Marie are an engineering marvel allowing the passage of massive freighters between the Great Lakes; it's easy to spend an hour watching the ships as they pass through the locks with just inches to spare.

Iconic parts of the Michigan landscapes that are just as important to its shipping industry are the picturesque lighthouses dotting the shoreline; in all, there are 100 or so that are still in good working condition. A tour of some of the most noteworthy lighthouses is a great way to explore the state's magnificent coast.

SAILBOAT PASSING HOLLAND HARBOR LIGHT

# BLACK HISTORY AND CULTURE IN DETROIT

Detroit's population is 81.6 percent Black, making it the most African American of major U.S. cities—and Black history and culture here are correspondingly rich. Much of Detroit's African American population immigrated north during the 20th century's Great Migration, for the promise of higher-paying jobs and less restrictive racial mores. Much of that promise remains unfulfilled. The exceptional **Charles H. Wright Museum of African American History** (315 E. Warren Ave.; 313/494-5800; www.thewright.org), one of the world's largest institutions dedicated to the African American experience, tells this story, from the Underground Railroad to the unrest and activism of the 1960s to icons such as Aretha Franklin and Joe Lewis.

As quintessential to the Motor City as automobiles, the Motown sound is one of Detroit's gifts to the world. The **Motown Museum** (2648 W. Grand Blvd.; 313/875-2264; www.motownmuseum.org), known across the country as Hitsville U.S.A., preserves the original Studio A, where Berry Gordy Jr.'s production gave us priceless recordings from The Supremes, The Temptations, Marvin Gaye, Stevie Wonder, the Jackson 5, and more.

While in Detroit, be sure to patronize its excellent **Black-owned businesses,** including wine retailer **House of Vin** (1433 Woodward Ave.; 313/638-2501; www.houseofpurevin.com), lifestyle brand **Détroit is the New Black** (1426 Woodward Ave.; 313/818-3498; www.detroitisthenewblack.com), and **Source Booksellers** (4240 Cass Ave. #105; 313/832-1155; www.sourcebooksellers.com), as well as restaurants like **Norma G's** (www.normagscuisine.com) and **Detroit Vegan Soul** (8029 Agnes St.; 313/649-2759; www.detroitvegansoul.com). **Baker's Keyboard Lounge** (20510 Livernois Ave.; 313/345-6300; www.theofficialbakerskeyboardlounge.com) is the world's oldest continuously operating jazz club, and you'll often hear live blues spilling from **Bert's Market Place** (2727 Russel St.; 313-567-2030; www.bertsentertainmentcomplex.com) near lively Eastern Market.

- The vibrant red **Holland Harbor Light,** erected in 1907, is known as "Big Red" by residents of its historically Dutch town in southwest Michigan.

- Thirty minutes up the Lake Michigan coast, the **Grand Haven South Pier Lighthouses** are also vivid red. Built in 1875 and 1905, they are still operational.

- On a peninsula jutting south from the UP into Lake Michigan, the **Seul Choix Point Lighthouse** (672 N. West Gulliver Lake Rd.; 906/283-3183; www.greatlakelighthouse.com) is an outstanding restored 1895 lighthouse and museum.

- On the knuckle of Michigan's "thumb," where Lake Huron drains into the St. Clair River, the **Fort Gratiot Lighthouse** (800/852-4242) stands 86 feet (26 meters) tall and is the state's oldest.

# BEST SCENIC DRIVES

From idyllic rural countryside to a coast that is by turns rugged and sandy white to thick, old-growth forest, Michigan is full of beautiful places to drive, especially when **fall foliage** is at its peak. For full color, the second week of September in the UP and the second week of October in the Lower Peninsula are usually the best times.

## TUNNEL OF TREES
### M-119 from Harbor Springs to Cross Village

The coastal stretch of M-119 is considered one of the prettiest drives in the country. The narrow lane twists and turns as it follows Lake Michigan from atop a high bluff. Yet it's the trees that take top billing, arching overhead to form a sun-dappled tunnel. The effect is spectacular on autumn afternoons, when the fiery oranges and bronzes glow in the angled sunlight like hot coals.

## THE M-22

The touted M-22 turns north off U.S. 31 just north of **Manistee,** and runs along the coast from there all the way around the **Leelanau Peninsula,** passing close to the **Sleeping Bear Dunes** and ending in **Traverse City,** a 116-mile (186-kilometer) stretch of highway. You'll pass inland lakes, rivers, dunes, rolling hills dotted with orchards and vineyards, and quaint towns, all in view of Lake Michigan.

# BEST PARKS AND RECREATION AREAS

Many of Michigan's parks and recreation areas require a state Recreation Passport (www.michigan.gov/dnr), available for purchase at the park entrance. Residents can purchase annual passes with their registration renewal through the Secretary of State.

## SLEEPING BEAR DUNES

Glaciers and a millennium of wind and water sculpted Sleeping Bear Dunes, rimming the east coast of the Leelanau Peninsula (the pinky of the Lower Peninsula's "mitten") with a crust of sand and gravel. Claiming center stage

SLEEPING BEAR DUNES NATIONAL LAKESHORE

are the perched dunes: immense pyramids of sand spiking up from the edge of Lake Michigan and climbing at seemingly impossible angles to the sky. Sleeping Bear measures close to 400 feet (121 meters), making it the world's largest freshwater dune.

It sounds cliché, but words really can't describe the Sleeping Bear Dunes. They can be a sunny, friendly playground for squealing children tumbling down the 130-foot (39-meter) **Dune Climb** (6748 S. Dune Hwy., Glen Arbor) or lunar and desolate like a bleak desert on a January day. They can be pale and white-hot at noon, then glow in pinks like white wine at sunset.

The **Sleeping Bear Dunes National Lakeshore** (9922 Front St., Empire, 231/326-4700; www.nps.gov/slbe), established in 1977, encompasses nearly 72,000 acres (291 square kilometers), including 35 miles (56 kilometers) of Lake Michigan shoreline. One of the best hikes to get you close to these unforgettable dunes is the **Pyramid Point trail,** a hilly 2.7-mile (4.3-kilometer) loop that leads to the park's northernmost point, with a high lookout over Lake Michigan and Sleeping Bear Bay. To reach the trailhead, take Highway 22 3 miles (4.8 kilometers) east of Glen Arbor to Port Oneida Road.

## ISLE ROYALE NATIONAL PARK
906/482-0986; www.nps.gov/isro

Isolated in the vast waters of Lake Superior, Isle Royale is perhaps the model of what a national park is supposed to be—wild, rugged, and remote. One of the least visited of the national parks, the 45-mile-long (72-kilometer) island annually receives the equivalent of a weekend's worth of visitors to Yellowstone. This presents some unique opportunities to protect the wilderness, allowing the National Park Service to enforce rules more effectively and preserve the backcountry solitude.

Those who make the trek by boat or seaplane to Isle Royale come primarily to **hike** its 165 miles (265 kilometers) of trails. Try the 4.2-mile (6.75-kilometer) Scoville Point loop or the 20-mile (32-kilometer) round-trip trek to Lookout Louise, **fish** its 46 inland lakes, and

# BEST BEACHES

Bordering four Great Lakes, Michigan is blessed with the most freshwater shoreline in the U.S. Fortunately, a high percentage of that coastline is pristine, sandy beach. Michigan's spectacular national lakeshores, **Sleeping Bear Dunes National Lakeshore** and **Pictured Rocks National Lakeshore,** both boast wonderful beaches. Here are some other top choices.

- **Belle Isle Beach** (844/235-5375; www.michigan.gov/dnr): This strip of sand on Belle Isle, Detroit's urban sanctuary in the middle of the Detroit River, is small but notable for its proximity to the city, and it's the place to be on a hot summer day. When you've had enough sunbathing, visit the park's other attractions, including a conservatory, aquarium, and lighthouse.

- **Holland State Park** (2215 Ottawa Beach Rd.; 616/399-9390): One of Michigan's loveliest and most accessible beaches, Holland State Park attracts sunbathers by the hundreds on weekends.

- **Grand Haven State Park** (1001 Harbor Ave.; 616/847-1309): Connected to downtown Grand Haven by a popular boardwalk, this sandy beach boasts great views of the park's lighthouses and Lake Michigan.

- **Lakeport State Park** (7605 Lakeshore Rd.; 810/327-6224): Located on the more peaceful Lake Huron shore of Michigan, this park offers a classic beach experience close to the urban centers in the southeast of the state, and it's not far from Fort Gratiot Lighthouse.

**paddle** its saw-toothed shoreline. (Five Fingers is a great option; it's a collection of fjord-like harbors and rocky promontories on the east end of the island. **Wildlife viewing** is also popular, especially for spotting moose, which swam to the island from Ontario; Eastern timber wolves later followed across on pack ice.

You can access Isle Royale by seaplane, ferry, or personal boat. Rustic campsites, requiring a free camping permit, are available on a first-come, first-served basis. For more information, visit the **Houghton Visitor Center** (800 E. Lakeshore Dr.; 906/482-0984).

## HARTWICK PINES STATE PARK

4216 Ranger Rd., Grayling; 989/348-7068

The majestic white pine may be the state tree, but few virgin stands remain today. One of the last can be seen in this state park, one of the largest in the state, where trees that have been here since before the Revolutionary War reach as high as 10 stories. The logging company charged with felling the trees in the mid-1890s was forced to suspend operations due to economic problems. In 1927, the trees and the surrounding 8,000 acres (3,237 hectares) were purchased from the lumber company and donated to the state for a park.

Long a popular stop for vacationers heading north, the state park has a superb **visitors center,** a walkway accessible to wheelchairs and strollers, and an extensive **logging museum.** But the 49-acre (19-hectare) virgin tract of white and red pines is the main attraction. Hiking and biking opportunities include 17 miles (27 kilometers) of easy **trails** open to mountain bikes in summer and cross-country skiers in winter.

# FESTIVALS AND EVENTS

## COLLEGE FOOTBALL

Though hockey is popular in many parts of the state and Detroit has its share of beleaguered sports fans, it's really college football that rules the roost, more specifically a rivalry the **University of Michigan** and **Michigan State University.**

The U of M Wolverines play out of **Michigan Stadium** (Stadium Boulevard and South Main Street) in Ann Arbor; known as the "Big House," it's the largest stadium in the Western Hemisphere, seating 105,000 fans. The MSU Spartans play at **Spartan Stadium** (1 Spartan Way) in Lansing. The teams meet once a year to vie for the Paul Bunyan Trophy, and at the time of writing, the record stands at 70 Wolverine wins, 36 Spartan wins, and 5 ties.

The annual games are hot-ticket events, sure to be an exciting day in Lansing or Ann Arbor, regardless of where the game is being played, as is any game day during football season (usually Oct.-Dec.). Between students and season ticket holders, **tickets** can be hard to come by, but check with https://mgoblue.com or https://msuspartans.com for more details. Finding a spot in a **local bar** can be just as much fun, and after the game, you'll have plenty of breweries, shops, and sights to visit in either town.

# BEST FOOD AND DRINK

## INTERNATIONAL EATS

Surprising to some, Michigan is home to a wide variety of immigrant populations, both historic and relatively recent. This means a wonderful diversity of cuisines can be found in the state; a few of the most delicious can be found below.

- **Polish in Hamtramck:** This small city surrounded by Detroit emerged as a Polish community after World War I. Try **Polonia Restaurant** (2934 Yemans St.; 313/873-8432; www.polonia-restaurant.net).

- **Middle-Eastern in Dearborn:** Dearborn, 20 minutes southwest of Detroit, is home to the largest population of Arabic-speaking people in the U.S. Try **Al Ameer** (12710 W. Warren Ave.; 313/582-8185; https://alameerrestaurant.com).

- **German in Frankenmuth:** Touristy Frankenmuth, in Michigan's thumb, is all about preserving its Bavarian heritage, perhaps nowhere more so than **Zehnder's of Frankenmuth** (730 S. Main St.; 800/863-7999; www.zehnders.com), famous for its family-style chicken dinners.

## GREAT LAKES SEAFOOD

Because Michigan is blessed to be surrounded by four of the Great Lakes, fresh lake fish can be found throughout the state, from **whitefish** to **lake trout**. Local fish is available at restaurants from fish shacks to fine dining establishments. Here are some places to seek it out.

- On the Leelanau Peninsula, visit **Carlson's Fishery** (205 W. River, Leland; 231/256-9801; www.carlsonsfish.com) for a taste of an old-school fisherman's shack.

- In the UP, **Fitzgerald's Restaurant** (5033 Front St., Eagle Harbor; 906/337-0666; www.fitzgerals-mi.com) offers upscale dining, including fresh fish, overlooking Lake Superior.

## CRAFT BEER

In a country that's craft beer-crazy, Michigan, with its seemingly endless access to freshwater and a notable history in the beer industry, has long been at the forefront. **Bell's Brewery** (8938 Krum Ave., Comstock; 269/382-2338; www.bellsbeer.com) outside Kalamazoo, for one, is regularly named one of the best in the U.S. No matter where you are in Michigan, a brewery is almost never far away, and a pint of craft ale is a common end to myriad activities, whether you're sightseeing, beachgoing, or skiing.

Many Michigan towns and cities have pub crawls or ale trails to guide drinkers through their brewery offerings; below are some of the best places to drink craft beer in the state.

- Not far from perennial award winner Bell's, **Kalamazoo** is home to the one-of-a-kind **Beer Exchange** (211 E. Water St.; 269/532-1188; https://thebeerexchange.com), where a rotating lineup of local brews are priced according to the principles of supply and demand. The city's **"Give a Craft" Beer Trail** (www.discoverkalamazoo.com) helps visitors discover its 13 breweries.

- **Grand Rapids** has styled itself Beer City USA, and its **Beer City Ale Trail** (www.experiencegr.com) boasts more than 40 breweries. **Founders Brewing Co.** (235 Grandville Ave. SW; 616/776-1195; https://foundersbrewing.com) is a favorite.

# BEST SOUVENIRS

## PETOSKEY STONES

Michigan's state stone isn't really a stone at all, but a piece of fossilized coral more than 350 million years old. You can find Petoskey stones at gift shops in the northwestern part of the Lower Peninsula, polished up and often turned into jewelry.

## LOCAL ART

Many towns in Michigan are known for their concentration of galleries and boutiques, selling handmade items ranging from sculptures for your garden to fine art. A few notable places to shop are **Ann Arbor** (www.mainstreetannarbor.org) and **Saugatuck** (www.saugatuck.com/explore/arts).

## FARM-STAND PRODUCE

Though much of Michigan is fairly industrialized, it's also a very agrarian state: you're likely to encounter dozens of farm stands lining local highways if you're doing any amount of driving in the state in summer. If you do, stop. Michigan is rightfully known for its **cherries,** most grown around Traverse City; **apples** and apple products, available for picking at orchards around the state; **maple syrup** from northern Michigan; and, of course, **wine.**

■ **Traverse City** has also become quite an oasis for beer lovers. The **Traverse City Ale Trail** (www.tcbrewbus.com) is a fun way to experience eight different microbreweries in the area. **Right Brain Brewery** (225 E. 16th St.; 231/944-1239; www.rightbrainbrewery.com) was recently named one of the top five local breweries in the nation.

# MAJOR AIRPORTS

■ **Detroit Metropolitan-Wayne County Airport:** DTW; I-94 and Merriman Rd., Detroit; www.metroairport.com

■ **Gerald R. Ford International:** GRR; 5500 44th ST. SE, Grand Rapids; www.grr.org

■ **Cherry Capital:** TVC; 727 Fly Don't Dr., Traverse City; www.tvcairport.com

# MORE INFORMATION

## TRAVEL AND TOURISM INFORMATION

■ **Pure Michigan Department of Tourism:** 888/784-7328; www.michigan.org

■ **Michigan Department of Natural Resources:** www.michigan.gov/dnr

## NEWSPAPERS AND MAGAZINES

■ *The Detroit News:* www.detroitnews.com

■ *The Detroit Free Press:* www.freep.com

■ *Michigan Blue Magazine:* www.mibluemag.com

■ *Experience Michigan:* http://experiencemichiganmag.com

# OHIO

There's no one way to define Ohio. Technically part of the Midwest, Ohio is on Erie, Kickapoo, and Shawnee land. The Buckeye State's northeastern environs echo the industrial centers of New England, Cincinnati is just a river away from the South, and much of the state's rugged southeast is the entryway into Appalachia. Ohio's official tourism slogan used to be "The Heart of It All," which accurately if not inspirationally told motorists where they'd arrived: the state where the country's cultures smash into each other.

> **AREA:** 44,825 square miles / 116,096 square kilometers (34th)
>
> **POPULATION:** 11,689,100 (7th)
>
> **STATEHOOD DATE:** March 1, 1803 (17th)
>
> **STATE CAPITAL:** Columbus

This mosaic of American temperament has produced some the country's greatest figures, including eight presidents, as well as astronauts, athletes, and inventors. You can find two top-shelf amusement parks, great museums, and the cosmopolitan offerings of the Three C's: Cleveland, Columbus, and Cincinnati. Holmes County is the center of the second largest Amish settlement in the world, the dense Appalachian foothills to the southeast conceal a world of cliffs, rock formations, and adventure sports, and Lake Erie's shoreline can either be a quiet retreat or a party. You'll be hard-pressed to find such a variety of things to do in a comparable amount of space.

▲ HOLMES COUNTY, ONE OF THE COUNTRY'S LARGEST AMISH SETTLEMENTS

## ORIENTATION

**Cleveland** is located on the shores of **Lake Erie,** which forms much of Ohio's northern border, as does **Toledo** farther west, at the border with Michigan. In between, **Cedar Point** sits on a spit of land jutting into the lake. The other two of the Three C's of Ohio's cities make a diagonal southwest of Cleveland, with **Columbus** in central Ohio and **Cincinnati** in the southwestern corner, right on the border with Kentucky. **Holmes County,** home of the Amish, lies between Cleveland and Columbus, while the **Cuyahoga River** twists and turns southeast out of Cleveland.

## WHEN TO GO

**Summer** is high season for Ohio's amusement parks, beaches, campgrounds, and events. This time of year is hot and humid. Try to visit in June before the real heat arrives, or after mid-August after schools reopen. **Fall** is a secondary high season: football is in full swing, peak foliage is mid-to-late October, and temperatures are comfortable.

**Winters** in Ohio are cold and varying degrees of snowy. The snow belt east of Cleveland sees upward of 100 inches of lake-effect snow every season. In **spring,** the weather can stubbornly oscillate between winter's last throes and warm fronts. .

# HIGHLIGHTS

## ROCK AND ROLL HALL OF FAME

1100 E. Ninth St., Cleveland; 216/781-7625; www.rockhall.com

I.M. Pei's postmodern, geometric Rock and Roll Hall of Fame is perhaps the most iconic building in Cleveland. Opened in 1995, the museum is much larger than it looks, with a significant portion underground. Start your tour by heading down the escalator to the permanent gallery, where a sensory feast awaits visitors with music, videos of live performances, costumes, memorabilia, and instruments from the biggest names in popular music. The gallery tells the story of rock and roll's evolution, starting by recognizing early influencers in blues, gospel, country, and folk and moving through every decade to the present. The actual Hall of Fame Gallery is on Level 3, with an exhibit on the year's inductees and the Power of Rock Experience, a 15-minute compilation of some of the induction ceremony's musical highlights. Elsewhere in the museum, try your hand at playing some classics, brand your own band logo, and shop in the massive gift shop. The All Access Café, a bit on the expensive side, has snacks, pizza, coffee, and alcohol with nice views of the harbor and city from the airy atrium.

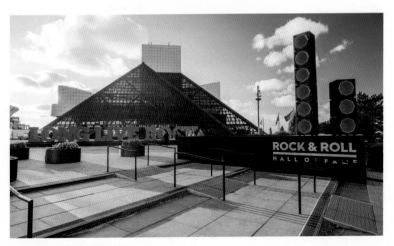

ROCK AND ROLL HALL OF FAME

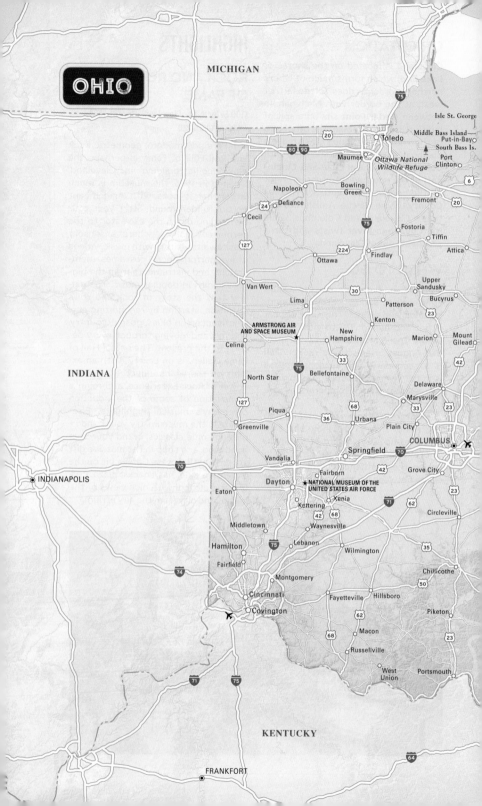

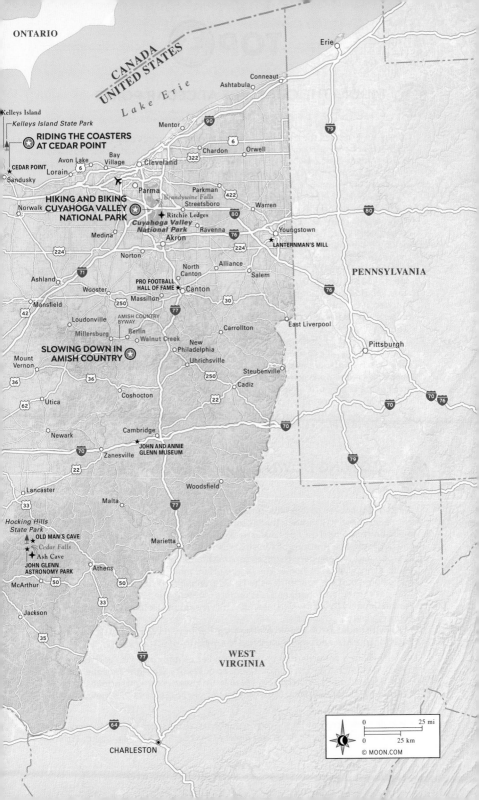

# RIDING THE COASTERS AT CEDAR POINT

1 Cedar Point Dr., Sandusky; 419/627-2350; www.cedarpoint.com

Consistently named the best amusement park in the world, Cedar Point is a glistening metropolis of roller coaster hills on Lake Erie. It is America's most visited seasonal amusement park and its second-oldest in operation, having opened its doors as a lakeside resort in 1870. This massive 364-acre (147-hectare) park is home to 17 roller coasters, the second-most of any park in the world, and each new addition seems to break a new record for height, twists, and screams. Standouts include **Millennium Force,** which broke the records for the tallest and faster roller coaster when it opened in 2000, and the **Top Thrill Dragster,** which launches riders to 120mph in less than four seconds. There are over 70 rides in total as well as live shows and a nightly laser show display.

ROLLER COASTER AT CEDAR POINT

If you can pull yourself away from the rides, there's a mile-long (1-kilometer) sand **beach** on the eastern edge of the peninsula that is open to ticketholders and guests of any of Cedar Point's accommodations. Included in admission are the 18 water attractions at **Cedar Point Shores Waterpark,** including various enclosed and open-air slides and a 500,000-gallon wave pool.

# SLOWING DOWN IN AMISH COUNTRY

Holmes County

Tucked in a pocket of low hills, Amish Country beckons 4 million tourists a year with hearty country dinners, made-from-scratch baked goods, and quality homemade crafts. Rivaled only by Lancaster, PA, **Holmes County** is the center of one of the largest concentrations of Amish in the world—nearly 50 percent of the county's population considers themselves Amish and a roughly equal number speak Pennsylvania Dutch at home. The region offers innumerable accommodations to make sure you take your time—the land's tranquility is lost on a whirlwind tour. Many of the region's shops and restaurants fall along the 160-mile (257-kilometer) **Amish Country Byway,** which meanders its way around Holmes County for bucolic country views.

All with under 3,000 people, **Millersburg, Berlin,** and **Walnut Creek** are the main hubs for tourists, and where you'll find the majority of attractions.

- Many visitors come here to browse an endless supply of shops and markets for renowned Amish goods, from antiques to quilts. Try **Starlight Antique and Gifts** (66 W. Jackson St., Millersburg; 330/674-5111; www.starlightantiques.com) and **Helping Hands Quilt Shop** (4818 W. Main St., Berlin; 330/893-2233; www.helpinghandsquilts.com).

- People come here just for the region's bakeries; there's something for everyone to enjoy at **Hershberger's Farm and Bakery** (5452 St. Rt. 557, Millersburg; 330/674-6096).

HOLMES COUNTY

- Cheese is one of the most popular items to shop for in Amish Country, with cheesemakers in the region offering free tours and samples—try **Walnut Creek Cheese** (2641 St. Rt. 39, Walnut Creek; 330/852-2888; www.walnutcreekcheese.com).

## HIKING AND BIKING CUYAHOGA VALLEY NATIONAL PARK

330/657-2752; www.nps.gov/cuva

In the 1960s, with the Cuyahoga River on fire upstream and urban sprawl encroaching on the land between Cleveland and Akron, locals sought to preserve the rural valley and the history within—most notably the remnants of the Ohio and Erie Canal, in use 1827-1913. In 1974, President Ford signed into existence the Cuyahoga Valley National Recreation Area, which was upgraded to a national park in 2000. What you get is a markedly different experience from most national parks, with small towns and farms intermittently scattered throughout. There are also miniature gorges, leafy woodland trails, waterfalls, and rock features all within an easy drive from Cleveland, Akron, and Canton. Combined, it's an altogether pleasing mix of wilderness, history, and culture, a recreational paradise, with ample options to hike and bike, including treks to **Brandywine Falls**, the crumbling cliffs of the **Ritchie Ledges**, and the **Ohio and Erie Canal Towpath Trail** (www.ohioanderiecanalway.com).

BRANDYWINE FALLS

# *Best* ROAD TRIP

**DAY 1**

Start in the heart of the state, **Columbus,** where you can walk through the picturesque **German Village neighborhood** and sample the craft beer scene.

**DAY 2**

Under 2 hours' drive northeast of Ohio's biggest city, you'll find yourself in the heart of **Amish Country,** where you'll have your pick of bakeries, artisan crafts, locally made cheese, and peaceful bed-and-breakfasts.

**DAY 3**

From here, make your way 2 hours north to **Cleveland,** and you can choose your own adventure en route, whether it's a stop at the **Pro Football Hall of Fame** or a hike in **Cuyahoga Valley National Park.** In the city, make a pilgrimage to the **Rock and Roll Hall of Fame** or the **Cleveland Museum of Art,** followed by a beer at **Great Lakes Brewing Company** in the vibrant **Ohio City** neighborhood.

**DAY 4**

Drive just an hour west to get your heart rate up on one of 70 rides at **Cedar Point.** Afterwards, choose a **Lake Erie** island to spend the night on: either keep the party going with an overnight stay in rowdy **Put-in-Bay,** or choose **Kelleys Island** for more peace and quiet.

**DAY 5**

It's a longer drive today, four hours south to **Cincinnati,** with a stop in **Dayton,** where you can grab a craft beer or explore some of the area's **aviation history.** In Cincinnati, wander the **Over-the-Rhine** neighborhood and be sure to try some Cincinnati chili.

**DAY 6**

Drive 2.5 hours east to hike Ohio's favorite outdoor destination, **Hocking Hills.** From here, it's only an hour drive north back to Columbus.

CRAFT BREWERY IN COLUMBUS

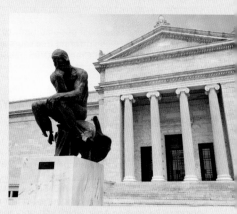

AUGUSTE RODIN STATUE, CLEVELAND MUSEUM OF ART

HOCKING HILLS

# *Major* CITIES

Together, the Three C's—Cleveland, the Gilded Age cultural powerhouse; Columbus, the polished, fashionable capital; and Cincinnati, the old-world river town—boast monumental museums and architecture, and tantalize with exciting food. One of the best ways to get to know them is walking through some of their most unique neighborhoods.

**CLEVELAND:** This former industrial powerhouse is undergoing a renaissance, with landmark museums and a necklace of greenspaces surrounding it. Arguably Cleveland's trendiest neighborhood and one of the most walkable and dynamic in Ohio, Ohio City shines as a model of Cleveland's resurgence, with a 21st-century building boom accommodating new breweries, restaurants, and cultural amenities.

**COLUMBUS:** Ohio's capital and largest city boasts a lineup of distinct urban neighborhoods, top-rated museums and cultural institutions, a burgeoning beer and restaurant scene, and one famous football program. The largest privately funded historic district in the United States, 233-acre (94-hectare) German Village is the city's preeminent historic neighborhood and the home of many of its favorite restaurants.

**CINCINNATI:** Founded in 1788, Cincinnati was the first true American boomtown. The impact of steamboats of German and Irish immigrants can still be seen in the city's distinctive architecture and unique culture, and at 362 acres (146 hectares), the Over-the-Rhine area claims to be the largest historic district in the United States.

## SPACE AND AVIATION HISTORY

With Orville and Wilbur Wright, John Glenn, and Neil Armstrong all hailing from the Buckeye State, sites belonging to and inspired by these and other historic figures are sprinkled across the state.

- Long before flight was possible, Ohioans observed the stars through the 19th-century **Cincinnati Observatory** (3489 Observatory Pl., Cincinnati; 513/321-5186; www.cincinnatiobservatory.org), home to one of the world's oldest working telescopes.

- **Dayton** is the epicenter of Ohio's aviation history, preserving sites relevant to Orville and Wilbur Wright and the birth of flight within the **Dayton Aviation Heritage National Historical Park.**

- The massive **National Museum of the United States Air Force** (1100 Spaatz Street, Wright-Patterson AFB; 937/255-3286; www.nationalmuseum.af.mil) chronicles the history of flight through the lens of armed conflict and science, featuring hundreds of fighter jets, space capsules, and presidential airplanes.

- North of Dayton is the **Armstrong Air and Space Museum** (500 Apollo Drive, Wapakoneta; 419/738-8811; www.armstrongmuseum.org) devoted to Apollo 11 astronaut and native son Neil Armstrong.

CINCINNATI OBSERVATORY

## MUSEUM MANIA

The Rock and Roll Hall of Fame often appropriately takes center stage, but Ohio is home to a number of other excellent museums, often overlooked.

### THE ARTS

With over 60,000 pieces of art, the **Cleveland Museum of Art** (11150 East Blvd., Cleveland; 216/421-7350; www.clevelandart.org) is one of the largest and finest art museums in the United States. The **Butler Institute of American Art** (524 Wick Ave., Youngstown; 330/743-1107; http://butlerart.com) was the first museum dedicated to American art and the best excuse to venture to Youngstown. The **Toledo Museum of Art** (2445 Monroe St., Toledo; 419/255-8000; www.toledomuseum.org), with more than 30,000 pieces of art, may have you asking "This is in Toledo?" And finally, there's more than 300 acres (121 hectares) of scenic woods, hills, and over 70 outdoor sculptures at **Pyramid Hill Sculpture Park and Museum** (1763 Hamilton Cleves Rd., Hamilton; 513/868-1234; www.pyramidhill.org).

### UNIQUE HISTORY

In Canton, the extravagant **Pro Football Hall of Fame** (2121 George Halas Dr. NW, Canton; 330/456-8207; www.profootballhof.com) highlights the National Football League's best players as well as its history and development. And in Cincinnati, the **National Underground Railroad Freedom Center** (50 E. Freedom Way, Cincinnati; 513/333-7739; https://freedomcenter.org) lays out in detail the evil of slavery and the Underground Railroad that rose to challenge the system.

▪ The **John and Annie Glenn Museum** (72 W. Main St., New Concord; 800/752-2602; http://johnandannieglennmuseum.org) celebrates John Glenn's achievements within the walls of John's boyhood home outside Cambridge. About an hour south is the **John Glenn Astronomy Park,** a designated dark sky park.

## LAKE ERIE ISLANDS

There are four primary inhabited islands in Lake Erie that belong to Ohio. Which you choose to visit depends on your preferences in terms of atmosphere, number of people, and activities. The two most visited are South Bass Island and Kelleys Island, with Middle Bass Island and Isle St. George quieter and less accessible.

### South Bass Island

The most popular destination is South Bass Island, known to most as **Put-in-Bay,** which is the name of the town on the north end of the island. The town is notable for its summer party scene, but there are quiet corners, with bed-and-breakfasts, wineries, and the commanding presence of **Perry's Victory and International Peace Memorial** (93 Delaware Ave.), lending some respectability.

### Kelleys Island

Kelleys Island is an altogether quieter experience than Put-in-Bay, with **Kelleys Island State Park** (920 Division St., Kelleys Island; 419/746-2546; https://ohiodnr.gov), which is home to a small beach and the island's most famous sight: a set of glacial grooves carved by retreating glaciers.

# BEST PARKS AND RECREATION AREAS

## OTTAWA NATIONAL WILDLIFE REFUGE

14000 St. Rt. 2, Oak Harbor; 419/898-0014; www.fws.gov/refuge/ottawa

A veritable safari for bird lovers, Ottawa National Wildlife Refuge harbors 6,500 acres (2,630 hectares) of wetlands, coastal grasslands, and woods frequented by flocks of migrating waterfowl, colorful songbirds, and several nesting pairs of bald eagles. Start at the large **visitor center,** where helpful rangers can tell you what to see and where to find them, then head out to hike atop the 10 miles (16 kilometers) of dikes that help control the water levels. While there's something to see in any season, spring is the busiest time of year as migratory birds stop on the lakeshore for a rest before continuing south.

## HOCKING HILLS

https://ohiodnr.gov

Arguably Ohio's favorite state park, Hocking Hills preserves unusual rock formations, cliffs, caves, waterfalls, and thickly forested land that epitomizes the dense foothills of Appalachian Ohio. The dominant formation is the recess cave, large cliff overhangs that are hundreds of feet long, especially **Ash Cave** (St. Rt. 56, Logan; 740/385-6841),

TRUMPETER SWANS, OTTAWA NATIONAL WILDLIFE REFUGE

## FALL FOLIAGE

In mid-late October, when autumn colors are at their peak, consider any of these locations for optimum fall foliage.

- **Lanternman's Mill** (1001 Canfield Rd., Youngstown) is a popular photo destination during peak autumn foliage.

- Sun shining through the autumn trees outside **Hocking Hills State Park's** Ash Cave make for a magical setting.

- Waterfalls and foliage combine for splendid views at **Cuyahoga Valley National Park**.

accessible by a short, 0.25-mile (0.4-meter) trail leads to the bottom of the stunning site, which also features a trickling waterfall depending on recent rainfall. A 0.5-mile (0.8-kilometer) trail travels alongside the rim, from which hikers can pick up the **Buckeye Trail** to **Cedar Falls** 2.3 miles (3.7 kilometers) away and on to **Old Man's Cave** (19988 St. Rt. 664, Logan; 740/385-6842) another 2 miles (3.2 kilometers).

# FESTIVALS AND EVENTS

## FOOTBALL

The **Ohio State Buckeyes** (https://ohiostatebuckeyes.com) football program is one of the most successful in the country, made even more legendary by the massive **Ohio Stadium** (411 Woody Hayes Dr., Columbus; 614/292-6330). Columbus lacks a National Football League team, though you would hardly notice; the city treats its Buckeyes, for better or worse, like its home team. The Buckeyes serve as a rallying point for the entire state; in some ways, the campus is the beating heart of Ohio.

Attending a game at Ohio Stadium is a bucket list item for many football fans, Buckeye or not. If you manage to grab tickets to a game, make sure to arrive early enough to watch the beloved

# BEST SOUVENIRS

- Cheese, jellies, or other delights from **Amish Country** make for good souvenirs. The Amish are also renowned for their quality furniture.

- Cheapest, most Ohioan souvenir you could buy? A can of **Skyline chili** at the supermarket.

**Ohio State University Marching Band,** known as "The Best Damn Band in the Land" (or TBDBITL) in their traditional pre-game performances. Be in your seat in the stadium at least 20 minutes before game time to watch the band march into the stadium for their pre-game show including the "Script Ohio" march.

# BEST FOOD AND DRINK

In the "Buckeye" state, bakers have concocted a popular peanut butter and chocolate confectionary that resembles a buckeye nut. The **buckeye** dessert is delectable. The buckeye nut is poisonous.

## CRAFT BEER

Breweries, walking tours, and the world's first craft beer hotel: Ohio has everything craft beer lovers need.

OHIO STADIUM

- In Dayton, taste beer history at **Carillon Brewing Company** (1000 Carillon Blvd. Dayton; 937/910-0722; www.carillonbrewingco.org), which brews using 19th-century recipes and techniques.

- Scottish company **BrewDog** (96 Gender Rd., Canal Winchester; 614/908-3051; www.brewdog.com) chose Columbus for its U.S. operations; its facility in suburb Canal Winchester sports a pub, a Craft Beer Museum, and the 32-room **DogHouse,** a craft beer hotel with taps in every guestroom. In the city's burgeoning, respected beer scene, **Land Grant Brewing Company** (424 W. Town St., Columbus; https://land-grantbrewing.com) and **Seventh Son Brewing Co.** (101 N. 4th St., Columbus; 614/421-BEER; www.seventhsonbrewing.com) top most lists.

- The big name in Cleveland is **Great Lakes Brewing Company** (2516 Market Ave, Cleveland; 216/771-4404; www.greatlakesbrewing.com), located in the Ohio City neighborhood, the epicenter of brewing in Cleveland and home to half a dozen breweries.

## GOETTA AND CINCINNATI CHILI

Cincinnati features not one, but two regional specialties that are worth a try.

To stretch their meat supply for the week, Cincinnati's 19th-century German immigrants added oats and onions to their pork, seasoned it with rosemary, thyme, or whatever else they had in their cupboard, and came up with **goetta** (pronounced 'get-uh'). Typically served for breakfast, goetta may also be found on sandwiches or topping a pizza.

More widely known is **Cincinnati chili,** developed by Greek immigrants in the 1920's looking to expand their

CINCINNATI CHILI

restaurant menus; the recipe includes an unusual array of ingredients including cinnamon and even chocolate, and is primarily eaten on spaghetti.

# MAJOR AIRPORTS

- **Cleveland Hopkins International Airport:** CLE; 5300 Riverside Dr., Cleveland; 216/265-6000; www.clevelandairport.com

- **John Glenn Columbus International Airport:** CMH; 4600 International Gateway, Columbus; 614/239-4000; https://flycolumbus.com

- **Cincinnati/Northern Kentucky International Airport:** CVG; 3087 Terminal Dr., Hebron, KY; 859/767-3151; www.cvgairport.com

# MORE INFORMATION

## TRAVEL AND TOURISM INFORMATION

- **TourismOhio:** https://ohio.org

- **Ohio Department of Natural Resources:** https://ohiodnr.gov/wps/portal/gov/odnr

## NEWSPAPERS

- *The Plain Dealer:* www.cleveland.com

- *Cincinnati Enquirer:* www.cincinnati.com

- *Columbus Dispatch:* www.dispatch.com

# NEW ENGLAND

◄ AUTUMN IN VERMONT

# NEW ENGLAND
## State by State

## MAINE

**Why Go:** Acadia National Park, lobster, and lighthouses sum up the Maine experience, and even just one of those would be worth the trip.

## NEW HAMPSHIRE

**Why Go:** The White Mountains, on many a hiker's bucket list, offer scenery for days.

## VERMONT

**Why Go:** Farm-fresh treats, from cheese to apples, are only some of the bucolic pleasures of the Green Mountain State.

## MASSACHUSETTS

**Why Go:** With history and culture galore, Boston is the nexus for the state—and all of New England—while beaches have their day on Cape Cod.

## RHODE ISLAND

**Why Go:** Providence's art scene and Newport's mansions steal the show, but the beaches of South County and Rhode Island's fun food items should also make the list.

## CONNECTICUT

**Why Go:** This little state is home to a variety of cultural attractions, from Yale University's museums and New England's foremost Native American research institute to the homes of Mark Twain and Harriet Beecher Stowe and the Philip Johnson Glass House.

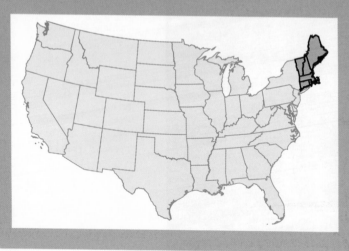

# New England ROAD TRIP

This road trip makes a loop through four states in about 10 days. With more time, you can add Connecticut and Rhode Island and check all the New England states off your list.

## MAINE

**Boston to Acadia National Park: 3 days / 280 miles (450 kilometers)**
From Boston, make a beeline to **Portland,** an easy, 2-hour drive up the interstate. Spend the next day winding your way to **Mount Desert Island,** the main area of **Acadia National Park,** a 4-hour drive if you take the coastal route. (**Bar Harbor** is the main town in the area.) The following day will be dedicated to exploring the park, starting with sunrise on **Cadillac Mountain.**

## NEW HAMPSHIRE

**Acadia National Park to the White Mountains: 2 days / 270 miles (435 kilometers)**
From Bar Harbor, the route to New Hampshire's **White Mountains** crosses the dark deep forests of inland Maine. You'll end up in **North Conway,** a little town with a scenic railway, in 4-5 hours. The next day, **Mount Washington,** the highest peak in the White Mountains, is your target an hour north. Make your way to the top, whether on foot, by twisty road, or by cog railway. Spend the night back in North Conway or Conway.

## VERMONT

**Conway to Grafton: 1 day / 185 miles (300 kilometers)**
Take the **Kancamagus Highway** (Rte. 112) from Conway for a scenic drive

PORTLAND HEAD LIGHT, MAINE

SKIING MOUNT MANSFIELD, VERMONT

through the New Hampshire mountains on your way west to Vermont. Cheese-taste in **Plymouth,** then head to the pretty village of **Grafton** for the night.

## MASSACHUSETTS

**The Berkshires and Boston: 3+ days / 220 miles (355 kilometers)**
After Grafton, spend a day in the gentle hills of the Berkshires in western Massachusetts. Stop in at **MASS MoCA** in North Adams, then continue south to **Edith Wharton's home** and spend the night in **Lenox.** The next day, make the 2.5-hour drive back to **Boston.** Spend at least a day visiting your pick of Boston's many sights. If you want to head out to **Cape Cod,** it's about 2 hours to reach Provincetown from Boston.

## MORE NEW ENGLAND

**Connecticut, Rhode Island, and Cape Cod: 2-4 days / 305 miles (490 kilometers)**
To see all the New England states, head south from Lenox through Connecticut's **Litchfield Hills** down to **New Haven,** about a 2-hour drive. Explore the Yale Campus and try the local specialty apizza. After spending the night in New Haven, make your way 2 hours east to **Newport,** Rhode Island, where a beautiful cliff walk and Gilded Age mansions await. From Newport, it's about 1.5 hours back to Boston, depending on traffic. Or you could head out to **Cape Cod** (2-3 hours) before heading back to Boston.

FRANCONIA NOTCH STATE PARK, NEW HAMPSHIRE

# MAINE

Set on the traditional lands of the Abenaki, Maliseet, Micmac, Passamaquoddy, and Penobscot people, Maine is an extraordinarily special place, where the air is clear, the water is pure, and the traditional traits of honesty, thrift, and ruggedness remain refreshingly appealing. From the glacier-scoured beaches of the southern coast, around spruce-studded islands and Acadia's granite shores, to the craggy cliffs Down East, Maine's coastline follows a zigzagging route that would measure about 3,500 miles (5,632 kilometers) if you stretched it taut. Each peninsula has its own character, as does each island, each city, and each village.

Maine's inland is just as exciting, with 6,000 lakes and ponds, 32,000 miles (51,499 kilometers) of rivers, and 17 million acres (6.8 million hectares) of timberlands for hiking and mountain biking, skiing and snowmobiling, paddling and fishing. This is where intrepid Appalachian Trail hikers finish at the summit of Katahdin, Maine's tallest peak. And then there's the food. Lobster, of course, is king, but don't overlook luscious wild blueberries, sweet Maine maple syrup, and delicious farmstead cheeses.

AREA: 35,385 square miles / 91,646 square kilometers (39th)

POPULATION: 1,344,212 (42nd)

STATEHOOD DATE:
March 15, 1820 (23rd)

STATE CAPITAL: Augusta

▲ ENJOYING THE VIEW IN ACADIA NATIONAL PARK

## ORIENTATION

Maine's 3,478 miles (5,597 kilometers) of coastline stretches diagonally from New Hampshire border in the southwest to the Canadian border in the northeast. **Portland** sits on the southern part of the coast, and although many travelers might think of **Acadia National Park** as the end of the road, there's still about 100 miles (160 kilometers) from there to the Canadian border. **Bangor** is the biggest city near the national park, while the state capital, **Augusta,** sits on the highway between Portland and Bangor. **Baxter State Park,** with its legendary **Katahdin,** and **Moosehead Lake** are in the northern wilds of the state, while the **Carrabassett Valley** and **Rangeley Lakes** are in western Maine.

## WHEN TO GO

**Late May to mid-October** is prime season, with **July** and **August,** the warmest months, being the busiest. Expect peak-season rates, congested roads, and difficulty getting reservations. Late June and late August tend to be a bit quieter.

**September-mid-October** is arguably the best time to travel in Maine. Days are warm and mostly dry, nights are cool, fog is rare, the bugs are gone, and the crowds are few. Foliage is turning by early October, usually reaching its peak by mid-month.

In **winter,** especially inland, skiing, snowshoeing, and ice skating replace hiking, biking, and boating. On the coast, choices in lodging, dining, and activities are fewer, but rates are generally far lower.

# HIGHLIGHTS

## OGUNQUIT

Located on Maine's southern coast, Ogunquit has been a holiday destination since the indigenous residents named it "beautiful place by the sea." What's the appeal? An unparalleled, unspoiled **beach,** a dozen art galleries, and the respected **Ogunquit Museum of American Art** (543 Shore Rd., Ogunquit; 207/646-4909; www.ogunquitmuseum.org), which boasts a 2,000-piece American art collection and incredible views.

No visit to Ogunquit is complete without a leisurely stroll along the **Marginal Way,** a mile-long (1.6-kilometer) paved footpath edging the ocean. En route are tidepools, intriguing rock formations, crashing surf, pocket beaches, and benches for absorbing the views. The route leads to **Perkins Cove,** a working lobster-fishing harbor where several old shacks have been

FISHING BOATS DOCKED IN PERKINS COVE

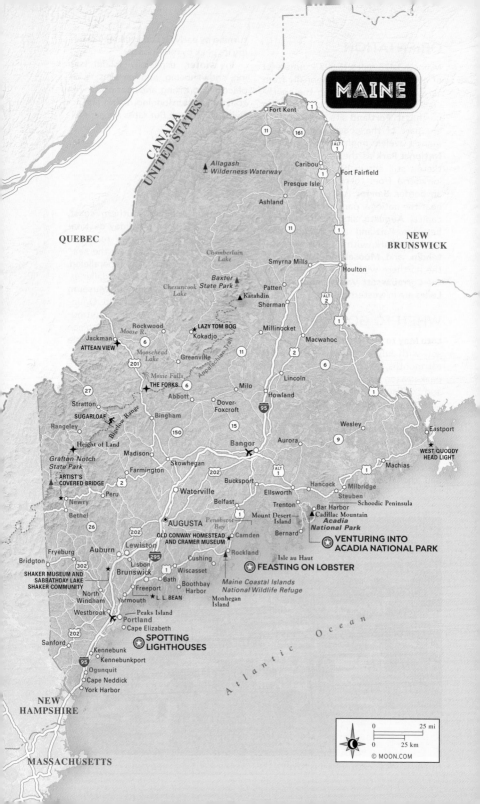

# *Major* CITIES

**PORTLAND:** Brine-scented air, cackling gulls, lobster boats, and fishing trawlers give notice that this is a seafaring town, but it's also Maine's cultural center. Portland is rich in museums and performing-arts centers, and it earns national kudos as a culinary destination.

**LEWISTON:** The state's second-largest city, home to Bates College, a private liberal arts school, is a magnet for visiting performers, artists, and lecturers. You'll also find rich Franco-American culture here, as the city has historically been home to Québécois and Acadian French immigrants.

**BANGOR:** This city features fine Victorian, Italianate, Queen Anne, and Greek Revival architecture. As you stroll alongside Kenduskeag Stream, duck into shops and restaurants, or catch some live music, you might even run into legendary horror author Stephen King, who calls Bangor home.

reincarnated as boutiques and restaurants. Photographers here go crazy shooting the quaint inlet spanned by a little pedestrian drawbridge.

## VICTORIA MANSION

109 Danforth St., Portland; 207/772-4841; http://victoriamansion.org

The jaws of first-time visitors drop when they enter the Italianate Victoria Mansion, also called the Morse-Libby Mansion. Built by Maine-born entrepreneur Ruggles Sylvester Morse in the late 1850s, it's widely considered the most magnificently ornamented dwelling of its period remaining in the country. The National Historic Landmark is rife with Victoriana: carved marble fireplaces, elaborate porcelain and paneling, a freestanding mahogany staircase, gilded glass chandeliers, and a restored 6x25-foot (1.8x7.6-meter) stained glass skylight. It retains more than 90 percent of its original interior, including almost all of Giuseppe Guidicini's unbelievable trompe l'oeil wall paintings. It's even more spectacular during the holidays, with yards of roping, festooned trees, and carolers.

## L. L. BEAN

95 Main St./Rte. 1, Freeport; 207/865-4761 or 800/341-4341; www.llbean.com

Established as a hunting and fishing supply shop, this giant sports outfitter now sells everything from kids' clothing to cookware on its ever-expanding downtown campus, with separate Hunting & Fishing (flagship); Bike, Boat & Ski; and Home stores. There's also the outlet store—a great source for deals on equipment and clothing—in the Village Square Shops across Main Street. The Bean reputation rests on a savvy staff, high quality, an admirable environmental consciousness, and a liberal return policy.

## MONHEGAN

Eleven or so miles (17 kilometers) from the mainland lies a unique island community with gritty lobstermen,

L.L. BEAN CAMPUS

# TOP

## VENTURING INTO ACADIA NATIONAL PARK

www.nps.gov/acad

Rather like an octopus, or perhaps an amoeba, Acadia National Park extends its reach here and there on **Mount Desert Island,** the most popular area of the park; the **Schoodic Peninsula** on the mainland; and the remote **Isle au Haut,** which caps visitors at 128 a day. The first national park east of the Mississippi River and the only national park in the northeastern United States, it was created from donated parcels that were slowly but surely fused into its present-day size of more than 46,000 acres (18,615 hectares).

Within the boundaries of this splendid space are mountains, lakes, ponds, trails, fabulous vistas, and several campgrounds. Each year more than 2 million visitors bike, hike, and drive into and through the park. Yet even at the height of summer, when the whole world seems to have arrived, it's possible to find peaceful niches and less-trodden paths.

MOUNT DESERT ISLAND, ACADIA NATIONAL PARK

Mount Desert Island's highlights include 27-mile (43-kilometer) **Park Loop Road,** a scenic drive that takes in most of the park's big-ticket sites, with plenty of trailheads and vistas along the way, and the **Carriage Roads,** a 57-mile (91-kilometer) car-free road system that sees see hikers, bikers, baby strollers, wheelchairs, and even horse-drawn carriages. Acadia is a great place to get into the water, too, with swimming at **Sand Beach** and **Echo Lake,** and **canoeing and kayaking** on the park's many ponds and waterways. Watching the sunrise from the summit of **Cadillac Mountain** is another must-do.

## **2** FEASTING ON LOBSTER

No Maine visit is complete without a "lobsta dinnah" at a lobster wharf, a rough-and-tumble operation within sight and scent of the ocean. If you spot a place with "Restaurant" in its name, keep going. You want to eat outside, at a picnic table, with a knockout view of boats, islands, and the sea. "Dinners" are served from noonish until around sunset. Dress casually so you can tackle the lobster without messing up your clothes. If you want beer or wine, call ahead and ask if the place serves it; you may need to bring your own. Lobster devotees cart picnic baskets with hors d'oeuvres, salads, and baguettes—even candles and champagne.

Here are some favorite lobster shacks (listed from south to north along the coast) to get you started:

LOBSTER DINNER FROM THE LOBSTER SHACK

- **The Lobster Shack** (222 Two Lights Rd., Cape Elizabeth; 207/799-1677; www.lobstershacktwolights.com): Ocean views, crashing surf, and a lighthouse have enticed lobster lovers to this location south of Portland since the 1920s.

- **Harraseeket Lunch and Lobster Company** (36 Main St., Town Wharf, South Freeport; lunch counter 207/865-4888, lobster pound 207/865-3535; www.harraseeketlunchandlobster.com): Take a break from L. L. Bean and head to this unfussy spot on the working harbor.

- **Thurston's Lobster Pound** (9 Thurston Rd., Bernard; 207/244-7600; www.thurstonforlobster.com): The two-story dining area tops a wharf above Bass Harbor.

## ③ SPOTTING LIGHTHOUSES

More than 64 beacons salt Maine's coastline from Kittery to Calais, and most can be viewed on the mainland or on a themed excursion cruise.

One of the state's most iconic lighthouses is **Portland Head Light** (1000 Shore Rd., Cape Elizabeth; 207/799-2661; www.portlandheadlight.com), located in Fort Williams Park, just 4 miles (6.4 kilometers) from downtown Portland in Cape Elizabeth. Commissioned by President George Washington and first lit in 1791, it has been immortalized in poetry, photography, and on stamps. There's no access to the 58-foot (17-meter) automated light tower, but the restored keeper's house has a **museum** filled with local history and lighthouse memorabilia.

On the southern coast in York is the distinctive 1879 lighthouse familiarly known as **Nubble Light** or "the Nubble." There's no access to the lighthouse's island, but a **welcome center** (Nubble Rd., York Beach; 207/363-7608; www.nubblelight.org) provides the perfect viewpoint. One of the icons of the Maine Coast, **Pemaquid Point Lighthouse** (www.lighthousefoundation.org) stands sentinel over some of the state's nastiest shoreline—rocks and surf that can reduce any wooden boat to kindling. It has been captured for posterity by gazillions of photographers and is even depicted on a Maine state quarter. Maine's only red-and-white-striped lighthouse, **West Quoddy Head Light,** is located in Quoddy Head State Park, the easternmost point of the United States. Views from the lighthouse grounds are fabulous, and whale sightings are common in summer.

NUBBLE LIGHT

# *Best* ROAD TRIP

**DAY 1** Begin your trip in **Portland.** Visit the **Portland Head Light,** a Cape Elizabeth landmark and Maine's oldest lighthouse, perched on the cliffs of 94-acre (38-hectare) Fort Williams Park. Spend a few hours in the **Portland Museum of Art** (7 Congress Sq., Portland; 207/775-6148; www.portlandmuseum.org). Make a pilgrimage north to giant sports retailer and outfitter **L. L. Bean,** hub of the hubbub in Freeport's outlet bonanza. End the day with a sunset cruise on **Casco Bay.**

MONHEGAN HARBOR

**DAY 2** Take a day trip to **Monhegan Island** from Port Clyde. This car-free, carefree gem, about a dozen miles (19 kilometers) off the coast, is laced with hiking trails and has earned renown as the Artists' Island. Continue up the coast to **Mount Desert Island** (100 miles/160 kilometers; 2.5 hours) and spend the night so you'll be ready for the next day's outdoor adventure.

SUNRISE FROM THE TOP OF CADILLAC MOUNTAIN

**DAY 3** In **Acadia National Park,** welcome the day by watching the sunrise from the summit of **Cadillac Mountain.** Afterward, before the crowds arrive, drive the **Park Loop Road,** which covers many of Acadia's highlights. Immerse yourself in the park by going hiking, bicycling, or sea kayaking, or take a carriage ride.

**DAY 4** Depart Mount Desert Island and head inland to **Greenville** and **Moosehead Lake** (120 miles/193 kilometers; 2.5 hours). This is a good place to spot moose—if you don't have a reservation for a **moose safari** (Northwoods Outfitters; www.maineoutfitter.com), head north to **Lazy Tom Bog,** where your moose sighting chances are good just before sunset (be sure to bring bug spray).

MOOSE IN GREENVILLE

**DAY 5** Depart Greenville and drive to **The Forks** via the **Moosehead Scenic Byway** and **Old Canada Road National Scenic Byway,** perhaps taking a break to stretch your legs on the easy hike into **Moxie Falls.** (Add a day here if you want to go **white-water rafting** on the Kennebec River.) Continue the scenic drive to **Rangeley** (130 miles/209 kilometers; 2.75 hours).

**DAY 6** After a morning hiking, paddling, or fishing, head south on Route 17 over **Height of Land** and the dazzling views. Detour off the main road in **Newry** to see the **Artist's Covered Bridge.** Snake southward through the White Mountain foothills, perhaps exploring the **Shaker Museum,** along the way. Make the one-hour drive back to **Portland.**

MOXIE FALLS

close-knit families, a longstanding summertime artists' colony, no cars, astonishingly beautiful scenery, and some of the best bird-watching on the Eastern Seaboard. Until the 1980s, the island had only radiophones and generator power; with the arrival of electricity and real phones, the pace has quickened a bit—but not much.

On the island, be sure to visit the **Monhegan Lighthouse** and the **Monhegan Historical and Cultural Museum** (207/596-7003; www.monheganmuseum.org) in the former keeper's house and adjacent buildings. Exhibits blend artwork by American icons such as Rockwell Kent and James Fitzgerald with historical photos and artifacts downstairs and an emphasis on flora, fauna, and the environment upstairs.

## ABBE MUSEUM

26 Mount Desert St., Bar Harbor; 207/288-3519; www.abbemuseum.org

The fabulous, Smithsonian-affiliated Abbe Museum is a superb introduction to prehistoric, historic, and contemporary Native American tools, crafts, and other cultural artifacts, with an emphasis on Maine's Maliseet, Micmac, Passamaquoddy, and Penobscot people. In creating the core exhibit, *People of the First Light,* museum staff worked with 23 Wabanaki curatorial consultants and four Native artists, among others. The **museum's original site** (2.5 miles/4 kilometers south of Bar Harbor at Sieur de Monts Spring), listed in the National Register of Historic Places, holds more displays; adjacent is the **Wild Gardens of Acadia,** which has more than 400 plant species native to Mount Desert Island.

## ASTICOU AZALEA GARDEN AND THUYA GARDEN

Northeast Harbor; 207/276-3727; www.gardenpreserve.org

One of Maine's best spring showcases is the **Asticou Azalea Garden,** a 2.3-acre (0.9-hectare) pocket where about 70 varieties of azaleas, rhododendrons, and laurels—many from the classic Reef Point garden of famed landscape designer Beatrix Farrand—burst into

## MOOSE-SPOTTING

Everyone loves Maine's bulbous-nosed and top-heavy state animal, *Alces alces americana.* Maine's wildlife department estimates that the state is home to more than 60,000 moose, most in the North Woods, the highest population in the lower 48 states. Moose are vegetarians, preferring new shoots and twigs in aquatic settings, so the best places to see them are wetlands and ponds fringed with grass and shrubs. These spots are likely to be buggy, so slather yourself with insect repellent. Try one of the following hot spots to get a glimpse:

- **Baxter State Park:** Sandy Stream, Grassy, and Russell Ponds
- **Lazy Tom Bog:** off Lily Bay Road, about 19 miles (30 kilometers) north of Greenville
- **Route 6/15:** Between Greenville Junction and Rockwood, on the west side of Moosehead Lake

bloom. Serenity is the key here, with a Japanese sand garden that's mesmerizing in any season, stone lanterns, granite outcrops, pink-gravel paths, and a tranquil pond. Behind a carved wooden gate on a forested hillside not far from Asticou lies **Thuya Garden,** designed as a semiformal English herbaceous garden, inspired by Beatrix Farrand and interpreted for coastal Maine. Special features of Thuya Garden are perennial borders and sculpted shrubbery. On a misty summer day, when few visitors appear, the colors are brilliant.

### THE ARTIST'S COVERED BRIDGE

Sunday River, Newry

Often called the Artist's Covered Bridge because so many artists have committed it to canvas, this 1872 wooden structure is one of Maine's nine covered bridges and stands alongside a quiet country road north of the Sunday River Ski Resort. It's located 5.7 miles (9.1 kilometers) northwest of Bethel off Route 2 in the western part of the state; the bridge is well signposted, just beyond a small cemetery.

### SHAKER MUSEUM AND SABBATHDAY LAKE SHAKER COMMUNITY

707 Shaker Rd., New Gloucester; 207/926-4597; http://maineshakers.com

Only a handful of Shakers remain in Sabbathday Lake Shaker Community, the world's last inhabited Shaker community. The members of the United Society of Shakers, an 18th-century religious sect, maintain a living-history museum, craft workshops, a store, and other activities. Guided tours of the community are offered, and the Shakers also welcome the public to their 10am Sunday Meeting worship.

## BEST SCENIC DRIVES

All of the scenic drives below feature beautiful **fall foliage.** Don't tell too many people, but Maine gets fewer leaf peepers than other New England states, so roads are less congested, and lodging and dining reservations are easier to score. (You can also access foliage info at www.mainefoliage.com.)

### MOOSEHEAD AND THE KENNEBEC RIVER

Leaf peepers who make it as far north as **Greenville** are amply rewarded. Loop from Greenville over to the **Kennebec River** and back on Routes 5 to **Jackman,** 201 south to **Bingham,** and 16 east to **Abbott,** and then Route 5 north to return to Greenville. You'll parallel the shorelines of **Moosehead Lake** and the **Moose River** on the **Moosehead Lake Scenic Byway** before arriving in **Rockwood.** As you head south, the views along the **Old Canada Road Scenic Byway** are spectacular. Dip into the **Attean View** rest area for vistas extending toward Canada. Need to stretch your legs? Consider the relatively easy hike to **Moxie Falls.** From here to Bingham, Route 201 can be truly spectacular as it snakes along the Kennebec River.

## BETHEL AND RANGELEY

Combine New England's trees with lakes and mountains and you have the best of nature's palette. From Bethel, take **Route 26** north to Errol, New Hampshire, then **Route 16** north to **Rangeley.** Return via **Route 17** south to **Route 2** west. Heading north, you'll cut through **Grafton Notch State Park** on the **Grafton Notch Scenic Byway;** the rest of the drive is speckled with mountains, lakes, and streams. Returning south from Rangeley, the **Rangeley Lakes National Scenic Byway** passes over **Height of Land,** providing dazzling views. The entire route is through prime **moose country,** so keep alert.

## ACADIA AND DOWN EAST

To the magic foliage mix, add the ocean and top it off with wild blueberry barrens, which turn crimson in foliage season. From **Hancock,** mosey inland on **Route 182** along the **Blackwoods Scenic Byway** to Cherryfield. Then head south **on Route 1A** to **Milbridge,** continuing south on **Route 1.** In **Steuben,** dip down Pigeon Hill Road to the Petit Manan section of the **Maine Coastal Islands National Wildlife Refuge** before continuing south on Route 1 to **Route 186,** which loops around the **Schoodic Peninsula** via the **Schoodic Scenic Byway.**

# BEST PARKS AND RECREATION AREAS

## BAXTER STATE PARK

Millinocket; www.baxterstateparkauthority.com

This fantastic recreational wilderness has 51 mountains, more than 225 miles (362 kilometers) of trails, and more than 60 named ponds. One rough unpaved road (limited to 20 mph) circles the park. No gasoline, drinking water, or food is available, but the rewards are worth it: rare alpine flowers, unique rock formations, pristine ponds, waterfalls, wildlife sightings (especially moose), dramatic vistas, and in late September, spectacular fall foliage. The **hiking** here is incomparable.

### Katahdin

Mile-high Katahdin, northern terminus of the Appalachian Trail, is the Holy Grail for most Baxter State Park hikers—and certainly for Appalachian Trail through-hikers, who have walked 2,158 miles (3,473 kilometers) from Springer Mountain, Georgia, to get here. Thousands of hikers scale the mountain annually via several different routes. Katahdin's other top experience is a traverse of the aptly named **Knife Edge,** a treacherous 1.1-mile-long (1.7-kilometer) granite spine (minimum width 3 feet/0.9 kilometers) between Baxter and Pamola Peaks. For a more family-friendly hike in the park, try **Roaring Brook Nature Trail.**

## CASCO BAY

When Portland city folks want to escape, they often hop a ferry for one of the islands of Casco Bay or head to one of the suburban preserves or beaches. With all the islands scattered through the bay, it's a **sea-kayaking** hotbed; the best place to start is out on **Peaks Island,** 15 minutes offshore via the **Casco Bay Lines ferry** (207/774-7871; www.cascobaylines.com). You can also book a **lobstering cruise,** where you'll learn lots of lobster lore and maybe even

SCENIC ROAD THROUGH ACADIA

catch your own dinner, and take a **boat excursion** where you can watch for lighthouses, seals, or whales. A real highlight is a tour of Casco Bay and its islands via a Casco Bay Lines **Mailboat Run,** during which you'll ride alongside mail, groceries, and island residents.

## WINDJAMMING IN PENOBSCOT BAY

In 1936, **Camden** became the home of the "cruise schooner" (sometimes called "dude schooner") trade when captain Frank Swift restored a creaky wooden vessel and offered sailing vacations to paying passengers. Now, more than a dozen sail Penobscot Bay's waters. **Rockland** wrested the Windjammer Capital title from Camden in the mid-1990s and has since held onto it.

Named for their ability to "jam" into the wind when they carried freight up and down the New England coast, windjammers trigger images of the Great Age of Sail. These windjammers head out for 3-11 days late May-mid-October, tucking into coves and harbors around Penobscot Bay and its islands. They set their itineraries by the wind, propelled by stiff breezes to Buck's Harbor, North Haven, and Deer Isle. Everything's totally informal and geared for relaxing. The **Maine Windjammer Association** (800/807-9463; www.sailmainecoast. com) is a one-stop resource for vessel and schedule information.

SCHOONER ON PENOBSCOT BAY

## ALLAGASH WILDERNESS WATERWAY

In 1966, Maine established a 92-mile (148-kilometer) stretch of the Allagash River as the Allagash Wilderness Waterway, a northward-flowing collection of lakes, ponds, and streams starting at Telos Lake and ending at East Twin Brook, about 6 miles (9.6 kilometers) before the Allagash meets the St. John River. Also recognized as a National Wild and Scenic River, the waterway's habitats shelter rare plants, 30 or so mammal species, and more than 120 bird species. **Canoeing** season usually runs from late May (after "ice-out") to early October.

## KENNEBEC RIVER

The focus of white-water rafting in this region is the **East Branch of the Kennebec River,** a 12-mile (19-kilometer) run from the Harris Station hydroelectric dam, below Indian Pond, to The Forks. Appropriately named, **The Forks** stands at the confluence of the Kennebec and Dead Rivers. Although neither looks particularly menacing from the Route 201 bridge, both draw legions of white-water rafters and kayakers for the Class III-IV rapids on the dam-controlled waters.

## CARRABASSETT VALLEY

The Carrabassett River winds its way through the smashingly scenic Carrabassett Valley in western Maine. On both sides of the valley, the **Longfellow** and **Bigelow Ranges** boast six of Maine's ten 4,000-footers (1,219 meters)—a paradise for **hiking. Mountain biking** is an excellent way to explore the area's mountains, streams, and forests: An ever-increasing network of world-class mountain-biking trails spans more than 100 miles (160 kilometers) here, with loop options for all abilities.

## SUGARLOAF

Carrabassett; 207/237-2000 or 800/843-5623; www.sugarloaf.com

The king of Maine's alpine resorts, Sugarloaf is a four-season destination resort with alpine skiing and snowboarding, snowshoeing, cross-country skiing, and ice skating in winter; golf, hiking, and mountain biking during warmer months; and zip-lining during all seasons. Well over 100 named trails and glades on more than 1,000 acres (404 hectares), served by 15 lifts ranging from a T-bar to detachable high-speed quads, ribbon the mountain's 2,820 vertical feet (859 meters). A compact base village has a hotel, an inn, and gazillions of condos as well as restaurants, a chapel, a few shops, and a base lodge housing a snow school and rental operations. The separate **Outdoor Center,** linked via shuttle and trails, houses cross-country skiing and mountain-biking operations and has an ice-skating rink.

# FESTIVALS AND EVENTS

## MOXIE FESTIVAL

Lisbon; www.moxiefestival.com; mid-July

The Moxie Festival, a certifiably eccentric annual celebration of the obscure soft drink Moxie, invented in 1884 and still not consigned to the dustbin of history, occurs in downtown Lisbon.

## MAINE LOBSTER FESTIVAL

Rockland; www.mainelobsterfestival.com; Aug.

August's Maine Lobster Festival is a five-day lobster extravaganza with live entertainment, the Maine Sea Goddess pageant, a lobster-crate race, crafts booths, boat rides, a parade, lobster dinners, and massive crowds. Hotels are full for miles in either direction.

## FRYEBURG FAIR

Fryeburg; www.fryeburgfair.com; Oct.

Maine's largest agricultural fair is held the first week of October, sometimes including a few days in September, and has been an annual event since 1851. A parade, a carnival, craft demonstrations and exhibits, harness racing, pig scrambles, children's activities, ox pulling, and live entertainment are all here, as are plenty of food booths (it's sometimes called the "Fried-burg" Fair). More than 300,000 turn out for eight days of festivities, so expect traffic congestion.

The fair runs Sunday-Sunday, and the busiest day is Saturday. Spectacular fall foliage and mountain scenery just add to the appeal.

# BEST FOOD

Everyone knows Maine is the place for lobster, but there are quite a few other foods that you should sample before you leave. In addition to those listed below, other must-try Maine favorites are **Moxie,** a carbonated beverage; **whoopie pies,** the state's official snack; and, especially in Down East Maine, **periwinkles,** a sea snail familiarly called wrinkles, and **smelts,** a small fish.

## BEANHOLE BEAN SUPPERS

A real live legacy of colonial times, beanhole bean suppers are generally a Saturday-night feast requiring plenty of preparation from its hosts and centered around beans baked in a hole in the ground. The supper also includes hot dogs, coleslaw, relishes, home-baked breads, and homemade desserts, and are typically alcohol-free. Check local newspapers for beanhole supper listings, but here are some annual favorites:

- **Broad Cove Church,** Cushing, mid-July
- **Patten Lumbermen's Museum,** Patten, second Saturday in August
- **Logging Museum Festival Days,** Rangeley, last weekend in July

## FIDDLEHEADS

For a few weeks in May, right around Mother's Day, a wonderful delicacy starts sprouting along Maine's woodland streams: fiddleheads, the still-furled tops of the ostrich fern (Matteuccia struthiopteris) that taste vaguely like asparagus. Don't go fiddleheading unless you're with a pro, though; the lookalikes are best left to the woods critters. If you find them on a restaurant menu, indulge.

## MAPLE SYRUP

We owe thanks to Native Americans for introducing us to maple syrup, one

## BEST SOUVENIRS

- Bring a taste of Maine home with you. You'll find **maple syrup,** as well as maple-flavored candies and other maple products, at local shops around the state. And don't forget about the blueberries—be sure to grab some **blueberry jam,** blueberry syrup, or a blueberry-flavored baking mix.

- Perusing the flagship **L. L. Bean** in Freeport for outdoor clothing and gear is a Maine must.

- **Deer Isle** is home to the renowned **Haystack Mountain School of Crafts,** so super-talented artists and artisans lurk in every corner of the island. To purchase an authentic craft for yourself, look for galleries tucked away on back roads, or try to catch an end-of-session auction at the school.

of Maine's major agricultural exports. The syrup comes in four different colors/flavors (from light amber to extra-dark amber), and inspectors strictly monitor syrup quality. The best syrup comes from the sugar or rock maple, Acer saccharum. On **Maine Maple Sunday** (usually the fourth Sunday in March), several dozen syrup producers open their rustic sugarhouses to the public for "sugaring-off" parties—to celebrate the sap harvest and share the final phase in the production process. **Old Conway Homestead and Cramer Museum** (Conway Rd., Camden; 207/236-2257; www.camdenrockporthistoricalsociety.org) opens its 1820 maple sugarhouse for demonstrations on Maine Maple Sunday.

### BLUEBERRIES

The best place for Maine maple syrup is atop pancakes made with Maine wild blueberries. Much smaller than the cultivated versions, wild blueberries are also raked, not picked. Although most of the Down East barren barons harvest their crops for the lucrative wholesale market, a few growers let you pick your own blueberries in mid-August. Contact the **Wild Blueberry Commission** (207/581-1475; www.wildblueberries.maine.edu) or the state **Department of Agriculture** (207/287-3491; www.getrealmaine.com) for locations, recipes, and other wild-blueberry information, or log on to the website of the **Wild Blueberry Association of North America** (207/570-3535; www.wildblueberries.com).

## MAJOR AIRPORTS

- **Portland International Jetport:** PWM; 1001 Westbrook St., Portland; 207/874-8877 https://portlandjetport.org

- **Bangor International Airport:** BGR; 287 Godfrey Blvd., Bangor; www.flybangor.com

## MORE INFORMATION

### TRAVEL AND TOURISM INFORMATION

- **Maine Office of Tourism:** www.visitmaine.com

- **Maine Tourism Association:** www.mainetourism.com

- **Maine Bureau of Parks and Lands:** www.maine.gov/dacf/parks

### MAGAZINES

- *Maine Magazine:* www.themainemag.com

# NEW HAMPSHIRE

Politically, this state on the land of the Abenaki, Pennacook, and Wabanaki people, might be best known for its fierce culture of independence, but it's the state's natural attractions that capture the traveler's imagination. The White Mountains, where bare rocky peaks emerge from the forest, form the rugged heart of New Hampshire. The Presidential Range sets the stage for Mount Washington, the tallest mountain in New England. A highlight of the 2,200-mile (3,540-kilometer) Appalachian Trail, the White Mountains are New England's top wilderness destination.

Venture out of the mountains, and the landscape turns into a rolling forest, broken by some of New Hampshire's endless lakes—the state claims nearly 1,000. Ranging from thumbprint ponds to vast bodies of water, they're pure nostalgia, lined with ice cream shops, lakeside cottages, penny arcades, and old-fashioned bandstands. The state even has a tiny sliver—just 18 miles (28 kilometers)—of coastline that shouldn't be overlooked.

**AREA:** 9,349 square miles / 24,213 square kilometers (46th)

**POPULATION:** 1,359,711 (41st)

**STATEHOOD DATE:** June 21, 1788 (9th)

**STATE CAPITAL:** Concord

FRANCONIA NOTCH STATE PARK, WHITE MOUNTAIN NATIONAL FOREST

## ORIENTATION

The **White Mountains,** within White Mountain National Forest, sit in northern New Hampshire, encompassing the **Presidential** and **Franconia Ranges. Lake Winnipesaukee** lies to the south of White Mountain National Forest. The state's three biggest cities are concentrated in southern New Hampshire, with **Concord** the farthest north, **Nashua** in the south near the border with Massachusetts, and **Manchester** in between. East of Manchester, the state stretches to the Atlantic, reaching it with its 18-mile (28-kilometer) coastline.

## WHEN TO GO

When schools let out in late June for **summer,** the New Hampshire's high season begins. Everyone heads to the beach—or the mountains—and prices spike around the region. **Autumn** brings cooler temperatures and one of New England's starring attractions: fall color. This season is a favorite for many, with warm, sunny days that alternate with crisp nights, and fall brings a host of fleeting pleasures: picking apples at local orchards, evenings cool enough for a crackling campfire, and outings fueled by cinnamon-scented cider donuts.

**Winter** weather begins in earnest at the end of December. Up north, New Hampshire can enter a deep freeze for weeks at a time, but for lovers of skiing, skating, and gorgeously frozen scenery, these winter months are a bonanza. March brings **spring** in fits and starts. Blooming lilacs scent the air, and in the forest a profusion of wildflowers appears.

# HIGHLIGHTS

## STRAWBERY BANKE MUSEUM

14 Hancock St., Portsmouth; 603/433-1100; www.strawberybanke.org

A cluster of 32 historic homes makes the open-air Strawbery Banke Museum among the best destinations in New England for exploring the daily lives of early colonial people. Part of the pleasure of visiting is that the museum is self-directed; in the summer you're invited to wander around, poke into houses, talk to costumed interpreters, and generally just explore colonial history for yourself. The homes are "inhabited" by enthusiastic docents, some costumed, who work to bring each place to life.

Among the museum's many highlights is the **Wheelwright House,** once home to an 18th-century ship captain active in the East Indies trade. His simple Georgian home is filled with furniture and ceramics from the period. Another must-see is the **Daniel Webster House,** which includes exhibits from the time that the great 19th-century statesmen spent in Portsmouth in the early part of his career. And if you are interested in seeing the actual items unearthed in the restoration of all the homes in the museum, stop by the **Jones Center,** which displays the findings from archaeological work on the neighborhood.

## PORTSMOUTH BLACK HERITAGE TRAIL

Portsmouth; www.blackheritagetrailnh.org

In recent years, Portsmouth has worked to acknowledge the history of enslaved people who lived and worked in the city through colonial times and beyond.

PORTSMOUTH BLACK HERITAGE TRAIL

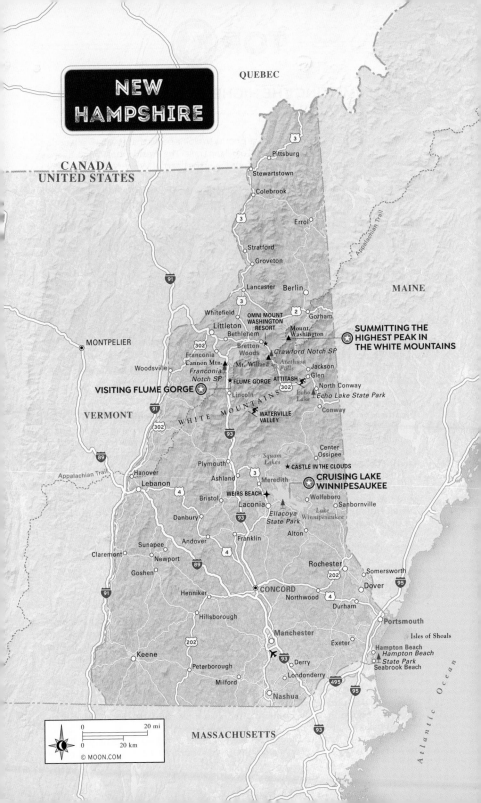

# TOP 3

## 1 SUMMITTING THE HIGHEST PEAK IN THE WHITE MOUNTAINS

New Hampshire's White Mountains are home to alpine peaks that tower over wooded valleys, mountain rivers, and a lifetime of hiking trails. The **Presidential Range,** a series of bare peaks pushing high above the tree line, is the heart of White Mountain National Forest, a rugged spine that culminates in **Mount Washington,** the highest summit in the White Mountains and northeastern United States.

THE MOUNT WASHINGTON COG RAILWAY AND DISTANT RIDGES OF THE WHITE MOUNTAINS

The most iconic hike in the White Mountains is the **Tuckerman Ravine Trail,** a 4.2-mile (6.75-kilometer) route to the summit of Mount Washington. Once you reach the top, you'll be rewarded with views across three states as you explore the summit's wind-whipped ridges. The mountaintop is also home to the **Mount Washington Observatory Weather Discovery Center**, where you can learn about the mountain's wild weather and the rare alpine plants that grow way up here. The oldest surviving building on the summit is the **Tip Top House,** a rustic stone lodge built in 1853, which became the office for a mountain newspaper in 1888-1915. Tiny bunks, communal tables, and a few dusty reproductions of the newspaper are on display.

On the opposite side of the mountain, two other trails ascend Mount Washington: the 4.4-mile (7-kilometer) **Ammonoosuc Ravine Trail,** which has gorgeous views as it works its way up the southwest face, and the 5.1-mile (8.2-kilometer) **Jewell Trail,** another stunner on clear days. You can also make it to the top via a ride on the **Mount Washington Cog Railway** (Base Rd., off Rte. 302, Bretton Woods; 603/278-5404; www.thecog.com), the world's first mountain-climbing train, or in a car on the **Mount Washington Auto Road.**

## 2 CRUISING LAKE WINNIPESAUKEE

Four-season, water-bound activities are everywhere you look around Winnipesaukee, the largest lake in New Hampshire. Known universally to residents as Lake Winni, the lake is a full 72 square miles (186 square kilometers) of spring-fed water, with upward of 200 miles (321 kilometers) of shoreline. Come summer, tourists descend on the lake from all over New England.

The villages surrounding the lake offer something for everyone: If you're looking for kitschy fun, the boardwalks of **Weirs Beach** have more than their fair share of waterslides, public beaches, arcades, and a great drive-in theater. Meanwhile, spots like **Meredith** and **Wolfeboro** offer quieter pleasures like antiquing, searching out galleries, and simply enjoying the scenery.

As soon as you catch a glimpse of Lake Winni's vast, folded shoreline, you'll think to yourself, "Why am I on dry land right now?" One of the best ways to get out on

*M/S MOUNT WASHINGTON AT ITS HOME PORT ON LAKE WINNIPESAUKEE*

the water is a **cruise** on the **M/S *Mount Washington*,** a rebuilt 1888 vessel that re-creates the era of old paddlewheel steamships. You can also zip around on a **Jet Ski,** rent a **pontoon boat,** or take to the lake in a **canoe, kayak,** or **sailboat.** And, of course, there's the beach. **Weirs Beach** is the most popular, and quieter **Ellacoya State Park** has a long, sandy stretch with views of the mountains.

 **VISITING FLUME GORGE**

Flume Gorge was formed before the last ice age, when a fin of basalt was forced into the vertically fractured granite; the basalt weathered away more quickly than the surrounding granite, leaving a winding slot in its place. Narrow, wooden walkways lead through this natural chasm, and high Conway granite walls shelter covered bridges, mossy walls, and waterfalls, including the spectacular 45-foot-high (37-meter) **Avalanche Falls.** A family-friendly 2-mile (3.2-kilometer) trail leads through the gorge, with a few places to duck off the path and explore, such as the **Wolf's Den,** a narrow, one-way route that involves squeezing yourself through cracks in the rock and crawling on hands and knees. It's cool

*AVALANCHE FALLS*

between the rock walls, and you'll see birch trees worm out of stony cracks.

Don't miss the **visitors center** (852 Rte. 3, Lincoln; 603/745-8391; www.nhstateparks.org) and its display case full of old-timey Flume Gorge postcards that 19th-century vacationers sent to their friends back home.

**DAY 1** Arrive in **Manchester,** New Hampshire's largest city and the location of its largest airport. In town, take a few hours to explore the **Currier Museum of Art** (150 Ash St.; 603/669-6144; https://currier.org), whose large collections include works by Pablo Picasso, Henri Matisse, and Georgia O'Keefe. Drive to Portsmouth (44 miles/70 kilometers; 45 minutes), where you'll be spending the night.

LAKE MASSABESIC

**DAY 2** In **Portsmouth,** get a taste of history at the **Strawbery Banke Museum,** a neighborhood of historic homes that brings colonial-era America to life. For even more history, follow the **Portsmouth Black Heritage Trail.** In the afternoon, take a cruise the **Shoals Islands,** where pirates, dreamers, and outcasts once made their escape. Oysters for dinner at **Row 34** is a must.

STRAWBERY BANKE MUSEUM

**DAY 3** Head over to **Hampton Beach** (16 miles/25 kilometers; 20 minutes) for fun in the sun. Lounge on the sand, visit the arcades, and play a round of mini golf. Feast on boardwalk favorites like fried clams and fried dough. Return to your accommodation Portsmouth for the night.

**DAY 4** Drive 1 hour (50 miles/80 kilometers) to **Wolfeboro,** your base for **Lake Winnipesaukee** and the Lakes Region. Take a **cruise** of Lake Wini and relax in the sand at **Ellacoya State Park.** For views of the entire Lakes Region, drive 30 minutes to the spectacular **Castle in the Clouds** mansion.

MOUNT WASHINGTON COG RAILWAY

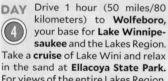

DAY **5** Up next: an adventure in the White Mountains. Drive 1 hour 40 minutes (70 miles/112 kilometers) to **Bretton Woods,** your base to summit the iconic **Mount Washington.** Hike up to the summit via the **Tuckerman Ravine Trail,** a full-day outing. Alternatively, sit back and take the **Mount Washington Cog Railway** up to the top. Back at the base of the mountain, visit the **Omni Mount Washington Resort.** Even if you're not staying at this grand historical hotel, stop for a drink on the deck or high tea in the Princess Room.

DAY **6** The next day, drive to **Franconia** (19 miles/30 kilometers; 25 minutes), your base for outdoor activities in the **Franconia Range.** If you have the time—and the stamina—hike the 6-hour, 8.2-mile (13-kilometer) **Franconia Ridge Loop,** the region's ultimate hike. There are several easier trails here, too. Whatever you do, don't miss a walk among the dramatic waterfalls and covered bridges of **Flume Gorge.**

DAY **7** Finish your road trip by driving back to **Manchester** (96 miles/154 kilometers; 1.5 hours). Along the way, you'll pass through **Concord,** the state capital.

THE FRANCONIA RANGE

Focusing on their stories, the Portsmouth Black Heritage Trail visits taverns, homes, and two burial grounds, including the moving **Portsmouth African Burying Ground** (1 Junkins Ave., Portsmouth; 603/610-7226; www.africanburyinggroundnh.org), which was rediscovered in 2003. The site is now inscribed with words from the 1799 Freedom Petition that a group of enslaved Africans submitted to the New Hampshire legislature, an eloquent document requesting that "we may regain our liberty and be rank'd in the class of free agents, and that the name of SLAVE be no more in a land gloriously contending for the sweets of freedom."

## ISLES OF SHOALS

A haven for fishermen, pirates, artists, and Unitarians, the nine rocky islands scattered off Portsmouth Harbor are thick with legend. This was a colonial-era escape from the Puritan strictures of the mainland, a prime spot for buried pirate treasure, and, they say, where Blackbeard honeymooned with his final bride. The 19th-century poet Celia Thaxter was raised in the Isles of Shoals, and later wrote of the islands that "there is a strange charm about them, an indescribable influence in their atmosphere, hardly to be explained, but universally acknowledged."

But the islands' most famous event is of the true crime genre—in 1873 two sisters were brutally murdered by an axe-wielding itinerant fisherman on the island of Smuttynose. A third woman managed to elude the killer and bring him to justice, but the story continues to haunt the area, inspiring florid books and movies ever since. Take a cruise that **tours** the islands to learn about all of the mist-enshrouded legends, from the 1614 arrival of Captain John Smith to a lineup of local ghosts.

## CASTLE IN THE CLOUDS

455 Old Mountain Rd., Moultonborough; 603/476-5900; www.castleintheclouds.org

Twenty-five minutes outside of Wolfeboro, Castle in the Clouds is a spectacular Arts and Crafts mansion set high on a hilltop with views of the entire Lakes Region. It's the former home of a shoe mogul, whose original estate

# *Major* CITIES

**MANCHESTER:** In New Hampshire's largest city, you'll find a bustling downtown, plenty of dining and shopping options, the respected **Currier Museum of Art,** the historic **Palace Theater,** and two homes designed by Frank Lloyd Wright. **Lake Massabesic** and **McIntyre Ski Area** offer outdoor recreation right in the heart of town.

**NASHUA:** Located at the intersection of the Nashua and Merrimack Rivers, Nashua is home to historic architecture and great dining options. **Mine Falls Park** right in the center of town offers walking paths and waterways for boating and fishing.

**CONCORD:** The state's capital, rich in history, is home to a **State House** that dates back to 1819 and a quintessential New England Main Street. Nearby trails and the Merrimack River mean that outdoor recreation is always within reach.

once covered 6,300 acres (2,549 hectares), stretching from the mountains to the edge of the lake. The view itself is worth the trip to the house, but the interior is beautifully restored, with decor and furnishings based on images of the original house or on written descriptions. The surrounding grounds feature 30 miles (48 kilometers) of hiking trails, too.

## OMNI MOUNT WASHINGTON RESORT

Rte. 302, Bretton Woods; 603/278-1000 or 800/843-6664; www.mountwashingtonresort.com

Of the dozens of grand hotels that dotted the White Mountains at the turn of the 20th century, the 1902 Omni Mount Washington Resort is the most perfectly preserved, and discovering the gorgeous historical touches throughout the building could easily occupy a rainy afternoon. A gracious veranda runs the length of the rambling hotel, with comfortable chairs that look straight out on Mount Washington. Even if you're not staying here, stopping by for a drink on the deck—or an utterly charming high tea in the Princess Room—is a wonderful experience, and a gracious counterbalance to the White Mountains' rugged scenery.

## CONWAY SCENIC RAILWAY

38 Norcross Circle, North Conway; 603/356-5251; www.conwayscenic.com

During the heyday of 19th-century travel to the White Mountains, rail lines threaded around the range, with spurs to each of the grand hotels in the area. Most of the tracks are quiet, but the Conway Scenic Railway sends vintage passenger trains from the charming, 1874 train station in North Conway Village. For rolling terrain and the finest views, opt for the five-hour round-trip on the **Notch Train** to Crawford Notch. Trips on the **Valley Train** range about 1-1.75 hours, linking North Conway with Conway or Bartlett. Some trips include lunch or dinner.

OMNI MOUNT WASHINGTON RESORT

# BEST SCENIC DRIVES

## MOUNT WASHINGTON AUTO ROAD

Rte. 16, Pinkham Notch; 603/466-3988; www.mountwashingtonautoroad.com

You'll see the bumper stickers as soon as you start driving around New England: "This Car Climbed Mount Washington." And you'll earn breathtaking views with every turn of the Mount Washington Auto Road. The 7.6-mile (12-kilometer) trip goes by at a snail's pace, taking about 30 minutes on the way up, 40 on the way down. Guided van tours are available for drivers and passengers who are unnerved by heights.

## KANCAMAGUS HIGHWAY

Rte. 112

Between Conway and Lincoln, 35 miles (56 kilometers) of tightly inscribed switchbacks, swooping valleys, and perfect mountain views make the Kancamagus Highway among the most iconic drives in New England. Route 112, affectionately known as "the Kanc," rolls through the heart of White Mountain National Forest, following the twists and curves of the Swift River and climbing to almost 3,000 feet (914 meters)—at 2,855 feet (870 meters), the Kancamagus Pass offers fabulous views, especially when autumn turns the surrounding forest into a riot of color.

There are plenty of places to stop along the way on the Kancamagus Highway—look for clusters of cars along the side of the road, which often signals a favorite local swimming spot—including a series of scenic overlooks, hiking trails, and historic sites. One worthy stop, where you can peer into daily life in 19th-century New Hampshire, is 12.7 miles (20.4 kilometers) in at the **Russell-Colbath House,** where docents are happy to share the mysterious story of Thomas Colbath's years-long disappearance and possible reappearance. Keep winding up to the **Kancamagus Pass,** which at 2,855 feet (870 meters) is the highest point on the road, then you'll find the **Otter Rock Rest Area** at 26 miles (41 kilometers), with restrooms and a short trail to another lovely swimming area in the Swift River.

# BEST PARKS AND RECREATION AREAS

## HAMPTON BEACH

Fried clams, penny arcades, sunburns, and mini golf—Hampton Beach is a rowdy and ramshackle beach town with the volume cranked to 11. Go for the people-watching or just dive into the honky-tonk fun, drifting up and

KANCAMAGUS HIGHWAY IN AUTUMN

## FALL FOLIAGE

New Hampshire, like its other New England neighbors, puts on a colorful display during fall foliage season, typically mid-Sept.-mid-Oct. These are the best leaf-peeping destinations in the state:

- Kancamagus Highway
- Mount Washington
- Flume Gorge

For in-depth and up-to-date foliage reports, visit www.visitnh.gov/foliage-tracker.

down the main drag alongside a crowd of slow-cruising teenagers checking out each other's tans. And when you've got enough sun, hit the arcades for some skee-ball, pinball, and vintage video games, then get your fortune told by a beachfront psychic.

Miles of sandy beach are the starring attraction at **Hampton Beach State Park** (Ocean Blvd., Hampton; 603/926-8990; www.nhstateparks.org), and on sunny days, the waterfront fills with families.

## SQUAM LAKES

Beyond the bustle of Lake Winnepesaukee, the forest closes in around a scattershot of ponds, lakes, and potholes—New Hampshire has almost 1,000 lakes altogether. Of these, Squam Lakes are among the most appealing. Morning breaks with the eerie loon call, or with the shushing rhythm of canoe paddles. There's not much to the town itself—a stamp-sized post office and a general store hold down the main crossroads—but that's just the idea. It's a place to pack a picnic lunch, maybe pick up some bait, and then spend the day exploring the shoreline.

To get out on the water, you can rent **canoes, kayaks,** and **paddleboards;** several backcountry and island campsites are amazing for overnight canoe trips. The most popular hike in the area is the 2-mile (3.2-kilometer) round-trip to the summit of **West Rattlesnake Mountain,** which leads through a forest of red oaks and red pines, then breaks from the trees for gorgeous views of Squam Lakes from a rocky summit. For a longer day on the trail, the **Squam Range Traverse** is a classic, 13.1-mile (21-kilometer) point-to-point that summits the seven named peaks in the Squam Range.

## CRAWFORD NOTCH STATE PARK

Crawford Notch State Park, also in the White Mountains, is home to the highest single-drop waterfall in New Hampshire, **Arethusa Falls.** The falls' musical name is said to be taken from a poem by Percy Bysshe Shelley about a Greek nymph who was transformed into a flowing spring. Reach the Arethusa Falls on a 2.6-mile (4.1-kilometer) round-trip hike along Bemis Brook, or extend your hike into a 4.7-mile (7.5-kilometer) loop by returning via **Frankenstein Cliff Trail,** which has lovely views of the valley. Another favorite trail is the 3.2-mile (5.1-kilometer) round-trip hike up **Mount Willard,** which earns fabulous views of Crawford Notch.

## THE FRANCONIA RANGE

A north-south ridgeline running from **Mount Lafayette** to Mount Flume, the Franconia Range is second only to the Presidential Range among New Hampshire's peaks. Following the valley (and highway) between the Kinsman Range

ENJOYING THE VIEW OF SQUAM LAKES FROM WEST RATTLESNAKE MOUNTAIN

# SKIING IN NEW HAMPSHIRE

With plentiful mountains, New Hampshire offers a wealth of skiing options. Here are a few of the best.

- **Bretton Woods Mountain Resort** (99 Ski Area Rd., Bretton Woods; 603/278-3320; www.brettonwoods.com): New Hampshire's biggest ski area is Bretton Woods Mountain Resort, which looks out at the southern edge of Mount Washington, with 97 trails, from beginner to expert, and 10 lifts on 464 acres (187 hectares) of terrain.
- **Attitash** (Route 302, Bartlett; www.attitash.com): With a prime location in the White Mountains, Attitash is one of the most popular ski resorts in New Hampshire. The resort has 68 trails and 11 lifts spread across two mountains, Attitash and Bear Peak.
- **Waterville Valley** (1 Ski Area Rd, Waterville Valley; 1-800-468-2553; www.waterville.com): Waterville Valley Resort considers itself the "gateway to the White Mountains." With 62 trails across 265 acres (107 hectares), skiers and snowboarders of all levels can catch fresh powder here.

and the Franconia Range, the beautiful **Franconia Notch State Park** has a bit of everything—including beaches, a campground, lots of hiking, and kid-friendly trails. This was the home of New Hampshire's most recognizable landmark, the **"Old Man of the Mountain,"** but the series of granite ledges came tumbling down in 2003, despite elaborate efforts to hold the stony face together.

Get your bearings from the top of **Cannon Mountain,** a bare granite dome—on a clear day, views stretch to four states and Canada. Reach the summit via the aerial tramway, or hike up along the 2.2-mile (3.5-kilometer) **Kinsman Ridge Trail.** Set just at the base of Cannon Mountain, **Echo Lake Beach** is sandy and scenic, with a lifeguard on duty during the day; it's possible to rent canoes, kayaks, and paddleboats here. For walking and biking, the **Franconia Notch State Park Recreation Path** is an 8.8-mile (14.1-kilometer) pedestrian trail that slopes gently downhill from the base of Cannon Mountain to the Flume Gorge. For the ultimate Franconia hike, plan for at least six hours on the 8.2-mile (13.1-kilometer) **Franconia Ridge Loop,** a rugged New Hampshire classic that goes up and over three peaks: **Little Haystack Mountain, Mount Lincoln,** and Mount Lafayette.

# FESTIVALS AND EVENTS

## LACONIA MOTORCYCLE WEEK

Laconia; www.laconiamcweek.com; mid-June

Packing the city with bikes, Laconia Motorcycle Week claims the title of World's Oldest Motorcycle Rally, with origins in a 1916 "Gypsy Tour" that landed on the shores of Lake Winnipesaukee. Those Gypsy Tours were organized to "create a more favorable opinion of the motorcycle and motorcycle rider," and after more than 100 years, the rally may be working—it's been said that the tradition of flashing bare breasts at or from a motorcycle has died down of late.

## AMERICAN INDEPENDENCE FESTIVAL

Exeter; 603/772-2622; www.independencemuseum.org; mid-July

"George Washington" addresses the crowds at the annual American Independence Festival, which takes place on the grounds of the American Independence Museum and is held in mid-July to celebrate the date that the Declaration of Independence was first read in Exeter, on July 16, 1776. Costumed

## BEST SOUVENIRS

- If you make the drive up the Mount Washington Auto Route, be sure to grab a **bumper sticker** to commemorate your feat. You'll see "This Car Climbed Mount Washington" stickers around the state.

- After a visit to the Strawbery Banke Museum, stop by the museum store, **Pickwick's at the Banke,** where you'll find vintage-style gifts.

- The classic Hampton Beach souvenir is a pile of saltwater taffy and caramel corn from **The Candy Corner** (197 Ocean Blvd., Hampton; 603/926-1740), which also does a brisk trade in fudge of all varieties.

interpreters also circulate through the event, which features helicopter rides, fireworks, music, craft vendors, and a specially brewed Independence Ale from Redhook Brewery.

### FROST DAY

Frost Place, Franconia; 603/823-5510; www.frostplace.org; early July

By governor's decree, each year in early July, Frost Place, the home of poet Robert Frost between 1915 and 1920, holds Frost Day, with poetry readings by the poet-in-residence and musical performances at the farmstead.

# BEST FOOD

New Hampshire doesn't disappoint when to comes to well-known New England dishes: You'll find lobster, clams, and other seafood near the coast, plus chowder and maple syrup all around the state.

### APPLES

New England is known for its apples, and New Hampshire is no exception. If you're visiting in autumn, head to an orchard where you can pick your own. A good choice is **Applecrest Farm** (133 Exeter Rd., Hampton Falls; 603/926-3721; www.applecrest.com), located 10 minutes from Hampton Beach, the state's oldest and largest apple farm. And don't forget to sip some **cider** and snack on an **apple cider doughnut** or two.

### OYSTERS

A visit to the coast would be incomplete without a seafood feast, specifically oysters. The place to try them is **Row 34** (5 Portwalk Pl., Portsmouth; 603/319-5011; www.row34nh.com), a shrine to the raw bar, and some of the oysters come from the restaurant's own farm. It's fascinating to try a lineup of oysters from neighboring farms, as the bivalves vary dramatically.

# MAJOR AIRPORTS

- **Manchester-Boston Regional Airport:** MAN; 1 Airport Rd., Manchester; www.flymanchester.com

# MORE INFORMATION

### TRAVEL AND TOURISM INFORMATION

- **New Hampshire Division of Travel and Tourism Development:** www.visitnh.gov

- **New Hampshire State Parks:** www.nhstateparks.org

### NEWSPAPERS AND MAGAZINES

- *New Hampshire Union Leader:* www.unionleader.com

- *New Hampshire Magazine:* www.nhmagazine.com

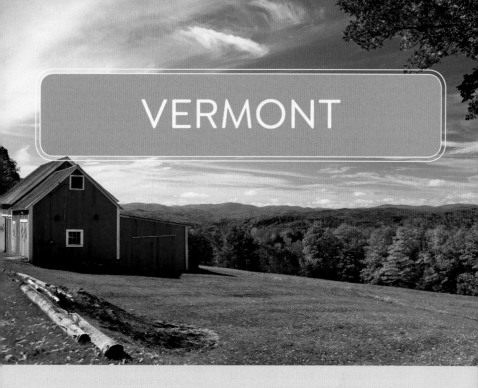

# VERMONT

Vermont is a blissfully rural state at the edge of densely populated New England. The state is on Abenaki land, and life here is wrapped around the seasons, recalling another era: Locals spend summer days in swimming holes, turn out for autumn's colorful display, then keep wintertime bright with sledding and pond skating. The rolling Green Mountains are dotted with sugar shacks and ski slopes. In the Northeast Kingdom, generations-old dairy families partner with young cheese makers. Maple syrup producers collect sap on horse-drawn sleds, gathering it into state-of-the-art sugarhouses powered by the sun. Vermont's intriguing blend of innovation and tradition means that visitors can weave between old and new as they explore.

AREA: 9,616 square miles / 24,905 square kilometers (45th)

POPULATION: 623,989 (49th)

STATEHOOD DATE: March 4, 1791 (14th)

STATE CAPITAL: Montpelier

▲ AUTUMN IN VERMONT

## ORIENTATION

The **Green Mountains** form a lengthwise ridge through the center of the state, and are themselves split into a northern portion, where **Montpelier** is the smallest state capital in the country and **Mount Mansfield** towers over the ski town of **Stowe,** and a southern portion with the vacation towns of **Manchester** and **Brattleboro.** In the northwest corner is the sparkling **Lake Champlain,** shared with New York State and with **Burlington** as its hub, and the wild and rural **Northeast Kingdom** in, well, the northeast.

## WHEN TO GO

If you don't mind the cold, Vermont is paradise in **winter.** This is the time to explore the Green Mountains on everything from skis to sleds and horse-drawn sleighs. **Spring** is "mud season," when outdoor adventures and backroad driving can be a challenge. But there's one sweet reason to come to Vermont this time of year: maple syrup.

In **summer,** sunny weather turns mountainsides lush and green, and the hills are traced with endless hiking and biking trails. **Autumn** is spectacular. The **fall foliage** is most dramatic in late September through October and leaf peepers arrive in droves.

# HIGHLIGHTS

## HILDENE

1005 Hildene Rd., Manchester; 802/362-1788; www.hildene.org

HILDENE, SUMMER HOME OF ROBERT TODD LINCOLN

Among those who once made Manchester their summer home was Abraham Lincoln's son, Robert Todd Lincoln, who entertained guests at Hildene, a Georgian Revival mansion with grounds overlooking the Battenkill River. The house is an intriguing glimpse of domestic life in Lincoln's time. It has a working Aeolian pipe organ that was installed in 1908 and still plays songs daily. The president's signature stovepipe hat retains its shine in an exhibit that illustrates the elder Lincoln's political life. There are also 12 miles (19 kilometers) of walking trails looping through the property and a working farm on the estate whose goats produce milk for a sharp aged cheese.

## PRESIDENT CALVIN COOLIDGE STATE HISTORIC SITE

3780 Rte. 100A, Plymouth; 802/672-3773; www.historicsites.vermont.gov/directory/calvin-coolidge

One of the best presidential historic sites in the country, the President Calvin Coolidge State Historic Site is situated on the grounds of the 30th president's boyhood home, a sprawling collection of houses, barns, and factories in a mountain-ringed valley. The exhibits inside give a rare intimate look into the upbringing of the president known as "Silent Cal" for his lack of emotion. The family parlor preserves the spot where Coolidge was sworn into office—by his father, a notary public. Even in 1924, when Calvin Coolidge ran for re-election, the homestead swearing-in must have seemed like a scene from a simple, earlier time.

## SHELBURNE MUSEUM

5555 Shelburne Rd., Shelburne; 802/985-3346; www.shelburnemuseum.org

The Shelburne Museum is less a museum than a city-state founded by a hoarder with exquisite taste. Its 38 buildings are full of extraordinary art and historical gewgaws, not to mention a Lake Champlain steamship and its own covered bridge. This is the work of art collector Electra Havemeyer Webb, who relocated buildings from across the country to display her collection,

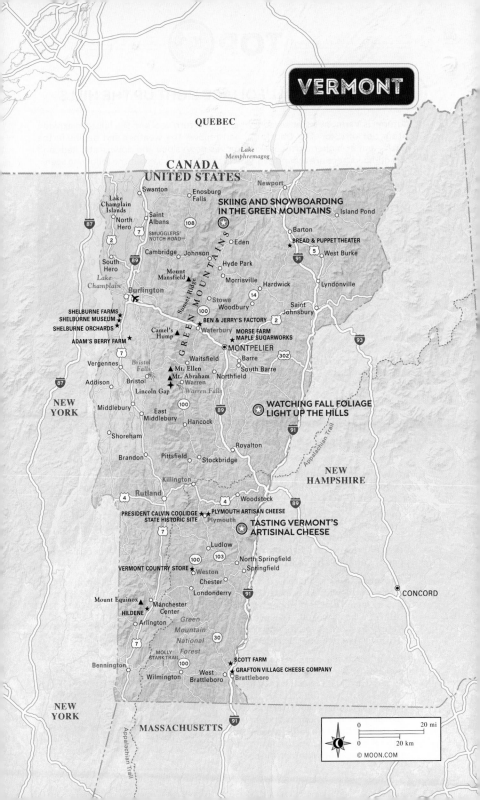

# VERMONT

QUEBEC

Lake
Memphremagog

CANADA
UNITED STATES

Newport

Lake
Champlain
Islands

Swanton        Enosburg
                Falls          **SKIING AND SNOWBOARDING
                                IN THE GREEN MOUNTAINS**        Island Pond

North      Saint
Hero       Albans                                              Barton
           108
                                            Eden                **BREAD & PUPPET THEATER**
South      Cambridge  Johnson                                   West Burke
Hero
Lake                        Mount         Hyde Park
Champlain                   Mansfield                Morrisville          Lyndonville
        Burlington                        Stowe              Saint
                                          Woodbury           Johnsbury
        SHELBURNE FARMS                    Ben & Jerry's Factory
        SHELBURNE MUSEUM                   Waterbury    MORSE FARM
        SHELBURNE ORCHARDS                              MAPLE SUGARWORKS
        ADAM'S BERRY FARM       Camel's        MONTPELIER
                                Hump                  Barre
        Vergennes                     Waitsfield              South Barre
                        Bristol              Northfield
        Addison         Falls    Mt. Ellen
                        Bristol   Mt. Abraham  Warren
                        Lincoln Gap   Warren Falls
        NEW             Middlebury
        YORK            East
                        Middlebury
                                  Hancock              **WATCHING FALL FOLIAGE
                                                       LIGHT UP THE HILLS**
        Shoreham
                        Royalton                        NEW
        Brandon   Pittsfield                            HAMPSHIRE
                        Stockbridge
                  Killington
        Rutland                     Woodstock
                        PLYMOUTH ARTISAN CHEESE
        PRESIDENT CALVIN COOLIDGE   Plymouth   **TASTING VERMONT'S
        STATE HISTORIC SITE                     ARTISINAL CHEESE**
                        Ludlow          CONCORD
        VERMONT COUNTRY STORE    North Springfield
                        Weston     Springfield
                        Chester
                        Londonderry
        Mount Equinox   Manchester
        HILDENE         Center    Green
                        Mountain
        Arlington       National
                        Forest
                        MOLLY
                        STARK TRAIL     SCOTT FARM
                                        GRAFTON VILLAGE CHEESE COMPANY
        Bennington      West       Brattleboro
                        Wilmington  Brattleboro

NEW
YORK

MASSACHUSETTS

0        20 mi
0        20 km

© MOON.COM

# TOP

## 1 WATCHING FALL FOLIAGE LIGHT UP THE HILLS

Autumn is Vermont's star season, when nights turn cool and the hillsides explode into a riot of color. The transformation follows the weather and begins in the north—and at higher altitudes—and moves downslope and downstate. Red- and orange-hued trees are around every bend this time of year, but the following scenic drives are two of the most spectacular ways to watch the show.

### MOLLY STARK TRAIL

Rte. 9

The scenic Molly Stark Trail connects artsy **Brattleboro** and historical **Bennington** (1 hour), rising up and over a mountain pass with long views of the **Green Mountain National Forest.**

FALL FOLIAGE IN STOWE

### ROUTE 100

The ultimate autumn road trip, this road follows the spine of the Green Mountains the whole length of the state. Start at the intersection with Route 9, and wind through **Plymouth, Warren, Stowe,** and **Newport** for a gorgeous 5-hour drive that cuts through the **Mad River Valley.**

## 2 SKIING AND SNOWBOARDING IN THE GREEN MOUNTAINS

Snowy Vermont shines in winter. All that powder turns the state into the perfect playground, whether that means skiing the moguls or taking in the silence on a cross-country jaunt.

- Tumbling down the slopes of **Mount Mansfield**—that's Vermont's highest peak—**Stowe** (5781 Mountain Rd./Rte. 108, Stowe; 888/253-4849; www.stowe.com) is the state's most glamorous place to hop a gondola. Tons of terrain mean that even on crowded days there's a place to ski and ride, and the adjacent village has one of Vermont's hottest post-slope scenes.

- **Killington** (4763 Killington Rd., Killington; 800/621-6867; www.killington.com) is a behemoth—with six peaks to choose from, the resort has something for everyone, including double diamonds, twisting glades, and family-friendly cruisers. This southern heavyweight also attracts Vermont's most devoted party scene, which fills nightclubs all week long.

- For a somewhat less crowded experience, many skiers head north to **Sugarbush** (102 Forrest Dr., Warren; 802/583-6300 or 800/537-8427; www. sugarbush.com), which is second only to Killington in the number and variety of trails; it boasts a large amount of natural snowfall thanks to the storms that come in from Lake Champlain.

KILLINGTON SKI RESORT

# ③ TASTING VERMONT'S ARTISANAL CHEESE

It's only fitting that a place speckled with dairy cows should have cheese makers to match, and Vermont's got more of them per capita than any other state. Cheddar has marquee appeal, but local artisans are producing everything from richly veined blues to creamy chèvres, and racking up international awards that have put Green Mountain cheese on the world stage. To try the state's best wedges all in one place, go to the annual mid-August **Vermont Cheesemakers Festival** (www.vtcheesefest.com), held at **Shelburne Farms.** It's also possible to visit individual cheese makers. The Vermont Cheese Council maintains a **Cheese Trail map** (www.vtcheese.com) of the cheese makers that welcome visitors. Here are a couple places to start your cheese tour.

## GRAFTON VILLAGE CHEESE COMPANY

400 Linden St., Brattleboro; 802/246-2221; www.graftonvillagecheese.com

At this factory and tasting room, you can graze samples at the retail store, and peek through a viewing window at the cheese makers' gleaming stainless-steel vats. While you're there, don't miss the firm, earthy **Shepsog,** a blended sheep's and cows' milk cheese that's cave aged for five months.

## PLYMOUTH ARTISAN CHEESE

106 Messer Hill Rd., Plymouth Notch; 802/672-3650; www.plymouthartisancheese.com

Located in a particularly pretty valley off Route 100, Plymouth Artisan Cheese has been operating continuously since John Coolidge (father to President Calvin Coolidge) founded it in 1890. Their distinctive granular curd cheeses are made with raw cows' milk, which you can learn about and sample in the on-site museum and store. Try the **Plymouth Original** or the sharp **Plymouth Hunter.**

GRAFTON VILLAGE CHEESE COMPANY

# *Best* ROAD TRIP

**DAY 1** Start in **Brattleboro**. Spend the day exploring Brattleboro's quirky **Main Street,** and try some Vermont cheese at **Grafton Village Cheese Company.**

**DAY 2** Head to **Weston** (40 miles/64 kilometers; 1 hour) to take in the kitschy charm of the **Vermont Country Store.** After lunch, continue north along scenic Route 100 to **Plymouth** (22 miles/35 kilometers; 35 min.), where you'll find the **President Calvin Coolidge State Historic Site** and some excellent cheese. Take the scenic **Route 100** north to end up in the picturesque Mad River Valley town of **Warren** (51 miles/82 kilometers; 1 hour), where **ski slopes** or **swimming holes** await, depending on the season.

DOWNTOWN BRATTLEBORO, VERMONT

**DAY 3** Head north along Route 100 to **Waterbury** (20 miles/32 kilometers; 30 min.), home of the **Ben & Jerry's factory.** After tasting ice cream, drive west along I-89 to the lakeside college town of **Burlington** (28 miles/45 kilometers; 30 min.). Head to the **Waterfront Park,** where you can take a spin on the bike path or go paddling on Lake Champlain.

HISTORIC BRIDGE IN WARREN

**DAY 4** Meander south down Route 7 to drive up the **Mount Equinox Skyline Drive** for a beautiful view of the Green Mountains. Then, head south down Route 7 to **Bennington** (40 minutes), and enjoy this quiet historical town. Finally, head back to Brattleboro along the **Molly Stark Trail** (40 miles/64 kilometers; 1 hour) to finish your loop.

BURLINGTON'S WATERFRONT

# *Major* CITIES

**BURLINGTON:** This lakefront community boasts forested trails, organic farms, and rocky coastlines within the city limits, and on snowbound winter mornings you can spot cross-country skis lined up outside coffee shops. It's a dynamic college town and culinary hot spot that's home to many academics and artisans.

**RUTLAND:** A 19th-century world leader in marble production, this working-class town has been down and out for generations. But there is a thread-bare charm to the once resplendent downtown, which is now home to a growing collection of tempting cafés and art galleries.

**BENNINGTON:** At the foot of the Green Mountains, this quiet, working-class town is best-known for the 1777 Battle of Bennington, a rebel victory that increased support for American independence during the Revolutionary War.

opening the museum in 1947. The buildings are as intriguing as their contents, and include a 19th-century jailhouse, a Methodist meeting house, and a beautifully restored round barn, one of just two dozen built in Vermont. Webb's own home was a Greek Revival mansion that now holds first-rate paintings by Cassatt, Degas, Monet, Corot, and Manet.

## WORKING FARMS IN THE CHAMPLAIN VALLEY

Though agriculture no longer dominates the Vermont economy as it once did, farming and agricultural life remain at the core of the state's identity. On summer weekends, families pick fruit at their local berry farms, dinners are held in barns and fields, and fall harvest feels like a statewide celebration. The farms range from elegant historic properties to down-home orchards.

### Shelburne Farms

1611 Harbor Rd., Shelburne; 802/985-8686; www.shelburnefarms.org

Shelburne Farms is a nonprofit that works for sustainability in the food system. Sights change with the season: Spring means maple sugaring and lambing—stopping by the farm to snuggle baby lambs is a yearly pilgrimage—and you can bundle up for horse-drawn sleigh rides in the winter. The on-site cheese-making operation is active

year-round, and the welcome center is stocked with samples.

### Shelburne Orchards

216 Orchard Rd., Shelburne; 802/985-2753; www.shelburneorchards.com

Shelburne Orchards is lined with undulating rows of trees that produce over a dozen varieties of apples, and it's a marvelous experience to visit in the early fall when the air is heavy with the scent of ripe fruit. The house-made cider doughnuts are delightful in a crust of cinnamon sugar, and the charismatic owner distills remarkably good apple brandy from his pressed apples.

### Adam's Berry Farm

985 Bingham Brook Rd., Charlotte; 802/578-9093; www.adamsberryfarm.com

Adam's Berry Farm brings crowds of families for pick-your-own organic blueberries, raspberries, and strawberries on a beautiful property in Charlotte. After you've stained your fingers blue (or red), head to the farm stand to pick up popsicles made with their own fruit as well as quince paste, jams, and sorbets.

## BEN & JERRY'S FACTORY

1401 Rte. 100, Waterbury; 802/882-2034; www.benjerry.com

This flagship factory offers a tour with an ice cream sample at the end, but many may just want to get a scoop at the ice cream shop outside, which features the entire flavor collection. And you don't have to join a tour to visit the Ben & Jerry's "Flavor Graveyard." Here, 30 tombstones are marked with flavors that didn't make it, including Lemon Peppermint Carob Chip, which just speaks for itself; and the ill-fated Sugar Plum, a plum ice cream with caramel swirl that was the worst-selling flavor in B&J history.

## BREAD & PUPPET THEATER

753 Heights Rd., Glover; 802/525-3031; www.breadandpuppet.org

FALL FOLIAGE IN SMUGGLERS' NOTCH

Bread & Puppet Theater is a barn-cum-museum and the home of a performing puppet troupe. With its mission that art should be accessible to the masses, B&P began more than 50 years ago with counterculture hand- and rod-puppet performances on New York's Lower East Side. Founder Peter Schumann moved back to the land in the 1970s, taking over an old farm and presenting bigger and more elaborate political puppet festivals every summer. The troupe virtually invented a new art form, pioneering the construction of larger-than-life papier-mâché puppets of gods and goddesses and other figures that now regularly spice up the atmosphere at left-of-center political protests around the world. On the grounds, the old barn has been transformed into a museum filled with 10-foot-tall (3-meter) characters from past plays, along with photographs and descriptions of the political context of the times. The troupe still performs on its original farm stage in Glover throughout the summer, and the rollicking shows are a classic Vermont experience.

# BEST SCENIC DRIVES

## SMUGGLERS' NOTCH ROAD

Rte. 108

Route 108 is an incredibly twisty, curving road that's hemmed in by high cliffs, granite boulders, and trees that turn bright gold in the fall. It winds through

**Smugglers' Notch,** the mountain pass that separates **Stowe** from Smugglers' Notch Resort (30 min.) and so named for the legend that it was used to bring contraband from Canada during the years of Prohibition. Oversize vehicles should stay away, and all drivers should approach this road with great care, as hikers, rock climbers, and cyclists are often hidden behind the sharp corners.

## MOUNT EQUINOX SKYLINE DRIVE

off Rte. 7A; 802/362-1115; www.equinoxmountain.com

This winding toll road climbs 3,800 feet (1,158 meters) to the summit of Mount Equinox for an unparalleled view of the surrounding peaks and occasional sightings of eagles and peregrine falcons. At the top of the mountain is the **Saint Bruno Viewing Center,** which tells the story of the nearby Carthusian Monastery, the only one of its kind in North America. A half-mile (0.8-kilometer) hiking trail starts at the viewing center and winds around the mountaintop.

# BEST PARKS AND RECREATION AREAS

## LAKE CHAMPLAIN

Lake Champlain is New England's grandest lake, with a meandering shoreline that offers expansive views of the mountains that line its flanks. The whalebones and shipwrecks beneath the lake's surface are clues to its former lives as an inland sea, trading hub, and site of fierce naval battles during the Revolutionary War. **Burlington** is the hub of the area, with a pedestrian-friendly Waterfront Park that's a great place to ride a bike, put in for a paddle, or watch the sun set over the Adirondacks.

On sunny summer days the lakefront fills with a cheerful flotilla of kayaks, canoes, and stand-up paddleboards, as locals and tourists alike head for the water. Paddling is a wonderful way to explore the ins and outs of the shoreline. For some swimming, head to sandy **North Beach** (60 Institute Rd., Burlington; 802/862-0942) or **Oakledge Park** (Flynn Ave., Burlington; 802/864-0123).

The northern end of the lake is home to the **Lake Champlain Islands,** which feels entirely separate from the rest of the state—if not the world. There's water on every end, along with farms, storm-weathered homes, and residents who lift their hands in a lazy wave as they pass on back roads. Given that the islands are home to more shoreline than anywhere else in Vermont, kayaks and canoes are perfect for nosing around the many crannies and nooks, and in warm weather you can take a stand-up paddleboard for a spin. For a great swimming beach on the islands, you can't beat the sand at **Knight Point State Park** (44 Knight Point Rd., North Hero; 802/372-8389; https://vtstateparks.com/knightpoint.html).

## THE LONG TRAIL

The oldest long-distance hiking trail in the United States, the 272-mile (437-kilometer) Long Trail follows the spine of the Green Mountains from Massachusetts to Canada, rising over some of Vermont's most beloved summits along the way. Vermont's highest peak, Mount Mansfield, is on the Long Trail, and even if you're not planning an end-to-end trek, it's a great place to start exploring alpine Vermont. Here are some hiking high points of Vermont's Long Trail:

- **Mount Mansfield:** At 4,393 feet (1,338 meters), this is the tippy top of the

SHELTER ON THE LONG TRAIL

Green Mountains, and on the Long Trail, it's just a 4.6-mile (7.4-kilometer) round-trip to the peak. There's more than one way to the top, and one favorite hike follows the lovely, bare **Sunset Ridge.**

- **Camel's Hump:** This distinctive silhouette has become a symbol of the state. An 18.7-mile (30-kilometer) section of the Long Trail traverses the summit, and it's a stout day of hiking—there are plenty of shorter alternatives, including the 7-mile (11.2-kilometer) round-trip via the **Monroe Trail.**

- **Mount Abraham:** The Long Trail climbs the 4,006-foot (1,221-meter) Mount Abraham on the 2.9-mile trail from **Lincoln Gap,** and the exposed rock that leads to the top is a favorite stretch of trail for many climbers. To tick off two of Vermont's "4,000 footers" (1,219 meters) on a single stretch of Long Trail, continue from Mount Abraham to **Mount Ellen,** an additional 3.7 miles (5.9 kilometers) from summit to summit.

## SWIMMING HOLES

Summer in Vermont can bring some hot, sticky days. When that happens, skip the air-conditioning and head for one of the state's many rivers, which stay blissfully cool no matter the weather. Searching out swimming holes is a passion for many locals, and there are endless "secret" places to swim that don't appear on any maps. These are some of the most beloved places to swim in the state.

- **Warren Falls** (Warren): A series of cascades drop into pools deep enough for a (cautious) dive—this is among the most beautiful swimming holes in Vermont, and it can get crowded on hot summer days.
- **Dorset Quarry** (Rte. 30 at Kelly Rd., Dorset): At this flooded, disused marble quarry, there's plenty of room to stretch out in the sun or find a cozy patch of shade. The daring line up to jump from the quarry's highest point.
- **Bristol Falls** (Lincoln Rd., Bristol): A mix of shallow and deep pools is interspersed with sections of fast-flowing river, but the star attraction of this spot is the 15-foot (4.5-meter) waterfall that drops into a churning pothole.

## KINGDOM TRAILS NETWORK

Kingdom Trails Association, 478 Rte. 114, East Burke; 802/626-0737; www.kingdomtrails.org

This is the best riding in Vermont, where carriage paths, railroad rights-of-way, and forest trails have been stitched together into a cyclist's wonderland. The **Tap and Die** trail is a rolling hoot as riders whip over quick ascents and swerve through curves lined with high berms. **Sidewinder** is a flowy classic, and one of the Northeast's most exhilarating rides. There are trails for every ability, and the mountain bike enthusiasts that staff the visitors center can tell you where to start and what to avoid.

# FESTIVALS AND EVENTS

## VERMONT BREWERS FESTIVAL

Burlington; 802/760-8535; www.vtbrewfest.com; July

Don't miss the Vermont Brewers Festival when a who's who of local and regional brewers set up shop right in Burlington's Waterfront Park. If you'd like to attend, check the website well in advance of your trip, as tickets often sell out the day they go on sale (usually in May).

# BEST FOOD AND DRINK

Vermonters are passionate about food, and recent years have seen an explosion of interest in farm-to-table dining, farmers markets, and everything local and sustainably produced.

## MAPLE SYRUP

Vermont bottles an estimated 500 million gallons (1,892,705,892 liters) of maple syrup each year—accounting for more than a third of the output of the entire country. It's a remarkable process that depends on precise weather conditions and sugar makers who tend to their trees all year.

In Vermont, you are never far from a sugarhouse, but one of the best is **Morse Farm Maple Sugarworks** (1168 County Rd., Montpelier; 800/242-2740; www.morsefarm.com). On the edge of Montpellier, this spot is a virtual museum of the industry, with old photographs and a movie theater that shows a film of the sugaring process.

MAPLE SYRUP FOR SALE IN BENNINGTON

# BEST SOUVENIRS

- Vermont **maple syrup** is a must. Pick up a jug of the sweet stuff, or grab some maple cream, maple kettle corn, or even spirits distilled from maple.

- To find the perfect souvenir, head to the original restored **Vermont Country Store** (657 Main St.; 802/824-3184; www.vermontcountrystore.com) in Weston. Browsing this old-fashioned store can be a transporting experience; penny candy, pickles, and sundry doodads are stocked alongside flannel nightgowns and quilts.

A cavernous gift shop sells maple kettle corn and that most Vermonter of treats, maple creemees (soft-serve maple ice cream cones).

## HEIRLOOM APPLES

Although Vermont farmers sell a range of heirloom produce, from tomatoes to zucchini, the state's blockbuster heirlooms are the hundreds of varieties of **apples** that are grown here, from tiny lady apples to the knobbed russet, whose lumpy exterior hides wonderfully crisp flesh. Apples don't get better than at **Scott Farm** (707 Kipling Rd., Dummerston; 802/254-6868; www.scottfarmvermont.com), where they grow 120 kinds of apples with intriguing names such as Lamb Abbey Pearmain and Zabergau Reinette.

## CRAFT BEER

The Green Mountain State is experiencing a golden age of brewing, with craft beers that have garnered national acclaim.

- **Long Trail Brewing Company** (5520 Rte. 4, Bridgewater Corners; 802/672-5011; www.longtrail.com): Those only familiar with the ubiquitous **Long Trail Ale** may be surprised by the wealth of beers on tap at this Bridgewater Corners brewpub.

- **Citizen Cider** (316 Pine St., Burlington; 802/448-3278; www.citizencider.com):

In the heart of Burlington, this cidery has been giving beer a run for its money. Try the **Full Nelson,** which is dry hopped with Nelson Sauvin hops.

- **The Alchemist** (100 Cottage Club Rd., Stowe; 802/882-8165; www.alchemistbeer.com): This Stowe-based brewery is known for its hop-heavy canned beer **Heady Topper,** which has been twice named the **Best Beer in the World.**

# MAJOR AIRPORTS

- **Burlington International Airport:** BTV; 1200 Airport Dr., South Burlington; 802/863-1889; www.btv.aero

# MORE INFORMATION

## TRAVEL AND TOURISM INFORMATION

- **Vermont State Parks:** https://vt-stateparks.com

- **Vermont Vacation:** www.vermontvacation.com

## NEWSPAPERS

- *Burlington Free Press:* www.burlingtonfreepress.com

# MASSACHUSETTS

On Massachusett, Pawtucket, Nipmuc, Pocumtic, Wampanoag, and Nauset land, Massachusetts is a contradiction and a confluence of the past and the present. In Boston, skyscrapers and modern architecture tower over—yet don't overshadow—Victorian brownstones, colonial graveyards, crooked streets, and gracious squares. Just over an hour from downtown Boston, Cape Cod unfurls into the ocean, a ragged hook of sand, bogs, and crashing waves. Cape Cod's blend of old, new, and wild offers the opportunity to weave between worlds. Inland, the Berkshires offer an unexpected mix of quaint villages and grand mansions, and one of New England's most vibrant arts communities.

Today, a new generation of creatives is bringing youthful energy to unexpected places in Massachusetts. Artists, musicians, and chefs are reinventing New England traditions for the 21st century. This thrilling blend of fresh takes and old ways is a standing invitation to explore.

**AREA:** 10,565 square miles / 27,363 square kilometers (44th)

**POPULATION:** 6,892,503 (15th)

**STATEHOOD DATE:** February 6, 1788 (6th)

**STATE CAPITAL:** Boston

CAPE COD NATIONAL SEASHORE

## ORIENTATION

**Boston** sits in the crevice in the middle of Massachusetts's Atlantic coastline, and **Cape Cod** is the hook of land curving out into the ocean from the southern part of the state. The islands of **Martha's Vineyard** and **Nantucket** sit off the Cape to the south. The **Berkshires,** with **Mount Greylock** and **MASS MoCA,** are in western Massachusetts.

## WHEN TO GO

Like all of New England, Massachusetts experiences all four seasons, offering reasons to visit in each one. **Summer**—especially after schools let out in June—is high season, when you can visit seasonal seafood shacks at the edge of the water and catch Red Sox games with the crowd at Fenway Park. In **autumn, the** temperature cools off, but visitors still flock here for fall foliage displays.

Winter is chilly, and Massachusetts usually experiences a few big snowstorms. Bring plenty of clothes and you'll be warm and cozy while skating on Boston Common or rolling through the hills on a horse-drawn sleigh. **Spring** means wildflowers and harvest season.

# HIGHLIGHTS

### FANEUIL HALL

Congress St., Boston; 617/523-1300; www.nps. gov/places/faneuil-hall.htm

Peter Faneuil built this landmark building for two purposes: The ground floor would serve as a public food market, and the upstairs meeting hall would be a "marketplace of ideas." When Faneuil Hall was built in 1742, the most pressing issues were taxation on goods by the British government, and it became the main meeting space for protests and discussions by the Sons of Liberty—earning it the nickname the "Cradle of Liberty." It was later expanded and became the main venue for talks by William Lloyd Garrison, Frederick Douglass, and other antislavery activists. Public talks and citywide meetings are still held in the upstairs hall.

Downstairs, the market stalls still exist, but most are now the venue for souvenirs and other made-in-Boston goods. The adjacent Faneuil Hall Marketplace (www.faneuilhallmarketplace. com) adds more indoor and outdoor shopping and dining opportunities. Just behind Faneuil Hall is **Quincy Market** (367 S. Market St.; 617/523-1300;), where farmers and butchers began selling their wares in 1826. Produce vendors have given way to food stalls, restaurants, and shops, making this a convenient place to grab a snack along the Freedom Trail.

## BOSTON PUBLIC LIBRARY

700 Boylston St., Boston; 617/536-5400; www. bpl.org

BOSTON PUBLIC LIBRARY COURTYARD

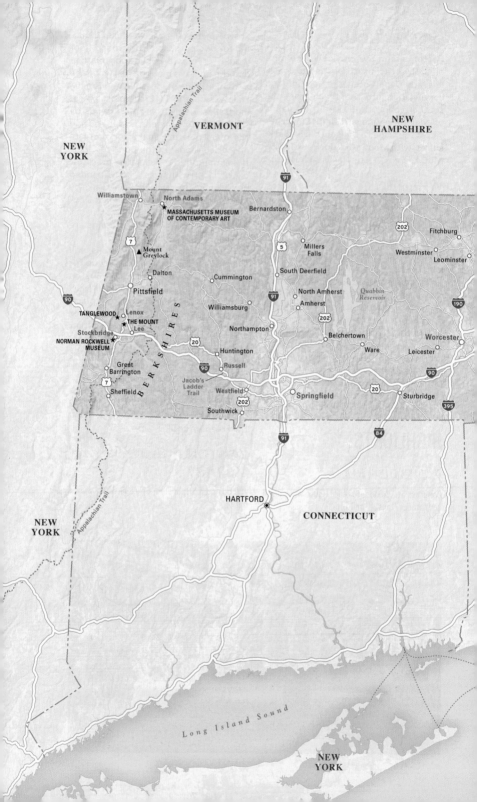

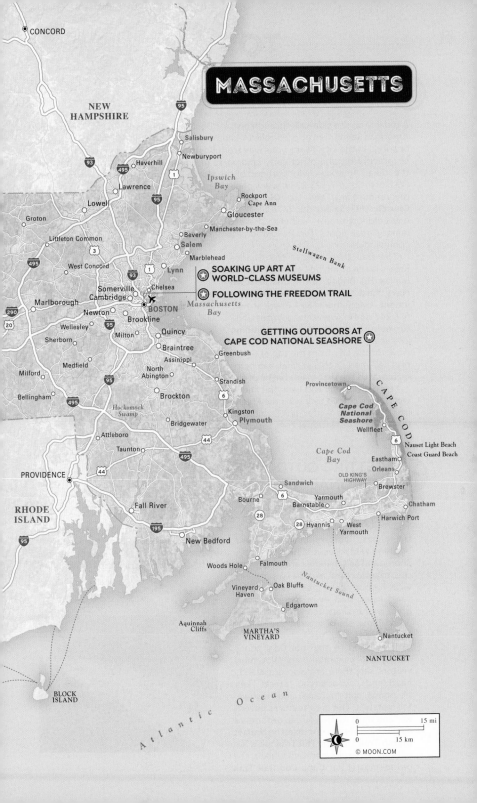

# MASSACHUSETTS

CONCORD

NEW HAMPSHIRE

Salisbury
Newburyport
Haverhill
Lawrence

*Ipswich Bay*

Lowell
Groton
Littleton Common
West Concord

Rockport
Cape Ann
Gloucester
Manchester-by-the-Sea
Beverly
Salem
Marblehead

*Stellwagen Bank*

Marlborough
Somerville
Cambridge
Newton
Brookline
Wellesley
Sherborn

Lynn
Chelsea
BOSTON

⊙ **SOAKING UP ART AT**
**WORLD-CLASS MUSEUMS**

⊙ **FOLLOWING THE FREEDOM TRAIL**

*Massachusetts Bay*

Milton
Quincy
Braintree
Assinippi
North
Abington
Brockton
Bridgewater

Greenbush
Standish

Medfield
Milford
Bellingham

Attleboro
Taunton

*Hockomock Swamp*

Kingston
Plymouth

☆ **GETTING OUTDOORS AT**
**CAPE COD NATIONAL SEASHORE**

Provincetown

*CAPE COD*

*Cape Cod National Seashore*

Wellfleet

Nauset Light Beach
Coast Guard Beach

Eastham

Orleans

*Cape Cod Bay*

Brewster

PROVIDENCE

RHODE ISLAND

Fall River

New Bedford

Sandwich

*OLD KING'S HIGHWAY*

Bourne
Barnstable
Yarmouth

Chatham

Harwich Port

Hyannis
West
Yarmouth

Woods Hole
Falmouth

Vineyard
Haven
Oak Bluffs

Edgartown

*Nantucket Sound*

Aquinnah
Cliffs

MARTHA'S
VINEYARD

Nantucket

NANTUCKET

BLOCK
ISLAND

*Atlantic Ocean*

0                    15 mi
0                    15 km

© MOON.COM

# TOP  3

## ① FOLLOWING THE FREEDOM TRAIL

A red line on the sidewalk through historic Boston connects 16 sites related to the American Revolution on a 2.5-mile (4-kilometer) walking trail ideal for getting your bearings in the city. Make your way from **Boston Common** to a series of churches, graveyards, and other early landmarks in downtown, then continue through the Italian American neighborhood of the **North End** to visit **Paul Revere's House** (19 North Sq.; 617/523-2338; www.paulreverehouse.org) and the **Old North Church** (193 Salem St.; 617/858-8231; www.oldnorth.com) where Revere hung signal lights for Revolutionary commanders.

BUNKER HILL MONUMENT

The trail then crosses the Charles River via the stunning Leonard P. Zakim Bunker Hill Bridge to the **Charlestown Navy Yard** and the **Bunker Hill Monument** (Monument Sq., Charlestown; 617/242-5641; www.nps.gov/bost/historyculture/bhm.htm), where climbing 294 steep steps earns you panoramic views of the city from the top of a 221-foot (67-meter) obelisk that has commemorated the first major battle of the Revolution since 1843.

You can set out and walk the line yourself, or, for more information along the way, take a guided tour with the **Freedom Trail Foundation** (Boston Common Visitor Information Center, 148 Tremont St., Boston; 617/357-8300; www.thefreedomtrail.org) or the **National Park Service** (www.nps.gov/bost).

## ② GETTING OUTDOORS AT CAPE COD NATIONAL SEASHORE

www.nps.gov/caco

The Cape Cod National Seashore is an utterly beautiful swath of coastline, with the longest unbroken beaches in New England. Coastal dunes are speckled with blushing wild roses, and historic lighthouses stand proudly at the edge of the sea. Shores and salt marshes are an important destination for migratory birds traveling the Atlantic coast, and the water teems with harbor seals, grey seals, whales, sea turtles, and even the occasional great white shark (contrary to Hollywood films, shark attacks are vanishingly rare).

In addition to the intertidal zones, dunes, and seagrass beds that most visitors see, there are also grasslands, heathlands, woodlands, forests, kettle ponds, salt marshes, and freshwater marshes. The area features several walking trails where you can experience all this biodiversity up close; the **Nauset Marsh Trail** and **Fort Hill Trail** are good options. To explore on two wheels, the paved, mostly flat **Cape Cod Rail Trail**

NAUSET LIGHT BEACH

follows 22 miles (35 kilometers) of former railroad track between South Dennis and Wellfleet, passing ponds, forests, and short spurs to reach the coast.

Of course, the real highlight here is the sand and the ocean. With a broad swath of sand backed by eroding cliffs, **Coast Guard Beach** is a strong contender for the best beach in New England. **Nauset Light Beach,** at the foot of its namesake lighthouse, is another good pick.

## 3  SOAKING UP ART AT WORLD-CLASS MUSEUMS

### MUSEUM OF FINE ARTS

465 Huntington Ave., Boston; 617/267-9300; www.mfa.org

This grand, neoclassical museum's art collection is one of the best and most beloved in the country. The MFA, as it's known, is particularly noted for its French Impressionist works, but it also has outstanding Asian and Egyptian collections, as well as many celebrated early American paintings and artifacts. The Museum of Fine Arts began its life as the painting collection of the Boston Athenaeum, the private library on Beacon Hill. Under its current leadership, the museum has taken some gambles to bring a new generation of viewers into the galleries, staging artistic exhibitions of guitars, race cars, and the World Series rings of Red Sox slugger David Ortiz alongside showstopping special exhibits featuring masterpieces by Monet, Van Gogh, and Gauguin.

### MASSACHUSETTS MUSEUM OF CONTEMPORARY ART

1040 MASS MoCA Way, North Adams; 413/662-2111; www.massmoca.org

Built on the sprawling campus of Sprague Electric, the size of the Massachusetts Museum of Contemporary Art is stunning. Composed of 27 redbrick former factory buildings and connected by an interlocking network of bridges, walkways, and courtyards, it has vast gallery spaces that allow for artwork of an unusually epic scale—from enormous installations to expansive performance art. The scale of the museum also affords more inclusiveness than many institutions, and MASS MoCA has a lack of pretension and takes an infectious delight in the creative process: Small, unexpected touches abound, like the sidewalk cracks that employees fill in with gleaming gold paint.

*THE APPEAL TO THE GREAT SPIRIT* MONUMENT (SCULPTOR CYRUS DALLIN), BOSTON MUSEUM OF FINE ARTS

**DAY 1**
Start your trip in **Boston,** the center of the action in Massachusetts. Walk the **Freedom Trail** to see historical sights, stopping for lunch and an Italian ice in the **North End.** For even more culture, head to the **Museum of Fine Arts.** Have a seafood feast for dinner and spend the night here.

**DAY 2**
Squeeze in a few more Boston sights today. Stroll through **Boston Common** and adjacent **Boston Public Gardens,** maybe hopping on one of the **swan boats** on the lagoon, and grab lunch from bustling **Quincy Market.** Now it's time to hop in the car. Drive 3 hours (130 miles/209 kilometers) to **Williamstown** and spend the night at **Clover Hill Farm** (249 Adams Rd., Williamstown; 413/458-3376; https://cloverhillfarm.net) for an authentic farm experience in the **Berkshires.**

**DAY 3**
To experience beautiful Berkshires scenery, there's no better way than a hike up **Mount Greylock.** There are many trails in the area, or you can simply drive to the summit. And a visit to the nearby **Massachusetts Museum of Contemporary Art** is a must. Return to Williamstown for dinner and a good night's sleep.

**DAY 4**
Dive 45 minutes (30 miles/48 kilometers) south to **Lenox,** where you can soak up some glamorous Gilded Age atmosphere. Don't miss a tour of **The Mount,** Edith Wharton's country home, and browse the boutiques on Lenox's main street. Afterward, drive 10 minutes south to nostalgic **Stockbridge** to visit the **Norman Rockwell Museum.** Spend the night back at your hotel in Lenox.

BOSTON'S FREEDOM TRAIL

SWAN BOATS, BOSTON PUBLIC GARDEN

BERKSHIRES VIEW FROM MOUNT GREYLOCK

**DAY 5** It's a long drive back to the coast—3.5 hours (200 miles/321 kilometers) to **Chatham,** a good base to enjoy **Cape Cod.** Explore this old-fashioned town and its lighthouse, or just head to the beach. Seafood for dinner—think oysters, fried clams, and creamy clam chowder—is a must.

**DAY 6** You can spend the whole day just relaxing on the beach before driving 1.5 hours (90 miles/144 kilometers) back to Boston. Or, for even more fun, head to **Provincetown** (1 hour; 35 miles/56 kilometers from Chatham) on Cape Cod's very tip. Here you'll find plenty of beaches and excellent **whale-watching** trips, but P-town's real showstopper is its LGBTQ+ nightlife scene. Catch a **drag show** before crashing for the night.

LIGHTHOUSE IN CHATHAM

The first municipal public library in the United States, the Boston Public Library fills two city blocks, dividing its treasures into two buildings. While the library's collection is vast, its art and architecture make it destination worthy as well; the exterior has classical proportions and is covered with names of great thinkers through the ages. One of the best-kept secrets of the city is the library's central courtyard, an Italianate plaza that wraps around a central fountain (high tea at the courtyard restaurant is a special treat). The hushed, studious heart of the original 1895 building is the Bates Reading Room, a 200-foot-long (60-meter) hall with a barrel-vaulted ceiling, high arched windows, and long tables lined with dimly lit green lamps.

## BLACK HERITAGE TRAIL

Boston; www.maah.org/trail.htm

The Black Heritage Trail traces the separate journey to freedom of African Americans, nearly 100 years after the events of the first Freedom Trail. Plaques at historic houses en route detail the lives of abolitionists and orators who lived on the back side of Beacon Hill, where Boston's more than 1,000 free African Americans lived and worked by the turn of the 19th century.

The trail begins at the **Robert Gould Shaw and Massachusetts 54th Regiment Memorial,** which depicts the commander of the Massachusetts 54th Regiment, the first all-black volunteer regiment to fight during the Civil War, marching out of Boston with his troops in March 1863. Follow the trail to the end to visit the African Meeting House, once headquarters of the New England Anti-Slavery Society. Considered the "Black Faneuil Hall," the church now houses the **Museum of African American History** (46 Joy St.; 617/725-0022; http://maah.org), which has exhibits and films dedicated to the story of Boston's abolitionists.

The trail is also part of the **Boston African-American National Historic Site** (617/742-5415; www.nps.gov/boaf), and the National Park Service runs free guided tours along the route.

# *Major* CITIES

**BOSTON:** The hub of New England is both modern and connected to its history—Revolutionary-era graveyards line busy streets, actors in 18th-century costume walk the Freedom Trail, and immigrant communities erupt with civic pride at festivals and parades.

**WORCESTER:** Pronounced WUH-stah, the state's second-largest city is home to a diverse population, several colleges, and a notable dining and art scene.

**SPRINGFIELD:** With a history in both the Revolutionary and Civil Wars, Springfield is known as the "City of Firsts"—it was home to the country's first armory, the first American-made car, and the birthplace of basketball.

## SALEM

With a grim history of deadly witch trials, Salem's tragedy has lingered through the centuries—a story of mass hysteria that's only underscored by the city's prim facade. To explore the town's dramatic history, visit the simple **Salem Witch Trials Memorial** (Liberty St.; www.salemweb.com/memorial), which displays the names of the victims on stone benches next to the central burying ground. There's also the **Salem Witch Museum** (Washington Sq. N.; 978/744-1692; www.salemwitchmuseum.com), whose basic displays lay the groundwork for the events of 1692-1693.

Salem might still be "Witch City," but it was also an important trading port, sending ships laden with salted codfish across the globe. These days, Salem is a bedroom community of Boston, and clusters of shops, cafés, and historic streets make the city an appealing place to explore.

## PLYMOUTH

Even as the Pilgrims landed in the "New World" they looked back toward the old one, naming their first settlement for the English port they left behind. For some, their arrival represents the dreams of the independent Puritans who risked everything for a new life, while others see the start of an era that brought tragedy to Native Americans and enslaved Africans.

The glacial erratic boulder that's known to every schoolchild, **Plymouth Rock** (79 Water St.) is located here and inscribed simply with "1620." For a vivid glimpse of the Pilgrims' daily lives, and at the lives of the Wampanoag people who helped them survive the harsh coastal winter, head to **Plimoth Patuxet Museums** (137 Warren Ave.; 508/746-1622; www.plimoth.org), a working replica of a Wampanoag village and their settlement. The **1627 Village** is the centerpiece of the site, and visitors can walk around to see the homes and hear stories from the costumed "pilgrims." At the **Wampanoag Homesite,** the staff are Indigenous people, whether Wampanoag or from another group, who help inform visitors about Wampanoag history and culture. There's also a wonderful replica of the *Mayflower*—it's dubbed *Mayflower II*.

To learn more about the history here, head to the **Mayflower Society House and Library** (4 Winslow St.; 508/746-3188; www.themayflowersociety.org), a mansion built by Edward Winslow, a *Mayflower* passenger. The small museum is filled with fascinating artifacts from the time, but the house alone is worth a stop, complete with period furnishings and artwork.

## LGBTQ+ NIGHTLIFE IN PROVINCETOWN

By the late 19th century, this village at "the end of the world" had become a destination for painters, playwrights, and novelists—think Eugene O'Neill, Jack Kerouac, Norman Mailer, and Jackson Pollock—who were drawn to the spot's scenic isolation. Full of creative spirit and spontaneity, P-town is also

# FIELD GUIDE TO THE BOSTON ACCENT

Listen closely on any inbound flight or train to Boston, and you're likely to hear a curious phrase from one of your fellow passengers: "park the car on Harvard yard." The sentence, sometimes called the **"Harvard Accent Test,"** isn't really a set of instructions on where to leave your vehicle. It's often used as a litmus test for the authenticity of one's Boston accent, or your ability to fake one. Pronounced properly, it comes out something like this: *pahk the cah on Hahvahd Yahd.*

According to historical linguists, the Boston accent has its roots in the language patterns of early British and Irish colonists. Notoriously hard to replicate, the Boston accent has diminished somewhat in recent decades, but you might hear it in a downtown bar.

While Bostonians lampoon many actors' attempts to imitate their distinctive accents, a few movies make the grade. Aficionados point to Michael Keaton's accent in *Spotlight* as well as Matt Damon's Southie accent in *Good Will Hunting* as prime examples. And for any visitors traveling with their own vehicle, it might be worth nothing that parking is *not* allowed on the Harvard Yard, a grassy stretch of the campus that's safely enclosed by fences.

one of America's most popular LGBT vacation spots, and has been for decades. On any summer Saturday evening, **Commercial Street** is a bustling mix of vacationing families, drag show touts, wedding processions, and revelers kicking off parties that will still be going strong at sunrise.

The drag scene is a classic P-town experience. You don't need to look for a drag show in Provincetown—watch for flamboyantly dressed performers careening down Commercial Street on foot, bicycle, and moped. Shows range from classic song and dance numbers to raunchy humor with big hair, big smiles, and outsized personalities. To get started, check out **Crown & Anchor** (247 Commercial St.; 508/487-1430; www.onlyatthecrown.com) or **The Art House** (214 Commercial St.; 508/487-9222; www.ptownarthouse.com). Drag queen residencies come and go; if there are performers you'd like to see, it's worth looking up where their show is now.

## MARTHA'S VINEYARD

On this wonderfully scenic island, quaint villages and tourist traps are interspersed with coastal dunes, pale beaches, and farmland. The Wampanoag tribe has a stronger presence here than elsewhere in the Cape and islands, and families of Vineyard sailors, farmers, and fishers still maintain deep roots.

A can't miss sight on the island is the **Aquinnah Cliffs.** Striped with wild layers of ochre clay, green sand, and glittering quartz, the dramatic cliffs have drawn mainland tourists for centuries. The walkway to the cliff overlook is lined with shops and information booths maintained by the Wampanoag, and is a great place to learn more about their history and culture.

## THE MOUNT

2 Plunkett St., Lenox; 413/551-5100; www.edithwharton.org

NIGHTLIFE IN PROVINCETOWN

Edith Wharton's incisive, prolific writing is among the best in American literature, but she once contended that she was "a better landscape gardener than novelist." Judge for yourself at The Mount, the gorgeously restored estate she designed from the ground up. With the exception of the library, most of the author's personal belongings and furniture are long gone, but Wharton's taste for symmetry, balance, and allusion are everywhere. And while visiting the house takes just an hour or so, the expansive grounds are an inviting place to linger—in the cool sunken garden, by a blossom-fringed fountain, or on the trails that pass through the woods and along neat lines of Tilia trees. On weekends in July and August, there are informal jazz sessions on the outdoor terrace, and professional actors perform readings of Wharton's writing on Wednesday in the summer.

## NORMAN ROCKWELL MUSEUM

9 Rte. 183, Stockbridge; 413/298-4100; www.nrm.org

Norman Rockwell charmingly depicted kids at soda fountains and quirky small-town characters, but images that resonate after a visit to the Norman Rockwell Museum also include six-year-old Ruby Bridges being escorted to school in 1960 and the iconic Four Freedoms. Don't miss the lower level, which displays all of Rockwell's *Saturday Evening Post* covers and shows a short film that includes real-life photos of his

NORMAN ROCKWELL MUSEUM

models, many of whom were his Stockbridge neighbors. The museum's pastoral 36-acre (14.5-hectare) site includes the artist's well-preserved barn studio. High-profile changing exhibitions include works by the likes of Warhol and Wyeth.

# BEST SCENIC DRIVES

## OLD KING'S HIGHWAY

Rte. 6A

For a route that blends American history with Cape Cod's coastal scenery, take a drive along Old King's Highway, aka Route 6A, a National Scenic Byway lined with cranberry bogs and antiques stores. Starting in **Sandwich**, 6A follows the bay side of the Cape until it reaches the town of **Orleans** (1 hour; 30 miles/48 kilometers). You can keep driving all the way until the end of the cape in **Provincetown**, though 6A merges with busier Route 6 along the way. Worthy stops along the drive include antique shops in Sandwich, Barnstable's **Old Jail**, which dates back to 1690, and the **Captain's Mile**, a stretch of historic captains' houses in Yarmouth.

## ESSEX COASTAL SCENIC BYWAY

To experience Massachusetts's scenic north coast, the Essex Coastal Scenic Byway follows 90 miles (144 kilometers) from **Lynn** to **Salisbury.** The route passes through 14 North Shore towns, including an especially scenic drive along Cape Ann. Along the way, you'll pass plenty of historic architecture and opportunities for recreation—hiking trails and beaches are just off the road.

## JACOB'S LADDER TRAIL

Rte. 20

This National Scenic Byway, dubbed "the first of the great mountain cross-overs," takes you through the southern Berkshire foothills. Route 20 starts in **Lee**, near Stockbridge, and ends in the towns of **Russell** and **Westfield** (50 minutes; 35 miles/56 kilometers). The small towns, beautiful nature, and unspoiled rural atmosphere along the way offer a scenic alternative to the busy Massachusetts turnpike.

# BEST PARKS AND RECREATION AREAS

## BOSTON COMMON AND BOSTON PUBLIC GARDEN

139 Tremont St. and 4 Charles St.; Boston

The Common feels like the city's collective backyard, with space for throwing Frisbees, spreading out picnics, and playing in the grass. Several monuments within the park are attractions in and of themselves: The **Brewer Fountain** is stunning, and you'll also find the **Robert Gould Shaw and Massachusetts 54th Regiment Memorial** here. The **Frog Pond** is an ice-skating rink in winter and a shallow fountain in summer, when it fills with kids cooling off. A bandstand is used as the site for summer concerts, political rallies, and **Shakespeare on the Common** (www. commshakes.org).

In contrast to Boston Common's open, parklike feel, the Boston Public Garden, right next door, is an intimate outdoor space, full of leafy trees and flower beds. The centerpiece is a lagoon, which is crossed by a fairy-tale bridge and surrounded by willow trees trailing their branch tips in the water. Tracing lazy circles in the lagoon are Boston's famous **swan boats** (617/522-1966; www.swanboats.com), a flotilla of six large paddleboats with the graceful white birds at the stern.

## WHALE-WATCHING TOURS

Just north of Cape Cod's Land's End is a shallow, sandy rise in the ocean floor called Stellwagen Bank, where a nutrient-rich upwelling and a U.S. National Marine Sanctuary attract a diverse population of dolphins, sea turtles, and whales. April-October, whales migrate to this coast to feed on schooling fish, and a dozen tour operators offer trips into the sanctuary to spot humpback, finback, minke, sei, and pilot whales. A good pick is the **Dolphin Fleet** (MacMillan Pier, Provincetown; 800/826-9300; www.whalewatch.com), which departs many times a day during the season from downtown Provincetown, with onboard naturalists help identify any fins and flukes you spot.

## MOUNT GREYLOCK

Rockwell Rd., Lanesborough; 413/499-4262; www.mass.gov/locations/mount-greylock-state-reservation

The 3,491-foot (1,064-meter) summit of Mount Greylock, the highest peak in Massachusetts, is both accessible and wild, and it and the surrounding peaks are favorites for overnight hikes or leisurely afternoon drives. Several trails lead up into the mountains from both **North Adams** and **Williamstown:** Trace some of Henry David Thoreau's 1844 hike to the peak on a challenging 9.6-mile (15.4-kilometer) loop from North Adams—follow **Bellows Pipe Trail** to the **Appalachian Trail** (AT), and return via the AT and **Bernard Farm Trail.** Or try the slightly easier, 6.2-mile (10-kilometer) round-trip **summit hike** from the Mount Greylock Campground.

If all that sounds a bit strained, you can take a scenic, winding road straight to the top of Mount Greylock, where there's a snack bar and visitors center

BOSTON PUBLIC GARDEN

## BEST SOUVENIRS

- To bring the energy of the American Revolution home with you, gift shops along the **Freedom Trail** sell prints of America's founding documents, merch to celebrate the founding fathers, and more.

- For a visit to Fenway Park, a **Red Sox baseball cap** is a must. Alternatively, pick up a jersey to represent one of Boston's other great sports teams—the Celtics, Patriots, or Bruins—or grab some apparel from one of the city's many **universities** (Harvard, Boston University, Boston College, Northeastern... the list goes on).

with information on short hikes and nature activities.

# FESTIVALS AND EVENTS

## RED SOX GAMES AT FENWAY PARK

4 Yawkey Way, Boston; 617/226-6666; www.redsox.com

Fenway has long been one of the most electric places to catch the national pastime. First opened in 1912, Fenway has a soul that none of the more modern parks can match. For the uninitiated, the geography of the park—with its Green Monster, Pesky's Pole, and Ted Williams's seat—can seem a little arcane, but you can get your bearings with a tour led by one of the Fenway faithful. As good as those tours may be, however, nothing quite beats taking a seat in the bleachers, grabbing a Sam Adams, and waiting for the first crack of the bat.

FENWAY PARK

## OTHER SPECTATOR SPORTS

Fans of all sports will find a great team to root for in Boston. The city hosts the **Boston Celtics** in the NBA, the **New England Patriots** in the NFL, the **Boston Bruins** in the NHL, and the **New England Revolution** in MLS.

## BOSTON MARATHON

Boston; www.baa.org; Apr.

Runners come from around the world to compete in the Boston Marathon, the oldest (and some say toughest) marathon in the United States, usually held in April on Patriots' Day. Spectators start lining the route to cheer along Beacon and Boylston Streets, all the way to Copley Square, where the finish line is painted in the street.

## TANGLEWOOD MUSIC FESTIVAL

297 West St., Lenox; 413/637-1600; www.bso.org; summer

During summer, the Boston Symphony Orchestra (BSO)—along with a suite of other performers—brings world-class music to Tanglewood, a sprawling venue named for a collection of stories by Nathaniel Hawthorne, who spent a summer writing on the property. The Tanglewood season runs late June-early September, and popular shows often sell out within days of their first availability in January, as do rooms in town. Music, however sublime, is only part of the experience. Elegant picnics at Tanglewood have been a tradition since the BSO performed here in the late 1930s.

Show up several hours early to stretch the picnic into an all-afternoon affair.

# BEST FOOD

## BOSTON BAKED BEANS

Not for nothing is Boston nicknamed Beantown. This dish—made of dried beans baked slowly with salt pork and molasses—was a staple in colonial times and remains a favorite today.

## CLAMS AND CLAM CHOWDER

Generally divided into types—hard shell or soft shell—clams are a true New England delicacy. Soft shells, or **steamers,** are usually eaten either steamed or fried. (If the clams are steamed, diners pull them from the shell, remove and discard the neck casing, and dip them in broth and drawn butter before eating.)

Hard shell clams are served differently: The smallest ones, known as **littlenecks** and **cherrystones,** are most frequently served raw with horseradish and cocktail sauce, while the largest hard shells are chopped up and used in chowders and stuffings.

Dating back to the 18th century, New England clam chowder is by far the most popular of the region's creamy fish stews. Most restaurants have their own recipes, using a bit more potatoes here, a different ratio of bacon to cream there (but not tomatoes—that is what distinguishes Manhattan clam chowder and is therefore heresy in New England). Sampling and finding your favorite is the real fun.

## BOSTON'S NORTH END CUISINE

Everyone from tour guides to locals will tell you the same thing about this historic neighborhood: "It's just like being in Italy!" The truth is, though, there's something essentially Bostonian about the Italian American North End—the home of the Celtics basketball team as well as numerous pastry shops, old-fashioned grocers, and classic red-sauce joints. It's a fascinating place to eat, drink, and explore with cannoli in hand. Top places to try include:

- **Regina Pizzeria** (11½ Thatcher St.; 617/227-0765; www.reginapizzeria. com): There's always a line out the door at this Neapolitan pizza place known for its crust.

- **Neptune Oyster** (63 Salem St.; 617/742-3474; www.neptuneoyster. com): This island of contemporary style in old-school North End has the best lobster rolls in town.

- **Mike's Pastry** (300 Hanover St.; 617/742-3050; www.mikespastry. com) and nearby **Modern Pastry** (257 Hanover St.; 617/523-3783; www.modernpastry.com) are locked in a fierce rivalry for Boston's best cannoli.

# MAJOR AIRPORTS

- **Boston-Logan International Airport:** BOS; One Harborside Dr., East Boston; 617/428-2800; www.massport.com/logan-airport

# MORE INFORMATION

## TRAVEL AND TOURISM INFORMATION

- **Visit Massachusetts:** www.visitma. com

- **Massachusetts State Parks:** www. mass.gov

## NEWSPAPERS

- *The Boston Globe:* www. bostonglobe.com

# RHODE ISLAND

On Narragansett, Niantic, Nipmuc, Pequot, and Wampanoag land, Rhode Island comprises only about 1,500 square miles (3,884 square kilometers), over one-third of which are in territorial waters, and one can easily drive from one end of the state to the other in about an hour. The ocean permeates everything in Rhode Island, from the sandy beaches and inland farms to city streets where seagulls can still be heard crying overhead and salty breezes blow in from the bay. Perhaps this is why Rhode Islanders live for summer, when rising temperatures and sunny skies make the coast that much more appealing. But Rhode Island has appeal in every season. Autumn means brilliant foliage, apple picking, and hayrides, while spring is an excuse to seek out cherry blossom trees. Even in the coldest winter months, visitors can enjoy the ineffable beauty of the Atlantic from behind the windowpanes of cozy seaside B&Bs or simply find warmth in the diversity and vibrancy of Providence or Newport—two of the nation's most historic cities.

**AREA:** 1,214 square miles / 3,144 square kilometers (50th)

**POPULATION:** 1,059,361 (44th)

**STATEHOOD DATE:** May 29, 1790 (13th)

**STATE CAPITAL:** Providence

SAILBOAT IN NEWPORT

## ORIENTATION

Cutting into the eastern side of Rhode Island, **Narragansett Bay** extends to an outlet of the Providence River. **Providence** sits at the top of the bay, while **Newport** is on Aquidneck Island in the bay, linked to the mainland by a series of bridges. After winding through the folds of Narragansett Bay, the coast turns toward the Atlantic—this is where the **South County** beaches are located. **Block Island** sits in the Atlantic off South County.

## WHEN TO GO

Rhode Island is a year-round destination, but **summer,** specifically mid-June through Labor Day, is high season for enjoying the water. The most bewitching and scenic seasons in Rhode Island are **spring,** when the entire state is abloom with greenery and flowers, and **fall,** when the foliage changes color. **Winters** are not brutal, but the state does get socked by the occasional snow or ice storm, and the wind and frigidity can be uncomfortable December through March.

The best compromise is to visit in the **shoulder season**—in May, before Memorial Day, when the days are often warm and sunny, or in September, after Labor Day, when the ocean is at its warmest.

# HIGHLIGHTS

## ROGER WILLIAMS PARK AND ZOO

1000 Elmwood Ave., Providence; 401/785-3510; https://rwpconservancy.org

Roughly 4 miles (6.4 kilometers) south of downtown is Providence's largest urban oasis, the 430-acre (174-hectare) Roger Williams Park. Visitors can bike, skate, or walk nearly 10 miles (16 kilometers) of paved roads. Unpaved trails also meander into the greenery around the 10 lakes (many where you can rent small boats). The park is best known for being the home of **Roger Williams Park Zoo** (www.rogerwilliamsparkzoo. org), which has more than 1,000 animals of more than 165 species. It's the third-oldest zoo in the nation and has been ranked among the nation's 10 best. You'll also find the **Museum of Natural History** (401/785-9457; http://www.providenceri.gov/museum) here, including a planetarium and more than 250,000 objects and artifacts.

## NEWPORT'S MANSIONS

Much has been written about Newport's vast marble halls, and not all of it positive. As the railroad and steel tycoons began constructing their

ROGER WILLIAMS PARK

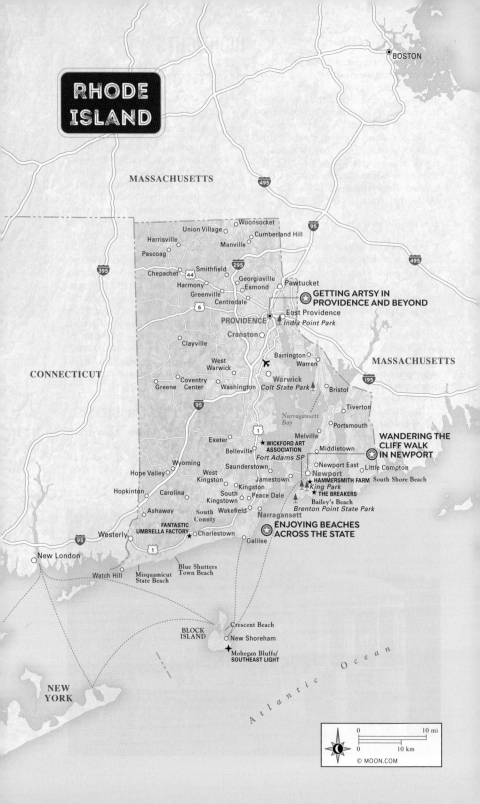

# RHODE ISLAND

BOSTON

MASSACHUSETTS

Woonsocket

Union Village
Cumberland Hill
Harrisville
Manville
Pascoag
Smithfield
Chepachet
Georgiaville
Esmond
Pawtucket
Harmony
Greenville
Centredale

**GETTING ARTSY IN PROVIDENCE AND BEYOND**

PROVIDENCE
East Providence
India Point Park

Cranston

Clayville

Barrington
Warren

West
Warwick

Warwick
Colt State Park

**MASSACHUSETTS**

**CONNECTICUT**

Coventry
Center
Greene
Washington
Bristol

Tiverton

Portsmouth

Narragansett
Bay

Exeter
Melville

**WICKFORD ART ASSOCIATION**
Belleville
Middletown

Wyoming
Saunderstown
Fort Adams SP
Newport East
Little Compton

**WANDERING THE CLIFF WALK IN NEWPORT**

Hope Valley
West
Kingston
Jamestown
Newport
South Shore Beach
**HAMMERSMITH FARM**

Hopkinton
Kingston
King Park
Carolina
Peace Dale
**THE BREAKERS**

Ashaway
South
Kingstown
Wakefield
Bailey's Beach
Brenton Point State Park

South
County
Narragansett

**FANTASTIC UMBRELLA FACTORY**
Charlestown
**ENJOYING BEACHES ACROSS THE STATE**

Westerly
Galilee

New London

Watch Hill
Misquamicut
State Beach
Blue Shutters
Town Beach

**BLOCK ISLAND**
Crescent Beach
New Shoreham
Mohegan Bluffs/
**SOUTHEAST LIGHT**

**NEW YORK**

_Atlantic Ocean_

0       10 mi
0       10 km

© MOON.COM

# *Major* CITIES

**PROVIDENCE:** Providence manages to feel like a cool college town while also maintaining a very genuine blue-collar vibe. It offers a stellar culinary experience, some beautifully preserved colonial and 19th-century architecture, and a youthful, unconventional, and thriving music, art, and club scene.

**WARWICK AND CRANSTON:** Rhode Island's most densely populated suburbs, Warwick and Cranston, lie immediately south of the capital and contain high concentrations of indoor and strip malls, chain restaurants, and motels. Both towns lie along Narragansett Bay and have several historic residential neighborhoods near the water, as well as nice public beaches.

**NEWPORT:** Known for posh luxury hotels and elite seaside estates, Newport is a small, well-preserved colonial seaport community and a living-history museum of the Gilded Age, with stunning mansions situated on rocky cliffs.

ostentatious summer homes at the end of the 19th century, they symbolized a new Renaissance in American architecture. Within a few short years, however, as the excesses of the Gilded Age spawned a Progressive backlash, novelist Henry James derided the Newport cottages as "white elephants"—beautiful but useless symbols of excess.

Still, there's nothing like the impact of walking into some of these homes, in which every element seems calculated to impress. There's not a single sconce or column that's free of adornment—each wall panel, and in some cases each ceiling tile, is decorated with some family crest or symbol. The **Preservation Society of Newport County** (401/847-1000; www.newportmansions.org) operates tours of most of the houses.

## The Elms

424 Bellevue Ave.; 401/847-1000; www.newportmansions.org

The Elms is a near-perfect copy of an 18th-century French château, built for coal tycoon Edward J. Berwind in 1901. The grounds comprise 10 acres (4 hectares) of landscaped parkland containing about 40 species of trees, plus dignified marble statuary and perfectly groomed shrubs. The interior, almost cozy compared to some mansions, abounds with gadgets as The Elms was among the earliest Newport homes to be lighted and run by electricity.

## The Breakers

44 Ochre Point Ave.; 401/847-1000; www.newportmansions.org

The most lavish of them all is The Breakers, completed in 1895 as the summer home of steamship and railroad giant Commodore Cornelius Vanderbilt II. The house has no less than 70 rooms and is a dead ringer for Italy's most opulent 16th-century palazzos. The impressive 13-acre (5.25-hectare) grounds overlook Cliff Walk and the Atlantic Ocean—it was the sound of the waves smashing against the rocks below that gave The Breakers its name. Inside, rooms feature semiprecious stones, rare marble, baccarat crystal chandeliers, and even platinum leaf on the walls.

## Rosecliff

548 Bellevue Ave.; 401/847-1000; www.newportmansions.org

French influence is evident at Rosecliff, built by Stanford White in 1902 and inspired by the Grand Trianon section of the palace at Versailles, France. It has been featured in a handful of movies, including the 1974 version *The Great Gatsby* and *Amistad*. The house is remembered for having hosted a magic-themed party at which Harry Houdini entertained the guests, as well as many other outlandish events hosted by Tessie" Fair Oelrichs, a colorful silver heiress from Nevada. A tour highlight is walking through the largest ballroom in

# TOP 3

## 1 WANDERING THE CLIFF WALK IN NEWPORT

www.cliffwalk.com

The two finest things Newport has to offer—its natural seaside beauty and the architectural relics of the Gilded Age—collide along the seaside Cliff Walk, arguably one of the country's grandest strolls.

Beginning at the western end of **Easton's Beach** (also known as First Beach), the 3.5-mi (5.6-kilometer) path runs between the rocky beach and many of the town's most impressive mansions. It's an opportunity to gaze at fancy estates and experience the same ocean views that mesmerized Newport's wealthy summer visitors at the turn of the 20th century. One of the first highlights on the walk is the **40 Steps,** a sharply descending stone stairway that goes nearly to the sea below. Soon after 40 Steps, the path meanders by some of Newport's most famous mansions, including **The Breakers.**

THE 40 STEPS ON THE NEWPORT CLIFF WALK

Past the mansions, the Cliff Walk cuts through two tunnels and becomes a scramble on the wild side, as it hugs the rocky shoreline by a series of large private homes. This span is aptly nicknamed **Rough Point**—wear sturdy shoes. Once you reach a dead end that seems to be the end of the walk, it's also possible to climb along the jagged rocks around the southwestern tip of this small peninsula. The official Cliff Walk resumes, and you'll see the exclusive **Bailey's Beach,** and before long you'll reach the eastern edge of this fabled stretch of sand.

## 2 GETTING ARTSY IN PROVIDENCE AND BEYOND

For generations, Providence has attracted artists and creative types of every ilk, many of whom attended institutions like the Rhode Island School of Design (RISD) and Brown University, and then stayed on after graduation to found small businesses, participate in public art projects, or simply live and work in a state that prides itself on supporting the arts. This is particularly evident in Providence, where there seem to be artist studios on every block, but it also extends throughout the state. Coastal art communities in Rhode Island tend to appeal to different sensibilities, with windswept watercolors, plein-air paintings, and whimsical sketchbook exhibits full of lighthouses and coastlines.

### PROVIDENCE

- No trip to Providence is complete without a stop at the **RISD Museum** (224 Benefit St.; 401/454-6500; www.risdmuseum. org), which houses more than 86,000 works of art, with galleries devoted to ancient Greek, Roman, and Egyptian artifacts; costumes and textiles; and Asian, decorative, and contemporary art.

RISD MUSEUM

- **WaterFire** (401/273-1155; www.waterfire.org), an ecological art installation created by a scientist-turned-artist, is the city's pièce de résistance. On select nights throughout the year, 80 fragrant bonfires are lit on Providence's rivers, creating a complete sensory experience that is not to be missed.

## BEYOND PROVIDENCE

- The **Wickford Art Association** (36 Beach St., Wickford; 401/294-6840; www.wickfordart.org) is a great resource for those looking to drop in on art classes, and the galleries here feature rotating exhibits by local artists.

- Newport is also home to the **National Museum of American Illustration** (492 Bellevue Ave., Newport; 401/851-8949; www.americanillustration.org), where you can view an impressive collection of art created for books, periodicals, advertisements, and new media.

 **ENJOYING BEACHES ACROSS THE STATE**

Rhode Island may be tiny, but it contains over 400 miles (645 kilometers) of coastline, along which you'll find more than 100 public and private beaches. If sunbathing and swimming are on your agenda, here are some suggestions to get you started.

- In Westerly, **Misquamicut State Beach** is one of the largest in the state. It's got a playground and a large concession stand, and is situated amidst the motels, gifts shops, candy stores, water slides, mini-golf courses, arcades, and other amusements along Atlantic Avenue. Nearby, **Charlestown and Blue Shutters Town Beaches** are both smaller with less commotion.

- An easily accessible beach break makes **Narragansett Town Beach** in South County a popular spot with both seasoned and beginner surfers. The swell here ranges 2-8 feet (0.6-2.4 meters), and a sunken barge just offshore along the northern stretch of the beach creates some nice right-breaking waves.

- **South Shore Beach** in Little Compton has fun waves to splash around in or surf, and crowds are relatively sparse even in the high season—it's also one of the only beaches that permits bonfires in the evenings.

MISQUAMICUT STATE BEACH

# *Best* ROAD TRIP

**DAY 1** Spend a day in **Providence** checking out the **RISD Museum** and **Roger Williams Park,** an easy 4-mile (6.4-kilometer) drive south from downtown. On many Saturday evenings from March through November you can also watch the dazzling *Waterfire,* a dramatic display of bonfires set in cauldrons along the river.

ROGER WILLIAMS PARK

**DAY 2** You should not visit **Newport** (40 minutes; 34 miles/54 kilometers from Providence) without taking a road trip along winding **Ocean Drive,** which meanders along the waterfront and affords close-up views of some of this small city's prettiest homes. In town, tour the massive summer homes of the Gilded Age along Bellevue Avenue, the most famous of which is **The Breakers.**

**DAY 3** Laid-back **South County** (about 1 hour from Newport; 40 miles/64 kilometers) contains some of Rhode Island's best beaches as well as opportunities for hiking, boating, swimming, and sunbathing. Pick a beach, whether it's surfer favorite **Narragansett Town Beach** or raucous **Misquamicut,** pull out that towel, and sunbathe. From South County, catch the ferry to beautiful and isolated **Block Island,** just 10 miles (16 kilometers) or so south of the mainland. You'll want to spend a night and really get the feel of the island.

LOBSTER BOATS IN A COVE OFF OCEAN DRIVE IN NEWPORT

**DAY 4** Go for a bike ride, hike along the grounds of **Southeast Light,** or simply laze away your time on Block Island reading in a lounge chair at **Crescent Beach** before driving back to Providence in the morning.

SOUTHEAST LIGHT, BLOCK ISLAND

Newport (and that's saying a lot in this city).

## THE FANTASTIC UMBRELLA FACTORY

4820 Old Post Rd./Rte. 1A, Charlestown; 401/364-6616; www.fantasticumbrellafactory.com

In South County, you'll find one of the more unusual sights in Rhode Island: the eclectic collection of shops, farmland, and animal exhibits known as The Fantastic Umbrella Factory. When the back-to-the-land movement was in full swing during the 1960s, a small group of hippies took up residence in the backwoods of Charlestown, where they created a curiosity shop and flower nursery that has grown over the years into a veritable Wonka-esque fantasyland. Guinea fowl and emus prowl the grounds among shops selling everything from handmade toys, crystals, and drums, to African masks, rain sticks, and samurai swords, while a greenhouse full of Technicolor perennials dazzles the eye. Be sure to check out the bamboo forest in the back.

# BEST SCENIC DRIVES

## OCEAN DRIVE

One of the most famous scenic drives on the East Coast, 9.5-mi (15.3-kilometers) Ocean Drive is a roughly C-shaped route that begins at the lower end of downtown Newport, on **Wellington Avenue** at the intersection of Thames Street. Ocean Drive isn't one road but rather the name of a well-marked route that connects several roads. At least half the fun of this journey, which can take from an hour to half a day, depending on how often you stop, is simply peering out the window at the stunning homes, sandy beaches, and ocean views.

Highlights at the start of the drive include **King Park,** Newport's small but pleasant in-town beach. Farther on is **Hammersmith Farm,** home to an 1887 mansion that was the site of Jacqueline Bouvier and John F. Kennedy's wedding reception in 1953. Farther on, you'll finally reach Ocean Avenue, which runs

right along the water. Stop at **Brenton Point State Park** for a picnic or a stroll along the beach.

Continue on Ocean Drive along the waterfront back toward Newport. Officially, Ocean Drive ends at **Coggeshall Avenue.** However, a short ways away is **Bellevue Avenue,** where you can tour the Newport mansions of the Gilded Age.

# BEST PARKS AND RECREATION AREAS

## BLOCK ISLAND

Block Island sits in the Atlantic, offshore from South County. Right off the Block Island ferry, the roads that flank downtown's shoreline are lined with shops, restaurants, bars, and hotels. But not far outside of these commercial boundaries is an island experience defined instead by lush green space, pristine shoreline, and well-preserved historical landmarks.

A hike along the **Greenway Trails** is the best way to observe the island's fiercely guarded woodland and wildlife. The trail network comprises about 28 miles (45 kilometers) and connects the various tracts of nature preserve that make up nearly 45 percent of the island. The **Block Island Bicycle Tour** is a self-guided, 7.5-mile (12-kilometer) loop that includes nine stops at island landmarks and attractions at the southern end of the island, with an option to extend the tour by 8.5 miles (13.7

BEACH ON BLOCK ISLAND

# NATIVE AMERICAN HISTORY IN RHODE ISLAND

The land that is now Rhode Island was occupied by a handful of Algonquin Native American groups through much of the early part of the last millennium—the **Narragansett, Niantic, Nipmuc, Pequot,** and **Wampanoag** people all lived here. The nations shared a common genealogical heritage and similar languages and other cultural traits, but they also observed their own distinct rituals, laws, and other practices.

By the 1620s, the area had a network of Indigenous villages, staked-out fishing areas, and cleared and tilled fields. Today, many Rhode Island place names have Indigenous roots: Conanicut Island, for example, is named for Canonicus, a 17th-century leader of the Narragansetts; Pawtucket translates as "place with the waterfall"; and Sakonnet means "land of the wild goose."

When Roger Williams, the "founder" of modern Rhode Island, settled in here, the area was home to perhaps 20,000 Native Americans. Within 50 years, the effects of European settlement almost wiped out the population. Tensions between settlers and Native people came to a head in the bloody conflict known as **King Philip's War**—Philip was the leader of the Wampanoag. By the time peace was agreed on in 1676, Philip and more than 5,000 Indigenous people had been killed, with many more sold into slavery. After the war, many Native Americans were permanently relocated to South County, near Charlestown, effectively ending autonomous Native American presence in the state. Eventually, of course, even those settlements were removed in the westward march of Europeans across America.

kilometers) with three stops on the north end. Block Island also offers excellent opportunities for sailing, paddling, surfing, fishing, and horseback riding. And, of course, there's always just relaxing on the beach. **Crescent Beach** is a top pick here, but 17 miles (27 kilometers) of beaches encircle the whole island.

Another top sight on Block Island is the 1873 **Southeast Light,** one of the most photographed lighthouses in New England, and in summer you can climb the 50-foot (15-meter) staircase to the top. Also not to be missed, the **Mohegan Bluffs** tower nearly 200 feet (60 meters) above the Atlantic Ocean on the island's southeast shore. Descend the steps to the secluded beach below, or enjoy breathtaking views from the top.

## EAST BAY BIKE PATH

The most scenic of the state's biking routes, the 14.5-mile (23.3-kilometer) East Bay Bike Path is a flat, 10-foot-wide (3-meter), paved trail that hugs many sections of eastern Narragansett Bay from **India Point Park** in Providence all the way to **Colt State Park** (off Hope St.; 401/253-7482; https://riparks.com/parks/colt.php) in Bristol. The path also welcomes joggers, strollers, in-line skaters, and anyone not using motorized vehicles. The path, which follows the former Penn Central rail bed, covers a tremendously varied landscape from undeveloped waterfront to the lively commercial districts of Warren and Bristol.

## WOOD RIVER

Rhode Island's network of pristine rivers, especially in the western and southern sections of the state, makes for some great kayaking and canoeing. One of the best spots is the crystalline Wood River in the state's southwest corner. Traveling its full length is an all-day affair through 14 miles (22.5 kilometers) of pristine woodland, with some good rapids along the way. Several good put-ins, however, offer shorter trips, including the relatively smooth 6-mile (9.7-kilometer) run from Hope Valley Road Landing to Alton Dam.

# FESTIVALS AND EVENTS

## ANNUAL CAPE VERDEAN INDEPENDENCE DAY CELEBRATION

India Point Park, Providence; 401/222-4133; July

In early July, one of the city's most vibrant ethnic communities throws an Annual Cape Verdean Independence Day Celebration, which gives attendees a chance to sample authentic Cape Verdean foods, observe arts and crafts exhibits, and listen to music and storytelling.

## NEWPORT FOLK AND JAZZ FESTIVALS

Fort Adams State Park, Newport; Aug.

Cofounded in 1959 by jazz producer George Wein and folk music heroes Pete Seeger, Theodore Bikel, Oscar Brand, and Albert Grossman, the **Newport Folk Festival** (www.newportfolk. org) went on to gain a reputation as a platform for introducing unknown talents to the world at large. Artists like Joan Baez, Bob Dylan, and Kris Kristofferson all got their starts at Newport Folk. Today the festival, which now includes alternative country, indie, folkpunk, world, and Americana genres, is one of the most popular outdoor music festivals on the Eastern Seaboard.

The following weekend in August, the hugely popular **Newport Jazz Festival** (401/848-5055; www.newportjazzfest.org) is also held at Fort Adams. Big international acts congregate here alongside promising up-and-comers.

## CHARLESTOWN SEAFOOD FESTIVAL

Charlestown; 401/364-4031; www.charlestownseafoodfestival.com; Aug.

In early August, the Charlestown Seafood Festival draws hundreds of chowder and quahog (hard-shell clam) aficionados to Ninigret Park. Just about every type of seafood popular in the Ocean State is available, including raw oysters and clams, steamed lobsters, clam cakes, fish-and-chips, and fried whole-belly clams.

# BEST FOOD AND DRINK

Rhode Island has a few quirky food items that locals find completely ordinary but which might cause confusion for the uninformed tourist. Here are some of the most commonly encountered—and uniquely delicious—items for which the Ocean State is known.

## QUAHOGS

Quahogs are hard-shell clams found in abundance on Rhode Island's sandy shores, inlets, and salt ponds. These tasty bivalves can be found on restaurant menus all over the state, but they taste even better if you dig them yourself. Popular "quahogging" spots include the **Point Judith Salt Pond** in Galilee, and **Ninigret Pond** in Charlestown. Note: Shellfishing licenses are required for out-of-state residents.

**Stuffies,** a common menu item at many restaurants, are quahog shells filled with a mixture of minced clams and a savory breadcrumb stuffing. They are especially delicious with a bit of fresh-squeezed lemon juice and hot sauce. Exceptional stuffies can be found at the **Matunuck Oyster Bar** (629 Succotash Rd., South Kingstown; 401/783-4202; www.rhodyoysters.com), where a gorgeous view of the salt pond makes them taste that much better.

NEWPORT FOLK FESTIVAL

# BEST SOUVENIRS

- As you celebrate Rhode Island's love of the arts on your trip to Providence, you'll want to take a piece home with you. Pop in to **Craftland** (212 Westminster St., Providence; 401/272-4285; www.craftlandshop.com), where an array of locally made crafts, gifts, prints, and jewelry can be found.

- The tendency of Rhode Islanders to stay put has become something of a joke over the years; local gift shops have taken to selling bumper stickers and T-shirts depicting an anchor chained to the phrase **"I never leave Rhode Island."**

## COFFEE MILK

Coffee milk is the official state drink; it's a rather self-explanatory mixture of milk and coffee syrup, which is a rarity in other states but can be found on grocery shelves throughout Rhode Island. Any Rhode Island diner worth its salt will have coffee milk on the menu—try the **Modern Diner** (364 East Ave., Pawtucket; 401/726-8390; www.moderndinerri.com), just over the Providence line.

## CABINETS

A "cabinet" is Rhode Island-ese for what is basically a milkshake: blended ice cream and milk. **Coffee cabinets** with Autocrat coffee syrup are a local favorite, but you can get them in a variety of flavors, locally made, at **Gray's Ice Cream** (16 East Rd., Tiverton; 401/624-4500; www.graysicecream.com).

## HOT WIENERS

Hot wieners, or New York System wieners, are famous staples of Rhode Island food culture and can be found at several New York System diners throughout the state. This strange, tiny hot dog is served on a steamed bun and tastes best when ordered "all the way," which means loaded with chopped onions, celery salt, yellow mustard, and seasoned meat sauce. The legendary **Olneyville New York System** (18 Plainfield St., Providence; 401/621-9500) is the best spot to enjoy them.

## DEL'S

Del's is the locally favored brand of frozen lemonade slush sold from trucks and lemonade stands all over the state. Look for the yellow and green striped Del's umbrella stands or trucks that park at beaches during the summer, or head to **1260 Oaklawn Avenue** in Cranston, where the first Del's Lemonade stand opened in 1948.

# MAJOR AIRPORTS

- **T. F. Green Airport:** PVD; 2000 Post Rd., Warwick; 401/691-2000; www.pvdairport.com

# MORE INFORMATION

## TRAVEL AND TOURISM INFORMATION

- **State of Rhode Island Tourism:** www.visitrhodeisland.com
- **State of Rhode Island Division of Parks and Recreation:** www.riparks.com

## NEWSPAPERS AND MAGAZINES

- *Providence Journal:* www.providencejournal.com
- *Rhode Island Monthly:* www.rimonthly.com

# CONNECTICUT

Connecticut, the "land of steady habits," is full of surprises. Drive the state's scenic coastal road and you'll find dreamy beaches, old-fashioned fishing villages, and an archipelago of tiny islands scattered across Long Island Sound.

On the land of the Pequot, Western Nehantick, Mohegan, Wangunks, Tunxis, Quinnipiad, Hammonassets, Wappinger, Paugussett, and Pequonnock people, Connecticut embodies great contrasts, and nowhere is that more apparent than in the eastern part of the state, which is home to big cities, rural farm country, and the state's largest tourist attractions: Mystic Seaport and a pair of behemoth casinos. East of the Connecticut River, the state looks more toward New England than New York, and much of the land here is—or was—devoted to farming. The remnants of stone walls and foundations are still visible through the trees in land that has been slowly reclaimed by forest.

**AREA:** 5,567 square miles / 14,418 square kilometers (48th)

**POPULATION:** 3,565,287 (29th)

**STATEHOOD DATE:**
January 9, 1788 (5th)

**STATE CAPITAL:** Hartford

ATLANTIC OCEAN NEAR NEW HAVEN

# CONNECTICUT

MASSACHUSETTS

NEW
YORK

Granby
Windsor
Locks

44
Winsted
44
202
Avon
7
Goshen
202
HARTFORD
Torrington
Burlington
West Hartford
East
Kent Falls
State Park
Litchfield Hills
Litchfield
Wethersfield
Newington
6
Thomaston
Bristol
New Britain
202
LAKE COMPOUNCE ★
84
7
Watertown
Wolcott
New Milford
Middletown
Waterbury
Meriden
84
Naugatuck
Cheshire
Durham
Wallingford
Center
Danbury
Seymour
North Haven
91
Derby
North Branford
New Haven
East Haven
95
Branchville
Trumbull
West Haven
Guilford
Thimble
Islands
684
Milford
Silver Sands State Park
PHILIP JOHNSON
GLASS HOUSE ★
Westport
Stratford
PADDLING THE
THIMBLE ISLANDS ★
New Canaan
Fairfield
Greens Farms
Norwalk
Darien
Long Island Sound
95
Stamford
Greenwich

NEW
JERSEY
95

LONG ISLAND

New York

NEW
YORK

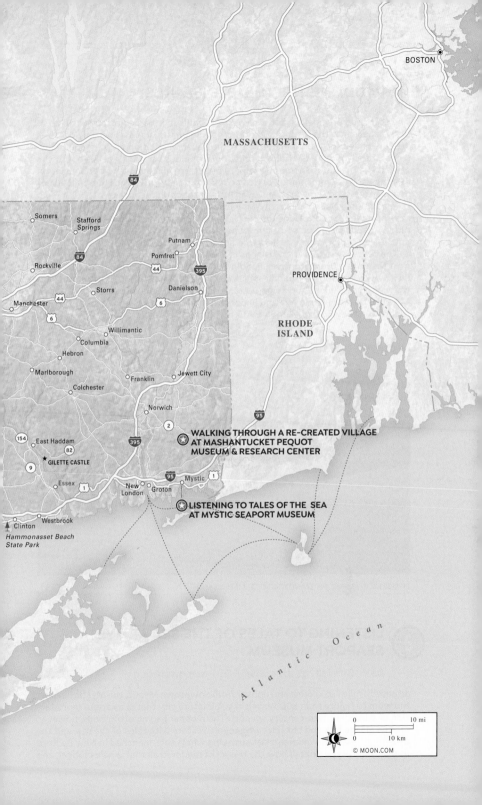

BOSTON

MASSACHUSETTS

84

Somers
Stafford
Springs
Putnam
Rockville
84
Pomfret
44
395
Storrs
Danielson
Manchester
44
6
6
Willimantic
Columbia
Hebron
Marlborough
Franklin
Jewett City
Colchester

PROVIDENCE

RHODE
ISLAND

Norwich
2
154
East Haddam
82
★ GILETTE CASTLE
9
395
95
Essex
95
Mystic
1
New
London
Groton
1
Westbrook
Clinton
⚓ Hammonasset Beach
State Park

◉ WALKING THROUGH A RE-CREATED VILLAGE
AT MASHANTUCKET PEQUOT
MUSEUM & RESEARCH CENTER

◉ LISTENING TO TALES OF THE SEA
AT MYSTIC SEAPORT MUSEUM

Atlantic Ocean

0                    10 mi
0          10 km

© MOON.COM

## 1 PADDLING THE THIMBLE ISLANDS

The scattered archipelago off the coast of Branford is named after the thimble-berry, a cousin to the raspberry that grows wild on the islands. They could just as well be named for their diminutive size, however; in addition to 24 populated is-lands, literally hundreds of pink granite outcroppings poke their peaks out of the waves. The islands are home to a variety of critters, including a winter population of seals—and a summer influx of rich people from New York, who have built elabo-rate mansions, tiny cottages, and even little gazebos on the rocks.

In addition to being unlike anything else on the New England coast, the islands have spawned dozens of legends, such as an enduring myth that the pirate Captain Kidd buried treasure on so-called Money Island. Keep your eyes peeled for pirate gold as you explore the tiny islets that speckle Long Island Sound.

The best way to take in the islands is at sea level, from the vantage of your very own sea kayak. **Branford River Paddle Sports** (50 Maple St., Branford; 203/980-8451; www.branfordriverpaddlesports.com) leads kayak and paddleboard expe-ditions to the Thimbles. Or sign up for a 45-minute narrated tour with "Captain Mike" on the *Sea Mist,* operating under the name **Thimble Island Cruise** (Thimble Island Rd., Stony Creek; 203/488-8905; http://thimbleislandcruise.com).

BRIDGE FROM ISLAND TO ISLAND AT THE THIMBLE ISLANDS

## 2 LISTENING TO TALES OF THE SEA AT MYSTIC SEAPORT MUSEUM

Rte. 27, Exit 90 off I-95, Mystic; 860/572-5315; www.mysticseaport.org

Situated a mile (1.6 kilometers) upriver from downtown Mystic, the Mystic Seaport Museum has more than 500 vessels in a miniature city that is a careful reproduc-tion of a bustling 19th-century seaport. The most engaging attractions, however, are the village folk and old salts who regale visitors with tales of the sea, and the *Charles W. Morgan,* America's last surviving whale ship, launched in New Bedford in 1841. Interpreters detail how the tryworks rendered all that whale blubber, and

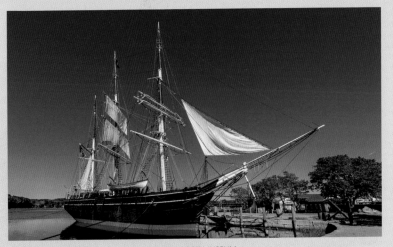

THE *CHARLES W. MORGAN* AT THE MYSTIC SEAPORT MUSEUM

also lead parties in hoisting sails, complete with authentic sea shanties. There are plenty of interactive experiences for kids, a boat-themed play area, a cooperage, and much more, with frequent demonstrations of old-fashioned sailor skills.

 ## WALKING THROUGH A RE-CREATED VILLAGE AT MASHANTUCKET PEQUOT MUSEUM & RESEARCH CENTER

110 Pequot Tr., Mashantucket; 860/411-9671; www.pequotmuseum.org

The foremost Native American research institute in New England is also a fascinating museum. A highlight of the visitor experience is walking through a re-created village where visitors can learn how the Pequot people built their homes, hunted, and cared for their sick. The museum doesn't mince words as it recounts the decimation of Native American tribes through warfare and disease. With a collection of some 150,000 books, the center's primary mission is researching, collecting, and preserving Native American artifacts from southern New England.

MASHANTUCKET PEQUOT MUSEUM & RESEARCH CENTER

**DAY 1** Start your trip in **Hartford;** Connecticut's capital is located just 20 minutes (15 miles/24 kilometers) south of the airport. Literature lovers can visit the **Mark Twain House & Museum** and adjacent **Harriet Beecher Stowe Center.** Afterward, head to the historic shipbuilding center of Mystic (1 hour; 54 miles/86 kilometers) for two nights.

**DAY 2** For this day, the **Mystic Seaport Museum** and **Mashantucket Pequot Museum & Research Center** are absolute musts. Grab a slice at **Mystic Pizza** (56 W. Main St., Mystic; 860/536-3700), made famous by the 1988 film of the same name starring Julia Roberts.

**DAY 3** Follow the coast 1 hour (55 miles/88 kilometers) to **New Haven.** In the morning, take a tour of the **Yale University** campus; make sure to stop by the **Yale University Art Gallery.** In the afternoon, get out on the water for some paddling among the nearby **Thimble Islands,** or spread a towel out on the beach at **Silver Sands State Park.** Make sure to try New Haven specialty **apizza** before spending the night.

**DAY 4** Head southwest to see the **Philip Johnson Glass House** (1 hour; 40 miles/64 kilometers from New Haven), then north to **Kent Falls State Park** (1.5 hours; 55 miles/88 kilometers), where you can hike to Connecticut's only covered bridges and the state's highest waterfall. To finish your loop, drive east (1.5 hours; 50 miles/80 kilometers) back to **Hartford.**

THE MARK TWAIN HOUSE & MUSEUM

CREW MEMBERS ABOARD THE *CHARLES W. MORGAN* AT THE MYSTIC SEAPORT MUSEUM

YALE UNIVERSITY ART GALLERY

## ORIENTATION

Connecticut's coast sits along Long Island Sound. **Mystic** is located on the eastern coast, near the border with Rhode Island, while **New Haven** sits a little west of center. **New Canaan** and the **Philip Johnson Glass House** is even farther west and a bit inland. **Hartford** sits in the center of the state, and the **Litchfield Hills** are are tucked into the state's northwestern corner.

## WHEN TO GO

New England experiences all four seasons, but there's no bad time to visit Connecticut. **Summer** is high season, when everyone heads to the beach to cool off. **Fall** brings dazzling colors as the leaves change. **Winter** weather begins at the end of December, when Connecticut might get a few snowstorms. **Spring** brings wildflowers, though the weather stays fitful until well into May.

# HIGHLIGHTS

## YALE UNIVERSITY CAMPUS

New Haven; www.yale.edu

Founded in 1701, Yale was the third college in the United States, and quickly established a rivalry with its northern neighbor Harvard, founding a tradition of one-upmanship that's alive and well. Many of Yale's buildings are done in a striking Gothic style, making a tour of the campus a genuine visual treat. Tours start at the **Yale University Visitor Center** (149 Elm St., New Haven; 203/432-2300; www.yale.edu/visitor) and include visits to several of Yale's libraries, including the rare-book library, which holds a copy of the Gutenberg Bible.

Yale also has several other outstanding museums. The **Yale Center for British Art** (1080 Chapel St., New Haven; 203/432-2800; http://ycba.yale.edu) is particularly worth singling out for its comprehensive collection of British art. The **Yale University Art Gallery** (1111 Chapel St., New Haven; 203/432-0600; http://artgallery.yale.edu) holds works from all over the world, as well as several fine canvases by American modernist Edward Hopper. Other highlights on campus include the **Yale Collection of Musical Instruments** (15 Hillhouse Ave., New Haven; 203/432-0822; http://collection.yale.edu) and the **Peabody Museum of Natural History** (170 Whitney Ave., New Haven; 203/432-5050 or 203/432-8987; www.yale.edu/peabody), which features famous dinosaur skeletons.

YALE UNIVERSITY CAMPUS

# *Major* CITIES

**BRIDGEPORT:** Located on the Long Island Sound coastline, Bridgeport is notable for having circus man P. T. Barnum as its mayor 1875-1876. Once an industrial center, Bridgeport fell on hard times in the mid-20th century in the wake of deindustrialization but is now making redevelopment efforts.

**NEW HAVEN:** One of the country's oldest cities and home to Yale University, this sprawling city is a blend of historic architecture, picturesque town greens, and some rough areas.

**HARTFORD:** The capital, sitting proudly in the middle of the state surrounded by a spider web of interstate highways, has a long history—the city was settled just after Boston and spent 200 years as a flourishing port city. Since then, however, Hartford has seen a long decline and rising crime.

## PHILIP JOHNSON GLASS HOUSE

Visitor Center, 199 Elm St., New Canaan; 203/594-9884; www.theglasshouse.org

The sleepy, leafy, New York City suburb of New Canaan seems an unlikely vanguard for modernist architecture, but this is where the renowned architect Philip Johnson built his groundbreaking Glass House in 1949. Tours, which take in the house, landscape design, and the sculpture and art sprinkled throughout the property, depart from the visitor center in downtown New Canaan.

Also featuring sublime glass architecture, **Grace Farms** (365 Lukes Wood Rd., New Canaan; 203/920-1702; www.gracefarms.org) has five buildings that are connected by an undulating covered walkway that rolls down the fall line of the hillside. Set on 80 acres (32 hectares) and used by nonprofit organizations, this relaxing space is especially beautiful in the autumn.

## LAKE COMPOUNCE

186 Enterprise Dr., Bristol; 860/583-3300; www.lakecompounce.com

Opened in 1846, Lake Compounce is the oldest continuously operating amusement park in the United States. With a wooden roller coaster and a triple-launch steel coaster, the park attracts families with older kids, but little ones can try the Dino Expedition and Flying Elephants. The adjoining water park has wave pools, waterslides, and a family rafting adventure.

## MARK TWAIN HOUSE & MUSEUM

351 Farmington Ave., Hartford; 860/247-0998; www.marktwainhouse.org

Samuel Langhorne Clemens—the writer who became known to the world as Mark Twain—is more often associated with the wide, muddy flow of the Mississippi River than urban Connecticut. But many of his masterpieces, including *The Adventures of Huckleberry Finn* and *The Adventures of Tom Sawyer*, were penned in this Victorian Gothic manse, now the Mark Twain House & Museum, just outside of downtown Hartford. Twain lived here for 16 years, and while he was here, he formed the nucleus of a literary group that included Harriet Beecher Stowe, Booker T.

PHILIP JOHNSON GLASS HOUSE

Washington, and other giants of the Gilded Age.

Inside, docents give tours of the house, including the billiards room where Twain did most of his writing; the elaborate Middle Eastern-inspired decor by Louis Comfort Tiffany; and Twain's telephone, one of the first installed in a private residence.

## HARRIET BEECHER STOWE CENTER

77 Forest St., Hartford; 860/522-9258; www.harrietbeecherstowecenter.org

Harriet Beecher Stowe lived in this Victorian "cottage" right next door to the Mark Twain House for 33 years. Through objects, photographs, and interactive media, docents tell the story of the author and the lasting impact of her novel *Uncle Tom's Cabin*. Exhibits explore the author's passion for social justice, including emancipation and women's rights, and a specially designed tour for children ages 5-12 provides a wonderful introduction to these concepts.

## GILETTE CASTLE

67 River Rd., East Haddam; 860/526-2336; www.ct.gov/deep/gillettecastle

The former residence of William Gilette, an American stage and silent film actor from the late 19th-early 20th centuries, resembles a stone medieval fortress. Highlights inside the 24-room mansion, built 1914-1919, include 47 unique doors with intricate puzzle-like locks, built-in couches, and carved-wood light switches. There is also a secret passageway and a secret room. The castle is located on a 184-acre (74-hectare) park, which includes hiking trails and picnic spots.

# BEST SCENIC DRIVES

## ALONG THE COAST

Visitors flock to Connecticut's coastal towns for colonial architecture, antiques stores, and restaurants serving freshly caught seafood with local flair. Beaches and clam shacks are big summer draws here, and the coast's sandy edges fill with umbrellas through the warm months. This part of Connecticut is also dreamy in autumn, when the gently changing colors make a picturesque contrast with the flanking ocean. Starting in Greenwich, the "Gateway to New England" near the New York border, the 100-mile (160-kilometer) drive east along I-95 to Mystic, near the Rhode Island border (or vice versa), takes 1.5-2 hours—without stops, of course.

**Greenwich,** your starting point, is known for mansions built on rolling lawns, high-end stores, and restaurants. Up next is **Norwalk,** where you'll find boutiques and cafés in the redeveloped and trendy South Norwalk neighborhood. Stop at **Silver Sands State Park** for the beach and **New Haven** for some culture at Yale University. Another worthy stop is the village of **Essex** and its quintessential New England vibe. Finally, you'll reach **Mystic,** with its excellent museums and maritime atmosphere.

# BEST PARKS AND RECREATION AREAS

## SILVER SANDS STATE PARK

1 Silver Sands Pkwy, Milford; 203/735-4311; www.ct.gov/deep/silversands

Located west of New Haven, the 297 acres (120 hectares) of beach, dunes, restored salt marsh, open areas, and

SILVER SANDS STATE PARK

KENT FALLS STATE PARK

woods of Silver Sands State Park includes the 14-acre (5.6-hectare) Charles Island, which is connected to the park by a sandbar that's submerged during high tide. Take time to wander the expansive salt marshes and dunes, but the beach is the real draw here, with gorgeous sand that invites lazy days by the water. Legend has it that Captain Kidd buried his treasure on this island, which is closed May-August to protect egrets and other bird rookeries. There are facilities such as a concession stand, restrooms, and a parking lot, and lifeguards are on duty.

## KENT FALLS STATE PARK

Rte. 7; www.ct.gov/deep/kentfalls

Kent Falls State Park in the Litchfield Hills is the home of the state's highest waterfall, a 250-foot (76-meter) cascade reached by an easy 0.25-mile (0.4-kilometer) trail with a few steep sections. It passes through a covered bridge that was built in 1974 for foot traffic only.

## HAMMONASSET BEACH STATE PARK

1288 Boston Post Rd. (Rte. 1), Madison; 203/245-2785; www.ct.gov/deep/hammonasset

Hammonasset Beach State Park features some of Connecticut's best coastline. There are more than 2 miles (3.2 kilometers) of beach, perfect for laying a towel out and swimming in the waves. There are also wetlands and woodlands, and plenty of opportunities for biking, kayaking, fishing, and bird-watching. Amenities include a boardwalk, restrooms, and boat launches.

# FESTIVALS AND EVENTS

## ANTIQUE AND CLASSIC BOAT RENDEZVOUS

Mystic; 888/973-2767; www.mysticseaport.org; July

A parade of antique and classic vessels set off from Mystic Seaport during the Antique and Classic Boat Rendezvous; the boats can be seen at the seaport that weekend.

## MATCHES AT GREENWICH POLO CLUB

1 Hurlingham Dr., Greenwich; 203/561-1639; www.greenwichpoloclub.com; June, July, and Sept.

If you're visiting Greenwich on a Sunday afternoon in June, July, or September, try to catch a polo match at the Greenwich Polo Club, a spectacular site for high-goal polo. Bring your own picnic, purchase snacks from food vendors, or buy a VIP ticket for reserved space and other amenities.

# BEST FOOD

Traditional New England fare revolves around the seafood of the area's coast,

# BEST SOUVENIRS

- Get into the Bulldog spirit with some Yale swag. The **Yale Bookstore** sells sweatshirts, hats, and more.

- Celebrate Connecticut's literary heroes with one of their **books.** Mark Twain, Harriet Beecher Stowe, and Booker T. Washington are the stars of Hartford. Gertrude Chandler, author of the popular children's book series *The Boxcar Children,* has her childhood home in Putnam, in northeastern Connecticut, while Madeline L'Engle, author of *A Wrinkle In Time,* grew up in Litchfield Hills, west of Hartford.

- A spot-on representative of a classic Connecticut **preppy clothing** retailer, **Island Pursuit** (23 W. Main St., Mystic; 475/777-3303; www.islandpursuit. com) sells items like brightly patterned shift dresses and ingenious waterproof espadrilles.

but pays homage to the cooking methods of its British origins—the likes of boiled lobsters, baked stuffed shrimp, fried cod, and steamed clams. Other foodstuffs native to the region also play a big part in the regional cuisine—cranberry sauce, maple syrup, corn bread, and baked beans, for starters.

## NEW HAVEN APIZZA

Neopolitan, New York style, Chicago style... in the oozy, blistered geography of pizza, New Haven's oddball flatbreads are unique and beloved. Strictly speaking, New Haven makes apizza, pronounced "ah-beets," and if you could sequence the apizza genome, it would point straight back to Naples—a century ago, the New Haven neighborhood of Wooster Square was known as Little Naples for the high concentration of immigrants who traced their roots to the city that invented pizza, and that's still where you'll find the city's top slices.

What makes it apizza? A classic New Haven pie is tossed by hand, stretched thin, then baked in a searing hot coal-fired oven. Order it plain and it comes topped with crushed tomatoes, olive oil, a dusting of pecorino cheese, and a bit of oregano—add some **mootz** to layer the pie with bubbling mozzarella.

The granddaddy of New Haven pizza is **Frank Pepe's Pizzeria Napoletana** (157 Wooster St., New Haven; 203/865-5762; www.pepespizzeria.com), where pies come crisp and sooty at the edges, with gorgeously toasted fillings in between. Fervent partisans of New Haven

pizza assert that Frank Pepe's invented **white clam pizza,** topped with fresh clams. Neck-and-neck for the best in the city is **Sally's Apizza** (237 Wooster St., New Haven; 203/624-5271; www. sallysapizza.com), where the tomato pie wins extra acclaim.

Something to drink with that pizza? Opt for a **Foxon Park** soda—it's been made in East Haven since 1922, with a long list of throwback flavors, including white birch, iron brew—a Scottish cross between cream soda and root beer—and *gassosa,* an Italian-style lemon-lime soda.

# MAJOR AIRPORTS

- **Bradley International Airport:** BDL; Schoephoester Rd., Windsor Locks; 860/292-2000; www.bradleyairport. com

# MORE INFORMATION

## TRAVEL AND TOURISM INFORMATION

- **Connecticut Tourism:** www.ctvisit. com
- **Connecticut State Parks and Forests:** https://portal.ct.gov/DEEP/ State-Parks

## MAGAZINES

- *Connecticut Magazine:* www. connecticutmag.com

# MID-ATLANTIC

◄ CHESAPEAKE BAY, MARYLAND

# THE MID-ATLANTIC
## State by State

### NEW YORK

**Why Go:** If the pulsing energy of New York City isn't for you, the Empire State also encompasses the pastoral Hudson Valley and the thundering Niagara Falls.

### NEW JERSEY

**Why Go:** The eclectic Garden State has kitsch, glitz, and Victorian architecture along the Jersey Shore, its very own mythical creature lurking in the Pinelands, and, yes, gardens.

### PENNSYLVANIA

**Why Go:** See where the foundations of the U.S. government were drafted and the art of Andy Warhol in his birthplace.

### WEST VIRGINIA

**Why Go:** River gorges and small towns show that the Mountain State has much to offer.

### DELAWARE

**Why Go:** The influence of one family looms large in the second-smallest state.

### MARYLAND

**Why Go:** The Chesapeake Bay infuses many of Maryland's sights with a maritime feel and is the source of its most famous food, Old Bay-seasoned crab.

### WASHINGTON DC

**Why Go:** The excellent—and free—museums are reason enough to visit the nation's capital, but everyone should see the buildings and landmarks dedicated to democracy at least once.

### VIRGINIA

**Why Go:** History permeates Virginia, from preserved colonial towns, presidential plantations, and Civil War battlefields to Civil Rights monuments and the birthplace of country music.

# Mid-Atlantic
# ROAD TRIP

This two-week route combines the coast with the major cities in the Mid-Atlantic. Given the large populations all along this corridor, traffic can be congested, so try to avoid driving during the busiest times. This trip starts with the cities but could easily be done in the opposite direction.

## NEW YORK

**New York City: 2 days**
Start with two days in New York City. On one day, combine the **Metropolitan Museum of Art** with **Central Park**, capped off with a **Broadway** show. On the second day, go out to the **Statue of Liberty** and take a walk over the **Brooklyn Bridge**. Be sure to have some pastrami at **Katz's Deli**.

## PENNSYLVANIA

**Philadelphia: 1 day / 100 miles (160 kilometers)**
You could drive from New York to Philadelphia, or you could take the train from Penn Station down to the City of Brotherly Love. When you arrive, walk around **Independence Hall** and have a Philly cheesesteak at **Jim's Steak** to avoid the Pat's versus Geno's rivalry.

## MARYLAND

**Baltimore: 1 day / 105 miles (170 kilometers)**
If you took the train to Philadelphia, pick up a rental car. Before leaving Pennsylvania, drive out to **Valley Forge** for a little break from all the cities. From there, drive 2.5 hours southwest to Maryland's largest city, **Baltimore,** where you'll explore the Inner Harbor, making sure to walk the waterfront promenade.

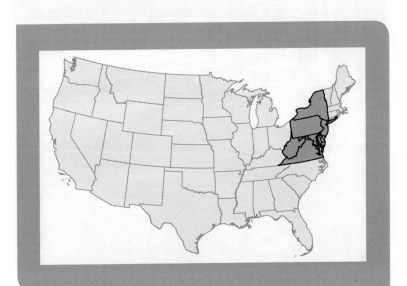

BRANDYWINE VALLEY, DELAWARE

## WASHINGTON DC

**2 days / 40 miles (65 kilometers)**
Get an early start out of Baltimore for the hour drive to DC. Over two days, divide your time between one or two of the excellent **Smithsonian** museums, the memorials of **National Mall,** and a walk around the **U Street** neighborhood. Be sure to have some **Ethiopian food** along the way.

## VIRGINIA

**Richmond, Virginia Beach, and Chincoteague: 3 days / 325 miles (525 kilometers)**
From DC, **Richmond** is about 2 hours south. Spend the rest of that day exploring Virginia's capital city. On the second day, your beach time starts. Head 2.5 hours east of Richmond to **Virginia Beach,** where the boardwalk, beach, and oceanfront hotels await. The next day, head north 2 hours to **Chincoteague National Wildlife Refuge** for a dose of nature.

## MARYLAND AND DELAWARE COAST

**Ocean City and Lewes: 2 days / 90 miles (145 kilometers)**
From Chincoteague, drive north into Maryland—**Ocean City** is about 1.5 hours away. After another beach-and-boardwalk day there, head north again to the Delaware beach town of **Lewes** (1 hour) with its quaint historic downtown.

## NEW JERSEY

**Cape May and the Jersey Shore: 1-2 days / 185 miles (300 kilometers)**
From Lewes, take the 1.5-hour ferry ride over Delaware Bay to New Jersey's **Cape May.** If you still want more beach time, you have many towns to choose from all along the **Jersey Shore,** especially if you're headed back up to New York City. Otherwise, head west 2 hours back to Philadelphia. Either way, be sure to stop in Margate to see **Lucy the Elephant.**

## ADDING WEST VIRGINIA

**Harpers Ferry: 1 day / 135 miles (220 kilometers)**
To get to all the Mid-Atlantic states, you could make a detour to **Harpers Ferry** between Baltimore and Washington DC. The historic town is about 1.5 hours away from either city.

BLACKWATER FALLS STATE PARK, WEST VIRGINIA

# NEW YORK

E ven those who have never strolled the streets of the Big Apple can instantly conjure its magic, having long been fed stories of the city through movies, novels, plays and melodies. But it's only a small part of what New York is.

New York is on Abenaki, Cayuga, Erie, Laurentian, Mohawk, Mohican, Mohegan, Delaware, Oneida, Onondaga, Poospatuck, and Seneca land. Along the state's labyrinth of scenic highways, you'll see a breathtaking landscape of rivers, lakes and mountains. The sublime falls of Niagara and the high peaks of the Adirondacks wait amid the largest semi-wilderness east of the Mississippi. There are pockets of arts and culture in the Finger Lakes, culinary excellence in the Hudson Valley, and historic locations, from Harriet Tubman's house to the rural communities of the Catskills.

All of these destinations are facets of New York, gems in the Empire State's crown.

**AREA:** 54,555 square miles / 141,296 square kilometers (27th)

**POPULATION:** 19,453,561 (4th)

**STATEHOOD DATE:** July 26, 1788 (11th)

**STATE CAPITAL:** Albany

▲ NIAGARA FALLS

## ORIENTATION

**New York City** sits in the crook of the arm of New York State that hits the Atlantic coast. The ribbon of land east of the city is **Long Island,** and the **Hudson Valley** is north of the city, along the river of the same name. To the west of the Hudson Valley rise the **Catskills.** North of the Hudson Valley is **Albany,** the state capital, and **Saratoga Springs,** and even farther north sprawl the **Adirondack Mountains.** The **Finger Lakes** are located in western New York, and **Buffalo** sits even farther west, on the shores of Lake Erie, and serves as the gateway to **Niagara Falls,** about 20 miles (32 kilometers) north.

## WHEN TO GO

**Late spring, early summer,** and **early fall** are the best times to visit much of New York. Temperatures generally hover in the 70s, and you're more likely to wake up to one of the state's precious cloudless days. **Midsummers** tend to be hot and humid; **winters** are overcast, wet, and cold.

# HIGHLIGHTS

## TIMES SQUARE

Btwn. 6th and 9th Aves., W. 40th and W. 54th Sts., New York City; www.timessquarenyc.org

With its crowds, chaos, and iconic larger-than-life billboards, Times Square radiates New York's energy and electricity, magnified exponentially. Named after *The New York Times,* which opened its offices at 43rd Street and Broadway in 1904, Times Square is usually packed no matter the season, although the crush of people hits a fever pitch in summer. Despite being avoided (and possibly despised) by locals, it is a place that everyone should see at least once.

## BROADWAY AND PERFORMING ARTS IN NEW YORK CITY

Attending a Broadway show is a quintessential New York experience. There's nothing quite like hurrying down the neon-splashed streets of Times Square along with thousands of other theatergoers. Discount tickets to same-day performances are sold at three **TKTS** booths (www.tdf.org) in the city. But the Big Apple has so many more entertainment options to offer, from opera and classical music at the **Lincoln Center for Performing Arts** (between 62nd and 65th Sts., and between Columbus and Amsterdam Aves.; 212/546-2656; www.lincolncenter.org) to an excellent jazz scene; the oldest and arguably best jazz club in the city is **Village Vanguard** (178 7th Ave. S. at 11th St.; 212/255-4037; www.villagevanguard.com).

BILLBOARDS IN TIMES SQUARE

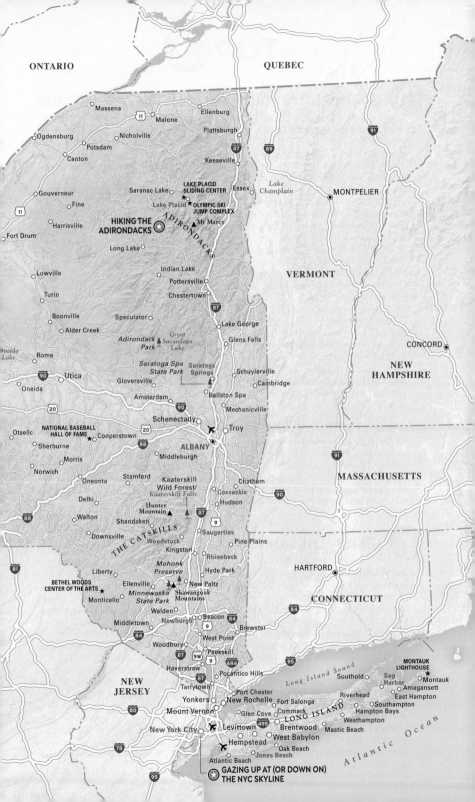

ONTARIO

QUEBEC

Massena

Malone

Ellenburg

Plattsburgh

Ogdensburg

Nicholville

Potsdam

Keeseville

Canton

Gouverneur

Saranac Lake

LAKE PLACID
SLIDING CENTER ★

Essex

Lake
Champlain

MONTPELIER

Fine

Lake Placid

OLYMPIC SKI
JUMP COMPLEX

Harrisville

HIKING THE
ADIRONDACKS

ADIRONDACKS

▲ Mt Marcy

VERMONT

Fort Drum

Long Lake

Lowville

Indian Lake

Pottersville

CONCORD

Turin

Chestertown

NEW
HAMPSHIRE

Boonville

Speculator

Lake George

Alder Creek

Adirondack
Park

Great
Sacandaga
Lake

Glens Falls

Oneida
Lake

Rome

Saratoga Spa
State Park

Saratoga
Springs

Schuylerville

Cambridge

Utica

Gloversville

Ballston Spa

Oneida

Amsterdam

Mechanicville

Schenectady

Troy

NATIONAL BASEBALL
HALL OF FAME ★ Cooperstown

Otselic

Sherburne

Middleburgh

ALBANY

MASSACHUSETTS

Morris

Norwich

Oneonta

Stamford

Kaaterskill
Wild Forest/
Kaaterskill Falls

Chatham

Delhi

Coxsackie

Hudson

Walton

Hunter
Mountain ▲

Downsville

Shandaken

THE CATSKILLS

Saugerties

HARTFORD

Woodstock

Kingston

Pine Plains

Rhinebeck

Liberty

Mohonk
Preserve

Hyde Park

CONNECTICUT

BETHEL WOODS
CENTER OF THE ARTS ★

Ellenville

Minnewaska
State Park

New Paltz

Shawangunk
Mountains

Monticello

Walden

Beacon

Middletown

Newburgh

Brewster

Woodbury

West Point

MONTAUK
LIGHTHOUSE ★

Peekskill

Haverstraw

Pocantico Hills

Long Island Sound

Southold

Montauk

Tarrytown

Sag
Harbor

Amagansett

NEW
JERSEY

Port Chester

Yonkers

New Rochelle

Fort Salonga

Riverhead

East Hampton

Mount Vernon

Glen Cove

Commack

Southampton

Hampton Bays

Westhampton

New York City

Levittown

Brentwood

West Babylon

Mastic Beach

Hempstead

Oak Beach

Jones Beach

Atlantic Beach

LONG ISLAND

Atlantic Ocean

GAZING UP AT (OR DOWN ON)
THE NYC SKYLINE

# TOP 3

## 1. GAZING UP AT (OR DOWN ON) THE NYC SKYLINE

When you're gazing at the New York City skyline from atop the **Empire State Building** (350 5th Ave., at 34th St.; 212/736-3100; www.esbnyc.com) or the **One World Observatory** (117 West St.; 212/602-4000; www.oneworldobservatory.com) on top of One World Trade Center, New York City feels like the center of the known universe. But you don't have to be on top of a dazzling skyscraper to can enjoy the spectacle. A cruise to and from Liberty or Ellis Islands or a stroll across the Brooklyn Bridge also offers stellar skyline views.

A gift from the people of France, the **Statue of Liberty** (www.nps.gov/stli) has become an indelible symbol of freedom and the United States. Across the water, **Ellis Island** (www.nps.gov/elis) was once the nation's primary immigration checkpoint, and its main building has been completely restored into an interesting museum displaying photos and artifacts from the island's past. **Statue Cruises** (877/523-9849; www.statuecruises.com) is the official provider of transportation to Liberty and Ellis Islands. Ferries depart several

NEW YORK CITY SKYLINE

times an hour from Battery Park and once or twice an hour from Liberty State Park in New Jersey—the ride alone is worth the trip, with glittering lower Manhattan rising up from the river before you.

**Brooklyn Bridge,** the celebrated link between Brooklyn and Manhattan, is a triumph of human ingenuity: its 1,595-foot (486-meter) span was the longest in the world when it was completed in in 1883, and the towers anchoring it were taller than any other structure in North America. Its elevated walkway, shared by pedestrians and cyclists, offers excellent views of the New York skyline.

## 2. HIKING THE ADIRONDACKS

**Adirondack Park** (581/846-8016; www.visitadirondacks.com) is the East's greatest wilderness, a 6-million-acre (2.4 million-hectare) refuge with an unusual mixture of public and private lands. Summer vacationers flock to its vast forests, gleaming lakes and ponds, and rushing rivers and streams, as well as the **45 High Peaks** (most over 4,000 feet/1,219 meters high).

**Mount Marcy,** elevation 5,344 feet (1,628 meters), is the highest mountain in the Adirondacks, and the one that draws the most hikers each year. **Adirondak Loj** (1002 Adirondak Loj Rd., Lake Placid; 518/523-3441; www.adk.org), 8 miles (12.8 kilometers) south of the town of Lake Placid, is the starting point of many trails that ascend in to the park, and the site of a first-rate information center, staffed by the nonprofit **Adirondack Mountain Club** (ADK; 814 Goggins Rd., Lake George; 518/668-4447 or 800/385-8080; www.adk.org) which can help you choose the hike that's right for you.

If you're short on time, a visit to the **Wild Center** (45 Museum Dr., Tupper Lake; 518/359-7800; www.wildcenter.org) will give you a sense of the area's natural wonders, with a highly interactive, 54,000-square-foot (5,017 square meters) museum and 81 acres (32 hectares) for visitors to wander.

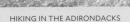

HIKING IN THE ADIRONDACKS

 **FEELING THE MIST OF NIAGARA FALLS**

The falls... ah, the falls. Despite the tourists, hoopla, and clichés, the falls are a sight to be seen. Stand in front of that white wall of water, and your breath will catch. Guaranteed.

Located along the Niagara River between the United States and Canada, Niagara Falls are actually three falls: **American Falls** and **Bridal Veil Falls** on the New York side, and **Horseshoe Falls** on the Ontario side. The falls and their accompanying attractions, including an interactive **visitors center** (716/278-1796), are located in **Niagara Falls State Park** (off Robert Moses Pkwy.; 716/278-1796; www.niagara-fallsstatepark.com), America's oldest state park, established in 1885. People come from all over the world to stroll through the park, enjoy the gardens, and, of course, see the falls. *Maid of the Mist* (716/284-8897; www.maidofthemist.com) and **Cave of the Winds** (716/278-1730) tours operate from the park; for visitors who don't want to get quite so close to the watery action, excellent views of the falls can be had from the park's **observation deck.**

AMERICAN FALLS AT NIAGARA FALLS

# *Best* ROAD TRIP

**DAY 1** In Manhattan, start your day early with a visit to the **Statue of Liberty** and **Ellis Island.** Grab a pastrami sandwich at the granddaddy of New York delicatessens, **Katz's,** followed by a visit to the **One World Observatory** atop **One World Trade Center** before braving the bustle of **Times Square** to take in a **Broadway** show.

**DAY 2** Grab a bagel at **Barney Greengrass,** then join legions of New Yorkers on a morning walk through **Central Park** before stepping into the **Metropolitan Museum of Art.** Head 40 minutes north out of the city for a special dinner at **Blue Hill at Stone Barns.**

**DAY 3** Continuing north along the Hudson, make stops to get your art fix at **Storm King Art Center** and **Dia:Beacon,** an hour's drive total. After another 45-minute drive, take a hike in the **Mohonk Preserve** before heading an hour west to the artsy town of **Woodstock** and catching a performance at the **Bethel Woods Center for the Arts** if the timing's right.

**DAY 4** Today, make a 3-hour beeline north to **Saratoga Springs,** where you can visit the famed racecourse and spa park, and maybe even see a show at the **Saratoga Performing Arts Center.**

**DAY 5** You're heading to the **Adirondacks** today, a 2-hour drive. Climb **Mount Marcy** if you're up to the challenge, or take on one of the shorter hikes from **Adirondak Loj** or the innovative **Wild Center.** To fuel up, stop at **ADK Food Hub** (320 Park St., Tupper Lake; 518/359-5112; www.adkfoodhub.com).

TIMES SQUARE

CENTRAL PARK

MOHONK PRESERVE

**DAY 6** Get an early start for your return trip back southward, to the Catskills. Budget about 4 hours to get to **Kaaterskill Wild Forest,** where you can stretch your legs with an hour-long hike to **Kaaterskill Falls.** Head back toward the river to **Saugerties** to enjoy its restaurants and shops. Spend the night in Saugerties or power through the last 2 hours back to **Manhattan.**

**Option:** Although the drive from New York City to **Niagara Falls** takes 7-8 hours (similar by train), the flight to **Buffalo,** the main gateway to the falls, is 1.5 hours. Take a couple days in western New York to see the falls, take an iconic cruise on the *Maid of the Mist,* and do a day trip or overnighter out to the **Finger Lakes** (2 hours by car), where you can visit the **Harriet Tubman Home** in Auburn and the **Women's Rights National Historical Park** in Seneca Falls, as well as taste some wines from the Napa Valley of the East.

WINERY IN THE FINGER LAKES

## LONG ISLAND

Long Island stretches east from New York City; remarkably, given its proximity, much of the island is still farmland, dunes, and beach. The most spectacular shores are along the southern coast, where white sands and dunes stretch out for an incredible, all-but-unbroken 123 miles (198 kilometers). Just 25 miles (40 kilometers) from Midtown Manhattan, **Jones Beach** (1 Ocean Pkwy., Wantagh; 516/785-1600; www.parks.ny.gov/parks/10) is Long Island's most famous and most accessible stretch of sand. West of Jones Beach are several smaller beaches, including **Long Beach** and **Lido Beach,** that are often less crowded and fun to explore.

Continuing east along Long Island, **the Hamptons** are known as New York City's playground, and everyone flocks here during the summer. A highlight is **Sag Harbor,** once a bustling, bawdy commercial town, and some of that lively atmosphere lingers, with shops and restaurants, 19th-century homes, huge old trees, and the weather-beaten 1,000-foot (305-meter) **Long Wharf.** At the island's easternmost point—windswept, barren, and wild—the still-operating **Montauk Lighthouse** (2000 Montauk Hwy., Montauk; 631/668-2544; www.montauklighthouse.com) is the oldest in New York State, commissioned by George Washington in 1792.

## NATIONAL BASEBALL HALL OF FAME AND MUSEUM

25 Maine St., Cooperstown; 607/547-7200; www.baseballhall.org

This museum was established in 1939 as an homage to America's favorite pastime. It's loaded with state-of-the-art displays covering every aspect of the sport, from famous ballparks and women's baseball, to the World Series, Negro League, and baseball in the Caribbean. Jackie Robinson's warm-up jacket, Hank Aaron's locker, Willie Mays's glove, and Yogi Berra's catcher's mitt are among the memorabilia on display.

# *Major* CITIES

**NEW YORK CITY:** New York is larger than life, a city of myth and legend. It's the country's center of commerce, and its cultural heart. Manhattan is the New York you've come to know through movies, but it is only one of the city's five boroughs, the other four being Brooklyn, the Bronx, Queens, and Staten Island.

**BUFFALO:** Maybe best known for its buffalo wings, after decades of economic decline, this formerly industrial steel town is undergoing an artistic and entrepreneurial comeback. It's also the main U.S. gateway to Niagara Falls.

**ALBANY:** The oldest city in New York and one of the oldest in the nation, Albany's main business is government; it's notorious for political wheeling and dealing.

## SARATOGA SPRINGS

For most of the year, Saratoga Springs is a charming Victorian town known for its first-rate arts scene, grand romantic architecture, sophisticated shops and restaurants, and therapeutic mineral springs. Come summer, though, the town turns itself upside down with buyers and sellers of dreams... all for the love of horses.

The **Saratoga Race Course** (267 Union Ave., Saratoga Springs; 518/584-6200; www.nyra.com/saratoga), built in 1864, is the country's oldest racetrack, and it has long represented the very best of what racing has to offer. Every mid-July through early September, the course has a race every day. The meet's highlight is the **Travers Stakes,** held on the fifth Saturday.

THE ERIE CANAL

Saratoga is slower but no less interesting once the horses are back in their stables. Arts thrive at the **Saratoga Performing Arts Center** (108 Ave. of the Pines; 518/584-9330; www.spac.org) and **Yaddo** (312 Union Ave.; 518/584-0746; www.yaddo.org), a renowned artists' retreat. The town also boasts **Saratoga Spa State Park** (off S. Broadway, just south of downtown; 518/584-2535; www.parks.ny.gov/parks/saratogaspa), spreading out over 2,200 pristine acres (890 hectares) of towering green-black pine trees and half-a-dozen mineral springs. The famous springs gurgle up from ancient seas trapped in limestone and shale, where visitors relax in bubbling golden-brown waters.

## THE ERIE CANAL

When it comes to bodies of water, the first one that may come to mind when you think of New York might be Niagara Falls, but it has tough competition. Another famous watery landmark is the Erie Canal: Facilitating trade and transport, it made New York City America's busiest port and transformed the state—almost every major city in New York falls along the route established by the Erie Canal. Made all but obsolete by the completion of the St. Lawrence Seaway, the canal can still be enjoyed by visitors in a number of ways. Rent a boat and cruise with **Lockport Locks & Erie Canal Cruises** (210 Market St., Lockport; 716/433-6155; www.lockportlocks.com) or **Erie Canal Adventures** (315/986-3011; www.eriecanaladventures.com); hike part of the

# ART, INDOORS AND OUT

You can easily lose yourself in the well-known wonders of New York City's art scene, but there are plenty of amazing arts institutions outside the city, too.

## NEW YORK CITY

- The **Museum of Modern Art** (11W. 53rd St., between 5th and 6th Aves.; 212/708-9400; www.moma.org) holds the largest collection of modern art in the world, including over 200,000 paintings, sculptures, drawings, prints, and photographs.

- One of the world's greatest museums, the **Metropolitan Museum of Art** (1000 5th Ave.; 212/535-7710; www.metmuseum.org) spreads out over about 1.5 million square feet (139,354 square meters), holding nearly 3 million works of art.

## UPSTATE

- **Dia:Beacon** (3 Beekman St., Beacon; 847/440-0100; www.diabeacon.org) is a huge contemporary art museum, just 30 minutes away from **Storm King Art Center** (Old Pleasant Hill Rd., off Rte. 32 a few miles south of Vails Gate; 845/534-3115; www.stormking.org), a 500-acre (202-hectare) setting for world-famous sculptures.

- The **Hyde Collection** (161 Warren St., Glens Falls; 518/792-1761; www.hydecollection.org) is a robust collection of masterworks by the likes of Cézanne, Rembrandt, Picasso, and Van Gogh.

- The **Corning Museum of Glass** (1 Museum Way, Corning; 607/937-5371; www.cmog.org) has the largest collection of glass in the world.

---

400-mile-long (643-kilometer) multiuse **Erie Canalway Trail** (www.eriecanalway.org); or visit Buffalo's revitalized **Canalside District** (www.buffalowaterfront.com), buzzing with festivals, concerts, recreation, and a naval and military park.

# BEST SCENIC DRIVES

New York is full of magnificent beauty, and one of the best ways to see it is by driving its many scenic highways and byways. They're pretty any time of year, but between late September and late October, they are just plain spectacular, when fall foliage sets the backdrops ablaze with flame-colored leaves.

## FINGER LAKES DRIVE AROUND SENECA LAKE

If you like your views reflected in water and punctuated with occasional stops for wine tastings, then this drive will tick all the boxes. It's short but impressive and ideal for a time-crunched traveler (35 miles/56 kilometers, 45 minutes-1 hour). Start in **Geneva,** at the northern end of Seneca Lake, and drive south on Rte. 14 to **Watkins Glen,** the southern end of Seneca Lake, tracing a path along the western side of the lake the entire way. Be sure to pull into the parking lot for **Watkins Glen State Park.**

## BEST OF THE CATSKILLS
### Rte. 23A

It's not the length of the drive; it's what there is to see along the way that matters when it comes to fall foliage. Plus, the short time in the car (9 miles/14 kilometers, 30 minutes) means you've got more time to explore each of the end points on this itinerary. Start in the **Kaaterskill Wild Forest** and hike toward the **Kaaterskill Falls,** which has a

# FOLLOWING THE FIGHT FOR RIGHTS

New York State is an activism hub and a cradle for movements that changed the nation, from suffrage to gay marriage.

## WOMEN'S RIGHTS

Elizabeth Cady Stanton and her abolitionist husband Henry Stanton moved to **Seneca Falls** from Boston in 1847. Often home alone, caring for her children, Stanton felt isolated and overwhelmed by housework. In July 1848, Stanton shared her discontent with four friends, who decided to convene a discussion on the status of women. About 300 people—men and women—showed up. During the meeting, the group's Declaration of Sentiments called for greater rights for women. Today, at the **Women's Rights National Historic Park,** you can visit **Wesleyan Chapel** (126 Fall St., Seneca Falls), where the historic convention took place, and the **house** where Stanton lived (32 Washington St., Seneca Falls). Start your visit at the **Visitor Center** (136 Fall St., Seneca Falls; 315/568-2991; www.nps.gov/wori).

## ABOLITION

The area of New York around Niagara Falls was a primary waypoint (and last stop, in most cases) on the Underground Railroad. Opened in 2018, the **Niagara Falls Underground Railroad Heritage Center** (825 Depot Ave. W., Niagara Falls; 716/300-8477; www.niagarafallsundergroundrailroad.org) is a vital addition to the region. It's located in an 1863 U.S. Customs House which, while not a stop on the Railroad itself, was located right next to the former International Suspension Bridge, which many freedom-seekers crossed.

About 2.5 hours to the east, the **Harriet Tubman Home** (180 South St., Auburn; 315/252-2081; www.harriettubmanhome.com) is where the "Moses of her people" settled after the Civil War. After escaping enslavement in 1849, Tubman risked 19 trips south to rescue more than 300 enslaved people. A visit to the Tubman property begins in the visitors center with interpretive panels that follow the timeline of Tubman's life, followed by a tour of the clapboard house where she tended to the elderly.

## GAY RIGHTS

New York City's **Greenwich Village** and **West Village** were once hotbeds of radical and artistic activity, antiwar rallies, and the Civil Rights Movement. In 1969, the Stonewall Riots marked the beginning of the national gay rights movement. In **Christopher Park,** at Christopher Street and 7th Avenue South, a statue commemorates the riots, which took place across the street at Stonewall Inn on June 27, 1969. The original Stonewall was at 51 Christopher Street and is now gone; the bar called **Stonewall** at 53 Christopher is a namesake and, as of 2016, a State and National Historic Landmark.

260-foot (79-meter) drop. Once you've had your fill of a hiking, hop back in the car and drive north to **Hunter Mountain,** where you can board the **Scenic Skyride,** a gondola that will slowly drift you up to a height of 3,200 feet (975 meters).

## HUDSON VALLEY

### Rte. 9W

Hugging the Hudson River's western shoreline, Route 9W makes for a beautiful fall foliage drive, as it passes through long stretches of hardwood forest between **Newburgh** and **Coxsackie.** Begin the day's drive at the **Bear Mountain Bridge,** and make your way

HUDSON VALLEY IN FALL

north, stopping for lunch and antiques shopping in **Saugerties.** Allow about 3 hours of driving time to reach downtown **Albany.**

# BEST PARKS AND RECREATION AREAS

## CENTRAL PARK

Between 5th and 8th Aves., 59th and 110th Sts., New York City; 212/310-6600; www.centralparknyc.org

Between the Upper East and the Upper West Sides lies that most glorious of New York spaces: Central Park. Without this vast, rolling green estate—the lungs of the city—life in New York would probably become unbearable. Walking through it is like walking through a carnival site. You'll see New Yorkers running, biking, or inline skating; oblivious lovers; stroller-pushing nannies; students lounging with textbooks; cashmere-clad matrons; professional dog-walkers; and musicians playing everything from concertos to rap.

An excellent way to tour the park is by bike. Several vendors can be found on the west side of 59th Street; if you're keen to try a **Citi Bike** (www.citibikenyc.com), the city's bike share program, there are several docking stations on the park's periphery. Among landmarks to seek out are the **Central Park Zoo** (830 5th Ave.; 212/439-6500; www.centralparkzoo.com), the 1908 **Carousel** (mid-park at 64th St.), and,

just north of the 72nd Street Transverse, **Bethesda Terrace, The Lake,** and **Loeb Boathouse,** which you'll probably recognize from the movies.

## MOHONK PRESERVE

847/255-0919; www.mohonkpreserve.org

In the heart of the Shawangunk Mountains, 2 hours north of New York City, there's a tilted ridge of translucent quartz cemented into sedimentary rock that's popular with rock climbers. The Mohonk Preserve is ideal for outdoor adventure with more than 30 miles (48 kilometers) of trails and carriage roads crisscrossing the preserve. One of the highlights of this area is **Mohonk Mountain House** (1000 Mountain Rest Rd., New Paltz; 855/883-3798; www.mohonk.com), an enormous castle-like structure on the edge of a deep-blue glacial lake. The last of the magnificent resort hotels that once lined the Hudson, Mohonk is an ultraromantic place, with grounds offering lovely scenic hikes, natural cave spelunking, impressive gardens, mountain biking, and crystal-clear lake swimming.

The use of the grounds is fee-based, so if the idea of spending $15-20 per person to hike the Mohonk Preserve sounds a bit steep, head farther west to **Minnewaska State Park** (5281 Rte. 44/55, Kerhonkson; 845/255-0752; www.parks.ny.gov/parks/127), filled with panoramic views, hiking trails, waterfalls, and lakes.

MOHONK MOUNTAIN HOUSE AT MOHONK PRESERVE

WATKINS GLEN STATE PARK

## WATKINS GLEN STATE PARK

1009 N. Franklin St. (off Rte. 14), Watkins Glen; 607/535-4511; https://parks.ny.gov/parks/watkinsglen

Created some 12,000 years ago during the last Ice Age is a wild and raggedy gorge flanked by high cliffs and strange, sculpted rock formations. **Glen Creek—** which drops some 700 feet (213 meters) in 2 miles (3.2 kilometers) over rapids, cascades, and 19 waterfalls—rushes through its center. Alongside the gorge runs the 1.5-mile (2.4-kilometer) **Gorge Trail,** made up of 832 stone steps, stone paths, and numerous bridges. The trail leads past tunnels, caves, and a natural stone bridge, all carved out of the sedimentary rock by Glen Creek.

### SKI AREAS

In winter, upstate New York transforms into a wonderland for skiers and snowboarders: the **Olympic Ski Jump Complex** (5486 Cascade Rd., Lake Placid; 518/523-2202; www.whiteface.com) and **Lake Placid Sliding Center** (518/523-4436) are places to see how the pros do it, but other popular places to get your adrenaline pumping include **Hunter Mountain Ski Area** (off Rte. 23A, Hunter; 518/263-4223; www.huntermtn.com) in the Catskills, and **Bristol Mountain Winter Resorts** (5662 Rte. 64, Canandaigua; 585/375-1100; www.bristolmountain.com) near the Finger Lakes.

# FESTIVALS AND EVENTS

## CHRISTMAS IN ROCKEFELLER CENTER

30 Rockefeller Plaza, New York City; 212/588-8601; www.rockefellercenter.com; Nov.-Jan.

Thanks to the myriad images of bundled-up ice skaters gliding under an enormous, festively decorated tree, Rockefeller Center has become synonymous with Christmas in the city. The famous Christmas tree arrives at the center in mid-November, with a **tree lighting** event taking place in early December, and stays up until just after New Year's. The skating rink is usually open October through April.

## BETHEL WOODS CONCERT SERIES

The legendary 1969 **Woodstock Music Festival** actually took place in Bethel, 60 miles (96 kilometers) away: The concert organizers wanted to hold the events closer to home, but Woodstock had no open space large enough, and last-minute ordinances imposed by nervous officials prevented the concert from taking place as originally planned. Today, the famed arts colony of Woodstock is still a picturesque and unusual spot, and the **Bethel Woods Center of the Arts** (200 Hurd Rd., Bethel; 866/781-2922; www.bethelwoodscenter.org), built on the festival site,

ICE SKATING AT ROCKEFELLER CENTER

attracts an ambitious lineup of performers ranging from the New York Philharmonic to ballet troupes, jazz greats, and pop music stars.

## SPECTATOR SPORTS

New York State has a full complement of professional sports teams, most in New York City, with a few in Buffalo, such as the NFL's **Buffalo Bills** (www. buffalobills.com). However, it's seeing the **New York Yankees** (Yankee Stadium, 1 East 161st St., Bronx; www.mlb. com/yankees) that appears on many sports fans' bucket lists.

# BEST FOOD AND DRINK

You could take a trip to New York just to eat, and many people do.

## ONLY IN NYC

There's a list of foods that are practically synonymous with New York City, from bagels to pizza: here are a few of the best places to eat them.

- **Bagels:** The competition for the city's best bagel is highly contested, but a few contenders are **Russ & Daughters** (179 E. Houston St., New York City; 212/475-4880; www.russanddaughters.com), **Barney Greengrass** (541 Amsterdam Ave., New York City; 212/724-4707; www.barneygreengrass.com), and **Ess-a-Bagel** (831 3rd Ave., New York City; 212/980-1010; www.ess-a-bagel.com).

- **Pastrami:** The place for a delicious and smoky pastrami sandwich is almost inarguably **Katz's Delicatessen** (205 E. Houston St., New York City; 212/254-2246; www.katzsdelicatessen.com).

- **Food trucks:** From classics like the **Halal Guys** (https://thehalalguys.com), who post up at 53rd St. and 6th Ave., to the village of carts that pops up at Brooklyn's **Smorgasburg** (www.smorgasburg.com), New York is fully in the age of the food truck.

- **Hot dogs: Gray's Papaya** (2090 Broadway, New York City; 212/799-0243; www.grayspapayanyc.com) sells New York-style hot dogs: snappy, grilled, and eaten standing up.

- **Pizza:** When there comes to NYC pizza, there are a few kinds: the big-as-your-head dollar slice, available on virtually every street corner in the city, and traditional crispy-thin coal-oven pies. **John's** (278 Bleecker St.; 212/243-1680; www.johnsbrickovenpizza.com) and **Patsy's Pizzeria** (2287 1st Ave.; 212/534-9783) serve some of the best of the latter.

## FARM-TO-TABLE

Many of us may think of the Midwest as the bread-basket of the United States, but New York State is an agricultural hotspot, too, with farms, dairies, and orchards generating exceptional products for consumption, both locally and beyond. Read on for some favorite farm-to-table experiences.

- **Blue Hill at Stone Barns** (630 Bedford Rd., Pocantico Hills; 914/366-9600; www.bluehillfarm.com): There are plenty of farm-to-table restaurants in the Hudson Valley, but none is more (justifiably) popular than Blue Hill at Stone Barns.
- **Culinary Institute of America** (1946 Campus Dr., Hyde Park; 845/452-9600; www.ciachef.edu): The nation's most prestigious cooking school is open for tours and has several first-rate student-staffed restaurants on its grounds.
- **Field Notes** (204 Lishakill Rd., Colonie; 518/400-2024; www.fieldnotes-ny.com): If the Capital-Saratoga region's farmers markets leave you hungry for more, weekly dinners here that feature locally grown and produced ingredients.
- **New York Kitchen** (800 S. Main St., Canandaigua; 585/394-7070; www.nykitchen.com): At New York Kitchen, you can take cooking classes that feature the grown and raised bounty of the Finger Lakes region.

## BUFFALO WINGS

Buffalo chicken wings got their name from the western New York city where they were invented. Try these morsels flavored with the signature spicy, sticky, orange sauce, served with celery sticks and blue cheese dressing, at their birthplace: **Anchor Bar** (1047 Main St., Buffalo; 716/886-8920; https://anchorbar.com).

## FINGER LAKES WINE

The hills of the Finger Lakes, covered with vineyards, glow pale green in spring, brilliant green in summer, and red-brown-purple in fall. Called the "Napa Valley of the East," the Finger Lakes region currently boasts more than 100 wineries (www.fingerlakeswinecountry.com). Stop by some of these standouts:

- **Fox Run Vineyards:** 670 Rte. 14, Penn Yan; 315/536-4616; www.foxrunvineyards.com
- **Hermann J. Wiemer Vineyard:** 3962 Rte. 14, Dundee; 607/243-7971; www.wiemer.com
- **Lamoreaux Landing Wine Cellars:** 9224 Rte. 414, Lodi; 607/582-6011; www.lamoreauxwine.com

## MAJOR AIRPORTS

- **La Guardia:** LGA; Elmhurst, Queens; 718/533-3400; www.panynj.gov/airports
- **John F. Kennedy:** JFK; Jamaica, Queens; 718/244-4444; www.panynj.gov/airports
- **Albany:** ALB; 737 Albany Shaker Rd., Albany; 518/242-2200; www.albanyairport.com
- **Buffalo Niagara:** BUF; 4200 Genesee St., Buffalo; 716/630-6000; www.buffaloairport.com

## MORE INFORMATION

### TRAVEL AND TOURISM INFORMATION

- **New York State Division of Tourism:** 800/225-5697; www.iloveny.com
- **New York State Parks Recreation & Historic Preservation:** https://parks.ny.gov

### NEWSPAPERS AND MAGAZINES

- *New York Times:* www.nytimes.com
- *Wall Street Journal:* www.wsj.com
- *The New Yorker:* www.newyorker.com
- *Time Out New York:* www.timeout.com/newyork

# NEW JERSEY

To the uninitiated, New Jersey is often known only as the butt of a joke comparing it to neighboring New York or Pennsylvania, but this understanding of the Garden State doesn't even scratch the surface. Get to know this relatively compact state long enough to get past its brashness and defensiveness, and you'll find extraordinary diversity.

**AREA:** 8,722 square miles / 25,182 square kilometers (47th)

**POPULATION:** 8,882,190 (11th)

**STATEHOOD DATE:** December 18, 1787 (3rd)

**STATE CAPITAL:** Trenton

There are the famous, rowdy boardwalks of the Jersey Shore, yes, but also quiet coastal towns with pristine beaches. On Munsee, Unalachtigo, and Unami land, New Jersey offers stimulating urban enclaves like Newark and Trenton, but also rural escapes great for hiking, canoeing, and cross country skiing. You'll find history around every corner, including the high ideals behind Liberty State Park and iconic figures from Edison to Springsteen. So don't disregard New Jersey: Come and see this beautiful, engaging state for yourself.

NEW JERSEY COAST

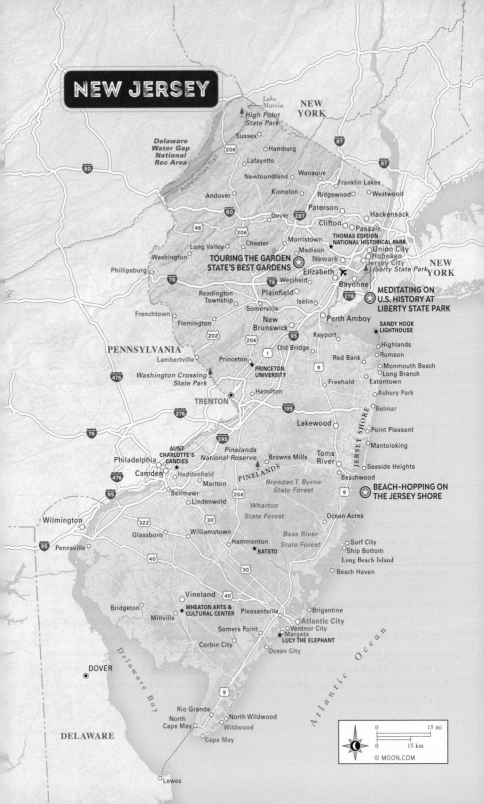

## ORIENTATION

**Newark, Jersey City,** and the other cities subject to the gravitational pull of New York City sit in the northeastern corner of the state. The **Jersey Shore** lines the eastern coast, the part of the state that hits the Atlantic Ocean, from Sandy Hook and its lighthouse in the north, through **Asbury Park, Long Beach Island,** and **Atlantic City,** down to **Wildwood** and **Cape May** at the far south end. The capital **Trenton** is inland in central New Jersey, separated from Pennsylvania by the Delaware River, and **Princeton** is nearby to the northeast. The sprawling **Pinelands** are located in the area between the Jersey Shore and the Delaware River.

## WHEN TO GO

New Jersey can be visited year-round, but **summer** is by far the busiest time, when the beaches and boardwalks of the Shore fill up with visitors. **Shoulder seasons** (May-Jun. and Sept.-Oct.), when many attractions are still open, can be a less hectic time to visit. **Winter** is the best for snow sports lovers, and in **autumn** trees put on a show of fall foliage.

# HIGHLIGHTS

## NEWARK MUSEUM

49 Washington St., Newark; 973/596-6550; www.newarkmuseum.org

The Newark Museum is a highlight of any trip to the state. With exhibits devoted to fires, brewing, art, and more—the Tibetan art collection is the largest in the western hemisphere—the museum is especially lively on Thursday night, when it stays open later for a usually more adult crowd who sip wine in the galleries.

## OLD BARRACKS MUSEUM

Barrack St., Trenton; 609/396-1776; www.barracks.org

This museum preserves barracks that are the last of their kind, surviving from the French and Indian War.

## PRINCETON UNIVERSITY

Princeton; www.princeton.edu

This Ivy League campus is almost like a museum. The **Princeton University Art Museum** (McCormick Hall;

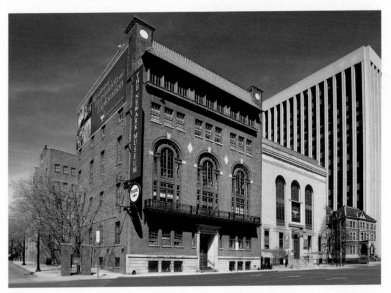

THE NEWARK MUSEUM

# TOP 3

## ① BEACH-HOPPING ON THE JERSEY SHORE

Sure, you can find the Jersey Shore of reality TV fame, but with 127 miles (204 kilometers) of coastline, New Jersey's Atlantic shoreline offers so much more. If you like...

- **Pristine beaches:** The 1.3-mile-long (2-kilometer) beach at **Belmar** is always bustling and one of the best on the Shore.

- **Surfing:** On **Long Beach Island,** you'll find waves for beginners as well as experts, and even a beach dedicated to surfers only.

- **Lighthouses:** The 1764 **Sandy Hook Lighthouse** is the oldest operating in the United States.

- **Architecture:** Lovers of Victorian architecture will adore **Cape May,** while **Wildwood** boasts a rare collection of mid-century buildings.

BELMAR BEACH

- **Music:** Known as the place where Bruce Springsteen got his start, **Asbury Park** is still the place to go for a Jersey Shore concert.

- **Boardwalks: Ocean City**'s boardwalk is a perfect mix of lively and relaxed, with enough rides and fried food to entertain you for hours.

- **Kitschy fun: Margate** is home to **Lucy the Elephant** (9200 Atlantic Ave.; 609/823-6473; https://lucytheelephant.org), a giant elephant statue built in 1881 as a sort of advertisement for the city. Tours inside the structure feature a chance to climb up to a viewing platform on Lucy's back.

- **Nightlife:** For dancing 'til dawn or trying your luck at blackjack, **Atlantic City** just can't be beat.

## ② MEDITATING ON U.S. HISTORY AT LIBERTY STATE PARK

Jersey City; www.libertystatepark.com

Though the Statue of Liberty is technically in New York, one of the best places to view it is from Jersey City's 1,200-acre (485-hectare) Liberty State Park. Two-mile (3.2-kilometer) waterfront **Liberty Walk** gives a unique profile view of Lady Liberty, as well as sweeping vistas of Manhattan across the Hudson River and great spots to picnic or throw a frisbee around.

Many people walk through Liberty State Park en route to the bridge to **Ellis Island,** where over 40 percent of Americans can trace their ancestry. The **Ellis Island Immigration Museum** (212/363-3200; www.ellisisland.org) honors the stories of the immigrants who came through this gateway to the U.S.; visitors can see the original baggage room, ticket office, and a dormitory, as well as exhibits filled with photos, letters, and other artifacts.

LIBERTY STATE PARK

 **TOURING THE GARDEN STATE'S BEST GARDENS**

The origin of New Jersey's nickname is somewhat obscure, based on a comment made by an 18th-century state attorney general. But even if they aren't the origin of the "Garden State" moniker, New Jersey does have some beautiful gardens.

▪ Calling **Branch Brook Park** (Newark; 973/268-2300; www.branchbrookpark.org) Newark's Central Park is apt, since it was designed by the same landscape architect, Frederick Law Olmstead. The best time to visit is in April, during the Cherry Blossom Festival.

▪ Beautiful, almost 3,000-acre (1,214-hectare) **Duke Farms** (Rte. 206 S., Somerville; 908/722-3700; www.dukefarms.org) is replete with greenhouses, tree-lined walkways, sculptures, and fountains.

▪ The inventive **Grounds for Sculpture** (18 Fairgrounds Rd., Hamilton; 609/586-0616; www.groundsforsculpture.org) was the idea of art collector and Johnson & Johnson heir J. Steward Johnson Jr., with over 200 artworks and 35 landscaped acres (14 hectares).

BRANCH BROOK PARK

# *Best* ROAD TRIP

**DAY 1** Start your Jersey journey in Jersey City's **Liberty State Park** for a view of the Statue of Liberty. From there, it's possible to walk over to the **Ellis Island Immigration Museum,** the gateway to the United States for many immigrants. For lunch, grab delicious Indian food in **Journal Square.** In nearby Newark, visit the **Newark Museum,** followed by a delicious Portuguese dinner in the **Ironbound District.**

ELLIS ISLAND IMMIGRATION MUSEUM

**DAY 2** Begin the day at the **Thomas Edison National Historical Park,** followed by a drive to **Duke Farms** in Hunterdon County. In the late afternoon, you should arrive in **Frenchtown,** a quaint place to spend the night and do some shopping.

**DAY 3** Today you'll drive down scenic **Route 29** to **Lambertville,** another great place to browse art and antiques. Be sure to take a walk or bike ride on the **D&R Canal Towpath,** along a 19th-century canal, or for earlier history, stop by **Washington Crossing State Park.** You'll finish your day in state capital **Trenton,** where you can see the 18th-century **State House** (State St.; 609/633-2709; www.njleg.state. nj.us), the second-oldest in the country, and eat some Italian food in the **Chambersburg** neighborhood.

THOMAS EDISON NATIONAL HISTORICAL PARK

**DAY 4** Spend today in the massive tract of forest that is the **Pinelands,** either hiking a portion of the **Batona Trail** or biking the **Pine Barrens River Ramble,** or **canoeing,** depending on your outdoor recreation preference.

D&R CANAL TOWPATH

**DAY 5** The last two days of your road trip will be devoted to the **Jersey Shore**. Start in picturesque **Cape May** and wind your way north on **Ocean Drive,** stopping in the coastal towns that pique your interest—**Wildwood, Ocean City,** and finally, **Atlantic City,** where you'll have your pick of great **nightlife.**

**DAY 6** Continuing north, stop in **Co-op Seafood Market** for lunch, then hit the beach in **Belmar** and wander **Asbury Park** for some Jersey music history. Make the trip all the way to **Sandy Hook Lighthouse** at the Shore's tip at before returning to the Newark area.

OCEAN CITY BOARDWALK

SANDY HOOK LIGHTHOUSE

609/258-3788; www.princetonartmuseum.org) is a gem, with pieces by Monet and Warhol.

## THOMAS EDISON NATIONAL HISTORICAL PARK

### Main St. and Lakeside Ave., West Orange

At the Thomas Edison National Historical Park, you can visit the preserved structures where technologies such as the phonograph, sound recording, movies, and batteries were developed and invented. Edison's Queen Anne-style home, Glenmont, was built in 1882 but later filled with all the bells and whistles technological development had to offer, from central heat and flushing toilets to electrical wiring.

# BEST SCENIC DRIVES

## OCEAN DRIVE

Scenic Ocean Drive runs much of the length of the Jersey Shore, from rowdy **Atlantic City** to the lovely Victorians of **Cape May** in the south. Actually a series of local roads, the 50-mile (80-kilometer) route is still easy to follow by keeping the Atlantic on one side, though speed limits and congestion can be somewhat inhibiting, especially in the summer. But the views are worth it: You'll pass picturesque Shore towns, marshes with waving, green tall grass, and postcard-perfect beaches. Though the road only takes about 2 hours to drive without traffic, consider breaking it up into a multiday trip, making stops at the best of the Shore on the way, from retro **Wildwood** to quaint, family-friendly **Ocean City.**

## ROUTE 29

This pretty route in western New Jersey follows along the Delaware River and Pennsylvania border, passing some of the state's most attractive river towns—**Lambertville** and **Frenchtown** are particularly charming, with art galleries, antique shops, restaurants, and 19th-century architecture. The route starts at **Washington Crossing State Park** (355 Washington

## *Major* CITIES

**NEWARK:** Many people only experience Newark on the way to and from the airport, but New Jersey's largest city has so much more to offer, from museums to excellent international food.

**JERSEY CITY:** Jersey City has great restaurants, skyline views, and green space to tempt even the snobbiest New Yorker to cross the Hudson.

**TRENTON:** With unique colonial history and wonderful Italian eateries, New Jersey's capital draws more than just politicians to the State House.

Crossing-Pennington Rd., Titusville; 609/737-0623; www.state.nj.us/dep/parksandforests/parks/washcros.html), where General George Washington crossed the Delaware with over 2,000 troops in December 1776. At several points along Route 29, you can stop to walk or bike on the **D&R Canal Towpath,** following along its namesake canal, which reached its heyday in the 1860s and '70s.

# BEST PARKS AND RECREATION AREAS

## HIGH POINT STATE PARK

1480 Rte. 23, Sussex; 973/875-4800; www.state.nj.us/dep/parksandforests/parks/highpoint.html

Home to New Jersey's highest elevation (1,803 feet/550 meters), High Point State Park is known as the state's

HIGH POINT STATE PARK

best cross country skiing destination at **High Point Cross Country Ski Center** (1480 Rte. 23, Sussex; 973/702-1222; www.xcskihighpoint.com), but it's a great place to visit year-round. There are more than 50 miles (80 kilometers) of multiuse trails for hiking and mountain biking, including a scenic stretch of the **Appalachian Trail.** Twenty-acre (8-hectare) **Lake Marcia** is open for swimming and fishing for trout, bass, and catfish in the summer.

## THE PINELANDS

www.nj.gov/pinelands

Also sometimes called the Pine Barrens, the 1.4-million-acre (566,560-hectare) **Pinelands National Reserve** is the East Coast's largest tract of forest, covering about 20 percent of New Jersey's total land area. Pitch pine, Atlantic white cedar, scrub oak, cranberry bogs, and blueberry bushels make a great habitat for rare tree frogs, orchids, and carnivorous plants. It's also supposedly home to the legendary Jersey Devil, a two-legged creature often described as having a goat-like head and bat-like wings, which has purportedly terrorized the area since the 18th century.

Eight state parks and forests are located within the Pinelands; among them, **Wharton State Forest** is the largest. The Pinelands are also full of cultural attractions, such as "forgotten towns" abandoned after the decline of the bog-iron and glass-making industries. Located in Wharton State Forest, the restored, 19th-century **Batsto** (31 Batsto Rd., Hammonton; 609/567-8116; www.batstovillage.org) shows the way these places looked in their heydays.

BATONA TRAIL, WHARTON STATE FOREST

For outdoor recreation, there's the 50-mile (80-kilometer) **Batona Trail** for hikers. This trail traverses Bass River, Wharton, and Brendan T. Byrne State Forests. For cyclists, the 42.6-mile (68-5-kilometer) **Pine Barrens River Ramble** starts at Batsto and passes by cranberry bogs and flowing rivers. Where the Barrens really shine is canoeing, and guided trips are available through **Pinelands Adventures** (1005 Atsion Rd., Shamong; 609/268-0189; www.pinelandsadventures.org).

# FESTIVALS AND EVENTS

## LAMBERTVILLE SHAD FESTIVAL

www.shadfest.com; Apr.

Charming Lambertville, known as a great place to shop for art and antiques, celebrates the restoration of the Delaware River with its annual Shad Festival during the last week of April. The humble shad, a river herring, was an important food source for New Jerseyans throughout the state's history, so its return to the revived Delaware from the Atlantic to breed in the 1980s was major cause for celebration. You can definitely try shad if you're here during the festivals—locals say it's best smoked—but this festival is about more than fish, with artists coming from across the region to show their work in booths and live music providing the soundtrack.

## QUICK CHEK FESTIVAL OF BALLOONING

Readington Township; 800/468-2479; http://quickchk.balloonfestival.com; July

With all its beautiful, wide-open scenery, Hunterdon County has become well-known for hot-air ballooning, and no time is this more evident than during the annual Quick Chek Festival of Ballooning in July. With up to 125 hot-air balloons in the air at any given time, the celebration is supplemented with music, fireworks, and amusement rides. If you're not in town for the festival, you still have plenty of ways to get up in the air: check out **American Balloon** (218 Dove Cote Ct., Whitehouse Station; 908/534-5220).

# BEST FOOD

New Jersey may be best known for its so-bad-it's-good **boardwalk food**—pizza, funnel cake, gyros, ice cream, cotton candy, and fudge—but that's certainly not all it has to offer. (Still, one **deep-fried Oreo** while walking along the beach may be hard to resist.)

## SEAFOOD

Not surprisingly, seafood along the Shore is excellent, especially crab cakes, flounder, and shellfish. You'll notice many towns and businesses named for clams and oysters. Visit Point Pleasant Beach's **Co-op Seafood & Market** (57

# BEST SOUVENIRS

- Some of the best places in the Garden State to buy **antiques** are quaint river towns **Lambertville** and **Frenchtown.**

- New Jersey offers a few iconic candies that make great souvenirs. **Saltwater taffy** is ubiquitous on the Shore, but **Aunt Charlotte's Candies** (5 W. Maple Ave., Merchantville; 856/662-0058; www.auntcharlottescandy.com), with its upstairs chocolate factory, is one in a million.

- The glass industry once ruled South Jersey, and you can still buy beautiful glass art in quaint towns like **Haddonfield** or the **Wheaton Arts & Cultural Center** (1501 Glasstown Rd., Millville; 856/825/6800; www.wheatonarts. org) today.

Channel Dr.; 732/899-2211) for fresh fish straight from the boats or **Dock's Oyster House** (2405 Atlantic Ave.; 609/345-0092; www.docksoysterhouse.com) in Atlantic City, family-owned for more than a century.

## INTERNATIONAL EATS

Italians are the state's largest ethnic group, making Italian food intrinsic to New Jersey culture, but a growing international population means you can find excellent example of many cuisines, from Indian to Spanish to Brazilian and Portuguese.

### Italian

**Trenton's Chambersburg District,** also known as its Little Italy, is full of classic Italian eateries. Pretty **Hoboken,** its streets lined with brownstones, is known for being Frank Sinatra's birthplace, with old-school Italian restaurants to live up to that reputation.

### Portuguese, Spanish, and Brazilian

**Newark's Ironbound District** is home to the largest Portuguese population in the country, along with many people of Spanish and Brazilian descent. It's a great place to find Spanish dishes like *mariscada,* the quintessential Brazilian all-you-can-eat meat fest, and typical, hearty Portuguese stews and chicken piri-piri.

### Indian

**Journal Square** in **Jersey City** is known as Little India, with dozens of Indian markets and eateries lining Newark Avenue.

## MAJOR AIRPORTS

- **Newark Liberty International Airport:** EWR; 888/397-4636; www. panynj.com

## MORE INFORMATION

### TRAVEL AND TOURISM INFORMATION

- **New Jersey Office of Travel and Tourism:** 800/847-4865; www. visitnj.org

- **New Jersey State Parks:** www.state. nj.us/dep/parksandforests/parks

### NEWSPAPERS AND MAGAZINES

- *Star-Ledger:* www.nj.com/starledger

- *Weird N.J.:* www.weirdnj.com

- *New Jersey Monthly:* www. njmonthly.com

# PENNSYLVANIA

Pennsylvania is on Delaware, Erie, Iroquois, Shawnee, and Susquehannock land. It's a wide expanse of mostly wilderness and farmlands flanked by two cosmopolitan cities. In the southeast corner is Philadelphia, the nation's birthplace and the sixth-largest city in the country. In the southwest corner, Pittsburgh, the former manufacturing powerhouse, is re-creating itself as a cultural hub.

**AREA:** 46,056 square miles / 114,101 square kilometers (33rd)

**POPULATION:** 12,801,989 (5th)

**STATEHOOD DATE:** December 12, 1787 (2nd)

**STATE CAPITAL:** Harrisburg

If there's one thing Pennsylvania's founder, William Penn, insisted on, it's that everyone feel welcome. It's thanks to Billy that Pennsylvania is home to the oldest Amish community in the world. The state that goes by "PA" is a magnet for history buffs, art enthusiasts, and nature lovers. It's where the nation's founders came up with "life, liberty, and the pursuit of happiness." It's where President Abraham Lincoln delivered the timeless speech that began: "Four score and seven years ago our fathers brought forth on this continent a new nation." And it's where you'll find the only U.S. museum dedicated to hiking and the largest herd of free-roaming elk in the Northeast.

▲ PHILADELPHIA SKYLINE

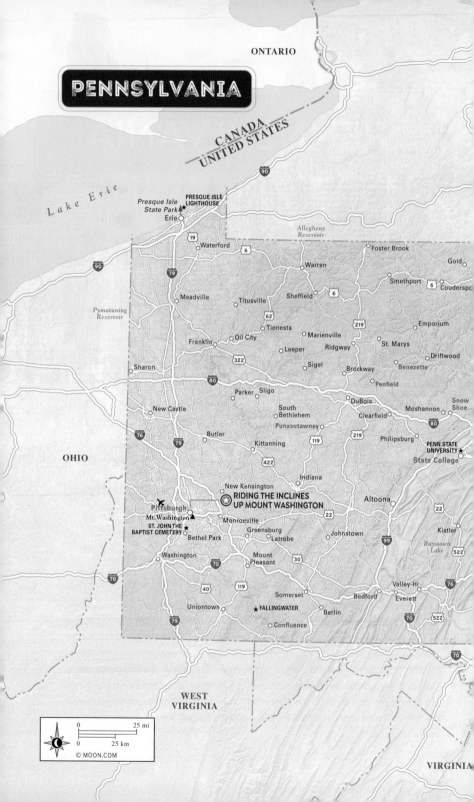

# PENNSYLVANIA

ONTARIO

CANADA
UNITED STATES

Lake Erie

Presque Isle State Park
**PRESQUE ISLE LIGHTHOUSE**
Erie

Allegheny Reservoir

Waterford

19

90

Pymatuning Reservoir

Meadville

Titusville

Sheffield

Warren

Foster Brook

Gold

Smethport

Couderspc

6

6

6

62

Tionesta

Marienville

219

Emporium

Oil City

Leeper

Ridgway

St. Marys

Driftwood

Franklin

Sigel

Benezette

322

Brockway

Penfield

Sharon

Parker

Sligo

DuBois

Moshannon

Snow Shoe

New Castle

South Bethlehem

Clearfield

80

80

76

Butler

Punxsutawney

119

219

Philipsburg

**PENN STATE UNIVERSITY**

79

Kittanning

422

State College

OHIO

Indiana

New Kensington

Altoona

⊛ **RIDING THE INCLINES UP MOUNT WASHINGTON**

22

22

Pittsburgh

Mt. Washington

Monroeville

Greensburg

Johnstown

Kistler

**ST. JOHN THE BAPTIST CEMETERY**

Bethel Park

Latrobe

99

Ruystown Lake

522

Washington

Mount Pleasant

30

70

40

119

Somerset

Bedford

Valley-Hi

Everett

76

Uniontown

★ **FALLINGWATER**

Berlin

70

522

79

Confluence

70

WEST VIRGINIA

0        25 mi

0        25 km

© MOON.COM

VIRGINIA

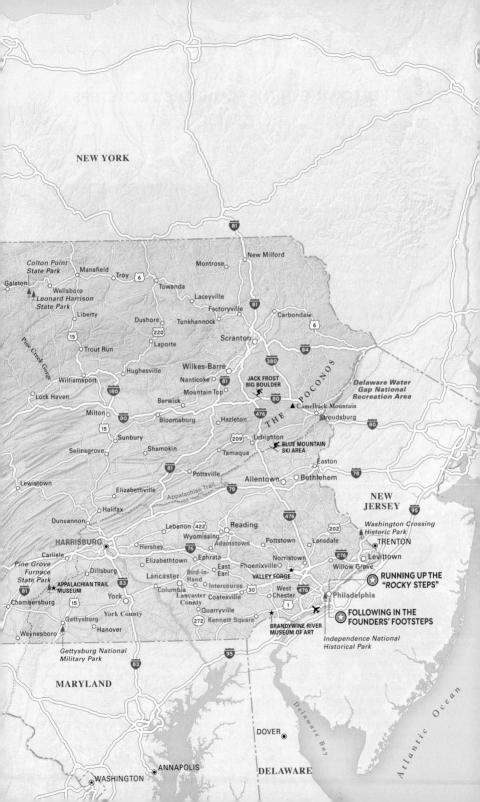

# TOP 3

## 1 FOLLOWING IN THE FOUNDERS' FOOTSTEPS

Philadelphia tells a vivid story of the fight for freedom from British rule: at **Independence Hall** (Chestnut St. between 5th and 6th Sts.; 215/965-2305; www.nps.gov/inde), where the Founding Fathers made so many important decisions; at **Valley Forge** (Rte. 23 and N. Gulph Rd., Valley Forge; 610/783-1099; www.nps.gov/vafo), where Washington and his troops spent the winter of 1777-1778 after Philadelphia fell to the British; at the **National Constitution Center** (525 Arch St.; 215/409-6600; www.constitutioncenter.org), which tells the story of the nation's supreme law; and at dozens of other historic sites and museums.

THE LIBERTY BELL

A good place to start is the **Museum of the American Revolution** (101 S. 3rd St.; 215/253-6731; www.amrevmuseum.org), where you'll get a crash course on the quest to end British rule in America. In **Independence National Historical Park,** which includes Independence Hall, you can also see the Liberty Bell at the **Liberty Bell Center** (Market St. between 5th and 6th Sts.); it's best to start your visit at the **Independence Visitor Center** (6th and Market Sts.; 800/537-7676; www.phlvisitorcenter.com), which can guide you to the numerous other Revolutionary sites throughout the city, such as the **Betsy Ross House** (239 Arch St.; 215/629-4026; www.historicphiladelphia.org). If you do decide to make your way to Valley Forge, 20 miles (32 kilometers) northwest of Philadelphia, make a day of it and add on **Washington Crossing Historic Park** (Rte. 32, between Rte. 532 and Aquetong Rd.; 215/493-4076; www.washingtoncrossingpark.org), 50 minutes northeast, where General George Washington and his ragged troops crossed the ice-choked Delaware River on December 25th, 1776.

## 2 RUNNING UP THE "ROCKY STEPS" AND VISITING THE MUSEUMS OF BENJAMIN FRANKLIN PARKWAY

Per William Penn's 17th-century plan, Philly is a city of parallel lines and right angles. Bucking the trend is the diagonal Benjamin Franklin Parkway, which starts near the city's distinctive **City Hall** (Broad and Market Sts.; 215/686-2840; www.phila.gov/virtualch) and ends at the magnificent **Philadelphia Museum of Art** (2600 Benjamin Franklin Pkwy.; 215/763-8100; www.philamuseum.org). The Philadelphia Museum of Art is known simply as the Art Museum, but it's not unusual for people to visit the main building without stepping foot inside. It sits on a granite hill, and the view from its east entranceway is one of the best in the city. The broad steps leading to the entrance are a tourist attraction in themselves, having appeared in an iconic scene in *Rocky,* the 1976 Best Picture Oscar winner starring Sylvester Stallone. Not everyone has the stamina to sprint up the steps à la Rocky, but almost every first-time visitor has an "Italian Stallion" moment at the top, posing with arms outstretched for a camera-wielding friend. A bronze statue of the movie character, commissioned by Stallone for a scene in Rocky III, can be found near the base of the so-called *Rocky* steps.

It's hard to sum up what you'll discover inside the museum, which is quite simply one of the preeminent cultural institutions in the country. Since its founding in 1876, the museum has amassed more than 240,000 objects representing 2,000 years of creative expression. It's worth a visit whether your passion is medieval armor, modern sculpture, or architecture and decorative arts.

PHILADELPHIA MUSEUM OF ART

Even without the Philadelphia Museum of Art, the Benjamin Franklin Parkway would be a cultural mecca. In addition to the Art Museum, it's home to the **Academy of National Sciences** (1900 Benjamin Franklin Pkwy.; 215/299-1000; www.ansp.org), the nation's oldest natural history museum; the **Franklin Institute** (222 N. 20th St.; 215/448-1200; www.fi.edu), a splendid science museum; the **Rodin Museum** (2151 Benjamin Franklin Pkwy.; 215/763-8100; www.rodinmuseum.org) the largest collection of Auguste Rodin sculptures outside Paris; and the **Barnes Foundation** (2025 Benjamin Franklin Pkwy.; 215/278-7000; www.barnesfoundation.org), with an extensive collection of works by the likes of Picasso, Matisse, Cézanne, and Renoir.

# RIDING THE INCLINES UP MOUNT WASHINGTON

Pittsburgh is famous for its hills, but the historic inclines of Mount Washington offer some of its best views.

Mount Washington was once called Coal Hill for its abundant coal seams, which supplied fuel to Pittsburgh's settlers and riverbank industries. Workers built houses on Pittsburgh's hillsides and for a while commuted on foot, trudging up steep paths after a hard day's work. The first people-moving incline opened in 1870; in the 25 years that followed, more than 15 others were built, but only two remain: the **Monongahela Incline** (lower station Carson St. near Smithfield Street Bridge; 412/442-2000; www.portauthority.org) and the **Duquesne Incline** (lower station 1197 W. Carson St.; 412/381-1665; www.duquesneincline.org).

THE DUQUESNE INCLINE

These inclines have been around so long that you might think twice about boarding the cable cars: Don't. The view more than compensates for the fear factor. Pittsburgh's skyline, with rivers, bridges, and uncommonly shaped buildings, is often ranked as one of the best in the world, and the scene from either of the inclines at night is especially enchanting.

# *Best* ROAD TRIP

**DAY 1** Begin in the nation's birthplace, **Philadelphia.** Pick up a timed ticket to **Independence Hall** and make your way to the **Liberty Bell.** After your tour, try a Supreme Court robe on for size at the **National Constitution Center.** Come sundown, head to the neon-lit, Cheez Whiz-stained intersection of 9th Street and Passyunk Avenue in South Philly, home to rival cheesesteakeries **Pat's King of Steaks** and **Geno's Steaks.**

GENO'S STEAKS

**DAY 2** Sprint up the so-called *Rocky* steps and get lost in the period rooms of the stunning **Philadelphia Museum of Art.** Then take a stroll along the picturesque **Benjamin Franklin Parkway** and visit your pick of **museums.** In the afternoon, get on I-95 south for the 30-mile (48-kilometer) ride to the **Brandywine River Museum of Art,** featuring works by three generations of Wyeths.

*WASHINGTON MONUMENT* BY RUDOLF SIEMERING, BENJAMIN FRANKLIN PARKWAY

**DAY 3** Factor in 45 minutes for the drive west toward **Lancaster County,** where you can head to a **smorgasbord** restaurant to eat your weight in **Pennsylvania Dutch food** and to shop for antiques and handmade goods in towns like Lancaster, Adamstown, and Bird-in-Hand. Head west 90 minutes on Route 30 to **Gettysburg,** site of the Civil War's bloodiest battle, and home to **Gettysburg National Military Park.**

**DAY 4** Today's destination—3 hours west of Gettysburg—is the Laurel Highlands, home to Frank Lloyd Wright's **Fallingwater** (be sure to reserve your ticket in advance). From Fallingwater, drive 90 minutes on Route 381 north and I-76 west to **Pittsburgh,** where you'll ascend **Mount Washington** via the **Duquesne Incline** for spectacular nighttime views.

GETTYSBURG NATIONAL MILITARY PARK

**DAY 5** Start the next day with a visit to the **Andy Warhol Museum,** then leave the steel and glass of Pittsburgh behind for a beach vacation. Head north on I-79 for 2 hours to **Presque Isle State Park,** a sandy peninsula jutting out into **Lake Erie.** Make the 7-hour drive back to Philadelphia the next day.

FRANK LLOYD WRIGHT'S FALLINGWATER

PRESQUE ISLE LIGHTHOUSE, PRESQUE ISLE STATE PARK

## ORIENTATION

Philadelphia and Pittsburgh, the state's two largest cities, sit at opposite ends of the state, with **Philadelphia** in the southeast and **Pittsburg** in the southwest. **Erie** is in the northeast corner of the state, right on Lake Erie. Lancaster County, the center of **Pennsylvania Dutch Country,** lies to the west of Philadelphia, and the capital **Harrisburg** is northeast of Lancaster. **Gettysburg** is east of Dutch Country, near the border with Maryland, while the **Poconos** are north of Philadelphia.

## WHEN TO GO

Like the rest of the northeastern United States, Pennsylvania experiences all **four seasons. Summer** is the season to loll on the beaches of Presque Isle. **Fall** is a fabulous time to visit this tree-blanketed state. Head to the northern half of the state for landscapes ablaze in color. **Winter** brings unique opportunities to enjoy snow sports in destinations like the Pocono Mountains. **Spring** is a good time to visit the state's largest city, Philadelphia, which gets crowded in summer.

# HIGHLIGHTS

## PENNSYLVANIA DUTCH COUNTRY

### Lancaster County

Lancaster County, west of Philadelphia, has the largest concentration of Amish in the world. After the 1955 Broadway production of *Plain and Fancy,* the story of two New Yorkers who travel to Lancaster County, the region found itself inundated by tourists. Today, Lancaster County is flush with information centers, attractions, and tour operators offering experiences to acquaint visitors with the ways of the Amish. **Plain & Fancy Farm** (3121 Old Philadelphia Pike, Bird-in-Hand; www.plainandfancyfarm. com) offers buggy rides through Amish countryside and the opportunity to visit an Amish family in their home. Shopping for antiques and handmade goods is another popular draw for this region. Lancaster County is also home to the

# *Major* CITIES

**PHILADELPHIA:** Philadelphia tells a vivid story of the fight for freedom from British rule. It's also an arts town, a sports town, and a food town.

**PITTSBURGH:** No longer an industrial powerhouse, Pittsburgh offers world-class museums and a skyline that inspires accolades.

**ERIE:** Erie's location on Presque Isle Bay made it a 19th-century naval ship-building center, and industry followed. Today, its waters and nearby beaches continue to attract water sports enthusiasts from all over the state.

oldest continually operated farmers market in the country, **Central Market** (23 N. Market St., Lancaster; 717/735-6890; www.centralmarketlancaster. com) and the oldest operating short-line railroad in the country, **Strasburg Rail Road** (300 Gap Rd., Ronks; 866/725-9666; www.strasburgrailroad. com). When traveling in Dutch Country, note that the Amish do not do business on Sundays, and also resist the urge to take pictures, as the Amish take offense at being photographed.

## FALLINGWATER

1491 Mill Run Rd., Mill Run; 724/329-8501; www.fallingwater.org

Frank Lloyd Wright's architectural masterpiece was designed in 1935 for the Kaufmann family of Pittsburgh, owners of the now-defunct Kaufmann's department store chain. The Kaufmanns wanted a vacation home with a view of their favorite waterfall. Wright decided

LANCASTER COUNTY

instead to cantilever the house directly over the 30-foot (9-meter) falls—killing the view, but creating an enchanting illusion the house sprung from nature. Concrete terraces and a glass-walled living room project over the water, which provides a constant soundtrack. The Kaufmanns used Fallingwater until 1963, when Edgar Kaufmann Jr. entrusted it to the Western Pennsylvania Conservancy. The family's artworks and furnishings, many of which were designed by Wright, still fill the house.

## THE ANDY WARHOL MUSEUM

117 Sandusky St., Pittsburgh; 412/237-8300; www.warhol.org

Andy Warhol was born and buried in Pittsburgh, which might have remained a little-known fact were it not for The Andy Warhol Museum. Opened in 1994, it is the largest U.S. museum dedicated to a single artist. The collection includes about 900 paintings and 2,000 drawings, along with sculptures, prints, photographs, films, videos, books, and even wallpaper designed by the artist. The "pope of pop" was born in 1928 to working-class immigrants from what is now Slovakia. After graduating with an art degree from the Carnegie Institute of Technology (now Carnegie Mellon University), Warhol moved to New York and gained recognition as a commercial illustrator. In the early 1960s, he shot to fame as a pop artist with paintings of consumer products such as Campbell's Soup and celebrities including Marilyn Monroe. He is buried at **St. John the Baptist Cemetery** in the Pittsburgh suburb of Bethel Park. Admirers still leave soup cans at the grave site.

# BRANDYWINE RIVER MUSEUM OF ART

**1 Hoffman's Mill Rd., Chadds Ford; 610/388-2700; www.brandywinemuseum.org**

In a converted Civil War-era gristmill, this museum on the banks of the Brandywine is home to an unparalleled collection of works by three generations of Wyeths. N. C. Wyeth moved to the Brandywine region in 1902 to study with famed illustrator Howard Pyle and became one of America's foremost commercial artists. Three of his five children also became artists, including daughters Henriette and Carolyn, who are well represented in the museum's collection. But it was his youngest child, Andrew, who was the first artist awarded the Presidential Medal of Freedom, the first living artist to have an exhibition at the White House, and the first living American artist to have an exhibition at London's Royal Academy of Arts. His 1948 painting *Christina's World* is one of the best-known images of the 20th century.

For even more insight into America's first family of art, tour the **N. C. Wyeth House and Studio,** where N. C. raised his talented brood; the **Andrew Wyeth Studio,** where Andrew painted from

INTERIOR OF THE BRANDYWINE RIVER MUSEUM OF ART

## SUPERLATIVE CITIES

The spaces in between Pennsylvania's largest cities, Philadelphia and Pittsburgh, jockey for distinction, often earning them some pretty unique nicknames. To name a few:

- **Hershey** is known as "The Sweetest Place on Earth," where the largest chocolate company in North America was founded.
- In Lancaster County, the center of Pennsylvania's Amish community, antiques enthusiasts will fall in love with **Adamstown,** aka "Antiques Capital USA."
- Just west of Lancaster County, **York County** touts itself as the "Factory Tour Capital of the World," where more than a dozen factories open their doors to visitors.
- Finally, there's **Punxsutawney,** a borough made famous by a groundhog.

1940 to 2008; or the **Kuerner Farm,** which inspired so many of Andrew's works.

## GETTYSBURG NATIONAL MILITARY PARK

**717/334-1124; www.nps.gov/gett**

Gettysburg earned its place in the history books as the setting for the Civil War's bloodiest battle and President Abraham Lincoln's most famous speech. The former took place July 1-3, with more than 165,000 soldiers converging on the crossroads town. Under the command of General George G. Meade, the Union army desperately defended its home territory from General Robert E. Lee's Confederate army. The war would continue for almost two years, but the Confederacy's hopes for independence effectively died on the Gettysburg battlefield. The human toll was astronomical: 51,000 soldiers were dead, wounded, or missing.

In the aftermath of the battle, a group of prominent residents convinced the state to help fund the purchase of a portion of the battlefield to serve as a final resting place for the Union's defenders, and invited President Lincoln to deliver "a few appropriate remarks" at the dedication ceremony on November 19, 1863. Lincoln's two-minute Gettysburg Address is regarded as the rhetorical zenith of his career and one of the greatest speeches in history.

Expect to spend the better part of a day at the 6,000-acre (2,428-hectare) park, which is not only one of the nation's most popular historical attractions but also an extraordinary sculpture garden, with more than 1,300 monuments, markers, and memorials. Begin at the **Museum and Visitor Center** (1195 Baltimore Pike/Rte. 97, Gettysburg; 717/338-1243; www.gettysburgfoundation.org). Tickets include admission to the on-site **Gettysburg Museum of the American Civil War,** which explores the causes and consequences of the deadliest war in American history. Museum-only tickets are available. **Gettysburg National Cemetery,** where President Lincoln delivered his famous Gettysburg Address, is a short walk from the visitors center.

To complete your experience, drive 50 minutes northwest to the **National Civil War Museum** (1 Lincoln Circle at Reservoir Park, Harrisburg; 717/260-1861; www.nationalcivilwarmuseum.org), whose focus is on the common soldier and the men and women on the home front. Particular attention is paid to the African American experience.

GETTYSBURG NATIONAL MILITARY PARK

# BEST SCENIC DRIVES

## ELK SCENIC DRIVE

Pennsylvania is today home to the largest herd of free-roaming elk in the northeastern United States. The animals we see today are descendants of 177 Rocky Mountain elk that were released in Pennsylvania between 1913 and 1926. Now almost 1,000 elk make their home in an 835-square-mile (2,162-square-kilometer) range stretching across Elk, Cameron, and Clearfield Counties. The heart of the elk region is the remote village of **Benezette.**

Elk Scenic Drive is a 127-mile (204-kilometer) route peppered with 23 sites of interest to nature lovers, including the viewing areas near Benezette. It winds through three state forests and three state game lands, starting and ending at points on **I-80.** From the west, leave I-80 at **Penfield** exit 111 at Route 153. From the east, take **Snow Shoe** exit 147 at Route 144. Look for distinctive signage. You can download a map of the route on the website of the **Pennsylvania Department of Conservation and Natural Resources** (www.dcnr.pa.gov). The journey can take a few hours or a few days, depending on your level of interest.

# BEST PARKS AND RECREATION AREAS

## PRESQUE ISLE STATE PARK

301 Peninsula Dr., Erie; 814/833-7424; www.dcnr.pa.gov/stateparks

Just 7 miles (11 kilometers) long, this park surrounded by Lake Erie boasts sandy beaches, a 19th-century lighthouse, and a remarkable diversity of plant and animal life. Stop at the **Tom Ridge Environmental Center** (301 Peninsula Dr., Erie; 814/833-7424; www.dcnr.pa.gov/StateParks/FindAPark/PresqueIsleStatePark/TRECPI), or TREC for short, to learn about Presque Isle's history and ecosystems and grab a map of the 3,200-acre (1,294-hectare) park. There's no better way to take in

# APPALACHIAN TRAIL

Pennsylvania is home to 230 miles (370 kilometers) of the famed Appalachian Trail, which passes through 14 states, and the Appalachian Trail Museum. The nation's first museum dedicated to hiking is located near the midpoint of the 2,180-mile (3,508-kilometer) footpath.

Housed in a former gristmill, the **Appalachian Trail Museum** (1120 Pine Grove Rd., Gardners; 717/486-8126; www.atmuseum.org) pays tribute to pioneer hikers such as Earl Shaffer, the first person to thru-hike the trail, and "Grandma" Gatewood, who was 67 when she became the first female to complete the journey alone. There's even an exhibit on Ziggy, the first feline to conquer the Georgia-to-Maine trail.

Visitors stand a good chance of rubbing shoulders with modern-day thru-hikers because the museum is located just off the Appalachian Trail in **Pine Grove Furnace State Park** (1100 Pine Grove Rd., Gardners; 717/486-7174; www.dcnr.pa.gov/stateparks).

Presque Isle than by biking the **Karl Boyes Multipurpose National Recreation Trail,** which makes a 13.5-mile (21.7-kilometer) circuit of the park. Maritime history buffs can retrace the steps of lighthouse keepers on the 1.25-mile (2-kilometer) **Sidewalk Trail.** At its north end is the **Presque Isle Lighthouse,** built in 1873 and raised to 68 feet (20 meters) in the 1890s. Various watercraft can be rented on Presque Isle, and more than 320 bird species have been spotted on the peninsula.

## PINE CREEK GORGE

Often referred to as the "Grand Canyon of Pennsylvania," Pine Creek Gorge starts near the Route 6 village of Ansonia and continues south for 47 miles (75 kilometers). Near its southern end, Pine Creek Gorge is as deep as 1,450 feet (441 meters) and a mile (1 kilometer) wide.

On the west rim of the gorge, there's **Colton Point State Park.** On the east, there's **Leonard Harrison State Park,** which offers superior views. You can stop at the **Tioga County Visitors Center** (2053 Rte. 660, Wellsboro; 570/724-0635; www.visitpottertioga.com) or the state **park office** at the entrance to Leonard Harrison (4797 Rte. 660, Wellsboro; 570/724-3061; www.dcnr.pa.gov/stateparks) for queries about both parks. The main overlook and an environmental interpretive center are 0.25 mile (0.4 kilometer) up the road.

The 60-mile (96-kilometer) **Pine Creek Rail Trail** brings hikers, bikers, horseback riders, cross-country skiers, and snowshoers to the region, while the swift waters of Pine Creek call to anglers and paddlers.

## THE POCONOS

Though not terribly tall, the Pocono Mountains are an appealing skiing, snowboarding, and snow tubing destination. Pennsylvania's first commercial ski area opened in the Poconos in the 1940s. Today there are seven major ski areas. These are some of the best:

- **Blue Mountain Ski Area:** 1660 Blue Mountain Dr., Palmerton; 610/826-7700; www.skibluemt.com

PINE CREEK GORGE

# ROOT FOR PENNSYLVANIA'S TEAMS

Pennsylvania is home to much-loved athletic franchises across the state, and some of the country's most rabid fan bases.

## PHILADELPHIA

- **Baseball:** In 2007 the **Philadelphia Phillies** became the first American professional sports franchise to lose 10,000 games. So you can imagine the city's elation when the team beat the Tampa Bay Rays in the 2008 World Series.

- **Basketball:** The **Philadelphia 76ers** have been very good and very bad. Local basketball fans also relish the intense rivalries between five area universities—the University of Pennsylvania, La Salle, Saint Joseph's, Temple, and Villanova—known as the **Big 5.**

- **Football:** In a fanatical sports town, no team inspires more passion than the **Philadelphia Eagles.**

- **Hockey:** The "Broad Street Bullies," as the **Philadelphia Flyers** were once known, are arguably the city's most successful franchise.

## PITTSBURGH

- **Baseball:** Pittsburgh's Major League Baseball club, the **Pirates,** is its oldest professional sports franchise.

- **Football:** In 2009, the **Steelers** became the first team in the National Football League to win six championships, causing the city to dub itself "Sixburgh."

- **Hockey:** The **Pittsburgh Penguins** captured the nation's attention in the early 1990s, bringing home the Stanley Cup twice in two years. They repeated the feat in 2016 and 2017 with back-to-back wins.

## PENN STATE

- **State College** is home to Pennsylvania State University and the mega parties that are **Nittany Lions** football games.

- **Camelback Mountain:** 301 Resort Dr., Tannersville; 570/629-1661; www.ski-camelback.com

- **Jack Frost Big Boulder:** 357 Big Boulder Dr., Lake Harmony; 570/443-8425; www.jfbb.com

# FESTIVALS AND EVENTS

## MUSHROOM FESTIVAL

610/925-3373; www.mushroomfestival.org; Sept.

In Brandywine Valley, Kennett Square is known as the Mushroom Capital of the World: More than 60 percent of the mushrooms consumed in the U.S. are grown in this area. The annual Mushroom Festival, held the weekend after Labor Day, showcases mushrooms in every imaginable form, including ice cream.

# BEST FOOD

## PHILADELPHIA CHEESESTEAK

These famous hot sandwiches comprised of sauteed ribeye steak and cheese on a roll are a Philadelphia staple. The best cheesesteak is truly a matter of personal preference. Some like the roll toasted and crispy, while others prefer it soft and chewy. Some like a cheesesteak dripping with grease, while others complain that too much grease makes the roll soggy. Some like the meat

# BEST SOUVENIRS

- People go out of their way for fresh ice cream produced by Penn State's **Berkey Creamery** (corner of Bigler and Curtin Rds., University Park; 814/865-7535; www.creamery.psu.edu). Quarts and half-gallons are so popular that Berkey sells travel bags and dry ice for the road.

- **Handicrafts** and **antiques** produced in Lancaster County Amish Country are deservedly popular. For quilts, **Intercourse** is a good place to go on a spree, with a number of shops on **Old Philadelphia Pike,** such as **Village Quilts** (3529 Old Philadelphia Pike, Intercourse; 717/768-2787; www.kitchenkettle.com/quilts).

diced as thinly as possible, while others prefer slightly larger slices or even small chunks. Some love yellow Cheez Whiz, but American or provolone cheese are just as common. The one indisputable fact is that cheesesteaks are just not the same anywhere else.

- **Pat's King of Steaks:** 215/468-1546; www.patskingofsteaks.com

- **Geno's Steaks:** 215/389-0659; www.genosteaks.com

- **Jim's Steaks:** 400 South St.; 215/928-1911; www.jimssouthstreet.com

## PENNSYLVANIA DUTCH FARE

If you're new to Pennsylvania Dutch cuisine, you should know a few things. Around here, **chicken potpie** isn't a pie at all. It's a stew with square-cut egg noodles. A **whoopie pie** isn't a pie either. Think of it as a dessert burger: creamy icing pressed between two bun-shaped cakes. The most iconic dessert, the **shoofly pie,** is, in fact, a pie with a crumb crust, packed with molasses and brown sugar. Other regional specialties include **egg noodles with browned butter, chow-chow** (a pickled vegetable relish), **scrapple** (a breakfast food made with pork scraps), and **schnitz un knepp** (a dish consisting of dried apples, dumplings, and ham). You can try them all at a **smorgasbord** restaurant.

- **Shady Maple Smorgasbord:** 129 Toddy Dr., East Earl; 717/354-8222; www.shady-maple.com/smorgasbord

- **Bird-in-Hand Family Restaurant & Smorgasbord:** 2760 Old Philadelphia Pike, Bird-in-Hand; 717/768-1500; www.bird-in-hand.com

## MAJOR AIRPORTS

- **Philadelphia International Airport:** PHL; 215/937-6937; www.phl.org

- **Pittsburgh International Airport:** PIT; 412/472-3525; www.flypittsburgh.com

## MORE INFORMATION

### TRAVEL AND TOURISM INFORMATION

- **Pennsylvania Tourism Office:** www.visitpa.com

- **Pennsylvania State Parks:** www.dcnr.pa.gov/StateParks

### NEWSPAPERS AND MAGAZINES

- *Philadelphia Inquirer:* www.inquirer.com

- *Pennsylvania Heritage:* www.paheritage.org

- *Pennsylvania Magazine:* www.pa-mag.com

# WEST VIRGINIA

"Almost Heaven" is the moniker chosen for this mountainous state by its tourism board. With deep river gorges and canyons and the Allegheny Mountains along its eastern flank, the state, on the land of the Massawomeck, Osage, Moneton, and Shawnee people, and its natural beauty have a claim on that lofty title. Although West Virginia's fortunes have long seemed inextricably linked to coal, with mine shafts dug into the ground and mountaintops flattened in search of the fossil fuel, travel and tourism have created a different source of revenue with incentives to preserve the forests, rivers, and peaks that draw people from nearby cities and beyond to hike, paddle, BASE jump, rock climb, and more. Designated in 2021, New River Gorge is one of the country's newest national parks, protecting an area that was once dotted with company mining towns. Add in towns and cities perfect for weekend getaways, and you'll start to see that you may want to stay awhile—something West Virginians have always known.

**AREA:** 24,038 square miles / 62,258 square kilometers (41st)

**POPULATION:** 1,792,147 (38th)

**STATEHOOD DATE:** June 20, 1863 (35th)

**STATE CAPITAL:** Charleston

HARPERS FERRY

## ORIENTATION

The state capital, **Charleston,** is located a little west of the center of the state, with **New River Gorge National Park and Preserve** to its southeast. Part of the Appalachians, the Allegheny Mountains, where **Monongahela National Forest** is located, cover much of eastern West Virginia. Historic **Harpers Ferry** sits at the tip of the sliver of West Virginia that's wedged between Virginia and Maryland and is closer to the nation's capital than the state capital.

## WHEN TO GO

Late **spring** (May and June) and **fall** (Sept. and Oct.) are usually the best times to explore West Virginia. The weather is most pleasant, and during the latter, the fall foliage is spectacular. **Summer** is the prime tourist season, but there is humidity to contend with. **Winter** is a slow season, with seasonal closures at some attractions and businesses and cessation of maintenance on mountain roads.

# HIGHLIGHTS

## BIENNERHASSETT ISLAND HISTORICAL STATE PARK

137 Juliana St., Parkersburg; 304/420-4800; http://wvstateparks.com/park/blennerhassett-island-historical-state-park

This unique park is located on an island in the middle of the Ohio River, and via self-guided walking tours and carriage rides, it offers insight into local history. The island is only accessible by riding on a sternwheeler, which departs from **Point Park** (2nd St.) in Parkersburg.

## APPALACHIAN TRAIL CONSERVANCY VISITOR CENTER

799 Washington St., Harpers Ferry; 304/535-6331; www.appalachiantrail.org

Harpers Ferry is one of the only West Virginia towns that the **Appalachian Trail (AT)** passes through in its 4-mile (6-kilometer) run through the state. The Appalachian Trail Conservancy Headquarters is just a quarter mile (0.4 kilometers) off the trail, and although it's not technically the midpoint of the Georgia-to-Maine hike, it serves as the symbolic halfway mark for many. The center is home to an enormous raised-relief map of the entire Appalachian Trail. It is one-of-a-kind and more than 10 feet (3 meters) long. In addition, pictures of more than 15,000 Appalachian Trail thru-hikers and section-hikers who have passed through the town since 1979 are kept in photo albums in the headquarters building. There are also maps, books, and other merchandise for sale, and staff can answer all types of questions regarding the AT.

APPALACHIAN TRAIL CONSERVANCY VISITOR CENTER

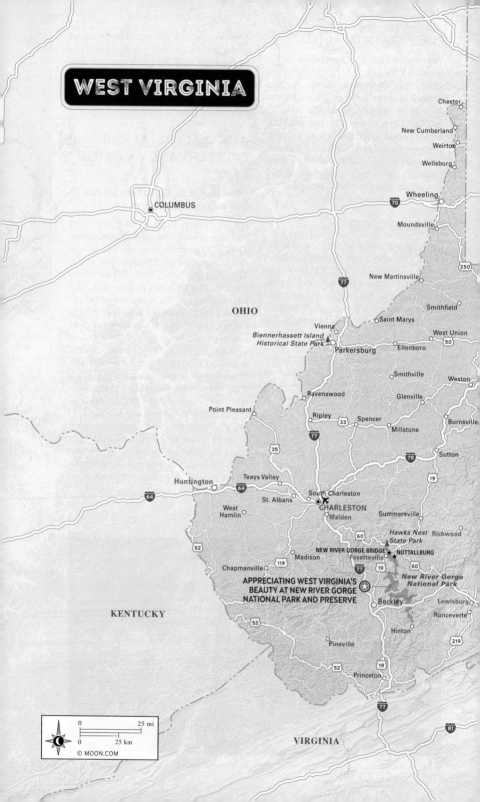

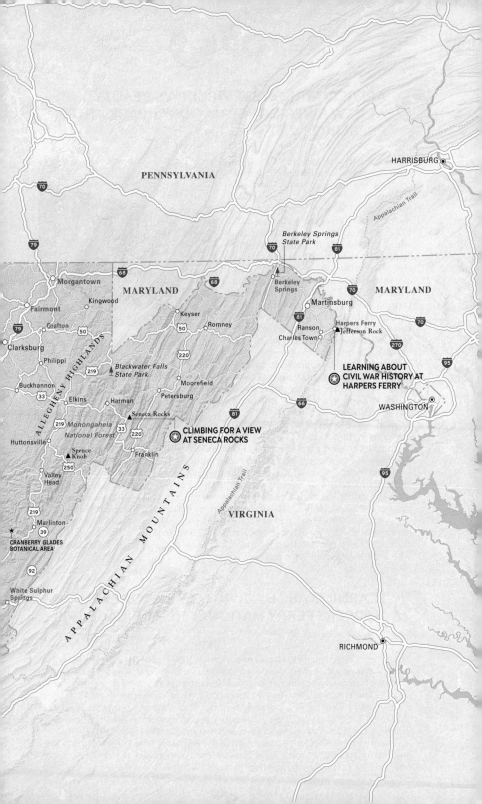

# TOP 3

## 1 APPRECIATING WEST VIRGINIA'S BEAUTY AT NEW RIVER GORGE NATIONAL PARK AND PRESERVE

Named a national park in 2021, New River Gorge National Park and Preserve contains the deepest and longest river-carved gorge in the Appalachian Mountains. The arch bridge over the river, the **New River Gorge Bridge** (U.S. 19), is the top attraction in the park, with its 3,030-foot (920-meter) length spanning 876 feet (267 meters) above the river. Views of this engineering marvel can be had from the **Canyon Rim Visitor Center** (162 Visitor Center Rd., Lansing; 304/465-0508; www.nps.gov/neri) and the upper overlook along the short (0.1 mile/0.2 kilometer) accessible **Canyon Rim Boardwalk,** which also has a lower overlook that involves 178

NEW RIVER GORGE BRIDGE

stairs to reach. For a longer distance view, hike the 1.6-mile (2.6-kilometer) **Long Point Trail,** and to see the bridge from below, drive **Fayette Station Road** from the Canyon Rim Visitor Center down through the gorge to the town of **Fayetteville,** a 40-minute trip. In addition to the bridge, white-water rafting is a popular activity on the New River, with gentler rapids (Class I-III) in the Upper Gorge and more difficult rapids (Class III-V) in the Lower Gorge. A number of outfitters are licensed to lead trips in the gorge.

The park also includes a number of sights with cultural significance to the state. Coal was and continues to be an important industry in West Virginia, and the New River and the surrounding area was a hub of mining at the turn of the 20th century. **Nuttallburg,** deep in the gorge, was one of the mining towns that was abandoned after the industry declined, but some of its structures still remain. Nuttallburg can be accessed via a 10-mile (16-kilometer) drive (including 4 miles/6 kilometers on unpaved road) from the Canyon Rim Visitor Center. The drive also highlights the heritage of Black Americans in the area, who came to work in the mines and the railroads that supported them, with informational placards posted along the road where the segregated living facilities stood.

## 2 LEARNING ABOUT CIVIL WAR HISTORY AT HARPERS FERRY NATIONAL HISTORICAL PARK

Harpers Ferry; 304/535-6029; www.nps.gov/hafe

The town of Harpers Ferry is best known for the 1859 raid of the **Harpers Ferry National Armory,** which mass-produced military arms for the United States, by abolitionist John Brown as part of an unsuccessful attempt to start a revolt of enslaved people. The National Park Service-managed park is technically located in three states—West Virginia, Virginia, and Maryland—but the main sights are located in the Lower Town of Harpers Ferry. The park features more than 25 historic buildings in the Shenandoah Street, High Street, and Potomac Street areas.

The armory site became the location of the **Harpers Ferry Train Station** in 1889 and remains as such today. **John Brown's Fort** (which was the armory's guardhouse) is the only surviving building from the Civil War. It was moved several times

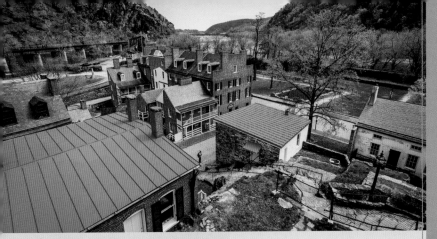

HISTORIC BUILDINGS IN HARPERS FERRY

and now sits approximately 150 feet (46 meters) east of its original location (the original site is now covered by the railroad). Another landmark is **White Hall Tavern** on Potomac Street. The tavern was owned by Frederick Roeder, the first civilian casualty of the Civil War in Harpers Ferry. Another historic building in the park is **Stipes' Boarding House** (Shenandoah St.), where Cornelia Stipes took in visitors during the Civil War. Other buildings include a mill, blacksmith shop, dry-goods store, and bookshop.

Harpers Ferry sits on a lovely triangle of land at the confluence of the Potomac and Shenandoah Rivers. Visitors can get a view of the water gap where the Potomac and Shenandoah Rivers meet by hiking up to the spot visited by Thomas Jefferson on October 25, 1783, now called **Jefferson Rock**. From the historic buildings, make your way to High Street and the stone steps that lead up to St. Peter's Church. The steps continue past the church and turn into a steep 5-minute climb. The view is spectacular, and you will find out why Jefferson said it was "worth a voyage across the Atlantic."

 ## CLIMBING FOR A VIEW AT SENECA ROCKS

Rte. 33 at Rte. 55, Seneca Rocks

Located within **Monongahela National Forest,** these dramatic 900-foot (274-meter) Tuscarora quartzite rock formations are a popular rock-climbing destination, with more than 375 routes of a range of difficulties (5.0-5.12). Climbers have the advantage here since they can scale up to the summit for a sweeping view of eastern West Virginia. Guide services lead guided climbs up the rocks as well.

Hikers can get up to a wooden observation deck on the steep **Seneca Rocks Hiking Trail** (2.6 miles/4.2 kilometers round-trip), which climbs 700 feet (213 meters) in elevation. The trail starts at

VIEW FROM SENECA ROCKS

the **Seneca Rocks Discovery Center,** which is a good place to see the rocks themselves as well as get information about the area. Adjacent to the center is the **Sites Homestead,** which is surrounded by gardens featuring 19th-century plants. Interpretive events highlighting period arts and crafts such as quilting or fiddling are held here on Saturdays in the summer.

**DAY 1** Start your trip in **Charleston.** Spend the morning browsing **Capitol Market,** and then head out of town on the **Midland Trail.** When you reach U.S. 19, take it to New River Gorge National Park. Stop at the **Canyon Rim Visitor Center** for views of the **New River Gorge Bridge** and do a short hike. Take **Fayette Station Road** for a view of the bridge from below. End up in **Fayetteville,** where you'll spend the night.

**DAY 2** Explore more of **New River Gorge National Park** in the morning, and then take U.S. 19 north to pick up the Midlands Trail again. Near the end of the scenic byway, you'll reach the small town of **Lewisburg,** where you'll spend the night.

NEW RIVER GORGE BRIDGE

**DAY 3** Get an early start into the mountains, heading to the dramatic **Seneca Rocks,** which you can admire from the base or work up a sweat hiking up to the observation deck. Not far away is the state's highest point, **Spruce Knob.** Afterward, drive 1.5 hours north to reach **Blackwater Falls State Park,** your last destination for the day. Check out the falls before turning in at the lodge or a cabin (reserve ahead of time).

BLACKWATER FALLS STATE PARK

**DAY 4** From Blackwater Falls, drive to **Harpers Ferry,** 2.5 hours away. (You can't help but to cross state boundaries on the way, as it's located on a thin arm of land between Maryland and Pennsylvania.) Wander the historic town and get a bite to eat. From there, drive an hour to **Berkeley Springs,** a town known for its mineral waters. Soak in the park's baths and spend the night in town.

**DAY 5** Make the 4.5-hour drive back to **Charleston.** On the way, stop at the **Country Club Bakery** in Fairmont for a pepperoni roll, a West Virginia original.

DOWNTOWN CHARLESTON

# *Major* CITIES

**CHARLESTON:** Featuring a gilded dome, the Cass Gilbert-designed capitol building sets the stage for the state capital's historic downtown area lined with restaurants and shops set in brick buildings.

**HUNTINGTON:** Located in western West Virginia just across the Ohio River from Ohio and a few miles east of the Kentucky state line, this former steamboat port has a lively downtown riverfront area centered around Pullman Square.

**MORGANTOWN:** Home to West Virginia University, Morgantown is located in northern West Virginia, south of the Pennsylvania border, on the banks of the Mon (Monongahela) River.

## BERKELEY SPRINGS STATE PARK

2 S. Washington St., Berkeley Springs; 304/258-2711; https://wvstateparks.com/park/berkeley-springs-state-park

The warm natural spring waters flowing in this state park have drawn visitors here since the birth of the United States, and even prior, with bathers that included George Washington. Today visitors to this patch of northern West Virginia near the Maryland border can see a re-creation of Washington's tub and partake of the waters and other spa services at the Main Bathhouse. The surrounding town of Berkeley Springs takes water quite seriously, hosting a water-tasting festival every June.

## THE GREENBRIER

101 Main St. W., White Sulphur Springs; www.greenbrier.com

First opened in 1778, this historic resort in southeast West Virginia has hosted U.S. presidents, politicians, professional sports figures, and others who came for the natural spring waters, luxury accommodations, and well-appointed grounds. During the Civil War, it was used by both Union and Confederate forces, and during World War II, diplomats from Axis nations were sequestered here in advance of being sent back to their home countries. Today, the property sprawls over 11,000 acres (4,452 hectares) with 582 rooms in its gleaming white main building, five golf courses, a casino, and a spa with the mineral-rich waters that were The Greenbrier's original draw.

# BEST SCENIC DRIVES

## MIDLAND TRAIL

U.S. 60; 866/ROUTE60; www.midlandtrail.com

Starting in the state capital, **Charleston,** this National Scenic Byway winds 117 miles (188 kilometers) through central and southeast West Virginia. It passes through small towns and natural areas, including **Malden,** the birthplace of Booker T. Washington; **Hawks Nest State Park** (49 Hawks Nest Park Rd., Ansted; 304/658-5212; https://wvstateparks.com/park/hawks-nest-state-park), with an aerial tramway descending into its deep canyon; and **Lewisburg,** a small town that draws weekenders. The route ends in the Greenbrier Valley, at **White Sulphur Springs,** home of the historic Greenbrier resort.

## MOTHER'S DAY

Grafton, a tiny town in northern West Virginia, is the birthplace of Mother's Day, first celebrated here in 1908. This claim to fame is commemorated in the **International Mother's Day Shrine** (11 E. Main St.; 304/265-1589) in an old church.

SPRUCE KNOB

## HIGHLAND SCENIC HIGHWAY

This 43-mile (69-kilometer) drive through **Monongahela National Forest** and **Allegheny Highlands** starts in **Richwood**, the purported "ramp (wild spring onions) capital of the world." It follows Routes 39/55 east, and then turns onto Route 150 near the **Cranberry Glades Botanical Area,** where you can stop to see bogs and their unique flora, such as carnivorous plants. The scenic highway ends when Route 150 meets U.S. 219. Avoid driving this route in winter, when the roads are not maintained.

# BEST PARKS AND RECREATION AREAS

## SPRUCE KNOB

Monongahela National Forest

Located in Monongahela National Forest, near Seneca Rocks, this 4,863-foot (1,482-meter) peak is the highest point in the state. There is an observation tower and parking lot at the top, and there are hiking trails and two campgrounds in the area.

## BLACKWATER FALLS STATE PARK

1584 Blackwater Lodge Rd., Davis; 304/259-5216; https://wvstateparks.com/park/blackwater-falls-state-park

Voted Best State Park several times by *WV Living* magazine, Blackwater Falls State Park offers hiking, biking, camping, and paddling, but its best attraction might be the 0.25-mile (0.4-kilometer) winter sled run and the Magic Carpet conveyer belt that takes sledders to the top of the run. There are several overlooks to see the falls themselves—the easiest is the on the 0.25-mile (0.4-kilometer) Gentle Trail, but those able to climb down and back up 200 stairs can get to the main viewing platform on the Boardwalk Trail.

# FESTIVALS AND EVENTS

## GEORGE WASHINGTON'S BATHTUB CELEBRATION

Berkeley Springs State Park; https://berkeleysprings.com/festivals/george-washingtons-bathtub-celebration; Mar.

This one-of-a-kind festival in March celebrates the outdoor tub said to have been used by George Washington during his visits to what is now Berkeley Springs State Park. The whole town of Berkeley Springs devotes itself to discounted items, themed foods, and

Find made-in-West Virginia items at **WV Marketplace** inside Charleston's **Capitol Market** (800 Smith St., Charleston; https://capitolmarket.net), which also hosts an outdoor farmers market with an all-West Virginia vendor lineup.

other specials over the three days of this festival.

## BRIDGE DAY

New River Gorge Bridge, U.S. 19; https://officialbridgeday.com; Oct.

Every third weekend in October since 1980, some sort of event involving daredevils jumping onto or from the New River Gorge Bridge has taken place. Today, the main event is watching BASE jumpers leaping off the bridge, but other activities, many of which involve registering beforehand, include a Bridge Walk along the catwalk, zip-lining from the catwalk, a 5K run starting on the bridge, and a chili cookoff.

# BEST FOOD

## PEPPERONI ROLLS

A pepperoni sausage (sliced or whole) baked into a white-bread bun is the basis for this West Virginia food, created as an easy-to-eat lunch for coal miners. The inventor, Giuseppe Argiro, was a coal miner himself until he opened **Country Club Bakery** (1211 Country Club Rd., Fairmont; 304/363-5690; www.countryclubbakery.net), which is still in business in northern West Virginia. If you can't make it to the bakery, you can order online and have a dozen (or three) to be shipped to you within the United States.

## GOLDEN DELICIOUS APPLES

The Golden Delicious apple, which originated in West Virginia, became the state fruit in 1905, and they taste the best here, of course. Find them in all manner of baked goods, or just bite into one in the way nature intended.

# MAJOR AIRPORTS

- **Yeager Airport:** CRW; 100 Airport Rd., Charleston; 304/344-8033; https://yeagerairport.com

# MORE INFORMATION

## TRAVEL AND TOURISM INFORMATION

- **West Virginia Tourism:** https://wvtourism.com
- **West Virginia State Parks and Forests:** https://wvstateparks.com

## MAGAZINES

- *WV Living:* https://wvliving.com

BRIDGE DAY

# DELAWARE

Delaware, on Nanticoke and Lenni-Lenape land, was the first state to ratify the U.S. Constitution, and thereby became the first state in the Union. In 2021, the first U.S. president from Delaware, Joseph R. Biden Jr., was inaugurated. (Yes, it's true that Biden was born in Scranton, Pennsylvania, but he served as a U.S. senator from Delaware for 36 years and is affiliated with the state politically.) Between those two historic events, the state struggled with divisions over enslavement—its location below the Mason-Dixon line meant that enslavement was allowed in Delaware, but many of its citizens supported abolition—saw the rise of the du Pont family and eponymous company in wealth and industry, and established itself as a corporation-friendly state, where the majority of Fortune 500 companies are incorporated.

Travelers can see this history throughout Delaware, from the red-brick buildings of the state capital, Dover, to the lavish properties built by generations of du Ponts. But Delaware is also a beach getaway, with its stretch of Atlantic coast leading toward Maryland.

**AREA:** 2,489 square miles / 6,446 square kilometers (49th)

**POPULATION:** 973,764 (45th)

**STATEHOOD DATE:** December 7, 1787 (1st)

**STATE CAPITAL:** Dover

▲ CAPE HENLOPEN STATE PARK

## ORIENTATION

Delaware shares the Delmarva Peninsula with Maryland and a semicircular northern boundary with Pennsylvania. The Delaware River, Delaware Bay, and Atlantic Ocean form its eastern border. **Wilmington** sits in the northern part of the state with the **Brandywine Valley** spreading north from the city. **Dover** is located near the center of the state, with **Atlantic beaches** lining the southeastern coast.

## WHEN TO GO

**Summer** is the **high season,** especially if your plans involve some beach time. **Late spring** (May and June) and **fall** (Sept. and Oct.) are good seasons to visit Delaware, with cooler temperatures. Some businesses, especially at the beach, close or have shorter hours for the **winter** season.

# HIGHLIGHTS

## DELAWARE HISTORICAL SOCIETY MUSEUMS

504 N. Market St., Wilmington; 302/655-7161; https://dehistory.org

Two museums of the Delaware Historical Society shed light on the history of the state. The **Delaware History Museum** tells the story of the state through permanent and temporary exhibits around themes such as immigration, agriculture, and industry. A sight on the Harriet Tubman Underground Railroad Byway, the **Jane and Littleton Mitchell Center for African American Heritage** focuses on the Black experience in Delaware, including the state's role in the era of enslavement (Delaware was below the Mason-Dixon line, and therefore, not a free state) and the Civil Rights Movement.

## NEMOURS MANSION & GARDENS

Rte. 141 and Alapocas Rd., Wilmington; 302/651-6912; www.nemoursmansion.org

Another great-grandson of DuPont founder E. I. du Pont, Alfred I. du Pont (1864-1935) built Nemours to please his second wife, a Francophile who also happened to be his cousin. The spectacular Louis XVI-style mansion and gardens, which are one of the finest examples of a formal French garden outside France, are modeled after those at Versailles's Petit Trianon.

## REHOBOTH BEACH BOARDWALK

Rehoboth Beach lies at the north end of Delaware's Atlantic beaches. Its mile-long boardwalk offers all the action you could want at the beach, including terrific views of the ocean, french fries, T-shirt shops, games, candy stores, and entertainment. The boardwalk is wide

NEMOURS MANSION & GARDENS

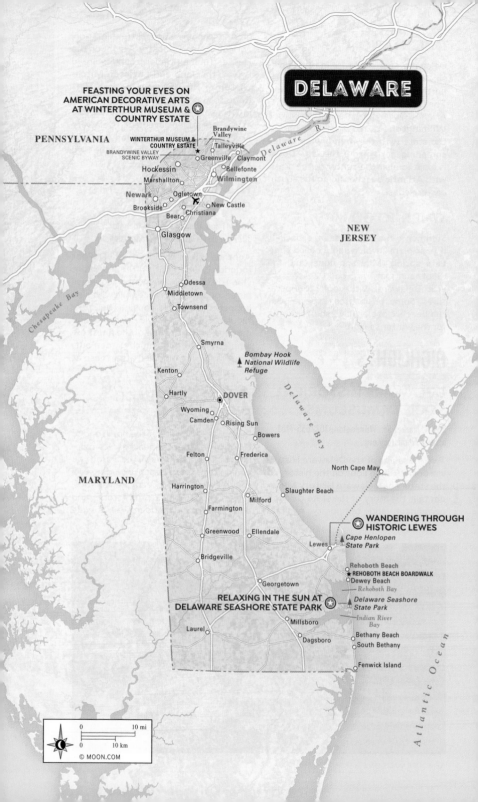

## *Major* CITIES

**WILMINGTON:** Set on the banks of the Delaware River with the Christina River and Brandywine Creek running through it, Wilmington is Delaware's largest city and the city of incorporation for half of all Fortune 500 companies.

**DOVER:** With its red-brick museums and government buildings, the state capital has an air of history to it. It's also home to Dover International Speedway, a NASCAR track that also hosts the annual Firefly Music Festival.

**NEWARK:** Not to be confused with the city in New Jersey, Newark, Delaware, is the home of the University of Delaware.

and clean and stretches from Penn Street at the south end to Virginia Avenue at the north end.

# BEST SCENIC DRIVES

## BRANDYWINE VALLEY SCENIC BYWAY

This short drive through the Brandywine Valley showcases the area that fueled the DuPont gunpowder company (today a chemical company) and the wealth of the du Pont family. As it winds its way from southeastern Pennsylvania to the northern Delaware city of Wilmington, Brandywine Creek crosses what geologists refer to as a fall line. In layman's terms, it takes a nosedive. That nosedive made the Brandywine Valley attractive to water-powered industries—flour mills, cotton mills, and the like—in days of yore. In 1802 a French immigrant by the name of Eleuthère Irénée (E. I.) du Pont began construction of a gunpowder works along the creek, often referred to as the Brandywine River. It wasn't long before his company was the nation's largest gunpowder producer, and the du Ponts grew wildly wealthy. The Brandywine Valley's present popularity as a tourist destination has much to do with their wealth, and this drive leads to one of the signature du Pont mansions, **Winterthur.** From **Wilmington,** take Highway 52 (Kennett Pike) northwest out of the city and, after a couple of miles, get onto Highway 100 (Montchanin Rd.). It's about 5 miles (8 kilometers) to the Pennsylvania state line, but you'll reach Winterthur before you get there. If you're not stopping at the estate, make a left on either Center Meeting Road or Twaddell Mill Road to take Highway 52 (Kennett Pike) 7.3 miles (11.7 kilometers) back to Wilmington.

# BEST PARKS AND RECREATION AREAS

## BOMBAY HOOK NATIONAL WILDLIFE REFUGE

2591 Whitehall Neck Rd., Smyrna; 302/653-6872; www.fws.gov/refuge/bombay_hook

Located on the coast of Delaware Bay, Bombay Hook National Wildlife Refuge is a tidal salt marsh that attracts a wide variety of birdlife, including migrating waterfowl, shorebirds lured by newly laid horseshoe crab eggs, black-necked stilts, herons, ibis, yellow warblers, and

GREAT BLUE HERON, BOMBAY HOOK NATIONAL WILDLIFE REFUGE

# TOP 3

## 1. RELAXING IN THE SUN AT DELAWARE SEASHORE STATE PARK

DE 1 between Bethany Beach and Dewey Beach; 302/227-2800; www.destateparks.com

Located between Rehoboth Beach and Bethany Beach, Delaware Seashore State Park covers a thin strip of land between the Atlantic and Rehoboth Bay. The primary attraction in the park is the beach itself—a 6-mile-long (10-kilometer-long) beach lover's paradise—where visitors can swim and relax along the shore. There are modern bathhouses with showers and changing rooms, and lifeguards are on duty during the day in summer. There are also snack vendors and beach equipment

DELAWARE SEASHORE STATE PARK

rentals such as chairs, rafts, and umbrellas. Fishing is popular in the park and can be done in the surf in designated locations or from the banks of the Indian River Inlet. There is also a special-access pier for the elderly or people with disabilities.

## 2. WANDERING THROUGH HISTORIC LEWES

The town of Lewes is on the Harbor of Refuge, just a short distance from the Atlantic. Its historic downtown is one of the prettiest spots on the mid-Atlantic coast, with historic homes (some dating back to the 17th century), a friendly atmosphere, and tidy, well-kept streets. The town's main thoroughfare, 2nd Street, offers wonderful dining and shopping with a cozy, friendly feel.

**Shipcarpenter Square** (www.shipcarpentersquare. com), bounded by 3rd and 4th

HISTORIC LEWES

Streets and Burton and Park Streets, is a community of delicately and accurately preserved and restored 18th- and 19th-century homes in the historic district. The homes in Shipcarpenter Square are mostly colonial farmhouses built in the late 1700s-late 1800s in other parts of Sussex County and moved to the site in the early 1980s. Other relocated buildings include three barns, a schoolhouse, an inn, a log home, a lifesaving station, a lighthouse, a market, and two Victorian houses.

THE CHINESE PAVILION AT THE WINTERTHUR MUSEUM & COUNTRY ESTATE

## **3** FEASTING YOUR EYES ON AMERICAN DECORATIVE ARTS AT WINTERTHUR MUSEUM & COUNTRY ESTATE

5105 Kennett Pike, Winterthur; 302/888-4600; www.winterthur.org

This estate of the du Pont family (of gunpowder company-turned-chemical company fame) is home to a vast collection of Americana and a splendid naturalistic garden. E. I. du Pont, the founder of DuPont, which made his family one of the wealthiest in America, purchased the land that would become Winterthur (pronounced "winter-tour") in the 1810s. But it wasn't until his great-grandson Henry Francis du Pont (1880-1969) got his hands on the property a century later that it evolved into the extraordinary estate it is today.

Henry doubled the size of the existing mansion and filled the rooms with his burgeoning collection of American decorative arts. By the time the mansion opened as a museum in 1951, he had created 175 period rooms. First Lady Jacqueline Kennedy was so wowed during a 1961 visit that she invited Henry to head the committee overseeing the restoration of the White House. General admission includes an introductory tour of the mansion, admittance to galleries displaying highlights from Winterthur's collection of more than 85,000 objects made or used in America from 1640 to 1860, and free rein of the Winterthur Garden.

# *Best* ROAD TRIP

**DAY 1** Start your trip in Wilmington, visiting **Delaware Historical Society** museums in the morning. In the afternoon, hop in the car for a drive through the **Brandywine Valley.** Even if you don't stop at the extravagant **Winterthur Museum & Country Estate,** the landscape is worth the short jaunt.

**DAY 2** Today, you're headed to the beach—the Atlantic Coast is about 1.5 hours south of Wilmington. On the way, stop at **Bombay Hook National Wildlife Refuge** for some bird-watching. Check into your accommodations in **Rehoboth Beach,** and then hit Rehoboth's **beach** and its **boardwalk** in the afternoon—pick up some beach food to snack on while you lounge.

**DAY 3** Head to **Lewes,** just 8 miles (13 kilometers) north, to stroll its cute historic downtown. Get in some more beach time or a hike at **Cape Henlopen State Park** before heading back up to Wilmington.

EXHIBIT AT THE WINTERTHUR MUSEUM & COUNTRY ESTATE

REHOBOTH BEACH AND BOARDWALK

BOMBAY HOOK NATIONAL WILDLIFE REFUGE

CAPE HENLOPEN STATE PARK

REHOBOTH BEACH

more. Open to cars, bikes, and pedestrians, the 12-mile (19-kilometers) Wildlife Drive weaves through a small portion of the protected area in the northeast corner.

## REHOBOTH BEACH

This beautiful strand of white sandy beach on the Atlantic is the attraction that made the town of the same name become known as "the Nation's Summer Capital," since so many visitors come from Washington DC each year.

## CAPE HENLOPEN STATE PARK

15099 Cape Henlopen Dr., Lewes; 302/645-8983; www.destateparks.com

This state park covers 5 miles (8 kilometers) of shoreline at the mouth of Delaware Bay where it meets the Atlantic. A military base was established at the cape in 1941, and bunkers were hidden among the dunes for protection. Observation towers built of cement, which are still standing, were also put in place along the shore to search for enemy ships. Today, the park provides many acres of seaside habitat and two swimming beaches. There's a nature center, hiking, fishing, a picnic pavilion, fishing pier, and camping in the park.

# FESTIVALS AND EVENTS

## FIREFLY MUSIC FESTIVAL

The Woodlands at Dover International Speedway, 1131 N. Dupont Hwy., Dover; https://fireflyfestival.com; June

Fans of popular rock music camp out at this annual festival that's usually held over three days in June at The Woodlands, part of the Dover International Speedway.

# BEST FOOD AND DRINK

## SEAFOOD

As with many seaside locales, the food in Delaware tends toward the marine. A good place to try it is **Off the Hook** (769 Garfield Pkwy., Bethany Beach; 302/829-1424; https://offthehookrestaurantgroup.com), which

THRASHER'S FRENCH FRIES, REHOBOTH BEACH

prides itself on supporting local farmers and anglers.

## CLASSIC BEACH FOOD IN REHOBOTH BEACH

Beach days are made for snacking, and Rehoboth Beach offers a nice array of goodies.

- **Fisher's Popcorn** (48 Rehoboth Ave., Rehoboth Beach; 302/227-2691; www.fishers-popcorn.com) is a staple on Maryland and Delaware beaches. You can buy the addicting little morsels by the bucket (0.5-6.5 gallons). Please note: It is easy to eat this until you feel sick. Stopping is hard to do. You've been warned.

- Local icon **Thrasher's French Fries** (26 Rehoboth Ave., Rehoboth Beach; 302/227-7366) serves up buckets of fresh fries from the walk-up window on the boardwalk. Even die-hard ketchup lovers will want to try them with salt and vinegar.

- **Kaisy's Delights** (70 Rehoboth Ave., Rehoboth Beach; 302/212-5360; www.kaisysdelights.com) offers delicious samples that may lure you into an Austrian Kaisy (actually *Kaiserschmarrn*, a treat made of sweet custardy dough with your choice of toppings such as ice cream or fruit sauce).

# MAJOR AIRPORTS

- **Wilmington/Philadelphia (New Castle) Airport:** ILG; 151 N. Dupont Hwy., New Castle; 855/FLY-ILG5; https://flyilg.com

# MORE INFORMATION

## TRAVEL AND TOURISM INFORMATION

- **Visit Delaware:** www.visitdelaware.com
- **Delaware State Parks:** www.destateparks.com

## NEWSPAPERS

- *The News Journal:* www.delawareonline.com

# MARYLAND

On Lenape, Nanticoke, Powhatan, Shawnee, Susquehannock, Tutelo, and Saponi land, Maryland has long been both witness and participant in the nation's most historic moments. Tread the hallowed ground at Antietam, the bloodiest battlefield of the Civil War, or see where abolitionist leader Frederick Douglass lived and worked. But there's also always something new to discover.

**AREA:** 12,407 square miles / 32,133 square kilometers (42nd)

**POPULATION:** 6,045,680 (19th)

**STATEHOOD DATE:** April 28, 1788 (7th)

**STATE CAPITAL:** Annapolis

Don't overlook the port city of Baltimore, whose Inner Harbor offers a slew of appealing sights. The state capital Annapolis boasts an enchanting historic district, trendy boutiques and taverns, a busy harbor, and the U.S. Naval Academy—not to mention an endless supply of blue crabs, oysters, and other delectable seafood. Not far from these thriving metropolitan areas, you'll find quaint fishing villages, sleepy mountain towns, Chesapeake Bay, and an abundance of natural beauty.

▲ CHESAPEAKE BAY

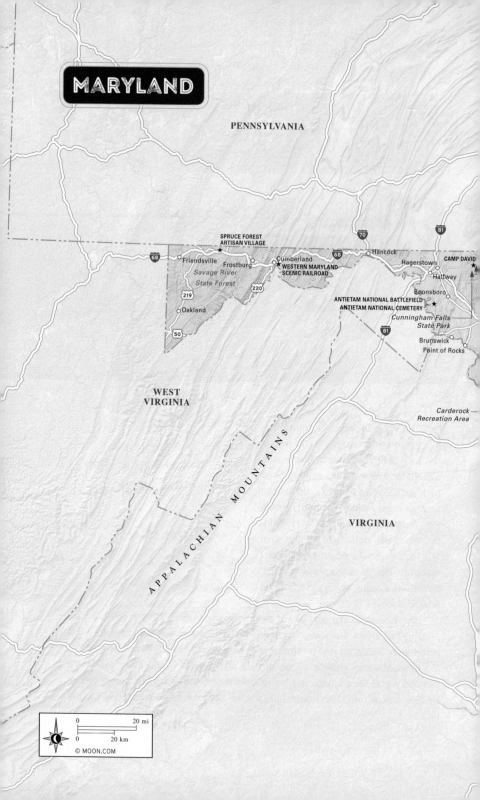

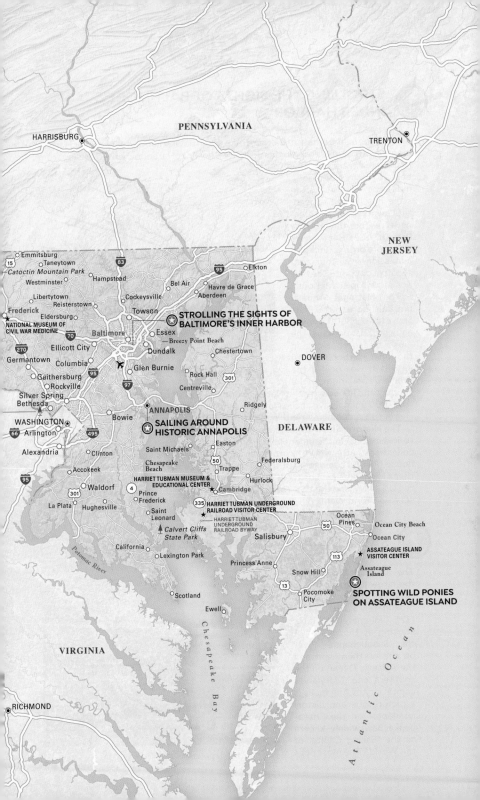

PENNSYLVANIA

HARRISBURG

TRENTON

NEW
JERSEY

Emmitsburg
Taneytown
15
*Catoctin Mountain Park*
83
Westminster
Hampstead
Libertytown
Reisterstown
Cockeysville
Frederick
Eldersburg
Bel Air
Elkton
95
★ Havre de Grace
NATIONAL MUSEUM OF
Towson
Aberdeen
CIVIL WAR MEDICINE
70
Baltimore
**STROLLING THE SIGHTS OF
BALTIMORE'S INNER HARBOR**
Ellicott City
Essex
DOVER
270
Breezy Point Beach
Germantown
Columbia
Dundalk
Chestertown
Gaithersburg
95
Glen Burnie
Rockville
97
Rock Hall
301
Silver Spring
Centreville
Bethesda
ANNAPOLIS
Ridgely
WASHINGTON
Bowie
**SAILING AROUND
HISTORIC ANNAPOLIS**
DELAWARE
66
Arlington
Saint Michaels
Easton
Alexandria
Clinton
Chesapeake
Federalsburg
Beach
50
Accokeek
Trappe
95
HARRIET TUBMAN MUSEUM &
Hurlock
EDUCATIONAL CENTER
Waldorf
4
★ Cambridge
301
Prince
Frederick
335 **HARRIET TUBMAN UNDERGROUND
RAILROAD VISITOR CENTER**
Ocean
La Plata
Saint
Pines
Hughesville
Leonard
HARRIET TUBMAN
50
UNDERGROUND
Ocean City Beach
RAILROAD BYWAY
Salisbury
▲ Calvert Cliffs
Ocean City
*State Park*
California
113
**ASSATEAGUE ISLAND
VISITOR CENTER**
Lexington Park
Princess Anne
Assateague
Island
Snow Hill
13
Scotland
**SPOTTING WILD PONIES
ON ASSATEAGUE ISLAND**
Pocomoke
City
Ewell

VIRGINIA

*Potomac River*

*Chesapeake Bay*

*Atlantic Ocean*

RICHMOND

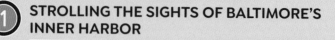

# TOP 3

## 1 STROLLING THE SIGHTS OF BALTIMORE'S INNER HARBOR

Most of the beauty shots of Baltimore are taken downtown and at the Inner Harbor, long the center of activity in this port city. The Inner Harbor benefited greatly from rejuvenation and became home to many attractions, museums, restaurants, upscale hotels, and a beautiful **waterfront promenade.** A four-day **Harbor Pass** (877/225-8466; www.baltimore.org) includes admission over four consecutive days into the harbor's four top attractions.

USS CONSTELLATION

The **National Aquarium, Baltimore** (501 E. Pratt St.; 410/576-3800; www.aqua.org) is perhaps the most treasured sight in the Inner Harbor. Opened in 1981, it was one of the first large aquariums in the country and joined with the National Aquarium in Washington, DC, in 2003. Close to 20,000 animals live at the National Aquarium, representing more than 660 species of fish, amphibians, reptiles, birds, and mammals in expertly designed habitats.

The **Historic Ships** (Inner Harbor Piers; 301 E. Pratt St.; 410/539-1797; www.historicships.org) in the Inner Harbor form one of the most impressive military ship collections in the world. Visitors can not only see four ships and the **Knoll Lighthouse** (Pier 5), but also 50,000 photographs, documents, and items that relate to them. Highlights include the **USS *Constellation*** (Pier 1), the last all-sail ship built by the U.S. Navy, and the **USS *Torsk*** (Pier 3), one of just 10 Tench Class submarines to serve in World War II.

## 2 SAILING AROUND HISTORIC ANNAPOLIS

The **Chesapeake Bay** is the largest estuary in the country. The bay is approximately 200 miles (321 kilometers) long, starting at the mouth of the Susquehanna River on the northern end and the Atlantic Ocean on the southern end. Maryland's capital city of Annapolis is a picturesque and historic seaport on the Chesapeake Bay, widely known as the "Sailing Capital of the World." The most pop-

WATERFRONT IN DOWNTOWN ANNAPOLIS

ular neighborhood for visitors is the Historic Downtown, where the scenic waterfront and **City Dock** (Dock Street) are located. Annapolis boasts more 18th-century buildings than any other American city, and many of these charming structures line the dock area, as well as locally owned shops, boutiques, souvenir stands, and waterfront restaurants beckoning visitors.

Heading northwest away from the dock, the **Maryland State House** (100 State Circle; 410/260-6445; www.msa.maryland.gov) is the oldest legislative house in the country that has been in continual use. Downtown you'll also find St. John's College (60 College Ave.; 410/263-2371; www.sjc.edu), on 32 scenic acres adorned with stately brick buildings, tree-lined paths, and sprawling lawns; **St. Anne's Episcopal Church** (1 Church Circle; 410/267-9333; www.stannes-annapolis.org), the first church in Annapolis; and **Hammond-Harwood House** (19 Maryland Ave.; 410/263-4683; www.hammondharwoodhouse.org), the best historic home to visit if you only have time for one.

Directly northeast of downtown, guided walking tours of the more than 300-acre (121-hectare) **U.S. Naval Academy** (121 Blake Rd.; 410/293-1000; www.usna.edu) provide a close-up look at the imposing marble buildings and monuments on campus, and cover topics such as history, architecture, traditions, and life as a midshipman. If you want to get out on the water yourself, 2-hour sailing cruises can be booked on two beautiful, 74-foot (22-meter) wooden schooners through **Schooner Woodwind Annapolis Sailing Cruises** (410/263-7837; www.schoonerwoodwind.com).

# SPOTTING WILD PONIES ON ASSATEAGUE ISLAND

Assateague Island National Seashore (www.nps.gov/asis) is a quiet place to calm your spirits, view wildlife, kayak, swim, fish, and bike, with a beautiful 37-mile (59-kilometer) beach, dunes, wetlands, and marsh. Protected as a natural environment, the island is a stopover for migrating shorebirds; more than 320 bird species can be viewed here during the year, including the piping plovers, great egrets, and northern harriers.

Assateague Island is also known for its wild ponies. It is widely believed that the ponies originally came to the island years ago when a Spanish cargo ship loaded with horses sank off the coast and the ponies swam to shore. In 1997, a Spanish shipwreck was discovered off the island, which supports this theory. The famous **Wild Pony Swim** (www.chincoteaguechamber.com) takes place each year in late July, when the herd is taken for a swim from Assateague Island across the channel to Chincoteague Island in Virginia.

Other mammals in Assateague include rodents as small as the meadow

WILD PONIES ON ASSATEAGUE ISLAND

jumping mouse, along with red fox, river otters, and deer. Several species of whales feed off the island's shore, along with bottlenose dolphins. The **Assateague Island Visitor Center** (Maryland District of Assateague Island, on the southern side of Route 611; 410/641-1441) offers a film on the wild ponies, brochures, aquariums, a touch tank, maps, and other exhibits.

# *Best* ROAD TRIP

**DAY 1** Start in Baltimore and spend the day learning more about Maryland's history at sites including **Frederick Douglass-Isaac Myers Maritime Park** and **Fort McHenry National Monument and Historic Shrine.** Finish the day walking the waterfront promenade of the **Inner Harbor.**

**DAY 2** Make the 1.5-hour drive west to **Antietam National Battlefield,** the site of the bloodiest single-day battle in U.S. history. The serene, rolling landscape invites quiet reflection. Afterward, head into nearby **Frederick,** where you can learn more Civil War history at the **National Museum of Civil War Medicine.** The town's historic district is a popular destination for antique hunters. Spend the night in Frederick.

**DAY 3** For a taste of DC without going into DC, head to Maryland's Capital Region, an hour away. With an early start, you can hike a section of the popular **Billy Goat Trail** along the Potomac. Keep heading east for another hour to reach **Chesapeake Beach,** a great place to try **blue crab.** Finish the day in **Annapolis,** another 45-minute drive north. Squeeze in a stroll of the downtown **City Dock** or a **cruise** around the bay before turning in for the evening.

**DAY 4** In the morning, see some more Annapolis sights, such as the **Maryland Statehouse,** the oldest continuously used legislative house in the country. Then drive 2 hours east to **Assateague Island,** where if you're lucky, you can spot wild ponies. After enjoying the seashore, head up to **Ocean City** for its boardwalk, beach, and theme parks.

CANNON DEMONSTRATION AT FORT MCHENRY

ANTIETAM NATIONAL BATTLEFIELD

HISTORIC SCHOOLHOUSE ON THE HARRIET TUBMAN UNDERGROUND RAILROAD BYWAY

**DAY 5** Head back across to the Eastern Shore to **Cambridge,** where you can start an exploration of the **Harriet Tubman Underground Railroad Byway** at the **Harriet Tubman Museum & Educational Center.** Make your way to some of the byway's 30-odd sights before heading across the bay toward Annapolis and back to Baltimore.

ANNAPOLIS HARBOR

OCEAN CITY BOARDWALK

## ORIENTATION

**Baltimore** sits on the northwestern end of **Chesapeake Bay,** the body of water that pierces into the eastern Maryland and divides the **Eastern Shore** from the rest of the state. **Frederic**k and **Antietam** lie to the west of Baltimore, while **western Maryland** is even farther west, past the crimp in the state where the Potomac River, which forms its southern boundary, veers north.

## WHEN TO GO

Late **spring** (May and June) and **fall** (Sept. and Oct.) are usually the best times to explore Maryland. The weather is most pleasant, and there are fewer tourists. Although **summer** is the prime tourist season, unless your plans involve some beach time or a stay in a mountain retreat, the humidity can be a bit overwhelming. If your focus is on historical sites and museums, the **winter** months (with the exception of the holiday season) can mean lighter crowds, though some sites may be closed or have shorter hours.

# HIGHLIGHTS

### FREDERICK DOUGLASS-ISAAC MYERS MARITIME PARK

1417 Thames St., Baltimore; 410/685-0295; https://livingclassrooms.org/programs/frederick-douglass-isaac-myers-maritime-park

The Frederick Douglass-Isaac Myers Maritime Park is a national heritage site/museum dedicated to African American maritime history. The site encompasses 5,000 square feet (464 square meters) of gallery space and features interactive exhibits, maps, photos, and artifacts that share the history of the African American community and how it influenced Baltimore in the 1800s. A series of exhibits chronicle the lives of Frederick Douglass and Isaac Myers. Douglass, who had been born enslaved, became a leader in the abolitionist movement and a successful statesman and orator. He lived and worked on the docks in Baltimore. Myers was a mason and labor leader who

# *Major* CITIES

**BALTIMORE:** A major port city since the 1700s, hardworking "Charm City" boasts world-class museums, fine dining, fierce spirit, and authenticity.

**FREDERICK:** Founded by German settlers in 1745, Frederick was an important crossroads during the Civil War, and today offers a lovely collection of shops, galleries, restaurants, and antique stores.

**ANNAPOLIS:** Maryland's quaint and historic state capital has a vibrant waterfront with many shops and restaurants, and is home to the U.S. Naval Academy.

created a first-of-its-kind union for African American caulkers just after the Civil War.

For more on the contributions of African Americans in Maryland throughout the state's history, visit the **Reginald F. Lewis Museum of Maryland African American History & Culture** (830 E. Pratt St., Baltimore; 443/263-1800; https://lewismuseum.org). Visitors can learn about the contributions of African Americans in Maryland throughout the state's history. The museum includes galleries, a genealogy center, recording studio, theater, café, and gift shop.

## FORT MCHENRY NATIONAL MONUMENT AND HISTORIC SHRINE

2400 E. Fort Ave., Baltimore; 410/962-4290; www.nps.gov/fomc

The Fort McHenry National Monument and Historic Shrine is a 43-acre

FORT MCHENRY NATIONAL MONUMENT AND HISTORIC SHRINE

(17-hectare) national park that houses Fort McHenry, known as the inspiration for the "Star-Spangled Banner." Francis Scott Key wrote the words to the anthem during the War of 1812 when he was held on a truce ship during the British attack on Baltimore. Key watched as the battle went on, and at "dawn's early light" on September 14, 1814, he could see the huge 30x42-foot (9x12-meter) U.S. flag still flying above Fort McHenry as a symbol that Baltimore had not surrendered.

You can also visit the **Star-Spangled Banner Flag House and Museum** (844 E. Pratt St., Baltimore; 410/837-1793; www.flaghouse.org) the home of Mary Pickersgill, the woman who made the enormous and famous flag that flew over Fort McHenry.

## NATIONAL MUSEUM OF CIVIL WAR MEDICINE

48 E. Patrick St., Frederick; 301/695-1864; www.civilwarmed.org

The National Museum of Civil War Medicine is tucked away on Patrick Street in the historic area of Frederick, Maryland. This interesting little museum started as a private collection. Exhibits cover many little-known facts about medicine and disease during the war (such as two-thirds of the 620,000 soldiers who died during the war succumbed to disease, not wounds, and doctors at the time had no knowledge of antiseptic practices or germ theory). It even explains the process used to embalm dead soldiers on the battlefield so they could be transported home.

WESTERN MARYLAND SCENIC RAILROAD

## ANTIETAM NATIONAL BATTLEFIELD

5831 Dunker Church Rd., Sharpsburg; 301/432-5124; www.nps.gov/anti

Antietam National Battlefield encompasses more than 3,200 acres (1,295 hectares) in the foothills of the Appalachian Mountains. On September 17, 1862, the Battle of Antietam was fought here. It was the first Civil War battle held on Union ground and was also the bloodiest battle ever to take place in a single day in U.S. history, with approximately 23,000 casualties. The day ended in a draw, but the Union Army checked the Confederates of any advancement into Northern territory. This tactical victory spurred Abraham Lincoln to issue the Emancipation Proclamation.

Near the battlefield is the **Antietam National Cemetery** (E. Main St., Sharpsburg; www.nps.gov/anti). After the battle, soldiers who died during the fight were buried by the hundreds in shallow graves extending miles in all directions. After the war, an effort was made to relocate the bodies to proper cemeteries, and the Antietam National Cemetery was formed.

## OCEAN CITY

Ocean City, stretching for 10 miles (16 kilometers) along the Atlantic Ocean between Delaware and the Ocean City Inlet, offers enough stimulation to keep kids of all ages entertained for days. The 3-mile (4.8-kilometer) wooden **boardwalk** is packed with shopping, restaurants, games, and amusements and is open all year. Seemingly every inch of real estate is claimed along the strip, a major East Coast destination for people who enjoy the beach, company, and entertainment.

**Ocean City Beach** is the main focus of Ocean City. It's wide and sandy, with brightly colored umbrellas lined up like soldiers. Outside of the beach and boardwalk, visit quirky attractions like the **Ocean City Life-Saving Station Museum** (813 S. Atlantic Ave.; 410/289-4991; www.ocmuseum.org), amusement park **Trimper's Rides** (S. 1st St. and the Boardwalk; 410/289-8617; www.trimpersrides.com) and **Jolly Roger at the Pier** (at the pier at the south end of the Boardwalk; 410/289-3031; www.jollyrogerpieroc.com).

## WESTERN MARYLAND SCENIC RAILROAD

13 Canal St., Cumberland; 301/759-4400; www.wmsr.com

Many historic railroad milestones occurred in the Cumberland area, including the use of the first iron rail made in the U.S. and the production of unique steam engines by the Cumberland & Pennsylvania Railroad. This fun 3.5-hour, 32-mile (51-kilometer) round-trip excursion from downtown Cumberland to nearby Frostburg is made by diesel locomotive on tracks that used to belong to the Western Maryland Railway. It's an entertaining and educational ride through a scenic Appalachian landscape. The train passes through the Narrows, a cut in the mountains that was considered at one time to be the gateway to the West.

# BEST SCENIC DRIVES

## HARRIET TUBMAN UNDERGROUND RAILROAD BYWAY

https://harriettubmanbyway.org

The Harriet Tubman Underground Railroad Byway is a scenic, self-guided driving route with more than 30 sites related to Harriet Tubman, the freedom fighter and former enslaved person who was known for leading many people to freedom through the Underground Railroad, and other African Americans seeking freedom in the 1800s. Among the stops, which start in Dorchester County where Tubman was born and head north through the Eastern Shore into Delaware and Pennsylvania, is the **Harriet Tubman Museum & Educational Center** (424 Race St., Cambridge; 410/228-0401; www.visit-dorchester.org). This small museum is dedicated to telling stories of Tubman's life and features exhibits on her work. Another stop is the **Harriet Tubman Underground Railroad Visitor Center** (4068 Golden Hill Rd., Church Creek; 410/221-2290; www.nps.gov/hatu), located 11 miles (17 kilometers) south of the museum. Run jointly by the National Park Service and the Maryland State Park Service, the visitor center showcases exhibits about Tubman and

provides information about surrounding attractions.

# BEST PARKS AND RECREATION AREAS

## CUNNINGHAM FALLS STATE PARK

14039 Catoctin Hollow Rd., Thurmont; 301/271-7574; www.dnr.maryland.gov

Located north of Frederick, this wonderful, 6,000-acre (2,428-hectare) park sits on Catoctin Mountain and offers swimming, hiking, a 43-acre (17-hectare) lake, fishing, canoeing, and a remarkable 78-foot (23-meter) waterfall. The park is made up of two primary areas. The Manor Area off U.S. 15 (3 miles/4.8 kilometers south of Thurmont) includes an aviary, camping, and the historic **Catoctin Iron Furnace,** where iron was made for more than 100 years. The second section, the William Houck Area, is 3 miles (/4.8 kilometers) west of Thurmont on Route 77 and encompasses the lake, falls, and a camping area.

Adjacent to Cunningham Falls State Park is a unit of the National Park Service called **Catoctin Mountain Park** (14707 Park Central Rd., Thurmont; 301/663-9388), best known as the site of presidential retreat **Camp David.**

## SAVAGE RIVER STATE FOREST

127 Headquarters Ln., Grantsville; 301/895-5759; https://dnr.maryland.gov/forests

The Savage River State Forest encompasses more than 54,000 acres (21,853 hectares). The forest is part of the Appalachian Plateau, the western section of the Appalachian Mountains, and offers the 360-acre (145-hectare) Savage River Reservoir, a boat launch, 100 miles (160 kilometers) of multiuse trails (hiking, biking, cross-country skiing, horseback riding, etc.), picnicking, and a shooting range.

SITE ON THE HARRIET TUBMAN UNDERGROUND RAILROAD BYWAY

# THE BILLY GOAT TRAIL

Hikers of all abilities can enjoy the popular Billy Goat Trail, running between the **C&O Canal** and the **Potomac River** in Maryland's Montgomery County near Great Falls. The trail is 4.7 miles (7.5 kilometers) long and has three sections. The three sections of the trail are not contiguous but are connected by the C&O Canal Towpath. The Billy Goat Trail is marked with light-blue blazes.

The northern section, **Section A** (1.7 miles/2.7 kilometers) is the most heavily traveled; pets are not allowed. Accessible from the **Great Falls Tavern Visitor Center** (11710 MacArthur Blvd., Potomac; 301/767-3714), Section A runs through rocky terrain on **Bear Island.** There is a steep climb along a cliff face bordering the Potomac River in Mather Gorge that requires scrambling in parts.

**Section B** (1.4 miles/2.2 kilometers) is less strenuous and has only one short segment where scrambling is required. **Section C** (1.6 miles/2.5 kilometers) is the easiest, with no scrambling. Sections B and C can be accessed from **Carderock Recreation Area** (off Clara Barton Pkwy., Carderock). Leashed dogs are allowed on these two sections.

## CALVERT CLIFFS STATE PARK

10540 H. G. Trueman Rd., Lusby; 301/743-7613; www.dnr.state.md.us

This day-use park is right on the Chesapeake Bay, and offers a sandy beach, playground, fishing, marshland, and 13 miles (20 kilometers) of hiking trails. The main attraction in this park, however, is fossil hunting along the beach. At the end of the **Red Trail** (1.8 miles/2.8 kilometers from the parking lot), the open beach area gives rise to the dramatic Calvert Cliffs. More than 600 species of fossils have been identified in the cliff area, dating back 10 to 20 million years, including oyster shells from the Miocene era and sharks teeth.

## CHESAPEAKE BEACH

The crown jewel of a charming coastal community of the same name, this beautiful Chesapeake Bay beach and nearby **Breezy Point Beach** often top lists of the best beaches in the state. Amenities include swimming areas, bathhouses, picnic areas, playgrounds, and historic fishing piers.

# FESTIVALS AND EVENTS

Perhaps Maryland's biggest event is the **summer season,** when colorful umbrellas decorate the beaches and old-fashioned amusement parks and boardwalks fill up with holidaymakers. Assateague Island's **Wild Pony Swim** is another summer highlight.

## PREAKNESS STAKES

5201 Park Heights Ave., Baltimore; 410/542-9400; www.preakness.com; May

The second leg of the famed Triple Crown horse races, the Preakness Stakes, is held on the third Saturday

THE PREAKNESS STAKES

## BEST SOUVENIRS

- **Frederick antiques:** The town of Frederick is a popular spot for a day trip of antiques hunting.

- **Spruce Forest arts and crafts:** In Western Maryland, Spruce Forest Artisan Village (177 Casselman Rd., Grantsville; 301/895-3332; www.spruceforest.org) is a dozen log-and-frame cabins housing artist studios that sell items such as carvings, stained glass, handloom weaving products, baskets, teddy bears, and pottery.

in May at **Pimlico Race Course**, northwest of Hampden in Baltimore. The historic racecourse is the second-oldest in the country, having opened in 1870. With more than a 140-year history, the Preakness Stakes are a big deal in Baltimore and in horse racing overall.

# BEST FOOD

Crabs are so ubiquitous in Maryland that they even have their own special seasoning to go with them. Outside of fruits from the sea, you should definitely pick up some **boardwalk favorites**

STEAMED BLUE CRABS

like French fries and other fried treats, and look for **National Bohemian,** or "Natty Boh," Baltimore's lager of choice with an iconic, one-eyed, mustachioed mascot.

## CRAB

From steamed, to crab cakes, to crab dip, to crab soup, this crustacean—the blue crab, to specific—is everywhere in Maryland. **Old Bay Seasoning,** developed in Baltimore, is one of the more common ways to spice the crustacean. Some of the best places to try it:

- **Abner's Crab House:** 3748 Harbor Rd., Chesapeake Beach; 410/257-3689; www.abnerscrabhouse.net

- **Bo Brooks Crab House:** 2780 Lighthouse Point, Baltimore; 410/558-0202; www.bobrooks.com

- **Cantler's Riverside Inn:** 458 Forest Beach Rd., Annapolis; 410/757-1311; www.cantlers.com

# MAJOR AIRPORTS

- **Baltimore Washington International Thurgood Marshall Airport:** BWI; 410/859-7040; www.bwiairport.com

# MORE INFORMATION

## TRAVEL AND TOURISM INFORMATION

- **Maryland Office of Tourism:** www.visitmaryland.org

- **Maryland Department of Natural Resources:** https://dnr.maryland.gov

## NEWSPAPERS

- *Washington Post:* www.washingtonpost.com

- *Baltimore Sun:* www.baltimoresun.com

# WASHINGTON DC

Washington DC is the seat of political power in the United States, home of the White House, the Supreme Court, and the U.S. Capitol, where all roads lead, quite literally. On Piscataway and Nacotchtank (Anacostan) land, the city today is home to vibrant neighborhoods like Dupont Circle and U Street, areas full of bars, shops, and restaurants of every persuasion. Washington has always had a unique flavor, a blend of soul food, Ethiopian food, and sizzling Chesapeake Bay seafood served in the backrooms of classic steakhouses where history was made over martinis. Beyond its presidents and elected representatives, the city claims such influential residents, past and present, as Frederick Douglass, Duke Ellington, Toni Morrison, Eleanor Roosevelt, Marvin Gaye, Katharine Graham, and José Andrés. Despite—or perhaps because of—the intoxicating political intrigue, the capital has drawn so many, power-hungry and idealistic alike, and enticed them to stay, not because they don't want to live anywhere else, but because they truly can't imagine a life without the pulse that only DC can bring.

AREA: 68 square miles / 176 square kilometers

POPULATION: 705,749

MARTIN LUTHER KING JR. MEMORIAL

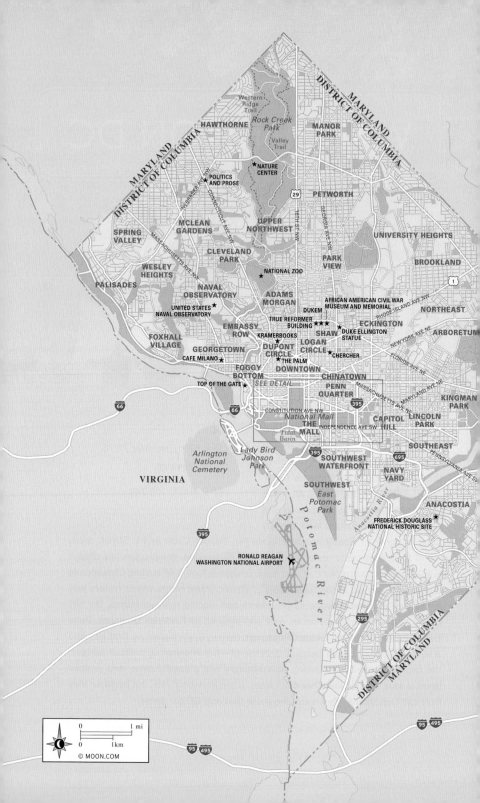

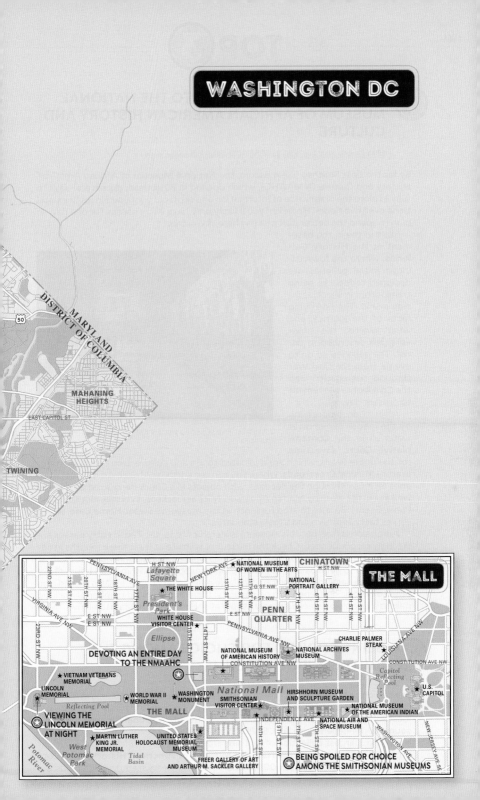

# WASHINGTON DC

## THE MALL

MARYLAND
DISTRICT OF COLUMBIA

50

MAHANING
HEIGHTS

EAST CAPITOL ST

TWINING

Potomac River

PENNSYLVANIA AVE
H ST NW
NEW YORK AVE
CHINATOWN
H ST NW

Lafayette Square

★ NATIONAL MUSEUM OF WOMEN IN THE ARTS

22ND ST NW
21ST ST NW
20TH ST NW
19TH ST NW
18TH ST NW
17TH ST NW
16TH ST NW
15TH ST NW
14TH ST NW
13TH ST NW
12TH ST NW
11TH ST NW

VIRGINIA AVE NW

★ THE WHITE HOUSE

G ST NW
F ST NW

NATIONAL PORTRAIT GALLERY ★

10TH ST NW
7TH ST NW
6TH ST NW
5TH ST NW
4TH ST NW
3RD ST NW

E ST NW
E ST NW

President's Park

PENN QUARTER

WHITE HOUSE VISITOR CENTER ★

23RD ST NW

E ST NW
E ST NW

PENNSYLVANIA AVE NW

Ellipse

CHARLIE PALMER STEAK

LOUISIANA AVE NW

CONSTITUTION AVE NW

DEVOTING AN ENTIRE DAY TO THE NMAAHC

NATIONAL MUSEUM OF AMERICAN HISTORY ★

★ NATIONAL ARCHIVES MUSEUM

CONSTITUTION AVE NW

Capitol Reflecting Pool

★ VIETNAM VETERANS MEMORIAL

National Mall

★ U.S. CAPITOL

LINCOLN MEMORIAL ★

Reflecting Pool

★ WORLD WAR II MEMORIAL

★ WASHINGTON MONUMENT

SMITHSONIAN VISITOR CENTER ★

HIRSHHORN MUSEUM AND SCULPTURE GARDEN

★ VIEWING THE LINCOLN MEMORIAL AT NIGHT

THE MALL

INDEPENDENCE AVE NW

★ NATIONAL MUSEUM OF THE AMERICAN INDIAN

★ MARTIN LUTHER KING JR. MEMORIAL

UNITED STATES HOLOCAUST MEMORIAL MUSEUM

10TH ST SW
9TH ST SW
7TH ST SW

★ NATIONAL AIR AND SPACE MUSEUM

NEW JERSEY AVE SE

WASHINGTON AVE

West Potomac Park

Tidal Basin

FREER GALLERY OF ART AND ARTHUR M. SACKLER GALLERY

★ BEING SPOILED FOR CHOICE AMONG THE SMITHSONIAN MUSEUMS

# TOP 3

## 1 DEVOTING AN ENTIRE DAY TO THE NATIONAL MUSEUM OF AFRICAN AMERICAN HISTORY AND CULTURE

1400 Constitution Ave. NW; 844/750-3012; http://nmaahc.si.edu

By far the best Smithsonian museum, the National Museum of African American History and Culture (NMAAHC), which opened in 2016, deserves several days to fully explore the magnitude of information and artifacts contained in its 12 exhibitions over five floors. However, you'll likely only have entry passes for one day, so plan to spend the better part of a day here, if you can.

Start in the in the basement at the **History Galleries,** where the low-ceilinged initial galleries are designed to feel like being transported in shackles inside a ship. The horrifying facts of the journey, and what awaited the survivors, are described in detail. The galleries go on to events from the Civil War through segregation and the Civil Rights Movement to present day.

After decompressing by the indoor rain-shower waterfall in the **Contemplative Court,** save time

NATIONAL MUSEUM OF AFRICAN AMERICAN HISTORY AND CULTURE

for the upper levels, which are dedicated to art and culture. Don't miss the celebratory **Musical Crossroads,** where you can see and hear African Americans' influence on music through the decades, with objects like Chuck Berry's red Cadillac as well as outfits worn by Marian Anderson, Michael Jackson, Whitney Houston, and Public Enemy. Be sure to stop for lunch at the museum's **Sweet Home Café,** which serves tasty Southern and Creole standards.

Admission is free, but this museum is incredibly popular. Timed entry passes are strongly recommended: Check the museum's website at least three months in advance to see when the next batch of passes will be released and log in at the first opportunity to get a pass—they are typically snapped up within a few hours of being released. Same-day passes are available online every day at 6:30am ET and also tend to go quickly. Depending on capacity, there are a limited number of walk-up passes available on weekdays only at 1pm at the entrance on Madison Drive.

## 2 BEING SPOILED FOR CHOICE AMONG THE SMITHSONIAN MUSEUMS

In addition to the NMAAHC, there are 12 other Smithsonian museums in DC, all of them free to enter and open to the public every day except Christmas Day. Many are located on the National Mall, including family favorite **National Air and Space Museum** (600 Independence Ave. SW; 202/633-2214; http://airandspace.si.edu), with the world's largest collection of real aircraft and spacecraft, including the Wright brothers' 1903 plane, and the **National Museum of American History** (1300 Constitution Ave. NW; 202/633-1000; http://americanhistory.si.edu), which holds the

200-year-old flag that inspired Francis Scott Key to write "The Star-Spangled Banner." In the five-story limestone building of the **National Museum of the American Indian** (4th St. SW and Independence Ave. SW; 202/633-6644; http://nmai.si.edu), the voices of American Indians relate Indigenous culture and spirituality across the Western Hemisphere, as well as the history of treaties between the United States and the American

NATIONAL AIR AND SPACE MUSEUM

Indian Nations, and the **Mitsitam Native Foods Café** is a great place for lunch.

Connected by a passageway, the **Freer Gallery of Art** and **Arthur M. Sackler Gallery** (12th St. SW at Independence Ave. SW; 202/633-4880; http://asia.si.edu) together showcase one of the most diverse collections of Asian art in the world. The quiet **Hirshhorn Museum and Sculpture Garden** (7th St. SW and Independence Ave. SW; 202/633-4674; http://hirshhorn.si.edu) is a local favorite for its contemporary art and 4-acre (1.6-hectare) Sculpture Garden.

Off the mall in downtown, the **National Portrait Gallery** (8th St. NW and F St. NW; 202/633-7970; http://npg.si.edu) is collocated (and more or less mixed together) with the **American Art Museum** (http://americanart.si.edu) and holds portraits of every U.S. president, as well as First Lady Michelle Obama, author Louisa May Alcott, groundbreaking astronomer Edwin Hubble, and many more.

To learn more about the Smithsonian and all its museums, visit the **Smithsonian Visitor Center** (1000 Jefferson Dr. SW; www.si.edu), located in a building known as the Castle.

 ## VIEWING THE LINCOLN MEMORIAL AT NIGHT

2 Lincoln Memorial Circle NW; 202/426-6841; www.nps.gov/linc

Located in a formerly swampy area at the west end of the National Mall, the 19-foot (5.8-meter) sculpture of a seated President Lincoln inside the Lincoln Memorial is most magnificent at night. After the crowds have dispersed, the interior lights cast a dramatic glow on the 16th U.S. president as he gazes across the 2,029-foot-long (618-meter-long) **Reflecting Pool,** which stretches from the Lincoln Memorial to the Washington Monument.

Symbolic details appear on the memorial, conveying Lincoln's dedication to keeping the Union intact: The 36 columns represent the 36 states in the Union when Lincoln died, and above the columns, 48 garland carvings represent the 48 states when the memorial was completed in 1922. Inside, the texts of two of Lincoln's most important speeches are etched on either side

THE LINCOLN MEMORIAL

of the statue: to the left, the 1863 Gettysburg Address, and to the right, the 1865 Second Inaugural Address, which he delivered months before his death. The most recent addition to the memorial was etched in 2003, on the 18th step below the top landing, marking the spot where Martin Luther King Jr. delivered his "I Have A Dream" speech on August 28, 1963.

# *Best* DC WEEKEND

**DAY 1** Base yourself in a central area, like **downtown** or the **Penn Quarter.** If you have tickets to the Smithsonian's **National Museum of African American History and Culture,** beeline to the museum: You'll need the better part of a day to see everything. If not, start your trip with a stroll through the monuments and memorials of the **National Mall** and pop into one of the other Smithsonian museums nearby, like the **Freer and Sackler Galleries** for Asian art or the contemporary **Hirshhorn.** In the afternoon, hop on the Metro to **U Street** for a walk through the area known as Black Broadway. Have Ethiopian for dinner at **Dukem.**

NATIONAL MUSEUM OF AFRICAN AMERICAN HISTORY AND CULTURE

**DAY 2** Take the Metro to the Anacostia neighborhood to visit the **Frederick Douglass National Historic Site,** about a 15-minute walk from the Anacostia station. (Take Howard Rd. SE one block south to Martin Luther King Jr Ave. SE and turn left. Walk four blocks to W St. SE and turn right. The site is three blocks down W St. SE.) After the tour, be sure to admire the view of the U.S. Capitol. Then, take the Metro to **Dupont Circle,** where you can spend some time people-watching in the park at the center of the circle before browsing **Kramerbooks,** one of DC's essential bookstores. Afterward, take a quiet walk up **Embassy Row.** In the evening, take a cab to the **Top of the Gate** for drinks, followed by and dinner at **Cafe Milano.** Then, get another taxi to the **Lincoln Memorial,** which absolutely must be seen at night.

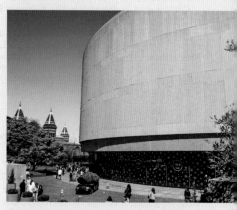

HIRSHHORN MUSEUM AND SCULPTURE GARDEN

DUPONT CIRCLE

## ORIENTATION

The District of Columbia is divided into quadrants—Northwest, Southwest, Northeast, and Southeast—with the U.S. Capitol as the nucleus. Most, but not all, of the streets are arranged in a grid around the **U.S. Capitol.** The numbered streets run north to south, the lettered streets run east to west, and the diagonal streets are named after states. The **Beltway,** the ring road that serves as an unofficial boundary for the city, doesn't actually fall within the District, but rather runs its circle through neighboring Maryland and Virginia.

The **National Mall** spreads west from the Capitol, and **downtown,** which includes the **Penn Quarter** and **Chinatown,** flanks the Mall to the north, between Capitol Hill and the White House. The historically Black neighborhoods of **U Street** and **Shaw** are north of downtown, with the historically gay neighborhood of **Dupont Circle** to the west. Preppy mecca **Georgetown** is west of Dupont Circle, across **Rock Creek.** The immigrant-rich **Adams Morgan** neighborhood sits north of Dupont Circle, while quiet **Upper Northwest** is north of Georgetown. These neighborhoods are all in Northwest, while **Anacostia,** with Frederick Douglass's former home, is in Southeast, across the **Anacostia River.**

Run by the **Washington Metropolitan Area Transit Authority** (202/637-7000; www.wmata.com), **Metrorail,** more commonly referred to simply as "Metro," is DC's network of underground and aboveground subway service. Simple to navigate, cheap, and efficient, the Metro can get you to most neighborhoods, with one famous exception being Georgetown.

## WHEN TO GO

Ask any local when you should visit DC, and they'll likely tell you **spring.** While these months are susceptible to unseasonably cold or hot weather and rain, you'll have plenty of mild, sunshine-filled days. The cherry blossoms bloom in March or April, and the **National Cherry Blossom Festival** is a bucket-list event. The **summer** months are hot, sticky, and jam-packed with tourists. The **fall** is crisp and lovely as the leaves begin to change colors and tourists disperse, and **winter** is even quieter, though often very cold.

# HIGHLIGHTS

## NATIONAL MALL

www.nps.gov/nama

Stretching from the U.S. Capitol in the east to the Lincoln Memorial in the

NATIONAL MALL

west, the National Mall is America's lawn, where people gather for major events like Independence Day and presidential inaugurations, as well as festivals, concerts, and protests for every issue imaginable. Smithsonian museums dominate the central section of the Mall, while the western side holds the many national monuments and memorials most associated with the National Mall. Here are a few to seek out.

- At 555 feet (169 meters) tall, the **Washington Monument** (15th St. NW and Madison Dr. NW; 202/426-6841; www.nps.gov/wamo; timed entry tickets required for observation deck) dominates the horizon as the world's tallest obelisk.

- At the eastern end of the Reflecting Pool is the **World War II Memorial** (1750 Independence Ave. SW; 202/426-6841; www.nps.gov/wwii), which honors the 16 million Americans who served during World War II and the 400,000 who died.

- Near the Lincoln Memorial, the two black granite walls of the **Vietnam Veterans Memorial** (5 Henry Bacon Dr. NW; 202/426-6841; www.nps.gov/vive) rise from the grassy earth, carved with the names of the 58,318 Americans who were killed or missing in action during the long, controversial war.

MARTIN LUTHER KING JR. MEMORIAL

- On the western banks of the Tidal Basin is the newest memorial on the Mall, the **Martin Luther King Jr. Memorial** (1964 Independence Ave. SW; 202/426-6841; www.nps.gov/mlkm), which is the first and currently only memorial on the National Mall dedicated to an African American, and the fourth dedicated to an individual who did not serve as U.S. president.

## THE WHITE HOUSE

1600 Pennsylvania Ave. NW; 202/456-7041; www.whitehouse.gov

America's most iconic home has served as the residence of every U.S. president except George Washington. Built in 1792-1800, the white neoclassical mansion made of painted sandstone includes the Executive Residence as well as the offices of the president in the West Wing, and reception rooms and the offices of the first lady in the East Wing. Seeing the inside of the White House requires the help of your member of Congress, although security concerns can change the availability of tours. The **White House Visitor Center** (1450 Pennsylvania Ave. NW; 202/208-1631; www.nps.gov/whho), a few blocks away, displays 100 artifacts and exhibits about the White House's history, architecture, and social events, as well as official White House memorabilia for sale.

To see the outside, there's an excellent photo op of the White House on Pennsylvania Avenue in **Lafayette Square,** a favorite gathering spot of protestors. Considered a part of the White House grounds, Lafayette Square provides a head-on view of the White House and North Lawn through a security fence. However, the park is occasionally blocked off for high-level diplomatic events, such as a state dinner, or the inauguration, as it's part of the day's parade route. The two-block stretch of 16th Street NW north of Lafayette Square is emblazoned with the words "Black Lives Matter" and is called **Black Lives Matter Plaza,** after the racial justice protests in 2020.

## NATIONAL ARCHIVES MUSEUM

Constitution Ave. NW between 7th St. NW and 9th St. NW; 202/357-5000; http://museum.archives.gov

The National Archives is the resting place of the precious founding documents of the republic—the Declaration of Independence, the U.S. Constitution, and the Bill of Rights—and holds them with the reverence and security of the Sistine Chapel. Every night, the documents are quickly lowered from the grand rotunda to a bomb-proof underground vault. The text-heavy exhibits provide important information about the nation's founding and the history of rights, freedoms, and the rule of law.

## UNITED STATES HOLOCAUST MEMORIAL MUSEUM

100 Raoul Wallenberg Pl. SW; 202/488-0400; www.ushmm.org

The permanent exhibition of this museum, "The Holocaust" (only recommended for ages 11 and up) spans three floors and follows a chronological timeline, from the rise of the Nazi Party to the horrifying treatment and murder of the Jews and, finally, to the liberation of the concentration camps and the end of World War II. The level of detail, personal artifacts, firsthand accounts, and multimedia are both amazing and challenging.

## NATIONAL MUSEUM OF WOMEN IN THE ARTS

1250 New York Ave. NW; 202/783-5000; www.nmwa.org

The National Museum of Women in the Arts is the only major museum in the world dedicated exclusively to women artists. Rotating exhibitions draw from the collection of nearly 5,000 pieces by more than 1,000 female artists, including Mary Cassatt, Clara Peeters, and Frida Kahlo, as well as hundreds of lesser-known artists.

## U.S. CAPITOL

U.S. Capitol Visitor Center, 1st St. SE and E. Capitol St. NE; 202/226-8000; www.visitthecapitol.gov

The imposing white neoclassical dome of the U.S. Capitol is visible for miles, rising 288 feet (88 meters) into the Washington skyline. Guided tours of the building can be arranged either by contacting the office of your senator or representative or by reserving tickets through the **U.S. Capitol Visitor Center,** although security concerns can change the availability of tours. The visitors center, underneath the Capitol's east plaza, is worth a stop for its historical artifacts and exhibits about the history of Congress. The visitors center has two gift shops on the upper level with exclusive Capitol merchandise, as well as a large **cafeteria** on the lower level, where you can try the famous Senate Bean Soup, which has been served in Senate dining rooms every day since the early 1900s.

## FREDERICK DOUGLASS NATIONAL HISTORIC SITE

1411 W St. SE; 202/426-5961; www.nps.gov/frdo

Located in Anacostia, the Frederick Douglass National Historic Site, also known as Cedar Hill, is the estate where Douglass lived from 1877, when he was

NATIONAL MUSEUM OF WOMEN IN THE ARTS

FREDERICK DOUGLASS'S LIBRARY AT THE FREDERICK DOUGLASS NATIONAL HISTORIC SITE

appointed U.S. Marshall by President Rutherford B. Hayes, until his death in 1895. Born into enslavement, Douglass would become a renowned (and mostly self-educated) abolitionist, author, and speaker. The home is only accessible by guided tour with a park ranger. You'll see rooms containing many of Douglass's personal belongings in the exact spots they would have been while he was alive, as well as artwork and photographs of the Douglass family. When you finish the tour, take in the view from his porch, located high above the city on a 51-foot (16-meter) hill and offering expansive views all the way to the U.S. Capitol.

# BEST NEIGHBORHOOD WALKS

## U STREET

Take a walk through U Street, a center of African American life and culture for much of the 20th century where the concentration of jazz clubs earned the area the name "Black Broadway." Starting at the 13th Street and U Street entrance of the **U Street/African-Amer Civil War Memorial/Cardozo Metro station,** head east on **U Street.** On the right before 12th Street, look for the **True Reformer Building,** the classical revival and Romanesque building designed in 1903 by John Anderson Lankford, the first registered African

American architect in Washington DC. Turn north onto 11th Street NW to see the gorgeous blue and purple mural depicting jazz legends (on the north side of the building). Return to U Street, and then walk 1.5 blocks toward Vermont Avenue. Enter the plaza on your right at the Metro station to view the **African American Civil War Memorial.** Continue southwest on Vermont Avenue to tour the **African American Civil War Museum** (1925 Vermont Ave. NW; 202/667-2667; www.afroamcivilwar.org), across the street from the memorial.

After the museum, double back to U Street NW, and two blocks to the east U Street becomes Florida Avenue NW after 9th Street. Keep walking on Florida Avenue to T Street NW, where the 20-foot (6-meter) stainless steel **Duke Ellington statue** pays homage to the musician, who grew up in the area and began his career in the jazz clubs of "Black Broadway." Go west on T Street half a block to see **The Howard Theatre** (620 T St. NW; 202/803-2899; www.thehowardtheatre.com), which hosts concerts from gospel to jazz, including DC's top go-go bands. Turn right on any of the numbered streets to get back to U Street and the Metro. If you get hungry, head to the legendary **Ben's Chili Bowl** (1213 U St. NW; 202/667-0909; www.benschilibowl.com), a historic spot that served activists during the 1968 riots and, more recently, President Obama, near the station.

ROCK CREEK PARK

## EMBASSY ROW

Massachusetts Ave. NW from Scott Circle northwest to the United States Naval Observatory

Crossing through several neighborhoods, Embassy Row is the stretch of Massachusetts Avenue NW lined with the stately international embassies and diplomatic missions where foreign ambassadors to the United States live and work. Beginning at **Scott Circle,** with the embassies of Australia and the Philippines, it heads northwest through **Dupont Circle** to the **United States Naval Observatory,** where the vice president lives. The buildings start getting really impressive just past the **embassy of India** in Dupont Circle, marked by a bronze Gandhi statue. Don't miss the former **embassy of Iran** (3003-3005 Massachusetts Ave. NW), known for some of the most lavish parties in Washington before diplomatic ties were severed in 1980; the shuttered building is still owned by Tehran but maintained by the U.S. State Department. The embassies are generally closed to the public, but every May, they open their doors for **Passport DC,** when you can go inside dozens of the mansions to experience the countries' art, culture, and food.

# BEST PARKS AND RECREATION AREAS

## WEST POTOMAC PARK

National Mall from about 17th St. NW west to the Lincoln Memorial and south to the Tidal Basin

Stretching from the Washington Monument west to the Lincoln Memorial and southeast to the Thomas Jefferson Memorial, West Potomac Park includes many of the major national memorials in its grassy fields. In addition to getting a history lesson, you can kick around in the JFK Hockey Fields south of the Reflecting Pool, which are perfect for a game of Frisbee or soccer. The park includes the **Tidal Basin,** an artificial inlet of the Potomac River surrounded by the cherry trees gifted to the United States by Japan in 1912. The trail around it is approximately 2 miles (3.2 kilometers). You can also rent **paddleboats** (1501 Maine Ave. SW; 202/479-2426; www.tidalbasinpaddleboats.com) from March to October.

## ROCK CREEK PARK

Covering more than 2,000 acres of parkland and historic sites around Rock Creek in Northwest DC, Rock Creek Park is an oasis for outdoors enthusiasts. The park essentially lines Rock Creek from Georgetown in the south to the Maryland border in the north, but the swath of parkland north of the

**National Zoo** (3001 Connecticut Ave. NW; 202/633-4888; http://nationalzoo.si.edu), roughly between Oregon Avenue NW/Broad Branch Drive NW and 16th Street NW, is the main section of trails and athletic facilities. The **Nature Center** (5200 Glover Rd. NW) has a visitors center. The park has two main hiking trails, which run from the DC-Maryland border at Beach Drive south toward the zoo. The **Western Ridge Trail** is 5.5 miles (8.9 kilometers) one way, and the **Valley Trail** on the eastern border is 7 miles (11.3 kilometers) one way; east-west trails connect them.

# FESTIVALS AND EVENTS

## NATIONAL CHERRY BLOSSOM FESTIVAL

Citywide; 877/442-5666; www.nationalcherryblossomfestival.org; mid-Mar.-mid-Apr.

In March and April, the city celebrates the bloom of the cherry trees, a gift from Japan in 1912. The festival includes many free events: the parade, kite festival, Japanese street festival, fireworks, museum events, and, of course, the showcase of the magnificent pink and white blossoms around the Tidal Basin and National Mall. This is one of the busiest, most expensive times to visit DC, and it's tough to predict peak bloom, but if you catch it, you'll be glad you braved the crowds.

FLOWERING CHERRY TREES ALONG TIDAL BASIN

## INDEPENDENCE DAY

National Mall; www.pbs.org/a-capitol-fourth; July 4

Celebrating Independence Day in the nation's capital begins with a mile-long **parade** (Constitution Ave. NW between 7th St. NW and 17th St. NW; www.july4thparade.com) down Constitution Avenue, featuring bands from across the country as well as military units. In the evening, PBS hosts **A Capitol Fourth** (U.S. Capitol West Lawn; www.pbs.org/a-capitol-fourth), the free concert on the West Lawn of the U.S. Capitol featuring celebrity musicians and military bands playing patriotic tunes. The concert builds anticipation for the spectacular **fireworks display** (National Mall; www.pbs.org/a-capitol-fourth), which can be viewed from the U.S. Capitol, National Mall, and anywhere you can see the Washington Monument. Crowds begin forming very early in the day on the National Mall; plan to arrive at the concert shortly after the gates open at 3pm to stake out a spot closer to the stage, and stick around to enjoy the fireworks with the soundtrack of Tchaikovsky's "1812 Overture" and live canon fire at the conclusion of the concert.

# BEST FOOD AND DRINK

## ETHIOPIAN FOOD

In the 1970s and 1980s, thousands of Ethiopians fled civil war to Washington DC, building the largest Ethiopian community outside Africa. While skyrocketing rents have led to many moving to suburbs like Silver Spring, Maryland, and Alexandria, Virginia, dozens of Ethiopian businesses remain in Adams Morgan and Shaw, and the area around 9th Street and U Street NW is known as **Little Ethiopia.** Here are a couple of places to get your *doro wat* (a spicy chicken stew) and *tibs* (sautéed beef or lamb).

- **Dukem Ethiopian Restaurant:** 1114-1118 U St. NW; 202/667-8735; www.dukemrestaurant.com

- **Chercher:** 1334 9th St. NW; 202/299-9703; www.chercherrestaurant.com

# SOUVENIRS AND COLLECTIBLES

Politically themed gifts are a DC specialty. Get official White House memorabilia at the **White House Visitor Center** gift shop. And while political books are available nationwide, DC's bookstores are particularly well stocked with them. Try **Kramerbooks** (1517 Connecticut Ave. NW; 202/387-1400; www.kramers.com) in Dupont Circle and **Politics and Prose** (5015 Connecticut Ave. NW; 202/364-1919; www.politics-prose.com) in Upper Northwest.

## THE POWER LUNCH AND HAPPY HOUR

For better or worse, Washington DC is all about who you know and—if you really want business to get done—how often you have a few drinks or a meal with them. Here are a few spots where VIPs go to do politics—and if you're lucky, you'll overhear well-oiled staffers exchanging snippets of political gossip.

- **The Palm** (1225 19th St. NW; 202/293-9091; www.thepalm.com) in Dupont Circle is where lobbyists and reporters go to shake hands with other VIPs whose faces are painted on the walls. (Yes, the person at the next table over was probably on CNN earlier.)

- **Charlie Palmer Steak** (101 Constitution Ave. NW; 202/547-8100; www.charliepalmer.com) is just a few blocks from the Capitol, so you're likely to see U.S. senators and representatives enjoying steak and American wine here.

- At **Cafe Milano** (3251 Prospect St.; 202/333-6183; www.cafemilano.com) in Georgetown, you may very well see a cabinet secretary or senator enjoying pasta or branzino on any given night.

- With a 360-degree view, including several monuments, the **Top of the Gate** (2650 Virginia Ave. NW; 202/322-6455; www.thewatergate-hotel.com), the sprawling, open-air rooftop bar at the infamous Watergate Hotel, is the best perch in the city—especially for happy hour, when the sun sets over the Potomac River.

## MAJOR AIRPORTS

There are no airports in Washington DC, but two airports in Virginia and one in Maryland serve the nation's capital.

- **Ronald Reagan Washington National Airport:** DCA; 2401 S. Smith Blvd, Arlington, Virginia; www.flyreagan.com

- **Washington Dulles International Airport:** IAD; 1 Saarinen Cir., Dulles, Virginia; www.flydulles.com

- **Baltimore/Washington International Thurgood Marshall Airport:** BWI; 7035 Elm Rd., Baltimore, Maryland; www.bwiairport.com

## MORE INFORMATION

### TRAVEL AND TOURISM INFORMATION

- **Destination DC:** www.washington.org

### NEWSPAPERS AND MAGAZINES

- *The Washington Post:* www.washingtonpost.com

- *Washington City Paper:* www.washingtoncitypaper.com

- *Washingtonian:* www.washingtonian.com

# VIRGINIA

Virginia embodies history like few other states in the Union. From the Iroquoian, Siouan, and Algonquian-speaking Indigenous tribes upon whose land Virginia rests to the first permanent English settlement in the New World at Jamestown to the tragedy and heroism of the Civil War, the Old Dominion has witnessed many of the major events that shaped this country. Most of the buildings, battlefields, and artifacts involved are now preserved in a host of parks, museums, and historic homes.

Virginia not only connects the storied past and thriving present—it's also a bridge between the mountains and the sea. Shenandoah is home to one of the most scenic roads in the country. Virginia Beach is one of the East Coast's premier resort destinations, with a bustling boardwalk and a bevy of great seafood restaurants. Detached from the rest of the state, the Eastern Shore is a time-warped land of unspoiled marshes, fishing towns, and the famous ponies of Chincoteague. Virginia offers the best of the many worlds it bridges—and then some.

**AREA:** 42,774 square miles / 110,784 square kilometers (35th)

**POPULATION:** 8,535,519 (12th)

**STATEHOOD DATE:** June 25, 1788 (10th)

**STATE CAPITAL:** Richmond

▲ SKYLINE DRIVE IN THE FALL

## ORIENTATION

Although a separate entity from the state of Virginia, **Washington DC** exerts a pull over northern Virginia, where **Arlington,** Alexandria, and the DC suburbs are located. Inland, to the west, is the Shenandoah Valley and the spectacular **Shenandoah National Park.** **Richmond** lies nearly due south of DC, about half-way between **Charlottesville** to the northwest and **Virginia Beach** to the southeast on the Atlantic Coast. The **Blue Ridge Parkway** weaves its 217-mile (349-kilometer) way south and west from the end of Shenandoah's **Skyline Drive** to hit the North Carolina state line in the western arm of the state.

## WHEN TO GO

**Late spring** (May and June) and **fall** (Sept. and Oct.) are usually the **best times** to explore Virginia. The weather is most pleasant, and there are fewer tourists to compete with. The fall foliage in the state is some of the most spectacular in the country—a drive through the Blue Ridge Mountains in October can lead to some of the most stunning scenery in the East. **Summer** is the **prime tourist season,** but unless your plans involve some beach time or a stay in a mountain retreat, the humidity can be a bit overwhelming. If your focus is on historical sites and museums, the **winter** months (with the exception of the holiday season) can mean **short or no wait times** for popular attractions. Just be prepared for some sites to be closed or to have shorter hours.

# HIGHLIGHTS

## ARLINGTON NATIONAL CEMETERY

1 Memorial Dr., Arlington; 877/907-8585; www.arlingtoncemetery.mil

This is, without a doubt, the most famous cemetery in the United States. It occupies a sprawling 624-acre (252-hectare) site where more than 400,000 soldiers from every U.S. military conflict are buried. The uniform white tombstones form an orderly quilt across the rolling green fields of the cemetery and are meticulously maintained. Called "Our Nation's Most Sacred Shrine," as the resting place for many generations of our nation's heroes, the cemetery grows daily: On average, more than two dozen funerals are held each weekday. In 1948, a group of women formed the Arlington Ladies, a volunteer group whose members attend services for all veterans and ensure that no member of the armed forces is ever buried alone.

There are several key sights within Arlington National Cemetery that are well worth a visit. The best known is the **Tomb of the Unknowns,** which houses

IWO JIMA MEMORIAL, ARLINGTON

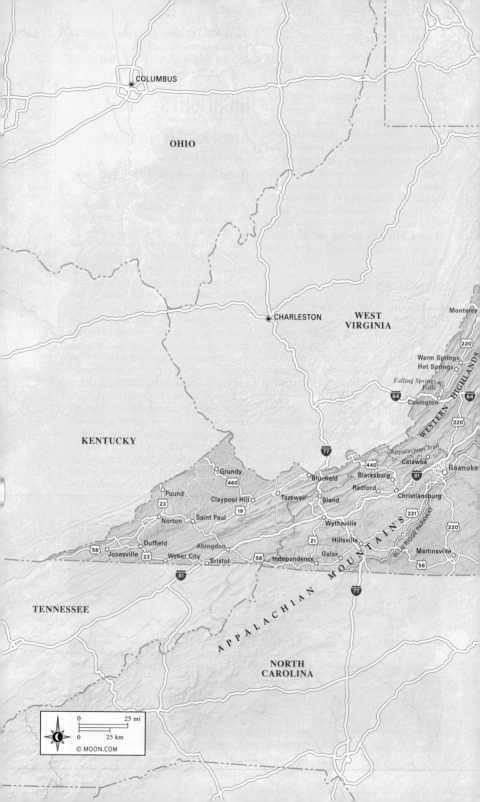

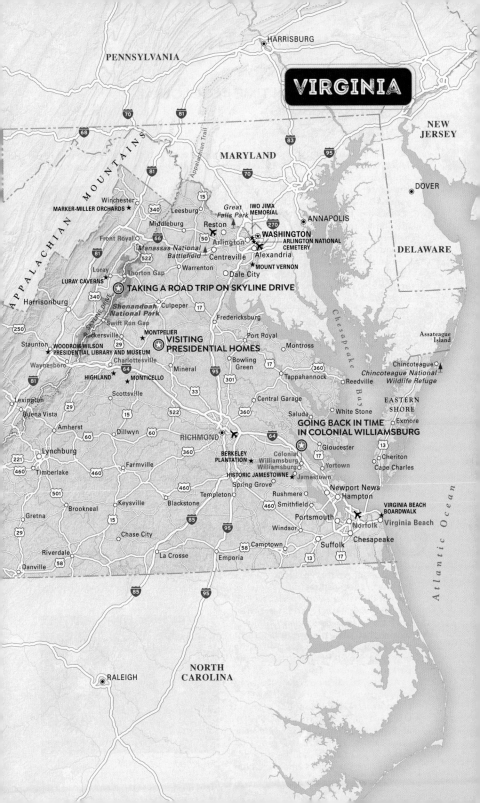

# TOP 3

## 1  GOING BACK IN TIME IN COLONIAL WILLIAMSBURG

888/965-7254; www.colonialwilliamsburg.com

Colonial Williamsburg is the largest **living museum** in the country, and it is truly a historical marvel. The museum encompasses the restored 18th-century colonial Virginia capital city, which was the center of politics in Virginia for 80 years. The site includes the real city streets and buildings that were erected during that time. As you explore historical exhibits, dine in **taverns** serving authentic colonial-style food, and peruse **shops** featuring original trades, you'll also interact with the staff, who are dressed in period clothing and play their roles very seriously. Visitors are considered "Residents of the City," and conversations between staff members and the public are always in character.

COLONIAL WILLIAMSBURG

Highlights of the site include **Duke of Gloucester Street,** which President Franklin D. Roosevelt called the "most historic avenue in all of America"; **Market Square,** the center of activity where residents would purchase goods and socialize; and the impressive **Governor's Palace.** Another interesting spot is the **Magazine,** well known for its role in the **Gunpowder Incident** of April 20, 1775, which occurred in the earliest days of the Revolutionary War.

Many craftspeople, some of whom have spent years learning the trade, create colonial-era crafts in dozens of shops throughout Colonial Williamsburg. Visitors can watch **blacksmiths** and armorers shape tools, weapons, and hardware out of iron and steel or visit the **Wigmaker** to learn the importance of 18th-century wigmakers and barbers. Other crafters include the **Shoemaker,** the **Weaver,** and the **Bindery.**

## 2  TAKING A ROAD TRIP ON SKYLINE DRIVE

Shenandoah National Park; 540/999-3500; www.nps.gov/shen

This stunning route runs along the mountain ridges of **Shenandoah National Park.** It's one of the most beautiful stretches of road in the East and is the most popular attraction in the national park. The 105-mile (168-kilometer) road takes travelers from vista to vista along a stunning byway that runs the entire length of the park from north to south—it is the only public road that goes through the park.

Access to Skyline Drive is from four entry points: from Front Royal at the northern terminus (near I-66 and U.S. 340), at Thornton Gap (U.S. 211), at Swift Run Gap (U.S. 33), and near Waynesboro at Rockfish Gap at I-64 and U.S. 250 (at the southern terminus). Skyline Drive ends where the **Blue**

SKYLINE DRIVE IN AUTUMN

Ridge Parkway begins. It takes approximately 3 hours to drive the entire road.

The most popular time to visit Skyline Drive is during the **fall.** Virginia is known for having one of the most spectacular leaf displays in the country, and this route showcases the best of the best. **Wildflowers** and other stunning blooms keep the area colorful throughout the warmer months. There are 75 overlooks along the route, from which you'll be able to see the beautiful Shenandoah Valley to the west and the Piedmont to the east. You'll also find popular **hiking** trails along the road.

# VISITING PRESIDENTIAL HOMES

Virginia has more claims to U.S presidents than any other state: Of the 45 people to hold that office, eight were born in Virginia, all before the Civil War, and seven owned or have a connection to a Virginia plantation that relied on the labor of enslaved people. Debate about these presidents' legacies—especially around the two most famous, George Washington and Thomas Jefferson—continues, and the plantation sights, after years of glossing over the role of slavery in their histories, are incorporating the stories of enslaved people into their narrative.

**Mount Vernon** (3200 Mount Vernon Memorial Hwy., Alexandria; 703/780-2000; www.mountvernon.org), George Washington's plantation house, is the most popular historic estate in the country. The estate, which highlights the first president's life and times, features the mansion and its meticulously restored interior, plus nearly 50 acres (20 hectares) of land where you'll find a dozen original structures and Washington's tomb. In addition to the Washington-centric exhibit, the *Lives Bound Together* exhibit focuses on the workers enslaved by Washington.

**Monticello** (931 Thomas Jefferson Pkwy., Charlottesville; 434/984-9880; www.monticello.org) is a plantation that was the home of Thomas Jefferson, the third president of the United States. The home, with its recognizable brick façade adorned by columns and a dramatic octagonal dome, sits on 5,000-acres (2,023-hectares). Visitors can take a tour of the first floor of the beautiful mansion and see original furnishings and personal items that belonged to Jefferson. In 2018, the plantation opened the *Life of Sally Hemings* exhibit, which describes the life of the enslaved woman who bore four children fathered by Jefferson.

The other presidential homes in Virginia include **Montpelier,** home to James Madison and his wife Dolley; **Highland,** a working farm that was home to James Monroe, the fifth president; the **Berkeley Plantation,** birthplace of William Henry Harrison and famous for being the site of the first official Thanksgiving. Unlike the others, the **Woodrow Wilson Presidential Library and Museum** is located in the manse where he was born during his father's tenure as the Presbyterian minister of Staunton.

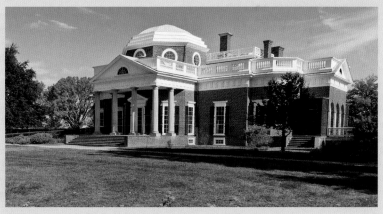

MONTICELLO

# *Best* ROAD TRIP

**DAY 1** From Dulles, drive 1 hour west to **Front Royal,** the gateway to **Shenandoah National Park.** Enter the park on the famed **Skyline Drive.** Spend the rest of the day meandering down the northern section of Skyline Drive to **Luray.** Be sure to stop along the way for a short hike and to take in the sights along this stunning section of road. Spend the night in Luray.

**DAY 2** Start your day by touring the incredible **Luray Caverns.** Then, take the 2-hour scenic route along the southern portion of Skyline Drive. At the end, take I-64 east to scenic **Charlottesville.** Visit **Monticello,** Thomas Jefferson's home, then pick a restaurant on the hip downtown mall in Charlottesville for dinner.

**DAY 3** Make the 3-hour drive to **Virginia Beach** early so you can enjoy a day on the Atlantic. Be sure to walk the famous **boardwalk** and enjoy fresh seafood before spending the night in a hotel right on the Atlantic Ocean.

**DAY 4** Drive 1.5 hours northwest to **Colonial Williamsburg.** Lose yourself in U.S. history by dedicating the day to exploring this unique living museum. Visit the **historic buildings,** shop in the authentic **colonial shops,** talk to the costumed interpreters, and have a refreshment in a colonial **tavern.**

**DAY 5** In the morning, drive an hour northwest to the capital city of **Richmond.** Spend the day learning about the city's Black history in the **Jackson Ward** neighborhood.

**DAY 6** On your final day, drive north about 2 hours to **Arlington.** Visit the **cemetery** and the **Iwo Jima Memorial.** Depending on your flight schedule, head back to Dulles or spend the night in Arlington.

SHENANDOAH NATIONAL PARK

LURAY CAVERNS

VIRGINIA BEACH

# *Major* CITIES

**VIRGINIA BEACH:** Virginia Beach is the state's premier beach destination. It is a thriving, year-round city with more than 442,000 full-time residents—and an influx of nearly 19 million visitors annually. The center of activity is the 3-mile-long boardwalk, and you'll find a variety of attractions, events, parks, and wildlife refuges in the area.

**NORFOLK:** A longtime navy town and home to the largest naval base in the world, Norfolk has undergone a rebirth in recent history that is most evident in the delightful restaurants and shops in the trendy Ghent village, located just northwest of downtown, not far from the Elizabeth River. The city also boasts numerous universities, museums, and a host of other attractions including festivals and shopping.

**ARLINGTON:** Densely populated Arlington, located across the Potomac River west of Washington DC, is known for its national landmarks, military memorials, and trendy restaurants and shopping areas.

the remains of unidentified American soldiers from World Wars I and II and the Korean War. Another popular sight is the **Women's Memorial,** which honors American servicewomen. A short walk uphill from the Women's Memorial is the eternal flame and burial site of **John F. Kennedy,** one of the most-visited graves in the cemetery.

## IWO JIMA MEMORIAL

Arlington Ridge, Arlington; 703/289-2500; www.nps.gov/gwmp

The Iwo Jima Memorial, also called the **U.S. Marine Corps War Memorial,** stands to honor those Marines who died in defense of the United States. This awe-inspiring memorial is a 32-foot-tall (9.7-meter) granite and bronze sculpture created in the likeness of a Pulitzer Prize-winning photograph depicting the raising of the American flag on Iwo Jima (a small island off the coast of Japan) in March 1945, near the end of World War II. The sculpture illustrates the U.S. flag being raised by five Marines and a Navy hospital corpsman. The detail in the memorial is stunning, and its enormous size adds to its inspirational appeal.

## MANASSAS NATIONAL BATTLEFIELD

6511 Sudley Rd., Manassas; 703/361-1339; www.nps.gov/mana

The premier attraction in Prince William County is Manassas National Battlefield Park, a great place for die-hard historians and tourists alike. This historic battlefield preserves the site of two well-known Civil War battles: the First Battle of Bull Run (July 21, 1861), which was the first major land battle in the war; and the Second Battle of Bull Run (Aug. 28-30, 1862), which was the biggest simultaneous mass assault of the Civil War and signaled the height of the Confederate army's power.

The park encompasses more than 5,000 acres (2,023 hectares) of meadows, woods, and streams. When visiting the battlefield, you can see the site

MANASSAS NATIONAL BATTLEFIELD

VIRGINIA BEACH BOARDWALK

where the battles took place and learn about the history via exhibits and artifacts, including uniforms from the era, weapons, and field gear. Other attractions in the park include the **Stone Bridge,** which the Union army retreated across after both battles; **Battery Heights,** where Confederate batteries fired on the attacking Union troops at the Brawner Farm; **Matthews Hill,** the site of the opening phase of the first battle; and **Groveton,** the remains of a Civil War-era village.

## HISTORIC JAMESTOWNE

1368 Colonial Pkwy., Jamestown; 757/856-1250; www.historicjamestowne.org

Step back in time at Historic Jamestowne, which occupies the site of the original Jamestown settlement on the banks of the James River. Historic Jamestowne is divided into "Old Towne," the original settlement site, and "New Towne," the part of the area that was developed after 1620. Highlights in Old Towne include the original Memorial Church tower, a burial ground (many of the first colonists died here), and a reconstructed sample of a "mud-and-stud" cottage. "New Towne" features replicas of homes from the time.

## VIRGINIA BEACH BOARDWALK

Between 1st St. and 42nd St., Virginia Beach

No trip to Virginia Beach is complete without a stroll along the 28-foot-wide (8.5-meter) boardwalk that runs parallel to the ocean for 3 miles (4.8 kilometers) on one of the longest recreational beach areas in the world. The boardwalk is perfect for getting some exercise with a view and is adorned with benches, grassy areas, play areas, amusement parks, arcades, hotels, restaurants, shops, and other entertainment. There is also a large fishing pier at 15th Street.

## BLACK HISTORY MUSEUM AND CULTURAL CENTER OF VIRGINIA

122 W Leigh St., Richmond; 804/780-9093; www.blackhistorymuseum.org

Housed in the old Leigh Street Armory in the heart of the **Jackson Ward** neighborhood of Richmond, this museum takes visitors on a journey from emancipation, reconstruction, and Jim Crow to desegregation, resistance, and the Civil Rights era, including the story of local heroes the Richmond 34, Virginia Union University students who staged a sit-in in 1960. This two-floor museum contains permanent exhibitions on the first floor and temporary exhibitions on the second floor. Throughout, artifacts, photos, videos, and interactive displays enhance the experience.

## MAGGIE L. WALKER HISTORIC SITE

600 N 2nd St., Richmond; 804/771-2017; www. nps.gov/mawa

Maggie L. Walker holds the honor of being the first Black woman in the United States to found a bank, St. Luke Penny Savings Bank, in 1903. Walker's rise was remarkable. Her mother was born enslaved, and her biological father was an Irish immigrant (and a Confederate soldier and hospital clerk). She also published a newspaper, *St. Luke Herald*, and used her voice to urge her community to buy Black.

Walker moved into this Jackson Ward row house with her family in 1905. The home had nine rooms when Walker moved in but was expanded into a 28-room Victorian mansion over time. More than 90 percent of Walker's things, including books, a porcelain bidet, and a baby grand piano, are still found inside as she left them. While Walker was alive, she welcomed Black thought leaders here, including W. E. B. DuBois, Booker T. Washington, and Mary McLeod Bethune. Poets Langston Hughes and Countee Cullen hung out in the kitchen around the same table and chairs you'll see on a tour of the site today.

## BIRTHPLACE OF COUNTRY MUSIC MUSEUM

520 Birthplace of Country Music Way, Bristol; 423/573-1927; www.birthplaceofcountrymusic. org

By the mid-1920s, a genre of music variously called "old Southern tunes," "hill-country tunes," and "hillbilly music" was gaining popularity. Beginning in 1926, record companies began to organize "field sessions" so artists could be recorded without having to make an expensive trip to New York. The sessions that took place in Bristol, on the Tennessee-Virginia border, in July and August 1927 proved that country music—as it eventually came to be called—both sounded good and could be a commercial success.

It is this story along with many more that is told at the Birthplace of Country Music Museum with archival material and interactive displays documenting the some of the artists discovered through the Bristol Sessions, including the Carter Family and Jimmie Rodgers. In the town of Bristol itself, you can tour the pleasant row of charming shops that line **State Street** and take pictures in front of the **Country Music Mural.**

# BEST SCENIC DRIVES

## BLUE RIDGE PARKWAY

www.blueridgeparkway.org

The Blue Ridge Parkway is one of the most popular units of the national park system. The parkway is 469 miles (754 kilometers) long and connects Great Smoky Mountains National Park in North Carolina and Tennessee with Shenandoah National Park in Virginia. The parkway was designed during the Great Depression, and its creators took advantage of the beautiful terrain and followed the natural contours of the ridgeline. Gorgeous scenery is the key ingredient to this outstanding park, and visitors can enjoy overlooks of the Blue Ridge Mountains, countless

HISTORIC STRUCTURE ALONG THE BLUE RIDGE PARKWAY

FALLING SPRING FALLS

vistas, beautiful old meadows, and picturesque farmland.

A 217-mile (349-kilometer) stretch of the Blue Ridge Parkway is in Virginia, with the prettiest part being the 114 miles (183 kilometers) between **Waynesboro** and **Roanoke**. This section follows the crest of the Blue Ridge Mountains. If it's beautiful mountain scenery you seek, then a ride down the Blue Ridge Parkway is a must—especially during the fall.

## COLONIAL PARKWAY

The "Historic Triangle," as it is known, consists of **Williamsburg, Jamestown,** and **Yorktown.** These three historic towns are just minutes apart and are the sites of some of our country's most important Revolutionary War history. The Colonial Parkway, a scenic, 23-mile-long (37-kilometer), three-lane road, connects the points of the Historic Triangle. Millions of travelers drive the road between Williamsburg, Jamestown, and Yorktown each year. The parkway is maintained by the National Park Service and was designed to unify the three culturally distinct sites while preserving the scenery and wildlife along the way.

## VIRGINIA'S WESTERN HIGHLANDS

U.S. 220

The western reaches of the state toward the West Virginia border include Highland County, Bath County, and parts of Augusta and Allegheny Counties. The Allegheny Mountains spill into West Virginia, and the area is split by river valleys. This region is scenic and sparsely populated. U.S. 220 from **Monterey** to **Covington** (55 miles/88 kilometers, 1.25 hours) is a particularly scenic drive. You'll pass through iconic mountain towns such as Warm Springs and Hot Springs, the location of the famed **Omni Homestead Resort** and by **Falling Spring Falls,** an 80-foot (24-meter) cascade.

# BEST PARKS AND RECREATION AREAS

## SHENANDOAH NATIONAL PARK

540/999-3500; www.nps.gov/shen

Shenandoah National Park is a popular escape for good reason: It offers superb outdoor recreation, stunning mountain scenery, the lovely Shenandoah River, and famous Skyline Drive. The park stretches 105 miles (168 kilometers) from north to south and has four primary entrances: from Front Royal (via I-66 and U.S. 340), at Thornton Gap (via U.S. 211), at Swift Run Gap (via U.S. 33),

SHENANDOAH NATIONAL PARK

and at Rockfish Gap (via I-64 and U.S. 250).

Shenandoah National Park is a prime location for **hiking.** There are more than 500 miles (804 kilometers) of trails here, mostly through lush forests. The most popular—and most challenging and dangerous—hike is **Old Rag Mountain,** where you'll be rewarded for your efforts with beautiful summit views. The park is also a great place to view **wildlife.** Some of the resident animals include coyote, black bear, bald eagles, and the timber rattlesnake.

## LURAY CAVERNS

970 U.S. 211 West, GPS 101 Cave Hill Rd., Luray; 540/743-6551; www.luraycaverns.com

There are many cavern attractions in the Blue Ridge Mountains, but the cream of the crop is Luray Caverns. This incredible natural wonder has been awing visitors since it was first discovered in 1878. Upon entering the caverns, you are transported into a subterranean world of mystery that took more than 4 million centuries to create. A series of paved walkways guide visitors through massive cavern "rooms" filled with natural stalagmites, stalactites, and, when the two join, columns or pillars. Some of the chambers have ceilings that are 10 stories high. There are many attractions along the paved route in the caverns, and one of the most famous is

the **Stalacpipe Organ,** considered the world's largest musical instrument—it's made up of stalactites covering 3.5 acres (1.4 hectares).

## CHINCOTEAGUE NATIONAL WILDLIFE REFUGE

8231 Beach Rd., Chincoteague; 757/336-6122; www.fws.gov/refuge/chincoteague

The Chincoteague National Wildlife Refuge is a 14,000-acre (5,665-hectare) refuge consisting of beach, dunes, marsh, and maritime forest on the Virginia end of **Assateague Island.** It was established in 1943, and the area is a thriving habitat for many species of waterfowl, shorebirds, songbirds, and wading birds. The popular herd of **wild ponies** that Chincoteague is known for also lives in the refuge.

# FESTIVALS AND EVENTS

## NORFOLK HARBORFEST

Norfolk; www.festevents.org; June

One of Norfolk's most popular events, the Norfolk Harborfest, is held annually for four days at the beginning of June and attracts more than 100,000 people. This large festival covers more than 3 miles (4.8 kilometers) on the Norfolk waterfront and offers visitors three sailboat parades, tall ships, the largest

NORFOLK HARBORFEST

## BEST SOUVENIRS

- Bring a piece of Colonial Williamsburg home with a visit to the **Williamsburg Craft House,** which sells pewter and ceramic gifts, jewelry, and folk art.

- Three miles (4.8 kilometers) south of Mount Vernon, stop by **George Washington's whiskey distillery and gristmill** to pick up whiskey, flour, and cornmeal. The facilities are still functioning today as they did in the 18th century and produce authentic products.

- You can also buy glassware made in the **Glasshouse at Historic Jamestowne,** where artisans create glass products as glassblowers did back in the early 1600s.

fireworks display on the East Coast, and seemingly endless entertainment.

## VIRGINIA HIGHLANDS FESTIVAL

Abingdon; www.vahighlandsfestival.org; Aug.

The town of Abingdon hosts one of the top 100 annual tourist events in the country: the Virginia Highlands Festival. This a 10-day event held in August showcases music, art, crafts, and writing indigenous to the Appalachians. The festival began in 1948 and started as a weeklong festival geared toward Appalachian arts and crafts and evolved into 10 days of festivities in a variety of venues. A large antiques market is also featured at the festival, and there is wine-tasting, gardening instruction, and even a hot-air-balloon rally.

## ANNUAL OLD FIDDLERS' CONVENTION

Galax; Aug.

The second week in August marks a very special time in the southern Virginia town of Galax. This town near the North Carolina border is the home of the largest old-time bluegrass fiddlers' convention in the country, which has been a main event in town since 1935. Hundreds of people from all over the country come with their instruments to compete for prize money totaling more than $10,000. Thousands more fans converge on the town to witness the contest and to hear up-and-coming bluegrass musicians.

# BEST FOOD

Virginia's colonial past, agricultural history, and proximity to water are all evident in the local cuisine. Many parts of southern and western Virginia embrace the culture of the southern United States. It is there you can find authentic Southern cuisine and Virginia-specific food such as Virginia ham (country ham produced in Virginia), Brunswick stew, and peanut soup. Additionally, although seafood is not unique to Virginia, it has certainly found a special place here, since it is harvested regionally.

## PEANUT SOUP

Peanuts, which were a popular plantation crop, have remained a staple in the Old Dominion. Try this signature dish at **The King's Arms Tavern** (416 E. Duke of Gloucester St., Williamsburg; 855/240-3278,) in Colonial Williamsburg or **The Red Fox Inn and Tavern** (2 E. Washington St., Middleburg; 540/687-6301; www.redfox.com).

## OYSTERS

Oyster lovers flock to the Chesapeake Bay region. For more than 100 years, this delectable yet peculiar-looking creature flourished in the bay and was one of the most valuable commercial fishing commodities. Get your fix at **AW Shucks Raw Bar & Grill** (2200 Colonial Ave., Norfolk; 757/664-9117; www.awshucksrawbar.com).

PEANUT SOUP

## COUNTRY HAM

In the 17th century, Virginia settlers learned how to smoke meat from the Indigenous residents. To this day, Virginia country ham has an international reputation. Try it at **The Homeplace Restaurant** (4968 Catawba Valley Dr., Catawba; 540/384-7252).

## APPLES

As one of the nation's top six producers of apples, Virginia makes sure to save room for dessert. Winchester, the state's top apple packaging location at the northern tip of the Shenandoah Valley, is often called "The Apple Capital of the World." Stop at **Marker-**

**Miller Orchards** (3035 Cedar Creek Grade, Winchester; www.markermillerorchards.com), a "pick-your-own" orchard, which begins September 1.

# MAJOR AIRPORTS

- **Ronald Reagan Washington National Airport:** DCA; 2401 Smith Blvd., Arlington; www.flyreagan.com
- **Washington Dulles International Airport:** IAD; 1 Saarinen Cir., Dulles; 703/572-2700; www.flydulles.com
- **Richmond International Airport:** RIC; 1 Richard E. Byrd Terminal Dr., Richmond; www.flyrichmond.com
- **Norfolk International Airport:** ORF; 2200 Norview Ave., Norfolk; www.norfolkairport.com

# MORE INFORMATION

## TRAVEL AND TOURISM INFORMATION

- **Virginia Is for Lovers:** www.virginia.org
- **Virginia State Parks:** www.dcr.virginia.gov/state-parks

## MAGAZINES

- *Virginia Living:* www.virginialiving.com

# SOUTH

◄ JONES LAKE, NORTH CAROLINA

# THE SOUTH
## State by State

## KENTUCKY

**Why Go:** Bourbon, horses, and Mammoth Cave National Park are big draws in Kentucky.

## TENNESSEE

**Why Go:** The music cities of Nashville and Memphis also have important sights connected to the Civil Rights Movement.

## ARKANSAS

**Why Go:** Where else can you dig for diamonds in a state park?

## LOUISIANA

**Why Go:** Jazz permeates the streets of New Orleans, and there are more food specialties than you can eat on one trip.

## NORTH CAROLINA

**Why Go:** Two great outdoors destinations—The Outer Banks and Great Smoky Mountains National Park—bookend the state, with lots of barbecue in between.

## SOUTH CAROLINA

**Why Go:** History-filled Charleston anchors a coast dotted with captivating natural wetland environments.

## GEORGIA

**Why Go:** The archetypal images of the South—hanging Spanish moss, sculpture-filled cemeteries, and dark-water swamps—plus the dynamic city of Atlanta can all be found in Georgia.

## ALABAMA

**Why Go:** With sights like the Birmingham Civil Rights Institute and the Edmund Pettus Bridge, Civil Rights history is front and center in Alabama.

## MISSISSIPPI

**Why Go:** Travel through time on the Natchez Trace Parkway, and revel in the blues in the Mississippi Delta.

## FLORIDA

**Why Go:** Unique doesn't even begin to describe this state that encompasses miles of beautiful beaches, three national parks, rivers with manatees, and wetlands with alligators.

# South
# ROAD TRIP

With 10 states, the South is an immense area. This road trip covers 6 of them over 21 days, with options to include all 10. It goes through mountains and along beaches, with plenty of music and history along the way.

## NORTH CAROLINA

**Raleigh to Great Smoky Mountains National Park: 3 days / 430 miles (690 kilometers)**
Starting in **Raleigh,** drive 3 hours to **Blowing Rock,** where you'll see a geologic curiosity and spend the night. Take the next day to weave along the **Blue Ridge Parkway** to **Asheville.** In the morning, finish the Blue Ridge Parkway at **Cherokee,** right outside **Great Smoky Mountains National Park.**

## TENNESSEE

**Nashville and Memphis: 5 days / 475 miles (765 kilometers)**
Drive **Newfound Gap Road** through Great Smoky Mountains into

Tennessee, taking the time to stop at viewpoints and do a hike. Stay the night in **Gatlinburg** or **Pigeon Forge.** The next day, drive out to **Nashville** (3.5-4 hours), where you'll spend two nights. From Nashville, make the 3-hour drive to **Memphis,** where you'll also spend two nights.

## MISSISSIPPI

**The Blues Trail and Jackson: 2 days / 255 miles (410 kilometers)**
Memphis is a great jumping-off point for the **Mississippi Blues Trail.** Take Highway 61 south to **Clarksdale,** stopping in **Tunica** on the way. In the morning, hit a couple more Blues Trail towns, **Cleveland** and **Leland,** on your way to **Jackson.**

## ALABAMA

**Birmingham, Selma, and Montgomery: 3 days / 380 miles (610 kilometers)**
Spend the morning in Jackson, then drive 3.5 hours to **Birmingham.** The

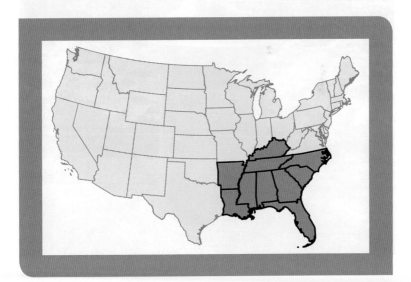

ELIZABETHAN GARDENS AT THE FORT RALEIGH NATIONAL HISTORIC SITE, NORTH CAROLINA

next day, visit your choice of Birmingham Civil Rights sights. In the morning, head south 2 hours to **Selma,** where you can walk across the historic Edmund Pettus Bridge. From Selma, drive to the state capital of **Montgomery,** where you'll spend the night.

## GEORGIA

**Atlanta: 1 day / 160 miles (355 kilometers)**
From Montgomery, drive 2.5 hours to **Atlanta.** Spend the rest of the day exploring the Georgia capital.

## SOUTH CAROLINA

**Congaree and Charleston: 3 days / 335 miles (540 kilometers)**
After a morning in Atlanta, drive 3 hours to the South Carolina capital of **Columbia.** The next morning, visit the nearby **Congaree National Park,** and after walking under the world's tallest forest canopy, make the 2-hour drive to **Charleston.** Spend a day enjoying the coastal city.

## NORTH CAROLINA COAST

**Wilmington to the Outer Banks: 4 days / 220 miles (355 kilometers)**
From Charleston, make the 3.5-hour drive to **Wilmington,** on the southern North Carolina coast. The next day, drive up to Cedar Island; make sure to time the 3-hour drive so you make your ferry (reserve ahead) to **Ocracoke Island,** where you'll stay the night. From Ocracoke, spend the day driving north along Highway 12 up to **Nags Head.** The next day, make the 3-hour drive back to Raleigh.

## ADDING KENTUCKY

**Mammoth Cave and Bowling Green: 2 days / 315 miles (510 kilometers)**
Instead of going straight to Nashville from Great Smoky Mountains National Park, head to **Mammoth Cave,** which is 3.5 hours away in southern Kentucky. Spend the night in **Bowling Green,** home of the Corvette, before heading an hour south to Nashville.

WILD HORSE AT DUNGENESS RUINS ON CUMBERLAND ISLAND NATIONAL SEASHORE, GEORGIA

## ADDING ARKANSAS

**Little Rock and Hot Springs National Park: 2 days / 395 miles (635 kilometers)**
**Little Rock** is 2 hours west of Memphis, and **Hot Springs National Park** is one hour west of Little Rock. To get to the Blues Trail towns from Little Rock is about 2.5 hours.

## ADDING LOUISIANA

**New Orleans: 3+ days / 535 miles (860 kilometers) or 395 miles (635 kilometers)**
From Jackson, **New Orleans** is 3 hours south. You'll want to spend at least a day there before making the 5-hour drive to Birmingham. Or you could head to Gulf Shores, Alabama, for some beach time before picking up the route again in Montgomery.

## ADDING FLORIDA

**St. Augustine and South: 2+ days / 490 miles (790 kilometers)**
From Charleston, **St. Augustine** in northern Florida is a 5-hour drive, with Savannah, Georgia, another lovely coastal city, along the way. From St. Augustine, **Fort Pierce,** north of West Palm Beach, is another 5.5 hours.

CIVIL WAR CANNONS AT SHILOH NATIONAL MILITARY PARK, TENNESSEE

CONGAREE NATIONAL PARK, SOUTH CAROLINA

# KENTUCKY

To put Kentucky into words is hard, because Kentucky is more than a collection of places. It's more than thoroughbred horses grazing on rich limestone-fed land in the rolling hills around Lexington. It's more than the bustling downtown streets of Louisville, where new enterprise lives in historic buildings. It's more than weathered tobacco barns, bourbon distilleries, record-length caves, and bluegrass festivals. Kentucky is a feeling, like sunshine in the winter or rain on a warm spring day.

Kentucky is on Shawnee, Cherokee, and Chickasaw land. It is a place of warm hospitality, where people treat neighbors like family, and are never too busy to sit on the porch for a glass of sweet tea and some gossip. But to assume that Kentucky is all country roads and simple pleasures would be wrong. The state has big urban areas, with innovative art galleries, award-winning restaurants, top-ranked hospitals, and first-rate universities. The birthplace of bluegrass music and home to the first integrated college in the south, Kentucky is at once traditional and progressive.

**AREA:** 40,408 square miles / 10,4656 square kilometers (37th)

**POPULATION:** 4,467,673 (26th)

**STATEHOOD DATE:**
June 1, 1792 (15th)

**STATE CAPITAL:** Frankfort

▲ KEENELAND RACETRACK IN LEXINGTON

## ORIENTATION

**Louisville** is located in the north-central part of the state, right on the Kentucky-Indiana state line. To the east is **Lexington,** which is surrounded by horse country, and the **Bourbon Trail** distilleries. The state capital, **Frankfort,** lies between Louisville and Lexington. **Mammoth Cave National Park** and **Bowling Green** are in south-central Kentucky. **Appalachia** is in eastern Kentucky, while the **Land Between the Lakes** is in western Kentucky.

## WHEN TO GO

The most popular time to visit Kentucky is **May-October.** The **Kentucky Derby** is held on the first Saturday in May. It's a celebratory and fun time to visit, although you'll have to deal with soaring hotel and flight prices as well as crowds in Louisville and surrounding areas. For those who don't mind heat and humidity, **summer** is the peak season for travel. However, many people declare **fall** their favorite season in Kentucky, when temperatures are mild, the trees burst into color, and crowds are down. **Winter** is a quiet time in Kentucky, when some parks and small-town attractions may be closed or have limited hours.

# HIGHLIGHTS

## HORSE COUNTRY

**Keeneland** (4201 Versailles Rd., Lexington; 859/254-3412; www.keeneland.com) is the state's (and maybe the world's) most beautiful racetrack, with lush, meticulously landscaped grounds and stone buildings. The live racing season is short, restricted to **April** and **October,** making every race day, especially those on weekends, feel like an event. If you find yourself in Lexington outside of racing season, you can make your way to the track to watch morning workouts. It's an intimate look at horse racing, and the park-like grounds look stunning in the early morning light. Most workouts end by 10am.

Around Lexington is where you'll find endless rolling hills of bluegrass, immense fields marked by wooden fences, and foals dancing in the morning sunlight. A combined working horse farm, equine competition facility, and horse-based theme park of sorts, the **Kentucky Horse Park** (4089 Iron Works Pkwy., Lexington; 859/259-4257; www.kyhorsepark.com) is the best place to get up close and personal with horses. A visit to the park is easily an all-day affair: start with a horse-drawn trolley

HORSES GRAZING ON KENTUCKY'S GREEN HILLS

# 1 HAVING A MINT JULEP AT THE KENTUCKY DERBY

Churchill Downs, 700 Central Ave., Louisville; www.kdf.org

The Kentucky Derby might be known as the most exciting two minutes in sports, but to Louisville, the Derby lasts far longer than two minutes. In fact, thanks to the **Kentucky Derby Festival,** Derby excitement lasts for a full two weeks, with events like **Thunder Over Louisville,** the largest annual fireworks display in the world; the **Great Steamboat Race;** and the **Pegasus Parade** leading up to the big race on the first Saturday in May. By Friday, locals, who often spend Derby Day itself at parties rather than at the track, flock to Churchill Downs for the running of the **Kentucky Oaks,** a premier race for fillies established alongside the Derby in 1875.

MINT JULEP

The grand finale, of course, is the Kentucky Derby, run every year since 1875 at Churchill Downs, making it the longest-running sporting event in the United States. The actual **Run for the Roses** is the 10th race of the day, with the traditional singing of "My Old Kentucky Home" and the call to the post taking place around 6pm. In the grandstands, women wear extravagant hats, men wear seersucker suits, and everyone enjoys at least one mint julep. When it's time to watch the best three-year-old thoroughbreds in the nation race, all eyes turn to the track.

Tickets for the Kentucky Oaks and Kentucky Derby are available at the gate. Reserved seats are the most difficult to come by. Tickets for the Derby and Oaks are sold together in a package. You can submit a ticket request to Churchill Downs via their website (www.churchilldowns.com), which will enter you into a lottery for tickets. Additionally, a few thousand tickets are released for public sale, again via the website, in December or January. Aside from the Oaks and Derby, most events are free to spectators with a Derby pin. Pins can be purchased at the entrance to all events, as well as at local grocery stores, drugstores, and other retailers.

If you can't make it to the Derby, experiencing it on the 360-degree high-definition screen at the **Kentucky Derby Museum** (704 Central Ave.; 502/637-7097; www.derbymuseum.org) is the next best thing. Interactive exhibits and authentic artifacts allow you to get a taste of Derby Day, and learn what it takes to create a champion thoroughbred. Your admission ticket also allows you to take a guided walking tour of **Churchill Downs** (502/636-4400; www.churchilldowns.com).

# 2 SPELUNKING AT MAMMOTH CAVE NATIONAL PARK

1 Mammoth Cave Pkwy., Mammoth Cave; 270/758-2180; www.nps.gov/maca

Kentucky's one national park is home to the most extensive cave system in the world. With nearly 400 miles (643 kilometers) of mapped passageways and perhaps hundreds of miles of undiscovered routes, Mammoth Cave is so big that no known cave in the world is even half as long as Mammoth. Evidence indicates that humans explored Mammoth Cave 4,000 years ago, although it wasn't until 1798 that the cave was "rediscovered." Established as a national park in 1941, Mammoth

THE HISTORIC ENTRANCE TO MAMMOTH CAVE

Cave was a tourist attraction as early as 1816, making it the second-oldest tourist site in the United States behind Niagara Falls.

To explore the cave, sign up for one of the many **tours** offered each day. Tours range in distance from 0.25 mile (0.8 kilometers) to 5.5 miles (8.8 kilometers) and in time from 1.25 hours to 6.5 hours; introductory and general tours give an overview of the cave, its history, and its formation. Tours can be reserved by phone (877/444-6777) or online (www.recreation.gov), and reservations are highly recommended in the summer.

Above ground, more than 60 miles (96 kilometers) of trails are open to hikers, mountain bikers, and horseback riders. Trail maps are available at the **visitors center.**

## ③ TASTING THE KENTUCKY SPIRIT ALONG THE BOURBON TRAIL

In 1999, the Kentucky Distillers Association decided to turn one of the state's most distinct industries into what is now one of its biggest tourist attractions, creating an official Bourbon Trail (https://kybourbontrail.com). **Bardstown,** the towns of **Loretto, Lebanon,** and **Lawrenceburg,** and state capital **Frankfort** make up the heart of bourbon country, a region of small towns and rolling countryside. Bourbon fanatics will want to go beyond the official trail to visit other major distilleries as well as craft distilleries, but below are a few highlights. All distillery tours end with a bourbon tasting.

- The **Willett Distilling Company** (1869 Loretto Rd., Bardstown; 502/348-0899; www.kentuckybourbonwhiskey.com), with wood ceilings and rough-hewn stone walls, is among the most handsome around and offers a nice range of bourbons to taste.

ORIGINAL COPPER STILLS AT MAKER'S MARK DISTILLERY

- Set on a village-like campus, **Maker's Mark Distillery** (3350 Burks Spring Rd., Loretto; 270/865-2099; www.makersmark.com) wins the award for most picturesque distillery.

- Authorized to produce "medicinal" liquor during Prohibition, **Buffalo Trace Distillery** (1001 Wilkinson Blvd., Frankfort; 502/696-5926; www.buffalotrace.com) owns the title of the oldest continually operating distillery in America.

# *Best* ROAD TRIP

**DAY 1** Start out in **Louisville**, where you can take a tour of **Churchill Downs** and visit some of the distilleries in town.

**DAY 2** Head about 45 minutes south on I-65 and KY-245 toward **Bardstown**, where you can base yourself in the heart of the official **Bourbon Trail.** You'll have your pick of distilleries to visit.

BOURBON TASTING IN LOUISVILLE

**DAY 3** Make your way east to **Lexington**, an hour east on scenic KY-9002. You're in prime horse country now; catch the races at **Keeneland** if you're lucky enough to be visiting during the spring or fall meets, and pay a visit to some of the area's famous equine residents at the **Kentucky Horse Park.**

**DAY 4** You'll find yourself heading into picturesque **Appalachia** on your 45-minute drive to **Berea** on I-75 South. Spend the day visiting the town's many **folk art galleries,** and catch a bluegrass show at **Renfro Valley** in the evening.

THE STABLES AT CHURCHILL DOWNS

**DAY 5** From Berea, it's over an hour's drive south through forested mountains to **Cumberland Falls State Resort Park.** If the timing isn't right to see the famous "moonbow," no matter; there are plenty of trails around the falls to keep you occupied. After hiking, make the two-and-a-half hour drive west to **Bowling Green,** where you'll stay the night.

HORSE RACE AT KEENELAND

**DAY 6** In Bowling Green, start the morning with a tour of the **National Corvette Museum,** pride of Kentucky's third-largest town. Head about 35 minutes north on 1-65 to **Mammoth Cave National Park,** where you can spend the afternoon on the cave tour of your choice. You can camp or stay in the hotel here for the night, or head another 1.5 hours north on 1-65 back to **Louisville,** completing your tour of Kentucky's highlights.

CUMBERLAND FALLS STATE RESORT PARK

MAMMOTH CAVE NATIONAL PARK

tour, then catch the Hall of Champions presentation, which introduces renowned horses to visitors.

Tours of the region are available with **Blue Grass Tours** (www.bluegrasstours. com), **Horse Farm Tours Inc.** (859/268-2906; www.horsefarmtours.com), **Thoroughbred Heritage Horse Farm Tours** (800/979-3370; www.seethechampions.com), or **Unique Horse Farm Tours** (800/259-4225; www.kyhorsepark. com).

## PORTAL 31 UNDERGROUND MINE

**KY 160, Lynch; 606/848-1530; portal31.org**

If you visit Appalachia, you will, at least once, end up behind a coal truck on a road that doesn't have a place to pass. This is coal country, where generations of men have spent their lives toiling in mines. Between 1917 and 1963, more than 120 million tons (108 million metric tons) of bituminous coal were mined from Portal 31, an underground drift mine owned by U.S. Steel. In October 2009, Portal 31 reopened for tours, offering visitors a fascinating look at life inside a coal mine. Participants on the 35-minute tour board a mine car for a jostling ride into the mine and through its history. Through animatronic displays featuring miners at work, you'll hear about the people who came to Lynch to work in the mines (33 different nationalities!), the process of mining and the safety measures taken, the unionization of the mine, the importance of the mines during World Wars I and II, and the evolution of the technology used in mining. The mine is rather dark and may be a bit scary for young children, but it's a must for all others.

## BOWLING GREEN CORVETTE ASSEMBLY PLANT

**600 Corvette Dr., Bowling Green; 270/745-8019; www.bowlinggreenassemblyplant.com**

The Bowling Green Corvette Assembly Plant is the one and only place in the world where Corvettes, America's sports car, are produced. The factory tour, which lasts a minimum of one hour and can last as long as two, allows

# *Major* CITIES

**LOUISVILLE:** Pronounced "LUH-vul" if you want to sound like a local, the biggest city in Kentucky is a fascinating mix of Southern hospitality, Midwestern modesty, and Northern sensibility. In addition to hosting the Kentucky Derby, Louisville is the birthplace of Muhammad Ali and the Louisville Slugger baseball bat.

**LEXINGTON:** Kentucky's second most populous city is a Southern-style metropolis, surrounded by the horse farms that make Lexington the center of the equine universe.

**BOWLING GREEN:** A college town that has grown into a city with the third largest population in the state, Bowling Green takes great pride in being the only place in the world where Corvettes are made.

participants to watch multiple steps of production, from the kitting out of the interiors to the final testing process as the cars are driven off the line.

Nearby, the **National Corvette Museum** (350 Corvette Dr., Bowling Green; 270/781-7973; www.corvettemuseum.com) is the only museum in the world dedicated solely to one specific model of car. Well-designed exhibits place the car into context in American history, discuss its role in performance sports, and celebrate the Corvette lifestyle.

## BEREA

Lots of towns have art galleries. What makes Berea unique is the fact that a huge portion of the artwork being sold in Berea is made right here in Berea. The backbone of Berea's status as the Folk Arts and Crafts Capital of Kentucky is the studio artist program, in which working artists operate combined studio galleries, not only selling their work to the public, but also sharing with them their creative process. Square purple signs bearing a four-hand design designate studio artists' galleries, where you can watch artists blow glass, weave, woodwork, throw pots, and more. The majority of studio artists are located in Old Town (Broadway), but a few are in College Square. Because Berea is so easy to walk, you can just wander the two districts, keeping an eye out for the studio artist signs. You can also pick up the Berea Working Artists Studio Map or the Map to Art in Berea brochure from the **Old Town Welcome Center** (201 N. Broadway; 800/598-5263; www.berea.com). Although it feels unfair to single out artists, as they all are truly exceptional, here are a couple of highlights:

- In College Square, visit **Warren May** (110 Center St.; 859/986-9293; www.warrenamay.com), a woodworker who creates beautiful pieces of furniture, but is most known for his Appalachian dulcimers.

- To learn about the process of weaving on a variety of looms, visit Mary Colmer at **Weaver's Bottom** (140 N. Broadway; 859/986-8661) in Old Town. Mary's husband Neil, who was a hand weaver for 50 years, retired and handed her the reins in 2018. The shop still turns out bed covers, blankets, rugs, shawls, and more in all kinds of colors and patterns.

## BLUEGRASS MUSIC

As the birthplace of bluegrass, Kentucky prides itself on its musical

NATIONAL CORVETTE MUSEUM

heritage and works hard to preserve the old-time music that has inspired generations. From front porches to concert halls, there are many places throughout the state where you can hear music. Here are a few favorites.

- No place has better preserved the tradition of country, bluegrass, and gospel music than **Renfro Valley Entertainment Center** (U.S. 25, Renfro Valley; 800/765-7464; www. renfrovalley.com. Here, the jamming still takes place in a barn, and performers address the audience as if it's made up of old friends.

- The International **Bluegrass Music Museum** (117 Daviess St., Owensboro; 270/926-7891; www.bluegrassmuseum.org), in western Kentucky, celebrates the tradition of bluegrass music, which got its start in this region before becoming popular around the globe. Artifacts, such as outfits worn by Bill Monroe, the father of bluegrass, and instruments that belonged to the Blue Grass Boys, trace the history of bluegrass.

- Every Friday night, a handful of bluegrass bands take to the stage at the **Rosine Barn Jamboree** (8205 U.S. 62E, Rosine; 270/274-5552). The feature entertainment starts at 7pm and rolls on into the night. The jamboree is literally held in a weathered old barn, plain except for a painted sign and a bronze plaque honoring Bill Monroe, who made one of his last appearances here.

# BEST SCENIC DRIVES

## LINCOLN HERITAGE SCENIC HIGHWAY

### U.S. 31E and U.S. 150

Abraham Lincoln was born in a tiny cabin in the knobs of Central Kentucky. This driving tour, which takes you on U.S. 31E and U.S. 150, begins in **Hodgenville,** where you can visit the **Abraham Lincoln Birthplace and Boyhood Home** (www.nps.gov/abli) and the **Lincoln Museum** (www.lincolnmuseum-ky.org). You'll then pass through **Bardstown,** the center of Kentucky's Bourbon Trail. The highway continues to **Springfield,** home of **Lincoln Homestead State Park; Perryville,** site of

## FALL FOLIAGE

Fall in Kentucky is a sensory experience, marked by crisp and cool mornings, pumpkin-flavored everything, the smell of bonfires, and, perhaps above all else, the colors of the changing leaves. Together, these beautiful trees—the bright reds and oranges of sugar maples; the plum purple of ash; the yellow of poplars, birches, and willows; and the dark red of dogwoods, redwoods, and sassafras—paint the landscape. Although one's mind naturally goes to the mountains when it's leaf-peeping time, every region of the state has wonderful sites for taking in the colors of fall.

- Within Louisville, head to the **Olmsted Parks.** If you're willing to go a bit farther afield, hike through the colorful forests of **Otter Creek Outdoor Recreation Area.**

- **Bernheim Arboretum** (www.bernheim.org), in Clermont along the Bourbon Trail, is a prime choice for fall beauty, especially if you venture out onto the Canopy Tree Walk.

- For an in-city escape in Lexington, take a stroll through the **University of Kentucky Arboretum,** where color abounds

- **Land Between the Lakes** is a kaleidoscope of color in fall.

Kentucky's biggest Civil War battle; and **Danville,** where Kentucky statehood was negotiated.

## RED RIVER GORGE SCENIC BYWAY

### KY 77

For downright beauty, nothing beats the Red River Gorge Scenic Byway (KY 77). This 46-mile (74-kilometer) drive through Appalachia, while short, can easily fill an entire day. You'll pass through the very cool **Nada Tunnel** as you enter **Red River Gorge Geological**

Area, and then you'll spend most of your day pulled over at hiking trailheads and viewpoints. Make sure your hiking shoes are in the trunk, because you'll want to visit **Sky Bridge** and **Angel Windows,** which are accessible by a short walk. You may also want to paddle Red River or take the sky lift at **Natural Bridge State Resort Park.**

## COVERED BRIDGES

Adding to Kentucky's idyllic scenery of fields and barns are 13 covered bridges, eight of which are concentrated in Northern Kentucky, particularly around Fleming County, northwest of Lexington. The majority of these bridges have long since been closed to traffic, but a few let you cross either by car or on foot, and all pose prettily for photos, transporting those who stop and take notice back to a different era. Eight of the region's bridges can be seen in a looping day's drive, in the order below. This entire loop totals 217 miles (349 kilometers), and it will take 5-5.5 hours to drive the whole circuit, not counting time spent at each bridge. It's certainly a full day's trip, but it's a very scenic route and a lovely way to explore the rural areas of this region. Start in Covington and drive east on AA Highway (KY 9) to reach the first bridge.

- **Walcott Covered Bridge:** N 38° 43.992 W 084° 05.868
- **Dover Covered Bridge:** N 38° 45.018 W 083° 52.719
- **Valley Pike Covered Bridge:** N 38° 40.470 W 083° 52.320

- **Cabin Creek Covered Bridge:** N 38° 36.574 W 083° 37.277
- **Goddard White Covered Bridge:** N 38° 21.738 W 083° 36.930
- **Ringo's Mill Covered Bridge:** N 38° 16.110 W 083° 36.624
- **Grange City Covered Bridge:** N 38° 15.294 W 083° 39.192
- **Johnson Creek Covered Bridge:** N 38° 28.950 W 083° 58.722

# BEST PARKS AND RECREATION AREAS

## NATURAL BRIDGE STATE RESORT PARK

2135 Natural Bridge Rd., Slade; 606/663-2214; http://parks.ky.gov

More than 20 miles (32 kilometers) of trails wind through the forested acres of Natural Bridge State Resort Park in eastern Kentucky. The 0.75-mile (1.2-kilometer) Original Trail climbs to the top of Natural Bridge, a 65-foot-high (19.8-meter) natural sandstone arch that spans 78 feet (23.7 meters). The arch can also be reached by a sky lift. Multiple other trails, many of them short and family-friendly, lead to other natural formations, such as Balanced Rock, Battleship Rock, Henson's Arch, and Whittleton Arch.

## CUMBERLAND FALLS STATE RESORT PARK

7351 KY 90, Corbin; 606/528-4121; http://parks.ky.gov

Ever seen a moonbow? If not, then you need to get yourself to Cumberland Falls State Resort Park in southern Kentucky during a full moon. On clear full-moon nights and the two nights before and after, the light from the moon creates a rainbow over Cumberland Falls, a 125-foot waterfall that drops 60 feet (18.2 meters). If you can't make it for the moonbow, the waterfall is beautiful year-round, arched over by rainbows in the mist on sunny days, framed by colorful trees in the fall, and magical in the snow and ice of winter. Hiking at the park is particularly excellent, with more

GRANGE CITY COVERED BRIDGE

CUMBERLAND FALLS STATE RESORT PARK

than 17 miles (27 kilometers) of trails tracing through the surrounding forests and down to the falls.

## LAKE CUMBERLAND

Lake Cumberland is houseboat heaven. At 101 miles (162 kilometers) long, Lake Cumberland is a long, narrow lake with many creeks and coves shooting off in all directions. These coves invite houseboats to tie up and establish camp. People throw out rafts and go for a float or a swim, and then return to the houseboat to take a ride down the slide or jump in the hot tub.

Two state parks and multiple private resorts and marinas line the shores of Lake Cumberland, offering options to rent boats and providing places to sleep on land. The lake has two main activity areas. The **Jamestown** area, which is on the northwest section of the lake, is home to **Cumberland Lake State Resort Park** (5465 State Park Rd., Jamestown; 270/343-3111; http://parks. ky.gov) and many of the most popular marinas. The **Burnside** area, at the far eastern end of the lake and close to the city of Somerset, is where you'll find the quieter **General Burnside State Park** (8801 S. U.S. 27, Burnside; 606/561-4104; http://parks.ky.gov) and a handful of other marinas.

## LAND BETWEEN THE LAKES NATIONAL RECREATION AREA

www.lbl.org

The thousands of acres of land at this national recreation area in western Kentucky welcome hiking, biking, camping, and other outdoor pursuits. Boat ramps are located up and down Land Between the Lakes, providing access to both Kentucky Lake and Lake Barkley. You must bring your own boat, as there are no marinas or rental facilities for motorboats in the area. The **Golden Pond Visitors Center** (100 Van Morgan Dr., Golden Pond; 270/924-2000) can provide permits for backcountry camping and arm you with maps, as can welcome stations are located at both the north and south ends of the park. There are no gas stations in the recreation area, so you should fill your tank before entering.

# FESTIVALS AND EVENTS

The Kentucky Derby Festival is Kentucky's most famous event, but there plenty of other festivals to spark a visit.

## KENTUCKY BOURBON FESTIVAL

Bardstown; 800/638-4877; www.kybourbonfestival.com; mid-Sept.

## BEST SOUVENIRS

- **Bourbon** is perhaps the most iconic taste of Kentucky you can bring home with you.
- Grab a fanciful **derby hat** at the gift shops at Keeneland or Churchill Downs.
- The authentic **folk art** made in the studios of Berea is another one-of-a-kind Kentucky keepsake.

Bardstown, the Bourbon Capital of the World hosts this six-day festival, an absolute must for lovers of America's native spirit. Highlights of the festival include the Great Kentucky Bourbon Tasting and Gala and the Kentucky Bourbon All-Star Sampler. Each of these events allows participants to meet with master distillers and taste the best bourbons being made.

### BLUEGRASS FESTIVALS

Kentucky has more than its share of bluegrass festivals across the state. The **Festival of the Bluegrass** (Lexington, www.festivalofthebluegrass.com, early June) and **Vine Grove Bluegrass Music Festival** (Vine Grove; 270/877-5636; www.vinegrovebluegrass.com; Sept.).

### COLLEGE BASKETBALL

College basketball's March Madness can be bigger than Christmas here, where the passion ignited by Kentucky's two teams is palpable. Lexington's **University of Kentucky Wildcats** men's basketball team (www.ukathletics.com), which has won multiple national titles, play inside **Rupp Arena** (430 W. Vine St., Lexington; www.rupparena.com). In mid-October, **Midnight Madness,** the first day that the NCAA allows formal basketball practice to be held, marks the beginning of what fans consider to be the best time of the year.

The **University of Louisville Cardinals** (502/852-5732; www.uoflsports.com) are Louisville's men's basketball team, playing their home games at the 22,000-seat **KFC Yum! Center** (S. 2nd St. and W. Main St). The basketball rivalry with the cross-state Kentucky Wildcats is rabid.

# BEST FOOD

## FRIED CHICKEN AND SOUTHERN HOME COOKING

Southern home cooking is probably the most popular style of food in the state. KFC doesn't have a stranglehold on fried chicken around here. It's found on many menus, along with country ham, fried catfish, pork chops, fried green tomatoes, okra, soup beans, and cornbread. Try it at these favorites:

- **Kurtz Restaurant:** 418 E. Stephen Foster Ave., Bardstown; 502/348-8964; www.kurtzrestaurant.com
- **Beaumont Inn Dining Room:** 638 Beaumont Inn Dr., Harrodsburg; 859/734-3381; www.beaumontinn.com

## BARBECUE

Barbecue is another Kentucky specialty, with Owensboro and Western Kentucky being the focal point and mutton being the meat of choice. Burgoo, a barbecue-style stew of meats and vegetables, is a uniquely Kentucky contribution to barbecue.

- **Moonlite Bar-B-Q:** 2840 W. Parrish Ave., Owensboro; 270/684-8143; www.moonlite.com
- **Old Hickory Bar-B-Q:** 338 Washington Ave., Owensboro; 270/926-9000; www.oldhickorybar-b-q.com

CRISPY FRIED CHICKEN

## MAJOR AIRPORTS

- **Cincinnati/Northern Kentucky International Airport:** CVG; 3087 Terminal Dr., Hebron; www.cvgairport.com
- **Louisville International Airport:** SDF; 600 Terminal Dr., Louisville; www.flylouisville.com
- **Blue Grass Airport:** LEX; 4000 Terminal Dr., Lexington; www.bluegrassairport.com

## MORE INFORMATION

### TRAVEL AND TOURISM INFORMATION

- **Kentucky Department of Tourism:** 800/225-8747; www.kentuckytourism.com
- **Kentucky State Parks:** https://parks.ky.gov

### NEWSPAPERS AND MAGAZINES

- *Courier-Journal:* Louisville; www.courierjournal.com
- *Lexington Herald-Leader:* www.kentucky.com
- *Kentucky Monthly:* www.kentuckymonthly.com
- *Louisville Magazine:* www.loumag.com

# TENNESSEE

Tennessee offers a suggestion for every season, every mood, and every personality. It's the cradle of country music and the birthplace of the blues. Creativity of all kinds seems to flow in the rivers and in the veins of the folks who call the Volunteer State home. It fosters an entrepreneurial energy that results in funky, offbeat music clubs, quirky boutiques, and one-of-a-kind roadside eateries: Allow us to introduce you to bluegrass, to Appalachian and African quilts, to meat-and-three, hot chicken, and barbecue.

Tennessee is on Cherokee, Chickasaw, Koasati, Quapaw, Shawnee and Yuchi land. From eastern Tennessee's mountains—real mountains that climb up to cloud-covered peaks and plunge down into valleys—moving west, the mountains become rolling hills of Middle Tennessee and the plains toward Memphis and the mighty Mississippi, Father of Waters.

Come to explore, to eat, to drink, to distill, to study, to shop, to hike and climb, to fish and run rivers, to hear music, to play music. No matter what brings you here, Southern hospitality ensures that you'll feel at home minutes after your arrival.

**AREA:** 42,144 square miles / 109,152 square kilometers (36th)

**POPULATION:** 6,829,174 (16th)

**STATEHOOD DATE:** June 1, 1796 (16th)

**STATE CAPITAL:** Nashville

BIG SOUTH FORK NATIONAL RIVER AND RECREATION AREA

## ORIENTATION

Tennessee's big cities zigzag across the state. **Knoxville** is in the east and serves as a gateway to **Great Smoky Mountains National Park,** which straddles the state's eastern border with North Carolina. **Chattanooga** sits in the southeast, right near the border with Georgia. In the central-north of the state is the capital and largest city of **Nashville,** while in the far southwest is **Memphis,** bordering Arkansas to the west and Mississippi to the south.

## WHEN TO GO

**Summer** is the season of hot weather, crowds, and some of the biggest music festivals and events. If you can, avoid the crowds and the heat. **Spring—** when the weather is mild and flora is in bloom—and **fall**—when the trees change color and temperatures drop— are the best times to explore Tennessee. Visitors in **winter** may encounter cold weather and snow, and some attractions close or cut back hours.

# HIGHLIGHTS

## GRACELAND

3717 Elvis Presley Blvd., Memphis; 901/332-3322; www.graceland.com

Attracting 650,000 visitors annually, Elvis Presley's Graceland mansion in south Memphis was declared a National Historic Site in 2006. Here you'll find a 200,000-square-foot (18,530-square-meter) complex housing a career museum, automobile collection, and several other exhibits featuring everything from fashion to the King's army gear. The portrait of Elvis that emerges is sympathetic and remarkably human for a man who is so often portrayed as larger than life.

Visitors can choose from five tours. High points include watching the press conference Elvis gave after leaving the army, witnessing firsthand his audacious taste in decor, and visiting the Meditation Garden, where Elvis, his parents, and his grandmother are buried. The exhibits gloss over some of the challenges Elvis faced in his life—his addiction to prescription drugs, his womanizing and failed marriage, and his unsettling affinity for firearms among them. But they showcase Elvis' generosity, his dedication to family, and his fun-loving character.

## SHILOH NATIONAL MILITARY PARK

1055 Pittsburg Landing Rd., Shiloh; 731/689-5696; www.nps.gov/shil

The Battle of Shiloh is one of the most remembered of the Civil War; it was the

GRACELAND, MEMPHIS

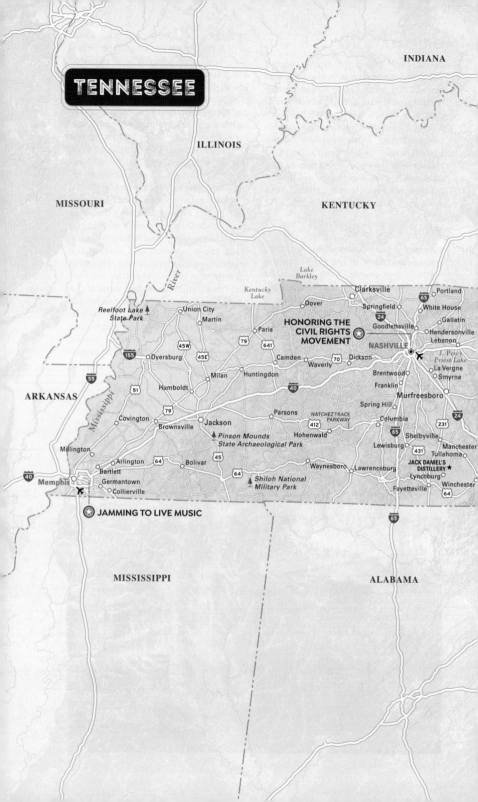

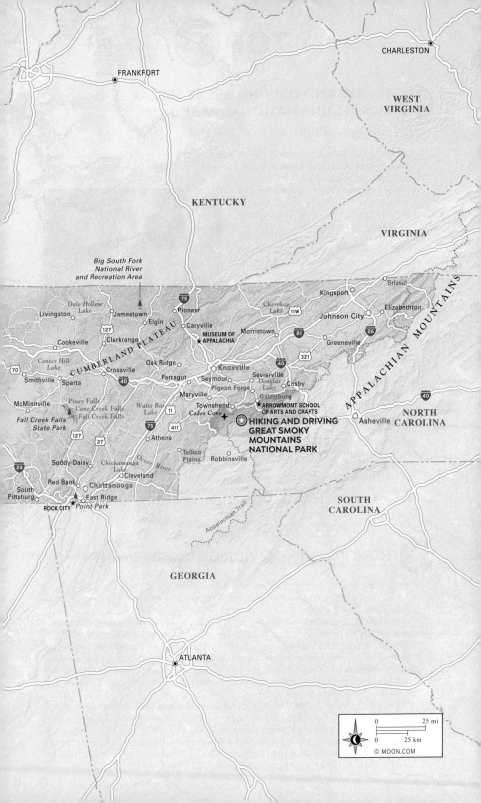

# TOP 3

## 1 HIKING AND DRIVING GREAT SMOKY MOUNTAINS NATIONAL PARK

Gatlinburg; 865/436-1200; www.nps.gov/grsm

Straddling the Tennessee-North Carolina border, the Great Smoky Mountains National Park is the single most popular national park in the United States, and for good reason. The park's iconic vistas of blue-green mountains topped by the namesake smoky mists are awesome, yet somehow comforting. The scenery in the Smokies is unrivaled.

CADES COVE

Once you start hiking the 800 miles (1,287 kilometers) of hiking trails within the park, you might never want to stop. On the Tennessee side, try **Grotto Falls Trail,** a popular hike to a picture-perfect waterfall, The Smokies are also more car-accessible than other national parks, meaning even those who can't or don't want to hike or bike can enjoy the sights. **Newfound Gap Road,** which connects Gatlinburg, Tennessee, to Cherokee, North Carolina, and the **Cades Cove Loop** are among the favorite places for exploring by car.

Spring in the Smokies is the season of variable weather; summer is generally hot, with lots of haze; winter snow is deep in the high elevations; autumn is the park's greatest season. In mid-May to mid-June, **synchronous fireflies** make their mating display. Although the timing of the peak varies, it's such a popular event that the park restricts evening visitation and conducts a lottery for a limited number of passes. Shuttles to the fireflies leave from Sugarland Visitor Center on the Tennessee side of the park.

Check the weather forecast before you pack. Temperatures in the park can be as much as 30 degrees colder than the surrounding area, and the park receives more rainfall than anywhere else in the United States except the Pacific Northwest—all that mist and fog is why they call them "the Smokies."

## 2 HONORING THE CIVIL RIGHTS MOVEMENT

The Civil Rights Movement can be traced across the state. From the Civil War to civil rights, baseball to Oprah, the African American experience is part of what made Tennessee the place it is.

If you do nothing else while you are in Memphis, or, frankly, in the state of Tennessee, visit the **National Civil Rights Museum** (450 Mulberry St., Memphis; 901/521-9699; www.civilrightsmuseum.org), built on the Lorraine Motel site, where Dr. Martin Luther King Jr. was assassinated on April 4, 1968. Exhibits display original letters, audio recordings, photos, and newspaper clippings from events including the Montgomery bus boycott, *Brown v. Board of Education*, Freedom Summer, and the march from Selma to Montgomery.

In Nashville, head to the **Civil Rights Room at the Nashville Public Library** (615 Church St., second floor; 615/862-5782; http://library.nashville.org) for a powerful exhibit on the movement in Nashville in the 1950s and 1960s. Large format photos show school desegregation, sit-ins, and a silent march to the courthouse that tell the story of the courageous men and women who helped make Nashville the first Southern city to desegregate public services.

NATIONAL CIVIL RIGHTS MUSEUM AT THE LORRAINE MOTEL

## ③ JAMMING TO LIVE MUSIC IN MEMPHIS AND NASHVILLE

Whether it's blues on Beale Street or classic country at the Grand Ole Opry, live music goes deep in Tennessee.

If you want to delve into the history and character of Memphis music, your starting point should be **Beale Street,** home of the blues. From the 1880s until the 1960s, Beale Street was the epicenter of African American life, not just for Memphians but also for the entire Mid-South region. Today, Beale Street has two distinct personalities. During the day it is a laid-back place to stroll, buy souvenirs, and eat. At night, Beale Street is a strip of nightclubs and restaurants, a great place to people watch, and the best place in the state, if not the country, to catch live blues seven nights a week. Nearly all Beale Street bars have live music, but a couple of the most popular are **B. B. King's Blues Club** (143 Beale St.; 901/524-5464; www.bbkings. com) and **Blues City Café** (138 Beale St.; 901/526-3637; www.bluescitycafe. com).

A couple hours east, Nashville is where America goes to make music. There is a song in the air all around the city—starting in Music Valley, modern home of the **Opry** (2802 Opryland Dr.; 615/871-6779; www.opry.com), with performances of its weekly radio country music showcase at least twice a week. The historic **Ryman Auditorium**

BLUES CITY CAFÉ

(116 5th Ave. N.; 615/889-3060; http://ryman.com) remains one of the best places in the United States to hear live music. But Nashville's most colorful country music establishments are the honky-tonks that line **Broadway.** For intimate views into songwriting and the roots of bluegrass and country music, try **The Bluebird Café** (4104 Hilsboro Pk.; 615/383-1461; http://bluebirdcafe.com) or **The Station Inn** (402 12th Ave. S.; 615/255-3307; www.stationinn.com).

# *Best* ROAD TRIP

**DAY 1**
Start in **Memphis,** where you can spend the day touring the **National Civil Rights Museum,** eating great **barbecue,** and at night, visiting the **blues joints** lining **Beale Street.**

**DAY 2**
Wake up early today to make two very different kinds of pilgrimages: First, drive 10 minutes south on I-69 to **Graceland,** the most famous home of the King, Elvis Presley. From here, it's a 2-hour drive on U.S. 72 E and TN-57 E to **Shiloh National Military Park,** site of one of the most remembered battles of the Civil War.

B.B. KING'S BLUES CLUB ON BEALE STREET

**DAY 3**
Continue east on U.S. 64 E toward **Chattanooga,** a 4-hour drive, with one important stop midway at **Jack Daniel's Distillery.** In Chattanooga, head up to **Lookout Mountain** in time for sunset.

**DAY 4**
Today make a beeline to **Smoky Mountains National Park.** It's a 3-hour drive via I-75 N to **Cades Cove,** which you should visit first to beat the crowds, followed by a nearby **hike.** Wrap up the day exploring Spend the night in **Knoxville,** 1.5 hours east on E Lamar Alexander Pkwy.

VIEW FROM LOOKOUT MOUNTAIN AT TWILIGHT

**DAY 5**
For the last big stop of the trip, head to **Nashville,** 3 hours away on 1-40 W. But first, make a worthy stop 20 minutes north of Knoxville at the **Museum of Appalachia.** When you arrive in Music City, be sure to spend an hour or two the **Civil Rights Room at the Nashville Public Library,** followed by a night out on the town at the **honky-tonks** of **lower Broadway.**

**DAY 6**
You'll likely wake up late after your night on the town; fuel up with biscuits at **Biscuit Love** or **Loveless Café,** followed by a tour of the **Grand Ole Opry.** It's a 4-hour drive to get back to Memphis.

CADES COVE

**NASHVILLE:** Tennessee's capital is where tomorrow's hits are written, but it's limiting to think that music is all there is to the city that also offers Civil Rights history and a vibrant dining scene.

**MEMPHIS:** Music has also defined this Southern metropolis on the banks of the Mississippi, famous for the blues and barbecue.

**KNOXVILLE:** Perhaps the state's most underappreciated city, Knoxville sits in the foothills of the Appalachian Mountains, with a lively downtown.

battle that demonstrated to both the North and South that the war would be a longer and harder fight than either had imagined. Shiloh today is a landscape of alternating open fields and wooded forest, populated by hundreds of monuments to soldiers who fought and died at Shiloh on April 6-7, 1862. The peacefulness of the present brings to even greater focus the violence of the battle that took place here more than 150 years ago and claimed nearly 24,000 lives.

Sights within the park include the **peach orchard,** now being regrown, where soldiers described the peach blossoms falling like snow on the dead and injured, and the **Hornet's Nest,** the site of some of the most furious fighting. The 10-acre (4-hectare) **Shiloh National Cemetery** is next to the visitors center; two-thirds of the 3,695 bodies here are unidentified. Most are Union soldiers killed at Shiloh; the Confederate dead were buried in five trenches around the battlefield and remain there today. Nearly 800 years before the Civil War, the riverbank near present-day Shiloh was home to a mound-building Mississippian Indian community. The **Shiloh Indian Mounds** that they left behind sit along the west bluff of the riverbank.

## JACK DANIEL'S DISTILLERY

133 Lynchburg Hwy./TN-55; 931/759-6457; www.jackdaniels.com

As you drive into or walk around the small town of Lynchburg in southern Tennessee, you might notice some odd-looking gray warehouses peeking

out above the treetops. These are barrel houses, where Jack Daniel's Distillery ages its whiskey.

Thousands of whiskey drinkers make the pilgrimage here every year to see how Jack Daniel's is made on one of the two tours. And what they find is that, aside from the use of electricity, computers, and the sheer scale of the operation, things have not changed too much since 1866, when Jack Daniel registered his whiskey still at the mouth of Cave Spring near Lynchburg, making this the oldest registered distillery in the United States. Daniel was introduced to the whiskey business by a Lutheran lay preacher named Dan Call, working with master distiller (and former enslaved person) Nathan "Nearest" Green. Perhaps less famous than the bourbon produced by Kentucky to the north, Tennessee whiskey is a specific kind of spirit, and getting to know its charcoal-filtered goodness is a must when visiting the Volunteer State.

## APPALACHIAN CULTURE

From authentic craftmaking to traditional Appalachian bluegrass, there's a rich heritage to explore in Tennessee's mountains. A good place to start is the **Museum of Appalachia** (2819 Andersonville Hwy., Clinton; 856/494-7680; www.museumofappalachia. org) outside Knoxville, a 250,000-artifact collection that contains more of the history of the mountainous eastern Tennessee region than any other place in the state, including precious musical instruments like fiddles and banjos. Indoor exhibits include the Appalachian Hall of Fame, a remarkable collection of items that were made,

DEMONSTRATION AT THE MUSEUM OF APPALACHIA

used, and treasured by the people who came and created a life in the rugged land of southern Appalachia; outside, the museum has a collection of mountain buildings.

Near Gatlinburg, the **Arrowmont School of Arts and Crafts** (556 Parkway, Gatlinburg; 865/436-5860; www.arrowmont.org) began in 1912 as a settlement school for mountain folks, opening the Arrowcraft Shop as a retail outlet for local crafts in 1926. Today, Arrowmont is known for its contemporary arts-and-crafts education, best experienced by taking a class, or with a visit to the Arrowmont Galleries.

## DOLLYWOOD

2700 Dollywood Parks Blvd., Pigeon Forge; 800/365-5996; www.dollywood.com

There is no way around it: Dollywood is just good clean fun. Owned and operated by Sevier County native Dolly Parton, the Dollywood theme park combines excellent rides with family-friendly entertainment. Mountain craft demonstrations keep Dolly's childhood alive. The park's wooden roller coaster, the Thunderhead, is thrilling and fun; and the Blazing Fury takes you through an 1880s frontier town engulfed in flames. The non-thrill ride Dollywood Express takes you on a 5-mile (8-kilometer) railroad journey through the foothills of the Smokies. There is also the Calico Falls Schoolhouse, a replica of a one-room mountain school, and the Southern Gospel Music Hall of Fame.

Dollywood also offers live music. Performers on various stages play bluegrass, country, gospel, and oldies. All shows are included with your admission to Dollywood. In addition, arts-and-crafts demonstrations are also a big part of Dollywood. You can watch glassblowers at work, see lye soap being made, and observe candles being dipped. A blacksmith shop produces metalwork, and a woodcarver makes one-of-a-kind pieces of artwork.

# BEST SCENIC DRIVES

There's a scenic drive for each season in Tennessee; fuel up the car and take the winding road on some of the best routes.

## NATCHEZ TRACE: TENNESSEE

Wildflowers bloom on the northern section of this 120-mile (193-kilometer) historic route from Nashville to the Tennessee/Alabama border in spring. The first people to travel what is now considered the Natchez Trace were probably Choctow and Chickasaw people, who made the first footpaths through the region. Early white settlers quickly identified the importance of a land route from Natchez, Mississippi to Nashville. Highlights on the trace near Nashville include the concrete **Double Arch Bridge** (milepost 438, 15 miles/24 kilometers northeast of Franklin), a beautiful feat of engineering; and the **Gordon House and Ferry Site** (milepost

DOUBLE ARCH BRIDGE

407.7, 25 minutes northeast of Columbia, just south of TN-50), a 200-year old former trading post, river crossing, and refuge.

## CHEROHALA SKYWAY
### Hwy. 165

This 54-mile (86-kilometer) scenic route starting in Tellico Plains and crossing the North Carolina border to Robbinsville also crosses three different national forests, climbs to more than 5,300 feet (1,310 meters), and provides stunning scenic views, especially at the **Turkey Creek, Lake View,** and **Brushy Ridge overlooks.** It's a pleasant alternative to congested highways through Great Smoky Mountains National Park, with sights and stops along the way including **Tellico Ranger Station** (250 Ranger Station Rd., Tellico Plains; 423/253-8400), a source of information about the area, and 100-foot-high (30-meter) **Bald River Falls** (off the skyway along Forest Service Road 210). The prettiest times for this drive are summer and fall (avoid the route in wintry weather), and the road is often extremely crowded during leaf season.

# BEST PARKS AND RECREATION AREAS

The purple mountain majesties of the Smokies tend to steal the show in Tennessee, but don't overlook the state's other great parks, which offer beauty and recreational variety—often without the crowds.

## PINSON MOUNDS STATE ARCHAEOLOGICAL PARK

460 Ozier Rd., Jackson; 731/988-5614; https://tnstateparks.com/parks/pinson-mounds

One of the largest complexes of mounds ever built by Woodland Indians is found on Tennessee's western plains, now a state park. A group of at least 17 mounds believed to have been built beginning around 50 BC were discovered in 1820, but it was not until 1961 that the first major investigation of the site

was completed by scientists from the University of Tennessee.

Despite continuing archeological study on the site, many mysteries remain. Among them is the significance of the design and arrangement of the mounds and why the builders abandoned the site around AD 500. Visitors to Pinson Mounds begin in a 4,500-square-foot (418-square-meter) mound replica, which houses a **museum** and **bookstore.** The mounds themselves are spread out along 6 miles (9.6 kilometers) of **hiking trails** that meander through the archaeological park.

## FALL CREEK FALLS STATE PARK

2009 Village Camp Rd., Pikeville; 423/881-5298; https://tnstateparks.com/parks/fall-creek-falls

Tennessee's largest state park is a prime area for outdoor recreation on the Cumberland Plateau. The 25,000-acre (10,117-hectare) park derives its name from 256-feet-tall (78-meter) **Fall Creek Falls,** the tallest waterfall east of the Rocky Mountains, where water plunges past millennia of rock layers and into a pool of water that is deep and mysterious. Visitors to the falls can take an easy stroll from the parking lot to the overlook, and there are other

FALL CREEK FALLS STATE PARK

# GETTING OUT ON THE WATER

In the summer when the weather is hot, Tennesseans all do the same thing: look for some cool water to put themselves in. Here are some of the best places in the state to swim, kayak, boat, raft, and float in the state.

- **Reelfoot Lake State Park:** A few hours north of Memphis, this flooded forest is a hauntingly beautiful landscape of knob-kneed cypress trees, gently rippling water, and open spaces great for boating and fishing.

- **Ocoee River:** White-water rafting is the most popular activity in the southern Cherokee Forest, which covers 650,000 acres (263,045 hectares) on the eastern edge of Tennessee.

- **Big South Fork National River and Recreation Area:** The river gorge carved into the Cumberland Plateau by the Big South Fork over millions of years is a lush playground for paddlers.

waterfalls in the state park, including **Cane Creek Falls, Cane Creek Cascade,** and **Piney Falls.** For information about the flora, fauna, and geological history of the Cumberland Plateau, visit the **nature center** (423/881-5708).

## LOOKOUT MOUNTAIN

Lookout Mountain extends 83 miles (133 kilometers) through Tennessee, Alabama, and Georgia, but the northernmost tip, which overlooks Chattanooga, is the most famous part. **Point Park** (110 Point Park Rd., Lookout Mountain), maintained by the National Park Service and part of the Chickamauga and Chattanooga National Military Park, offers the best views. Several Civil War battles, including the Battle Above the Clouds, took place on Lookout Mountain; students of the Civil War should visit the **Battles for Chattanooga**

**Electric Map and Museum** (1110 E. Brow Rd., Lookout Mountain; 423/821-2812). Chattanooga's most famous attraction may well be **Rock City** (1400 Patten Rd., Lookout Mountain; 800/854-0675; www.seerockcity.com), a remarkable yet hokey rock garden with exceptional views, and **Ruby Falls** (1720 S. Scenic Hwy., Chattanooga; 423/821-2544; www.rubyfalls.com) is an underground waterfall deep within Lookout Mountain that claims to be the tallest underground waterfall in the country.

# FESTIVALS AND EVENTS

In a state with more than 1,000 annual festivals, how do you choose? Start with **Bonnaroo Music and Arts Festival** (Manchester; www.bonnaroo.com; June), which started as a jam-band festival on a Tennessee farm and has grown into one of the most diverse and well-organized music festivals in the United States. Elvis mania always exists in Memphis, but it reaches a fever pitch during **Elvis Week** (Memphis; www.graceland.com/elvisweek; Aug.), the annual remembrance of the King's death.

For your taste buds as well as your ears, the **National Cornbread Festival** (South Pittsburg; www.nationalcornbread.com; Apr.) is a celebration of the iconic Southern side dish that includes bluegrass music, cook-offs, and lots and lots of cornbread. And for something totally different, watch the world's greatest show horses compete in the heart of horse country at the 11-day **Tennessee Walking Horse National Celebration** (Shelbyville; www.twhnc.com; ends the Saturday before Labor Day).

# BEST FOOD

Food is the way Southerners stay connected to their history, show their love, and spend their free time. You can get a good sense of Tennessee by tasting these staples.

## BARBECUE

**Memphis** barbecue is known for being tangy and sweet. Wherever you go,

# BEST SOUVENIRS

- **Traditional crafts:** The folk art and other handicrafts made by Appalachian artisans are some of the most precious objects you can take home with you from Tennessee.

- **Tennessee whiskey:** Distinct from Kentucky bourbon, a bottle of Volunteer State spirits makes a fun souvenir.

- **Music memorabilia:** Grab an Elvis figurine or a record from the band you just saw at the Ryman, or go whole-hog and invest in cowboy boots from **Robert's Western World** (416B Broadway, Nashville; 615/244-9552; https://robertswesternworld.com).

though, it should be cooked low and slow. Try it at **Coletta's** (1063 Parkway East; 901/383-1112; www.colettas.net). On the other side of the state in **Bristol,** there's no pork shoulder or brisket at **Ridgewood Barbecue** (900 Elizabethton Hwy., Old 19E; 423/538-7543), where it's all about the ham.

## HOT CHICKEN

Deep-fried chicken is a Southern favorite, but hot chicken, served panfried and spicy, is the Nashville way. **Prince's Hot Chicken Shack** (123 Ewing Dr., Nashville; 615/226-9442) is the original.

## BISCUITS

Made with baking soda or baking powder instead of yeast, the biscuit is a Southern staple that has stood the test of time. **Biscuit Love** (316 11th Ave. S., Nashville; 615/490-9584; http://biscuitlove.com) and **Loveless Café** (8400 TN-100, Nashville; 615/646-9700; www.lovelesscafe.com) in Nashville serve some of the state's best-known biscuits, and **J.C. Holdway** (501 Union Ave., Knoxville; 865/312-9050; www.jcholdway.com) serves biscuits with pork belly in a James Beard Award-winning setting.

## MEAT-AND-THREES

At its most basic, a meat-and-three is a cafeteria-style restaurant where you choose one meet and three "vegetables" (mac 'n' cheese can be a vegetable here). More so, the meet-and-three is an affordable tradition, and one of the places you're likely to see folks from all walks of life eating together.

The menu at **Big Al's Deli** (1827 4th Ave. N., Nashville; 615/242-8118; www.bigalsdeliandcatering.com) changes daily. Founded in 1919, **Zarzour's Café** (1627 Rossville Ave., Chattanooga; 423/266-0424) shows how immigrants to Tennessee adapted Southern tastes with their own experiences. And everyone who is anyone stands in line for fried chicken and sides at **Chandlers** (3101 E. Magnolia Ave., Knoxville; 865/595-0212; www.chandlersstore.com).

# MAJOR AIRPORTS

- **Nashville International Airport:** BNA; 1 Terminal Dr., Nashville; flynashville.com

- **Memphis International Airport:** MEM; 2491 Winchester Rd., Memphis; flymemphis.com

# MORE INFORMATION

## TRAVEL AND TOURISM INFORMATION

- **Tennessee Department of Tourism:** www.tnvacation.com

- **Tennessee State Parks:** www.tnstateparks.com

## NEWSPAPERS

- *The Tennessean:* www.tennessean.com

# ARKANSAS

Anyone unfamiliar with the humble state of Arkansas might consider its Crater of the Diamonds State Park a fitting metaphor for the state itself. Buried in the park's soil are actual diamonds any visitor can dig for—an experience that's only possible a very few places in the world.

Beyond its literal diamonds, Arkansas, on Osage, Quapaw, Oceti Sakowin land, also holds gems of all other sorts. Bordered by the Ozark Mountains in the northwest and the mighty Mississippi to the east, the aptly named Natural State boasts features ranging from placid swimming holes and relaxing hot springs to churning rivers and towering mountain peaks. Befitting a place with a designated state instrument—the fiddle—Arkansas nurtures its local artists and artisans, celebrating their work at music festivals and handicraft markets. The state also holds important sites that commemorate (or, in some cases, confront) its sometimes complicated history, including Little Rock Central High, which was famously desegregated by nine Black students in 1957, and the historic Dyess community, which sprung from an economic-recovery initiative after the Great Depression, and where Johnny Cash was reared. Both are well worth a visit.

**AREA:** 53,179 square miles / 137,732 square kilometers (29th)

**POPULATION:** 3,032,812 (33rd)

**STATEHOOD DATE:** June 15, 1836 (25th)

**STATE CAPITAL:** Little Rock

▲ WATERFALL IN THE OZARK MOUNTAINS

## ORIENTATION

**Little Rock** is located near the center of Arkansas. Most of the state's attractions are located in its forested western half, including **Hot Springs National Park** and **Crater of the Diamonds State Park** in the southwest, and the southern portion of the **Ozark Mountains** in the northwest. Arkansas's eastern half is adjacent to the Mississippi River and is generally flatter than the western half.

## WHEN TO GO

Arkansas offers pretty pleasant weather year-round and doesn't regularly experience the kinds of major weather events that can derail travel plans. Mild weather and light rainfall in September and October make **fall** is a great time to visit Arkansas. **Spring,** especially April and May, is also pleasant. **Winter** is relatively mild, with lows just below freezing. **Summer** is hot and humid.

# HIGHLIGHTS

## WILLIAM J. CLINTON PRESIDENTIAL LIBRARY AND MUSEUM

1200 President Clinton Ave., Little Rock; tel. 501/374-4242; www.clintonlibrary.gov

Arkansas is one of just a handful of states that feature a presidential library. Arkansas native Bill Clinton lived in Little Rock for 16 years while he was governor of the state. Housed in a modernist, LEED-certified building, the William J. Clinton Presidential Library and Museum includes exhibits, artifacts, and archives from Clinton's two terms as president, as well as artifacts from Hillary Clinton. An exact replica of the Oval Office—down to the last inch—allows you to mimic the experience of sitting behind the big desk.

On the second floor of the museum, African Americans can find their places in this presidential narrative. Here, a permanent exhibit on the Little Rock Nine includes a display of their Congressional Gold Medals, awarded by Clinton in 1999 during a special White House ceremony. This medal is considered the highest civilian honor given by Congress.

## ESSE PURSE MUSEUM

1510 Main St., Little Rock; 501/916-9022; www.essepursemuseum.com

Yes, this is a purse museum, only of three in the world and the only one in the United States. But this little museum is really about women's experiences. Purses are arranged chronologically, with items that would have been in women's purses during that decade. Makeup changed, fashion changed, and women's lives changed as they gained more freedom, worked outside the home, and pushed against the restrictions of society. A fun exhibit allows you to weigh the contents of your purse and write about what you carry. The gift shop, of course, is spectacular,

WILLIAM J. CLINTON PRESIDENTIAL LIBRARY AND MUSEUM

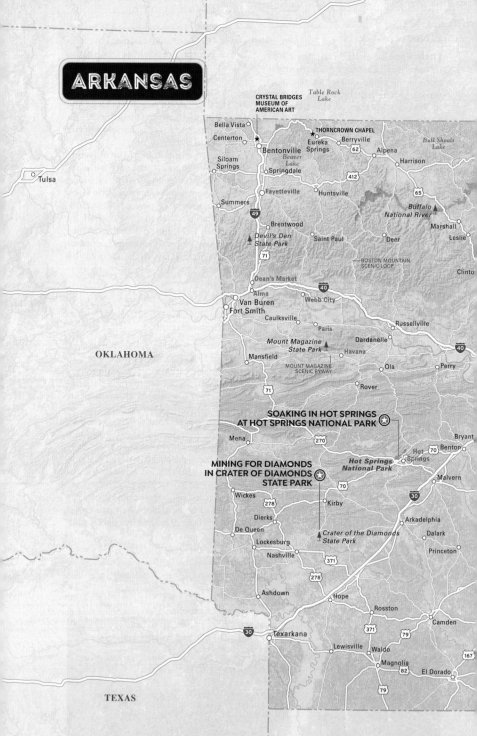

# ARKANSAS

CRYSTAL BRIDGES
MUSEUM OF
AMERICAN ART

*Table Rock Lake*

Bella Vista
Centerton

★ THORNCROWN CHAPEL

Bentonville
*Beaver Lake*
Eureka Springs
Berryville
*Bull Shoals Lake*

Siloam Springs

62
Alpena

Harrison

Springdale

412

Fayetteville
Huntsville

65

Summers

49

*Buffalo National River*

Marshall

Brentwood

*Devil's Den State Park*

Saint Paul
Deer

Leslie

71

*BOSTON MOUNTAIN SCENIC LOOP*

Clinto

Dean's Market

40

Alma
Webb City

Van Buren
Fort Smith

Caulksville
Paris
Russellville

**OKLAHOMA**

Mansfield

*Mount Magazine State Park*

Dardanelle
Havana

40

Ola
Perry

*MOUNT MAGAZINE SCENIC BYWAY*

71

Rover

**SOAKING IN HOT SPRINGS
AT HOT SPRINGS NATIONAL PARK** ⦾

Bryant

Mena

270

*Hot Springs National Park*

Hot Springs

70
Benton

**MINING FOR DIAMONDS
IN CRATER OF DIAMONDS
STATE PARK** ⦾

Malvern

Wickes

278

Kirby
70

30

De Queen

Dierks

*Crater of the Diamonds State Park*

Arkadelphia
Dalark

Lockesburg

Nashville

371

Princeton

278

Ashdown

Hope

Rosston

Camden

30

371
79

El Dorado

167

Texarkana

Lewisville
Waldo

Magnolia

82

79

Tulsa

**TEXAS**

**LOUISIANA**

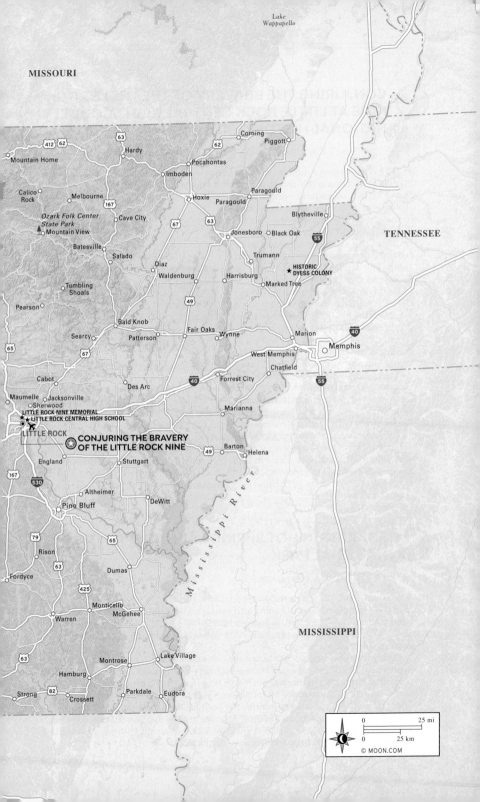

# TOP 3

## 1 CONJURING THE BRAVERY OF THE LITTLE ROCK NINE AT LITTLE ROCK CENTRAL HIGH SCHOOL NATIONAL HISTORIC SITE

2120 W. Daisy L. Gatson Bates Dr., Little Rock; 501/374-1957; www.nps.gov/chsc

In 1957, nine African American students enrolled in Little Rock's all-white Central High School, testing the *Brown v. Board of Education* Supreme Court ruling that found school segregation unconstitutional. The school became a flash point in the struggle for civil rights. The Arkansas National Guard was ordered not to allow the students to enter, while federal troops were ordered to protect them. The students, who came to be known as the Little Rock Nine, faced years of violence and protests. President Barack Obama invited them to his inauguration in 2009, citing their bravery as one of his personal inspirations.

LITTLE ROCK CENTRAL HIGH SCHOOL

You can learn this detailed history at the Little Rock Central High School National Historic Site, which is managed by the National Park Service. Start your visit across the street from the school at the **visitors center,** which includes historical video and photographs. **Little Rock Central High** itself is still a public school, so you can only enter the building with one of the guides, several of whom are Little Rock natives with firsthand memories of this tumultuous time.

Tours include the restored **Mobil gas station,** to the south across Daisy L. Gatson Bates Drive/14th Street, which had the only public telephone at the time. This was where national news media used to file reports on the conflict. Other nearby landmarks include a memorial to the Little Rock Nine across Park Street east of the school, and a bus bench at 13th and Park Streets, where one student sought refuge from the violent crowds.

## 2 SOAKING IN HOT SPRINGS AT HOT SPRINGS NATIONAL PARK

501/620-6715; www.nps.gov/hosp

More than 4,400 years ago, rainwater soaked deep into the earth here, more than 1 mile (1.6 kilometers) down. Coming into contact with a hot fault, the water heated, boiling to the surface again. In today's Hot Springs National Park, this hot water gushes at 700,000 gallons (2.6 million liters) per day, a unique phenomenon in the eastern United States.

This once luxurious spot attracted the rich and famous to Arkansas to enjoy the health benefits of the minerals in these waters—and the most sumptuous cluster of natural hot spring bathhouses in North America. The historic architecture, with marble buildings surrounded by fountains, speaks to the affluence of those times. Today, the buildings house museums, the **Fordyce Bathhouse Visitor Center** (369 Central Ave., Hot Springs; 501/620-6715), and even the **Superior Bathhouse Brewery** (329 Central Ave., Hot Springs; 501/624-2337; www.superiorbathhouse.com), but are still lauded for their architectural distinction.

QUAPAW BATHS & SPA

You'll want to take some time to appreciate the architecture, but of course, the best experience to be had here is a relaxing soak in the springs, which two of the historic bathhouses still offer. For a traditional soak, walk inside the 1912 **Buckstaff** (509 Central Ave., Hot Springs; 501/623-2308; www.buckstaffbaths.com) for a dip in your own individual tub. **Quapaw Baths & Spa** (413 Central Ave., Hot Springs; 501/609-9822; http://quapawbaths.com) offers a more modern spa experience with covered indoor thermal pools and a steam cave.

## 3 MINING FOR DIAMONDS IN CRATER OF DIAMONDS STATE PARK

209 State Park Rd, Murfreesboro; 870/285-3113; www.arkansasstateparks.com/parks/crater-diamonds-state-park

Crater of Diamonds State Park is the country's only diamond-producing mine, and one of very few places in the world where visitors can mine for diamonds themselves. The diamonds are in the soil here, so you can search for them with a shovel (rent tools from the park, or bring your own), or by simply walking across the 37-acre (15-hectare) field and looking for anything that glints. The soil hides other gemstones, too, including amethyst, peridot, and garnets. Your chances of finding an actual diamond are slim—some say around one in 250—but it's thrilling

SEARCHING FOR GEMSTONES AT CRATER OF DIAMONDS STATE PARK

hunt, especially when you consider that more than 30,000 diamonds have been unearthed at Crater of Diamonds since the site was designated a state park in 1972. And yes, you do get to keep any gems you find.

**DAY 1** Begin your trip in Little Rock. Spend the morning touring historic **Little Rock Central High School** and its associated visitors center and historic gas station. Have lunch at a spot that serves cheese dip—the local specialty—then look around the **Esse Purse Museum** or the **William J. Clinton Presidential Library and Museum.**

DIGGING FOR DIAMONDS AT CRATER OF DIAMONDS STATE PARK

**DAY 2** From Little Rock, drive 110 miles southwest (177 kilometers; 2 hours) to **Crater of the Diamonds State Park,** where you can mine for the precious gems—this is one of the only places in the world where the general public can do so. From there, drive 60 miles (96 kilometers; 1.5 hours) to **Hot Springs.** Check into **The Arlington Resort Hotel & Spa** (239 Central Ave., Hot Springs; 800/643-1502; www.arlingtonhotel.com) for two nights.

**DAY 3** Spend the day in **Hot Springs National Park,** spending the night back in The Arlington.

BOSTON MOUNTAINS PANORAMA

**DAY 4** Leave Hot Springs and head to Dean's Market (145 miles/233; 3 hours), where you can jump on U.S. 71. It's one of the two highways that comprise the **Boston Mountain Scenic Loop,** which leads through the highest part of the Ozarks. You'll end up in **Fayetteville,** where you'll spend the night.

**DAY 5** From **Fayetteville,** take the other half of the Boston Mountain Scenic Loop, U.S. 49 South, back to Dean's Market (40 miles/64 kilometers; 45 minutes). On the way, you'll pass through **Devil's Den State Park,** where you can stop for a mountain hike. It's a 2.5-hour drive (150 miles/241 kilometers) back to Little Rock from Dean's Market.

DEVIL'S DEN STATE PARK

# *Major* CITIES

**LITTLE ROCK:** Arkansas's state capital and largest city, Little Rock is a city of Southern traditions and modern food, of makers and outdoors-folk, of politicians and entrepreneurs. It's also a city that acknowledges and remembers its past, from Native American roots to civil rights struggles.

**FAYETTEVILLE:** Proud home of the University of Arkansas, Fayetteville is located in the Ozark Mountains and has a cute downtown area and a thriving restaurant and brewery scene.

with purses of all shapes, sizes, colors, and price points.

## THORNCROWN CHAPEL

12968 Hwy. 62 West, Eureka Springs; 479/253-7401; https://thorncrown.com

Constructed in 1980 by architect E. Fay Jones, an apprentice of Frank Lloyd Wright, this award-winning chapel feels like a natural extension of its Ozark surroundings. Jutting 48 feet (14.6 meters) into the sky, the chapel contains more than 425 windows and thousands of square feet of glass. Thanks to its airy construction, the leafy foliage that peeks through feels as much a part of the design as the building itself. In fact, some say the chapel is at its most beautiful in the spring, when the surrounding leaves glow a brilliant green. In any season, it's a meditative, ethereal space.

## CRYSTAL BRIDGES MUSEUM OF AMERICAN ART

600 Museum Way, Bentonville; 479/418-5700; https://crystalbridges.org

Crystal Bridges Museum of American Art houses one of the country's largest collections of American art, including pieces by Georgia O'Keeffe, Andy Warhol, and Norman Rockwell. The museum itself is tucked into a ravine, its architecture taking cues from the surroundings; for example, concrete-and-cedar curves mimic the surrounding hillsides. After viewing the art, you can take a stroll into the surrounding Ozark forests, thanks to 4 miles (6.4 kilometers) of trails that surround the museum.

## HISTORIC DYESS COLONY AND JOHNNY CASH BOYHOOD HOME

110 Center Dr., Dyess; 870/764-2274; http://dyesscash.astate.edu

Created in 1934 as part of President Franklin D. Roosevelt's New Deal, the **Historic Dyess Colony** was a community planned to encourage economic recovery from the Great Depression. Almost 500 families moved here for a chance at a better life, working the land to grow soybeans and cotton. One of those families was that of Ray and Carrie Cash, who had five children, one of whom grew up to be famous: Johnny Cash, aka the Man in Black.

Cash lived here until he graduated from high school. Even as he became musical royalty, he remembered his hardscrabble roots in Dyess and often sang about those living in poverty. His song "Five Feet High and Rising" refers to the 1937 floods in Dyess.

These days, Dyess (located in eastern Arkansas, just 45 minutes outside

JOHNNY CASH BOYHOOD HOME

Memphis) is no longer inhabited and functions exclusively as a tourist site. The **Johnny Cash Boyhood Home** has been restored to the 1940s period, with input from Cash's siblings, Joanne Cash Yates and Tommy Cash. Artifacts include a piano adorned with sheet music and family photos, period furniture, and a pantry filled with canned goods. The Historic Dyess Colony also includes a museum, which shouldn't be skipped, even if your primary interest is Johnny Cash. It offers insight into history, economic development—and yes, country music.

# BEST SCENIC DRIVES

## MOUNT MAGAZINE SCENIC BYWAY

Hwy. 309

The 45-mile (72-kilometer) Mount Magazine Scenic Byway makes a dramatic ascent to the state's highest peak at Mount Magazine (2,753 feet/839 meters). The climb up the mountainside begins in **Havana**. At the top of the mountain is **Mount Magazine State Park** (www.arkansasstateparks.com/parks/mount-magazine-state-park), where you can park your car and continue on foot to the tippy top of the state (or simply enjoy impressive vistas of lakes, mountains, and rivers from the park's overlooks). Leaving the state park, you'll drop into the city of **Paris,** then pass through a rural landscape

MOUNT MAGAZINE STATE PARK OVERLOOK

of pastures, trees, and hayfields before ending the drive in **Webb City,** near the Arkansas River.

## BOSTON MOUNTAIN SCENIC LOOP

The 80-mile (128-kilometer) Boston Mountain Scenic Loop twists through the Boston Mountains, passing through the highest part of the Ozarks. The appeal of the drive is the gorgeous mountain scenery, plus the chance to stop for hiking or to explore the city of Fayetteville.

Beginning in **Dean's Market** near Alma, on **U.S. Highway 71,** the route winds through the wild terrain of the Boston mountains. **Fayetteville,** 42 miles (67 kilometers) outside Dean's Market, is a good place to stop for a bite to eat and to take in the vibrant town. Leaving Fayetteville, exit onto **U.S. 49 South.** You'll pass through **Devil's Den State Park,** which offers good hiking, before finishing your drive back in Dean's Market.

# BEST PARKS AND RECREATION AREAS

## BUFFALO NATIONAL RIVER

www.nps.gov/buff

Buffalo National River is one of just a few rivers in the Lower 48 that have not been dammed. It runs more than 130 miles (209 kilometers) through the Ozark Mountains, with huge limestone bluffs skirting its banks.

The area surrounding the river is popular for hiking, and as a designated **International Dark Sky Park,** there are stargazing programs throughout the year. But of course, the best way to experience it is to get out on the water itself. The Buffalo is split into upper, middle, and lower districts, with the paddling season beginning on the upper district in spring. Depending on which section and time of year you choose to paddle, you can find anything from shaded swimming holes to challenging, churning rapids suited for expert paddlers only. This ability to choose your

BUFFALO NATIONAL RIVER

own adventure is very much part of the river's beauty. You can return to the river again and again, exploring a different section every time, and never feel like you've seen it all.

## DEVIL'S DEN STATE PARK

www.arkansasstateparks.com/parks/devils-den-state-park

Located in the Lee Creek Valley, Devil's Den was designated a state park in the 1930s. In addition to its beautiful mountain scenery, the park contains structures that were built by the Civilian Conservation Corps using native wood and stone. It's considered to be among the most intact CCC sites in the country. There are also more than 60 miles (96 kilometers) of hiking trails that are open to hikers, mountain bikers, and horses.

# FESTIVALS AND EVENTS

## OZARK MOUNTAIN MUSIC FESTIVAL

Eureka Springs; www.ozarkmountainmusicfestival.com; Jan.

This four-day winter festival celebrates a regional sound that draws on folk and bluegrass, among other musical genres. Unique among music festivals, OzMoMu is held indoors, at the Basin Park Hotel. It's a raucous sing-and dance-along with performances on multiple stages. With no backstage area, performers and festival-goers mix and mingle, so who knows? You might even end up dancing with your new favorite musician.

# BEST FOOD

## CHEESE DIP

If there is one claim to fame on which Little Rock residents agree, it is that cheese dip was invented in North Little Rock in 1935. Consisting mostly of cheese (or processed cheese), it might also include meat, vegetables, or dairy. It's served warm or hot, with a side of crisp tortillas or chips. One popular local version stars Velveeta or Kraft cheese spiced up with chili sauce.

Blackie Donnelly, owner of Mexico Chiquito restaurants, is credited with

OZARK MOUNTAIN MUSIC FESTIVAL

## BEST SOUVENIRS

Find local handicrafts at the northern Arkansas **Ozark Folk Center State Park** (1032 Park Ave., Mountain View; 870/269-3851; www.arkansasstateparks. com), which has a unique mission among state parks: to protect the culture—primarily music and crafts—of the region. More than 20 artists offer on-site demonstrations at the **Craft Village** and sell their wares in the **Homespun Gift Shop.** Items on offer include everything from jewelry and pottery to wood carvings and spun yarn.

the creation of cheese dip, and you can still order it at the chain's single surviving location, **Mexico Chiquito To Go** in Little Rock (11406 W Markham St., Little Rock; 501/217-0647). **Dizzy's Gypsy Bistro** (200 River Market Ave #150, Little Rock; 501/375-3500) is another popular place to taste. And every October in Little Rock, contestants prepare their favorite recipes for the **World Cheese Dip Festival** (Clinton Presidential Center, 1200 President Clinton Ave., Little Rock; www.cheesedip.net), and attendees vote for their favorites. Hot tip: Bring an empty muffin tin. The small samples of dip fit perfectly in the tray, so you can carry them with one hand and chips with the other.

## MAJOR AIRPORTS

- **Bill and Hillary Clinton National Airport:** LIT; 1 Airport Rd., Little Rock; 501/372-3439; www.clintonairport. com

## MORE INFORMATION

### TRAVEL AND TOURISM INFORMATION

- **Arkansas Tourism Department:** www.arkansas.com

- **Arkansas State Parks:** www.arkansasstateparks.com

### NEWSPAPERS

- *Pine Bluff Commercial:* www. arkansasonline.com/pb/news

- *Arkansas Times:* www.arktimes.com

# LOUISIANA

ouisiana is not all New Orleans, and New Orleans is not all cheap beads and giant drinks on Bourbon Street. This is a sensory place: the smell of jasmine or the spicy scent of crawfish boiling in someone's backyard, the sound of music floating on the humid air, a school marching band practicing for next year's parades, or the refreshing feel of condensation clinging to a can of cold soda or beer. Go beyond the city to explore swamps, islands, bayous, and other singular Louisiana cities and Cajun cultural communities that have added as much to the cultural dialogue as New Orleans has.

On Atakapa, Caddo, Chitimacha, Choctaw, Houma, Natchez, and Tunica land, you can feel the history flowing through this place, in its music, food, celebrations, and most importantly, its people. Louisiana is not an orderly or easily digested place, but underneath the wonderful chaos, there's a raw beauty that you won't want to miss.

AREA: 52,069 square miles / 134,858 (31st)

POPULATION: 4,648,794 (25th)

STATEHOOD DATE: April 30, 1812 (18th)

STATE CAPITAL: Baton Rouge

LOUISIANA SWAMP

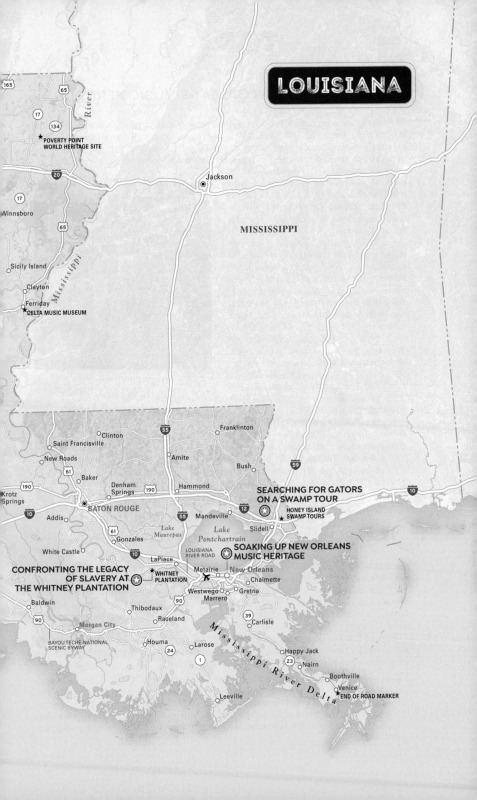

## LOUISIANA

**165**
**65**
River
**17**
**134**
★ POVERTY POINT
WORLD HERITAGE SITE
**20**

● Jackson

**MISSISSIPPI**

**17**

○ Winnsboro

**65**

○ Sicily Island

Mississippi

○ Clayton
★ Ferriday
★ DELTA MUSIC MUSEUM

● Clinton
○ Saint Francisville
○ Franklinton
**55**
○ New Roads
○ Amite
**61**
○ Baker
○ Bush
**59**
○ Denham
Springs
**190**
**190**
○ Hammond
Krotz ○
Springs
**10**
● BATON ROUGE
**12**
**SEARCHING FOR GATORS
ON A SWAMP TOUR**
**10**
○ Addis
**55**
○ Mandeville
★ HONEY ISLAND
SWAMP TOURS
○ White Castle
Lake
Maurepas
Lake
Pontchartrain
○ Slidell
**61**
○ Gonzales
**10**
○ LaPlace
LOUISIANA
RIVER ROAD
★ **SOAKING UP NEW ORLEANS
MUSIC HERITAGE**
**CONFRONTING THE LEGACY
OF SLAVERY AT
THE WHITNEY PLANTATION**
★ WHITNEY
PLANTATION
○ Metairie
✈
New Orleans
○ Chalmette
○ Baldwin
Westwego ○
Marrero
○ Gretna
○ Thibodaux
**90**
○ Raceland
**39**
○ Carlisle
Morgan City ○
○ Houma
**24**
○ Larose
**23**
○ Happy Jack
○ Nairn
BAYOU TECHE NATIONAL
SCENIC BYWAY
Mississippi River Delta
○ Boothville
○ Venice
★ END OF ROAD MARKER
**1**
○ Leeville

# ① SOAKING UP NEW ORLEANS MUSIC HERITAGE

There's perhaps no better introduction to New Orleans music than **Preservation Hall** (726 St. Peter St.; 504/522-2841; www.preservationhall.com), formed in 1961 expressly to keep the legacy of the city's distinctive style of jazz music alive for generations to come. Visiting musicians continue to come to this surprisingly in-timate concert hall, housed in a weath-ered, 1750s era house, to sit in with the Preservation Hall Band. Right off **Bourbon Street,** it's without question the most authentic music venue in the French Quarter.

For a nightlife district more fo-cused on music than the Quarter's fa-mous party street, head to **Frenchmen Street,** a three-block stretch of musical excess—over a dozen bars and music clubs are jammed in together here. You can find old-school big band jazz, brass band, traditional jazz, R&B, klezmer, rock, acoustic folk... sometimes all in the same bar if you stay in one place long enough. **d. b. a.** (618 Frenchmen St.; 504/942-3731; www.dbaneworleans.com) and **The Spotted Cat Music Club** (623 Frenchmen St.; 504/943-3887;

THE SPOTTED CAT MUSIC CLUB

www.spottedcatmusicclub.com) are perennial favorites.

For live music a bit more off the beaten path, check out the lineup at one of these venues: **Bacchanal Fine Wine & Spirits** (600 Poland Ave.; 504/948-9111; www.bac-chanalwine.com), at once a unique live music venue, a wine and cheese shop, and bistro; **Le Bon Temps Roule** (4801 Magazine St.; 504/895-8117; https://lbtrnola.com), a neighborhood juke joint open 24 hours a day; and **Candlelight Lounge** (925 N. Robertson St.; 504/906-5877), an unassuming cinderblock building that offers good music, good food, good people, and good times.

# ② SEARCHING FOR GATORS ON A SWAMP TOUR

On a tour through the unique swamp environments of Southern Louisiana, you'll feel far away from civilization, sharing a flat-bottomed boat with other passengers and your guide, usually an old-school, funny, folksy character who knows the wa-terways and inhabitants of the area (both human and animal) like the back of their hand. It's a fascinating look at the area's wildlife and plant life, and the people who exist alongside them.

Part of the fun of a swamp tour is spotting gators. If there's a swamp, there's likely a gator nearby, swimming and sunning themselves on logs especially outside of winter when it warms up.

- **Cajun Pride Swamp Tours** (110 Frenier Rd., LaPlace; 504/467-0758; www.ca-junprideswamptours.com) operates in a privately owned wildlife refuge in the Manchac Swamp. If there are gators around, your captain will throw them marsh-mallows to draw them close to the boat so you can snap photos. The tour also includes a history of the Manchac Swamp, and Frenier, the tiny Cajun town that sits within it.

SWAMP TOUR

- **Honey Island Swamp Tours** (41490 Crawford Landing Rd., Slidell; 985/641-1769 or 504/242-5877; www.honeyislandswamp.com) will take you on small boats past cypress tress dripping with moss into one of the most pristine river swamps in the U.S.

 ## CONFRONTING THE LEGACY OF SLAVERY AT THE WHITNEY PLANTATION

5099 LA-18, Edgard; 225/265-3300; https://whitneyplantation.com

A required stop for understanding the realities of slavery, the Whitney Plantation Museum is dedicated to educating visitors without white-washing history by fo-cusing on the pretty houses and gardens built on enslaved people's backs. It's a context that should be a part of every antebellum narrative, since it was this inhumane and barbaric practice that created and supported the economy of the South (and this country, as a whole) for generations.

The 90-minute tour covers the restored plantation and a series of memorials that draw on the oral history provided by the post-Depression WPA (Works Progress Administration) Federal Writer's Project of enslaved people's narratives. The stops on the tour focus on the daily lives of the enslaved

FORMER RESIDENCE OF ENSLAVED PEOPLE ON THE WHITNEY PLANTATION

men, women, and children who worked here harvesting sugarcane and tending to the big house for centuries. There's a stunning exhibit on the largest (but failed) slave rebellion in Louisiana, and another that discusses the post-Emancipation sharecropper culture that effectively continued slavery practices. It's sobering, enlightening, educational, and crucial to understanding the foundational history of the United States of America.

**DAY 1** Ease into your time in Louisiana in **New Orleans**, with a stroll through one of the city's beloved parks, either **City Park** or **Audubon Park**. After getting a sense of how the city's living spend their recreation time, visit one of its cities of the dead: **Lafayette Cemetery No. 1** and **St. Louis Cemetery No. 1** offer fascinating glimpses into New Orleans's history. Cap off your day with a pilgrimage to jazz mecca **Preservation Hall**.

AUDUBON PARK

**DAY 2** Head out in search of alligators with **Honey Island Swamp Tours**; afterward, grab a refreshing beer at **Abita Brewing Company**. Back in New Orleans, grab a classic po'boy from **Frady's One Stop Food Store** and head to **Bacchanal** for low-key cheese, wine, and live music.

**DAY 3** Leave the city for **Acadiana**, driving on the **Bayou Teche Scenic Byway** with a detour to the **Tabasco Factory** for a tour. Spend the night in cultural capital **Lafayette**, heading to Cajun dance hall **La Poussiere** in nearby **Breaux Bridge** for the evening's entertainment.

AMERICAN ALLIGATOR IN HONEY ISLAND SWAMP

**DAY 4** Today you'll drive deeper into the country through 600,000-acre (242,811-hectare) **Kisatchie National Forest**, a great place to take a hike through the unique longleaf pine forest. You're heading for history in small-town **Natchitoches**; for dinner, try one of the regional specialty meat pies.

WELCOME SIGN AT THE TABASCO FACTORY

**DAY**
**5**

Backtracking south from Natchitoches, stop at **Melrose Plantation,** one of the only existing structures of its kind built by and for free Black people. It's a long drive today to **Baton Rouge** (get boudin from **Billy's Mini-Mart** on the way), where you can tour the old and new capitol buildings, each quirky in its own way.

**DAY**
**6**

You'll return to **New Orleans** today, but not without another stop at **Whitney Plantation,** an unmissable education on the legacy of slavery in the U.S. Back in the Crescent City, visit the **Backstreet Cultural Museum,** followed by a decadent last night out on **Frenchmen Street.**

EVENING IN NATCHITOCHES

OLD STATE CAPITOL, BATON ROUGE

## ORIENTATION

**New Orleans** is located in southeastern Louisiana, bordered by **Lake Pontchartrain** and the **Mississippi River. Baton Rouge,** also on the Mississippi, is northwest of New Orleans, and **Cajun Country,** also known as Acadiana, sits to the west of Baton Rouge. **Kisatchie National Forest** and **Natchitoches** are farther north in central Louisiana.

## WHEN TO GO

Louisiana is almost always hot, but there are variations: there's **festival season,** usually between March and May; the **very hot and humid season** (also hurricane season), late May through early October; **football season,** mid-October through early December, when there's usually terrific weather; and a lull with some potential for **damp and cold weather** in January and February, until Mardi Gras when the whole cycle starts over again.

# HIGHLIGHTS

### NEW ORLEANS CEMETERY TOURS

Touring one of New Orleans's cemeteries is a great way to learn about the history of the city. Even their unique appearance is indicative of the city's geography: because New Orleans is at such a low elevation, all bodies are interred aboveground.

Dating back to 1832, **Lafayette Cemetery No. 1** (1416-1498 Washington Ave.; 504/658-3781; www.saveourcemeteries.org) is the oldest of New Orleans's municipal cemeteries and takes up an entire city block. Its proximity to the working-class Irish Channel neighborhood ensured that a wide variety of individuals and families rest here; it's non-denominational and non-segregated, with immigrants from over 25 different countries and natives of 26 states interred in its tombs over the centuries. There's a whole lot to learn about the city by reading the cemetery's various engravings.

Arguably the most famous of New Orleans's "cities of the dead," **St. Louis Cemetery No. 1** (Basin St. between

# Major CITIES

**NEW ORLEANS:** In the Crescent City, music and tempting food are everywhere, and you'll find beautiful architecture and unforgettable memories just walking down the street.

**BATON ROUGE:** The state capitol is a distinctively Louisianan city with Cajun and Creole influences, as well as being the home of the beloved Louisiana State University Tigers.

**SHREVEPORT:** Located in northwest Louisiana, the third-largest city in the state once hosted the radio program that first broadcast Elvis Presley. It experienced a decline after the oil companies headquartered there departed, but a number of casinos downtown have spurred revitalization efforts.

Conti St. and St. Louis St.; 504/482-5065) was established in 1789, outside what was then the city border. The cemetery currently contains more than 700 tombs and thousands interred; most of these aboveground structures are owned by families and designed to hold multiple sets of remains. The elaborate brick tombs are often covered in concrete or stucco; some of the oldest are little more than crumbled ruins. Famous residents here include Homer Plessy (of *Plessy v. Ferguson*) and the much-loved voodoo priestess Marie Laveau.

## NATCHITOCHES

Louisiana's oldest permanent settlement, Natchitoches (pronounced NA-CK-a-tish), was founded in 1714 as a French outpost, named for the Indigenous residents. Its Queen Anne and Victorian architecture mixed with

NATCHITOCHES

Creole-style cottages may look familiar to you not only because they are so historic, but also because it served as the set of the move *Steel Magnolias*.

With so many years of history, Natchitoches has its own cultural institutions, from the meat pie, a staple of central and northern Louisiana cuisine—try it at **Lasyone's Meat Pie Restaurant** (622 Second St.; 318/353-3353; http://lasyones.com)—to a world-famous Christmas festival, celebrated for almost 100 years with more than 300,000 lights decorating the downtown district.

One of the town's most fascinating, complicated sites is **Melrose Plantation** (3533 LA-119, Melrose; www.melroseplantation.org), one of the largest plantations in the U.S. built by and for free Black people. These descendants of a former enslaved woman who became a wealthy business owner in the area, who in turn enslaved people themselves, and built structures including the African House, one of the only examples of Congolese architecture in the U.S.; today, it also houses the art of Black folk artist Clementine Hunter.

## OLD STATE CAPITOL

100 North Blvd., Baton Rouge; https://louisianaoldstatecapitol.org

This national historic landmark served as the home for the Louisiana State Legislature from the mid-1800s until the 1930s, and was built to look like an actual gothic castle, turrets and all. After the state government fled Baton Rouge during the Civil War, what is sometimes called the Louisiana Castle was rebuilt to include the stained-glass dome that can still be seen today. The Old State Capitol has seen a lot of history, including the saga of infamous Governor Huey P. Long, who ultimately opted to build a new state capitol (the nearby art deco **Capitol Tower**, 900 N 3rd St.; 225/342-7317; www.crt.state.la.us/tourism/welcome-centers/state-capitol) after surviving an impeachment attempt based on his alleged bribery and misuse of state funds. Today the Old State Capitol serves as a museum of Louisiana's political history, with exhibits on everything from women's suffrage to a resident ghost.

# BEST SCENIC DRIVES

Fittingly for a state that is often below sea level, many of the best drives in Louisiana follow major waterways. **Louisiana Byways** (https://byways.louisianatravel.com) is a great resource for all kinds of road trips through the state.

## BAYOU TECHE NATIONAL SCENIC BYWAY

This route follows several different state highways, most prominently LA 31 and LA 182, closely following the Bayou Teche waterway through three parishes (the Louisiana version of counties): St. Mary, Iberia, and St. Martin. Traveling through this region, known as **Acadiana,** is a great way to experience authentic Cajun, or Acadian, culture; it's filled with communities that are home to unique festivals and small-town eateries. Running from **Morgan City** in the south to **Arnaudville** in the north, the entire route is about 184 miles (296 kilometers). It can be done in a day or over two days if you want to take your time and spend the night somewhere along the route. On the way, you'll pass **Lafayette,** considered the capital of Cajun country; **Breaux Bridge,** home of the Breaux Bridge Crawfish Festival in early May; and historic **Vermilionville** (300 Fisher Rd., Lafayette; 337/233-4077; https://bayouvermiliondistrict.org), a living history compound devoted to Cajun culture.

One of the true pleasures of traveling in this part of Louisiana is finding authentic Acadian food, like boudin, and zydeco music—try **Billy's Mini-Mart** (24467 U.S. 190, Krotz Springs; 333/566-2318; http://billysboudincracklin.com) for the former and Cajun dance hall **La Poussiere** (1301 Grand Point Ave., Breaux Bridge; 337/332-1721; https://lapoussiere.com) for the latter. For a vibrant, contemporary view into Cajun country, visit **Bayou Teche Brewing** (1094 Bushville Hwy., Arnaudville; 337/754-5122; https://bayoutechebrewing.com), which bills itself as a "cultural brewery," incorporating the sounds, language, arts, and history of Acadiana into everything they do.

## LOUISIANA RIVER ROAD

The mighty Mississippi is arguably the most powerful force in shaping Louisiana's history. Follow its course along the Louisiana Great River Road Byway, a section of the Great River Road, which travels all the way up to the Mississippi's mouth in Minnesota. The more than 300-mile-long (482-kilometer) stretch of this road in Louisiana crosses over the great river several times, passing various locks, levees, and other water control mechanisms that illustrate the long struggle to harness and control the power of this body of water and fertility of its delta, while avoiding the catastrophic damage that can be caused by flooding.

ZYDECO MUSIC AT THE CRAWFISH FESTIVAL IN BREAUX BRIDGE

The route passes historical landmarks like the **Poverty Point World Heritage Site** (6859 LA-577, Pioneer; www.povertypoint.us), a prehistoric earthwork built between 1700 and 1100 BC; and the **Delta Music Museum** (218 Louisiana Ave., Ferriday; 318/757-4297; www.deltamusicmuseum.com), an off-the-beaten-path museum dedicated to music legends like Jerry Lee Lewis who grew up in the area; as well as those from Baton Rouge and New Orleans. Only purists may follow River Road all the way to the **End of Road Marker,** in fittingly named, tiny and watery Venice, Louisiana, but getting there truly feels like you've reached the end of the world.

# BEST PARKS AND RECREATION AREAS

## NEW ORLEANS'S GREEN SPACES

New Orleans's often dense grid of streets lined by historic buildings is punctuated by many urban retreats, where locals gather to walk, bike, and picnic.

### City Park

1 Palm Dr.; 504/482-4888; www.neworleanscitypark.com

City Park is a haven for bikers, hikers, music lovers, art aficionados, and anyone looking to for captivating nature within New Orleans. From the **New Orleans Botanical Garden** (1 Palm Dr., City Park; 504/483-9386; www.neworleanscitypark.com) and the **New Orleans Museum of Art** (City Park, 1 Collins C. Diboll Cir.; 504/658-4100; noma.org) with its accompanying sculpture Garden, to the beautifully designed bridges and walking paths, the thousands of lush and tangled oak trees (the nation's largest collection), and the wildlife that lives here, City Park is a gem.

### Audubon Park

6500 Magazine St.; 504/861-2537; https://auduboninstitute.org

One of New Orleanians' favorite places for strolling, Audubon Park's 340 acres (137 hectares) encompass the Audubon Zoo, a pleasant lagoon, moss-draped live oak trees, lush lawns, three playgrounds, a golf course, a swimming pool, and the 1.8-mile (2.9 kilometer) **Audubon Park Trail.** The centuries-old **Tree of Life** is a popular meeting spot and peaceful place to meditate and people-watch.

## KISATCHIE NATIONAL FOREST

www.fs.usda.gov/kisatchie

If you've seen enough of the enthralling swamps and marshes of coastal Louisiana, head to the Kisatchie National Forest, with over 604,000 acres (244,430 hectares) of piney and hardwood forests to bird-watch, canoe, fish, and camp in, as well as over 100 miles (160 kilometers) of trails for hiking and mountain biking. Try **Longleaf Vista Interpretive Trail** for a short (1.5-mile/2.4-kilometers) hike with a great view, or any part of the 24-mile (38-kilometer) **Wild Azalea Trail,** whose namesake flowers bloom there in spring. The protected land is a habitat for a vital population of longleaf pines, which in turn provide a home for fauna including deer, armadillo, wild turkeys, racoons, the rare Louisiana black bear, red-cockaded woodpeckers, and more. Stop by the **Catahoula Hummingbird and Butterfly Garden** in Bentley, Louisiana, to see some of the park's fluttering and hovering inhabitants. The forest's **headquarters** (2500 Shreveport Hwy.; 318/473-7160) are located in Pineville and can provide more information about this unique Louisiana landscape.

KISATCHIE NATIONAL FOREST

# MARDI GRAS EVERY DAY

If you can't get a hotel room during the packed Mardi Gras festivities in New Orleans, or the extra crowds on Bourbon or Frenchmen Streets aren't your thing, not to worry: There are ways to get a taste of Fat Tuesday all year long.

- Meant to be enjoyed only from January 6 (Three Kings Day, hence the name) through Mardi Gras, the traditional **king cake** is very simple: braided sweet dough, topped with icing and purple, gold, and green sugar. Inside you'll find a "baby"—plastic, or a bean, or a pig, or a ceramic token—hidden in the cake. Whoever gets the piece with the baby is on the hook for bringing a king cake to the next gathering.

- **Mardi Gras Zone** (2706 Royal St.; 504/947-8787; mardigraszone.com) sells everything: Masks, beads, souvenirs, groceries, prepared food, and booze. Just browsing the place is an experience that everyone should have at least once.

- **Blaine Kern's Mardi Gras World** (1380 Port of New Orleans Pl.; 504/361-7821; www.mardigrasworld.com) is the largest builder of Carnival sculptures and parade floats in the country. Tour the cavernous warehouse facility to see the kaleidoscopic floats and the artists working on them: you might see them shaping the oversized frames with wire and plaster or painting the float to bring it to life.

- The **Backstreet Cultural Museum** (1116 Henriette Delille St.; 504/522-4806; www.backstreetmuseum.org) contains a comprehensive collection of costumes, films, and photographs, especially of Carnival-related groups like the Mardi Gras Indians.

# FESTIVALS AND EVENTS

Rather than asking when you can find a party in Louisiana, the better question might be, when isn't there a party going on? This question is particularly hard to answer in New Orleans. In addition to huge festivals like Mardi Gras and Jazz Fest, there are smaller ones, at least one festival to attend just about any weekend of the year (yes, even during the dog days of summer). Halloween and Christmas are special times here too. Louisiana's innate hospitality welcomes people from every background to celebrate.

## MARDI GRAS

New Orleans; www.mardigrasneworleans.com; Feb. or Mar.

Few festivals exemplify the joyous spirit of New Orleans more than Mardi Gras, the French term for "Fat Tuesday." If you're a fan of colorful, exciting festivals, there's no better time to visit New Orleans than during Mardi Gras season, which usually falls in February or early March and lasts 2-3 weeks prior to Lent (from Epiphany to Ash Wednesday). Festivities include everything from colorful street masks and costumes to gala balls and events. Most famous parts are the free public parades sponsored by krewes, or long-standing social organizations that prepare all year for the colorful floats, marching bands, motorcycle squads, dancers, entertainers,

MARDI GRAS

and, sometimes, royal court (the king, queen, maids, and dukes of a krewe) that make Mardi Gras so special.

## JAZZ FEST

Fair Grounds Race Course & Slots, 1751 Gentilly Blvd., New Orleans; 504/410-4100; www. nojazzfest.com; Apr. and May

Established in 1970, this musical extravaganza, which takes place at the Fair Grounds Race Course, has grown to be nearly as popular as Mardi Gras. Usually on two long weekends in late April and early May, this event features music workshops, artisanal and culinary demonstrations, Native American powwow performances, arts-and-crafts vendors, an unbelievable array of food stalls, and numerous stages that buzz with jazz, blues, zydeco, rock, gospel, and folk musicians.

## FESTIVAL INTERNATIONAL DE LOUISIANE

Downtown Lafayette; 337/232-8086; www. festivalinternational.org; Apr.

Outside New Orleans, no part of the state enjoys a good festival more than Acadiana. Scores of engaging events are held in towns throughout the region, practically year-round. Lafayette hosts the annual Festival International de Louisiane, a massive five-day music festival and street fair in late April that showcases all kinds of local and French/French-speaking countries' music, French-language plays, and other Francophone fun, plus more local food

JAZZ FEST

than you can shake a stick at. Check out dishes like sweet potato beignets, Cajun egg rolls, and praline chicken. It's a local favorite due to the music performances and the fact that Lafayette is laissez-faire.

## FOOTBALL SEASON

Weekends in the fall in Louisiana usually mean one thing: football. It's without a doubt the state's favorite sport, with New Orleans's NFL team, the **Saints,** having a devoted fanbase.

New Orleans's **Mercedes-Benz Superdome** (1500 Sugar Bowl Dr.; www. mbsuperdome.com) is a part of the cultural landscape; when the Saints won the Super Bowl in 2010, just a few harrowing years after Hurricane Katrina, it was a cause for national celebration, not just in the Crescent City. On Saints game days, it seems the whole city is dressed up in black and gold. Head to **Champions Square** (Lasalle St.; 504/597-3663; www.champions-square.com), where thousands of fans congregate before the game with drinks, food vendors, and sometimes live music.

# BEST FOOD AND DRINK

## FOOD SPECIALTIES

New Orleans and Louisiana have the country's most specialized and unique food culture, with more regional specialties than you can count—much less eat on one trip. What follows below is just a brief overview.

- **Beignets:** These deep-fried, powdered-sugar-covered donuts are New Orleans staples; the ones at **Café Du Monde** (800 Decatur St., New Orleans; 504/587-0833; https://shop. cafedumonde.com) are the archetype, delicious with a cup of chicory coffee.

- **Po'boys:** The traditional Louisiana sandwich involves French bread filled with meat or seafood, often fried. In New Orleans, try neighborhood spot **Frady's One Stop Food Store** (3231 Dauphine St.; 504/949-9688); in Acadiana, the po'boys at **Bon Creole** (1409 E. St. Peter St., New Iberia; 337/367-6181; https://bon-creole. com) are beloved and overstuffed.

# BEST SOUVENIRS

- **Hot sauce** is ubiquitous in Louisiana, which even has its own style, typically heavy on the vinegar. Perhaps the most famous is Tabasco; visit the **Tabasco Factory** (32 Wisteria Rd., Avery Island; 337/373-6129; www.tabasco.com) to see where it's made.
- **Abita Brewing Company** (21084 LA-36, Covington; 985/893-3143; www.abita.com) is Louisiana's best-known brewery, beloved by locals and drinkers around the country. You'll find it in bars throughout the state, or visit Abita at the source for a pint and a tour.

- **Gumbo and jambalaya:** You'll find both of these hearty, soul-warming stews throughout Louisiana; the main difference is that rice is cooked with the other ingredients in jambalaya, while with gumbo it's served on the side. The gumbo at **Gabrielle Restaurant** (2441 Orleans Ave., New Orleans; 504/603-2344; www.gabriellerestaurant.com) is an institution.
- **Crawfish boils:** Lovingly known as mudbugs, these delectable crustaceans are served boiled with potatoes and spices during spring when they are in season. For an unforgettable experience, stay at **Crawfish Haven/Mrs. Rose's Bed and Breakfast** (6807 LA-35, Kaplan; 337/652-8870; www.crawfishhaven.net), where you can catch and boil them yourself.
- **Muffaletta:** Italian immigrants brought this layered sandwich of olives, salami, ham, mortadella, provolone, and Swiss cheese to New Orleans. Those from **Central Grocery** (923 Decatur St., New Orleans; 504/523-1620; https://centralgrocery.com) in the French Quarter are considered some of the best.
- **Vietnamese:** With a significant Vietnamese immigrant population, Vietnamese cuisine is as much a part of the New Orleans's culinary history as any other. No-frills **Lilly's Café** (1813 Magazine St.; 504/599-9999) is perfect for a bowl of pho or a banh mi.

## COCKTAILS

New Orleans has been a cocktail town since its inception. It's sometimes called the "cradle of civilized drinking" and is home to many historically significant cocktail bars.

- **Sazerac:** The official cocktail of New Orleans includes two locally created ingredients: Peychaud's bitters and Herbsaint (an absinthe substitute). Best Place to Get It: **Sazerac Bar** (The Roosevelt, 130 Roosevelt Way; 504/648-1200; www.therooseveltneworleans.com).
- **Ramos Gin Fizz:** This classic cocktail once got its iconic egg-white froth from 12 minutes of vigorous shaking. These days, no one shakes it for that long—a few minutes at the most. Best Place to Get It: **Bourbon O Bar** (730 Bourbon St., New Orleans; 504/571-4685; www.bourbono.com).

## MAJOR AIRPORTS

- **Louis Armstrong New Orleans International Airport:** MSY; 1 Terminal Dr., Kenner; 504/303-7500; flymsy.com

## MORE INFORMATION

### TRAVEL AND TOURISM INFORMATION

- **Louisiana Office of Tourism:** www.louisianatravel.com
- **Louisiana State Parks:** www.crt.state.la.us/louisiana-state-parks

### NEWSPAPERS AND MAGAZINES

- *The Times-Picayune* and *New Orleans Advocate:* www.nola.com
- *The Louisiana Weekly:* www.louisianaweekly.com
- *64 Parishes:* https://64parishes.org

# NORTH CAROLINA

S tay here long enough, and North Carolina—on the land of many Indigenous peoples, including the Cherokee, Catawba, Pee Dees, Tutelo, Saura, Cheraw, Waccamau, and Tuscarora—will start to color everything you see. Somewhere between a sip of sweet tea and a bite of barbecue sandwich, you'll see blue everywhere. The sky, more often than not, is Tarheel Blue. The Atlantic Ocean: turquoise near shore but growing to a deeper sapphire as it approaches the horizon, a line invisible in the evenings when the sky and sea seem as one. On maps, blue veins of rivers and creeks draw the unseen contours of the land. And west, where the mountains rise high and rugged, you can see their crenellations grow blue with distance.

The state may be surrounded by blue, but the palette changes depending on where you go. White sands cover the shore, and winter's snowy cap tops the tallest mountains. Half a hundred shades of autumn jewel the mountainsides and half a hundred more burst out in spring's wildflower bloom. There's a map of the state waiting for you to fill it in with your colored pencils; all you need to bring is a sense of adventure.

**AREA:** 53,819 square miles / 139,390 square kilometers (28th)

**POPULATION:** 10,488,084 (9th)

**STATEHOOD DATE:** November 21, 1789 (12th)

**STATE CAPITAL:** Raleigh

▲ VIEW FROM THE BLUE RIDGE PARKWAY NEAR ASHEVILLE

## ORIENTATION

The ribbon of shore that is the **Outer Banks** lines the northeast coast of North Carolina. The coast continues beyond the Banks, with **Wilmington** anchoring the southern coast. The Triangle of university towns, **Raleigh, Durham,** and **Chapel Hill,** are just east of the center of the state, where **Greensboro** is located. **Charlotte** is in the middle of southern North Carolina, while **Asheville** is to the west, about an hour away from **Great Smoky Mountains National Park,** which sits on the western border with Tennessee.

## WHEN TO GO

**Summer** is the high season: Beaches are jam-packed, traffic is slow in the mountains, and across the state you'll find festivals and events. Heat and humidity can be brutal, and the cooler mountains and coast draw the most visitors for this reason. **Spring** brings nice weather, but some regional events are so large that entire cities or corners of the state may be booked.

**Fall foliage** in **autumn** accounts for the mountains' second high season, running from late September through early November. Water along the coast stays swimmably warm past Halloween most years. **Winter** is milder here than in many parts of the country, but

many businesses along the coast and in the mountains, where temperatures are much colder and snow falls a few times a year, reduce their hours or close entirely.

# HIGHLIGHTS

## BILTMORE ESTATE

1 Lodge St., Asheville; 800/411-3812; www.biltmore.com

The architectural crown jewel of Asheville, the Biltmore Estate, was built in the late 1800s for George Vanderbilt, grandson of Gilded Age robber baron Cornelius Vanderbilt. He engaged celebrity architect Richard Morris Hunt to build the home and hired esteemed Frederick Law Olmsted, creator of New York City's Central Park, to design the landscape for the grounds.

Asheville's most popular attraction is not only an awe-inspiring mansion—the square footage is nearly 4 acres (1.6 hectares), and there are 65 fireplaces and more than 250 rooms—but the grounds are also home to a collection of great little restaurants, shops, and a popular winery, all in a beautiful riverside setting. Visitors can eat, shop, tour, explore, relax, and unwind without leaving the grounds, and there's easily enough here to fill a weekend.

BILTMORE ESTATE

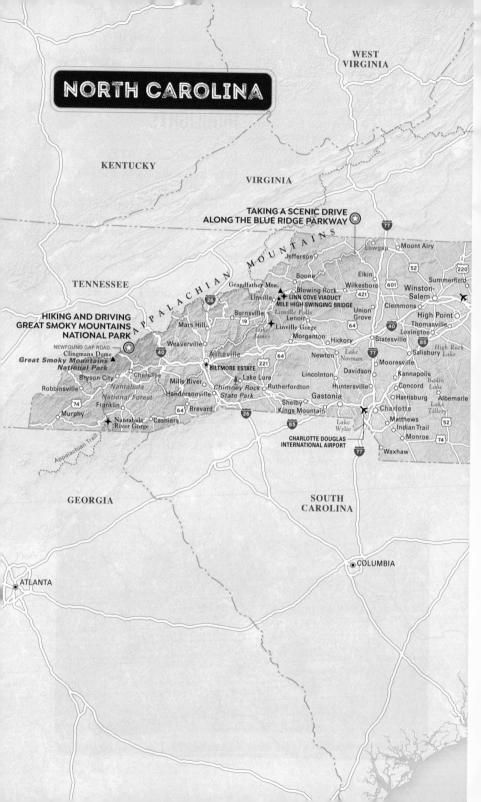

# NORTH CAROLINA

**WEST VIRGINIA**

**KENTUCKY**

**VIRGINIA**

**TAKING A SCENIC DRIVE ALONG THE BLUE RIDGE PARKWAY**

Lowgap  Mount Airy

Jefferson

**TENNESSEE**

Boone

Elkin

52

220

Summerfield

Grandfather Mtn.  Blowing Rock  Wilkesboro  601

Winston-Salem

Linville  **LINN COVE VIADUCT**  421

26  **MILE HIGH SWINGING BRIDGE**  Clemmons

**HIKING AND DRIVING GREAT SMOKY MOUNTAINS NATIONAL PARK**

Burnsville  19  Linville Falls  Lenoir  Union Grove  High Point

Mars Hill  Linville Gorge  Morganton  64  40  Lexington

NEWFOUND GAP ROAD  Lake James  Hickory  Statesville  85  High Rock Lake

Clingmans Dome  Weaverville  Salisbury

*Great Smoky Mountains National Park*  40  Asheville  Newton  Lake Norman  77  Mooresville

Bryson City  Cherokee  **BILTMORE ESTATE**  221  Lincolnton  Davidson  Kannapolis

Robbinsville  *Nantahala*  Mills River  **Lake Lure**  Concord  Hartisburg  Badin Lake

*National Forest*  Hendersonville  **Chimney Rock**  Rutherfordton  Huntersville  Albemarle

74  Franklin  **State Park**  Shelby  Gastonia  Charlotte  Lake Tillery

Murphy  Nantahala  64  Brevard  Kings Mountain  Matthews  52

*Appalachian Trail*  **River Gorge**  Cashiers  26  85  Indian Trail  Monroe  74

Lake Wylie  **CHARLOTTE DOUGLAS INTERNATIONAL AIRPORT**  Waxhaw

77

**GEORGIA**

**SOUTH CAROLINA**

**COLUMBIA**

**ATLANTA**

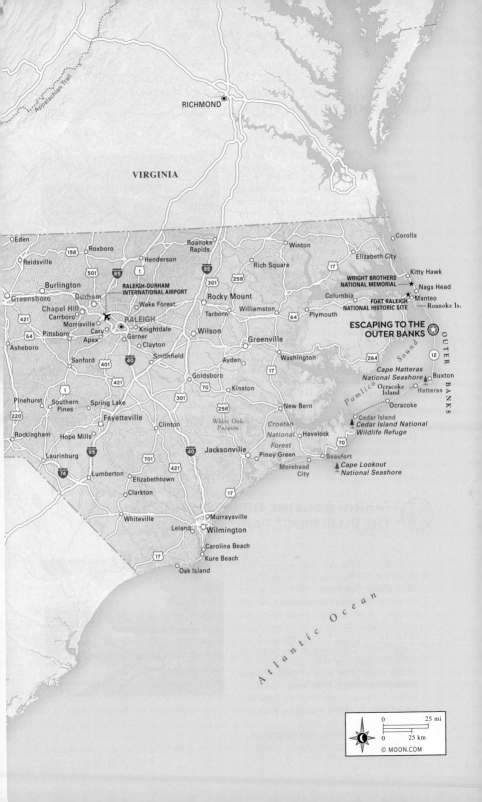

# TOP 3

## 1 HIKING AND DRIVING GREAT SMOKY MOUNTAINS NATIONAL PARK

865/436-1200; www.nps.gov/grsm

The Great Smoky National Park straddles the North Carolina/Tennessee state line, and the slightly larger North Carolina side of the park is wilder and less developed than the Tennessee side. The Smokies are the land of the Cherokee people, who have roots here going back centuries, and today they draw more than 10 million visitors annually. It's easy to see why: These mountains are laced with trails, rivers, and waterfalls, and populated with diverse wildlife—from rare salamanders to huge elk.

VIEW FROM NEWFOUND GAP ROAD

The best way to explore the park is on foot: It is home to more than 800 miles (1,287 kilometers) of hiking trails, ranging from easy walks around major attractions to strenuous wilderness paths suited to experienced backpackers. A section of the **Appalachian Trail** goes through the park, tracing the state border. Top hikes on the North Carolina side of the park include **Andrews Bald** at **Clingmans Dome,** the highest peak in the Smokies, and **Mount Cammerer Trail,** which bounces over the NC/TN line a number of times, has some of the best views in the park.

Another great way to explore the park is via a scenic drive. **Newfound Gap Road** traverses the park from Cherokee, North Carolina, to Gatlinburg, Tennessee. When driving it, be sure to stop at a scenic overlook that has a hiking trail (more than half of them do).

## 2 TAKING A SCENIC DRIVE ALONG THE BLUE RIDGE PARKWAY

Running more than 450 miles (725 kilometers) between Shenandoah National Park in Virginia and Great Smoky Mountains National Park in North Carolina, the Blue Ridge Parkway is the mother of all scenic roads. It covers more than 200 miles (321 kilometers) in North Carolina, from **Lowgap** at the state line to **Cherokee** in the Smokies. In North Carolina, the mountains take center stage. The peak of **Grandfather Mountain** looms high over the Blue Ridge Parkway, and the spectacular **Linn Cove Viaduct** seems to float off its mountainside.

TRAIL AND OVERLOOK AT GRANDFATHER MOUNTAIN

Between Asheville and Cherokee is the highest and most crooked part of the drive. **Asheville** is home to the lauded **Biltmore Estate** and some of the best restaurants in the South. **Cherokee,** where the Blue Ridge Parkway ends, is the ancestral home of the Eastern Band of the Cherokee Nation.

You can travel along the parkway from the North Carolina line to **Great Smoky Mountains National Park** in one day, but two days will allow you to enjoy the countless sights along the way. Traffic on the parkway is always slow—the maximum speed limit never exceeds 45 mph—and can be congested in summer and during leaf season.

## ③ ESCAPING TO THE OUTER BANKS

From the Virginia border in the north to Ocracoke Island in the south, the Outer Banks act as barrier islands, protecting the mainland, marshlands, and towns of the Inner Banks from a storm's brunt. This series of islands traces a path some 125 miles (201 kilometers) long along the northeastern coast of the state. In summer, visitors come from all over to enjoy the beaches and numerous warm-weather festivals. This is where you'll also find stretches of untamed shore, wild horses, and iconic lighthouses.

A highlight of the region is **Cape Hatteras National Seashore,** which stretches into the Atlantic and brushes the warm waters of the Gulf Stream. **Hatteras** draws surfers, anglers, divers, bird-watchers, and beach-loving vacationers by the thousands. You'll want to climb **Cape Hatteras Lighthouse,** with its black-and-white spiral exterior, and pay a visit to **Ocracoke Island,** which was a favorite haunt of the pirate Blackbeard.

In the Lower Outer Banks, **Cape Lookout National Seashore** is 56 miles (90 kilometers) of beach stretched out across four barrier islands, a one-stop shop for all this region has to offer. **Wild horses** roam the beaches and dunes, **dolphins** frequent both the ocean and sound sides of the islands, and it's a great place for **bird-watching.** Don't miss the black-and-white diamond-spangled **Cape Lookout Lighthouse,** one of the most iconic symbols of North Carolina, which has stood watch here since 1859.

For a scenic drive, **Highway 12** traces the Outer Banks from the mainland onto the barrier islands and all the way up to the Virginia border. Take the ferry (reservations required) at **Cedar Island** on the mainland across to **Ocracoke;** another ferry takes you to the village of **Hatteras** at the southern end of Hatteras Island, part of the Cape Hatteras National Seashore. From there, keep heading north on the highway until you reach **Corolla,** where the paved highway ends. If you're adventurous and have a 4WD vehicle and beach driving experience, head north a few miles toward the Virginia border. A herd of wild horses (and not much else) lives here.

CAPE HATTERAS NATIONAL SEASHORE

# *Best* ROAD TRIP

**DAY 1** Start your North Carolina adventure in **Raleigh,** the state capital, which is home to a number of excellent museums. Be sure to get your first taste of North Carolina barbecue at **Clyde Cooper's Barbecue.**

**DAY 2** Travel west on I-40 to **Greensboro** to see one of the most important sites in civil rights history: the Woolworth's Lunch Counter where a peaceful sit-in ignited the Civil Rights Movement in North Carolina. **The International Civil Rights Center and Museum** is housed in the former F. W. Woolworth building where the protest took place.

**DAY 3** From Greensboro, make your way to **Lowgap** (about 1.5 hours), where the Blue Ridge Parkway starts in North Carolina. Spend the day driving the parkway to **Asheville.** Slow your pace past **Grandfather Mountain** and across the precariously perched **Linn Cove Viaduct.**

**DAY 4** In Asheville, head directly to the **Biltmore Estate.** Tour the **Biltmore Winery** and watch the **blacksmith** at Antler Hill Village make music with the anvil. Spend the evening enjoying the fruits of a growing array of chefs and brewers.

**DAY 5** Complete your Blue Ridge Parkway road trip at **Great Smoky Mountains National Park,** 1 hour away from Asheville. You're as likely to see a bear as a deer as you drive the park's stunning **scenic roads,** and you'll also pass a number of trailheads. The trails around **Clingmans Dome**—the highest point in the Smokies—are popular. Beat a retreat back to **Cherokee,** outside the park, and rest up.

DOWNTOWN RALEIGH

INTERNATIONAL CIVIL RIGHTS CENTER AND MUSEUM

VIEW FROM THE TOP OF CLINGMANS DOME

**DAY 6**

Start making your way back east. Break up the drive with a night in **Charlotte,** home of the **NASCAR Hall of Fame** (400 E. Martin Luther King Jr. Blvd., Charlotte; 704/654-4400; www.nascarhall.com).

**DAY 7**

Head back to **Raleigh,** 2.5 hours away from Charlotte. If you want to get some beach time, add a day or two for an out-and-back to the **Outer Banks,** which are a 3-hour drive east from Raleigh.

NASCAR HALL OF FAME MUSEUM

THE OUTER BANKS

# WRIGHT BROTHERS NATIONAL MEMORIAL

Milepost 7.5, U.S. 158, 1000 N. Croatan Hwy, Kill Devil Hills; 252/473-2111; www.nps.gov/wrbr/index.htm

In 1903, Orville and Wilbur Wright changed the world in just 12 seconds. Their first flight was short, but it was the culmination of more than three years of failed designs, tests, and travels between their Dayton, Ohio, home and Kitty Hawk, North Carolina, where they tested their gliders on Kill Devil Hill, then the tallest dune on the Outer Banks. The feat is honored at the Wright Brothers National Memorial, where replica gliders, artifacts from the original flight, and tools the Wright brothers used are on display. In the adjacent field a wooden runner and stone markers show their runway, takeoff point, and the spots where their first four flights landed. Climb nearby Kill Devil Hill to see the 60-foot (18-meter) monument honoring their achievement. At the foot of the hill, a life-size bronze sculpture of the *Wright Flyer* seconds after liftoff lets you get a sense of the excitement of the moment.

# FORT RALEIGH NATIONAL HISTORIC SITE

1401 National Park Dr., Manteo; 252/473-2111; www.nps.gov/fora/index.htm

In the 1580s, the first white residents of North Carolina's Outer Banks moved in and established Fort Raleigh. Shortly thereafter, the community vanished, earning the name many now know them by: The Lost Colony. Fort Raleigh National Historic Site on **Roanoke Island** marks the last known location of the Lost Colony, and sections of the earthworks associated with the settlers' original 1580s fort remain and have been preserved. Archaeologists still conduct digs here, and as you explore the site, you'll learn about the missing colonists as well as the freedman's colony—a colony of freed and displaced enslaved people established on the island during the Civil War.

Where the settlers went and why is unknown to this day, but it's explored

# *Major* CITIES

**CHARLOTTE:** A Southern city at heart, Charlotte is also one of the most diverse cities in the Southeast, home to immigrants from Africa, Latin America, Southeast Asia, and India. In addition to two major sports franchises and a booming NASCAR scene, you'll find amazing city parks, outstanding art museums, and first-class dining.

**RALEIGH, DURHAM, AND CHAPEL HILL:** This tri-city area is called "The Triangle," which originally referred to the three major universities here, the University of North Carolina at Chapel Hill, Duke University in Durham, and North Carolina State University at Raleigh. In addition to these three universities, there are more than a dozen other institutions of higher education, including several historically Black colleges and universities, resulting in booming biotech, pharmaceutical, and high-tech industries, and deep roots in the arts.

**GREENSBORO:** Greensboro is the home of several universities, including the University of North Carolina Greensboro and North Carolina Agricultural and Technical State University (A&T), and as befits a college town, you'll find a lively arts and music scene and a creative, engaged population. The city also played a key role in the Civil Rights Movement of the 1960s.

in the outdoor drama *The Lost Colony,* performed at the **Waterside Theatre** in the park (1409 National Park Dr., Manteo; 252/473-6000; http://thelostcolony.org). In the park you'll also find **Elizabethan Gardens** (1411 National Park Dr., Manteo; 252/473-3234; http://elizabethangardens.org), a permanent memorial to the settlers of Roanoke Island that features the types of gardens and plants that would have been common in the colonists' native England in the 16th century.

## INTERNATIONAL CIVIL RIGHTS CENTER AND MUSEUM

134 S. Elm St., Greensboro; 336/274-9199 or 800/748-7116; www.sitinmovement.org

This museum occupies the former F. W. Woolworth's building where four students now known as the Greensboro Four staged a trailblazing sit-in in February 1960. When students David Richmond, Franklin McCain, Ezell Blair Jr. (Jibreel Khazan), and Joe McNeil took their seats on these red-topped stools and refused to move—instead of standing at the end of the counter and waiting for their orders, which would be consumed elsewhere, as African Americans were permitted to do—history

was made. The original full-scale lunch counter is still here, and screens along the counter's back wall show reenactments of the day the sit-in took place.

Other exhibits relating to the Greensboro Four include a replica of a room in Scott Hall Dormitory, where the four students lived on the campus of North Carolina Agriculture & Technical State University. The museum's signature exhibition, called The Battlegrounds, delves further into the lived experience of segregation.

## BLOWING ROCK

U.S. 321 S.; 838/295-7111; www.theblowingrock.com

The Blowing Rock is a strange rock outcropping purported by Ripley's Believe It or Not to be the only place in the world where snow falls upward. Indeed, light objects thrown off Blowing Rock—not allowed, by the way, to prevent the valley from filling up with litter—do tend to come floating back up. The nearby town of the same name has a pleasant downtown, as well as food and accommodations in proximity of the Blue Ridge Parkway.

## CHEROKEE

Cherokee is the seat of government of the Eastern Band of the Cherokee, who have lived in the Great Smoky Mountains for centuries. Today, their traditional arts and crafts, government, and cultural heritage are very much alive.

As you drive around, take a look at the road signs: Below each English road name is that same name in Cherokee, a beautiful script created by Sequoyah, a 19th-century Cherokee silversmith. This language, once nearly extinct, is being taught to the community's youth now, and there is a Cherokee language immersion school on the Qualla Boundary, a large tract of land owned and governed by the Cherokee people.

### Museum of the Cherokee Indian

589 Tsali Blvd., Cherokee; 828/497-3481; https://cherokeemuseum.com

This well-regarded modern museum is a locus of community culture. In the exhibits that trace the long history of the Cherokee people, you may notice the realistic mannequins. Local community members volunteered to be models for these mannequins, allowing casts to be made of their faces and bodies so that the figures would not reflect an outsider's notion of what Indigenous people should look like. The museum traces their history from the Paleo-Indian people of the Pleistocene, when the ancestral Cherokee were hunter-gatherers, through the ancient days of Cherokee civilization and into contact with European settlers.

### Qualla Arts and Crafts Mutual

645 Tsali Blvd., Cherokee; 828/497-3103; http://quallaartsandcrafts.com

Ancient craft traditions still thrive among Cherokee artists in western North Carolina. At the Qualla Mutual, a community arts co-op where local artists sell their work, visitors can learn about and purchase the work of today's masters. The gallery's high standards and the community's thousands of years of artistry make for a collection of very special pottery, baskets, masks, and other traditional art. The double-woven baskets are especially beautiful, as are the carvings of the masks representing each of the seven clans of the Cherokee people (the Bird, Deer, Longhair, Blue, Wolf, Paint, and Wild Potato).

### Oconaluftee Indian Village

778 Drama Rd., Cherokee; 828/497-2111; http://visitcherokeenc.com

Oconaluftee Indian Village is a recreated Cherokee Village tucked into the hills above the town. Here, you'll see how the tribe lived in the 18th century. Tour guides in period costumes lead groups on walking lectures with stops at stations where you can see Cherokee cultural, artistic, and daily-life activities performed as authentically as possible. From cooking demos to flint knapping (for arrowheads and spear points) to wood carving and clay work, you'll get a look at how the Cherokee lived centuries ago. The highlight of the tour is the ritual dance demonstration showing a half-dozen dances and explaining their cultural significance.

# BEST SCENIC DRIVES

The **Blue Ridge Parkway** and the Outer Banks's **Highway 12** are two of North Carolina's best scenic drives.

CARVING OUTSIDE THE MUSEUM OF THE CHEROKEE INDIAN

# DOWN EAST ON U.S. 70

U.S. 70 runs almost the entire length of North Carolina, from Asheville to Core Sound. The farthest-east section, a dogleg through Craven, Jones, and Carteret Counties, gives you a taste of life Down East. Drive southeast through the **Croatan National Forest**, then east through seafood central—**Morehead City.** When you cross the bridge into the colonial port of **Beaufort**, leave U.S. 70 for to explore historic downtown Beaufort, where you'll find attractions and 18th-century architecture. From Beaufort, U.S. 70 winds up along **Core Sound** through fishing communities and marshes full of herons and egrets. Just past Stacy, you can either backtrack on U.S. 70 or proceed to the **Cedar Island National Wildlife Refuge** at the end of the peninsula and catch the Ocracoke Ferry at Cedar Island.

This drive is just over 70 miles (112 kilometers) and can be done about 1.5 hours with no stops—but, of course, the point is to dawdle and enjoy the scenery and small towns. It's an attractive drive any time of year, but old coastal cities like Beaufort are most gorgeous in spring when the azaleas are in bloom.

# BEST PARKS AND RECREATION AREAS

## WRIGHTSVILLE BEACH

About 8 miles (12 kilometers) east of Wilmington is one of the nicest beaches on the Carolina coast: Wrightsville Beach. Wide and easily accessible, it is one of the most visitor- and family-friendly beaches you'll find. Wrightsville benefits from proximity of the Gulf Stream; here the warm ocean current sweeping up the Atlantic seaboard lies only 30-40 miles (30-64 kilometers) offshore, which means warmer waters that are colored more like the Caribbean. A number of lodging and rental choices along the beach make it an easy place to stay, and numerous public beach access points (www.towb.org), some of which are disabled-accessible and some with showers or restrooms, line Lumina Avenue.

## U.S. NATIONAL WHITEWATER CENTER

5000 Whitewater Center Pkwy, Charlotte; 704/391-3900; www.usnwc.org

The U.S. National Whitewater Center features "the world's only multichannel recirculating white-water river"—that is, a complex of artificial rapids—designed for training athletes at the Olympic level; it is the home of the U.S. Olympic canoe and kayak team. Visitors can try white-water rafting, kayaking, stand-up paddleboarding, and white-water kayaking. The center's 300 acres also (121 hectares) feature mountain biking trails, a climbing center, concession area (with beer), and area for bands to perform.

## GRANDFATHER MOUNTAIN

U.S. 221, 2 miles/3.2 kilometers north of Linville; 828/733-4337; www.grandfather.com

Grandfather Mountain, at a lofty 5,964 feet (1,817 meters), is the highest peak in the Blue Ridge Mountains and is a United Nations-designated biosphere reserve. The main attraction is the summit and the **Mile High Swinging Bridge.** It is indeed a mile (1.6 kilometers) high, and it swings a little in the breeze—but it should be called the "Singing Bridge" because of the somewhat unnerving sound of the constant wind moving through the steel cables holding it in place. The view from Grandfather Mountain is stunning, and the peak is

WRIGHTSVILLE BEACH

MILE HIGH SWINGING BRIDGE, GRANDFATHER MOUNTAIN

easily accessible via the scenic road that traces the skyward mile.

Aside from the view, many come to Grandfather Mountain for the **hiking.** There are a few short hikes along the drive to the top and more hikes that will test your stamina and mettle as you climb to the true summit of Grandfather Mountain. The **Wildlife Habitats** are also popular, where you'll find large enclosures that provide a place for white-tailed deer, eagles, river otters, black bear, and cougars to live.

## LINVILLE GORGE AND FALLS

The deepest gorge in the United States—often called the Grand Canyon of the East—is Linville Gorge, located near Blue Ridge Parkway milepost 316 in a 12,000-acre (4,856-hectare) federally designated Wilderness Area. It's genuine wilderness, and some of the hollers in this preserve are so remote that they still shelter virgin forests—a rarity even in these wild mountains. Linville Falls (BRP milepost 316) is one of the most photographed places in North Carolina, a spectacular series of cataracts that fall crashing into the gorge. It can be seen from several short trails that depart from the **Linville Falls Visitors Center** (BRP milepost 316; 828/765-1045). Linville Gorge has some great climbing spots, including Table Rock, parts of which are popular with beginning climbers, and other parts which should only be attempted by experts.

Other extremely strenuous options are the Hawksbill cliff face and Sitting Bear rock pillar.

## CHIMNEY ROCK STATE PARK

U.S. 64/74A, Chimney Rock, MP 384.7 via U.S. Alt. 74 East; 800/277-9611; www.chimneyrockpark.com

Chimney Rock State Park is among the many geological beauties you'll find along the Blue Ridge Parkway corridor. The 315-foot (96-meter) tower of stone that is Chimney Rock stands on the side of the mountain. To get to the top of the chimney, you can take a 26-story elevator ride, or hike the **Outcroppings Trail,** a 0.25-mile (0.4-kilometer) trail nicknamed "The Ultimate Stairmaster." No matter how you get there, the view is spectacular. There are number of additional dizzying views to take in and mountain-hugging trails to hike in the park, and you'll also find rock climbers tackling bouldering, top-rope, and multipitch climbs.

# FESTIVALS AND EVENTS

## LOCAL MUSIC FESTIVALS

In September, Raleigh is filled with music as the **Hopscotch Music Festival** (various venues; http://hopscotchmusicfest.com; early Sept.) delivers a genre-rich lineup of artists, and the **Wide Open Bluegrass Festival** (Red Hat Amphitheatre, Raleigh Convention Center, City Plaza; http://wideopenbluegrass.com; late Sept.) brings hundreds of banjo pickers into the state capitol.

In the Northern Blue Ridge you'll find a few great fiddlers conventions, including the **Bluegrass and Old-Time Fiddlers Convention** (691 W. Lebanon St., Mount Airy; 336/345-7388; www.mountairyfiddlersconvention.com; first full weekend in June) and the **Fiddler's Grove Ole Time Fiddlers and Bluegrass Convention** (Fiddlers Grove Campground, Union Grove; 828/478-3735; www.fiddlersgrove.com; Memorial Day weekend) in Union Grove near Wilkesboro.

WIDE OPEN BLUEGRASS FESTIVAL

In Wilkesboro, what began as a small folk festival more than 20 years ago has grown into **MerleFest** (www.merlefest.org; late Apr.), one of the premier roots-music events in the country. It draws thousands of visitors every year for many of the top-name performers in folk, country, and bluegrass music.

## FULL FRAME DOCUMENTARY FESTIVAL

Durham; 919/687-4100; www.fullframefest.org; Apr.

In April, Durham hosts the Full Frame Documentary Festival, identified by the *New York Times* as the premier documentary film festival in the country before it was even in its 10th year. Venues around downtown host screenings, workshops, panels, and soirees where documentary fans and aspiring filmmakers can mingle with the glitterati of the genre.

## BARBECUE FESTIVAL

Lexington; www.barbecuefestival.com; Oct.

October is officially Barbeque Month in Davidson County, and late in the month every year, up to 100,000 people descend on Lexington for the Barbecue Festival. Lexington No. 1, Speedy's, and a host of other local honeymonkeries provide the eats, while concerts, contests, and children's activities fill the city. It's your chance to sample the full array of Carolina 'cue in one place. Considering that more than 15,000 pounds of barbecue are served each day, there's plenty of each style to go around.

# BEST FOOD AND DRINK

## BARBECUE

In North Carolina, barbecue can be a divisive topic, yet it always brings people back together. There are two primary styles within the state and hundreds of regional and family recipe variations on seasonings, sauce, and sides, but let's keep it simple and say that in North Carolina, barbecue is either Eastern-style or Lexington-style.

**Eastern-style** barbecue uses whole hogs that, once cooked over oak wood coals (sometimes as long as overnight) are chopped or pulled apart, seasoned with a dash or splash of thin sauce made from vinegar and peppers, then served on sandwiches and platters. You'll find the highest concentration of Eastern-style 'cue restaurants east of I-95. **Lexington-style** barbecue uses shoulders and butts, cooks them over a hickory-dominant blend of woods, and is chopped coarsely before being served on platters and sandwiches. The sauce builds off the vinegar and pepper from the East and adds something thick and sweet—sometimes tomato paste, other times brown sugar, and still other times molasses—to give it body. Throughout the state, you'll hear friendly (or borderline heated) discussions on the merits of each style and

# BEST SOUVENIRS

- Be sure to pick up **handmade wares** made by the **craftspeople of the Appalachian Mountains.** You'll find beautiful textiles, pottery, jewelry, furniture, dolls, and more at **Southern Highland Craft Guild** stores (828/295-7938; www.southernhighlandguild.org), or stop by the gallery at the **Penland School of Crafts** (67 Doras Trail, Bakersville; 828/765-2359; www.penland. org), a folk arts instruction center of international renown.

- The tiny town of **Seagrove** is home to a generations-old tradition of folk **pottery.** Start at the **North Carolina Pottery Center,** then move onto the 100-plus studios tucked along lovely country roads.

- Featured in a memorable scene in the 2006 movie *Junebug*, **Replacements Ltd.** in Greensboro (1089 Knox Rd., off I-85 exit 132; 800/737-5223; www.re-placements.com) is an incredible place to shop as well as simply to gawk. Replacements is five football fields of retail and behind-the-scenes space dedicated to what is surely the world's largest collection of tableware and flatware. If you want to replace your great-grandmother's 1865 baby spoon that you accidentally mangled in the garbage disposal, Replacements is at your service.

how sides like slaw, hush puppies, or potato salad should be prepared.

Here are some places where you can try it for yourself.

- **Skylight Inn** (4618 S. Lee St., Ayden; 252/746-4113; www.skylightinnbbq. com), one of the oldest and most lauded barbecue joints in the state, uses the whole hog all the time. Dishes are served with dense, fried cornbread and slaw.

- **Clyde Cooper's Barbeque** (327 S. Wilmington St., Raleigh; 919/832-7614; www.clydecoopersbbq.com) is a Raleigh institution that has been serving Eastern-style barbecue since the 1930s. They're always busy—which is a good thing.

- **Lexington No. 1** (100 Smokehouse Lane, Lexington; 10 U.S. 29/70 S; 336/249-9814; www.lexbbq.com) is the pinnacle of Lexington-style barbecue. Order a plate of coarse chopped brown—the crispy, barky bit on the outside of the meat—and you'll be hooked.

- **Stamey's Old Fashioned Barbecue** (2206 W. Gate City Blvd., Greensboro; 336/299-9888; www.stameys.com) is family-run, and they've been running for a long time, so you know their barbecue game is strong. Traditional, rootsy, and delicious, Lexington-style Stamey's is a must.

## CRAFT BREWS

You can't go far without passing a brewery in North Carolina. There are nearly two-dozen breweries in **Wilmington,** and they've racked up accolades, awards, and stellar writeups, putting the city on the map as one of North Carolina's great beer destinations. Stop by **Flying Machine Brewing Company** (3130 Randall Pkwy., Wilmington; 910/769-8173; www.flyingmachine.beer) or **New Anthem Beer Project** (116 Dock St., Wilmington; 910/399-4683; www.ne-wanthembeer.com) to get started.

In the **High Country** corner of the state, the breweries tend to be smaller, which means styles and flavors that really reflect local palates and, for the bold, allows for more experimentation. While you're here, **Fonta Flora Brewery** (317 N. Green St., Morganton; 828/475-0153; www.fontaflora.com) and **Skull Camp Brewing** (1980 N. Bridge St., Elkin; 336/258-8124; www.skullcampbrewing. com) are good spots to try first.

**Asheville** is regarded as the epicenter of North Carolina's beer and culinary scenes, and it's well deserved. Winner of the title "Beer City USA" and perpetually at the top of any beer geek's list of cities to visit, Asheville's brewery scene is exemplary in terms of variety, innovation, and sheer volume. When you're in town you'll have no problem finding a brewery to visit, but you could start with **Burial Beer Co.** (40 Collier Ave., Asheville; 828/475-2739; www.burial-beer.com) or **Green Man Brewery** (23 Buxton Ave., Asheville; 828/252-5502; www.greenmanbrewery.com).

## BOILED PEANUTS

Few snacks are more viscerally craved by locals, and more revolting to non-Southerners, than boiled peanuts. The recipe is simple: Green peanuts are boiled in their shells in bulk in water as salty as the chef deems necessary. Once they're soft and slimy, the peanuts are dumped into a strainer and are ready to eat. All you need to make them is a big kettle and a fire, so boiled peanuts are often made and sold in small

BOILED PEANUTS

bags at roadside stands, primarily in the Lowcountry and coastal plain, but increasingly in the mountains as well. Often these roadside stands are themselves folk art, with handmade signs reading "Boilt P-Nuts Here," with a collection of carvings or sculptures for sale in the bed of a truck nearby.

# MAJOR AIRPORTS

- **Charlotte Douglas International Airport:** CLT; 5501 Josh Birmingham Pkwy., Charlotte; www.charmeck.org
- **Raleigh-Durham International Airport:** RDU; 2400 W. Terminal Blvd., Morrisville; www.rdu.com
- **Piedmont Triad International Airport:** GSO; 1000 Ted Johnson Pkwy., Greensboro; www.flyfrompti.com

# MORE INFORMATION

## TRAVEL AND TOURISM INFORMATION

- **Visit North Carolina:** www.visitnc.com
- **North Carolina State Parks:** www.ncparks.gov

## NEWSPAPERS

- *Charlotte Observer:* www.charlotteobserver.com
- *Raleigh News & Observer:* www.newsobserver.com

# SOUTH CAROLINA

Even by Southern standards, South Carolina is bathed in a certain mystique. The Spanish moss hangs low, people catch their own seafood for dinner, and the creeks are like highways in the marsh. You can traverse its entire width in half a day, going from a beautiful white-sand beach to a stunning mountain overlook. Along the way, you'll find the oldest cypress stands in the world, a wealth of mountain waterfalls, and some of the best fishing, kayaking, and white-water rafting in the country. The state, on Waccamaw, Chicora, Winya, Sewee, Kusso, Yamasee, Santee, Congaree, Wateree, Lumbee, Cheraw, Waxhaw, Sugaree, Catawba, and Cherokee land, is famous for its historic sites, which are as diverse as the landscape, including a seemingly endless supply of colonial and Civil War sites along with St. Helena Island, the center of Gullah history and culture.

Once here, you'll quickly tune in to a particularly South Carolinian vibe that's easygoing yet flamboyant, laid-back yet cocksure: a sort of assertive niceness that's a unique twist on the proverbial Southern hospitality.

**AREA:** 32,020 square miles / 82,931 square kilometers (40th)

**POPULATION:** 5,148,714 (23rd)

**STATEHOOD DATE:** May 3, 1788 (8th)

**STATE CAPITAL:** Columbia

BEACH NEAR THE COASTAL CITY OF CHARLESTON

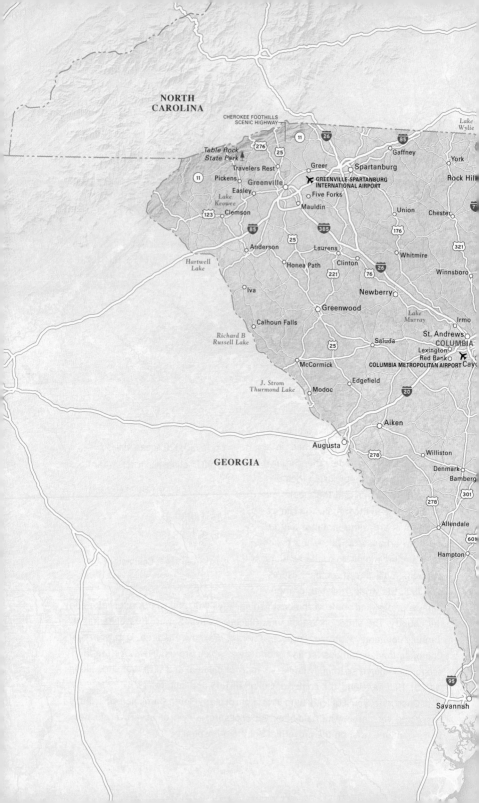

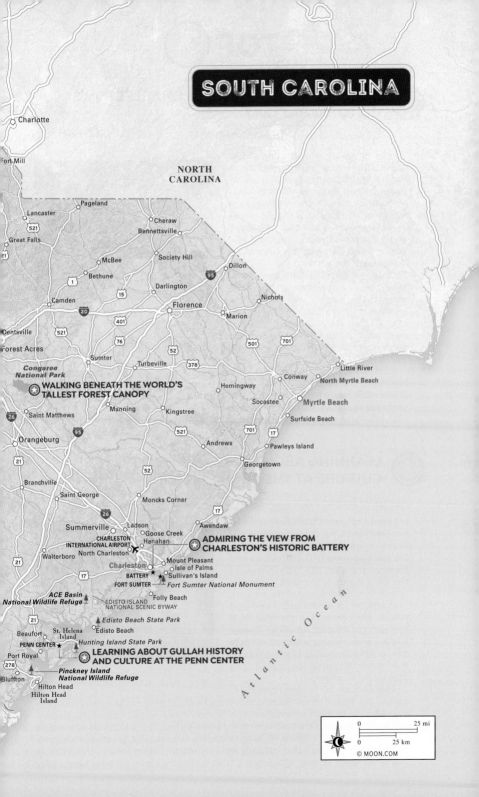

# SOUTH CAROLINA

NORTH CAROLINA

Charlotte

Fort Mill

Lancaster
521
Great Falls
21

Pageland
Cheraw
Bennettsville

McBee
Society Hill
Bethune
1
Darlington
Dillon
95
Camden
20
15
Nichols
Florence
401
Marion
Dentsville
521
76
Sumter
Turbeville
501
701
Little River
Conway
North Myrtle Beach

Congaree
National Park
WALKING BENEATH THE WORLD'S
TALLEST FOREST CANOPY
Hemingway
Socastee
Myrtle Beach
Surfside Beach

Saint Matthews
Manning
Kingstree
26
Orangeburg
95
521
701
17
Pawleys Island
21
52
Andrews
Georgetown

Branchville
Saint George
52
Moncks Corner
17

Summerville
Ladson
Awendaw
CHARLESTON
INTERNATIONAL AIRPORT
Goose Creek
Hanahan
ADMIRING THE VIEW FROM
CHARLESTON'S HISTORIC BATTERY
Walterboro
North Charleston
21
Charleston
Mount Pleasant
Isle of Palms
BATTERY
Sullivan's Island
FORT SUMTER
Fort Sumter National Monument
ACE Basin
National Wildlife Refuge
Folly Beach
EDISTO ISLAND
NATIONAL SCENIC BYWAY
Edisto Beach State Park
Beaufort
St. Helena
Island
Edisto Beach
21
PENN CENTER
Hunting Island State Park
Port Royal
LEARNING ABOUT GULLAH HISTORY
AND CULTURE AT THE PENN CENTER
278
Pinckney Island
National Wildlife Refuge
Bluffton
Hilton Head
Hilton Head
Island

Atlantic Ocean

0        25 mi
0    25 km
© MOON.COM

# TOP 3

## ① ADMIRING THE VIEW FROM CHARLESTON'S HISTORIC BATTERY

S. Battery St. and Murray Blvd. Charleston; 843/724-7321

The Battery is arguably the single most iconic Charleston spot, drenched in history and boasting dramatic views. South is the Cooper River, with views of Fort Sumter, Castle Pinckney, and Sullivan's Island; north is the old carrier *Yorktown* moored at Mount Pleasant; and landward is the adjoining, peaceful White Point Gardens, the sumptuous mansions of the Battery.

Once the bustling (and sometimes seedy) heart of Charleston's maritime activity, the Battery was where "the gentleman pirate" Stede Bonnet and 21 of his men were hanged in 1718. The area got its name for hosting cannons

THE BATTERY

during the War of 1812, with the current distinctive seawall structure built in the 1850s.

Contrary to popular belief, no guns fired from here on Fort Sumter, as they would have been out of range. However, many inoperable cannons, mortars, and piles of shot still reside here, much to the delight of kids. This is where Charlestonians gathered in a giddy, party-like atmosphere to watch the shelling of Fort Sumter in 1861, blissfully ignorant of the horrors to come.

## ② LEARNING ABOUT GULLAH HISTORY AND CULTURE AT THE PENN CENTER

16 Martin Luther King Jr. Dr., St. Helena Island; 843/838-2474; www.penncenter.com

Located between Charleston and Hilton Head on St. Helena Island, itself the nexus of Gullah culture, Penn Center is the spiritual home of Gullah culture and history—and a key site in the history of the Civil Rights Movement. Once the site of Penn School, one of the nation's first schools for emancipated enslaved people, the center now provides legal counsel to African American homeowners in St. Helena, where developers are constantly making shady offers so that ancestral land can be opened up to upscale development.

PENN SCHOOL HISTORIC DISTRICT

The 50-acre (20-hectare) campus is part of the Penn School Historic District, a National Historic Landmark comprising 19 buildings, most of historical significance. A self-guided tour of the grounds will teach you about the history of freed enslaved people who resided in Beaufort County during the Civil War. Walking among the live oaks and humble but well-preserved buildings, you'll also instantly see why Martin Luther King Jr. chose this as one of his major retreat and planning sites during the civil rights era. Lessons for formerly enslaved people were taught inside **Darrah Hall,** the oldest building on campus. The **Retreat House** was intended for Dr. King to continue his strategy meetings, but he was assassinated before being able to stay there. Learn more in the **York W. Bailey Museum,** situated Cope Building right along MLK Jr. Drive. Just across the street from the Penn Center is **Brick Baptist Church.** Built by enslaved people in 1855, it is the oldest church on St. Helena Island.

## ③ WALKING BENEATH THE WORLD'S TALLEST FOREST CANOPY AT CONGAREE NATIONAL PARK

100 National Park Rd., Hopkins; 803/776-4396; www.nps.gov/cong

There's literally nothing like it on the planet. Set on a pristine tract of land close to Columbia's sprawl but seemingly a galaxy away, Congaree National Park contains the most ancient stands of old-growth cypress left in the world.

A system of elevated boardwalks and trails, 20 miles (32 kilometers) in total, takes you through a good portion of Congaree's 22,000 acres (89 hectares). You'll see cypresses towering over 130 feet (39 meters) into the air—taller than the boreal forests of Canada and the Himalayas. At ground level you'll see hundreds of cypress "knees," parts of the trees' root systems that jut aboveground. You'll see unbelievably massive loblolly pines—a larger, immeasurably grander species than the sad slash pine tree farms that took over much of the South's available acreage with the arrival of the big paper plants in the 1930s.

You'll have the rare experience of seeing what an old-growth forest actually looks like and why it's so peaceful: Because the canopy shuts off so much light, there is almost no understory. You can walk among the great trees as if you were in a scene from *Lord of the Rings*. You'll view gorgeous Weston Lake, actually an oxbow lake that was once part of the Congaree River, isolated as the river changed course over time. You'll see—and much more often, hear—a wide range of wildlife, including owls, waterfowl, and several species of woodpecker. In mid-May to mid-June, **synchronous fireflies** make their mating display, drawing thousands of visitors. During the two-week peak period, the park may restrict evening visitation via a lottery system.

CYPRESS FOREST IN CONGAREE NATIONAL PARK

# *Best* ROAD TRIP

**DAY 1** Spend your first morning walking or biking around peaceful **downtown Beaufort.** In the afternoon, take a short drive to **Hunting Island State Park** and walk on the windswept beach. Then enjoy dinner at **Saltus River Grill** (802 Bay St., Beaufort; 843/379-3474) on the scenic waterfront. Spend the night at one of Beaufort's many classic B&Bs, such as the **Beaufort Inn** (809 Port Republic St., Beaufort; 843/379-4667; www.beaufortinn.com).

**DAY 2** Visit the relaxing **Pinckney Island National Wildlife Refuge,** then stop at the **Penn Center** on St. Helena Island before heading up to **Charleston** and checking into a romantic room at **The Vendue** (19 Vendue Range, Charleston; 800/845-7900; www.thevendue.com).

**DAY 3** Do a little shopping in Charleston at **Old City Market,** perhaps picking up a sweetgrass basket. Have a hearty Southern-style lunch, then take an afternoon trip to **Fort Sumter.** In the evening, take a sunset stroll around **the Battery** and admire **Rainbow Row** before diving right into a seafood meal at one of the city's fine restaurants.

**DAY 4** Drive 2 hours northwest and spend the rest of the day touring South Carolina's capital, **Columbia,** focusing on the include the **South Carolina State Museum,** downtown. Spend the night at the venerable **Inn at USC** (1619 Pendleton St., Columbia; 866/455-4753; www.innatusc.com).

**DAY 5** Get up bright and early and drive out of town to **Congaree National Park** to walk along its primordial cypress swamp and old-growth forest. Getting back to Beaufort takes about 2.5 hours.

HUNTING ISLAND STATE PARK

THE VENDUE

FORT SUMTER NATIONAL MONUMENT

## ORIENTATION

**Charleston** is situated on the Atlantic, with the coastal tourist attractions of **Myrtle Beach** to the north and **Hilton Head** to the south. **Columbia,** the state capital, is situated right in the middle of the state. To the east, the northern-most part of the South Carolina, including the city of **Greenville,** is located along the fringes of the Blue Ridge Mountains.

## WHEN TO GO

South Carolina is at its peak of natural beauty during spring (**mid-March** to **mid-May**). **November,** when the tourist crush subsides, is also a good time for a visit; the days are delightful, the nights are crisp but not frigid, and you can also get a room at a good price. **June-October** is **hurricane season** on the coast, with **September** in particular the time of highest risk.

# HIGHLIGHTS

## RAINBOW ROW

79-107 East Bay Street, between Tradd and Elliot Streets, Charleston

One of the most photographed sights in the United States, colorful Rainbow Row comprises nine pastel-colored mansions facing the Cooper River in Charleston. The bright, historically accurate colors are one of the vestiges of Charleston's Caribbean heritage, a legacy of the English settlers from the colony of Barbados who were among the city's first citizens.

The homes are unusually old for this fire-, hurricane-, and earthquake-ravaged city, with most dating from 1730 to 1750. These houses were originally right on the Cooper River, their lower stories serving as storefronts on the wharf. The street was created later on top of landfill, or "made land" as it's called locally.

## FORT SUMTER NATIONAL MONUMENT

Charleston Harbor; 843/883-3123; www.nps. gov/fosu

This is the place that brought about the beginning of the Civil War. Though many historians insist the war would have happened regardless of President Lincoln's decision to keep Fort Sumter in federal hands, the stated casus belli was Major Robert Anderson's refusal to surrender the fort when requested to do so in the early-morning hours of April 12, 1861. A few hours later came the first shot of the war, fired from Fort Johnson by Confederate captain

RAINBOW ROW

## *Major* CITIES

**CHARLESTON:** One of America's oldest cities and the birthplace of the Civil War, the coastal city of Charleston is now a vibrant, creative hub with excellent restaurants and a number of historic sites.

**COLUMBIA:** South Carolina's state capital has a distinct college-town vibe, thanks to the University of South Carolina. The South Carolina State Museum, located here, contains a comprehensive history of the Palmetto State.

**GREENVILLE:** Fast-growing Greenville is nestled in the foothills of the Appalachians on what used to be the heart of the Cherokee Nation, with South Carolina's Blue Ridge region just a short drive away.

George James. That 10-inch (25-centimeter) mortar shell, a signal for the general bombardment to begin, exploded above Fort Sumter.

Today the battered but still-standing Fort Sumter remains astride the entrance to Charleston Harbor. You can only visit by boat. Once at the fort, you can be enlightened by the regular ranger talks on the fort's history and construction, take in the interpretive exhibits throughout the site, and enjoy the view of the spires of the Holy City from afar.

## OCEAN DRIVE BEACH

### North Myrtle Beach

Just north of **Myrtle Beach** (which, with its golf courses, resorts, and 60-mile/96-kilometer Grand Strand, remains the number one travel destination in the state) you'll find a spot that's less an actual place than a state of

mind: The "OD," which is notable for its role in spawning one of America's great musical genres, beach music. Don't confuse beach music with the Beach Boys or Dick Dale—that's surf music. Beach music, simply put, is music to dance the shag to. Think the Drifters, the Platters, and the Swingin' Medallions.

To experience the OD, go to the intersection of Ocean Boulevard and Main Street in North Myrtle Beach and take in the vibe. There's still major shag action going on up here, specifically at several clubs specializing in the genre. The two main ones are **Duck's** (229 Main St., North Myrtle Beach; 843/249-3858; www.ducksatocean-drive.com) and **Fat Harold's** (210 Main St., North Myrtle Beach; 843/249-5779; www.fatharolds.com). Another fondly regarded spot is the **OD Pavilion** (91 S. Ocean Blvd., North Myrtle Beach; 843/280-0715), aka the Sunset Grill or "Pam's Palace," on the same site as the old Roberts Pavilion that was destroyed by 1954's Hurricane Hazel. Legend has it this was where the shag was born.

## SOUTH CAROLINA STATE MUSEUM

301 Gervais St., Columbia; 803/898-4921; www.scmuseum.org

The mother lode of all history of the Palmetto State, the South Carolina State Museum occupies the 1893 Columbia Mill textile building. Open since 1988, the museum has collected more than 70,000 artifacts. There's a constant menu of rotating exhibits as well as a standing collection of art, archaeology, and natural history. Kids love the giant

MYRTLE BEACH

shark display, a 43-foot-long (13-meter) replica of a prehistoric shark skeleton typical of the species that once roamed this area back when water levels were significantly higher than today. But the real highlights are the detailed and vibrant exhibits on particular segments of the human history of South Carolina.

Housed within the State Museum complex is the small but well-tended **South Carolina Relic Room & Military Museum** (301 Gervais St., Columbia; 803/737-8095), which maintains an interesting collection of artifacts and memorabilia highlighting the state's significant contributions to American military history, with a strong focus on the Civil War era.

# BEST SCENIC DRIVES

## CHEROKEE FOOTHILLS SCENIC HIGHWAY

### Hwy. 11

While the landscape is not as stark as north of the border, the Blue Ridge in South Carolina has the dual advantages of being both more easily accessible and much less expensive than the increasingly upscale area of the North Carolina mountains. The main route through the area, Cherokee Foothills Scenic Byway runs roughly 118 miles (189 kilometers) east-west along the base of the Blue Ridge. It's a stunning drive in autumn. The key stop is **Table Rock State Park,** whose namesake chunk of granite dominates the northern sky-scape and compels hikers like a magnet.

## EDISTO ISLAND NATIONAL SCENIC BYWAY

### Hwy. 174

One of the last truly unspoiled places in the Lowcountry, Edisto Island has been highly regarded as a getaway spot since the Edisto people first started coming here for shellfish. In fact, locals here swear that the island was settled by English-speaking colonists even before Charleston was settled in 1670.

The 16-mile (25-kilometer) Edisto Island National Scenic Byway cuts across the island, beginning at **ACE Basin National Wildlife Refuge** and passing a shifting rural landscape of marshes, creeks, and corn fields along with historic buildings produce stands before ending at **Edisto Beach State Park.** Popular stops include **McKinley Washington, Jr. Bridge,** and **Russell Creek Bridge,** two prime birdwatching spots with beautiful views.

# BEST PARKS AND RECREATION AREAS

## HUNTING ISLAND STATE PARK

2555 Sea Island Pkwy., Sea Island Pkwy.; 866/345-7275; https://southcarolinaparks.com/hunting-island

Rumored to be a hideaway for Blackbeard himself, Hunting Island is home to an abundance of wildlife, including dolphins, loggerheads, alligators, and deer, and is one of the East Coast's best birding spots. A true family-friendly outdoor adventure spot, it still retains a certain sense of lush wildness—so much so that it doubled as Vietnam in the movie *Forrest Gump.*

The island's main landmark, the historic **Hunting Island Light** (no longer in operation) dates from 1875. While the 167-step trek to the top is strenuous, the view is stunning.

EGRET IN ACE BASIN

## ACE BASIN

Occupying pretty much the entire area between Beaufort and Charleston, the ACE Basin—the acronym signifies its role as the collective estuary of the Ashepoo, Combahee, and Edisto Rivers—is one of the most enriching natural experiences in the country. The ACE Basin's three core rivers, the Edisto being the largest, are the framework for a matrix of waterways crisscrossing its approximately 350,000 acres (141,639 hectares) of salt marsh. Despite 6,000 years of human presence, the basin manages to retain much of its untamed feel. Experience it by kayak: **Outpost Moe's** (843/844-2514; www.geocities.ws/outpostmoe) is a good service for rentals and knowledgeable guided tours.

## EDISTO BEACH STATE PARK

8377 State Cabin Rd., Edisto Island; 843/869-2156; https://southcarolinaparks.com/edisto-beach

Edisto Beach State Park is one of the world's foremost destinations for shell collectors. Largely because of fresh loads of silt from the adjacent ACE Basin, there are always new specimens, many of them fossils, washing ashore. The park stretches almost 3 miles (4.8 kilometers) and features the state's longest system of fully accessible hiking and biking trails, including one

EDISTO BEACH STATE PARK

leading to a 4,000-year-old shell midden, now much eroded from past millennia. The well-done **interpretive center** has interesting exhibits about the nature and history of the park as well as the surrounding ACE Basin. Sources online suggest that the shell midden may fall into the creek, and also that it's being professionally excavated.

## PINCKNEY ISLAND NATIONAL WILDLIFE REFUGE

912/652-4415; www.fws.gov/refuge/pinckney_island

Consisting of many islands and hammocks, Pinckney Island National Wildlife Refuge is the only part of this small but very well-managed 4,000-acre (1,618-hectare) refuge that's open to the public. Almost 70 percent of the former rice plantation is salt marsh and tidal creeks, making it a perfect microcosm for the Lowcountry as a whole, as well as a great place to kayak or canoe. Some of the state's richest birding opportunities abound here.

# FESTIVALS AND EVENTS

## SPOLETO FESTIVAL USA

Charleston, 843/579-3100; www.spoletousa.org; Memorial Day-mid-June

This performing arts extravaganza features plenty of music (including orchestral, opera, jazz, and avant-garde), along with dance, drama, and spoken word, in traditions from Western to African to Southeast Asian. For 17 days from Memorial Day weekend through mid-June, a variety of Charleston venues hop and hum nearly 24 hours a day to the energy of this vibrant celebration. It's the city's largest event. **Piccolo Spoleto** (843/724-7305; www.piccolospoleto.com), literally "little Spoleto," runs concurrently, emphasizing local and regional performers.

## GULLAH FESTIVAL OF SOUTH CAROLINA

Beaufort; www.theoriginalgullahfestival.org; Memorial Day Weekend

PICCOLO SPOLETO

Now over 20 years old, the Gullah Festival of South Carolina celebrates Gullah history and culture on Memorial Day weekend at various locations throughout Beaufort, mostly focusing on Waterfront Park. The event features music, storytelling, handicrafts, and Gullah cuisine.

# BEST FOOD

## SEAFOOD

South Carolina—especially the coastal region—is a paradise for seafood lovers. Here are some highlights you shouldn't miss.

- **Shrimp and grits:** The most iconic South Carolina seafood dish features delectable shrimp and stoneground hominy. Enjoy this classic entrée at **Poogan's Porch** (72 Queen St., 843/577-2337; www.poogansporch.com) and **Slightly North of Broad** (192 E. Bay St.; 843/723-3424; www.snobcharleston.com), both in Charleston.

- **Lowcountry boil:** Also called Frogmore stew after the township on St. Helena Island where it originated, this deceptively simple dish, commonly found in family-style neighborhood restaurants, offers all the basic nutrients you need boiled together in one big pot: shrimp, sausage, potatoes, and corn on the cob, all with a spicy kick.

- **Fried catfish:** The lowly catfish is a renowned freshwater fish in South Carolina, and fried up right it's a treat.

This is what to order when you're inland and need a fresh-seafood fix.

- **May River oysters:** Though most of the great South Carolina stocks are long gone, the well-preserved May River at Bluffton still provides some of the best-quality oysters in the world. Buy them fresh at Bluffton's **Bluffton Oyster Company** (63 Wharf St., Bluffton; 843/757-4010; www.blufftonoyster.com), which brings them in right off the boat during the season (Sept.-Apr.).

## BARBECUE

South Carolina holds a rare distinction in the world of Southern barbecue: It's the only state in the union that represents all known variants of **barbecue sauce:** vinegar and pepper, light tomato, heavy tomato, and the Palmetto State's own contribution, a hot, sweet mustard-based sauce. This indigenous mustard sauce, a culinary legacy of German settlers in the state, is found mostly in the central Midlands portion of the state from Newberry almost to Charleston.

Sides are important in South Carolina, especially the item known as **hash,** made from pork byproducts served over rice. In any genuine barbecue place you'll also encounter **cracklins** (fried pork skin), whole loaves of **white bread,** and, of course, **sweet tea.**

Key purveyors of the culinary art form include:

- **Henry's Smokehouse** (240 Wade Hampton Blvd., Greenville; 864/232-

# BEST SOUVENIRS

**Sweetgrass baskets:** Once used in rice cultivation, these baskets, handmade by Gullah artisans, are now considered works of art. Purchase in Charleston at **Charleston City Market** (Meeting St. and Market St., Charleston; 843/973-7236) or from a street vendor at the **"Four Corners of Law,"** as the intersection of Broad and Meeting Streets is famously known.

7774; www.henryssmokehouse.com) serves sauces on the side, both a to-mato-based version and a mustard-based version.

- **McCabe's Bar-B-Que** (480 N. Brooks St., Manning; 803/435-2833) serves up a vinegar and pepper sauce.

- **Duke's Barbecue** (949 Robertson Blvd., Walterboro; 843/549-1446) of-fers a range of sauces.

## MAJOR AIRPORTS

- **Charleston International Airport:** CHS; 5500 International Blvd., Charleston; 843/767-1100; www. iflychs.com

- **Columbia Metropolitan Airport:** CAE; 3250 Airport Blvd, West Columbia; 803/822-5000; www. columbiaairport.com

- **Greenville-Spartanburg International Airport:** GSP; 2000 GSP Dr., Greer; 864/877-7426; www. gspairport.com

## MORE INFORMATION

### TRAVEL AND TOURISM INFORMATION

- **Discover South Carolina:** http:// discoversouthcarolina.com

- **South Carolina State Parks:** www. southcarolinaparks.com

### NEWSPAPERS

- *The State:* www.thestate.com

# GEORGIA

When people around the world think of the American South, it's some archetypal image from Georgia that comes to mind, whether they know it or not. Spanish moss hanging from a live oak, a tangy barbecue sandwich, hiking the Appalachian Trail...This is the vivid, iconic backdrop of a real or imagined experience of the South, both for the people who've always yearned to visit as well as for those who call it home.

> **AREA:** 59,425 square miles / 153,910 square kilometers (24th)
>
> **POPULATION:** 10,617,423 (8th)
>
> **STATEHOOD DATE:**
> January 2, 1788 (4th)
>
> **STATE CAPITAL:** Atlanta

Georgia, which is set on Muscogee (Creek) land, defies easy labels. It's located in the Deep South and contains one of the nation's most cosmopolitan cities. This state, with a history of intolerance, became the epicenter of the U.S. Civil Rights Movement and was the birthplace of its key leader. Physically, Georgia's landscapes range from the swamps in the southeast to the mountains in the north that mark the beginning of the Appalachian Trail.

▲ CUMBERLAND ISLAND NATIONAL SEASHORE

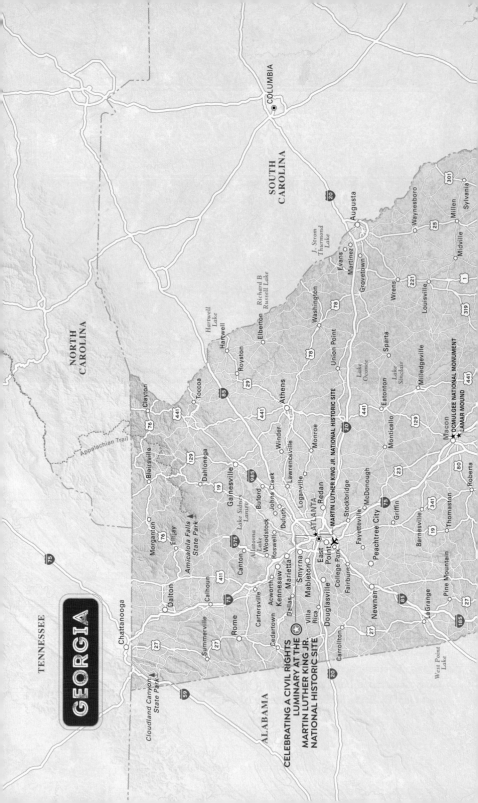

# TOP 3

## 1 CELEBRATING A CIVIL RIGHTS LUMINARY AT THE MARTIN LUTHER KING JR. NATIONAL HISTORIC SITE

450 Auburn Ave., Atlanta; 404/331-5190; www.nps.gov

In 1929, the man who would become the most prominent leader of the Civil Rights Movement was born here in Atlanta. King lived with his family in a home on Sweet Auburn Avenue, a historically African American neighborhood, until he was 12, and was later ordained at nearby Ebenezer Baptist Church. King's funeral was held at Ebenezer, too, following his assassination in 1968.

THE TOMB OF MARTIN LUTHER KING, JR. AND CORETTA SCOTT KING

The Martin Luther King Jr. National Historic Site isn't only a moving elegy to the great Atlantan but an overview of the most crucial epoch of the Civil Rights Movement itself. The facility comprises several wide-ranging features, all within a single block of Auburn Avenue. The **visitors center** (450 Auburn Ave.) focuses on the sacrifice of King and his family, with an entire room devoted to a display of the humble wagon that served as his hearse. Stop inside the restored original sanctuary of **Historic Ebenezer Baptist Church** (corner of Auburn Ave. and Jackson St.; www.ebenezeratl.org), where King preached, and the **King Birth Home** (501 Auburn Ave.), which is presented in a slice-of-life manner, with games and clothes strewn around the children's rooms. The nearby **Fire Station Number 6** played a key role in the desegregation of Atlanta's fire department.

Most visitors also save time to pay their respects at the tomb of Dr. King and his wife, Coretta Scott King, across the street at the **King Center for Nonviolent Social Change** (449 Auburn Ave.). The tomb is situated at the end of a beautiful reflective pool and marked by an eternal flame.

## 2 WANDERING HAUNTINGLY BEAUTIFUL BONAVENTURE CEMETERY

330 Bonaventure Rd., Savannah; 912/651-6843

One of Savannah's most distinctive sights, Bonaventure Cemetery was used as a burial ground as early as 1794. In the years since, this achingly poignant vista of live oaks and azaleas has been the final resting place of such local and national luminaries as Johnny Mercer, Conrad Aiken, Noble Jones, and, of course, the Trosdal plot, former home of the famous *Bird Girl* statue (the original is now in the Telfair Academy of Arts and Sciences). Fittingly, the late great Jack Leigh, who took the *Bird Girl* photo for the cover of *Midnight in the Garden of Good and Evil,* is interred here as well.

Free guides of the cemetery are available at the visitors center. By all means, do the tourist thing and pay your respects at Johnny Mercer's final resting place, and go visit beautiful little "Gracie" in Section E, Lot 99. Then, do as the locals do: Set yourself beside the breezy banks of the Wilmington River with a picnic lunch, taking in all the lazy beauty and evocative bygone history surrounding you.

BONAVENTURE CEMETERY

## ③ GLIMPSING WILD HORSES ON CUMBERLAND ISLAND NATIONAL SEASHORE

912/882-4335, reservations 877/860-6787; www.nps.gov/cuis

Not only one of the richest estuarine and maritime forest environments in the world, Cumberland Island National Seashore is one of the most beautiful places on the planet. With more than 16 miles (25 kilometers) of gorgeous beach and an area of over 17,000 acres (6,879 hectares), there's no shortage of scenery. The Indigenous Timucuan people revered this site, visiting it often for shellfish and for sassafras, a medicinal herb common on the island.

Famously, the seashore also hosts a band of beautiful but voracious wild horses. The current population of about 140 or so is descended from horses brought to the island by the Carnegie family in the 1920s. Frankly, these gorgeous, magnificent animals are not the best thing for this sensitive barrier island ecosystem. But their beauty and visceral impact on the visitor is undeniable, and, responding to overwhelming public opinion, the National Park Service leaves the herd virtually untended and unsupervised.

You're not guaranteed to see wild horses on Cumberland, but the odds are heavily in your favor. They often congregate to graze around the Dungeness ruins, and indeed any open space, and can often be seen cavorting on the windy beach in the late afternoon and early evening.

WILD HORSES AT CUMBERLAND ISLAND NATIONAL SEASHORE

**DAY 1** Begin in **Atlanta,** birthplace of Martin Luther King, Jr. Tour King's birth home and Historic Ebenezer Baptist Church, both part of the **Martin Luther King Jr. National Historic Site.** If there's time left in the day, visit the **Georgia Aquarium.**

**DAY 2** Begin the 250-mile/402-kilometer journey east to Savannah, breaking up the 4-hour drive mid-way with a stop to view ancient Indian mounds at **Ocmulgee National Monument.** Once arrived in **Savannah,** check into a hotel for your first of three nights.

HISTORIC EBENEZER BAPTIST CHURCH

**DAY 3** Stroll Savannah's downtown squares, maybe adding a tour of the historic **Owens-Thomas House** or the **First African Baptist Church,** the oldest Black congregation in North America and a staging area for the Underground Railroad.

**DAY 4** Ride out to **Bonaventure Cemetery** (about 15 minutes outside downtown Savannah) to enjoy its calming beauty, and then visit **Fort Pulaski** (another 30-minute drive) to take in both the history and the scenic grounds. For dinner in Savannah, splurge on a meal at **Elizabeth on 37th** (105 E. 37th St., Savannah; 912/236-5547; www.elizabethon37th.net).

OCMULGEE NATIONAL MONUMENT

**DAY 5** Leave Savannah via the scenic **U.S. 17,** aka the Coastal Highway, heading south to **Jekyll Island** (95 miles/152 kilometers; 1.5 hours). Spend a leisurely afternoon cycling around the island, then stay at the legendary **Jekyll Island Club** (371 Riverview Dr., Jekyll Island; 800/535-9547; www.jekyllclub.com).

FORT PULASKI NATIONAL MONUMENT

**DAY**  This morning, drive an hour south to St. Marys and walk around the cute little downtown area before heading out on the ferry to **Cumberland Island National Seashore.** The 45-minute ferry ride takes you to a full day of biking or hiking the many trails among the ruins and dunes—plus a chance to spot the island's resident wild horses.

**DAY** **7** Make the half-hour drive into Folkston and the Suwanee Canal Recreation Area at **Okefenokee National Wildlife Refuge.** Take a guided tour up and down the blackwater canal, or walk the trails out to the swamp's prairie vistas and drink in this unique natural beauty. Stay the night in nearby **Folkston,** and return to Atlanta (5 hours away) the next day.

JEKYLL ISLAND CLUB

OKEFENOKEE NATIONAL WILDLIFE REFUGE

## ORIENTATION

From the Blue Ridge mountains of North Georgia to the sandy barrier islands of the coast, Georgia's geography is impressively varied. Most roads seem to radiate out from **Atlanta,** which is located in the northeastern part of the state. Outside Atlanta, many tourist attractions are located on the Atlantic Coast, between **Savannah,** which is situated very near the South Carolina border, and the **Okefenokee Swamp,** situated right on Florida's doorstep.

## WHEN TO GO

Generally speaking, the shoulder seasons of **spring** and **fall** are the best times to visit Georgia. In North Georgia, leaf-peeping is extremely popular in fall. The state gets very hot in the **summer,** especially August, while **winters** are mild. (North Georgia is the exception in both seasons, staying comfortable in August but experiencing ice and snow in winter.) The hurricane threat on the coast is highest in **August** and **September.**

# HIGHLIGHTS

## GEORGIA AQUARIUM

225 Baker St. NW, Atlanta; 404/581-4000; www.georgiaaquarium.org

Unlike research-educational aquariums you might visit around the country, the Georgia Aquarium's main purpose is to entertain, and it's quite good at that. Its focal point is the huge **Ocean Voyager** exhibit, the largest single aquarium tank in the world at 6.3 million gallons (23.8 million liters). You observe the hundreds of species inside during a walk through a 100-foot (30-meter) viewing tunnel around which the tank is formed. For an even more up-close experience, the Georgia Explorer area has touch pools with horseshoe crabs, stingrays, and other coastal creatures.

## FIRST AFRICAN BAPTIST CHURCH

23 Montgomery St., Savannah; 912/233-2244; http://firstafricanbc.com

# *Major* CITIES

**ATLANTA:** One of America's most dynamic cities, Atlanta is a burgeoning multiethnic melting pot. For every snarled intersection, a delightfully bucolic neighborhood tantalizes with cafés, shops, and green space. Adventurous restaurants and quirky nightlife venues are Atlanta's specialties.

**SAVANNAH:** Georgia's grand old city isn't just full of history (though that aspect remains very much worth exploring): It's also found new life as an arts and culture mecca. With a liberal open-container law, it's also a good place to find a party.

**MACON:** Located smack in the middle of the state, Macon is in many ways it's the archetypal Georgia town: laid-back, churchified, heavy on fried food, built by the railroad, surrounded by seemingly endless farmland, and a center of cross-pollinating musical traditions.

First African Baptist Church is the oldest Black congregation in North America, dating from 1777. The church also hosted the first African American Sunday school, begun in 1826. The church's founding pastor, George Liele, was the first Black Baptist in Georgia and perhaps the first Black missionary in the country. The present building dates from 1859 and was built almost entirely by members of the congregation themselves, some of whom redirected savings intended to purchase their freedom toward the building of the church.

A key staging area for the **Underground Railroad,** First African Baptist still bears the scars of that turbulent time. In the floor of the fellowship hall—where many civil rights meetings were held—you'll see breathing holes, drilled for use by escaped enslaved people hiding in a cramped crawlspace.

## OWENS-THOMAS HOUSE

124 Abercorn St., Savannah; 912/233-9743; www.telfair.org

Widely known as the finest example of Regency architecture in the United States, the Owens-Thomas House was designed by brilliant young English architect William Jay for cotton merchant Richard Richardson, who lost the house in the Depression. The house's current name is derived from Savannah mayor George Owens, who bought the house in 1830.

When built, the Owens-Thomas House had the first indoor plumbing in Savannah, and its complex plumbing system, including rain-fed cisterns, flushing toilets, sinks, and a shower, remains one of its most interesting features. In 1825, Revolutionary War hero Marquis de Lafayette addressed a crowd of starstruck Savannahians from the cast-iron veranda on the south facade. The associated quarters for enslaved people are in a surprisingly intact state, including the original "haint blue" paint.

HISTORICAL MARKER OUTSIDE FIRST AFRICAN BAPTIST CHURCH

# FORT PULASKI NATIONAL MONUMENT

U.S. 80 E; 912/786-5787; www.nps.gov/fopu

This Civil War fort located on Cockspur Island fell in April 1862, when a Union force successfully laid siege using rifled artillery, a revolutionary technology that instantly rendered the world's masonry forts obsolete. A visit here is a delight for any history buff. Begin by crossing the drawbridge over the moat and see a cannon pointed at you from a narrow gun port. Inside, the fort is huge—Union occupiers regularly played baseball on the grassy parade ground. Take a walk around the perimeter, underneath the ramparts, to see where the soldiers lived and worked, and where Confederate prisoners of war were held after the fort's surrender. Cannon firings happen most Saturdays.

The fort is also situated in a beautiful setting. Take the steep corkscrew staircase up to the ramparts themselves and take in the jaw-dropping view of the lush marsh, with the Savannah River and Tybee Island in the distance. Afterward, stroll all the way around the walls and see the power of those Yankee guns. Some sections of the wall remain in their damaged state—you can even pick out a few cannonballs still stuck in the masonry.

# JEKYLL ISLAND

www.jekyllisland.com

In the late 1800s and 1900s, Jekyll Island was a home away from home for the country's richest industrialists, including J. P. Morgan, William Rockefeller, and William Vanderbilt. Today, it's a great place for a relaxing vacation that retains some of the perks of luxury of its Gilded Age pedigree. The smallest of Georgia's barrier islands, it's a paradise for bicyclists and walkers, with a safe and well-developed system of paths totaling about 20 miles (32 kilometers) and running the circumference of the island. The paths go by all major sights, including the **Historic District,** one of the largest ongoing restoration projects in the southeastern United States and a living link to the Gilded Age, with its croquet grounds and manicured gardens. The historic district essentially comprises the buildings and grounds of the old **Jekyll Island Club,** a full-service resort complex that includes several amazing "cottages" that are mansions themselves.

After the historic district, steer your bike toward **Driftwood Beach.** With the help of ocean currents, the soil has eroded from under the large trees here, causing them to fall and settle into the sand and creating a naturalist's wonderland.

It's worth remembering that the history of this island is not all Gilded Age glamor: The island was the final port of entry for the infamous voyage of *The Wanderer,* the last American slave ship. After intercepting the ship and its contraband manifest of 409 enslaved Africans—the importation of enslaved people having been banned in 1808—its owners and crew were put on trial and acquitted in Savannah.

# OCMULGEE NATIONAL MONUMENT

1207 Emery Hwy.; 478/752-8257; www.nps.gov/ocmu/index.htm

There are somewhat better-preserved Native American mounds elsewhere, but none quite so extensive as the sprawling and entirely fascinating Ocmulgee National Monument. To the Mississippian people that lived here from about 900 to 1650, it was a bustling center of activity, from the enormous temple mound to the intimate and striking Earth Lodge, which, though completely restored, boasts the only

DRIFTWOOD BEACH, JEKYLL ISLAND

original and unchanged lodge floor in North America. Some scholars say that at its peak this site was more populous than modern-day Macon.

Perhaps the most amazing offering at the monument is actually some distance away from the rest of the mounds at the younger **Lamar Mound.** Built around 1350 during a later incarnation of the Mississippian culture, the Lamar site is the only known example of a spiral mound in North America. It is accessible only when the water level in the Ocmulgee River is low, and only by a Ranger-led tour.

# BEST SCENIC DRIVES

## COASTAL HIGHWAY U.S. 17

Many travelers take I-95 south from Savannah to the Golden Isles, but U.S. 17, also known as the Coastal Highway, roughly parallels the interstate and is a far more scenic and enriching drive for those with a little extra time to spend. Indeed, U.S. 17 is an intrinsic part of the life and lore of the region.

Leaving Savannah, you'll pass the smallest church in North America, **Memory Park Christ Chapel,** and can make a stop in the bird-watching haven of **Harris Neck National Wildlife Refuge.** Further south is Brunswick, a

STORK, HARRIS NECK NATIONAL WILDLIFE REFUGE

port city, from which it's an easy detour over to **Jekyll Island.** The whole drive is around 130 miles (209 kilometers). Along the way, you'll pass old military forts, marshes, and other pretty scenery.

# BEST PARKS AND RECREATION AREAS

## AMICALOLA FALLS STATE PARK

418 Amicalola Falls State Park Rd., Dawsonville; 706/265-8888; https://gastateparks. org/amicalolafall

Home of the tallest cascade east of the Mississippi River, Amicalola Falls State Park also happens to be a main gateway to the **Appalachian Trail,** 76 miles (122 kilometers) of which run through Georgia. It's an extremely popular park, especially during leaf-viewing season in the fall. The magnificent 730-foot (222-meter) fall is one of the "Seven Natural Wonders of Georgia" and is worth braving the crowds.

There is a total of 12 miles (19 kilometers) of trails in the park, with the most popular and famous being the 8.5-mile (13.6-kilometer) **Southern Terminus Approach Trail** from the falls to Springer Mountain, the bottom tip of the AT. You can stay overnight at the **Len Foote Hike Inn** (www.hike-inn.com), an eco-friendly hiker's lodge that's a 5-mile (8-kilometer) trek from the main park area.

## CLOUDLAND CANYON STATE PARK

122 Cloudland Canyon Park Rd., Rising Fawn; 706/657-4050; https://gastateparks.org/ CloudlandCanyon

With its namesake 1,000-foot (304-meter) canyon, Cloudland Canyon State Park is quite simply one of the most striking of all Southern state parks. Its steep sandstone walls are the remnants of a 200-million-year-old shoreline. From the various lookout points along the West Rim Loop Trail, skirting the edge of the main picnic area and parking lot along the canyon's edge,

CLOUDLAND CANYON STATE PARK

you can also see the entrances to some of the canyon's many limestone caves. You can also hike to the bottom of the canyon via some steep but well-maintained and staircase-augmented trails.

## HARRIS NECK NATIONAL WILDLIFE REFUGE

5000 Wildlife Dr. NW, Townsend; 912/832-4608; www.fws.gov/refuge/harris_neck

In addition to being one of the single best sites in the South from which to view wading birds and waterfowl in their natural habitat, Harris Neck National Wildlife Refuge also has something of a poignant backstory. For generations after the Civil War, an African American community descended from the area's original enslaved population quietly struggled to eke out a living here by fishing and farming.

The settlers' land was taken by the federal government during World War II to build a U.S. Army Air Force base. Now a nearly 3,000-acre (1,214-hectare) nationally protected refuge, Harris Neck gets about 50,000 visitors a year to experience its mix of marsh, woods, and grassland ecosystems, and for its nearly matchless bird-watching.

Most visitors use the 4-mile (6.4-kilometer) "wildlife drive" to travel through the refuge. Kayaks and canoes can be put in at the public boat ramp on the Barbour River. Near the landing is the **Gould Cemetery,** an old African American cemetery that is publicly accessible. Handmade tombstones evoke the post-Civil War era of Harris Neck before the displacement of local citizens to build the airfield.

## OKEFENOKEE NATIONAL WILDLIFE REFUGE

Folkston; 912/496-7836; www.fws.gov/okefenokee

Nearly the size of Rhode Island, the massive and endlessly fascinating Okefenokee National Wildlife Refuge is one of the lesser-visited national public lands—but it remains one of the most intriguing natural areas on the planet.

Native Americans used the swamp as a hunting ground and gave us its current name, which means "Land of the Trembling Earth," a reference to the floating peat islands, called "houses," that dominate the landscape. It features a wide variety of ecosystems, including peat bogs, sand hills, and black gum and bay forests. Perhaps most

OKEFENOKEE NATIONAL WILDLIFE REFUGE

# BRUNSWICK STEW

Virginians insist that the distinctive Southern dish known as Brunswick stew was named for Brunswick County, Virginia—but all real Southern foodies know the dish is named for Brunswick, Georgia. (Hey, there's a plaque in downtown Brunswick to prove it!) The stew is likely based on an old colonial recipe, adapted from Native Americans, that relied on the meat of small game—originally squirrel or rabbit but nowadays mostly chicken or pork—along with vegetables like corn, onions, and okra simmered over an open fire. Today, this tangy, thick, tomato-based delight is a typical accompaniment to barbecue throughout the Lowcountry and the Georgia coast, as well as a freestanding entrée on its own. Try it in central Georgia at **Vanna's Country Barbecue** (Hwy. 17 S., Royston; 706/246-0952), in western Georgia at **The Whistlin' Pig Cafe** (572 S. Main Ave., Pine Mountain; 706/663-4647), or at the **Brunswick Stewbilee,** held on the second Saturday in October in Brunswick itself.

BRUNSWICK STEW

surprising are the wide-open vistas of the swamp's many prairies or extended grasslands, 22 in all. You'll also notice the water is all very dark, due to natural tannic acid released into the water from the decaying vegetation. The Okefenokee hosts a huge variety of animal life, including over 200 varieties of birds and more than 60 types of reptiles, alligators among them.

For most visitors, the best way to enjoy the Okefenokee is to book a guided tour through **Okefenokee Adventures** (866/843-7926, www.okefenokeeadventures.com), the designated concessionaire of the refuge. They offer a 90-minute guided boat tour that leaves hourly, and a 2.5-hour tour that takes you to see the gorgeous sunset over Chesser Prairie.

# FESTIVALS AND EVENTS

## MARTIN LUTHER KING JR. BIRTHDAY CELEBRATION

Atlanta; 404/526-8900; www.thekingcenter.org; Jan.

King's birthday is a huge focus in his hometown of Atlanta. A variety of events take place, most centering on the MLK Jr. National Historic Site (www.nps.gov/malu/index.htm). Ebenezer Baptist Church typically hosts an annual memorial service, and the MLK Jr. Birth Home often holds an open house. The keynote event is the annual march down Auburn Avenue from Peachtree Street to Jackson Street.

## GEORGIA APPLE FESTIVAL

Ellijay; www.georgiaapplefestival.org; Oct.

Although Georgia is the Peach State, one of its most popular festivals celebrates a different fruit. Happening over two weekends each October in the tiny mountain town of Ellijay, the Apple Festival celebrates the harvest of the area's chief crop—over 600,000 bushels a year. For a scenic look at the farms where the apples are grown, take a drive down **"Apple Alley"** (Highway 52). Many farms are open in the autumn harvest season for tours, hayrides, and pick-your-own apples.

# BEST FOOD AND DRINK

## SAVANNAH'S "TO-GO" COCKTAILS

Certainly one of the things that most sets Savannah apart is the glorious old tradition of the "to-go cup." Like New Orleans, the city legally allows those 21 and over to walk the streets downtown with an open container of their favorite adult beverages. (There are boundaries to where to-go cups are legal, but the quick and easy rule of thumb is to keep your to-go cups north of Jones Street.)

Every downtown watering hole has stacks of cups at the bar for patrons to use. You can either ask the bartender for a to-go cup—a.k.a. a "go cup"—or just reach out and grab one yourself. Don't be shy; it's the Savannah way.

# MAJOR AIRPORTS

- **Hartsfield-Jackson Atlanta International Airport:** ATL; 6000 North Terminal Pkwy., Atlanta; 404/530-6600; www.atl.com
- **Savannah/Hilton Head International Airport:** SAV; 400 Airways Ave., Savannah; 912/964-0514; www.savannahairport.com

# MORE INFORMATION

## TRAVEL AND TOURISM INFORMATION

- **Explore Georgia:** www.exploregeorgia.org
- **Georgia State Parks:** http://gastateparks.org

## NEWSPAPERS

- *Atlanta Journal-Constitution:* www.ajc.com

# ALABAMA

Alabama is perhaps best known for its role in the Civil Rights Movement, and a visit to the state is the chance to walk in the footsteps of heroes. In Selma, you can walk across the Edmund Pettus Bridge toward Montgomery—just as John Lewis did when he was advocating for voting rights. Montgomery offers the opportunity to visit the church where Martin Luther King accepted his first pastorship at the age of 25, and to visit the transformative Legacy Museum. Birmingham, another movement hotbed, remembers Rosa Parks and others in its Civil Rights Institute, drawing connections from the Civil Rights Movement to other movements around the world.

Alabama is on Muscogee (Creek) land. Often overlooked, this sunbaked Southern state offers much beyond its civil rights legacy, too, from white-sand beaches and world-class fishing on the Gulf Shores to some surprising cultural finds in the Shoals region, including an impressive piece of Frank Lloyd Wright architecture, a pair of sights that pay homage to the state's musical history, and a monument commemorating the Trail of Tears.

**AREA:** 52,419 square miles / 135,760 square kilometers (30th)

**POPULATION:** 4,903,185 (24th)

**STATEHOOD DATE:** December 14, 1819 (22nd)

**STATE CAPITAL:** Montgomery

▲ 16TH STREET BAPTIST CHURCH IN BIRMINGHAM

## ORIENTATION

**Birmingham** is located near the center of Alabama, with **Montgomery** and **Selma** about 1.5 hours south, and **Huntsville**, a large city with the University of Alabama-Huntsville, about 1.5 hours to the north. The **Natchez Trace Parkway** grazes the state's northwestern corner.

Tucked between Mississippi to the west, Georgia to the east, Tennessee to the north, and Florida to the south, Alabama does have a slice of shoreline, too: the southwestern corner of the state lies directly on the Gulf of Mexico. This is where **Mobile** is located, along with the popular vacation destinations of **Gulf Shores** and **Orange Beach**.

## WHEN TO GO

**Fall,** which tends to be dry and mild, is generally a good time to visit Alabama. **Summers** are among the hottest in the country, with average temperatures above 90 degrees F (32 degrees C). Tropical storm season lasts November through May, with most tornadoes taking place in **spring** (Mar.-Apr.). **Winter** is relatively mild, though average night temperatures can dip below freezing, particularly in the northeastern part of the state.

# HIGHLIGHTS

## BIRMINGHAM CIVIL RIGHTS INSTITUTE

520 16th St. N, Birmingham; 205/328-9696; www.bcri.org

Opened in 1992, this institute is the centerpiece of the Birmingham Civil Rights Historic District. Through photos, video, and narratives, visitors meet courageous Black residents who galvanized Birmingham's Black community—including children—to embrace nonviolent direct-action tactics. The museum also covers civil rights events outside Birmingham, including the Montgomery Bus Boycott.

The institute is separated into five themed galleries. "Barriers" covers social norms before the Civil Rights Movement kicked off, when segregation seeped into every corner of life and affected everything from water fountains to barbershops, while "Movement," showcases the Montgomery bus boycott sparked by Rosa Parks. You'll also see original steel bars from the jail cell from which King wrote "Letter from a Birmingham Jail." The bars stand in a moodily lit room that is motion-activated to play King's reading of the famous letter.

The "Human Rights" gallery links the U.S. Civil Rights Movement to the larger quest for equality and access globally. In "Resource," the final gallery, you can listen to an oral history collection, including voices of foot soldiers who marched in the 1963 Children's Crusade.

## 16TH STREET BAPTIST CHURCH

1530 6th Ave. N., Birmingham; 205/251-9402; www.16thstreetbaptist.org

BIRMINGHAM CIVIL RIGHTS INSTITUTE

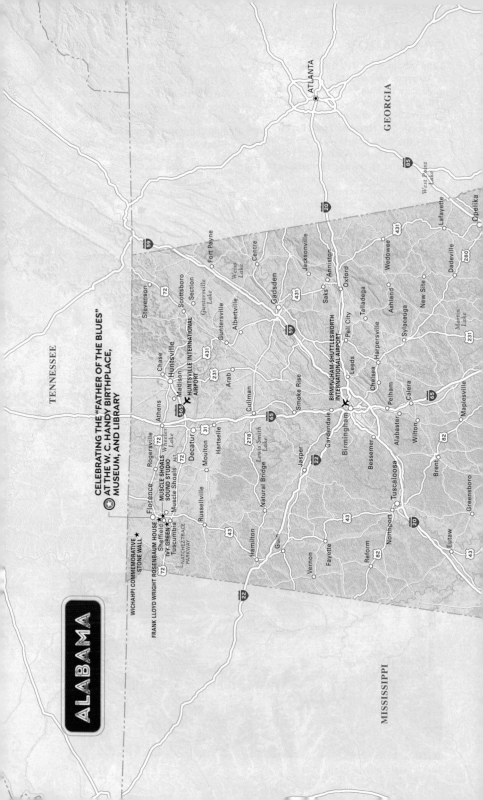

# ALABAMA

★ CELEBRATING THE "FATHER OF THE BLUES" AT THE W. C. HANDY BIRTHPLACE, MUSEUM, AND LIBRARY

★ WICHAHPI COMMEMORATIVE STONE WALL

TENNESSEE

GEORGIA

MISSISSIPPI

ATLANTA

West Point Lake

Opelika
Lafayette
Dadeville
New Site
Wedowee
Ashland
Sylacauga
Martin Lake
Harpersville
Chelsea
Pelham
Calera
Maplesville
Wilton
Alabaster
Brent
Bessemer
Greensboro
Eutaw

Fort Payne
Stevenson
Scottsboro
Section
Guntersville Lake
Weiss Lake
Centre
Jacksonville
Saks
Anniston
Oxford
Talladega
Pell City
Leeds
Gadsden
Albertville
Guntersville
Arab
Cullman
Smoke Rise
Gardendale
Jasper
Birmingham
BIRMINGHAM-SHUTTLESWORTH INTERNATIONAL AIRPORT
Tuscaloosa
Northport
Reform
Vernon
Fayette
Gu
Hamilton
Russellville
Moulton
Hartselle
Natural Bridge
Lewis Smith Lake
Decatur
Wheeler Lake
Rogersville
Athens
Madison
Chase
Huntsville
HUNTSVILLE INTERNATIONAL AIRPORT
Florence
MUSCLE SHOALS SOUND STUDIO
Muscle Shoals
FRANK LLOYD WRIGHT ROSENBAUM HOUSE
Sheffield
IVY GREEN
Tuscumbia
NATCHEZ TRACE PARKWAY

59
72
72
565
72
72
231
431
31
278
43
82
22
20
65
65
43
431
59
431
20
85
280
231
22

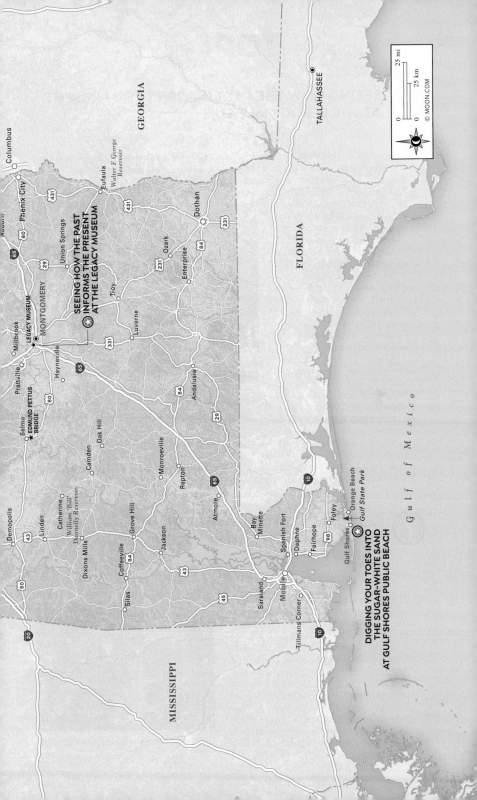

MISSISSIPPI

GEORGIA

FLORIDA

Columbus

Phenix City

Auburn

Eufaula

Walter F George
Reservoir

TALLAHASSEE

Union Springs

Dothan

431

431

231

Ozark

84

Enterprise

231

SEEING HOW THE PAST
INFORMS THE PRESENT
AT THE LEGACY MUSEUM

LEGACY MUSEUM

MONTGOMERY

Troy

29

Luverne

331

Millbrook

Prattville

Hayneville

65

Andalusia

84

Selma

EDMUND PETTUS
BRIDGE

80

29

Oak Hill

Demopolis

Linden

Catherine

Camden

Monroeville

William "Bill"
Dannelly Reservoir

Grove Hill

Repton

65

Atmore

Dixons Mills

Jackson

Bay
Minette

Coffeeville

84

Spanish Fort

Daphne

Fairhope

Silas

43

Saraland

Mobile

Tillmans Corner

45

10

98

Foley

Gulf Shores

Orange Beach

Gulf State Park

DIGGING YOUR TOES INTO
THE SUGAR-WHITE SAND
AT GULF SHORES PUBLIC BEACH

Gulf of Mexico

20

85

80

80

10

43

25 mi

25 km

© MOON.COM

# TOP 3

## 1 SEEING HOW THE PAST INFORMS THE PRESENT AT THE LEGACY MUSEUM

115 Coosa St., Montgomery; 334/386-9100; https://museumandmemorial.eji.org

Opened in 2018, the 11,000-square-foot (1,021-square-meter) Legacy Museum: From Enslavement to Mass Incarceration draws a critical and irrefutable through-line from Black enslavement to contemporary policies that continue to oppress. The museum is housed on the grounds of a former warehouse where Black people were held prisoner. Inside, exhibits unfurl like a timeline, leading visitors chronologically through periods of U.S. history. You'll see holograms of enslaved Black people held in pens, soil samples from cities where people were lynched, and a wall of Jim Crow signs reminding us of how the color line was reinforced in daily movements and interactions.

THE LEGACY MUSEUM

After you've explored the museum, head to the haunting **National Memorial for Peace and Justice** (417 Caroline St., Montgomery; 334/386-9100; https://museumandmemorial.eji.org/memorial)—the nation's first-ever memorial to the victims of lynching—located about a mile (1.6 kilometers) away from the museum on 6 acres (2.4 hectares) that overlook the city. Taken together, the museum and memorial are a heavy, but worthwhile experience. You will be transformed.

## 2 CELEBRATING THE "FATHER OF THE BLUES" AT THE W. C. HANDY BIRTHPLACE, MUSEUM, AND LIBRARY

620 W. College St., Florence; 256/760-6434; www.wchandymuseum.org

The modest cabin that was musician W. C. Handy's birthplace in 1873 is now the site of this museum, which houses considerable memorabilia from the man who created St. Louis Blues, Beale Street Blues, and Memphis Blues. The African American composer had a significant impact not just on blues, but on the music that eventually would become rock 'n' roll. Knowledgeable tour guides impart a lot of information about Handy's roll in modern music. Artifacts include Handy's piano and lots of sheet music.

W. C. HANDY BIRTHPLACE, MUSEUM, AND LIBRARY

GULF SHORES PUBLIC BEACH

## 3  DIGGING YOUR TOES INTO THE SUGAR-WHITE SAND AT GULF SHORES PUBLIC BEACH

100 Gulf Shores Pkwy., Gulf Shores; 251/968-1420; www.gulfshoresal.gov

The stretch of coast from **Orange Beach** to **Gulf Shores** contains 32 miles (51 kilometers) of beautiful shoreline. The region is a natural extension of the Florida Gulf Coast in both geography and culture, and the beaches here are just as beautiful and sugar-white. Gulf Shores Public Beach is the most popular beach in the area. To find huge crowds of beachgoers, just drive to the end of Highway 59. There are volleyball courts, plenty of bars and restaurants, three open-air pavilions, and restrooms with showers. Lifeguards are on duty during summer, making this an excellent choice for families for swimming, surfing, or boogie-boarding.

A sprawling, laid-back beach bar and restaurant, **The Hangout** (101 E. Beach Blvd., Gulf Shores; 251/948-3030; www.thehangout.com), is impossible to miss, and features live music most nights in summer. Once the band starts up, the place draws a heavy-drinking college crowd, but before then it's an excellent choice for families—kids love playing in the large sand pit.

# *Best* ROAD TRIP

**DAY 1**
Begin in **Montgomery,** Alabama's state capitol, where Martin Luther King, Jr. helmed his first church, **Dexter Avenue King Memorial Baptist Church.** Tour the church to learn about its history, along with **Dexter Parsonage Museum,** where the King family lived.

**DAY 2**
Spend the morning visiting Montgomery's **Legacy Museum** and the **National Memorial for Peace and Justice,** the nation's first memorial to the victims of lynching. In the afternoon, start the drive to Selma (52 miles/83 kilometers; 1 hour). As you approach the town, you'll cross the **Edmund Pettus Bridge,** where peaceful voting rights demonstrators met violence at the hands of law enforcement on what came to be known as Bloody Sunday.

**DAY 3**
From Selma, drive 90 miles/144 kilometers (2 hours) to Birmingham. Learn about the Birmingham Campaign, a local civil rights initiative, at the **Birmingham Civil Rights Institute.** Then go across the street to **Kelly Ingram Park,** a site where some of the most critical events took place.

**DAY 4**
Spend a second day in Birmingham touring **16th Street Baptist Church** and finding something good to eat at the **Historic 4th Avenue Business District.**

DEXTER AVENUE KING MEMORIAL BAPTIST CHURCH

NATIONAL MEMORIAL FOR PEACE AND JUSTICE

KELLY INGRAM PARK

**DAY 5** From Birmingham, it's about a 2-hour drive to The Shoals region, sometimes called the Quad Cities: Tuscumbia, Muscle Shoals, Sheffield, and Florence. Swing by **Muscle Shoals Sound Studio** for a photo op, then spend the afternoon touring the **W. C. Handy Birthplace, Museum, and Library** in Florence. The **Frank Lloyd Wright Rosenbaum House** is also here in Florence, and **Ivy Green,** Helen Keller's birth home, is located nearby.

**DAY 6** From Florence, it's a 20-minute drive to **Wichahpi Commemorative Stone Wall.** Built to commemorate one woman's journey on the Trail of Tears, it's quite a moving landmark. From there, driving back to Montgomery takes about 4 hours.

PLAQUE OUTSIDE 16TH STREET BAPTIST CHURCH

WICHAHPI COMMEMORATIVE STONE WALL

A longtime gathering center for African American Birmingham residents, 16th Street Baptist Church was the site of mass meetings and rallies during the Civil Rights Movement. The church was also the site of tragedy on September 15, 1963, when a Ku Klux Klan bombing killed four young girls who were preparing for a day of youth-focused activities in the basement bathroom.

Travelers can visit the church, which was designed by Black architect Wallace Rayfield, on tours led by church members, many of whom have a connection to the movement: Some can even provide firsthand experiences of the day of the bombing and surrounding events. The centerpiece of the church is the **Wales Window,** presented to the church by the people of Wales in memory of the bombing in 1963. The window features a crucified man resembling a Black Christ—a bold statement that continues to show parishioners that they are the image of God. The figure's right hand pushes away hatred and justice while the left offers forgiveness. A rainbow above his head represents the covenant between God and His people.

## DEXTER AVENUE KING MEMORIAL BAPTIST CHURCH

**454 Dexter Ave., Montgomery; 334/263-3970; www.dexterkingmemorial.org**

In 1954, at the age of 25, Martin Luther King, Jr. became minister of the church that's now known as Dexter Avenue King Memorial Baptist in Montgomery. This was King's first pastorate, and it's where he was launched into the limelight. Montgomery Bus Boycott organizing activity occurred in the church basement, where King had an office.

The church is home to a thriving congregation today, but visitors are welcome to partake in a tour to learn about its history, and to walk where King walked and see where he preached. See King's basement office and his high-backed pulpit chair in the upstairs sanctuary, which is awash with sunlight beaming through colored window panes. The **Dexter Parsonage Museum** (303 S Jackson St.; 334/261-3270; www.dexterkingmemorial.org), where

# *Major* CITIES

**BIRMINGHAM:** The state's most populous city, Birmingham was the site of an intense, multifaceted campaign against segregation in 1963. Visitors today can learn about the city's role in the Civil Rights Movement by visiting museums, memorials, and churches.

**MONTGOMERY:** Alabama's capital city was the site of a famous bus boycott during the Civil Rights Movement. Like Birmingham, it's home to a number of sites where visitors can learn about this pivotal moment in national history.

**MOBILE:** The port city of Mobile, known for seafood and French architecture, is situated on Alabama's Gulf Coast, about 1.5 hours northwest of Gulf Shores.

the King family lived, is also open to visitors, and is frozen in time, with King family mementos throughout.

## EDMUND PETTUS BRIDGE

Selma

The Edmund Pettus Bridge stretches across the Alabama River, designating the entrance into the city of Selma. When voting rights activists attempted to cross the bridge to leave Selma in a march to Montgomery in 1965, violence ensued. Today, the bridge is an enduring symbol of the Civil Rights Movement, and a site for the annual commemorative march that takes place every March.

Ironically, the bridge, a powerful symbol for voting rights, is named for a Confederate general and Ku Klux Klan leader. Some have argued the bridge should be renamed for the late civil rights leader and longtime House Representative John Lewis, a key player in the marches; others surmise that a landmark representing Black triumph over White supremacy suits the Pettus legacy well.

For many, the bridge with the controversial name will always be a site of pilgrimage and purpose. If you're in good shape, it should take about 10-15 minutes to get across the quarter-mile (0.4-kilometer) bridge and back.

## FRANK LLOYD WRIGHT ROSENBAUM HOUSE

601 Riverview Dr., Florence; 256/718-5050; http://wrightinalabama.com

Rosenbaum House, the only Frank Lloyd Wright building in the state of Alabama, is an example of Wright's utilitarian Usonian-style architecture, and perhaps one of its best examples. The L-shaped red brick house was designed to be affordable and functional and was built for Mildred and Stanley Rosenbaum and their family. It is one of the few Wright homes with an addition designed by Wright himself (the Rosenbaums had four boys who needed a little more room to roam than the original design afforded). Mildred donated the house to the city of Florence in 1999, and some of her weavings are on display inside. The house has a strong connection to the outdoors, where the large lot blends with the house through the tall glass windows.

EDMUND PETTUS BRIDGE

## IVY GREEN

300 N. Commons St., West Tuscumbia; 256/383-4066; www.helenkellerbirthplace.org

Ivy Green is the birthplace and historic home of Helen Keller, the brilliant woman who would become a leader for education and rights for the blind and deaf. The clapboard house has been left mostly how it was in Keller's time, and tours are available for the home and grounds. One of the highlights of the 640-acre (258-hectare) property is the well pump where "Miracle Worker" Anne Sullivan taught the young Keller to spell out "water" with hand symbols, connecting those symbols to a concrete meaning. By the end of that day, Keller, who had been largely unable to communicate, knew 30 words. Six months later she knew the alphabet and 625 words.

While the building itself is interesting, it is the stories told here of Sullivan and Keller's friendship and hard work that are compelling for kids and adults alike. *The Miracle Worker* is performed here each summer as part of the annual Helen Keller Festival.

## MUSCLE SHOALS SOUND STUDIO

3614 Jackson Hwy., Sheffield; 256/978-5151; http://muscleshoalssoundstudio.org

Muscle Shoals Sound Studio (also known by its address, **3614 Jackson Highway**) may look familiar: It's appeared on the cover of a Cher album named after the famous address. Between 1969 and 1978, this was the place musicians including Bob Seger, Paul Simon, and the Rolling Stones came to record. After closing, it fell into disrepair. After the *Muscle Shoals* documentary, music executives and producers Dr. Dre and Jimmy Iovine from Beats Electronics decided to make a sizeable philanthropic gift toward its restoration. Muscle Shoals Sound Studio reopened in 2017, fully restored to its 1969 glory down to its retro plaid couches. Musicians such as The Black Keys have come to record here since.

In addition to nabbing the requisite selfie in front of the famous sign, you should take a **tour of the studios.** In addition to viewing memorabilia, you'll hear stories about the music history made here—for instance about the rift between Rick Hall and The Swampers that led them to leave FAME Studios and create this one.

## WICHAHPI COMMEMORATIVE STONE WALL

Natchez Trace milepost 341.8; 256/764-3617

One of the country's most compelling landmarks, this mile-long (1.6-kilometer) wall is a monument to builder Tom Hendrix's great-great grandmother, Te-lah-nay, and her journey on the Trail of Tears. Each stone, hand-placed by Hendrix (or visitors) beginning in 1988, symbolizes a single step Te-lah-nay took. Today the wall includes stones from more than 120 different countries.

# BEST SCENIC DRIVES

## NATCHEZ TRACE: ALABAMA

The Natchez Trace runs through just a small corner of Alabama, only 33 miles (53 kilometers) of the parkway's total 444 (231 kilometers). This section of the Trace, while short, was essential for General Andrew Jackson's soldiers to travel south during the Battle of New Orleans. Long before, Native

NATCHEZ TRACE

Americans used this route as a thoroughfare for traversing the region.

There are just eight stops on this section of the Trace, but they are some of the Trace's most powerful and most scenic. Among them is a moving monument to the Trail of Tears, the **Wichahpi Commemorative Stone Wall,** which is the first stop while heading south on the Trace after crossing the Alabama-Tennessee state line (milepost 341.8). Other stops include the sites of several former inns that sheltered soldiers, Native Americans, and other travelers.

The Trace's short hikes and overlooks and wooded oases offer a shady respite to what can be hot summer temperatures in Alabama. Wildflowers bloom in spring and early summer, leaves change to oranges and reds in fall.

# BEST PARKS AND RECREATION AREAS

## GULF STATE PARK

www.alapark.com/parks/gulf-state-park

The biggest draw of Alabama's Gulf Coast—apart from the miles of sugar-white beaches—is the abundant freshwater and saltwater spring-fed lakes that dot the coast for fishing. Most are found within the 6,150 acres (2,488 hectares) of Gulf State Park, which also features rare maritime forest, coastal beaches, and vital dune habitat. The park is around 900-acre

GULF STATE PARK

(364-hectare) **Lake Shelby,** and as you drive along the coast, you will discover large stretches of beach and preserved dune habitat. The park also offers the best camping in the Gulf Shores and Orange Beach area.

Located within the park, **Gulf State Park Pier** (20800 E. Beach Blvd.; 251/967-3474; www.alapark.com/parks/gulf-state-park/fishing-and-education-pier), the largest pier on the Gulf Coast, extends 1,500 feet (457 meters) into emerald waters and is the best place in the area to reel in Spanish mackerel, bluegill, and more. Even if you don't fish, you can still walk the length of the pier and enjoy the view. The wide beach around the pier is just as popular, with plenty of room to spread out and enjoy the sand and surf with the family. The break on both sides of the pier pilings is popular with surfers and boogie boarders, while the rest of the beach is excellent for swimming.

# FESTIVALS AND EVENTS

## SELMA BRIDGE CROSSING JUBILEE

Selma; 334/526-2626; http://selma50.com; Mar.

Every year, the tiny population of Selma (around 17,000) swells with people from around the globe returning to re-enact the Sunday, March 7, 1965, attempted crossing of the Edmund Pettus Bridge known as Bloody Sunday. This annual event is billed as the largest civil rights commemoration in the world and takes place the first weekend in March, Friday-Sunday.

This weekend-long event is staged in venues throughout Selma. Activities include talks, film screenings, and inductions into the Hall of Resistance, which honors those who fought (and those who continue to fight) for social justice. The big day, however, is Sunday, when the bridge walk reenactment takes place. For the march's 50th anniversary in 2015, 40,000 people, including President Barack Obama, Congressman John Lewis, and activist Amelia Boynton Robinson, participated.

EDMUND PETTUS BRIDGE

SELMA BRIDGE CROSSING JUBILEE

In Selma, **Lannie's BBQ Spot** (2115 Minter Ave.; 334/874-4478), in operation since 1944, is notable for its role in feeding foot soldiers in the Selma voting rights movement. The pulled pork sandwiches here just might change your life: They're topped with cracklins, so you get a crunch in every moist, juicy bite.

During segregation, **Brenda's Bar-B-Que Pit** (1457 Mobile Rd.; 334/264-4517) in Montgomery was a safe haven for secret NAACP meetings. Now, the pit is a member of the Alabama Barbecue Hall of Fame. They're big on plates here, so try a pig ear plate, or a pork rib, fish, or chicken plate. It's all good.

# BEST FOOD

## SOUL FOOD

Alabama cuisine is heavily influenced by the state's African American population, with dishes such as pulled pork, black-eyed peas, and sweet potato pie taking center stage. Soul food, Southern food, American food—whatever you call it, it's all served with a smile and good feeling that reaches all the way down into your belly. Some of the state's long-standing soul-food restaurants played a role in Civil Rights Movement by feeding activists or serving as meeting places. Eating at them today is a powerful way to honor that connection.

In Birmingham's **Historic 4th Avenue Business District,** businesses serve up the best soul food traditions and more, with dishes ranging from baked chicken to bean pie. During the Civil Rights Movement, **Nelson Brothers Café** (312 17th St. N; 205/254-9098) served foot soldiers based on what they could afford to pay; today the café is a go-to for pork chops, rice and gravy, and sweet potato pie.

# MAJOR AIRPORTS

- **Huntsville International Airport:** HSV; 1000 Glenn Hearn Blvd SW, Huntsville; 256/772-9395; www.flyhuntsville.com
- **Birmingham-Shuttlesworth International Airport:** BHM; 5900 Messer Airport Hwy, Birmingham; 205/595-0533; www.flybirmingham.com

# MORE INFORMATION

## TRAVEL AND TOURISM INFORMATION

- **Alabama Tourism Department:** https://alabama.travel
- **Alabama State Parks:** www.alapark.com

## NEWSPAPERS

- *The Birmingham News:* www.al.com/birmingham
- *Mobile Press-Register:* www.al.com/mobile
- *The Huntsville Times:* www.al.com/huntsville

# MISSISSIPPI

You don't need a particularly active imagination to picture the significance Mississippi has had on the country. The Natchez Trace Parkway, a trail worn by the footsteps of thousands of Native Americans, settlers, and travelers, cuts a diagonal route through the state. On Acolapissa, Biloxi, Pascagoula, Bayougoula, Houma, Natchez, Chakchiuma, Ibitoupa, Koroa, Ofogoula, Taposa, Tiou, Tunica, Yazoo, Chickasaw, and Choctaw land, the state has seen some of the bloodiest Civil War battles, the forcible removal of Native Americans from their land via the Trail of Tears, the murder of Emmett Till, and the assassination of Medgar Evers. Mississippi is also the home of the Delta Blues Trail, which holds both the past and the present of this very American form of music. And Tupelo is known for one specific contribution to the American music scene—it's the birthplace of Elvis Presley.

Today, Mississippi holds a reverence for its history, its lush green landscapes and rolling hills along the banks of the mighty Mississippi River, its love of music and literature, and, of course, its delicious food.

> AREA: 48,430 square miles / 125,433 square kilometers (32nd)
>
> POPULATION: 2,976,149 (34th)
>
> STATEHOOD DATE: December 10, 1817 (20th)
>
> STATE CAPITAL: Jackson

▲ RED'S BLUES CLUB, CLARKSDALE

## ORIENTATION

**Jackson** is located near the center of Mississippi, with **Vicksburg** due west. **Natchez**, the beginning of the **Natchez Trace Parkway**, is south of Vicksburg, as the Mississippi River flows. The beach cities of **Gulfport** and **Biloxi** line the southeastern arm of the state that stretches to the Gulf of Mexico, with the Mississippi portion of **Gulf Islands National Park** just offshore. Located in the northwestern corner of the state, the **Mississippi Delta** is the triangle of land between the Mississippi and Yazoo Rivers that cradles the blues. Northeastern Mississippi, which includes **Tupleo**, is the part of the state known as "the hills."

## WHEN TO GO

**Spring** is the most desirable time to visit Mississippi, when the weather is temperate, without the oppressive heat of **summer. Fall** is also popular, as the Natchez Trace Parkway is one of the best places in the South to see the leaves change. **Winter** is generally low season; the weather is mild as the state sees little snow.

# HIGHLIGHTS

## CHICKASAW VILLAGE SITE

Natchez Trace Parkway Milepost 261.8, Tupelo; www.nps.gov/places/chickasaw-village-site.htm

Archaeologists believe that the Chickasaw people had a fort and several summer dwellings at this site in the 1700s, in what's now a wildflower-strewn meadow. A modern covered shelter has artist renderings of how the fort would have looked.

There are several options for hikes here. The first is an easy, sun-dappled 15-minute loop walk with signage pointing out the various plants that the Chickasaw used in their daily life for food and medicine. The 0.3-mile (0.48-kilometer) loop is slightly hilly but relatively easy. Stay to the right and you'll end up back behind the information shelter where you started. If you are up for a longer hike, you can take the trail to the right of the shelter (in the left corner if you are in the parking lot) 2 miles to Old Town Overlook.

## ELVIS PRESLEY BIRTHPLACE

306 Elvis Presley Dr., Tupelo; 662/841-1215; http://elvispresleybirthplace.com

If there is one thing for which Tupelo is known, it is the Elvis Presley Birthplace, which includes the house Elvis was born in, a museum, his childhood chapel, a gift shop, and much more. Elvis Aaron Presley was born on January 8, 1935, in this two-room house that's been restored to its original condition, although the family didn't live in the house long—hard financial times befell them.

CHICKASAW VILLAGE SITE

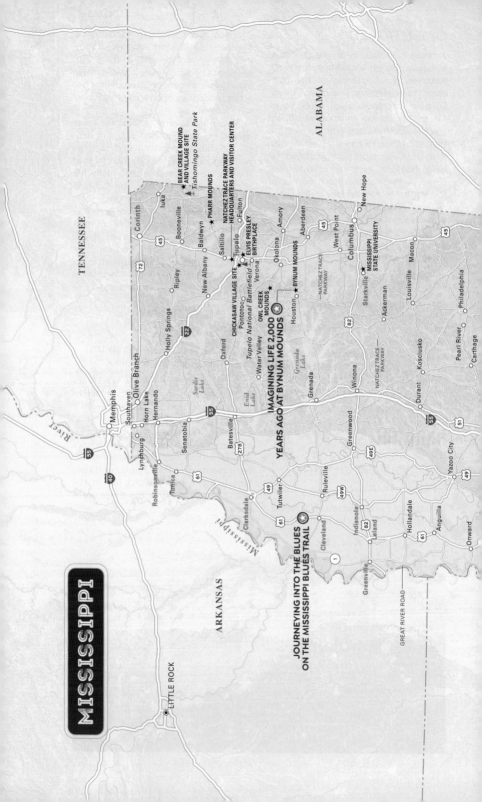

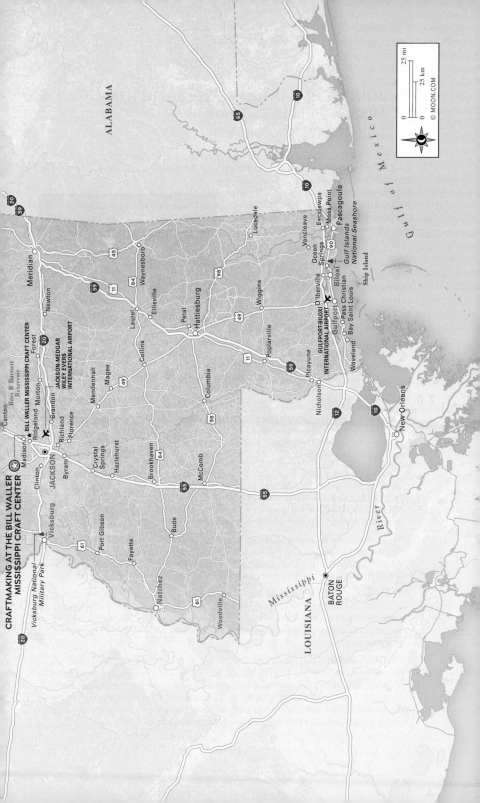

CRAFTMAKING AT THE BILL WALLER
MISSISSIPPI CRAFT CENTER

**BILL WALLER MISSISSIPPI CRAFT CENTER**

**JACKSON-MEDGAR
WILEY EVERS
INTERNATIONAL AIRPORT**

**GULFPORT-BILOXI
INTERNATIONAL AIRPORT**

ALABAMA

Gulf of Mexico

LOUISIANA

Mississippi River

BATON
ROUGE

New Orleans

Ross R Barnett
Reservoir

Vicksburg National
Military Park

**Places labeled on map:**

Meridian
Newton
Forest
Morton
Brandon
Ridgeland
Canton
Madison
Richland
Florence
Clinton
JACKSON
Byram
Vicksburg
Crystal Springs
Hazlehurst
Brookhaven
Bude
Port Gibson
Fayette
Natchez
Woodville
McComb
Columbia
Magee
Mendenhall
Collins
Laurel
Ellisville
Petal
Hattiesburg
Wiggins
Waynesboro
Poplarville
Picayune
Nicholson
Lucedale
Vancleave
Escatawpa
Moss Point
Pascagoula
Ocean Springs
D'Iberville
Biloxi
Gulfport
Pass Christian
Bay Saint Louis
Waveland
Gulf Islands National Seashore
Ship Island

Highways: 20, 59, 45, 11, 84, 98, 49, 55, 61, 10, 90, 12

25 mi
25 km

© MOON.COM

# TOP 3

## 1 JOURNEYING INTO THE BLUES ON THE MISSISSIPPI BLUES TRAIL

www.msbluestrail.org

There are nearly 200 sites included as part of the Mississippi Blues Trail, and visiting all of them is a considerable undertaking. Must-see stops delve into the history and influence of blues greats, while others are mere markers or plaques about artists from the town or what happened on that spot. **The Blues Trail app** (www.msbluestrail.org/app) gives details on them all.

VISITORS CENTER IN TUNICA

A selective tour of the Blues Trail travels through the Mississippi Delta and hits sights in the towns of Tunica, Clarksdale, Cleveland, Indianola, and Leland in about 170 miles 273 kilometers) of driving.

- The must-stop 3,500-square-foot (325-square-meter) **Gateway to the Blues Museum** (13625 U.S. 61 N., Tunica; 888/488-6422; www.tunica-travel.com) has six different galleries, where you can learn about the history of the blues and how the geography contributed to the genre. There's even an exhibition where you can record your own blues song (which will be emailed to you).

- Created in 1979, the **Delta Blues Museum** (1 Blues Alley Ln., Clarksdale; 662/627-6820; www.deltabluesmuseum.org) is the state's oldest music museum. The cabin where Muddy Waters was born has been relocated here from its original site a few miles northwest.

- Juke joints, lively, no-frills places with great music and cheap drinks, have long been associated with the blues but tend to come and go. An authentic juke joint with an erratic schedule, **Red's Blues Club** (390 Sunflower Ave., Clarksdale; 662/627-3166) offers live blues by some of the best local musicians behind a hard-to-find entrance—it's the door to your right as you approach the building.

- The spectacular **Grammy Museum Mississippi** (800 W. Sunflower Rd., Cleveland; 662/441-0100; www.grammymuseumms.org) is the institution's first outside Los Angeles and has more than 12 different interactive exhibits that do an excellent job of linking the blues to other genres.

- The impressive **B. B. King Museum and Delta Interpretive Center** (400 2nd St., Indianola; 662/887-9539; http://bbkingmuseum.org) chronicles the legend's rise to fame. In addition to showing his importance as a musician, it also lets his personality shine through (and if you don't know why he named his guitars Lucille, you'll find out).

- The **Highway 61 Blues Museum** (307 N. Broad St., Leland; 662/686-7646; www.highway61blues.com) is a labor of love, jam-packed with blues artifacts and info compiled by local enthusiasts. This particular museum has more visual art, including paintings and photography by Delta artists, than most music museums. If you call ahead, they'll do their best to have some musicians show up to play while you peruse, an experience no blues fan should miss.

## 2 IMAGINING LIFE 2,000 YEARS AGO AT BYNUM MOUNDS

Natchez Trace Parkway Milepost 232.4; www.nps.gov/places/bynum-mounds.htm

Bynum Mounds' six burial mounds were built between 100 BC and AD 100 (known as the Middle Woodland period). Just two of the mounds, the two largest, have been restored to their original appearance and are available for public viewing. Detailed signage and displays give you an in-depth archaeological information.

BYNUM MOUNDS

Stop at the simple shelter off of the parking lot that has illustrated signage about what life would have been like in the Middle Woodland period. The southernmost of the two restored mounds, called Mound A, contained the remains of a woman, with copper spools at each wrist, placed between two burned oak logs at the mound's base. In addition, cremated remains of two other adults and a child were found. The largest mound, Mound B, covered a log-lined crematory pit. Here the Park Service found greenstone axe heads, copper spools, and other objects that didn't come from Mississippi. These finds demonstrate the long-distance trade networks used by the people living at the time.

Other mound sites can be found along the Natchez Trace Parkway, including the nearby **Owl Creek Mounds** (Milepost 243.1), which are ceremonial, not burial, mounds built much later around AD 1100-1200; **Pharr Mounds** (Milepost 286.7) farther north, where eight burial mounds date back to AD 1-200; and **Bear Creek Mound and Village Site** (Milepost 308.8) with a mound intended either for ceremonial use or as a residence for an elite member of the tribe. These are all sacred spaces and should be treated with respect. Stay on the well-marked paved pathways to circle the mounds and read the signage.

## 3 CRAFTMAKING AT THE BILL WALLER MISSISSIPPI CRAFT CENTER

950 Rice Rd., Ridgeland; 601/856-7546; https://mscrafts.org

Run by the Craftsmen's Guild of Mississippi, the Bill Waller Mississippi Craft Center is a surprising cornucopia of art. This large building houses local events, artisan demos, and fine art exhibitions. The center also offers an array of classes where members of the guild teach skills from knitting, crochet, and basic jewelry making to creating stained-glass ornaments. The large gallery store is also fun to browse for quilts, wood-carvings, ceramics, baskets, sculpture, jewelry, and metalworking made by local and regional craftspeople. Outside the building, there are some outdoor sculptures and a sizable deck.

BILL WALLER MISSISSIPPI CRAFT CENTER

# *Best* ROAD TRIP

**DAY 1** Start in **Jackson,** and head to the **Two Mississippi Museums,** one devoted to the state's civil rights history and the other covering the state's 200-year history. Check to see if the **Eudora Welty House** is open, and take a tour to see the home the way the writer set it up.

**DAY 2** From Jackson, embark on a brief jaunt on the **Natchez Trace Parkway** heading north, heading to the **Bill Waller Mississippi Craft Center,** just east of Jackson, and browse the items made by local artisans. Stop for lunch in **Starkville,** home to **Mississippi State University.** While you're there, be sure to pick up a cowbell to show you're a true fan. After lunch, go to **Bynum Mounds** to see 2,000-year-old Indigenous burial mounds. From there, hop back on the Trace to **Tupelo,** where you'll spend the night.

THE EUDORA WELTY HOUSE

**DAY 3** This morning is devoted to Elvis, with a tour of his birthplace home. Afterward, drive west 2 hours to **Clarksdale,** your first stop on the Mississippi Blues Trail. Check out the **Delta Blues Museum,** and hit **Red's Blues Club,** an authentic juke joint, for live music.

**DAY 4** It's more blues today: Drive south to **Cleveland,** home of the **Grammy Museum Mississippi,** and then to **Indianola** for the **B. B. King Museum and Delta Interpretive Center.** Make sure to try some Delta tamales while you're in the area. If you can squeeze in one more museum, head to Leland's **Highway 61 Blues Museum,** before calling it a day in nearby **Greenville.**

GRAMMY MUSEUM MISSISSIPPI

**DAY 5** From Greenville, take the **Great River Road** along the Mississippi to **Vicksburg,** where there is a famous Civil War battlefield. From there, turn east to go inland back to Jackson.

VIEW OF THE MISSISSIPPI RIVER NEAR VICKSBURG

# *Major* CITIES

**JACKSON:** Named after President Andrew Jackson, Mississippi's energetic, complicated, and historic capital and biggest city is known for its blues music, museums, and complex civil rights history.

**GULFPORT:** The biggest city on Mississippi's Gulf Coast attracts visitors to its beaches constructed over the wetlands in the area.

**BILOXI:** Just 20 miles (32 kilometers) east of Gulfport, Biloxi is the Gulf Coast's other main city. In addition to the beaches, casinos are a big draw to the city.

You can stop by the birthplace and see the exterior of the small home, as well as the chapel and one of the family's cars, without taking the **Grand Tour.** If you go on the tour, you'll hear about how the blues and gospel influenced Elvis and how he created his signature sound, leading him to be the best-selling solo artist in history. With the tour, you'll also be able to go inside the museum, which is full of artifacts that celebrate his life and music. The grounds are lovely and include walking trails, gardens, a reflective pond, and a dynamic sculpture called *Becoming* depicting Elvis as a child and then as a larger-than-life star.

## TWO MISSISSIPPI MUSEUMS

222 North St., Jackson; 601/576-6800; www.mdah.ms.gov/2MM

A complex coined the Two Mississippi Museums was developed as part of a celebration of Mississippi's bicentennial in 2017. In the short time it has been open, the **Mississippi Civil Rights Museum** has become an international destination. The interactive museum fully documents the history of the state and its civil rights struggles. The subject matter, of course, can be upsetting, as the content doesn't shy away from the atrocities that took place, including lynchings, arrests, and church burnings. However, there are also elements that are uplifting and inspiring, particularly the central This Little Light of Mine gallery, which is filled with song and the opportunity for crowds to interact with a light sculpture.

The connected **Museum of Mississippi History** (mmh.mdah.ms.gov) covers everything that has happened in the state the last 200 years, with lots of memorabilia and artifacts, and even a replica of the sunken Natchez Trace Parkway.

## MEDGAR EVERS HOME MUSEUM NATIONAL MONUMENT

2332 Margaret Walker Alexander Dr., Jackson; 601/977-7839

Medgar Evers was the first field secretary for the NAACP in Jackson. He was assassinated in his own driveway in June 1963 during Jackson's difficult and violent fight for civil rights. The Medgar Evers Home Museum National Monument was named a National Historic Landmark in 2017 and became a National Monument in 2019. Both inside and outside the home are panels detailing Evers's life, death, and work. Bullet holes are visible in the walls. Neighbor and local author Eudora Welty was moved by Evers's death, and during a sleepless night that followed his assassination, she wrote one of her most powerful stories, "Where Is the Voice Coming From?" from the point of view of Evers's killer.

# BEST SCENIC DRIVES

## NATCHEZ TRACE: MISSISSIPPI

The Natchez Trace Parkway, which connects Natchez, Mississippi, with

# LITERARY LEGENDS

Some of the South's most celebrated writers have deep roots in Mississippi.

- Playwright Tennessee Williams lived in Clarksdale when his grandfather, Reverend Walter E. Dakin, served as rector of St. George's Episcopal Church. Their home, next to the still-active, still-lovely church, is now the restored **Tennessee Williams Rectory Museum** (106 Sharkey Ave., Clarksdale; 646/465-1578; http://tennesseewilliamsrectorymuseum.com), which is chock-full of information about the writer, his life, and his work.

- **Rowan Oak** (916 Old Taylor Rd., Oxford; 662/234-3284; www.rowanoak.com) is the former family home of the Nobel and Pulitzer Prize-winning writer William Faulkner. The grounds of the Greek Revival-style house are said to be the inspiration for Yoknapatawpha County, the fictional setting for all but three of Faulkner's works.

- The **Eudora Welty House and Garden** (1119 Pinehurst St., Jackson; 601/353-7762; http://eudorawelty.org), where the prolific author grew up and lived until her death, preserves everything—the exterior, interior, and furnishings—is as it was in 1986 when she donated it to the State of Mississippi.

Nashville, Tennessee, runs diagonally through the state for roughly 365 miles (587 kilometers), from the southwest, at its southern terminus of **Natchez,** to the northeast, where it enters Alabama near **Corinth.** The scenic parkway passes through the capital city of **Jackson,** the civil war **Tupelo National Battlefield** (2083 Main St., Tupelo; www.nps.gov/tupe), and numerous Native American mound sites. For more information and a wealth of Trace information, stop at the **Natchez Trace Parkway Headquarters and Visitor Center** (2680 Natchez Trace Pkwy., Tupelo; 800/305-7417 or 662/680-4027; www.nps.gov/natr) at Milepost 266, north of Tupelo.

## GREAT RIVER ROAD

The Great River Road follows the Mississippi River, which forms Mississippi's western boundary, from the Gulf Coast in the south to the U.S. border with Canada. Within Mississippi, the route mostly follows **U.S. 61** in the south and **Highway 1** in the north, depending on which is closer to the river. From the south, it enters the state near **Woodville** and exits into Tennessee north of **Robinsonville.** Along the way, it passes through **Natchez,** the famous civil war battlefield at **Vicksburg** (3201 Clay St., Vicksburg; 601/636-0583; www.nps.gov/vick), and parts of the **Blues Highway,** such as Tunica.

# BEST PARKS AND RECREATION AREAS

## GULF ISLANDS NATIONAL SEASHORE

www.nps.gov/guis

Barrier islands off the coast of Mississippi and Florida comprise the majority

GREAT RIVER ROAD

SWINGING BRIDGE IN TISHOMINGO STATE PARK

of Gulf Islands National Seashore. Only two areas of the Mississippi portion, Davis Bayou and Ship Island, are accessible without a private boat. You can drive to **Davis Bayou,** the only part of the park on the mainland, via I-10 or U.S. 90, and once there you can hike along short trails through the beautiful wetlands environment. There are seasonal public ferries that run from Gulfport (from Jones Park, 1022 23rd Ave.) and Biloxi (Margaritaville Resort, 195 Beach Blvd.,) to **Ship Island,** which has a nice beach along the gulf and a historic D-shaped former fort.

## TISHOMINGO STATE PARK

105 County Road 90, Tishomingo; 662/438-6914; www.mdwfp.com

Named for Chief Tishomingo, once leader of the Chickasaw Nation, Tishomingo State Park offers lots of outdoor recreation options, including canoeing on 45-acre (18-hectare) Bear Lake, fishing on well-stocked Bear and Haynes Lakes (license required), swimming, rock climbing, and hiking on the park's 13 miles of trails. Limestone outcroppings provide the backdrop in this scenic park. One of the most popular paths is the **Bear Creek Outcropping Trail,** which starts at a 200-foot (60-meter) swinging bridge and continues for 3.5 miles (5.6 kilometers). Rock climbing is allowed in the park, but you must bring your own gear and obtain a permit when you pay the park entrance fee.

# FESTIVALS AND EVENTS

## TUPELO ELVIS FESTIVAL

Tupelo; http://tupeloelvisfestival.com; June

This festival hosted by Elvis's birthplaces honors The King with live music for four days in early June.

## OXFORD CONFERENCE FOR THE BOOK

University of Mississippi, Oxford; www.oxford-conferenceforthebook.com; Mar.

This celebration of all things related to the written word is held for three days in March each year at Ole Miss.

## COLLEGE FOOTBALL

The football teams of **University of Mississippi** (Oxford; https://olemisssports.com/sports/football), called Ole Miss by locals, and **Mississippi State University** (Starkville; https://hailstate.com/sports/football), the Bulldogs, are incredibly popular in the state. Home games in the fall fill up their respective cities and make hotel rooms hard to come by.

# BEST FOOD

## DELTA TAMALES

Tamales are as intrinsic a part of the Mississippi Delta as the Mississippi River is. As far back as 1928 Reverend

# BEST SOUVENIRS

**Cowbells** have been rung at Mississippi State football games since at least 1940, when the football team had an undefeated season. People debate which styles are best and which best help cheer the Bulldogs to victory, but a popular choice is a long-handled, bicycle-grip bell made of thin and tightly welded shells. Pick one up anywhere in Starkville—you'll see them in every store, bar, and even gas station.

Moses Mason sang about them; and in 1936, blues legend Robert Johnson sang about tamales in "They're Red Hot." Today, you can find a variety of tamales in the area, but most don't stray too far from the signature recipe: pork, beef, or turkey, encased in corn meal (which makes them a little gritty), and then wrapped in a corn husk and tied with string. In general they are spicier and smaller than a tamale you'd find in Latin America. They're usually sold in paper bags of 3, 6, or 12. To find your favorite, here are some options, from north to south:

- **Ground Zero Blues Club:** 387 Delta Ave., Clarksdale; 662/621-9009; www. groundzerobluesclub.com
- **Airport Grocery:** 3606 U.S. 61, Cleveland; 662/843-4817; www. airportgrocerycleveland.com
- **Doe's Eat Place:** 502 Nelson St., Greenville; 662/334-3315; www. doeseatplace.com

# MAJOR AIRPORTS

- **Jackson-Medgar Wiley Evers International Airport:** JAN; 100 International Dr., Jackson; www. iflyjackson.com
- **Gulfport-Biloxi International Airport:** GPT; 14035-L Airport Rd., Gulfport; 228/863-5951; www.flygpt. com

# MORE INFORMATION

## TRAVEL AND TOURISM INFORMATION

- **Visit Mississippi:** https:// visitmississippi.org
- **Mississippi State Parks:** www. mdwfp.com/parks-destinations

## NEWSPAPERS

- *The Clarion Ledger:* www. clarionledger.com

# FLORIDA

Ask any longtime resident of Florida how they feel about their state, and they'll get a gleam in their eyes. They'll tell you about a spot off a nearby river, along a beautiful beach, or amid the buzzing electricity of the city. This spot, they'll say, could only be found in Florida. And it's places like that, wonderful spots so numerous that it seems nearly every resident has their own private collection, that continue to make Florida unique among places in all of the United States, if not the world.

Florida is on Seminole, Mayaimi, Tocobaga, Guarungumbe, Cuchiyaga, Matecumbe, Jeaga, Guacata, Calusa, Ais, Timucua, and Muscogee (Creek) land. Sitting on the beach watching the sun rise above the Atlantic, with nothing but the squawks of gulls and the crashing of the waves disturbing the peace, you'll see why people have been drawn to the Sunshine State for centuries. The sense of boundless opportunity, the awe-inspiring natural beauty, the numerous opportunities for recreation and relaxation, the sun, the sand, the swamps... Florida still inspires even the most hard-hearted souls with its beguiling promise of paradise.

**AREA:** 65,758 square miles / 170,312 square kilometers (22nd)

**POPULATION:** 21,944,600 (3rd)

**STATEHOOD DATE:** March 3, 1845 (27th)

**STATE CAPITAL:** Tallahassee

▲ MIAMI BEACH

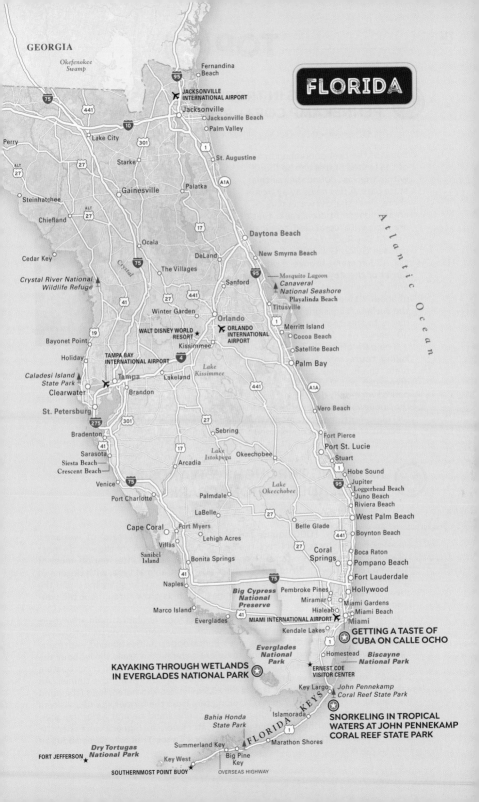

GEORGIA

*Okefenokee
Swamp*

Fernandina
Beach

95

✈ JACKSONVILLE
INTERNATIONAL AIRPORT

441

75

Jacksonville

Lake City

10

● Jacksonville Beach

● Palm Valley

Perry

301

27

1

● St. Augustine

Starke

ALT
27

Gainesville

Palatka

A1A

ALT
27

Steinhatchee

Chiefland

17

Daytona Beach

Ocala

DeLand

● New Smyrna Beach

Cedar Key

75

*Crystal*

The Villages

95

*Mosquito Lagoon*

*Canaveral
National Seashore*

Sanford

Playalinda Beach

*Crystal River National
Wildlife Refuge*

41

Winter Garden

Titusville

1

Orlando

● Merritt Island

Bayonet Point

19

WALT DISNEY WORLD
RESORT ★

✈ ORLANDO
INTERNATIONAL
AIRPORT

● Cocoa Beach

Holiday

Kissimmee

● Satellite Beach

TAMPA BAY
INTERNATIONAL AIRPORT

4

● Palm Bay

*Caladesi Island
State Park*

*Lake
Kissimmee*

Tampa

Lakeland

441

A1A

Clearwater

✈

Brandon

St. Petersburg

275

● Vero Beach

Bradenton

301

Sebring

● Fort Pierce

41

Sarasota

17

Port St. Lucie

Siesta Beach

*Lake
Istokpoga*

Arcadia

Okeechobee

Stuart

Crescent Beach

75

Venice

Palmdale

1

Hobe Sound

Port Charlotte

*Lake
Okeechobee*

Jupiter

27

Loggerhead Beach

Juno Beach

Cape Coral

LaBelle

Riviera Beach

Fort Myers

● West Palm Beach

95

Villas

Lehigh Acres

27

441

● Boynton Beach

*Sanibel
Island*

Bonita Springs

Belle Glade

Coral
Springs

● Boca Raton

41

Naples

75

● Pompano Beach

● Fort Lauderdale

Marco Island

*Big Cypress
National
Preserve*

Pembroke Pines

● Hollywood

Miramar

Miami Gardens

41

Everglades

MIAMI INTERNATIONAL AIRPORT ✈

Hialeah

● Miami Beach

Miami

Kendale Lakes

◎ GETTING A TASTE OF
CUBA ON CALLE OCHO

*Everglades
National
Park*

● Homestead

*Biscayne
National
Park*

KAYAKING THROUGH WETLANDS
IN EVERGLADES NATIONAL PARK ◎

★ ERNEST COE
VISITOR CENTER

1

Key Largo

*John Pennekamp
Coral Reef State Park*

◎ SNORKELING IN TROPICAL
WATERS AT JOHN PENNEKAMP
CORAL REEF STATE PARK

*Bahia Honda
State Park*

● Islamorada

*FLORIDA KEYS*

*Dry Tortugas
National Park*

Summerland Key

1

Marathon Shores

FORT JEFFERSON ★

Key West

Big Pine
Key

SOUTHERNMOST POINT BUOY

OVERSEAS HIGHWAY

*Atlantic
Ocean*

# TOP 3

## 1 SNORKELING IN TROPICAL WATERS AT JOHN PENNEKAMP CORAL REEF STATE PARK

102601 Overseas Hwy., Key Largo; 305/451-6300; http://pennekamppark.com

Some of the best snorkeling in all of the United States can be found within the vast boundaries of this state park. A few miles away from shore, clear, shallow waters house an abundance of coral reefs that are rich with coral and tropical fish. At Dry Rocks reef, snorkelers can see Guido Galletti's 8.5-foot-tall (2.5-meter) bronze statue, **Christ of the Abyss,** extending its arms to the heavens from a depth of about 20 feet (6 meters) below the surface. This sight has drawn divers to this spot for more than 40 years.

JOHN PENNEKAMP CORAL REEF STATE PARK

The park offers 2.5-hour **snorkeling tours** that leave for the reefs three times daily. **Scuba divers** can avail themselves of the park's twice-daily deep-dive tours. Visitors who prefer to stay dry can still glimpse the underwater beauty of the park on the **Spirit of Pennekamp,** a 65-foot (19-meter) glass-bottomed catamaran that can carry more than 100 passengers. Advance reservations highly recommended.

## 2 KAYAKING THROUGH WETLANDS IN EVERGLADES NATIONAL PARK

www.nps.gov/ever

Comprising nearly 4,000 square miles (10,359 square kilometers) of wetlands, swamps, scrub forests, and rivers, the Everglades make up one of the world's most treasured wetland ecosystems. Despite decades of human intervention, most of the area remains wild: **Birds** are the most abundant animal type, with dozens of species calling the 'Glades home. **American alligators** hug the shoreline under the cover of **mangroves,** and nearly 50 species of **orchids** grow throughout the wetlands.

Getting a glimpse into wild, untamed Florida is the Everglades' main attraction. By far, the best way to do this is in a kayak, which allows you to navigate narrow waterways and dense thickets of mangroves. Rental opportunities abound, with many agencies offering guided tours, and there are several boat trails throughout the park. The challenging 8-mile (12.8-kilometer) **West Lake Canoe Trail** takes boaters through some impressive (and occasionally claustrophobic) mangrove tunnels. An easier option, **Nine Mile Pond Trail** is only 3.5 miles/5.6 kilometers long (the pond it's named after is located 9 miles/14 kilometers from the former site of a visitors center), guiding paddlers through mangrove tunnels and several wider marshes. It's best explored during the summer, when water levels are higher. Even easier, the 2-mile (3-kilometer) loop of the **Noble Hammock Canoe Trail** only takes about an hour to traverse.

NAVIGATING THE MANDGROVES IN EVERGLADES NATIONAL PARK

## 3 GETTING A TASTE OF CUBA ON CALLE OCHO

SW 8th Street, Miami

Miami's **Little Havana** is the heart of the U.S. Cuban American community: Some observers have even said that walking along its main drag, the 23-block-long stretch of SW 8th Street famously known as **Calle Ocho,** is a reasonable facsimile for a stroll through the Cuban capital. In fact, nobody's going to mistake the low-slung mid-20th-century buildings here for the crumbling majesty of Habana Vieja anytime soon, but what Little Havana lacks in architectural beauty, it more than makes up for in its vibrant sense of community.

There are very few sights on Calle Ocho (or in Little Havana, for that matter). A great way to spend your time here is to simply park your car and take a half day to wander up and down the street, stopping into places like the dozen or so cigar shops and **Maximo Gomez Park** (801 SW 15th Ave. at Calle Ocho), where old-timers play dominoes. You'll quickly realize that Calle Ocho—and, more generally, Little Havana—is not a tourist-ready trapped-in-amber re-creation of a mystical Cuban homeland, but rather a busy communal neighborhood filled with folks shopping, running errands, and living their lives.

Of course, you'll also have to eat. Legendary **Versailles** (3555 SW 8th St.; 305/444-0240; www.versaillesrestaurant.com), a favorite among locals and tourists alike, serves the best Cuban food in the U.S.

COFFEE SHOP WINDOW IN LITTLE HAVANA

# *Best* ROAD TRIP

**DAY 1** Start in **Miami** and spend your daylight hours exploring the Cuban American community of **Little Havana.** Grab dinner at one of the many excellent restaurants at **South Beach.**

**DAY 2** Once you've shaken off the night before, hit **Miami Beach,** where the sunbathers next to you might be famous. In the afternoon and evening, hit **Ocean Drive** to shop, eat, and gawk at the **art deco buildings.**

OCEAN DRIVE, MIAMI

**DAY 3** Slather yourself in sunscreen and bug spray and head south to **Everglades National Park,** spend the day exploring the swamps and nature trails that are accessible from the convenient **Ernest Coe Visitor Center** (40001 State Rd. 9336, Homestead). When dusk falls, point your car south on the **Overseas Highway** for a 3-hour drive to **Key West,** where you'll be able to whoop it up in the clubs and bars of **Duval Street.**

**DAY 4** Spend the early morning strolling the sidewalks of **Key West,** exploring the historic buildings and soaking up the tropical vibe before the sun makes the heat and humidity unbearable. Then make the 2.5-hour drive to **John Pennekamp Coral Reef State Park** in Key Largo, arriving by mid-afternoon to join a snorkeling tour. Head back to Miami once your tour ends.

DUVAL STREET, KEY WEST

**DAY 5** Get up early for the 3-hour drive from Miami to **Sanibel Island,** which will take you through the northern edge of the Everglades. Spend a relaxing hour gathering shells on the beach before leaving for **Fort Myers,** arriving early enough to explore the **Edison & Ford Winter Estates** before they close.

SHELL-STREWN BEACH ON SANIBEL ISLAND

**DAY (6)** From Fort Myers, drive about 2.5 hours north to **Tampa.** Check into your hotel, then drive 30 minutes to **St. Petersburg** to take in the **Salvador Dalí Museum** and the walkable waterfront area.

**DAY (7)** Wake up early for a 90-minute drive from Tampa to **Crystal River,** a small rural town on the Gulf Coast with a network of warm waterways that are favored by manatees. Spend the day canoeing or kayaking, keeping an eye out for the sea cows that lumber along just beneath the surface.

**DAY (8)** Depart as early as possible for the **Walt Disney World Resort,** which is an hour east of Tampa. Once you arrive, take the rest of the day to explore the fairy-tale fantasies of the **Magic Kingdom** or the eco-minded **Animal Kingdom**.

**DAY (9)** Spend a second day at Walt Disney World digging into the international food-and-drink possibilities in the World Showcase section of **Epcot Center.** It's about a 4-hour drive back to Miami.

MANATEE IN CRYSTAL RIVER

## ORIENTATION

Florida is located in the southeastern corner of the United States, its southernmost point in **Key West** a mere 90 miles (144 kilometers) from Cuba. Its eastern shore is lapped by Atlantic; it's western shore by the Gulf of Mexico.

Many of the main tourist attractions, including the **Everglades, Florida Keys, Miami,** and **Palm Beach** (on the Atlantic Coast) are located on the southern end of the state. **Orlando,** home to **Disney World,** is roughly in the center of Florida, with **Tampa** about halfway up the Gulf Coast. **Jacksonville** and the state capital of **Tallahassee** are in the far northern part of the state, not far from the Georgia border. (Alabama also borders Florida to the north.)

## WHEN TO GO

**Tampa** and **Orlando** have activities year-round. Miami, the South Atlantic Coast, the Keys and the South Gulf Coat are popular in **winter.** The beach towns of the north Atlantic coast are crowded during **summer, spring break,** or any other time when schools aren't in session. As a general rule, holiday weekends—regardless of the time of year—are busy throughout the state.

Florida has three basic climate zones. **North Florida** sees four-season weather patterns: brutally hot and humid summers, chilly and largely snowless winters, and temperate, unpredictable springs and autumns. The **Central Florida** region sees its seasons reduced to three. Summer (late April-late September) brings blistering heat, humidity, and thunderstorms; autumn (October-mid-December), mild temperatures and clear skies; and spring (December-late April), dry air, sunny days, and temperatures that generally hover in the mid-60s to mid-70s, occasionally dropping down to the mid-30s. Tropical **South Florida** sees only two seasons: oppressive (mid-March-mid-October) and pleasant (the rest of the year, when highs are in the mid-70s-low 80s and lows click in comfortably around 60°F every night).

The official season for Atlantic **hurricanes** is June 1-November 1, with peak activity August-September. Although almost every region of Florida has been

# *Major* CITIES

**MIAMI:** Informed by the culture of its substantial Latin American population, by the tropical sea breezes that blow in over Biscayne Bay, and by its stature as the state's largest metropolitan area, Miami manages to be urban and stylish while maintaining the laissez-faire sort of cool that comes with year-round gorgeous weather.

**TAMPA:** Urban explorers will enjoy the nightlife and urban scruffiness of Tampa, whose surrounding Bay area is rich in outdoor activities and boasts some of the most consistently enjoyable weather in the state.

**ORLANDO:** A visit to Florida is incomplete without a trip to Orlando's world-famous theme parks. The city itself combines the urban flair of a growing metropolis and the tranquility of sprawling suburbs.

impacted by hurricanes, the Florida Keys and South Florida are most often in their direct path.

# HIGHLIGHTS

## SOUTH BEACH'S ART DECO ARCHITECTURE

Miami

No matter how many semi-celebs flock to Miami's South Beach, the area's stunning art deco buildings—the crown jewels of Florida's architecture—are the real showstoppers. The stories of how these 1930s icons were rescued from dilapidation and decay are legendary, but the effect of seeing so many refurbished treasures in one place—especially at night, when many of them are lit with clean lines of green, pink, and

ART DECO ARCHITECTURE ON OCEAN DRIVE

purple neon—is spectacular. The vintage cars parked along **Ocean Drive** add to the appeal.

The **Miami Design Preservation League** offers a **walking tour** from the **Art Deco Gift Shop** (1001 Ocean Dr., Miami Beach; 305/531-3484; www.mdpl.org) that points out and contextualizes the numerous examples of art deco architecture on and around Ocean Drive. There are guided and non-guided tours, as well as bike and cell phone tours.

## KEY WEST

Key West is the libertarian heart of the Florida Keys, a city as devoted to bacchanalian pleasures as it is proud of its beautiful and historic scenery. Historic buildings, tropical landscapes, quirky residences (and residents), and a deep sense of individuality combine to create a powerful atmosphere in which people are strongly encouraged to be themselves.

The historic district of Old Town is where you'll find the city's romance and fun. **Duval Street's** range of shopping, dining, and drinking options can easily occupy an entire day, but make sure to take time to notice the unique and beautiful architecture, too: The building that houses **St. Paul's Episcopal Church** (401 Duval St.) dates from 1901, while the old **Strand Theater** (527 Duval St.), currently a chain drugstore, still evokes the glory of its 1930s roots. Built in 1871 by Cuban exiles, the ornate **San Carlos Institute** (516 Duval St.) is a museum, library, art gallery, and theater

THE SAN CARLOS INSTITUTE IN KEY WEST

focusing on Cuban and Cuban American culture.

A block east of Duval Street, the colorful **Southernmost Point Buoy** (South St. and Whitehead St.) is close to the heart of historic Key West., as it notes the fact that you're not only at the southernmost point in the continental United States, but also only 90 miles (144 kilometers) from Cuba. Nearly all visitors make their way here for a snapshot.

## KENNEDY SPACE CENTER VISITOR COMPLEX

State Rd. 405 E., Titusville; 866/737-5235; www.kennedyspacecenter.com

For most of us, the Kennedy Space Center Visitor Complex and Astronaut Hall of Fame is as close as we'll get to extraterrestrial action. Somewhere between a museum and a theme park, its exhibits are all about the innovative thinking that put humans into orbit. When you stand next to a full-sized rocket in one of the main exhibit halls, the effect is truly awe-inspiring. IMAX films and the daily "astronaut encounter," in which one of the 500 people who have ever flown in space shares stories and answers questions, helps give visitors a real sense of the history of American space travel. Although rocket launches aren't as frequent as they were during the shuttle era, if one is scheduled during your visit, you can now view them from the visitors center. Otherwise, you are still able to see the Vehicle Assembly Building, where the shuttles used to be prepared for launch, as well as the launch pads where rockets leave the earth. Kids also love many of the other exhibits, especially the stomach-churning reality of the launch simulator.

## WALT DISNEY WORLD

Orlando; http://disneyworld.disney.go.com

A visit to Florida is incomplete without a trip to the Orlando's world-famous theme parks, and the Walt Disney World Resort is, of course, the theme-park center of gravity in the area. Not only was it the first, it's still the largest and most popular. The place holds a

KENNEDY SPACE CENTER VISITOR COMPLEX

captivating spell over children, but the resort also caters to grown-up tastes with exceptional fine-dining experiences, luxurious spas, and even award-winning cocktails.

The resort encompasses four "kingdoms." The **Magic Kingdom,** the first park built in Orlando by Walt Disney, is where most of the resort's signature attractions—from the spires of Cinderella Castle and to Adventureland and Frontierland—are located. At **Epcot,** Disney's vision of a futuristic city has been supplanted by science-fact displays of technology, a "parade of nations," thrill rides, and a voyage through the food and culture of several different countries. **Disney's Hollywood Studios** combines the magic of Disney with the magic of the movies. **Disney's Animal Kingdom** deftly blends live animal habitats, ecofriendly messages, and a handful of excellent rides.

## SALVADOR DALÍ MUSEUM

1 Dali Blvd., St. Petersburg; 727/823-3767; www.thedali.org

Located just a few blocks outside St. Petersburg's downtown core, the Salvador Dalí Museum is an essential stop for even the most casual art lover. Housing the largest collection of the infamous surrealist's paintings in the United States, it's a somewhat surprising find in this sedate waterfront town. Visitors travel chronologically and thematically through the collection.

SALVADOR DALÍ MUSEUM

Several of Dalí's more famous pieces are often on loan to other museums, and others are not part of this collection, so don't have your heart set on seeing any specific works. What's most impressive is the spacious area devoted to the painter's large-scale masterworks, like the 14-foot-tall (4-meter) *The Discovery of America by Christopher Columbus.* Smaller pencil pieces and various sketches provide considerable insight into his formative years.

## EDISON & FORD WINTER ESTATES

2350 McGregor Blvd., Fort Myers; 239/334-7419; www.edisonfordwinterestates.org

**Thomas Edison** was so taken by the beach town of Fort Myers that he not only built a large winter residence here, he also convinced his friend **Henry Ford** to do the same. Today, while there are dozens of historic homes throughout Florida, none captures the imagination or evokes an era as completely as the Edison & Ford Winter Estates.

Guests to the estates can explore the gardens and grounds as well as a 15,000-square-foot (1,393-square-meter) museum that's filled with various inventions and memorabilia from both men's illustrious pasts, including a Model T. While Thomas Edison's house and labs are available to tour, Henry Ford's house is not. Edison's lab has been kept as is, reflecting its state during the inventor's final days, and is included as part of the museum-style tour of the main house. From the period furnishings and Edison's swimming pool (one of the first concrete swimming pools in Florida) to the impressive banyan trees and verdant gardens, it's certainly worthwhile splurging for the full guided tour of the entire estate.

## ST. AUGUSTINE'S OLD TOWN

St. Augustine is the oldest continually occupied city settled by Europeans in the United States. Walking through Old Town, you'll see 400-year-old residences abutting beer bars, and gorgeous churches within sight of taco stands and wax museums. The narrow streets are remarkably well-preserved

OVERSEAS HIGHWAY TO THE FLORIDA KEYS

in some respects, and the dregs of tourist claptrap in others. This juxtaposition is what makes St. Augustine so fascinating. As you explore, duck into sights like the **Colonial Quarter Museum** (53 St. George St.; 904/825-6830; http://colonialquarter.com), which valiantly re-creates the life of the town's early colonists.

# BEST SCENIC DRIVES

## OVERSEAS HIGHWAY

### U.S. 1

The only way in and out of the Florida Keys, the Overseas Highway links **Miami** with **Key West,** home to the southernmost point in the continental U.S. The 160 miles/257-kilometer (3-hour) drive is stunning, with endless expanses of ocean on either side.

As you pass Florida City and leave the mainland to enter the **Upper Keys,** the transformation of the atmosphere, topography, and attitude is both immediate and overwhelming: The worn-out gas stations and fast-food outlets recede in the rearview, and an open expanse of sea and a slender road spread out in front of you. A bit more developed than their southern counterparts, the Upper Keys include the famous **Key Largo** and snorkeling and diving paradise of **Islamorada.**

Leaving Islamorada, you'll soon enter the **Lower Keys,** a region that has withstood hurricanes, pushed back against development, and maintained a laid-back lifestyle that's richly evocative of Old Florida's charms. The road terminates in **Key West,** the southernmost island and the best known and most visited of all the Keys. Its historic architecture and bustling counterculture make it a must-see.

## STATE ROAD A1A

State Road A1A is the main road through most of Florida's Atlantic beach towns. The beach-hugging route runs the length of the coast, from the Georgia border all the way down to Key West. In some sections, such as the one between Fort Lauderdale and West Palm Beach, choosing this route over an inland one will double your travel time and exponentially add to your traffic anxiety. But you'll definitely want it to get from **Fort Pierce** to **Vero Beach;** it takes about the same amount of time as U.S. 1 or I-95 (about a half hour) but provides superlative views of the ocean. In fact, you'll want to use A1A and U.S. 1 for most of your northerly journey along the coast; from Fort Pierce, it's about 3.5 hours (140 miles/225 kilometers or so) to **Daytona Beach,** and **Cocoa Beach, Titusville,** and **New Smyrna Beach** are all along the way. It will take nearly 2 hours to make the 70-mile (112-kilometer) journey from Daytona north to **St. Augustine,** but the tree-lined vistas and occasional beach views along the way are worth it; it's a surprisingly relaxing drive, which continues an hour (30 miles/48 kilometers) north to get to **Jacksonville Beach,** and from there, it's a half-hour trip (about

CALUSA BEACH

20 miles/32 kilometers) to downtown **Jacksonville.**

# BEST PARKS AND RECREATION AREAS

## CANAVERAL NATIONAL SEASHORE

Visitors center at 7611 S. Atlantic Ave., New Smyrna Beach; southern entrance at 212 S. Washington Ave., Titusville; 386/428-3384; www.nps.gov/cana

Combining isolated and near-meditative beaches, an expansive wildlife sanctuary, legendary fishing spots, and extensive hiking trails, Canaveral National Seashore is a geographical snapshot of what Florida once was, and a haven for those longing for an outdoors adventure. It's one of the best national parks in Florida.

The land on which Canaveral sits was purchased as a buffer zone for NASA's Kennedy Space Center, which abuts the park. Soon, however, the area's biodiversity and unspoiled beaches became a point of pride in the region. Although quite a few people pass through the gates during the summer, even the busiest day at Canaveral never feels crowded. In fact, whether making your way to **Mosquito Lagoon** for some fishing or sneaking off to the unofficial nude beach at the northern end of **Playalinda Beach,** the thing that impresses most about Canaveral is just how spacious and calming it is.

There are half a dozen hiking trails around the park, all of which are brief, fairly easygoing, and well-marked. One of the best, the **Turtle Mound** trail winds through tidal flats and Mosquito Lagoon, and contains several shell mounds left by Timucuan Indians. Many visitors opt to drive along **Black Point Wildlife Drive,** a 6-mile (9.6-kilometer) route that takes in marshland, wildlife, and slash pine copses. Your best chance at wildlife sightings is 1-2 hours after sunrise and 1-2 hours before sunset.

## BAHIA HONDA STATE PARK

36850 Overseas Hwy., Big Pine Key; 305/872-2353; http://bahiahondapark.com

The Keys may seem to be lacking in the beach department—that is, until you hit Bahia Honda, one of the best beach areas in the state. The park offers three gorgeous beaches. **Sandspur,** at the southeast end of the island, is the largest, while **Loggerhead Beach** area has shallow waters that make it great for families. Still, the best beach here is **Calusa Beach,** which offers not only the beautiful sands and blue waters of the other beaches, but also a great view of the cars zooming by on the Overseas Highway bridge. (Be advised that the underwater surface here quickly shifts from smooth, shallow sand to jagged rocks.) There are ample snorkeling opportunities just a few hundred feet from the shore of all three beach areas. Snorkeling trips can be arranged at the visitors center.

Beyond the beaches, Bahia Honda has plenty of opportunities for bird-watching and hiking along two fantastic nature trails, one of which takes visitors up to the ruins of the old Bahia Honda Bridge, a vantage point that provides fantastic ocean views.

The on-site nature center and the butterfly garden are both great educational detours for curious kids and adults.

# DRY TORTUGAS NATIONAL PARK

305/242-7700; www.nps.gov/drto

One of the most unique destinations in the entire National Parks system, Dry Tortugas National Park is a group of seven tiny isolated islands located about 70 miles (112 kilometers) west of Key West. Named the "Dry" Tortugas due to the absence of fresh water on the scrub-lined islands, these islands were used for most of the late 19th and early 20th centuries as the southern edge of the United States' naval defense strategy. Accordingly, the heart of the park, and the sole indicator of human habitation, is **Fort Jefferson,** one of the largest and most remote coastal forts in the country.

The fort, the largest masonry structure in the Western Hemisphere, is the only artificially constructed sight in the Tortugas. It's certainly impressive, but the majority of visitors to the Tortugas use their time here to explore the abundant marine life. Expansive coral reefs are home to blindingly colorful tropical fish and the predators who feed on them, as well as lobsters, anemones, sea turtles, and more. The park contains a recently established 46-square-mile (119-square-kilometer) Research Natural Area, basically a well-protected no-anchor zone, that provides endless opportunities for exploration in the clear blue waters and

helps maintain this fragile ecosystem. There are also ample fishing and boating opportunities in and around the Tortugas, and camping is available at an 11-site campground located near Fort Jefferson. (Camping at Fort Jefferson is primitive.)

# CALADESI ISLAND STATE PARK

727/469-5918, ferry 727/734-1501; www. floridastateparks.org/parks-and-trails/caladesi-island-state-park

Caladesi's perennial ranking at or near the top of every rundown of America's best beaches immediately makes sense, thanks to unspoiled views and the population-controlled atmosphere. Four miles (6.4 kilometers) of white sand on this small barrier island provide plenty of space for beach activities and relaxed sunbathing. The views from nearly every vantage point are stunning. The shallow warm water is extremely calm, and the sand itself manages the soft whiteness expected of Gulf beaches while being firmly packed like many Atlantic-side beaches. Rent a kayak on the island to explore the verdant 3-mile (4.8-kilometer) **kayak trail,** which is excellent for bird spotting.

The only way to get to Caladesi Island State Park is by boat. A ferry departs hourly from near the entrance of Honeymoon Island State Park. The ride takes 20 minutes. The parks department caps daily admissions, and visitors are limited to 4-hour excursions, keeping the beaches from ever feeling too crowded.

# CRYSTAL RIVER NATIONAL WILDLIFE REFUGE

1502 SE Kings Bay Dr., Crystal River; 352/563-2088; www.fws.gov/crystalriver

The 46-acre (18-hectare) refuge Crystal River National Wildlife Refuge is one of the best places on earth to watch **manatees** (who converge on the waters in and around the Crystal River in winter) go about their business. November-March, several areas are designated as no-entry zones, which allows the manatees to eat and mate in peace

TROPICAL WATERS SURROUNDING DRY TORTUGAS NATIONAL PARK

## BEST SOUVENIRS

**Sanibel Island** sees a large amount of empty marine-life homes washing up on its shores. More than 400 different species of **shells**—from bivalves to conchs—can be found on its beaches. As long as they don't contain an inhabitant (either living or dead), it's perfectly fine to collect them, and many visitors do. Sanibel shells can make a nice gift or memento of your trip.

for at least part of the year. During that time the area is so flush with sea cows you'd be hard-pressed to not find one in other parts of the wildlife refuge.

The wildlife area is accessible only by boat. Rent a kayak or canoe from **Crystal River Manatee Tour and Dive** (36 NE 4th St., Crystal River; 888/732-2692; www.manateetouranddive.com) to get here. The company also organizes manatee-watching tours, during which you can commune with the gentle giants from the top of the water or by snorkeling alongside them.

## SIESTA KEY BEACHES

Located on the South Gulf Coast, the wide beaches of Siesta Key boast soft, white sand that seamlessly merges into calm, crystal-blue waters that are largely unaffected by tidal action (this is the Gulf, after all). The gentle wave

action is perfect for inveterate snorkelers and families with small kids.

You'll find lots of people at the main beach, **Siesta Beach** (948 Beach Rd., Sarasota)—but its size means that it somehow still feels spacious, with a wide-open beach vista that's one of Siesta Key's biggest appeals. Snorkelers should head to the southernmost tip of **Crescent Beach** (at the western end of Point of Rocks Rd.), where the "point of rocks," an outcropping of coral formations, is home to a wide variety of fish and marine life.

# FESTIVALS AND EVENTS

### ART BASEL

Miami; www.artbasel.com; first weekend in Dec.

Although Art Basel is consistently referred to as a "sister festival" to the original prestigious Art Basel in Switzerland, it could be argued that this younger sibling has eclipsed its predecessor in terms of both its impact on the art world and on the Miami social scene. For three days Miami Beach becomes the beating heart of the visual arts world as more than 200 galleries from around the world converge on museums and other display spaces throughout the area (as well as Wynwood, the Design District, and other locations) to exhibit the best in contemporary art. Those exhibits are complemented by scores of installations, parties, and innovative art shows that, for a weekend at least, disprove stereotypical notions of Miami's lack of culture.

# BEST FOOD

### KEY LIME PIE

The tiny and super-tart yellow limes that are indigenous to the Florida Keys are quite different from the more common green Persian limes. A true key lime pie is one that utilizes that tang as a counterpoint to the pillows of light sugary meringue that top them. Where to try it? The key lime pie at **Sundowners** (103900 Overseas Hwy., Key Largo;

CRESCENT BEACH AT SIESTA KEY

## CUBAN SANDWICHES

Made with salty ham, succulent roasted pork, pickles, and tangy mustard, Cuban sandwiches are a Miami staple. In fact, the quickest way to start an argument here is to posit that you know the place that prepares the best one. Located in the Wynwood District downtown, **Enriqueta's Sandwich Shop** (2830 NE 2nd Ave.; 305/573-4681) makes theirs with fresh bread and offers a version stuffed with *croquetas* (breaded and fried ham). Another excellent choice, **Sarussi Cafeteria** (6797 SW 8th St.; 305/264-5464), slathers a "secret" mojo sauce on its ham-stacked Cubans. The sandwiches here are so good that they caught the eye of the Travel Channel's *Man v. Food*.

305/451-5566; www.sundownerskeylargo.com) in Key Largo is close to famous.

## FLORIDA STONE CRABS

Stone crabs are abundant all along the coast of the Gulf of Mexico, down to the Keys, and then back up the Atlantic coast to North Carolina. However, the stone crabs that are prevalent along the southwest coast of Florida and in the Keys are known as Florida stone crabs, rather than Gulf stone crabs. Although any stone crab claw is highly prized in kitchens throughout the world, Florida stone crabs have a reputation as being both sweeter and meatier than Gulf stone crabs.

Feasting on stone crab while in the area during harvest season (mid-October and mid-May) is nearly mandatory. **The Fish House** (7225 Estero Blvd.; 239/765-6766; www.thefishhouserestaurants.com) in Fort Myers Beach specializes in stone crab claws, or try them at Naples's **Stone Crab Festival** in October. Try dipping one in mustard; it's better than butter.

## MAJOR AIRPORTS

- **Miami International Airport:** MIA; 2100 NW 42nd Ave., Miami; 305/876-7000; www.miami-airport.com

- **Orlando International Airport:** MCO; 1 Jeff Fuqua Blvd., Orlando; 407/825-2001; www.orlandoairports.net

- **Tampa Bay International Airport:** TPA; 4100 George J Bean Pkwy., Tampa; 813/870-8700; www.tampaairport.com

- **Jacksonville International Airport:** JAX; 2400 Yankee Clipper Dr., Jacksonville; 904/741-4902; www.flyjacksonville.com

## MORE INFORMATION

### TRAVEL AND TOURISM INFORMATION

- **Florida Board of Tourism:** www.visitflorida.com

- **Florida State Parks:** www.floridastateparks.org

### NEWSPAPERS

- *Miami Herald:* www.miamiherald.com

- *Tampa Bay Times:* www.tampabay.com

- *Orlando Sentinel:* www.orlandosentinel.com

# ISLANDS

RAINBOW FALLS, BIG ISLAND OF HAWAI'I

# THE ISLANDS
## *State by State*

## HAWAII

**Why Go:** Hawaii is the island getaway of the imagination—soft, white-sand beaches; swaying palm trees; warm, clear waters for snorkeling; juicy tropical fruits—with the ever-present welcoming spirit of aloha.

## PUERTO RICO

**Why Go:** With natural wonders like bioluminescent bays and a rich cultural life formed of Indigenous, African, and Spanish influences, not to mention the lovely beaches and the various preparations of plantains, Puerto Rico lives up to its nickname: Isla del Encanto, or Island of Enchantment.

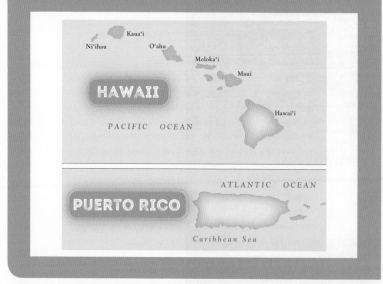

MOUNT BRITTON TRAIL, EL YUNQUE NATIONAL FOREST, PUERTO RICO

WAIPI'O VALLEY OVERLOOK, BIG ISLAND OF HAWAI'I

MAUNA KEA OBSERVATORY COMPLEX, BIG
ISLAND OF HAWAI'I

MUSEO DEL CEMÍ, PUERTO RICO

VIEJO SAN JUAN, PUERTO RICO

# HAWAII

As the most isolated archipelago on the planet, Hawaii is a place of geologic and biological extremes. Active volcanoes and erosion continually redefine a land populated by myriad endemic and native plant species found nowhere else on earth. With more than a quarter of the population identifying as native Hawaiian or part Hawaiian, the islands hold many cultures and attract immigrants from all over the globe who contribute to Hawaii's eclectic cultural heritage, cuisine, and lifestyle.

**AREA:** 10,931 square miles / 28,311 square kilometers (43rd)

**POPULATION:** 1,415,872 (40th)

**STATEHOOD DATE:** August 21, 1959 (50th)

**STATE CAPITAL:** Honolulu

This is a place to escape the world you know. Wander beautiful stretches of white sand. Swim in warm, crystal-clear water. Explore colorful reefs teeming with marine life. Lose yourself in tropical rain forest. Cool off in passing rain showers and enjoy the rainbows that follow them. At the heart of Hawaii's ambiance is aloha, a gift of hospitality from native Hawaiian tradition ingrained with deep reverence for nature, respect for the land, the ocean, family, and friends, that resonates among all who live and travel here.

HALEAKALA NATIONAL PARK, MAUI

## ORIENTATION

There are four main islands in Hawaii. From northwest to southeast, they are Kaua'i, O'ahu, Maui, and the Big Island of Hawai'i. In addition, two smaller islands off the coast of Maui, Moloka'i and Lana'i, can be visited. **O'ahu** is the home of the state capital, Honolulu, as well as many of the state's well-known places: Waikiki, Pearl Harbor, and Diamond Head. **Maui** is the second-largest island, and its main town is Lahaina. Haleakala National Park is also located on Maui. The biggest island is the **Big Island**, with Hawai'i Volcanoes National Park and two main cities, Kona and Hilo. **Kaua'i** is the oldest of the islands and feels more remote: only 90 percent of the island is inhabited.

## WHEN TO GO

Hawaii has a beautiful, comfortable tropical climate all year long. Ocean and air temperatures vary by only a few degrees between seasons. **Winter** and **spring** are known for more rain, but showers and squalls are always possible. Surf-wise, north shores see higher waves October-March, when south shores are flat, better for snorkeling and diving. The opposite is true during the **summer** (May-Sept.). Hawaii does have defined high and low seasons, with an influx of visitors from **Memorial Day to Labor Day,** and from the **late March to the end of April,** thanks to spring break holidays. The busiest time to visit is around **Christmas and New Year.**

# HIGHLIGHTS

### WHALE-WATCHING

Maui

December through April, any vessel that floats is going to be offering whale-watching in the waters off Maui, home to the highest concentration of humpback whales on the planet. Head out for an up-close encounter with these 50-ton creatures. The peak of the season is January-March, when simply being out on the water turns any trip into whale-watching. The choice ultimately comes down to what sort of vessel best suits your comfort level. **Lahaina Harbor** is the departure point for most trips.

- Small rafts from Lahaina Harbor place you the closest to the water; try **Ultimate Snorkel Adventure** (808/667-5678; www.ultimatewhale-watch.com).

- Sailboats also offer whale-watching trips from both Lahaina Harbor and Ka'anapali Beach; **Trilogy** (808/874-5649; www.sailtrilogy.com) is a good option.

- Large 149-passenger diesel boats run by **Pacific Whale Foundation** (612 Front St., Lahaina; 808/942-5311;

HUMPBACK WHALE NEAR LAHAINA HARBOR

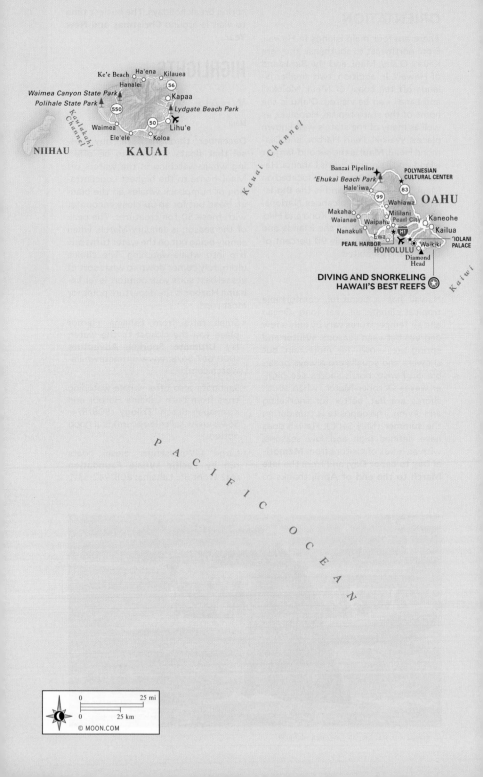

NIIHAU

KAUAI

Ke'e Beach  Ha'ena  Kilauea
Hanalei
Waimea Canyon State Park
Polihale State Park
550
Waimea
Ele'ele  Koloa
Kapaa
Lydgate Beach Park
Lihu'e
56
50

Kaulakahi Channel

Kauai Channel

OAHU

Banzai Pipeline
'Ehukai Beach Park
Hale'iwa
99
Wahiawa
Makaha
Waianae
Waipahu
Nanakuli
Ewa
PEARL HARBOR
Mililani
Pearl City
Kaneohe
Kailua
HONOLULU
Waikiki
Diamond Head
'IOLANI PALACE
POLYNESIAN CULTURAL CENTER
83

Kaiwi

**DIVING AND SNORKELING HAWAII'S BEST REEFS** ✪

PACIFIC OCEAN

0          25 mi
0          25 km
© MOON.COM

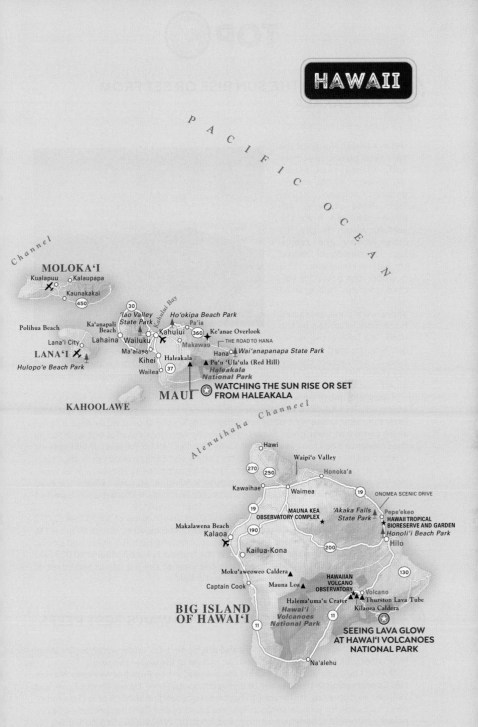

**HAWAII**

PACIFIC OCEAN

Channel

**MOLOKA'I**

Kualapuu   Kalaupapa
        Kaunakakai
        450

Kahului Bay

**'Iao Valley State Park**

Ho'okipa Beach Park
Pa'ia
30
Ka'anapali Beach
Polihua Beach
Lana'i City
**LANA'I**
Hulopo'e Beach Park
Lahaina   Wailuku   Kahului
Ma'alaea
360   Ke'anae Overlook
        THE ROAD TO HANA
Kihei
Wailea
37   Haleakala
Hana   Wai'anapanapa State Park
Makawao

**KAHOOLAWE**

**MAUI**

Pu'u 'Ula'ula (Red Hill)
*Haleakala National Park*

⊛ WATCHING THE SUN RISE OR SET
   FROM HALEAKALA

*Alenuihaha Channeel*

Hawi
Waipi'o Valley
270   250   Honoka'a
Kawaihae   Waimea   19   ONOMEA SCENIC DRIVE
**MAUNA KEA OBSERVATORY COMPLEX**
'Akaka Falls State Park   Pepe'ekeo
        **HAWAII TROPICAL BIORESERVE AND GARDEN**
        *Honoli'i Beach Park*
19
Makalawena Beach
Kalaoa
190
Kailua-Kona   200   Hilo

Moku'aweoweo Caldera
                130
Captain Cook   Mauna Loa
        **HAWAIIAN VOLCANO OBSERVATORY**
        Volcano
        Thurston Lava Tube
**BIG ISLAND OF HAWAI'I**
Halema'uma'u Crater   Kilauea Caldera
*Hawai'i Volcanoes National Park*
11   11

⊛ SEEING LAVA GLOW
   AT HAWAI'I VOLCANOES
   NATIONAL PARK

Na'alehu

# TOP 3

## 1 WATCHING THE SUN RISE OR SET FROM HALEAKALA

Maui; www.nps.gov/hale

"Hale-a-ka-la," House of the Sun. Few places are more aptly named than Maui's 10,023-foot (3,055-meter) dormant volcano, 30,000 feet (9,144 meters) tall when measured from the seafloor. Given its size, it's little wonder the mountain is considered sacred to native Hawaiians. This is where the powerful volcano goddess, Pele, crafted her colorful cinder cones, and a *wahi pana,* or sacred place, only inhabited by the gods. It's where the demigod Maui lassoed the sun to

SUNRISE OVER HALEAKALA VOLCANO CRATER

slow its path across the sky so his people could have time to grow their crops and dry their cloth in the sun. It's also a fragile ecological treasure, with more endangered species than any other national park.

Today, the most popular activity for visitors to Maui is visiting for sunrise, which requires advance reservations. But there's far more to **Haleakala National Park** than simply the light of dawn, although everyone should experience a Haleakala sunrise at least once. Sunset is a display nearly as colorful but without all the crowds or need for a reservation. Over 30 miles (48 kilometers) of hiking trails crisscross the crater, where backcountry cabins and campgrounds provide a classic wilderness experience. The sunsets and stargazing are as spectacular as viewing the crater at sunrise, and even the drive leading up to park—where the road gains 10,000 vertical feet (3,048 meters) in only 38 miles (61 kilometers)—is part of the magical, mystical experience of standing atop Haleakala.

Stop at **Park Headquarters** (808/572-4400) at an elevation of 6,800 feet (2,072 meters), and the **Visitors Center,** at 9,740 feet (2,968 meters), about 10 miles (16 kilometers) up the mountain, for information, camping permits, maps and books, and guided tours. **Pu'u 'Ula'ula** (Red Hill) is the highest point on Maui at 10,023 feet (3,055 meters), with a glass-sided where the view of the Big Island and coast of Maui is even better than at the Visitors Center below.

## 2 DIVING AND SNORKELING HAWAII'S BEST REEFS

Hawaii's reefs teem with marine life and are perfect for underwater exploration. No matter which island you visit, you can marvel at life under the sea.

**O'ahu:** The most abundant marine life is found in the **Pupukea-Waimea Marine Life Conservation District,** home to diving hot spots Three Tables, Sharks Cove, and Waimea Bay, covering 100 acres (40 hectares) of coastline about a mile (1.6 kilometers) long. Look for wrasse, surgeonfish, reef squid, puffer fish, the spotted eagle ray, palani, unicorn fish, harlequin shrimp, and frogfish. Waimea Bay is also known for pods of spinner dolphins that frolic in the middle of the bay. Flourishing reefs have an array of endemic fish, as well as lava tubes, caverns, and walls to explore.

**Maui:** When it comes to snorkeling along Maui's shore, **Honolua Bay** is the gold standard. This wide, scenic cleft in the coast is a biodiverse marine reserve, the valley's lush green foliage and shimmering turquoise waters exuding a supernatural beauty. Tracing the shore, rather than heading to the center of the bay, is best for viewing marine life, including Hawaiian green sea turtles. During winter, dive a few feet underwater to listen for the distant song of humpback whales.

**Kaua'i:** Breathtakingly beautiful **Ke'e Beach** is known for great underwater views inside a large natural swimming pool. Outside in the open ocean the views get even better. Advanced snorkelers find that heading a bit to the left and snorkeling along the reef offers the best views.

GREEN SEA TURTLE NEAR MAUI

## ③ SEEING LAVA GLOW AT HAWAI'I VOLCANOES NATIONAL PARK

Big Island of Hawai'i; www.nps.gov/havo

The indomitable power of Hawai'i Volcanoes National Park is apparent to all who come here. Wherever you stop to gaze, realize that you are standing on a thin skin of cooled lava in an unstable earthquake zone atop one of the world's most active volcanoes.

The park's heart is **Kilauea Caldera,** almost 3 miles (4.8 kilometers) across, 400 feet (121 meters) deep, and encircled by 11 miles (17 kilometers) of **Crater Rim Drive.** You'll pass steam vents, sulphur springs, and tortured fault lines that always seem

KILAUEA CALDERA

on the verge of gaping wide and swallowing the landscape. On the way, peer into the mouth of **Halema'uma'u Crater,** home of the fire goddess, Pele. You'll also pass **Hawaiian Volcano Observatory** (http://hvo.wr.usgs.gov), which has been monitoring geologic activity since the turn of the 20th century, and the adjacent **Thomas A. Jaggar Museum** (808/985-6049), an excellent facility where you can educate yourself on the past and present volcanology of the park. The **Devastation Trail** is a paved path across a desolate cinder field where gray, lifeless trunks of a suffocated forest lean like old gravestones. Within minutes is **Thurston Lava Tube,** a magnificent natural tunnel overflowing with vibrant fern grottoes at the entrance and exit. Sweating in the hot lava fields, you'll see snowcapped, difficult to access, 13,680-foot (4,169-meter) **Mauna Loa** in the distance; its mighty **Moku'aweoweo Caldera** is more than 3 miles (4.8 kilometers) long, 1.5 miles (2.4 kilometers) wide, and 600 feet (182 meters) deep.

The park covers 333,000 acres (134,760 hectares), a UNESCO International Biosphere Reserve and World Heritage Site. With a multitude of ways to access the park—on foot, by car, by bike, and by helicopter—Hawai'i Volcanoes National Park truly does offer something for everyone. Start at the park's **Kilauea Visitor Center** (808/985-6000; www.nps.gov/havo/planyourvisit/kvc.htm) to plan your visit.

# *Best* HAWAII TRIP

A week only gets you so far in the Hawaiian islands; this itinerary focuses on O'ahu, the Big Island of Hawai'i, and Maui.

**DAY 1** After arriving on **O'ahu,** tour **'Iolani Palace,** followed by a taste of authentic Chinese food at **Little Village Noodle House.** Then head to Waikiki and the bustling hub of **Kuhio Beach Park** for some beach time.

**DAY 2** Start the day with a climb up to **Diamond Head State Monument.** Then venture further out to snorkel in the **Pupukea-Waimea Marine Life Conservation District.** Afterward, attend the Ali'i Lu'au at the **Polynesian Cultural Center.**

KUHIO BEACH PARK, O'AHU

**DAY 3** Today, you're **Big Island** bound. Base yourself in **Hilo,** the start of a scenic drive on **Highway 19,** passing **Honoli'i Beach** (a great surf spot), the **Hawaii Tropical Botanical Garden,** and **'Akaka Falls State Park,** ending in the beautiful **Waipi'o Valley.** For sustenance, grab fresh malasadas (Portuguese pastries) from **Tex Drive In,** or loco moco from **Hawaiian Style Café.**

**DAY 4** Spend today in **Volcanoes National Park,** driving **Crater Rim Drive** around the **Kilauea Caldera,** stopping at the **Halema'uma'u Crater** and the **Thurston Lava Tube.**

'AKAKA FALLS, BIG ISLAND

**DAY 5** You'll be in **Maui** for the last leg of your trip. Keep it leisurely and relax on famous **Ka'anapali Beach.** For dinner, grab Vietnamese at **A Saigon Café.**

**DAY 6** Start your last full day in Hawaii by watching the sunrise from **Haleakala.** Afterwards, grab a filling lunch plate at **Sam Sato's** (you earned it) and post up at **Keawakapu Beach** until the sun goes down.

KEAWAKAPU BEACH, MAUI

# *Major* CITIES

**HONOLULU:** The economic and political center of the state, the capital of Hawai'i, which is on O'ahu, is known for its historic district and Chinatown, and historic sites such as 'Iolani Palace and Pearl Harbor.

**PEARL CITY:** This O'ahu community borders Pearl Harbor, a placid, deepwater harbor that still evokes a military presence and sense of reverence for the people who lost their lives during the attack on December 7, 1941.

**HILO:** Hilo, the only major city on the Big Island's east coast, feels like old Hawaii, boasting Honoli'i Beach (the best place to watch surfing) and the mesmerizing 'Akaka Falls State Park.

www.pacificwhale.org) provide the most affordable rates, but you'll won't get the same 360-degree views.

## PEARL HARBOR

O'ahu

The USS *Arizona* Memorial, USS *Bowfin* Submarine Museum and Park, USS *Oklahoma* Memorial, and the Battleship *Missouri* Memorial comprise the Pearl Harbor Historic Sites. Over 1.7 million people visit the USS *Arizona* Memorial and the historic sites each year, making this one of the most heavily toured areas in the state. The four sites together tell the story of Hawaii's and U.S. involvement in World War II, from the surprise attack on Pearl Harbor to the surrender of the Japanese. Pearl Harbor also serves as the central point of the **World War II Valor in the Pacific National Monument.** Entering the 17-acre (6.8-hectare) park, where you'll first see the **visitors center** (808/454-1434; www.pearlharborhistoricsites.org), where you can get a ticket for a tour time.

## 'IOLANI PALACE

364 S. King St., Honolulu, O'ahu; 808/522-0822; www.iolanipalace.org

Set on a grassy 11 acres (4.5 hectares), shaded by canopy trees in the heart of the Capitol District, 'Iolani Palace is the second royal palace to grace the grounds. The building, with its glass and ironwork imported from San Francisco and its Corinthian columns, is the only true royal palace in America. Begun in late 1879 under orders of King Kalakaua,

it was completed in December 1882 at a cost of $350,000. It was the first electrified building in Honolulu, having electricity and telephones even before the White House in Washington DC. The palace served as the official residence of the monarch of Hawai'i until the overthrow of the Hawaiian kingdom in 1893. It then became the main executive building for the provisional government, with the House of Representatives meeting in the throne room and the Senate in the dining room, until 1968. It has since been elevated to a state monument and National Historic Landmark.

## MAUNA KEA OBSERVATORY COMPLEX

Big Island of Hawai'i

As you climb the Big Island's Mauna Kea (White Mountain), the tallest peak in

'IOLANI PALACE

# HAWAII'S MOST SPECTACULAR BEACHES

## O'AHU

- **To mix and mingle: Kuhio Beach Park** is the thumping heart of **Wakiki**'s legendary 2.5-mile (4-kilometer) strip of coastline, with a ton of amenities, iconic statues of Duke Kahanamoku and Prince Kuio, and great surf waves like Canoes to boot.

- **To watch expert surfers:** Banzai Pipeline, off **'Ehukai Beach Park** is one of the most dangerous waves in the world; breaking just 75 yards (68 meters) off the beach, it's a surfer's delight.

- **To relax:** With sandy beaches, grassy parks, a fair bit of shade from palms and trees, and a meandering pathway, the **Ko Olina Lagoons** provide a sheltered, resort-style beach experience.

## MAUI

- **To see and be seen:** Few stretches of Maui shore are more famous than **Ka'anapali Beach,** a long, uninterrupted expanse of sand lined from end to end with world-class resorts and island beach activities.

- **To windsurf and kitesurf:** In the afternoon, the cobalt waves of **Kanaha Beach Park** become flecked with whitecaps and dozens of colorful sails as windsurfers and kitesurfers race across the water.

- **To watch the sunset:** In morning, before the wind picks up, **Keawakapu Beach** is a bustle of snorkelers entering the water and kids splashing in the surf, and by late afternoon, it changes into the perfect perch for the sunset.

## LANA'I

- **To hang with locals:** If you want to make your friends back home jealous, snap a picture of **Hulopo'e Beach Park,** the undisputed favorite hangout for islanders.

the Pacific, you pass through the clouds to a barren world devoid of vegetation. The earth is a red, rolling series of volcanic cones. You get an incredible vista of Mauna Loa peeking through the clouds and what seems like the entire island lying at your feet. In the distance the lights of Maui flicker.

Atop the mountain is a mushroom grove of astronomical observatories, like a futuristic earth colony on a remote planet. Crystal-clear air and lack of dust and light pollution make the observatory complex the best in the world. At close to 14,000 feet (4,267 meters), it is above 40 percent of the earth's atmosphere and 98 percent of its water vapor. Temperatures hover around 40-50ºF (10ºC) during the day,

with only 9-11 inches (22-28 centimeters) of precipitation annually, mostly in the form of snow. Scientists from around the world book months in advance for a squint through one of these phenomenal telescopes, and institutions from several countries maintain permanent outposts there.

At present, only the **Subaru Telescope** (www.naoj.org) allows visitors on organized tours, and you must reserve at least one week ahead of time through the National Astronomical Observatory of Japan website. While the **Keck telescopes** do not offer tours, the visitors gallery at the telescope base is open on weekdays.

- **To escape the crowds: Polihua Beach** is so remote that even Lana'i residents consider it "out there." A vast, windswept, and often completely empty stretch of sand, utterly unrivaled in its seclusion.

## BIG ISLAND

- **To hike to the beach: Makalawena Beach** is an authentic Big Island experience, because it requires a little bit of hiking to get there. If you make the 30-minute trek to the beach, you'll be rewarded with isolated white sand and turquoise water.

- **To surf:** While black-sand beach **Honoli'i Beach Park** is not great for swimming, it is a great surfing spot. If you're not a seasoned surfer, no worries: there is a "kiddie" area, and lifeguards if any issues should arise.

MAKALAWENA BEACH, BIG ISLAND

## KAUA'I

- **To bring kids:** At **Lydgate Beach Park,** the pools are protected by lava rock barriers that create perfect places to swim and snorkel, safe for young children and anyone else who prefers to relax in the water worry-free.

- **For dramatic scenery:** Imagine sitting on a long white-sand beach, a distant island in view, clear blue sky overhead, looming cliffs behind you, and waves rolling in as your soundtrack. This is **Polihale State Park.**

# BEST SCENIC DRIVES

## THE ROAD TO HANA

Maui

The Road to Hana is the most loved and loathed section of Maui. Most people who don't enjoy the trip didn't know what they were getting themselves into. Three words will make or break your trip: Don't rush Hana.

Devote a full day to the experience at a minimum. You're visiting one of the most beautiful places on earth; two or three days are even better. Here are some mile-by-mile highlights along the road:

- **Hana Highway Mile Marker 7:** Starting in the town of Pa'ia, where you can go for a stroll on long, wide Baldwin Beach.

- **Hana Highway Mile Marker 13.5:** Turnoff for Pe'ahi, also called Jaws, quite possibly the world's most famous surf break.

- **Highway 360 Mile Marker 6.5:** Na'ili'ili Haele (Bamboo Forest) is one of the most popular hikes in East Maui.

- **Highway 360 Mile Marker 17:** The Ke'anae Overlook provides a vista of the peninsula's mosaic of green taro fields.

- **Highway 360 Mile Marker 32:** Turnoff for Wai'anapanapa State Park, also known as "black-sand beach."

- **Highway 330 Mile Marker 42:** Here you'll find a bridge overlooking the stunning Pools of 'Ohe'o.

## ONOMEA SCENIC DRIVE
Hwy. 19, Big Island of Hawai'i

Highway 19 heading from **Hilo** to **Honoka'a** on the Big Island of Hawai'i has magnificent inland and coastal views, one after another. Only 5 minutes from Hilo, just past mile marker 7, a road posted as the scenic drive dips down toward the coast. Take it. Almost immediately, signs warn you to slow your speed because of the narrow winding road and one-lane bridges; start down this meandering lane past some modest homes and into the jungle that covers the road like a living green tunnel. Stop, and you can almost hear the jungle growing. Along this 4-mile (6-kilometer) route are sections of an ancient coastal trail and the site of a former fishing village. This road runs past the **Hawaii Tropical Bioreserve and Garden** (27-717 Old Mamalahoa Hwy.; 808/964-5233; https://htbg.com), attracting lovers of plants, flowers, and photography, before heading up to higher ground to rejoin Highway 19 at **Pepe'ekeo.**

Continuing further on Highway 19, you'll pass Highway 220, which leads to the entrance to **'Akaka Falls State Park,** everybody's idea of a pristine Hawaiian valley, as well as the abandoned plantation remnants in **Hakalau Bay.** At Honoka'a, Highway 19 branches off into Highway 240, where you'll find the **Waipi'o Valley.** Waipi'o, which means curved or arched waters, is known to Hawaiians as the Sacred Valley of the Kings. Locals know it as one of the best views on all of the Big Island—the valley

is postcard perfect, with a river running through deep green hills and waterfalls (the two most recognizable ones are **Hi'ilawe** and **Hakalaoa**).

# BEST PARKS AND RECREATION AREAS

## KAPI'OLANI PARK AND DIAMOND HEAD STATE MONUMENT
O'ahu

Kapi'olani Park (intersection of Kapahulu and Kalakaua Avenues; www.kapiolanipark.net) is the oldest public park in Hawai'i, established in 1877 by King David Kalakaua, monarch of Hawai'i. What was once marshland and lagoons is now a 300-acre (121-hectare) expanse of grass, sports fields, and canopy trees. The park attracts all types of sports, from rugby and cricket to soccer and softball and has four lit tennis courts. It's a hub for picnics, birthdays, large family gatherings, and barbecues. The park also draws runners and walkers, who circle it on the 3-mile (4.8-kilometer) running path, and is the best spot for bird-watching on the South Shore.

Just east of Kapi'olani Park is Diamond Head State Monument (www.hawaiistateparks.org). **Diamond Head Lookout,** with views of the waves crashing on shallow reefs to the west and the surfers at Diamond Head's popular surf spots, is accessible by car, trolley, or tour bus. The historic **Diamond Head Summit Trail,** built in 1908, climbs 560 feet (170 meters) from the crater floor to the summit in just 0.8 miles (1.25 kilometers), up the inner southwestern rim of the crater on a combination of concrete walkway, switchbacks, stairs, uneven natural terrain, and lighted tunnels. On the ocean side of Diamond Head Road, the **Diamond Head Lighthouse** (3399 Diamond Head Rd.), constructed in 1899, then rebuilt in 1917, makes for a great Kodak moment.

HAWAII TROPICAL BIORESERVE AND GARDEN

or ocean swells. When done properly, it feels like you're surfing on a wave that virtually has no end.

Paddlers begin at Maliko Gulch to the east of Hoʻokipa Beach Park on Maui, and paddle downwind to either Kahului Harbor or the beach at Kanaha Beach Park. Maliko Runs are a favorite weekend activity of the island's water sports enthusiasts, and over 200 racers gather each year for the professional races, with one of the largest being the **OluKai** race at the end of April. A Maliko Run isn't an activity for anyone who isn't an avid stand-up paddler, but for stand-up paddling enthusiasts, this is the Holy Grail.

'IAO VALLEY, MAUI

## 'IAO VALLEY STATE PARK

### Maui

The journey to 'Iao Valley State Park on Maui begins the moment you leave the streets of nearby Wailuku and make the turn down 'Iao Valley Road through a thick canopy of trees. You'll find chickens crossing the road, rural houses, fields, and farms at the base of vertical cliffs. Before you hike to see the famous 'Iao Needle, take a moment to read the history of the park, where Maui's tribal army lost to King Kamehameha I and his forces in the 1790 Battle of Kepaniwai, allowing for the unification of the Hawaiian archipelago. A 133-step walkway leads you to Kukaʻemoku—better known as **'Iao Needle**—rising 2,250 feet (685 meters). Rugged ridgelines line the valley, sacred and untouched because it's believed the bones of Hawaiian royalty are buried deep inside the caves.

## THE MALIKO RUN

### Maui

In the sport of downwind stand-up paddling, there's no stretch of water more legendary than the 9-mile-long (14.4-kilometer) Maliko Run. It's where downwind racing was born, and the place where the world's best paddle surfers train for the professional tour. In a "downwinder," paddlers position the wind at their backs and glide on the open ocean, connecting "bumps,"

## WAIMEA CANYON STATE PARK

### Kauaʻi

Waimea Canyon State Park on Kauaʻi is home to vast, breathtaking canyons and decorated with numerous trails weaving through the forest from ridgeline to the canyon floor, from serious hikes to short walks. The canyon's colors change throughout the day with the sun, so if you gaze into the 10-mile-long (16-kilometer), 3,000-foot-deep (914-meter) canyon for any length of time, different photo opportunities usually present themselves. Once you've gazed at the views on the drive up to **Waimea Canyon State Park Overlook** (make sure to take Waimea

WAIMEA CANYON STATE PARK OVERLOOK

POLYNESIAN CULTURAL CENTER

Canyon Drive rather than Koke'e Road), take a hike to immerse yourself in the natural splendor of the canyon. One of the park's best is the 10-minute **Cliff Trail** to the semi-strenuous 1.8-mile (2.9-kilometer) **Canyon Trail.** This leads to the upper section of the 800-foot (243-meter) **Waipo'o Falls** before going up and along the canyon's eastern edge, down into a gulch, and weaving along the cliff to the Koke'e Stream and the falls. The reward of swimming in freshwater pools makes it a choice hike. It all takes about 3 hours.

# FESTIVALS AND EVENTS

## ALI'I LU'AU AT THE POLYNESIAN CULTURAL CENTER

55-370 Kamehameha Hwy., La'ie, O'ahu; 800/367-7060; www.polynesia.com; lu'au year-round

On the northern end of O'ahu, the Polynesian Cultural Center introduces visitors to the people and cultures of Hawai'i, Samoa, Maori New Zealand, Fiji, Tahiti, Marquesas, and Tonga as you walk through and visit the different villages and interact with the people demonstrating their specific arts and crafts. There is a canoe ride that explores the villages as well. Dining is paramount to the experience; choose the famous Ali'i Lu'au, with authentic Hawaiian food, including traditional imu pork, a large pig cooked in an earthen oven. An evening show called "Ha: Breath of Life" is a culmination of story, dance, Polynesian music, and fire.

# BEST FOOD

One of the pleasures of traveling around Hawaii is the proliferation of **fruit stands** and **farmers markets** selling the bounty grown on the islands—including pineapples, coconuts, bananas, papayas, and many more—and things made from them, from smoothies to fresh-made banana bread.

## INTERNATIONAL CUISINE

Immigrants from around the world brought their cuisine to the islands, and many of the dishes remain local favorites to this day.

- **Chinese: Little Village Noodle House** (1113 Smith St.; 808/545-3008; http://littlevillagehawaii.com), in Honolulu's Chinatown, is the quintessential place to pick from over 100 menu items, covering meat, seafood, rice, and noodle dishes.

- **Vietnamese:** At one of Maui's most popular Vietnamese venues, **A Saigon Café** (1792 Main St., Wailuku; 808/243-9560), opt for clay pot dishes with rice, chicken, and vegetables, or try the pho, banh hoi, or tasty Vietnamese soup.

- **Portuguese: Tex Drive In** (Hwy. 19 at the corner of Pakalana St., Honoka'a; 808/775-0598) is a Big Island insti-

# BEST SOUVENIRS

## ART

With Hawaii's unbeatable scenery, it's no wonder artists have settled here, making this a great place to find one-of-a-kind pieces. Some towns with a high concentration of artists include **Volcano Village** on the Big Island and historic **Makawao** on Maui.

## COFFEE AND MACADAMIA NUTS

At the **Hamakua Macadamia Nut Factory** (Maluokalani St., off Hwy. 270 between mile markers 4 and 5; 808/882-1690; www.hawnnut.com) on the Big Island, imagine a room full of macadamia nuts and coffee of every variety imaginable that can be sampled and purchased to take home.

tution, known for fresh malasadas: sugared Portuguese pastries filled with passion fruit cream, chocolate, or strawberry.

- **Japanese: Goma Tei** (4211 Waialae Ave., G07, Honolulu; 808/732-9188; www.gomatei.com) has some of the best ramen on O'ahu, with flavorful broths, fresh vegetables, soft noodles, rich cuts of meat, and crispy gyoza.

## LOCAL HAWAIIAN

While local Hawaiian food is rooted in Polynesian techniques and flavors, it is also an amalgam of the cuisine from the immigrants who became an integral part of Hawaiian culture.

### Plate Lunches

Plate lunches, found mainly at drive-in restaurants (island-style fast food), are served with two scoops of rice, macaroni salad, and a protein, including chicken katsu, kalbi, or kalua pork. This affordable and filling meal incorporates Japanese, Korean, American, and Hawaiian cooking. Try it at **Sam Sato's** (1750 Wili Pa Loop, Wailuku; 808/244-7124) on Maui or at **Lana'i City Grille** (828 Lana'i Ave.; 808/565-7211; www.hotellanai.com) on Lana'i.

Loco moco is another favorite plate for lunch as well as breakfast: two fried eggs, a hamburger patty over rice smothered in gravy—talk about East meets West. Try it at **Kualapu'u Cookhouse** (102 Farrington Ave., Kualapuu; 808/567-9655) on Moloka'i or at **Hawaiian**

**Style Café** (65-1290 Kawaihae Rd./Hwy. 19 between mile markers 57 and 58, Waimea; 808/885-4295) on the Big Island.

### Lu'au

The food served at lu'au is very similar to what you'll find at a Hawaiian food restaurant, and there are several staple dishes no matter where you go. Among others, there's **kalua pig,** a smoky-flavored pulled pork tossed with cabbage, traditionally cooked in an imu (an underground earthen oven); **lau lau**—fish, pork, or chicken wrapped in taro leaves and steamed in ti leaves; and **poke,** a raw fish salad made with ahi tuna, soy sauce (called shoyu in Hawaii), and sesame oil. No Hawaiian lu'au is complete

HAWAIIAN PLATE LUNCH

without **poi,** a staple starch made from pounded taro root, or **haupia,** a coconut milk-based dessert usually served as a congealed pudding.

# MAJOR AIRPORTS

- **Honolulu International Airport:** HNL; 300 Rodgers Blvd., Oʻahu; 808/836-6411; http://hawaii.gov/hnl
- **Kona International Airport:** KOA; 73-200 Kupipi St., Hawaiʻi; 808/327-9520; http://hawaii.gov/koa
- **Kahului Airport:** OGG; 1 Kahului Airport Rd., Maui; 808/872-3830; http://hawaii.gov/ogg
- **Molokaʻi Airport:** MKK; 3980 Airport Loop, Hoʻolehua; 808/567-9660; http://hawaii.gov/mkk
- **Lanaʻi Airport:** LNY; Lanaʻi; 808/565-7942, hawaii.gov/lny
- **Lihue Airport:** LIH; 3901 Mokulele Loop, Lihue, Kauaʻi; 808/274-3800; http://hawaii.gov/lih

# MORE INFORMATION

## TRAVEL AND TOURISM INFORMATION

- **Hawaii Visitors and Convention Bureau:** www.gohawaii.com
- **Hawaii State Parks:** https://dlnr.hawaii.gov/dsp

## NEWSPAPERS AND MAGAZINES

- *Midweek Oahu:* www.midweek.com
- *Honolulu Star-Advertiser:* www.staradvertiser.com
- *Hawaii Free Press:* www.hawaiifreepress.com
- *Hawaiʻi Magazine:* www.hawaiimagazine.com

# PUERTO RICO

Puerto Rico's nickname is Isla del Encanto, or Island of Enchantment, and for good reason. Sandy beaches, palm trees, and tropical breezes make it a favorite getaway for the sun and surf crowd, and rugged mountains and a verdant rain forest attract adventure travelers. But Puerto Rico is more than a picture postcard. Centuries of Indigenous, African, and Spanish influences can still be experienced as part of Puerto Rico's vibrant cultural life today. San Juan is a hip, bustling metropolis, but a simple stroll through the cobblestone streets of Viejo San Juan steeps visitors in a concentrated dose of the island's history and cultural life.

Life is vivid in Puerto Rico, where beauty abounds in the many protected coves, lagoons, caves, and three bioluminescent bays. Indigenous Taíno culture, ancient ruins, and petroglyphs, can be found throughout the lush central mountain region. The sun shines brightly, rainbow-hued buildings pop with color, and tropical music fills the air. Prepare to be enchanted.

AREA: 3,515 square miles / 9,103 square kilometers

POPULATION: 3,142,799

BECAME A U.S. TERRITORY: October 18, 1898

CAPITAL: San Juan

▲ BEACH NEAR GUÁNICA

# PUERTO RICO

ATLANTIC OCEAN

AEROPUERTO INTERNACIONAL
RAFAEL HERNÁNDEZ ✈

Isabela
San Antonio
Camuy   Hatillo
Arecibo
Vega Baja
Balneario
Cerro Gordo
Dorado

Quebradillas
Manatí
22

Bahía de Aguadilla
Aguadilla
119
Ciales
Corozal

Aguada
Domes
111
San Sebastián
10
Naranjito

Rincón
109
111
Utuado
Orocovis
San
Cristóbal
Cañón

Bahía de Añasco
Jayuya
LA PIEDRA ESCRITA
CAFÉ HACIENDA
SAN PEDRO TIENDA Y MUSEO

Mayagüez
105
Maricao
LA RUTA PANORÁMICA   MUSEO DEL CEMÍ
Adjuntas
HACIENDA
POMARROSA
MIRADOR
OROCOVIS-VILLALBA

Joyuda
Bosque Estatal
de Maricao
CORDILLERA   CENTRAL
143
Bosque Estatal
de Toro Negro
MIRADOR
PIEDRA DEGETAU

Cabo Rojo
2
10
Coamo

Boquerón
San
Germán
Yauco
Guayanilla
Juana Díaz
52

El Combate
La Parguera
116
Guánica
Ponce
Salinas

FUERTE CAPRÓN ★
Bosque Estatal
de Guánica
Santa Isabel

Cabo Rojo
Bahía Fosforescente
Punta Brea
Caja de
Muertos
Bahía de Rincón

Caribbean Sea

**STROLLING VIEJO SAN JUAN**

CASA MELAZA
CASA BACARDÍ
Cataño

Viejo San Juan
SAN JUAN
Bosque Estatal de Piñones

Bayamón

52

Carolina

Loíza

Canóvanas

**PORTALITO HUB**

**KIOSKOS**
Playa Luquillo
Luquillo

3

Coca Falls
El Yunque
El Yunque Nat'l Forest

**DIVING DEEP INTO EL YUNQUE NATIONAL FOREST**

**YOKAHU TOWER**
**BAÑO GRANDE**

SIERRA DE LUQUILLO

Caguas

30

San Lorenzo

52

EL MOJITO

BARRIO GUAVATE

LA RUTA DEL LECHÓN

182
Charco Azul

Cayey

Reserva Forestal de Carite

Cidra

Fajardo

Ceiba

53

Naguabo
Punta Puerca

Punta Lima
Punta Santiago

Humacao

53

SIERRA DE CAYEY

Yabucoa

Patillas

Maunabo

Guayama

3

Jobos

Pasaje de San Juan

Cayo Icacos

Pta. de Molinos

Playa Flamenco

**SOAKING UP THE SUN AND SURF**

Playa Carlos Rosario

Dewey

**CULEBRA**

Sonda de Vieques

Isabel Segunda

Punta Este

**VIEQUES**

Esperanza

Mosquito Bay

Pasaje de Vieques

0                    5 mi

0              5 km

© MOON.COM

# TOP 3

## 1 STROLLING VIEJO SAN JUAN

Viejo San Juan is the heart and historic center of Puerto Rico. The 500-year-old walled city is a 45-block grid of blue cobblestone streets lined with pastel-colored 16th-, 17th-, and 18th-century buildings trimmed with ornamental ironwork, flanked by two Spanish fortresses and surrounded by a 400-year-old wall. Art and history museums, plazas, shops, and ship docks: Many of the island's must-see sites are located here. At night it throbs with locals and tourists alike at some of the city's finest restaurants and bars. The best way to see Viejo San Juan is on foot. A few of the top sights to look out for:

CASTILLO DE SAN FELIPE DEL MORRO

- **Castillo San Felipe del Morro** (501 Calle Norzagaray; 787/729-6777; www.nps.gov/saju) is a daunting display of military defense featuring four levels of cannon-bearing batteries that rise 140 feet (42 meters) from the sea. Inside is a maze of rooms, connected by tunnels, ramps, and a spiral stairway.

- **Castillo de San Cristóbal** (Calle Norzagaray at the entrance to Viejo San Juan; 787/729-6777; www.nps.gov/saju) is the large fortress, built by the Spanish, at the entrance to Viejo San Juan by Plaza de Colón. Today, a section of the fort is open to the public to explore.

- **Catedral de San Juan Bautista** (151-153 Calle del Cristo; 787/722-0861; http://catedralsanjuanbautista.org) is the second-oldest church in the western hemisphere, first built of wood and straw in 1521 and destroyed by hurricanes and rebuilt multiple times.

- **Museo de las Americas** (Cuartel de Ballajá, 2nd Fl., on Calle Norzagaray beside Plaza del Quinto Centenario; 787/724-5052; www.museolasamericas.org) contains a fantastic collection of Latin American folk art.

## 2 DIVING DEEP INTO EL YUNQUE NATIONAL FOREST

787/888-1880; www.fs.usda.gov/elyunque

El Yunque National Forest is the crown jewel of Puerto Rico's natural treasures, the only tropical forest in the U.S. National Forest System, and home to some of the only virgin forest remaining on the island. It's also home to hundreds of native plant and animal species. The name El Yunque, also the name of the forest's second-highest peak (3,469 feet/1,057 meters), is believed to be a Spanish derivation of the Taíno Indian name for the area, Yuke ("white earth"), referring to the clouds that often encase the mountaintops. The Taíno believed that El Yunque to be sacred, home to their gods, and visited the forest to harvest trees, vines, and palm fronds to make canoes, baskets, and roofing thatch, and to gather its abundant fruits, roots, and medicinal plants. Petroglyphs can be found carved into rocks and boulders throughout the forest, signs of the religious ceremonies and rituals that were often held here.

It's possible to take a drive-by tour of El Yunque in about an hour, but spending the day immersed in this natural wonderland is recommended. Start at **Portalito Hub** (54 Calle Principal, Palmer, Río Grande; 787/809-0534), the National Forest Service visitors center, to pick up a map, then drive south on PR 191, the main road through the forest, to view dramatic **Coca Falls;** climb **Yokahu Tower,** a 69-foot (27-meter) observation tower with a 360-degree view of the island; and see **Baño Grande,** a picturesque stone pool with an arched bridge constructed in the 1930s. In the afternoon, try the strenuous 45-minute hike on **Mount Britton Trail,** and if you have time, continue another hour to the summit of **El Yunque** (allow 4-5 hours round-trip).

THE SUMMIT OF EL YUNQUE

## ③ SOAKING UP THE SUN AND SURF

No two beaches are alike in Puerto Rico. **Balnearios** are large, government-maintained beaches with bathroom and shower facilities, picnic tables, and snack bars. Some have lounge-chair rentals, lifeguards, and campsites. There are also many **wilderness beaches,** which are typically remote and devoid of development and facilities. Some beaches have big waves best suited to **surfing,** and others are as calm as bathwater and ideal for **swimming.** Some, especially along the north coast, are rife with strong currents, beautiful to look at, but not safe for swimming. One thing all the beaches have in common is their accessibility to the public. There is no such thing as a private beach in Puerto Rico. Below is a list of some favorites.

- **Playa Luquillo** is considered one of the island's most beautiful beaches. It features a wide flat crescent of sand, a shady palm grove, calm shallow waters, and a couple of food vendors selling fritters and piña coladas.

- Culebra is the lucky site of **Playa Flamenco,** named one of America's best beaches by the Travel Channel, a wide, mile-long (1.6-kilometer), horseshoe-shaped beach with fine white sand and calm, aquamarine water. An abandoned graffiti-covered tank is a reminder of U.S. Navy presence.

PLAYA FLAMENCO

- **Balneario Cerro Gordo** in Vega Alta on the north coast is a large protected cove with calm waters and a pristine sandy beach surrounded by hills covered in lush vegetation. It boasts one of the best campgrounds of any of the balnearios and great surfing too.

- **Rincón** is the surfing capital of Puerto Rico, thanks to literally dozens of popular surf sites. By far the favorite is **Domes,** located in front of the green domes of an abandoned nuclear power plant, an easy-to-access spot featuring long hollow waves.

- For easy access to a site rich in marine life, visit **Playa Carlos Rosario,** a narrow beach flanked by boulders and a protruding coral reef in Culebra. The underwater visibility is usually quite good here, so you can see all kinds of colorful fish and coral formations.

# *Best* ROAD TRIP

At approximately 100 miles long by 35 miles wide (160x56 kilometers), Puerto Rico is small enough that many of the destinations on this road trip could be done as day trips, if you prefer to base yourself in a city like San Juan or Ponce.

**DAY 1** There's no better way to begin your trip to Puerto Rico than by exploring **Viejo San Juan,** wandering cobblestone streets, looking up at pastel-painted buildings from as far back as the 16th century, and taking in the view from the **Castillo de San Felipe del Morro.** In the evening, dine on Puerto Rican fare at **Punto de Vista,** then join the festivities on party street **Calle San Sebastián.**

VIEJO SAN JUAN

**DAY 2** Start your second day in **Bosque Estatal de Piñones,** which offers undeveloped, lovely beaches just east of San Juan, before continuing east to **Luquillo** to lounge on the lovely beach and eat Puerto Rican Street food at the **kioskos.**

**DAY 3** Plunge into **El Yunque National Forest** today, driving past captivating pools and waterfalls, taking in views from **Yohaku Tower,** and maybe even hiking **El Yunque,** the island's second-highest mountain. After dark, take a kayaking tour on glittering green **Laguna Grande,** 25 miles (40 kilometers) away.

PLAYA LUQUILLO

**DAY 4** You'll take in parts of **La Ruta Panorámica** and **La Ruta del Lechón** today, starting in **Yabucoa,** passing **Charco Azul** (a great place to take a dip), and numerous **lechoneras** to try the beloved Puerto Rican roast pork. You'll pass scenic overlooks en route to **Ponce** on the island's southern coast; enjoy the early evening bustle of **Plaza las Delicias** and search for authentic Puerto Rican food at **La Casa del Chef.**

PLAZA LAS DELICIAS, PONCE

**DAY 5** Spend today in the island's mountainous **Cordillera Central,** learning about Puerto Rico's Indigenous Taínos at **Museo del Cemí** and **La Piedra Escrita,** and the legacy of its coffee plantations at **Café Hacienda San Pedro Tienda y Museo.**

**DAY 6** Return to San Juan on your final day, stopping at lovely **Balneario Cerro Gordo** on the way to lounge on the sand and maybe enjoy some surfing. Back in the capital, try a **rum tasting** or Viejo San Juan's **Museo de las Americas,** before dinner at **La Casita Blanca** and dancing your last night away in nightlife district **La Placita.**

LA PIEDRA ESCRITA

MUSEO DE LAS AMERICAS

## ORIENTATION

Puerto Rico's capital and largest city, **San Juan,** is situated on the northeast coast. The east coast of Puerto Rico contains some of its most popular tourist sights, such as **El Yunque National Forest** and **Playa Luquillo.** Off the east coast are another two small islands, **Vieques** and **Culebra.** The island's second-largest city, **Ponce,** is located on the south coast. Within the west coast region are fun-loving surf towns and the colonial city of **Mayagüez.** The north coast is more off the beaten path, with rocky beaches and seaside cliffs. The **Cordillera Central** mountain range runs through the interior of the island, with **Jayuya** holding many Taíno cultural sites.

## WHEN TO GO

The climate in Puerto Rico is classified as tropical marine, which means it is **sunny, hot, and humid year-round.** The average year-round temperature ranges from 80°F (26°C) on the coast to 68°F (20°C) in the mountains. There are two seasons: **Dry season** (Jan.-Apr.), when humidity is lowest and airline tickets and hotel room rates tend to be higher, and **rainy season** (May-Nov.), also hurricane season, when an average of 4-6 inches (10-15 centimeters) of rain falls each month.

# HIGHLIGHTS

## BIOLUMINESCENT BAYS

Puerto Rico is home to three of the world's five bioluminescent bays, created by the single-celled microorganisms called dinoflagellates, which live in the water and light up when disturbed. Though bioluminescent dinoflagellates exist throughout the ocean, it's rare for them to be concentrated enough to create the biological lightshow you'll see in Puerto Rico's bioluminescent bays. By day, you'll see what looks like any other body of still water; the only way to see bioluminescence is by taking a boat ride or paddling a kayak into the lagoon at night. For the best visibility, go when there's a new moon.

▪ If you see only one bio-bay, make it

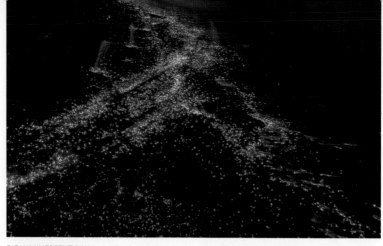

BIOLUMINESCENT BAY

Mosquito Bay in Vieques. When it's at its best, the water here glows an electric blue.

- Laguna Grande in Fajardo traverses a mangrove canal, and the only way to access it is by kayak tours. When conditions are optimum, the water glows a glittery green.

## PONCE

Elegant, cultured Ponce was an economic and cultural rival to San Juan back in the day, experiencing great growth and wealth during the 18th and 19th centuries, thanks to its international shipping trade, lucrative rum distilleries, and plantations growing coffee and sugarcane. All that wealth translated into hundreds of gorgeous, ornate homes and buildings that combine rococo, neoclassical, and Spanish Revival architecture with traditional *criolla* (creole) building styles, with broad balconies, large doorways, and open-air patios.

At the city's core is **Plaza las Delicias** (bounded by Calle Isabel, Atocha, Unión, and Simon Bolívar), an enormous, shady plaza anchored by the **Fuentes de Leones** and impressive **Catedral de Nuestra Señora de Guadalupe** (787/842-0134). The streets around the plaza are lined with many thriving businesses, and street vendors. Also of note on a visit to the city are the **Museo de Arte de Ponce** (2325 Blvd. Luis A. Ferre Aguayo; 787/848-0505 or 787/840-1510; www.museoarteponce.org), the crown jewel of Puerto Rico's cultural institutions, with more than 3,000 pieces of European, North American, and Puerto Rican art from the 14th century to the present; and **Castillo Serrallés** (17 Calle El Vigía; 787/259-1774, 787/259-1775, or 800/981-2275; www.castilloserralles.org) built in 1934 for Eugenio Serrallés, a leader in the local sugarcane industry and offering a grand view of the city.

## MUSEO DEL CEMÍ

PR 144, km 9.3, Jayuya; 787/828-1241 or 787/828-4618

Museo del Cemí is located in the mountainous interior municipality of Jayuya, which is the place to get a glimpse of

CATEDRAL DE NUESTRA SEÑORA DE GUADALUPE

# Major CITIES

**SAN JUAN:** Arguably the most cosmopolitan city in the Caribbean and the second-oldest European settlement in the Americas, San Juan offers world-class restaurants and luxury hotels in Spanish colonial and neoclassical buildings lining cobblestone streets, and you're never very far from the beach.

**PONCE:** The south coast's biggest city rivals San Juan as the island's cultural, historical, and architectural center.

**MAYAGÜEZ:** Mayagüez is a lovely colonial city and a bustling mini-metropolis that has resisted the siren's call of tourism and mainland influence.

vestiges of Taíno culture in the environment where the culture once had deep roots. The building makes quite a statement as you approach. It's shaped like a huge cemí—a triangular artifact with animal characteristics, believed to have represented a deity and to have contained many powers. Downstairs is a small collection of Taíno artifacts: necklaces of stone and shells, ceremonial maracas, and the mysterious stone collar/belt, the purpose of which is unknown. Upstairs are poster-size photographs of petroglyphs found throughout the island.

Within a couple of miles of the museum on the PR144, the enormous granite boulder of **La Piedra Escrita,** measuring 32 feet high and 13 feet wide (9.75x4 meters), is located smack-dab in the middle of Río Saliente, creating a natural pool. The rock is one of Puerto Rico's most revered reminders of Taíno culture. On the rock's surface are 52 petroglyphs carved into the rock by members of Indigenous groups sometime between AD 600 and 1200. Some symbols clearly depict faces of humans and animals while others are geometric or abstract. Because of the quantity of petroglyphs on the rock, some believe La Piedra Escrita was an important ceremonial site.

# BEST SCENIC DRIVES

## LA RUTA PANORÁMICA (VIEW ROUTE)

You couldn't ask for a better way to explore Cordillera Central, the island's mountainous inland, than to drive this 167-mile (270-kilometer) route from **Mayagüez** on the west coast to **Yabucoa** on the southeast coast. The route takes visitors to breathtaking heights on the island's highest peaks, revealing panoramic views of both the Atlantic and the Caribbean, as well as the dramatic mountains and valleys that make up the island's spine. The well-maintained, well-marked route traverses a network of secondary roads beginning on **PR 105** in Mayagüez and ending on **PR 182** in Yabucoa. From end to end, the journey takes about 6 hours, not including stops, so plan to spend two days to see all the landscape has to offer.

Highlights along the way include several state forests and reserves, including **Reserva Forestal de Carite** (PR 184, kilometer marker 17.8, Cayey; 787/747-4510 or 787/747-4545), **Bosque Estatal de Toro Negro** (along Ruta Panorámica on PR 143, south of Jayuya), and **Bosque Estatal de Maricao** (PR 120, kilometer marker 13.2, Maricao; 787/838-1040), as well as impressive overlooks such as **Mirador Piedra Degetau** in Aibonito and **Mirador Orocovis-Villalba** (PR 143 between Orocovis and Villalba).

## LA RUTA DEL LECHÓN (ROAST PORK ROUTE)

### PR 184

South of San Juan is a terrific scenic drive along PR 184 through **Barrio Guavate** in the municipality of **Cayey.** Not only does this route provide spectacular views of the mountains, but it also passes by the many popular lechoneras that make this area a popular

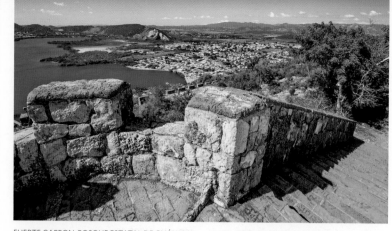

FUERTE CAPRON, BOSQUE ESTATAL DE GUÁNICA

destination for foodies. Specializing in pork cooked whole hog-style over a wood fire, lechoneras are casual, open-air restaurants that also serve other authentic Puerto Rican dishes and even sometimes have live salsa music on the weekends.

From **San Juan,** proceed south on PR 52, turn left on PR 184, and for the next 9 miles (15 kilometers) you will drive past panoramic views of the mountains and lechoneras including **El Mojito** (PR 184, kilometer marker 32.9; 787/738-8888; www.lechoneraelmojito.com) and **Los Pinos** (PR 184, kilometer marker 27.7, Cayey; 787/286-1917). A good end point is **Charco Azul,** a natural freshwater swimming hole with a small waterfall. On weekends, street vendors sell crafts, homemade cheese, candied fruits, and mavi champagne along the roadside. Without stops, the drive takes about 30 minutes one way, but for the best experience, devote a full day to the drive.

# BEST PARKS AND RECREATION AREAS

## BOSQUE ESTATAL DE GUÁNICA

PR 334; 787/821-5706, 787/724-3724, or 787/721-5495

The primary draw for visitors to Guánica is the astounding landscape of Bosque Estatal de Guánica. This 10,000-acre (4,046-hectare) subtropical dry forest sits atop petrified coral reefs

millions of years old and features a variety of environments, from dry scrub forest, featuring sun-bleached rocky soil, cacti, and stunted, twisted trees, to evergreen forest, where you can find Spanish moss, mistletoe, bromeliads, and orchids. The rest of the forest is deciduous, and agave and campeche trees are common too.

There are nearly 37 miles (60 kilometers) of trails in the forest. From the main entrance off PR 334, follow the long narrow road to the **information center,** where you'll find the trailheads and where you can obtain trail maps and tips from the helpful English-speaking rangers. One of the most popular hikes is a trek to the ruins of **Fuerte Capron** (3 miles/5 kilometers, 1.5 hours), once a lookout tower for the Spanish Armada. For a breathtakingly beautiful drive through the forest, take the **PR 333** scenic route, which starts in the town of Guánica and traverses eastward for 6.5 miles (10.5 kilometers) along the southern rim of the forest.

## SAN CRISTÓBAL CAÑON

PR 162/PR 725, between Aibonito and Barranquitas

San Cristóbal Cañon is the biggest canyon in the Caribbean, at 4.5 miles (7.2 kilometers) long and 500-800 feet (152-243 meters) deep. It's hard to believe this beautiful deep hole in the earth, now filled with verdant green vegetation, was once a garbage dump. Today it's a popular site for adventure seekers who want to get away from it all and

CALLE SAN SEBASTIÁN, VIEJO SAN JUAN

witness the canyon's natural beauty, including a spectacular river, waterfalls, and shoals. **Montaña Explora** (PR 191, kilometer marker 27.9, Camino Viejo, Charco El Hippie; 787/516-6194; www.facebook.com/mexplorapr) provides guided extreme adventure tours of San Cristóbal Cañon. A challenging 6-hour hiking and rappelling tour is $175 and is only for the physically fit and truly adventurous, although no previous rappelling experience is required. Other tours include hiking and swimming in a freshwater pond on the less-touristy southern side of El Yunque.

# FESTIVALS AND EVENTS

Though visiting Puerto Rico during a festival is bound to be an unforgettable experience, you can find a party almost any evening in one of its party districts, like **La Placita** in Santurce, **Boca de Cangrejos** in Piñones, and **Calle San Sebastián** in Viejo San Juan. Before you go, brush up on Puerto Rican music: The island is world renowned for **salsa,** a lively fusion of jazz, African polyrhythms, and Caribbean flair, that's as fun to dance to as it is to listen to. The roots of salsa music can be heard in Puerto Rico's earliest known musical styles, **bomba** and **plena,** which originated in African culture, both propelled by hand drummers.

## FESTIVAL DE MÁSCARAS (FESTIVAL OF MASKS)

Hatillo; Dec.

**Hatillo,** on the island's north side, 1.5 hours west of San Juan, hosts one of the island's most celebrated annual festivals. Originating in 1823 with the Spaniards who settled this part of the island, Festival de la Máscaras is a three-day costumed celebration held December 26-28. Originally it was meant to retell the story of King Herod's attempt to kill the infant Jesus by ordering the death of all male babies. Men would don elaborate costumes and masks and travel house-to-house on horseback. After playfully harassing the residents and demanding money, which was donated to the church or a civic organization, they would receive homemade treats and beverages. Today, festivities revolve around street parades, music, dance, food, and crafts on the main plaza. The last day is reserved for **Día de Inocentes,** a festival specifically for children.

## COFFEE FESTIVALS

In the 19th century, Puerto Rico was a major exporter of coffee. The industry has waxed and waned since, notably taking a big hit from Hurricane Maria in 2017, but the industry is slowly building back, and there are plenty of ways to experience the history and the flavors of Puerto Rico's coffee heritage. The best time to see coffee farms is during harvest season (Sept.-Dec.), or visit during

# BEST SOUVENIRS

- A bag of Puerto Rican **coffee** is a piece of island heritage, and you get to support local growers. Pick one up at a working coffee farm in Jayuya, like **Café Hacienda San Pedro Tienda y Museo** (PR 144, kilometer marker 8.4, Jayuya; 787/828-2083; www.cafehsp.com) or **Hacienda Pomarrosa** (PR 511 at PR 143, near Jayuya; 787/844-3541; http://pomarrosacoffeelodge.com).

- Edible souvenirs don't get much better than the **brazo gitanos,** or jelly rolls, from **Ricomini Panadería** (131 Calle Méndez Vigo, Mayagüez; 787/832-0565 or 787/831-3217), a Mayagüez speciality.

- Rum is another traditional Puerto Rican export, a product of the bounty of sugarcane that's integral to the island's history. You can try it at distilleries from well-known **Casa Bacardí** (PR165, kilometer marker 6.2, Cataño; 787/788-8400; www.bacardi.com/casa-bacardi) to "rum boutique" **Casa Melaza** (74 Caleta de San Juan, San Juan; 787/462-4782; www.casamelaza.com).

a coffee festival. **Festival del Café** is an annual weeklong celebration of coffee held in March in the southern town of Yauco. In Cordillera Central, Maricao has celebrated the end of coffee harvest since the 1800s with the three-day **Fiesta del Acabe del Café** in mid-February. Both festivals have parades, award ceremonies, dance and musical performances, arts, crafts, and food vendors.

# BEST FOOD

Puerto Rican cuisine is a hearty fare called *cocina criolla,* which means creole cooking. A typical *criolla* dish contains fried or stewed meat (especially pork, so popular Puerto Rico has a tourist driving route dedicated to it, the **Ruta de Lechón**), chicken, or seafood, combined with or accompanied by rice and beans.

## PLANTAINS AND BANANAS

The plantain is a major staple of the Puerto Rican diet, similar to a banana but larger, firmer, and less sweet. Bananas are also popular, especially **guineitos en escabeche,** a green-banana salad marinated with pimento-stuffed olives in vinegar and lime juice.

- **Tostones** are a popular plantain dish. The fruit is sliced into rounds, fried until soft, mashed flat, and fried again until crisp, often served with the ubiquitous Puerto Rican condiment, mayo ketchup. Try it at **La Casita Blanca** (351 Calle Tapía, San Juan; 787/726-5501; www.facebook.com/lacasitablancapr).

- Probably the most popular way plantain is served is in **mofongo,** a mashed mound of fried green plantain, garlic, olive oil, and chicharrón (pork cracklins). You'll find it on the menu of just about every restaurant on the island. Try it at **Punto de Vista** (Hotel Milano, 307 Calle Fortaleza, San Juan; 787/307-2970; www.facebook.com/pdvosj), or **La Casa del Chef** (Callejon Fagot, Ponce; 787/843-1298).

MOFONGO

## LUQUILLO'S *KIOSKOS*

**PR 193 at PR 3**

The Kioskos de Luquillo are nearly as popular an attraction as Playa Luquillo. This long stretch of 50-plus side-by-side kiosks is one of the best places to experience Puerto Rico's array of traditional fritters. Shaped like discs, halfmoons, cigars, boats, and balls, these crispy deep-fried goodies come stuffed with a varied combination of meat, fish, crab, poultry, or cheese. Most kiosks serve similar fare at stand-up bars where you can eat on your feet or seated at a table nearby. Pick one of each and wash it all down with a cold beer, a cocktail, or coco frio (ice-cold coconut water served from the shell). Be sure to buy a bag of coco dulce—sinfully rich patties of sugary coconut—for later. The following are some favorites:

- **La Parrilla #2** (787/889-0590)
- **El Jefe Burger & Mojito Factory #12** (787/604-0644; www.facebook.com/jefeburgershackmojitofactory)
- **Tattoo Tavern #17** (787/889-1189; www.facebook.com/tavern17)

# MAJOR AIRPORTS

- **Aeropuerto Internacional Luis Muñoz Marín:** SJU; San Juan; http://aeropuertosju.com
- **Aeropuerto Internacional Rafael Hernández:** BQN; Aguadilla; https://aguadilla.airport-authority.com

# MORE INFORMATION

## TRAVEL AND TOURISM INFORMATION

- **Tourism Company of Puerto Rico:** www.discoverpuertorico.com

## NEWSPAPERS

- *El Nuevo Día:* www.elnuevodia.com/english
- *San Juan Daily Star:* www.sanjuandailystar.com

# ESSENTIALS

BAR HARBOR, MAINE

is the most common way to obtain this proof.

When renting a car, you can opt to purchase insurance from the rental agency for the duration of the vehicle rental. If you already have private auto insurance, check with your carrier to see if the policy covers rentals. During the trip, keep all insurance and vehicle-related paperwork in a secure place.

## Road Rules and Driving Tips

In the United States, motorists drive on the right side of the road, and speed limits are displayed in miles per hour, including in Puerto Rico. Distance is measured in miles, except in Puerto Rico, where kilometers are used. Road signs are in English, except in Puerto Rico, where they are in Spanish. Vehicle speedometers display both miles and kilometers. Drivers should be familiar with the road regulations and laws for each state they visit. More information can be found at www.usa.gov/motor-vehicle-services.

### CELL PHONES

Many states prohibit drivers from using handheld cell phones while operating a vehicle, and outright ban the use of a cell phone by teen drivers. If you're caught breaking one of these laws, there could be steep fines. Always have a hands-free option available. Find state-by-state rules here: www.ncsl.org/research/transportation/cellular-phone-use-and-texting-while-driving-laws.aspx.

### SPEED LIMITS

Speed limits vary from state to state and are posted in increments of five miles per hour. Maximum speed limits tend to be higher (75-80 miles per hour in some areas) in the West compared to states east of the Mississippi River (generally 65-70 miles per hour).

### CROSSING STATE LINES

In general, the rules of the road throughout the country are the same. Notable exceptions relate to **speed limits, motorcycle helmet laws, seat belts,** and **child restraints.** Get specific state road rules at www.

dmv-department-of-motor-vehicles.com.

Drivers entering California must stop at **Agricultural Inspection Stations.** You don't need to present a passport, visa, or a driver's license, but be prepared to present fruits and vegetables, even those purchased within neighboring states. Other items that may be illegal to transport across state lines include **fireworks, exotic animals,** and **certain plants.**

Federal law allows travelers who can legally carry **firearms** under federal, state, and local laws to bring a gun across state lines. However, states have their own laws governing the transportation of firearms, so be sure to comply with the legal requirements in each state. When in doubt, carry firearms unloaded, locked in a case, and stored in the trunk. Store ammunition in a separate, locked container.

### FUEL

There are remote areas within the country where **service stations** are few and far between. A good rule of thumb for road-tripping is to keep the gas tank level above the **half-full** line, and fuel up in major towns whenever possible. Gasoline in Puerto Rico is sold in liters, whereas elsewhere in the United States, gallons are used.

### ROAD CONDITIONS AND NAVIGATION

Road conditions can be affected by closures, accidents, traffic jams, construction, and weather. Most states provide real-time road conditions, construction updates, and road closure information via the **U.S. Department of Transportation's Federal Highway Administration.** To access this information on the road, **dial 511.** Of the 50 states, 11 do not have active 511 access. These are: Michigan, Indiana, Illinois, Texas, Oklahoma, Missouri, Arkansas, Alabama, Rhode Island, Connecticut, and Delaware.

Never rely solely on your GPS for navigation. Always have a **printed map** or a **road atlas** in the vehicle to use as a backup.

## DRIVING RVS, CAMPERVANS, OR VEHICLES WITH TRAILERS

When driving an RV, campervan, or a vehicle pulling a trailer, remember that these are heavy pieces of machinery. This means they will take longer to slow down, so give yourself time to **brake** and maintain a greater distance between you and other vehicles.

To **park** safely, use a spotter, use your mirrors, and take your time. Try to park in designated RV spots whenever possible; these are larger and often let you pull in straight on.

**Slow down** when driving on hills and mountains. Use **low gears** going uphill and downhill, and always stay in the right lane.

Make **turns** long and wide, especially right turns. Make good use of your side and rearview mirrors. Keep as close to the center lane as possible.

Pay attention to **height clearances** for parking garages, overpasses, and bridges. Know the maximum height of your vehicle.

## PUBLIC TRANSPORTATION

Most big cities and many midsize cities in the United States have some form of public transportation, such as buses, light rail, or a metro system. Outside cities, however, it can be hard, if not impossible, to get around without a car.

# HEALTH AND SAFETY

## EMERGENCIES

For emergencies in the United States, including Alaska, Hawaii, and Puerto Rico, **dial 911** on your phone for immediate assistance.

## CRIME

Crime in the United States varies from location to location. Crimes against travelers are often theft-related crimes.

Given the large number of guns in the United States (the highest per capita in the world) and the frequency of shootings, mass or otherwise, the United States may seem dangerous to visit or travel around. In 2019, about 4 deaths in 100,000 in the United States were caused by gun violence, according to the Institute of Health Metrics and Evaluation (www.healthdata.org) at the University of Washington. This places the United States at 32nd in the world in rate of gun violence deaths.

## HAZARDS

When out in nature, be aware of your surroundings and the conditions of the area. Beyond the hazards listed below, falls, hypothermia, or simply getting lost are very real threats that can happen almost anywhere.

### Poison Oak, Ivy, and Sumac

Poison oak, ivy, and sumac are vines or shrubs that inhabit forests. Common in western states, poison oak has three scalloped leaves. Found across the United States except for tropical islands and Alaska, poison ivy has three spoon-shaped leaves and grows along rivers, lakes, and oceans. With 7-13 leaflets, poison sumac grows in wet, swampy zones in the north and Florida. Contact with these plants may cause a rash and itching, which can be transferred to your eyes or face via touch. Your best protection is to wear long sleeves and long pants when hiking, no matter how hot it is. Washing exposed skin with Tecnu cleanser can prevent a rash from poison oak and ivy. Calamine lotion or a topical antihistamine can help ease the rash and itching.

### Giardia

Lakes and streams can carry parasites like *Giardia lamblia*. If ingested, it causes cramping, nausea, and severe diarrhea for up to six weeks. Avoid giardia by boiling water (for one minute, plus one minute for each 1,000 ft./305 m of elevation above sea level) or using a one-micron filter. Bleach also works (add two drops per quart and wait 30 minutes).

### Hantavirus

Hantavirus infection is contracted by inhaling dust from deer mice droppings. When camping, store food in rodent-proof containers. If you contract the virus, which results in flu-like

# WILDLIFE SAFETY TIPS

While you may see bison, elk, moose, or bears, remember that wildlife is just that... *wild*. Though animals may appear tame, they are not and gorings and maulings are common. Here are a few tips to remain safe.

- **Do not approach wildlife.** Crowding wildlife puts you at risk and endangers the animal, often scaring it off. Seemingly docile bison and elk have suddenly gored people who come too close. Stay at least **100 yards away** (91 meters, the length of a football field) from bears and wolves. For all other wildlife, stay at least **25 yards (23 meters) away.** For spying wildlife up close, use a good pair of **binoculars** or a **spotting scope.** Use telephoto lenses for photography.

- **Take safe selfies.** Many injuries are related to people trying to take selfie photos with tablets or cell phones. Avoid getting too close to large creatures and maintain a distance of 25-100 yards (23-91 meters) between yourself and all wildlife.

- **Do not feed any animal.** Because human food is not part of their natural diet, animals may become less healthy if humans feed them, and they may begin to seek humans' supplies rather than forage on their own. As they rely on people for handouts, they become aggressive, endangering both human visitors and themselves.

- **Follow instructions for food storage.** Bears, wolves, and coyotes may become more aggressive when acquiring food, and ravens can strew food and garbage, making it more available to other wildlife.

- **Let the animal's behavior guide your behavior.** If an animal appears twitchy or nervous, or points eyes and ears directly at you, back off: You're too close. If you behave like a predator stalking an animal, the creature will assume you are one.

  If you see **wildlife along a road,** use pullouts or broad shoulders to drive completely off the road. Use the car as a blind to watch wildlife, and keep pets inside. Watch for cars, as visitors can be injured by inattentive drivers whenever a wildlife traffic jam occurs. Animals are more active at **dusk and dawn,** especially in the fall and spring, so watch out for road crossings when driving through wildlife-rich areas.

symptoms, seek immediate medical attention.

## Bears

Bears are dangerous around food, be it a carcass in the woods, pack on a trail, or cooler in a campsite. Proper use, storage, and handling of food and garbage helps prevent bears from being conditioned to look for food around humans and turning aggressive.

On the trail, pick up any dropped food, including wrappers and crumbs, and pack out all garbage. When camping, use low-odor foods, keep food and cooking gear out of sleeping sites in the backcountry, and store them

inside your vehicle in front-country campgrounds.

## Mountain Lions

Because of their solitary nature, it is unlikely you will see a mountain lion, even on long trips in the backcountry. These large cats rarely prey on humans, but they can—especially small kids. Hike with others, keep children close, and make noise on the trail. If you do stumble upon a cougar, do not run: Remain calm and gather your group together to appear bigger. Look at the cat with peripheral vision, rather than staring straight on, and back away slowly. If the lion attacks, fight back with rocks and sticks, or by kicking.

## Spiders, Mosquitoes, and Ticks

Spiders, mosquitoes, and ticks can carry diseases such as West Nile virus and Rocky Mountain spotted fever. Protect yourself by wearing long sleeves and pants, and use insect repellent in spring-summer when mosquitoes and ticks are common. If you are bitten by a tick, carefully remove it by the head with tweezers, disinfect the bite, and then see a doctor. Some spiders, such as the brown recluse, carry poison in their bites. If symptoms are severe (breathing difficulty, nausea, sweating, and vomiting), seek medical attention immediately.

## Snakes

Rattlesnakes are ubiquitous in prairies and deserts across the West. When hiking, keep your eyes on the ground and an ear out for the telltale rattle—a warning to keep away. Should you be bitten, seek immediate medical help.

## Altitude

Some visitors from sea-level locales feel the effects of altitude at high elevations, such as in the Rocky Mountains. Watch for light-headedness, headaches, or shortness of breath. To acclimate, drink lots of fluids and increase elevation slowly, if possible. If symptoms spike, descend in elevation as soon as possible. Altitude also increases UV radiation exposure and the chance of sunburn.

## Ocean Safety

The ocean is beautiful but can present hazards. Avoid swimming alone, and obey all warning signs. When at an unfamiliar beach, ask lifeguards or beach attendants about conditions and follow their advice. Be aware of undertows (the waves drawing back into the sea), as they can knock you off your feet.

Stay out of the water during periods of high surf, which can create riptides. Riptides are powerful currents, like rivers in the sea, that can drag you out to sea. If caught in a "rip" don't fight to swim directly against it, which will only exhaust you. Instead, swim diagonally across it, while going along with it, and try to stay parallel to the shore until you are out of the strong pull. The last rule is, if in doubt, stay out.

If you encounter a shark, don't panic. Never thrash around because this will trigger their attack instinct.

## Hunting Season

Where hunting is allowed, such as in many state parks and some federal lands, visitors should be aware of hunting seasons, which vary depending on the location and the bird or animal, and take necessary precautions, such as wearing blaze orange and avoiding popular hunting times (opening day, dusk, and dawn), when engaging in recreation.

# ACCOMMODATIONS

During busy summer months and other high tourist periods, such as holidays and special events, accommodations can get booked up early, especially in popular destinations. Rates also go up during these times.

## HOTELS

From luxury to budget, small to sprawling, hotel accommodations span coast to coast. The benefits of properties owned by major brands (Marriott, Hilton, Best Western, etc.) is that you can find them anywhere; they usually have room availability or can refer you to a sister property that does; and they offer consistent amenities.

## MOTOR LODGES AND MOTOR COURTS

Vintage and full of charm, these retro gems are often found on scenic byways and in tiny towns. Because they are older, they may offer small guest rooms, no Wi-Fi, and limited amenities. But for travelers who desire one-of-a-kind accommodations, a motor lodge or court is the way to go.

## BED-AND-BREAKFASTS

Plan to reserve a B&B well in advance, especially during peak season, as they

# CORONAVIRUS IN THE UNITED STATES

At the time of writing in April 2021, the United States was starting to reopen after the large-scale shutdowns in response to the coronavirus. The situation was constantly evolving, and conditions and regulations varied from state to state. Some states lifted mask mandates, while others planned to keep them in place even after all businesses would reopen.

Now more than ever, Moon encourages its readers to be courteous and ethical in their travel. We ask travelers to be respectful to residents, and mindful of the evolving situation in their chosen destination when planning a trip.

## BEFORE YOU GO

- Check local websites for **local restrictions** and the **overall health status** of the destination and your point of origin. If you're traveling to or from an area that is currently a COVID-19 hotspot, you may want to reconsider your trip.

- Moon encourages travelers to get **vaccinated** if your health status allows, and to take a **coronavirus test** with enough time to receive your results before your departure if possible. Some attractions, events, and businesses may require proof of vaccination or a negative COVID test result to allow entry. Check requirements for places you want to visit and factor these into your plans.

- If you plan to fly, check with your airline and the Centers for Disease Control and Prevention website (www.cdc.gov) for updated **travel requirements.** Some airlines may be taking more steps than others to help you travel safely, such as limited occupancy; check their websites for more information before buying your ticket, and consider a very early or very late flight and flying direct to limit exposure. Flights may be more infrequent, with increased cancellations.

- Check the website of any museums and other venues you wish to patronize to confirm that they're open, if their hours have been adjusted, and to learn about any specific visitation requirements, such as **mandatory reservations or face coverings,** or **limited occupancy.**

- Pack **hand sanitizer, a thermometer,** and plenty of **face masks.** On road trips, consider packing **snacks, water,** a **cooler,** or anything else you might need to limit the number of stops along your route, and to be prepared for possible closures and reduced services over the course of your travels.

- **Assess the risk** of entering crowded spaces, joining tours, and taking public transit.

- Expect **general disruptions.** Events may be postponed or canceled, and some tours and venues may require reservations, enforce limits on the number of guests, be operating during different hours than the ones listed, or be closed entirely.

## RESOURCES

- **Centers for Disease Control and Prevention** (www.cdc.gov/coronavirus/2019-ncov/travelers/index.html): Start here when planning a trip in the United States. The Travel Planner allows you to look up specific destinations by city, zip code, or address and get links for the local health departments.

usually offer only a few guest rooms. The benefit is a white-glove experience in a thoughtfully appointed home, complete with a gourmet breakfast.

## CAMPING

National parks provide a safe—and beautiful—way to camp. Book campsites months in advance during the summer, except for in the Southwest, when many campsites shut down because of extreme heat. Always check with park rangers about campfire regulations, information on local wildlife, and **Leave No Trace** (www.lnt.org) policies.

## VACATION RENTALS

Short-term rentals from companies such as **Airbnb** (www.airbnb.com), **VRBO** (www.vrbo.com), and **HomeAway** (www.homeaway.com), or from regional companies that manage privately owned properties, let you lease a private home or room. These tend to offer affordable options in highly desirable areas, such as big cities or beach towns. Homeowners provide essentials, such as toilet paper, linens, and basic kitchen and pantry staples; you're responsible for everything else.

## HOSTELS

For the budget-conscious traveler, hostels are a great option. Typically found in major metropolises, hostels offer a bed in a shared room or single room in a dorm-like setting. You might also share bathrooms, showers, and a community kitchen with other guests. **American Hostels** (http://americanhostels.us) lets you search by region within the United States.

# TRAVEL TIPS

## WI-FI AND CELL SERVICE

**Wi-Fi** is available at most accommodations, attractions, restaurants, and welcome centers throughout the country.

**Cell phone service** is widely available around the country, especially around population centers. However, the more remote the area, usually the less you can rely on having service.

# TIME AND MEASUREMENTS

The time zones in the United States are Hawaii, Alaska, Pacific, Mountain, Central, and Eastern. Each is separated by one hour. Arizona and Hawaii don't observe daylight saving time. Puerto Rico observes Atlantic standard time and does not practice daylight saving time. This means that it's one hour later than Eastern time November-March, and the same as Eastern time March-November.

The United States uses the imperial system of measurements (miles, feet, pounds, gallons, etc.) and Fahrenheit for temperatures. Puerto Rico uses the metric system, except for speed limits, which are in miles per hour.

# TRAVELING TO NATIVE AMERICAN RESERVATIONS

A Native American reservation is a sovereign nation within the borders of the United States. Take special care when driving on Native American lands. Each community has its own guidelines, rules, and judicial system. The website **NativeAmerica.travel** (https://nativeamerica.travel) by the American Indian Alaska Native Tourism Association provides travel tips, as well as destination listings and other travel information.

## Attending a Powwow

Attending a powwow is a wonderful way to interact with Native American culture. It is important to respect the ceremony and the celebration of the tribes and remember that as a visitor, you are a guest. The participants in the dance will be wearing their finest regalia. Honor this and refrain from wearing grungy, torn clothing.

Many powwows, particularly on reservation lands, are held outdoors where there is very little in the way of public seating. Bring lawn chairs or blankets for seating. There are sometimes benches set up around the arena. These benches are reserved for dancers only. Sometimes the areas just behind the benches are reserved for family members, so ask before you set up chairs.

Some of the outfits worn by the dancers are breathtakingly beautiful. Remember to ask permission before you take pictures. Listen to the master of ceremonies for cues. Certain songs and ceremonies require the attendees to stand with heads uncovered while they are played. The Grand Entry Song, Flag Songs, Veteran Songs, and Memorial Songs all require that you stand. Attendees are free to participate in intertribal dances whether wearing regalia or not, but should not try to dance at any other time. Blanket dances are held at traditional powwows to help defray the costs of the powwows and the travel costs of some of the drums. If you see a blanket placed on the grounds and dancers start leaving money on the blanket, feel free to contribute by asking a dancer to place money on the blanket for you. If a dancer drops or loses something off their regalia, particularly an eagle feather, do not pick it up. There are ceremonies for retrieving items that have touched the ground. Ask a dancer or other person in authority for assistance.

It sounds like a lot of rules, but the guiding principle behind attending a powwow is respect.

## NATIONAL PARKS AND FEDERAL RECREATIONAL LANDS PASSES

National parks and other areas and attractions managed by the National Park Service (www.nps.gov) are among the most popular destinations in the United States. Entry fees to these sites vary, and if you are planning to visit a number of them in a year, you may want to get a pass.

The **Annual Pass** ($80) admits entrance to all national parks and federal fee areas for up to one year. All U.S. fourth graders are eligible to receive a free annual pass. This pass can be purchased online (https://store.usgs.gov/pass) or at a federal recreation site. Fares for tours, transportation, and campgrounds are not covered by the Annual Pass.

U.S. citizens or permanent residents aged 62 and older have two pass options: an **Annual Senior Pass** ($20, $10 processing fee), good for one year, or a

**Lifetime Senior Pass** ($80, $10 processing fee), which is valid for life. To purchase either pass, apply online (https://yourpassnow.com) or bring proof of age (state driver's license, birth certificate, or passport) in person to any national park entrance station (processing fee waived at park entrance). In a private vehicle, the card admits four adults, plus all children under age 16. Four annual senior passes can be traded in for the lifetime senior pass. Both senior passes grant the passholder discounts on fees for federally run tours and campgrounds; however, discounts do not apply to park concessionaire services like hotels, boat tours, and bus tours.

Blind or permanently disabled U.S. citizens or permanent residents can request a lifetime **National Parks and Federal Recreational Lands Access Pass** (free, $10 processing fee) for access to all national parks and other federal sites. The pass admits the passholder plus three other adults in the same vehicle; children under age 16 are free. Passholders also receive a 50 percent discount on federally run tours and campgrounds. Proof of medical disability or eligibility is required for receiving federal benefits.

U.S. military personnel can get a lifetime **National Parks and Federal Recreational Lands Access Pass** (free) for access to all national parks and other federal sites. The pass admits the passholder plus three other adults in the same vehicle; children under age 16 are free. Passholders also get 50 percent discounts on federally run tours and campgrounds. Passes must be acquired in person at entrance stations; proof of service is required.

## ACCESSIBILITY

The Americans with Disabilities Act (ADA) requires public places to provide facilities to accommodate disabled patrons. Most major restaurants and accommodations are wheelchair-accessible, but small businesses located in older properties were grandfathered in and do not have to abide by the new laws. Chain motels generally have rooms with larger doors for wheelchair access, but it's best to call ahead and reserve the room you need.

The **Society for Accessible Travel and Hospitality** (www.sath.org) publishes links to major airlines' accessibility policies and publishes travel tips for people with various disabilities, including blindness, deafness, mobility disorders, diabetes, kidney disease, and arthritis. The society publishes *Open World*, an online magazine about accessible travel.

## SENIOR TRAVELERS

For discounts and help with trip planning, the **AARP** (800/454-5768, www.aarp.org) offers a full-service travel agency, trip insurance, a motor club, and the AARP Passport program, which provides seniors with discounts for hotels, car rentals, and other things.

Travelers over 55 should always check for a senior discount. Most attractions and some hotels and restaurants have special pricing for senior citizens. There are two national parks and federal recreational lands passes for U.S. citizens and permanent residents age 62 and older: the Annual Senior Pass ($20, $10 processing fee) and the Lifetime Senior Pass ($80, $10 processing fee).

## LGBTQ TRAVELERS

Several guidebooks and websites specialize in LGBTQ-friendly listings of hotels, restaurants, bars, and other establishments. The **Damron LGBT Travel Guides** (www.damron.com) sells print guides and publishes an online calendar of events, and the **International Gay and Lesbian Travel Association** (IGLTA, www.iglta.org) is a trade organization with listings of gay-friendly hotels, tour operators, and much more.

A number of states have passed or are considering laws that restrict LGBTQ rights. The **Transgender Law Center** publishes a National Equality Map (https://transgenderlawcenter.org/equalitymap) that rates each state and territory on its policies regarding LGBTQ rights.

## TRAVELERS OF COLOR

The **Open to All** campaign (www.opentoall.com) encourages businesses to take a pledge of nondiscrimination, and it's possible for search **Yelp** (www.yelp.com) for businesses who self-report having taken this pledge.

Online resources for travelers of color include:

- **Wanderful** (https://sheswanderful.com) is a travel community for women with a focus on making travel more equitable for all. The blog (https://blog.sheswanderful.com) includes lists of travel influencers of various backgrounds.

- **Travel Noire** (https://travelnoire.com) offers travel guides to various cities, with an emphasis on Black-owned businesses.

# SUSTAINABLE TRAVEL

## TRANSPORTATION

### Air Travel

Economy class seats increase the per-passenger mile efficiency of a plane trip; first and business class seats decrease it. Fly direct whenever possible. For short flights, consider taking a train or bus instead.

### Car Travel

When going on a road trip, get a pre-trip tune-up to aid in better fuel efficiency. Plan your route so you don't waste gas by backtracking. Use cruise control to maintain efficient speeds. Check your tire pressure. Tires that are not operating at the optimum pressure use more fuel.

If you're not driving your own car, rent an electric car or a hybrid.

In cities, ride the metro or buses, bike, or walk, rather than traveling by car.

## REUSE AND RECYCLE

Pack reusable water bottles to fill up at hotels, welcome centers, rest areas, campsites, and parks. Bring reusable food containers. Bring your own toiletries rather than using the small bottles provided at your accommodation.

Buy cans instead of bottles. They're easier to crush, thus saving space.

Use fabric grocery bags for shopping. If you have to use plastic grocery bags, save them to reuse.

Keep recyclables separate. Stop at retailers with recycling bins or at rest stops to recycle. Access Google Maps to locate recycling centers wherever you are.

## FOOD AND WATER

To create less food waste, plan out your meals. If you have food in the cooler, eat it instead of ordering at a restaurant or fast-food joint. Buy in bulk when it's feasible.

Bring reusable water bottles to avoid wasting plastic. If you must buy water, purchase gallon-size containers rather than individual bottles, then fill your reusable water bottle.

## WATER CONSERVATION

Do a full load of laundry instead of several small ones. Rewear clothes, or wash single items in your hotel sink.

Shower, don't bathe. Turn off the water when shampooing and soaping.

# RESOURCES

## TRAVEL BOOKINGS

**Kayak**
www.kayak.com

**Hotels.com**
www.hotels.com

## FEDERAL LANDS AND DESIGNATIONS

**National Park Service**
www.nps.gov

**U.S. Forest Service (National Forests)**
www.fs.usda.gov

**National Wildlife Refuge System**
www.fws.gov/refuges

**National Scenic Byways**
www.fhwa.dot.gov/byways

## MAPS

**American Automobile Association**
www.aaa.com

**National Geographic**
www.natgeomaps.com

**Rand McNally**
www.randmcnally.com

# INDEX

## A

Acadia National Park: 420
accessibility: 768-769
accommodations: 765, 767
Adirondacks: 498
air travel/airports: 760, 769; *see also specific state*
Alabama: 592, 593, 595, 688-699; map 690-691
Alaska: 36, 39, 40-54; map 42-43
Albany: 502
Albuquerque: 153, 156, 162
alligators: 24, 638-639, 671, 686, 714
altitude sickness: 765
Amish Country (Ohio): 402-403
Anchorage: 41, 48
Annapolis: 554-555, 558
Ann Arbor: 392, 395-396
Apostle Islands National Lakeshore: 350
Arches National Park: 140
Arizona: 106, 109, 122-136; map 124-125
Arkansas: 592, 596, 624-634; map 626-627
Arlington: 577, 583
Assateague Island: 23, 555
Atlanta: 678, 681, 682, 686
Austin: 19, 168, 175, 176

## B

Badlands National Park: 17, 260
Badwater Basin: 28, 98
bald eagles: 25, 50, 118, 195, 342, 407, 587
Baltimore: 554, 557-558, 561-562
Bangor: 419

barbecue: 30; Alabama 699; Illinois 372; Kansas City 291, 318; Kentucky 610; Memphis 622-623; North Carolina 660-661; South Carolina: 673-674; Texas: 176
Baton Rouge: 642-643
beaches: 22-23; California 91; Hawaii 738-739; Illinois 369; Michigan 395; New Jersey 512; Puerto Rico 749; Rhode Island 471
bears: 25; Alaska 45; Montana 206; safety 764; Wyoming 218-219
beef sandwiches: 30
beer: 31; Colorado 231; Indiana 382; Michigan 396-397; Missouri 321; North Carolina 661-662; Ohio 408; Oregon 84; Vermont 451; Wisconsin 359-360
Benjamin Franklin Parkway Museums: 522-523
Bennington: 447
*bierock*: 30, 292
Big Bend National Park: 168-169
Big Island of Hawai'i: 735, 737-738, 739, 740
Billings: 206
Bill Waller Mississippi Craft Center: 705
Biloxi: 707
BIPOC travelers: 769
Birmingham: 689, 695, 696
Bismarck: 253
bison: 24, 218
Black history/culture: Alabama 689, 692, 695-696; Arkansas 628; Delaware 543; Georgia 678, 681-682; Illinois 367; Kansas

286; Louisiana 639, 642; Maryland 560; Massachusetts 459; Michigan 393; Missouri 323; Nebraska 275; New Hampshire 430, 435; New York 504; North Carolina 656; Ohio 406; Oklahoma 296; South Carolina 666-667; Tennessee 616; Texas 176; Virginia 584-585; Washington DC 566, 570, 571-572, 574
Bloomington: 380
bluegrass music: 19; Annual Old Fiddlers' Convention 588; Kentucky 606-607, 610; North Carolina 659; Telluride Bluegrass Festival 238
Blue Ridge Parkway: 585-586, 652-653
blues music: 19; Alabama 692; Austin 168; Chicago 369; Detroit 393; Memphis 617; Mississippi Blues Trail 704
Boise: 185, 192
Bonaventure Cemetery: 678
Boston: 453, 456, 457, 459, 460, 461, 463, 464, 465
Boundary Waters Canoe Area: 336
Bourbon Trail: 603
Bowling Green: 605-606
Branch Brook Park: 513
Bridgeport: 484
bridges: 26-27
Browning: 202
*Brown v. Board of Education* National Historic Site: 286
Bryce Canyon National Park: 12, 140-141
Buffalo: 502, 508

# LIST OF MAPS

# PHOTO CREDITS

# TEXT CREDITS

## WEST COAST

Text adapted from *Moon Alaska*, second edition, by Lisa Maloney; *Moon British Columbia*, 11th edition, by Andrew Hempstead; *Moon California*, first edition, by Elizabeth Linhart Veneman; *Moon California Road Trip*, third edition, by Stuart Thornton; *Moon Oregon*, 13th edition, by Judy Jewell & W. C. McRae; *Moon Pacific Coast Highway Road Trip*, third edition, by Ian Anderson; and *Moon Washington*, 11th edition, by Matthew Lombardi.

## SOUTHWEST

Text adapted from *Moon Arizona*, 15th edition, by Tim Hull; *Moon Nevada*, first edition, by Scott Smith; *Moon New Mexico*, 11th edition, by Steven Horak; *Moon Southwest Road Trip*, second edition, by Tim Hull; *Moon Texas*, 10th edition, by Andy Rhodes; and *Moon Utah*, 13th edition, by W. C. McRae & Judy Jewell.

## ROCKY MOUNTAINS

Text adapted from *Moon Colorado*, 10th edition, by Terri Cook; *Moon Idaho*, seventh edition, by James P. Kelly; *Moon Montana*, first edition, by Carter G. Walker; *Moon Montana & Wyoming*, fourth edition, by Carter G. Walker; *Moon Wyoming*, third edition, by Carter G. Walker; *Moon Yellowstone & Grand Teton*, ninth edition, by Becky Lomax; and *Moon Yellowstone to Glacier National Park Road Trip*, first edition, by Carter G. Walker.

## GREAT PLAINS

Text adapted from *Moon Baseball Road Trip*, first edition, by Timothy Malcolm; *Moon Mount Rushmore & the Black Hills*, fourth edition, by Laural A. Bidwell; *The Open Road*, first edition, by Jessica Dunham; *Moon Oregon Trail Road Trip*, first edition, by Katrina Emery; *Moon Route 66 Road Trip*, second edition, by Jessica Dunham; and *Moon USA National Parks*, second edition, by Becky Lomax

## GREAT LAKES

Text adapted from *Moon Illinois*, second edition, by Christine des Garennes; *Moon Michigan*, seventh edition, by Paul Vachon; *Moon Minneapolis & St. Paul*, fourth edition, by Tricia Cornell; *Moon Minnesota*, fourth edition, by Tricia Cornell; *Moon Ohio*, first edition, by Matthew Caracciolo; *Moon USA National Parks*, second edition, by Beck Lomax; and *Moon Wisconsin*, eighth edition, by Thomas Huhti

## NEW ENGLAND

Text adapted from *Moon Maine*, eighth edition, by Hilary Nangle; *Moon New England*, first edition, by Jen Rose Smith; *Moon New England Road Trip*, first edition, by Jen Rose Smith; *Moon Rhode Island*, fifth edition, by Liz Lee; and *Moon Vermont*, fifth edition, by Jen Rose Smith

## MID-ATLANTIC

Text adapted from *Moon Drive & Hike Appalachian Trail*, first edition, by Timothy Malcolm; *Moon Hudson Valley & the Catskills*, fifth edition, by Nikki Goth Itoi; *Moon New Jersey*, second edition, by Laura Kiniry; *Moon New York State*, eighth edition, Julie Schwietert Collazo; *Moon Pennsylvania*, sixth edition, by Rachel Vigoda; *Moon*

*U.S. Civil Rights Trail,* first edition, by Deborah D. Douglas; *Moon Virginia,* eighth edition, by Michaela R. Gaaserud; *Moon Virginia & Maryland,* third edition, by Michaela R. Gaaserud; *Moon Washington DC,* second edition, by Samantha Sault

## SOUTH

Text adapted from *Moon Florida,* second edition, by Jason Ferguson; *Moon Florida Gulf Coast,* sixth edition, by Joshua Lawrence Kinser; *Moon Georgia,* eighth edition, by Jim Morekis; *Moon Kentucky,* second edition, by Theresa Dowell Blackinton; *Moon Memphis,* second edition, by Margaret Littman; *Moon Nashville to New Orleans,* second edition, by Margaret Littman; *Moon New Orleans,* first edition, by Nora McGunnigle; *Moon North Carolina,* seventh edition, by Jason Frye; *Moon South Carolina,* seventh edition, by Jim Morekis; *Moon South Florida & the Keys Road Trip,* first edition, by Jason Ferguson; *Moon Tennessee,* eighth edition, by Margaret Littman; *Moon USA National Parks,* second edition, by Becky Lomax; and *Moon U.S. Civil Rights Trail,* first edition, by Deborah D. Douglas

## ISLANDS

Text adapted from *Moon Hawaii,* second edition, by Kevin Whitton, and *Moon Puerto Rico,* fourth edition, by Suzanne Van Atten

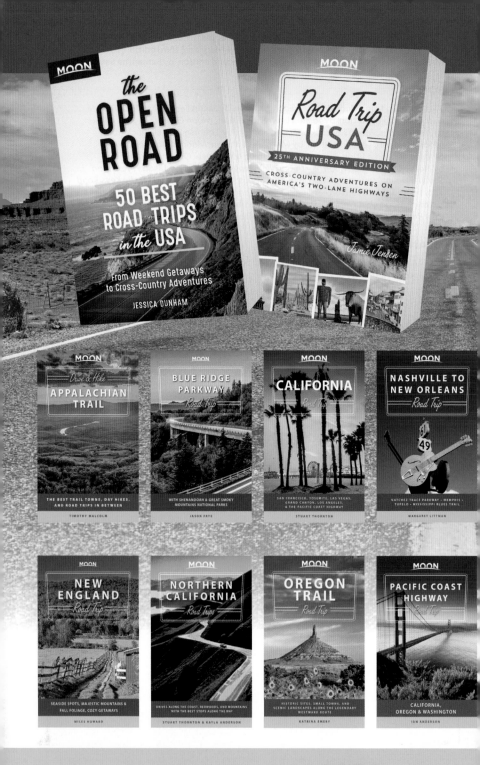

# ROAD TRIP GUIDES FROM MOON

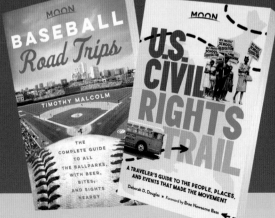

Explore the US with expert authors like baseball writer Timothy Malcolm and journalist Deborah D. Douglas!

# National Parks Travel Guides from Moon

**ACADIA NATIONAL PARK**
SEASIDE TOWNS · FALL FOLIAGE
CYCLING & PADDLING
HILARY NANGLE

**ARCHES & CANYONLANDS NATIONAL PARKS**
HIKING · BIKING
SCENIC DRIVES
JUDY JEWELL & W. C. McRAE

**BANFF NATIONAL PARK**
HIKE · CAMP
SEE WILDLIFE
ANDREW HEMPSTEAD

**CANADIAN ROCKIES**
WITH BANFF & JASPER NATIONAL PARKS
HIKE · CAMP
SEE WILDLIFE
ANDREW HEMPSTEAD

**DEATH VALLEY NATIONAL PARK**
HIKING SCENIC DRIVES
DESERT SPRINGS & HIDDEN OASES
JENNA BLOUGH

**GLACIER NATIONAL PARK**
HIKING · CAMPING
LAKES & PEAKS
BECKY LOMAX

**GRAND CANYON**
HIKE · CAMP
RAFT THE
COLORADO RIVER
TIM HULL

**GREAT SMOKY MOUNTAINS NATIONAL PARK**
HIKING · CAMPING
SCENIC DRIVES
JASON FRYE

**JOSHUA TREE & PALM SPRINGS**
JENNA BLOUGH

**MOUNT RUSHMORE & THE BLACK HILLS**
Including the Badlands
LAURAL A. BIDWELL

**ROCKY MOUNTAIN NATIONAL PARK**
HIKE · CAMP
SEE WILDLIFE
ERIN ENGLISH

# MAP SYMBOLS

| | | | | | | | |
|---|---|---|---|---|---|---|---|
| ═══ | Expressway | ○ | City/Town | 🛈 | Information Center | ♠ | Park |
| ═══ | Primary Road | ◉ | State Capital | P | Parking Area | ⛳ | Golf Course |
| ═══ | Secondary Road | ⊛ | National Capital | ♦ | Church | ✦ | Unique Feature |
| ▪▪▪▪ | Unpaved Road | ★ | Top 3 | ❦ | Winery/Vineyard | ⟆ | Waterfall |
| ---- | Trail | ★ | Point of Interest | TH | Trailhead | Λ | Camping |
| ···· | Ferry | ● | Accommodation | 🚉 | Train Station | ▲ | Mountain |
| ━•━ | Railroad | ▼ | Restaurant/Bar | ✈ | Airport | ⛷ | Ski Area |
| ▦▦▦ | Pedestrian Walkway | ▪ | Other Location | ✈ | Airfield | ⬯ | Glacier |
| ▨▨▨ | Stairs | | | | | | |

# CONVERSION TABLES

°C = (°F - 32) / 1.8
°F = (°C x 1.8) + 32
1 inch = 2.54 centimeters (cm)
1 foot = 0.304 meters (m)
1 yard = 0.914 meters
1 mile = 1.6093 kilometers (km)
1 km = 0.6214 miles
1 fathom = 1.8288 m
1 chain = 20.1168 m
1 furlong = 201.168 m
1 acre = 0.4047 hectares
1 sq km = 100 hectares
1 sq mile = 2.59 square km
1 ounce = 28.35 grams
1 pound = 0.4536 kilograms
1 short ton = 0.90718 metric ton
1 short ton = 2,000 pounds
1 long ton = 1.016 metric tons
1 long ton = 2,240 pounds
1 metric ton = 1,000 kilograms
1 quart = 0.94635 liters
1 US gallon = 3.7854 liters
1 Imperial gallon = 4.5459 liters
1 nautical mile = 1.852 km

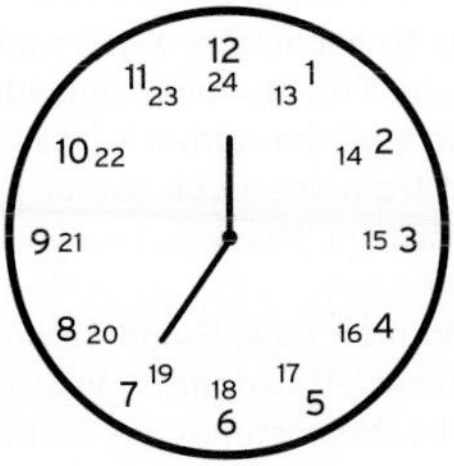

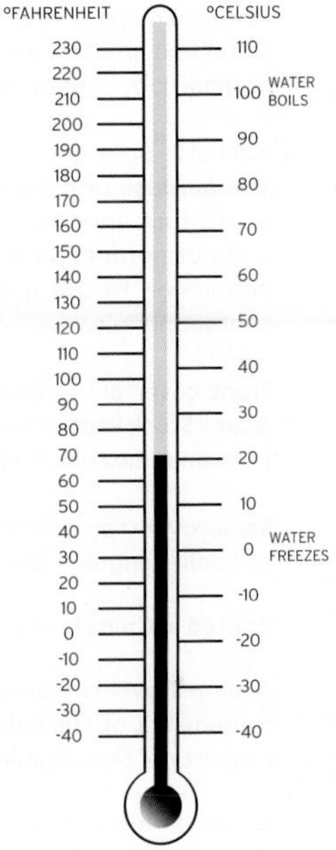

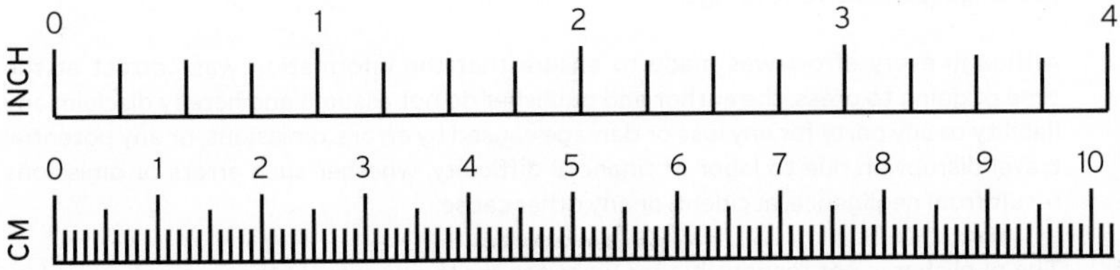

°FAHRENHEIT  °CELSIUS

230 — 110
220 — 
210 — 100  WATER BOILS
200 — 
190 — 90
180 — 80
170 — 
160 — 70
150 — 
140 — 60
130 — 
120 — 50
110 — 
100 — 40
90 — 30
80 — 
70 — 20
60 — 
50 — 10
40 — 
30 — 0  WATER FREEZES
20 — -10
10 — 
0 — -20
-10 — 
-20 — -30
-30 — 
-40 — -40

INCH 0 1 2 3 4

CM 0 1 2 3 4 5 6 7 8 9 10

**MOON USA STATE BY STATE**
Avalon Travel
Hachette Book Group
1700 Fourth Street
Berkeley, CA 94710, USA
www.moon.com

Editors: Grace Fujimoto, Hannah Brezack, Megan Anderluh, and Nikki Ioakimedes
Copy Editor: Barbara Schultz
Production Coordinators: Suzanne Albertson, Jane Musser
Graphics Coordinator: Kathryn Osgood
Cover Design: Erin Seaward-Hiatt
Interior Design: Megan Jones Design
Moon Logo: Tim McGrath
Map Editors: Mike Morgenfeld, Karin Dahl
Cartographers: Moon Street Cartography, Durango, CO., Karin Dahl, and Mike Morgenfeld

ISBN-13: 978-1-64049-597-5

Printing History
1st Edition — October 2021
5 4



Front cover photo (top): Mormon Row, Grand Tetons, Wyoming, All Canada Photos / Alamy Stock Photo; (bottom row, left to right): © Ventdusud | Dreamstime.com; © Mkopka | Dreamstime.com; © Hellen8 | Dreamstime.com; © Filtv | Dreamstime.com

Back cover (top to bottom): © NPS/Daniel A. Leifheit; © Stealthc4 | Dreamstime.com; © Adeliepenguin | Dreamstime.com

Printed in China by R.R. Donnelley



All recommendations, including those for sights, activities, hotels, restaurants, and shops, are based on each author's individual judgment. We do not accept payment for inclusion in our travel guides, and our authors don't accept free goods or services in exchange for positive coverage.

Although every effort was made to ensure that the information was correct at the time of going to press, the author and publisher do not assume and hereby disclaim any liability to any party for any loss or damage caused by errors, omissions, or any potential travel disruption due to labor or financial difficulty, whether such errors or omissions result from negligence, accident, or any other cause.

The publisher is not responsible for websites (or their content) that are not owned by the publisher.